KNOWLEDGE LOST

Knowledge Lost

A NEW VIEW OF EARLY MODERN
INTELLECTUAL HISTORY

MARTIN MULSOW

TRANSLATED BY
H. C. ERIK MIDELFORT

PRINCETON UNIVERSITY PRESS
PRINCETON & OXFORD

Published by Princeton University Press
41 William Street, Princeton, New Jersey 08540
6 Oxford Street, Woodstock, Oxfordshire OX20 1TR

press.princeton.edu

Orignially published as *Prekäres Wissen: Eine andere Ideengeschichte der Frühen Neuzeit*
© Suhrkamp Verlag Berlin 2012.

ISBN 9780691208657
ISBN (e-book) 9780691244129

Library of Congress Control Number: 2022938285

British Library Cataloging-in-Publication Data is available

Editorial: Ben Tate and Josh Drake
Production Editorial: Karen Carter
Jacket/Cover Design: Layla Mac Rory
Production: Danielle Amatucci
Publicity: Charlotte Coyne and Alyssa Sanford

Jacket/Cover Credit: Cover image by Suzy Hazelwood

This book has been composed in Arno

Printed on acid-free paper. ∞

Printed in the United States of America

10 9 8 7 6 5 4 3 2 1

A Carlo

Il miglior fabbro

CONTENTS

List of Illustrations ix

Preface xiii

Introduction: Precarious Knowledge, Dangerous Transfers,
and the Materiality of Knowing 1

PART I. TACTICS OF THE INTELLECTUAL PRECARIAT 25

SECTION I. THE RADICAL PERSONA 27

1 The Clandestine Precariat 31

2 The Libertine's Two Bodies 46

3 Portrait of the Freethinker as a Young Man 69

4 The Art of Deflation, or: How to Save an Atheist 101

5 A Library of Burned Books 139

*SECTION II. TRUST, MISTRUST, COURAGE: EPISTEMIC
PERCEPTIONS, VIRTUES, AND GESTURES* 167

6 Threatened Knowledge: Prolegomena to a Cultural History
of Truth 171

7 Harpocratism: Gestures of Retreat 200

8 Dare to Know: Epistemic Virtue in Historical Perspective 224

**PART II. FRAGILITY AND ENGAGEMENT IN THE
KNOWLEDGE BOURGEOISIE**   237

SECTION III. PROBLEMATIC TRANSFERS   239

9   A Table in One's Hand: Historical Iconography   243

10 Family Secrets: Precarious Transfers within Intimate Circles   281

11 The Lost Package: The Role of Communications in the
    History of Philosophy in Germany   295

*SECTION IV. COMMUNITIES OF FASCINATION AND THE
INFORMATION HISTORY OF SCHOLARLY KNOWLEDGE*   325

12 Protection of Knowledge and Knowledge of Protection:
    Defensive Magic, Antiquarianism, and Magical Objects   331

13 Mobility and Surveillance: The Information History of
    Numismatics and Journeys to the East under Louis XIV   355

14 Microscripts of the Orient: Navigating Scholarly Knowledge
    from Notebooks to Books   381

    Concluding Word   417

Index   423

ILLUSTRATIONS

1. Salvator Rosa, *The Lie*   55

2. Attributed to Ary de Vois, *Portrait of Adrian Beverland*   70

3. Copy of a painting attributed to Jacob Huysmans, *Portrait of the Earl of Rochester*   72

4. *Portrait of Theodor Ludwig Lau*   74

5. Lau, *Portrait*, detail: "Haec mysteria"   76

6. Lau, *Portrait*, detail: "Rationis & Revelationis Objecta"   87

7. Lau, *Portrait*, detail: "Sunt mihi curae, utraque Salus"   88

8. Lau, *Portrait*, detail: "Vobis, Tales Eos Facere Monstro"   89

9. Lau, *Portrait*, detail: "Tondereque docui non deglubere"   91

10. Wilhelm Schröder, *Fürstliche Schatz- und Rentkammer* (Königsberg and Leipzig, 1752), frontispiece   92

11. Lau, *Portrait*, detail: "Aerem feriunt Cornua vestra"   93

12. Lau, *Portrait*, detail: "Pro re nata, sum usus utroque"   94

13. Michael Moscherosch, *Philander von Sittewald*, part II (Strasbourg, 1650), frontispiece   95

14. Lau, *Portrait*, detail, "Palingenesia"   96

15. Peter Friedrich Arpe, marginal additions to his *Apologia pro Vanino*   114

16. Friedrich Wilhelm Stosch, marginal additions to his *Concordia rationis et fidei*   133

17. Satirical stove, Stift Mattsee   140

18. Heubel's list   152

19. *La vie de Spinosa*, "Hambourg," 1735   155

20. Marcolino's printer's emblem   172

21. Pietro della Vecchia, *Allegory*, Accademia Carrara, Bergamo   174

22. Pietro della Vecchia, *Allegory*, Vicenza, Museo Civico   177

23. Abraxas gem   178

24. "Sapiens supra Fortunam"   180

25. Pietro della Vecchia, grotesque of the sense of hearing   182

26. Francesco Ruschi, title engraving for Giovan Francesco
    Loredano, *Dianea*   183

27. Successor of Frans Floris, *Truth Protected by Time*   184

28. Pietro della Vecchia, *The Kingdom of Love*   186

29. Pietro della Vecchia, *Socrates and Two Pupils*   187

30. Achille Bocchi, *Symbolicae quaestiones*   188

31. Pietro della Vecchia, *Ius in Armis*   196

32. Harpocrates images   207

33. Political Harpocrates   209

34. Jan Müller, *Harpocrates*   210

35. Hermann von der Hardt, *Justitia* and *Silentium*   213

36. Hermann von der Hardt, *Harpocrates*   215

37. Hermann von der Hardt, *Aenigmata prisci orbis*   215

38. "Veritas premitur non opprimitur"   221

39. Medal of the Alethophiles   228

40. Florentius Schoonhovius, *Emblemata partim moralia,
    partim etiam civilia*   234

41. Pietro della Vecchia, *Portrait of a Young Man*   248

42. Johann Baptist Großschedel, detail from *Calendarium naturale
    magicum perpetuum profundissimam rerum secretissimarum
    contemplationem totiusque philosophiae cognitionem complectens*   251

43. Dice, detail from della Vecchia, *Portrait of a Young Man*   265

44. Pietro della Vecchia: *Mathematics Lesson*   269

45. Double portrait of father and son van Helmont in Johann
    Baptist van Helmont, *Ortus Medicinae*   277

46. Postal route to the northwest of Leipzig   319

47. Certificate from the Brunswick postal authorities from 1751   321

48. Natalitio Benedetti, drawing of a gnostic Mercury   340

49. Valentin Ernst Löscher (praes.)/Johann Sigismund Koblig
(resp. et auctor), *Disquisitio antiquaria de talismanibus*   348

50. Hermann von der Hardt to Zacharias Nolte concerning
magical coins   350

51. Peter Friedrich Arpe, *De prodigiosis naturae et artis operibus
Talismanes et Amuleta dictis*   351

52. Ottavio Falconieri, *De nummo Apamensi Deucalionei diluvii
typum exhibente dissertatio*   359

53. Charles-César Baudelot, *L'utilité des voyages*   363

54. Relief of Lamia of Athens, Charles-César Baudelot, *Histoire de
Ptolemée Auletes*   365

55. Silver tetradrachm of Demetrios Poliorketes, ca. 290/289 BCE   366

56. Claude Petit, *De amazionibus dissertatio*   368

57. Andreas Morell, letter, Forschungsbibliothek Gotha   374

58. Johann Christoph Wolf's private copy of Johannes Leusden,
Onomasticum sacrum   383

59. Johann Christoph Wolf's private copy of Georg Matthias
König, *Bibliotheca vetus et nova*   390

60. Johann Christoph Wolf, *Oracula Sibyllina*   395

61. *Oracula Sibyllina*, detail: "Habet Cl. Arpius"   402

62. Pieter Claesz, *Vanitas Still Life*   418

63. Jan Davidszoon de Heem, *Still Life with Books*   419

PREFACE

THE INTELLECTUAL history of modern Europe, its history of knowledge, needs to be corrected. First, we need case histories that do not just emphasize the well-known intellectual giants and dominant trends but deploy current theoretical insights to examine hitherto unknown materials. But second, we have already celebrated sufficiently the growth, organization, and diffusion of new information and knowledge. It is high time to recognize the vulnerability and loss of knowledge, the uncertain and endangered states of some bodies of knowledge and theory, the precarious condition of those who transmitted these bodies, their reactions to danger and loss, and the risk involved in disseminating heresy. All this needs to be reclaimed and added to our understanding of the history of knowledge. This material is rich enough to show how much philosophy and the history of philosophy can benefit from welcoming the cultural sciences, including especially the "material turn" and the "iconic turn" in the history of communication and information.

The case studies brought together in this volume emerged during the years 2005–12 in Princeton, Munich, Rutgers, and Erfurt/Gotha. They share a concern for tracing an "alternative" intellectual history that steps off the well-trodden paths and offer a different narrative, one that emanates from the situation of those I am calling the intellectual precariat (*Wissensprekariat*). In many respects this book continues my earlier studies, *Enlightenment Underground* (German 2002, English 2015) and *Die unanständige Gelehrtenrepublik* (2007), but there are new themes, too, especially in the exploitation of pictorial evidence and manuscripts, as well as a sharper attention to gestures and attitudes.

I wish to thank Eva Gilmer for her intensive editorial work as well as Asaph Ben-Tov, Michael Multhammer, Kristina Petri, and Stefanie Kießling for their help with the final version of the manuscript.

This book is dedicated to Carlo Ginzburg, a friend who more than anyone else is for me a model of how to go beyond pure historical research to combine contemporary ways of thinking with underground history.

KNOWLEDGE LOST

Introduction

The Loss of Knowledge

We seem to be sure of what we know. But that is deceptive. Knowledge can be endangered. Information can also suddenly go missing. Everyone knows from experience the bitter loss of a data file—or the discovery that a valued text has been erased or even that one's hard disk has crashed, eliminating in a flash the whole content of one's personal computer. What happens then? Thoughts that seemed stable or perhaps even beautiful and well formulated have suddenly lost their vehicle and do not exist anymore. They no longer exist if they can no longer be remembered or reconstructed. It is painful to see the contrast between the timelessness that propositions claim to have and our inability to recover these propositions in all the order or complexity they once had.

Something similar happens when a species of plants or animals goes extinct. Here again the genetic code is bound up with its physical carrier, and if the carrier can no longer reproduce, a sort of "knowledge" in nature is lost—a complex that stored experiences of survival, of accommodation, and of further evolutionary developments.

Like the genetic code of rare tigers, of whom only a few survive, manuscripts and printed books can contain insights that can disappear with their vehicle. When the antitrinitarian Michael Servetus was burned to death at the urging of Calvin in Geneva, all available copies of his work were burned as well. Only three copies of *Christianismi restitutio* escaped destruction, but then a feeble stream of transmission developed, a new life, but at first only in manuscript, until these copies provided the basis for a new printed edition in the eighteenth century.[1] Far different was the case of Kazimierz Lyszcynski, who was executed in 1689—one of the many whose works were so successfully exterminated that literally nothing of his thinking survives.[2]

What does this kind of scarcity and endangeredness mean for our concept of knowledge? When we speak of "knowledge"—especially in composite terms like "cultures of knowledge," the history of knowledge, or knowledge management—it becomes essential to clarify whether we are speaking of knowledge in a broad or narrow sense. In the narrow, epistemological meaning, knowledge should no longer be simply identified with Plato's idea of true and justified opinion. Recent discussions suggest further conditions that may be internalist, externalist, or limited in some other way.[3] But this purely epistemological concept of knowledge is too strict for many problems that depend on context, like those treated in this book. So I will be using a broader idea of knowledge, one that depends more on the subjective side and means essentially "reasonable convictions or beliefs." It presents more complex, theoretical deliberations than the smaller units of knowledge that we call information.[4] Thus knowledge is the "dinner" prepared from the raw ingredients of

1. See Jerome Friedman, *Michael Servetus: A Case Study in Total Heresy* (Geneva, 1978); Jean Jacquot, "L'Affaire de Servet dans les controverses sur la tolérance au temps de la Révocation de l'Édit de Nantes," in *Autour de Michel Servet et de Sébastien Castellion*, ed. Bruno Becker (Haarlem, 1953), 116–29; for a popular treatment, see Lawrence Goldstone and Nancy Goldstone, *Out of the Flames: The Remarkable Story of a Fearless Scholar, a Fatal Heresy, and One of the Rarest Books in the World* (New York, 2002).

2. Only a few fragments of his treatise *De non existentia Dei* are known from court records. Cf. Andrzej Nowicki, "Pięć fragmentów z dzieła De non existentia dei Kazimierza Łyszczyńskiego" (from the document held in the library of Kórnik No. 443), *Euhemer* 1 (1957): 72–81; idem, "Studia nad Łyszczyńskim," *Euhemer, Zeszyty Filozoficzne* 4 (1963): 22–83.

3. For an introduction, see Matthias Steup and Ernest Sosa, eds., *Contemporary Debates in Epistemology* (Oxford, 2004); Timothy Williamson, *Knowledge and Its Limits* (Oxford, 2000); Gerhard Ernst, *Das Problem des Wissens* (Paderborn, 2002). The problem of the loss of knowledge has also been treated by Peter Burke, *A Social History of Knowledge*, vol. 2: *From the Encyclopédie to Wikipedia* (Cambridge, 2012), 139–59. Robert N. Proctor and Londa Schiebinger have suggested a whole new discipline, dedicated specifically to not knowing; see idem, eds., *Agnotology: The Making and Unmaking of Ignorance* (Palo Alto, 2008). But they are concerned less with the loss of knowledge than with the problem of dealing with unknown facts and with the suppression of expert knowledge.

4. On the concept of information, see Arndt Brendecke, Markus Friedrich, and Susanne Friedrich, eds., *Information in der Frühen Neuzeit, Status, Bestände, Strategien* (Berlin, 2008).

information: it is organized information soaked in the context of experience and is therefore connected to many other sorts of information and not at all isolated.[5] Naturally, information and "small facts" come with their own load of theory, but it would make little sense to go into such detailed problems at this point. But it is clear that the "knowledge" of actors is similar to the notion of meaning as understood by Max Weber and Alfred Schutz: as an orientation to action.[6] Because meaning is mainly derived from society, that is, adopted, stored, and classified by others, knowledge can be understood as meaning that has become social. One can also speak of subjective bodies of knowledge and reflect on its relations with knowledge that is both institutionalized and socialized. In this way knowledge no longer has to be true because even "false" knowledge and erroneous theories can motivate and guide action.

Regardless of all that, even the masses of data and information that are transmuted into knowledge can disappear if their vehicle disappears. As the Renaissance philosopher Charles Bovelles wrote, the world contains a maximum of substantiality but a minimum of knowledge.[7] And he added that man has a maximum of knowledge but a minimum of substance. It would be hard to imagine a better image to express the fragility of human knowledge. The material basis is thin—it could hardly be thinner. If an individual person disappears, so does his world.

Would that be thinking of knowledge in terms that are too individualistic? If knowledge is socially transmitted meaning, then isn't it more the group, the institution, society itself that should be regarded as the medium or bearer of knowledge rather than the individual person? Isn't knowledge stored securely in the common language and culture and therefore immune to the dangers of losses in individual embodiments?[8] Even if single libraries burn down, societies can surely preserve the fundamentals of their knowledge. Yes, but this insight does not apply to "smaller," counterintuitive, specialized, or revolutionary

---

5. Cf. Peter Burke, *Papier und Marktgeschrei: Die Geburt der Wissensgesellschaft* (Berlin, 2001), 20; idem, *The Social History of Knowledge: From Gutenberg to Diderot* (Cambridge, 2000).

6. Cf. Hubert Knoblauch, "Was ist Wissen?" in idem, *Wissenssoziologie*, 2nd ed. (Constance, 2010), 359–66 (afterword).

7. Charles Bovelles, *De sapiente* (Paris, 1510), fol. XIX: "Mundus maxima substantia, scientia nullus. Homo scientia amplissimus, substantia pusillus. Uterque stat in utroque; uterque utriusque capax." Cf. Martin Mulsow, "Wissen III," in *Historisches Wörterbuch der Philosophie*, vol. 12 (Basel, 2004), cols. 876–80.

8. Cf. Ernest Gellner, *Language and Solitude: Wittgenstein, Malinowski and the Habsburg Dilemma* (Cambridge, 1998); Alvin I. Goldman, *Knowledge in a Social World* (Oxford, 1999).

units of knowledge, which are rare and may possibly not even exist in printed or in any other "communal" form.

Perhaps our experience of computer crashes has sensitized us to the loss of knowledge, but no one has yet drawn out all the consequences. We have not yet realized that the "material turn" in intellectual history highlights not just the means of storing information but also the ways in which knowledge can be endangered. That means that wonder cabinets and exotic objects are relevant to our topic, but so are charred paper and faded ink. When is knowledge itself endangered? Who threatens it? What is the difference between the loss of knowledge in a person and the loss of a text? How do we react to the loss of knowledge? These are the questions taken up in this book. According to an ancient tradition, the descendants of Seth (the third son of Adam and Eve) inscribed all knowledge onto two pillars that would withstand destruction from a global fire or flood. Similarly, the Pioneer 10 spacecraft launched in 1972 carries a special plaque with a pictorial message intended to be read by extraterrestrial aliens, conveying crucial information about the earth and human beings. These fantasies from ancient to modern times appear to represent or encapsulate the entirety of human knowledge.[9] But early modern times handled such questions in a more granular manner; preserving knowledge was often just a practical problem. How could one guarantee that a secret message, a letter, or a package actually reached its intended recipient? How could a certain message get past the censors to a potential reader? How could one make sure that the police did not confiscate and destroy the whole print run of a book?

Precarity

I am subsuming all of these phenomena under the concept of "precarious knowledge." Precarious means unsure, tenuous, awkward, problematic, revocable. These descriptions do not refer mainly to the content of some kinds of knowledge but to their status. Of course it is clear that this status is itself often the result of content that is controversial and objectionable to a powerful elite,

---

9. Cf. Carl Sagan, ed., *Communication with Extraterrestrial Intelligence* (Cambridge, MA, 1975); Douglas A. Vakoch, ed., *Communication with Extraterrestrial Intelligence* (Albany, 2011). On the columns of Seth, see Jan Assmann, "Das gerettete Wissen: Flutkatastrophen und geheime Archive," in *Sintflut und Gedächtnis*, ed. Martin Mulsow and idem (Munich, 2006), 291–301.

but for the time being we'll ignore that fact. Instead, let us note three ways in which knowledge can be precarious: (1) the precarious status of certain media of knowledge; (2) the precarious social status of certain thinkers; and (3) the precarious status of certain forms of expression.

The Precarious Status of Knowledge Transmitters

The medium of knowledge is precarious if it can easily be lost or destroyed. This occurs if texts or images exist only in unique specimens; or if they survive only in a few manuscript copies instead of in printed works; or if a communication exists only orally instead of in writing, and then perhaps without the memory of a group of some firmly established form of transmission,[10] or if it survives only subjectively in the mind of the messenger.

A perfect example can be found in the samizdat literature of Eastern Europe during the Cold War, works that were distributed only as typewritten pages,[11] or in their predecessors, the clandestine underground literature of the seventeenth and eighteenth centuries, when manuscript copies of tracts criticizing religion were "published" (i.e., distributed) in France and many other European countries.[12] All such texts were extremely vulnerable: they were forbidden; the authorities of church and state pursued them; and often they were destroyed once they were confiscated. For example, just three copies survive of *Theophrastus redivivus*, the comprehensive, scholarly, clandestine work from the 1650s, a philosophical text that seems to be the very first explicitly atheistic

10. Cf. Jack Goody, *Literacy in Traditional Societies* (Cambridge, 1975); idem, *The Logic of Writing and the Organization of Society* (Cambridge, 1986).

11. Cf. Wolfgang Eichwede, ed., *Samizdat: Alternative Kultur in Zentral- und Osteuropa: Die 60er bis 80er Jahre* (Bremen, 2000); Friederike Kind-Kovacs, "'Out of the Drawer and into the West': Tamizdat from the Other Europe and Its Reception in the West during Cultural Cold War (1956–1989)" (PhD diss, University of Potsdam, 2008); idem and Jan Behrends, "Vom Untergrund in den Mainstream: Samizdat, Emigrationsliteratur und Tamizdat und die Neuerfindung Mitteleuropas in den achtziger Jahren," *West-Ost-Verständigung im Spannungsfeld von Gesellschaft und Staat seit den 1960er-Jahren: Archiv für Sozialgeschichte* 45 (2005): 427–48.

12. See Gianni Paganini, *Introduzione alle filosofie clandestine* (Bari, 2008); Miguel Benitez, *La face cachée des lumières: Recherches sur les manuscrits philosophiques clandestins de l'âge classique* (Paris, 1996). Winfried Schröder provides a survey of the most important texts in *Ursprünge des Atheismus: Untersuchungen zur Metaphysik- und Religionskritik im 17. und 18. Jahrhundert* (Stuttgart, 1998).

treatise.[13] An accident could easily have annihilated these three. But even texts as harmless as the notes for opera arias were precarious. In the early modern period the notes of a piece were sometimes guarded as the secrets of an orchestra, performed but not printed or distributed in order to preserve an opera ensemble's claims of exclusivity. If an opera company dissolved, all traces of its music usually evaporated.[14] Other forms of exclusive knowledge included alchemical recipes and scientific or technical inventions.[15]

Let us also recall the philosophical "literature" dating back to the origins of literacy, such as the teachings of pre-Socratics like Pythagoras, whose work survives only in fragments assembled by later writers. Other forms of knowledge found in many oral cultures up to just before our time no longer survive because the representatives of those cultures died off.

Precarious Social Status

The social status of persons can also be precarious if they hold certain views that are regarded as offensive, dangerous, or forbidden. These persons may be forced to communicate their ideas secretly either by hiding their identity or at least by hiding their intentions and opinions.[16] Wide dissemination of their views can provoke repression, and they may even be persecuted, so that they jeopardize their careers, their freedom, and even their lives. For them there is no easy way to publicize their ideas institutionally by teaching at universities and instructing students. To be sure, it became easier for such persons to have their works printed during the early modern period, but often only at specific places and by using various defensive measures such as anonymity, concealment of the publisher's name, and the use of clandestine distribution networks.[17] This was and is a high-risk activity.

13. See *Theophrastus redivivus: Edizione prima e critica*, ed. Guido Canziani and Gianni Paganini, 2 vols. (Florence, 1981, 1982).

14. See, in general, Isolde Schmid-Reiter, ed., *L'Europe Baroque: Oper im 17. und 18. Jahrhundert. L'opéra aux XVIIe et XVIIIe siècles* (Regensburg, 2010).

15. William Eamon, *Science and the Secrets of Nature: Books of Secrets in Medieval and Early Modern Culture* (Princeton, 1996); Daniel Jütte, *Das Zeitalter des Geheimnisses: Juden, Christen und die Ökonomie des Geheimen (1400–1800)* (Göttingen, 2011).

16. See generally Perez Zagorin, *Ways of Lying: Dissimulation, Persecution, and Conformity in Early Modern Europe* (Princeton, 1990).

17. Ira O. Wade, *The Clandestine Organization and Diffusion of Philosophic Ideas in France from 1700 to 1750* (Princeton, 1938).

The Precarious Status of Certain Forms of Expression

To avoid persecution, if they did not publish secretly, such persons often discovered highly refined methods of making their views available, at least indirectly, to a wider public without becoming liable or responsible for these opinions; examples include the use of masking, constructing a doubled persona, and "pseudonymization."

Without claiming to speak the truth directly one could also publish precarious knowledge within a framework that disguised it, for example in a literary fiction, or by putting ideas into the mouths of one or several dialogue partners, or by masking them in a joco-serious burlesque that made it difficult to tell if an utterance was to be taken seriously or only as a joke. Was it just an obscure performance within a riddle or an ambiguous reference or perhaps some "abstruse" form of speech, like those expressed in deliberately enigmatic academic "*dubia*"?[18] The intention was always to avoid or obfuscate any clear responsibility of a speaker for any specific statement so that one could always pull back—in case of denunciation, persecution, or legal accusation—and claim that one had not meant anything offensive.

If we are thus speaking of such "problematic" forms of speech, knowledge should be understood in the old sense of Kant's understanding of the problematical as applying to judgments in which the affirmation or denial is accepted as merely possible (ad libitum).[19] A matter may be put forward for discussion, for example, without making any claim of a final resolution, no fixed conclusion within the semantic net. So here there would be no truth or falsehood because it's only the propositional content that is at stake, a content that also tests the semantic net for the implications it would have if it were integrated into the net. But this knowledge is therefore precarious. The French word *précaire*, from which the English word "precarious" is derived, includes the meaning of fluctuating and revocable.[20] The word stems from "precarius," a Roman legal concept that described trading options and property relations that were guaranteed only by personal favor (cf. Latin *prex*,

---

18. Martin Mulsow, *Die unanständige Gelehrtenrepublik: Wissen, Libertinage und Kommunikation in der Frühen Neuzeit* (Stuttgart, 2007), 200ff.; Pävi Mehtonen, *Obscure Language, Unclear Literature: Theory and Practice from Quintillian to the Enlightenment* (Helsinki, 2003).

19. Kant, *Critic der reinen Vernunft* (Riga, 1781), A, p. 74; *The Critique of Pure Reason*, trans. J.M.D. Meiklejohn (London, 1855), SS 5, sec. II, para. 4 on "The Modality of Judgments."

20. Translator's note: The same can be said of the German word *prekär*.

precis) and could be revoked whenever the grantor wished.[21] Applied to our context this meant that precarious knowledge was uncertain; it had not been decided whether it was valid or if its claim to truth might have to be taken back, perhaps for internal reasons but perhaps because some powerful authority decided so. For example the Roman Inquisition could place certain books on the Index of Prohibited Books, or the imperial *Hofrat* (i.e., Aulic Court) might condemn a book and declare to the whole empire that its author should be prosecuted.[22]

The early modern history of these sorts of "problematic" matters encompasses a multitude of genres and expressive strategies that made possible a state of uncertainty; one of the most common was the joco-serious forms of half-joking speech.[23] When people began to consider that perhaps the philosophy of Epicurus might actually possess a certain truth, writers cautiously suggested so in comic jest books.[24] When Copernicus published his revolutionary idea of a heliocentric cosmos, Andreas Osiander famously declared that it was only a mathematical hypothesis that occupied a problematic status beyond any claims of being empirically true or false.[25]

The Precariat of Knowledge

These various forms of precarious status can be said to produce an "intellectual precariat." The neologism "precariat" is an amalgam of "precarious" and "proletariat" used by modern sociologists to indicate that increasingly insecure forms of working and living have led to a sort of lower class, but not one that

21. Karl Ernst Georges, *Ausführliches lateinisch-deutsches Handwörterbuch*, 8th ed. (Hanover, 1918; reprint, Darmstadt, 1998), vol. 2, cols. 1908–9.

22. Franz Heinrich Reusch, *Der Index der verbotenen Bücher: Ein Beitrag zur Kirchen und Literaturgeschichte*, 2 vols. (Bonn, 1883–85); Hubert Wolf, *Index: Der Vatikan und die verbotenen Bücher*, 2nd ed. (Munich, 2006).

23. Cf. Martin Mulsow, "Libertinismus in Deutschland? Stile der Subversion im 17. Jahrhundert zwischen Politik, Religion und Literatur," *Zeitschrift für historische Forschung* 31 (2004): 37–71.

24. André Arnauld, "Apologia Epicuri," in idem, *Joci* (Avignon, 1605).

25. Bruce Wrightsman, "Andreas Osiander's Contribution to the Copernican Achievement," in *The Copernican Achievement*, ed. Robert S. Westman (Berkeley, 1975), 214–43; Lutz Danneberg, "Schleiermacher und das Ende des Akkommodationsgedankens in der hermeneutica sacra des 17. und 18. Jahrhunderts," in *200 Jahre "Reden über die Religion,"* ed. Ulrich Barth et al. (Berlin, 2000), 194–246, here at 209ff.

was confined to just one level or economic class; rather it can apply to all sorts of people, even including the traditionally elevated levels of the highly educated.[26] This amounts to a transformation of our understanding of social stratification by using the new criterion of income security. If we extend this understanding to the cultures of knowledge, we can speak of an "intellectual precariat." But we must also pay attention to the durable forms of knowledge transmitted by those who habitually use clandestine practices, camouflage their forms of expression, and partially even conceal their own identity. This precariat extended, as we will see, up into the "higher" layers of academic scholarship. Their opposites could then be called something like the "intellectual bourgeoisie," signifying those bearers of culture who can rely on secure institutions, open publications, and academic discipleship that provide space for acceptance of their pronouncements so that they need not resort to dissimulation. But we should not describe this intellectual bourgeoisie (actually we should be calling it the "knowledge securiat") as a social class with any clearer borders than those of the precariat; they were both amorphous.

Taking this view of things transforms our conventional intellectual history, which usually focuses on radical, moderate, and orthodox streams of thought.[27] Our new approach concentrates not on the classification of ideas but on the status of the carriers of knowledge, and specifically on whether that status was

26. Cf. Robert Castel, *Les métamorphoses de la question sociale, une chronique du salariat* (Paris, 1995) (English translation by Richard Boyd, *From Manual Workers to Wage Laborers: Transformation of the Social Question* [New Brunswick, 2002]); Évelyne Perrin, *Chômeurs et précaires au cœur de la question sociale* (Paris, 2004); Robert Castel, *Prekarität, Abstieg, Ausgrenzung: Die soziale Frage am Beginn des 21. Jahrhunderts,* ed. Klaus Dörre (Frankfurt, 2009); Heinz Bude and Andreas Willisch, eds., *Exklusion: Die Debatte über die "Überflüssigen"* (Frankfurt, 2007); idem, eds., *Das Problem der Exklusion: Ausgegrenzte, Entbehrliche, Überflüssige* (Hamburg, 2006); Heinz Bude, *Die Ausgeschlossenen: Das Ende vom Traum einer gerechten Gesellschaft* (Munich, 2008); Claudio Altenhain et al., eds., *Von "neuer Unterschicht" und Prekariat: Gesellschaftliche Verhältnisse und Kategorien im Umbruch* (Bielefeld, 2008); Alessandro Pelizzari, *Dynamiken der Prekarisierung: Atypische Erwerbsverhältnisse und milieuspezifische Unsicherheitsbewältigung* (Constance, 2009).

27. Cf., e.g., Margaret C. Jacob, *The Radical Enlightenment: Pantheists, Freemasons and Republicans* (London, 1981); Jonathan Israel, *Radical Enlightenment: Philosophy and the Making of Modernity, 1650–1750* (Oxford, 2001); idem, *Enlightenment Contested: Philosophy, Modernity, and the Emancipation of Man, 1670–1752* (Oxford, 2006); idem, *Democratic Enlightenment: Philosophy, Revolution, and Human Rights, 1750–1790* (Oxford, 2011). For further discussion, see Catherine Secretan et al., eds., *Qu'est-ce que les lumières radicales? Libertinage, athéisme et spinozisme dans le tournant philosophique de l'âge classique* (Amsterdam, 2007).

secure and by what means it was secure. Such security was usually the result of the social acceptance of the ideas of these carriers, who could therefore depend on professorships and on firm bonds of patronage that produced groups of disciples and students and the certainty that their writings would be printed and published. Yet that was not always the case. Occasionally radicals too might—at least for a time—develop their ideas under the protection of a prince's patronage (as in the case of the rationalist biblical translator Johann Lorenz Schmidt at the court of Countess von Löwenstein-Wertheim-Virneburg),[28] but moderate thinkers could also fall into precarious circumstances. Often the border between the precariat and the bourgeoisie ran straight through one person, for example, when a theoretician had to divide his works, as Isaac Newton clearly did, between those in physics that he published and those on alchemical or religious-historical topics that remained unpublished.[29] Another example might be Hermann Samuel Reimarus, who acted on the surface like a distinguished Hamburg professor, who published many philosophical works, but who also had one foot in the precariat because he secretly wrote his *Apologie*, an attack on ideas of Christian revelation.[30] Initially we should regard the intellectual precariat and the intellectual bourgeoisie as just a group of persons; but it is also sensible to think in terms of Bruno Latour's notion of "ensembles" of persons, manuscripts, and pictures; they are all "carriers of knowledge" in a neutral sense that points to its pure potential for updating knowledge.[31]

The trichotomy describing a radical, a moderate, and an orthodox Enlightenment sets things up differently, because concentrating on precarity does not

28. Ursula Goldenbaum, *Appell an das Publikum: Die öffentliche Debatte in der deutschen Aufklärung 1687–1796* (Berlin, 2004).

29. Cf. B.J.T. Dobbs, *The Foundations of Newton's Alchemy* (Cambridge, 1983); James E. Force and Richard H. Popkin, eds., *Newton and Religion: Context, Nature and Influence* (Dordrecht, 1999); Richard S. Westfall, *Never at Rest: A Biography of Isaac Newton* (Cambridge, 1983).

30. Hermann Samuel Reimarus, *Apologie oder Schutzschrift für die vernünftigen Verehrer Gottes*, 2 vols., ed. Gerhard Alexander (Frankfurt, 1972). Cf. Dietrich Klein, *Hermann Samuel Reimarus (1694–1768): Das theologische Werk* (Tübingen, 2009); Martin Mulsow, ed., *Between Philology and Radical Enlightenment: Hermann Samuel Reimarus (1694–1768)* (Leiden, 2011).

31. I refer, e.g., to Bruno Latour, "The Berlin Key, or How to Do Words with Things," in *Matter, Materiality and Modern Culture*, ed. P. M. Graves-Brown (London, 1991), 10–21; idem, *Reassembling the Social: An Introduction to Actor-Network Theory* (Oxford, 2007). But one could also think of Foucault's broad concept of discourse and *dispositif*. Michel Foucault, *The Archaeology of Knowledge*, trans. Alan Sheridan (New York, 1972); idem, *The Order of Things*, trans. Alan Sheridan (New York, 1973).

allow for any clearly defined exclusions; instead we must distinguish zones of weaker integration[32] with divided knowledge and divided convictions from zones of stronger integration, in which radicalization resulted in the "casualization" of knowledge (*Wissensprekarisierung*). Chapter 3 will show that this transformation is helpful for understanding cases like that of the "freethinker" Theodor Ludwig Lau, who was able to integrate his ideas as a cameralist into the debates of his social circle, but his thinking as a philosopher could not be so easily integrated.

Knowledge in Niches

If we seriously apply Gregory Bateson's metaphor describing an "ecology of the intellect" to intellectual history, we can think fruitfully about protecting "endangered species" of knowledge.[33] In contrast to the ideas of the evolution of ideas[34] based on normal cases, we will be examining borderline cases of catastrophes and near catastrophes in which knowledge goes extinct or nearly does so. Only then do all the niches come into view, ranging from persecuted freethinkers, to women, to innovative scholars; then we can protect their insights and see how they spread despite their being endangered.[35] It might concern a Spinoza, who entrusted the manuscript of his *Ethics* to his closest friends, asking them to publish it after his death,[36] or perhaps a Reimarus, who left his *Apologie* to certain trusted members of his family, as we'll see more clearly in chapter 10. In each case we need to reconstruct the exact historical circumstances that made the construction of such niches necessary. Publishing and not publishing (or posthumous publishing) are speech acts; they were

---

32. Borrowing from Castel, *Prekarität, Abstieg, Ausgrenzung*, ed. Dörre, 15.

33. Gregory Bateson, *Steps to an Ecology of Mind* (Chicago, 1972). Markus Völkel has urged the adoption of Bateson's concept for intellectual history: "Historiker oder Narr: Das Lächerliche in Theorie und Praxis frühneuzeitlicher Geschichtsschreibung (16. und 17. Jahrhundert)," *Zeitschrift für historische Forschung* 21, no. 4 (1994): 483–511.

34. Niklas Luhmann, *Ideenevolution* (Frankfurt, 2008).

35. Mulsow, *Die unanständige Gelehrtenrepublik*.

36. Koenraad O. Meinsma, *Spinoza et son cercle* (1895 [Dutch]; Paris, 1984). Cf. Leen Spruit and Pina Totaro, *The Vatican Manuscript of Spinoza's "Ethica"* (Leiden, 2011). Generally, Manfred Walther and Michael Czelisnski, eds., *Die Lebensgeschichte Spinozas: Zweite, stark erweiterte und vollständig neu kommentierte Auflage der Ausgabe von Jakob Freundenthal 1899* [with a bibliography] (Stuttgart, 2006).

ways of acting; and we have to discover the intentions that made it one way and not another.[37]

Niches were not just a means for the concealment of manuscripts; they could also be institutional or textual. The so-called Averroists at the University of Paris in the thirteenth century were trying to carve out an institutional niche for philosophy by separating philosophical from theological truth by faculties (or departments, as we might call them).[38] Religious dissidents in the sixteenth century and the philosophical libertines of the seventeenth used equivocation about categories in order to make themselves invulnerable to the assaults of their critics, or they constructed strategies similar to those of their spiritual forefathers among the medieval Jews and Muslims, ways of saying things between the lines that were different from the surface of the text.[39]

In such niches knowledge was rare almost by definition. It was elite knowledge, not in the sense that only an upper class had access to it but because only a limited, initiated circle could acquire it. It possessed a different logic from knowledge that flourished in unendangered circumstances and hotly contested situations, knowledge that was part of the mainstream of the Great Tradition. The fundamental differentiation of knowledge according to who carried and transmitted it was well known. The humanist Mario Nizolio, who was writing in the wake of Lorenzo Valla and centuries before Ludwig Wittgenstein, unmasked the language traps of professional philosophers—whom he labeled "pseudophilosophers." In 1553 he distinguished the artificial way of knowing (*idios*) among philosophers who did not use any language from the way of knowing embodied in the common language (*koinos*) of normal people and from the specially elaborated language (*kyrios*) of the spiritual elite. He described the elite as those who "understand one or more things that are

---

37. Cf. Quentin Skinner, "Meaning and Understanding in the History of Ideas," *History and Theory* 8 (1969): 3–53.

38. Cf. chapter 2, where the literature is listed.

39. Cf. Laurent Jaffro et al., eds., *Leo Strauss: Art d'écrire, politique, philosophie* (Paris, 2001); Jean-Pierre Cavaillé, *Dis/simulations: Jules César Vanini, François La Mothe Le Vayer, Gabriel Naudé, Louis Machon et Torquato Accetto; religion, morale et politique au XVIIe siècle* (Paris, 2002). Moshe Halbertal, *Concealment and Revelation: Esotericism in Jewish Thought and Its Philosophical Implications* (Princeton, 2007). See also the clear critique of Strauss's views by scholar of Islam Dimitri Gutas, "The Study of Arabic Philosophy in the Twentieth Century: An Essay on the Historiography of Arabic Philosophy," *British Journal of Middle Eastern Studies* 29 (2002): 5–25.

worth knowing, are hard to know, and are unknown by the common people."[40] This is the way in which Averroes distinguished between common and uncommon knowledge when he claimed that philosophers could digest more knowledge and truth than simple people could. And for that reason it was legitimate to withhold certain truths from the people: they should not be given a stomachache.[41]

But withholding certain kinds of knowledge from certain groups is not a real sign of its precarious status. Rather, it could also be a sign of privileged information controlled by the authorities, such as the church or the state—the Arcana *imperii*.[42] Only if a piece of knowledge was regarded as "hot" information, that is, an item that (in contrast to "cold" or preserved dogmas) was totally open for further internal development, was it really true that it might need the sort of robust intellectual "digestion" in the sense that Averroes was speaking of; only then could it be integrated into expanding knowledge that might go in unexpected or even undesirable directions. Below we will develop the concept of "inferential explosiveness" to describe the quality found in "hot" information. If one desired to carve out a protective niche for such knowledge, one might have to confront the paradox that one was trying to confine something whose content could not be limited, except at best formally or temporarily. This could be achieved with language, using Latin that the common people could not read,[43] or institutionally by confining specific knowledge to the philosophical faculty. And yet conflict was unavoidable, and the barriers of language and institutions could all too easily be ruptured, especially when they were attacked by fanatics or zealots for the truth. Sincerity, which along with accuracy is one of the two cardinal virtues of truth as identified by Bernard Williams, frequently rejects any communicative barriers.[44]

One curious niche for knowledge is the footnote.[45] In these underground vaults of scholarship one finds not only the "choicest bottles," as Robert

40. Mario Nizolio, *De veris principiis et vera ratione philosophandi* (Parma, 1553), III,1,1 (German translation: *Vier Bücher über die wahren Prinzipien und die wahre philosophische Methode, gegen die Pseudophilosophen* [Munich, 1980]).

41. Averroes, *Kommentar zum 3. Buch der aristotelischen Physik*; cf. chapter 2.

42. Andreas Gestrich, *Absolutismus und Öffentlichkeit: Politische Kommunikation in Deutschland zu Beginn des 18. Jahrhunderts* (Göttingen, 1994).

43. Françoise Waquet, *Le latin ou l'empire d'un signe, XVIe–XXe siècle* (Paris, 1998).

44. Bernard Williams, *Truth and Truthfulness: An Essay in Genealogy* (Princeton, 2002).

45. On the footnote, see Anthony Grafton, *The Footnote: A Curious History* (Cambridge, MA, 1999).

Minder once said, but also the hidden contraband that one hoped to preserve safe from the prying eyes of hasty inspectors. Jacob Soll has shown that Amelot de Houssayes used his annotations and footnotes to ancient historians such as Tacitus or political theorists such as Machiavelli to express a sort of critical thinking that was a seventeenth-century forerunner of the Enlightenment. This critical thinking did not develop on the periphery of power but at its very center, in Paris. That was possible only because the indirect forms of commentary and annotation permitted certain liberties that would not have survived in the main text.[46] Footnotes provided a space in which one could experiment with explosive ideas or import impudence and hijinks because they did not attract as much close attention as the main text. So we find here a precarious knowledge that literally submerged sensitive material in the "preconscious" level at the foot of the page.

This is even truer in the case of handwritten marginalia, which constitute quasi-private footnotes or intimate messages offered to those who might borrow an annotated copy for private reading. John Toland communicated in this manner with his friend Robert Molesworth.[47] Thus the privacy or "domesticity"[48] of marginalia can provide a key to this sort of preconscious. So we can suggest that the materiality and uniqueness of handwritten comments offer insights into the emotional side of scholarship, the history of fascination with the exotic, the problematic, and the highly controversial.

Risky Transfers

The precarious status of knowledge had obvious consequences for communication. Every transfer can run a risk, both for the transmitter and for the recipient. Frequently just being found in possession of forbidden writings such as *De tribus impostoribus* or the *De vindiciis contra tyrannos* could lead to draconian punishments. Simply transmitting a report could be risky. Just as the claims of knowledge to possess a sort of universal truth were no guarantee that it would survive materially, so it was no guarantee that it could be transferred

46. Jacob Soll, *Publishing the Prince: History, Reading, and the Birth of Political Criticism* (Ann Arbor, 2005).

47. Justin Champion, *Republican Learning: John Toland and the Crisis of Christian Culture, 1696–1722* (Manchester, 2003).

48. Michael McKeon, *The Secret History of Domesticity: Public, Private, and the Division of Knowledge* (Baltimore, 2005).

successfully from one insider to another. Naturally and in general the history of communication in the early modern period was a history of success. With the invention of printing came standardization, comparability, and objectivity, as well as toleration and public opinion.[49] We learned that long ago. But a little skepticism is in order, and certain distinctions need to be made. The print media according to Adrian Johns did not simply foster uniform standards, as Elizabeth Eisenstein claimed, because it also produced variation and deviation.[50] If we look more closely, the history of communicating knowledge appears much less orderly. Printers used to switch whole passages around between work sessions, pages got lost, and authors rushed to insert a couple of additions at the last minute.

The same thing is true if we divide knowledge into "normal" and "precarious," for it's clear that all the precarious knowledge hidden in niches during the early modern period had to survive a whole series of problematic transfers. Let's recall an example much closer to our times, the samizdat literature of Eastern Europe during the Cold War. It was typed on private typewriters, and mimeographed writings and pamphlets were handed around under the table, "published," in a sense; but such communications were suppressed and authors were sent to the gulag. Every transfer ran huge risks of failure, which could plunge both the sender and the recipient of a message into danger.

These problems in transfer implicitly raise questions about the nature of knowledge. For one thing, the ensemble of practices, convictions, generational experiences, and individual appropriations can be hard to disentangle and can seem merely old-fashioned to a younger generation; certain abilities such as being able to read Latin can wither, and certain cultural practices, such as writing down the fruits of one's reading in special notebooks of "loci communes," can die out. But there are also transfer problems that apply specifically to controversial knowledge: censorship and persecution made secrecy crucial; they promoted clandestine means of distribution or the use of allusions as a means of disguising an author's meaning.[51] Pseudonyms were used, and publishers posted false information about the printer or place of publication; titles were falsified as well. All too often these tactics did no good. Books were confiscated

49. Elizabeth Eisenstein, *The Printing Press as an Agent of Change: Communications and Cultural Transformations in Early Modern Europe* (Cambridge, 1979).

50. Adrian Johns, *The Nature of the Book: Print and Knowledge in the Making* (Chicago, 1998).

51. Martin Mulsow, "Die Transmission verbotenen Wissens," in *Kulturen des Wissens im 18. Jahrhundert*, ed. Ulrich Johannes Schneider (Berlin, 2008), 61–80.

and print runs were destroyed, authors were jailed or even killed. But these techniques could also lead to serious misunderstanding or obscurity. And so the underground scene was itself cloaked in a certain opacity, especially because the actors themselves had difficulties in learning who had really written a book, where they could find a copy, and what certain allusions meant.[52]

Research over the past two decades into cultural transfers has developed a series of concepts that can be usefully applied to the special case involving the transfer of knowledge. Thus we need to distinguish "structures" from "cultures" and the culture of origin from the culture into which something is being translated. Scholars have stressed how much meanings change if knowledge developed in one culture is reconstituted in new national or cultural contexts.[53] Such reconstitutions can lead to gross distortions with regard to precarious knowledge. For example, statements that in one culture may be completely unproblematic can suddenly be explosive in another culture, in a place with a different confession or religion. Thus anti-Christian arguments that circulated unproblematically in manuscript among the seventeenth-century Jews of Amsterdam became ticking time bombs when they came by chance into the hands of intellectuals outside these circles or were printed, as sometimes happened.

The transfer of knowledge is also risky or fragile in the simple sense that packages sometimes just do not arrive. A historical reconstruction of intellectual exchange that is oriented to practices cannot ignore such contingencies. In a case study in this book I will show that a packet of notes on the history of philosophy that went astray (or was perhaps wantonly destroyed by opponents) crucially influenced philosophical historiography in Germany. If one agrees with Bruno Latour in describing the consequences of actions in such a way that things can also be reckoned as agents, then the intellectual history of an epoch should see manuscripts as actors and take censorship regulations and postal routes into account.[54] For the history of precarious information this would mean that endangered species of knowledge move to the very

52. Martin Mulsow, *Enlightenment Underground: Radical Germany, 1680–1720*, trans. H. C. Erik Midelfort (Charlottesville, 2015).

53. Wolfgang Schmale, ed., *Kulturtransfer: Kulturelle Praxis im 16. Jahrhundert* (Vienna, 2003); Michel Espagne and Michael Werner, eds., *Transfers: Les relations interculturelles dans l'espace franco-allemand (XVIIIe–XIXe siècles)* (Paris, 1988).

54. For a critical discussion of this approach, see Georg Kneer, Markus Schroer, and Erhard Schüttpelz, eds., *Bruno Latours Kollektive* (Frankfurt, 2008).

center of our concern, shaping our understanding of functional but especially of dysfunctional communications. Where did the Republic of Letters get stuck? Where were packages pulled out of circulation instead of proceeding on their way?

Tacitness: Intellectual History and Cultural Studies

The discipline of "knowledge management" has adopted Michael Polanyi's notion of tacit knowledge and used it for questions of business management.[55] I have already alluded to the role of tacitness in transfer problems. I think that Polanyi's reasoning can also be deployed to pull various forms of knowledge into the description of the intellectual precariat. We must especially consider whether paratextual, visual, and practical forms of knowledge could be described as tacit. Polanyi understands "tacit knowledge" as knowing *how* something is done, even if the actor does not explicitly indicate (or may not be able to indicate) just what this "knowing how" consists of. This may be because tacit knowledge often consists of habitual automatisms, but also because such knowledge may not be focused and thus may form only the background of one's consciously guided attention.

Both kinds of tacitness can serve to integrate new directions in cultural studies into the history of knowledge. Intellectual history has become to no small degree a cultural history of intellectual practices.[56] The acquisition of certain practices anchors knowledge in human thought and behavior, and in this way tacit sorts of knowledge exercise a real influence. This accords well with one of Michel Foucault's central insights: that these tacit factors (or, as he calls them, discursive formations) shape the content of what we know.

The category of tacit knowledge also opens up the history of knowledge to other suggestions coming from cultural studies. Our use of images, our emotionality and gestures can all be seen as corporeal or unfocused expressions of knowledge, even if they can later become the objects of focus and then explicit topics for discussion. According to Nonaka and Takeuchi the constant alternation between explicitness and tacitness is one of the keys to successful

55. Ikujiro Nonaka and Hirotaka Takeuchi, *The Knowledge Creating Company: How Japanese Companies Create the Dynamics of Innovation* (New York, 1995).

56. Peter Burke, "The Cultural History of Intellectual Practices," in *Political Concepts and Time: New Approaches to Conceptual History*, ed. Javier Fernández Sebastián (Santander, 2011), 103–28.

communication in business. And maybe we need to imagine communication among members of the intellectual precariat in a similar manner: as an alternation between the tacit, personal transmissions in the small circle of trusted confidants and the explicit formulations of written documents that are saturated with allusions, textual gestures, and unspoken practices.

The knowledge tied up in images is also tacit insofar as the (verbal) description of pictures never fully encompasses their meaning. Realizing that precarious knowledge is rare enables us to learn from "visual studies," which has broken down the old barriers of art history. Art historians used to concentrate on a restricted canon of works recognized as "art," but visual studies have turned our scholarly attention to all sorts of visual images from films and news photos to comics, graffiti, and scientific illustrations, without regard to whether they are art.[57] But taking a cue from visual scholars, what happens to "historical textual studies" if they no longer concentrate only on what can be found in books or manuscripts? As the case study in chapter 9 will show, certain philosophical thoughts from texts long considered lost can be reconstructed from paintings that have survived. So here historical visual studies come together with textual studies, because the text can only be conceived as something that was precariously or tacitly embedded in a picture; the picture will not be interpreted as art but as a historical document that was itself integrated with the needs of a learned culture for visual representation.

Pictures from the world of learning are interesting for our study in yet another way. They can display the status of the knower and the endangered status of his or her knowledge. In allegorical form—that is, deliberately obfuscated—they show us that cultures of knowledge are structured by trust or by distrust: trust in small groups of the like-minded, who produce new knowledge; and distrust of the powerful, who do not want to accept this new knowledge, who misunderstand, despise, and threaten it. From this meta-perspective on the conditions set by the world, allegories and gestures speak more loudly than texts. In emblems, portraits, and staged images of actions the double character

57. W.J.T. Mitchell, *Picture Theory: Essays on Verbal and Visual Representation* (Chicago, 1994); Gottfried Boehm, ed., *Was ist ein Bild?* (Munich, 1994); Horst Bredekamp, "Bildwissenschaft," in *Metzler Lexikon Kunstwissenschaft*, ed. Ulrich Pfisterer (Stuttgart, 2003); Hans Belting, *Bild-Anthropologie: Entwürfe für eine Bildwissenschaft* (Munich, 2001); Jörg Probst, Jost Philipp Klenner, and Christian Berndt, eds., *Ideengeschichte der Bildwissenschaft* (Frankfurt, 2009).

of "representation" is vividly present as both an imagined scene and a portrayal of the social world.[58]

The largely unconscious portions of bodies of knowledge and their emotional "colors" make up another tacit aspect of life, shaping the lives of individuals. This tacit dimension reaches deeply into the ambivalences of modern life: fascination, dread, feelings of disgust—all play a role even in the apparently abstract occupations of many a scholar sitting at a desk or the researcher in the laboratory.

We penetrate the layers of tacit knowledge most easily when we can read the manuscript evidence, where a scholar transcribed his reading into notes directly, sometimes with a trembling hand, or recorded his enthusiasm or rejection in the manuscript marginalia written in a book. In such cases we can sense a reader's reactions in all their full cognitive and emotional variety. Knowledge about the East, for example—concerning the language of the Ethiopians, or the legendary Prester John, or the gods of the Syrians—could be both fascinating and controversial. As we will see in chapter 14, such information cast a spell over many an early modern scholar because it promised to disclose an exotic, unknown world, but it was dangerous because of the new perspectives contained in these subjects: from possible political alliances against the Ottoman Empire to insights that could devalue the Christian religion.[59] At the same time it sharply challenged old or habitual scholarly practices because, after all, who could expect to master the Arabic, Syrian, Coptic, and Amharic languages? How could one expect to digest the flood of information that was pouring from these manuscripts? How was it all to be incorporated into the semantic network?

In the early modern period knowledge about magic had an ambivalent force of dramatic proportions. Humanists extracted some of it from Kabbalist treatises or necromantic handbooks and created connections with various ancient philosophies, trying to make sense of the weird diagrams, names of angels, and magical formulas contained in them. As we will see in chapter 12, they were both attracted to and repelled by this material. They began to collect talismans but did not know what to do with these "alien things."[60] Even if they

58. Roger Chartier, *Cultural History: Between Practices and Representations*, trans. Lydia G. Cochrane (Ithaca, 1988).

59. Cf. Wilhelm Braun, *Die Verwandlungen des Mythos vom Reich des Priesterkönigs Johannes* (Klagenfurt, 1999).

60. Michael C. Frank et al., eds., *Fremde Dinge* (= *Zeitschrift für Kulturwissenschaft* 1/2007).

eliminated virtually every trace of this fascination from the learned treatises they finally wrote, it would be a serious mistake to pay attention only to the end product, the published book, because the explicit knowledge exposed there rested on deep layers of tacit knowledge that testified to the quivering or marveling attraction these authors felt toward magic, their unacknowledged experiments and their passionate collecting of magical objects.

Inferential Explosiveness

Up to this point we have left to one side the content of precarious knowledge both in determining what made the status of certain knowledge precarious and in considering the questions that emerge from cultural studies. But it would be a mistake to completely ignore the content because often enough it was the content that determined its precarious status. What were the typical sorts of precarious knowledge?

In the early modern period Enlightenment thinkers often accused the Orthodox elites of "hunting after the supposed consequences" of anything out of the ordinary ("*Konsequenzenmacherei*"), of discovering supposedly atheistic, heretical, or socially dangerous implications in certain authors. And indeed all too often the Orthodox did go too far in their effort to define and defend truth ever more narrowly and ruthlessly. Even so, this hunt for consequences did have a real point: a deviant statement might not have been explosive in itself but an assertion might have upsetting implications for an established body of knowledge.

For that reason it will be important to supplement Polanyi's notion of tacitness with another, entirely different and philosophically much broader meaning of "implicit." Robert Brandom[61] has developed a position that he calls "rationalistic pragmatism" because he understands assertions and convictions pragmatically as social practices of giving or demanding reasons. Broadly speaking for him, asserting something is the tacit knowledge of how something is to be done. There's a connection between practicality in intellectual history and rationalistic pragmatism. The first concentrates on the learned practices that are characteristic for the forms of knowledge: collecting texts, concealing and secretly distributing manuscripts, excerpting books, and smuggling radical notions into the footnotes. The latter, in contrast, concentrates

61. Robert B. Brandom, *Articulating Reasons: An Introduction to Inferentialism* (Cambridge, MA, 2001), 11; idem, *Begründen und Begreifen: Eine Einführung in den Inferentialismus* (Frankfurt, 2001); idem, *Reason in Philosophy: Animating Ideas* (Cambridge, MA, 2009).

on the practices of giving reasons and drawing conclusions—the provision of so-called inferential determinations. "Saying or thinking that things are thus-and-so is undertaking a distinctive kind of inferentially articulated commitment: putting it forward as a fit premise for further inferences, that is, authorizing its use as such a premise, and undertaking responsibility to entitle oneself to that commitment, to vindicate one's authority, under suitable circumstances, paradigmatically by exhibiting it as the conclusion of an inference from other such commitments to which one is or can become entitled."[62]

The concept of assuming responsibility is the decisive one for us. For one can say that some tactics dealing with precarious knowledge consisted specifically in not taking responsibility, in refusing to make oneself explicit. Above all, as chapter 2 will show, certain quasi-juridical constructions were invented in order to avoid having to take responsibility for atheistic statements. Precarious forms of speech were used to utter certain sentences, as we have seen, that could not be clearly attributed to the speaker.

Why should radicals have hesitated to make explicit statements? Well, because then the consequences of their theses would become visible. Thus one can say that precarious knowledge often had a certain inferred explosiveness. Knowledge was tacitly explosive if its integration into the larger body of knowledge would lead to overturning a significant number of established truths within that body.[63] Explosive ideas are like black swans, extremely rare and always unexpected events or facts, which once they appear or are recognized have massive effects.[64] It is therefore awkward to accept such knowledge or such information.

Cognitive scientists speak of "semantic networks" to refer to knowledge that is so organized that the elements of knowledge get stored at certain "knots," to which one can then refer and which are inferentially connected with other knots.[65] The knowledge landscape can be seriously disturbed if central "knots," for instance certain political or theological notions, are occupied differently. To give just one example, Michael Servetus's arguments

62. Brandom, *Articulating Reasons*.

63. Cf. the reflections on Donald Davidson's semantic holism in Mark Bevir, *The Logic of the History of Ideas* (Cambridge, 2002).

64. Nassim Nicholas Taleb, *Der schwarze Schwan: Die Macht höchst unwahrscheinlicher Ereignisse* (Munich, 2010).

65. Allan M. Collins and Ross Quillian, "Retrieval Time from Semantic Memory," *Journal of Verbal Learning and Verbal Behaviour* 8 (1969): 240–47; and more generally, Robert Solso, *Cognitive Psychology*, 6th ed. (Boston, 2001).

against the Christian doctrine of the trinity—such as the factual claim that the New Testament had no passages on which belief in the trinity could be based—were explosive by inference, for if they had been accepted, a key element of Christianity over against the other monotheistic religions would have had to be abandoned; but also the divinity of Jesus Christ would have collapsed and many other consequences would have been necessary as well.

A second example is Isaac La Peyrère's claim in 1655 that there was human life before Adam.[66] At first sight this seems to be only a bizarre and isolated exegetical thesis. But it was deeply embedded in the knowledge cosmos of the seventeenth century, and that meant, for example, that the peoples of the newly discovered American continent could well be the descendants of pre-Adamite people; but then, further, that the whole system of original sin and salvation did not apply to them; and that even before Creation there may have been even older peoples, whose existence demolished the chronology of the Bible. If the biblical chronology of the six thousand years since Creation was no longer valid, however, then a whole series of other assumptions were thrown into question.

Because the arguments of Servetus and those of La Peyrère were hardly weak and could not be dismissed out of hand, they were explosive; and so an attempt was made to isolate these assertions and to pull them out of circulation. Against such attempts were ranged the many sorts of tactics by authors who, despite the dangers, distributed them anyway. Other pieces of knowledge, however, could be explosive even if they were not directly opposed to the currently orthodox views but merely exhibited an erratic character that could not easily be fitted into the existing framework of accepted wisdom. Lorraine Daston has researched the "strange facts" found in Francis Bacon and has drawn the conclusion that just their rarity and oddity made them potentially destructive of the traditional Aristotelian Worldview.[67]

Precarious Elements in the Intellectual Bourgeoisie

In my view it's always important to see the intellectual precariat within the context of the larger intellectual bourgeoisie and thus to resist the temptation of succumbing to the social romanticism that emphasizes only the "outsiders," the "radicals,"

66. Isaac La Peyrère, *Praeadamitae* (Amsterdam, 1655). Cf. Richard H. Popkin, *Isaac La Peyrère (1596–1676): His Life, Work and Influence* (Leiden, 1987).

67. Lorraine Daston and Katherine Park, *Wonders and the Order of Nature, 1150–1750* (Cambridge, MA, 1998), 253–300.

the "freethinkers," and "dissidents."[68] Otherwise we run the risk of regarding iso-lated individuals or small groups, which for very different reasons found them-selves in the wilderness or part of a protest, as somehow constituting a large group and of imagining them as having a homogeneity they did not at all possess. There-fore I'm learning from current sociological research on the precariat but trying to identify small units and areas in which precarious knowledge is dominant, where, in Robert Castel's words, there were deficits of integration or in our case where links to traditional knowledge were deficient.[69] But of course there are also zones within secure cultures of knowledge where precarious elements could create seri-ous wounds. In those cases we may speak of real fragility.

In my view, one of the most important conclusions of my book *Enlighten-ment Underground* is that especially in the late seventeenth century and the early eighteenth, in a decisive period of moving toward modernity,[70] radicalized in-tellectual debates broke out only in the context of debates within established scholarship. Far from trying to establish a separate, independent tradition (e.g., some sort of proto-Marxism), it was mostly the actual dynamics of debates that created space for radical commentary. Methodologically this implies that even early modern scholars with exalted positions, whose scholarly production was "secure," could become enmeshed in zones containing precarious knowledge. We will see that it was mainly implicit factors such as ambivalences and fascina-tions that made the knowledge of established groups so vulnerable. But external circumstances such as foreign travels or just putting certain materials in the post could also expose knowledge or its carrier to a variety of risks.

This book therefore seeks to develop the elements of a theory and practice of precarious knowledge in the early modern period, using examples from entirely different zones of such knowledge. Although certain forms of the in-tellectual precariat can be found in earlier or later periods, I will confine myself here (owing to my limited competence) to the time from the Renaissance to the Enlightenment. Trying to tell the whole history of precarious knowledge in the early modern period would be a hopeless task at this point. So this book works from case studies that are almost always based on distinctive sources. It draws conclusions from these specific sources and does not pretend to offer

---

68. This is the risk encountered in many older Marxist or neo-Marxist works, e.g., Gottfried Stiehler, ed., *Beiträge zur Geschichte des vormarxistischen Materialismus* (Berlin, 1961).

69. Castel, *From Manual Workers to Wage Laborers*, 395.

70. Paul Hazard, *The Crisis of the European Mind: 1680–1715*, trans. J. Lewis May (London, 1953).

universal claims in some abstract space. It intentionally descends into the everyday problems of tacit knowledge, exploring the obscure settings of controversial statements and the key junction points of dysfunctional transfers.

The trick is choosing the right guides who can provide the "index fossils" (to use Hans Blumenberg's image) that can lead us into the hidden layers of intellectual history. For this task the most useful thinkers are second- and third-rate theorists, who until now have never been given much attention, because they can show us the typical intellectual and behavioral models of an age; but they can also guide us into areas that lie off the beaten track of ordinary research. I have located some of these guides in the Italy of the early seventeenth century, especially in the libertine circles of Venice, concentrating especially on the painter Pietro della Vecchia, a little-known imitator of Titian and Giorgione, and one of the few artists who had contacts with libertine intellectuals, as well as travelers to Italy such as Gabriel Naudé, Jacques Gaffarel, Otto Tachenius, and Johann Michael Wansleben. I have found other guides in the Germany of the early Enlightenment, such as Theodor Ludwig Lau, a student of Christian Thomasius, who became so radicalized that his teacher could no longer approve of him; and the jurists of Hamburg and Kiel, Peter Friedrich Arpe and Johann Heinrich Heubel, who both exhibited a sort of sublimated radicalism, as we will see. In addition, certain "index fossils" of the intellectual bourgeoisie will play a leading role in this book: the pastor and Hebrew scholar Johann Christoph Wolf, who was banished for a time and watched the precarious heretics surrounding him with the anxiety of a rabbit staring at a snake; the antiquarian and numismatist Charles-César Baudelot; and the Göttingen literary historian Christoph August Heumann, who had obtained a professorship but had had his own brush with precarity because he had long been excluded from academia owing to a youthful "sin"—having expressed too dangerous an interpretation of the Bible. For members of the intellectual bourgeoisie the books and ideas produced by precarious intellectuals presented disturbingly "strange facts," as I will show in chapter 14: weird and repellent speculations that secure scholars had to know about if they hoped to gauge what was possible in their world.

The "alternative intellectual history of the early modern period" that I present here does not, therefore, treat such major figures as Descartes, Spinoza, Leibniz, Locke, or Hume. It describes forgotten or half-forgotten scholars; and not the great topics of metaphysics and epistemology but fringe areas like magic and numismatics, biblical interpretation and natural law, the history of philosophy and Oriental studies; and not just theories but also the emotions, fears, fascinations, and encouragements. For they too existed and helped shape this alternative history.

PART I

Tactics of the
Intellectual Precariat

SECTION I

The Radical Persona

For some time now intellectual historians have spoken of the "scientific persona."[1] Adopting a concept from Marcel Mauss's essay "A Category of the Human Mind: The Notion of Person; The Notion of Self," these scholars have concentrated on the modern scientific and disciplined self that embodies certain rules, a type of scholar who, shaped by his circumstances, develops him- or herself within the space between the individual and the social institution, forming a connection between them.[2]

In using this notion, however, we need to avoid an ambiguity. "Persona" can also be used in a sociological or legal sense to mean a role or a function. I will take that up in chapter 2, where we will examine several quasi-juridical roles that radicals used to help them express their views. We have to keep this meaning separate from that of the persona as self, which focuses more on the complex disposition of the scientist or scholar, shaped by learned practices, exemplary models, the acceptance of authorities, ideals of behavior, and methods of arguing. Of course, in practice the two meanings of persona sometimes blend into each other. An assumed role can become habitual.

The Australian historians of philosophy Ian Hunter, Stephen Gaukroger, and Conal Condren have been studying the persona of the philosopher. In particular Hunter has reconstructed philosophical personae as an alternative

---

1. See *The Cambridge History of Science*, vol. 3: *Early Modern Science*, ed. Katherine Park and Lorraine Daston (Cambridge, 2006), part 2; and *Science in Context* 16 (March 2003), ed. Lorraine Daston and H. Otto Sibum.

2. Marcel Mauss, "A Category of the Human Mind: The Notion of Person; The Notion of Self," trans. W. D. Halls, in *The Category of the Person: Anthropology, Philosophy, History*, ed. Michael Carrithers, Steven Collins, and Steven Lukes (Cambridge, 1981), 1–25 (original French publication, 1938).

to the concentration by Skinner and Pocock on textual events understood as speech acts.[3] Hunter argues that the Cambridge School's concentration on texts amounts to a severe truncation of historical reality. The rivalry of philosophical schools did not mainly depend on different mutually incomprehensible "paradigms"; instead, they often stemmed from a quite tangible competition between personae, on forms of scholarly reproduction, which were bound up with social and intellectual practices and their embodiments.

Hunter's goal is to eliminate the last remnants of transcendentalism from history, and so it's not accidental that he uses the example of Christian Thomasius and the early Enlightenment in Halle; he can use Thomasius not just methodologically but also topically, because Thomasius replaced the metaphysical speculations of his predecessors with a non-metaphysical conception.

> Thomasius thus drew on Christian doctrines of the damage done to man's faculties at the Fall, together with Epicurean doctrines of the helplessness of human reason in the face of the corporeal passions, in order disqualify knowledge of metaphysical objects and man's supposed capacity for rational self-governance. He also developed a contextualist history of philosophy, drawn in part from his father, Jacob, and in part from Gottfried Arnold's massive history of heresy, which viewed metaphysics and theology as products of the historical corruption of Christian faith by Platonic and Aristotelian philosophy.[4]

In Hunter's view this enabled Thomasius to throw into question the claims to truth made by both metaphysics and theology and to conceive of them rather as just historical phenomena, whose influence in the spheres of law, politics, and bourgeois society one could investigate.

Above all, moral philosophy showed which practices one should use to make up a persona.

> Thomasius also made moral-therapeutic use of his Epicurean *Affektenlehre*, deploying it as an ethical exercise designed to induce skepticism in his law students regarding their capacity for knowledge of transcendent objects,

---

3. Ian Hunter, "The History of Philosophy and the Persona of the Philosopher," *Modern Intellectual History* 4, no. 3 (2007): 571–600; see also Conal Condren, Stephen Gaukroger, and Ian Hunter eds., *The Philosopher in Early Modern Europe: The Nature of a Contested Identity* (Cambridge, 2006).

4. Hunter, "The History of Philosophy and the Persona of the Philosopher," 581; http://www.ched.uq.edu.au/docs/persona2papers/HunterRevised2.pdf, p. 12.

thence requiring them to concentrate on ethical self-restraint and to make the best use of the sensory and historical knowledge of which humans are capable. He thus sought to cultivate a psycho-cognitive attitude that was inimical to metaphysics and theology and receptive to an array of more recent disciplines—public law, political history, Hobbesian-Pufendorfian political philosophy, and the history of theology and philosophy—all with a view to undermining the intellectual infrastructure of the early modern confessional state.[5]

Hunter thus gives an example of how the Halle early Enlightenment consciously constructed a new philosophical persona. Students were given practice with fresh examples and historical views, rehearsed with a new combination of disciplines, and were even given different clothing so that they could behave in a new way and thus become accustomed to a new view of philosophy.

If we apply this proposal to the precarious intellectual cultures of libertine and "radical" authors, it is immediately apparent that their persona was more than just a special case of the philosophical persona. Radicals were never able to establish schools of thought like those of the academics of Halle, who could shape their students' personas. But in intimate settings they adopted suggestions from their predecessors, such as the ideal of the wise man, of the "prud'homme," the "sapiens," who could stand above the opinions of the masses and take the liberty of holding unorthodox views.[6] Chapter 4 uses the example of Peter Friedrich Arpe to show how this sort of ideal persona could blend with a socialized early Enlightenment persona and how an actual antimetaphysical attitude could lead to new interpretations of libertine texts— even if it meant moderating their metaphysically grounded critique of religion. Later in chapter 6 we will take up the way that certain visual artists approached the theme of the ideal "wise man."

One essential element of the persona of the early modern radicals—and one that distinguishes it from the persona of philosophic members of the intellectual bourgeoisie—was that it was especially familiar with tactics, indeed that it was specifically dependent on tactics, as understood by Michel de Certeau's distinction between the strategic options enjoyed by the establishment

5. Ibid., 581–82; online version, p. 13.

6. See Lorenzo Bianchi, "Sapiente e popolo nel Theophrastus redivivus," *Studi storici* 24 (1983): 137–64; Jean Daniel Charron, *The Wisdom of Pierre Charron: An Original and Orthodox Code of Morality* (Chapel Hill, 1960); René Pintard, *Le libertinage érudit dans la première moitié du XVIIe siècle* (Paris, 1943; reprint, Geneva, 1989).

and the opposing tactics of the non-established.[7] Such tactics could, as we'll see in chapter 1, shape the precarious manners of speaking and acting of clandestine authors, and partially shape even their personas as well, when an author maintained a distinction between his various roles, carving out a niche for his assertions (chapter 2). But then a bewildering variety comes into view. For example, with Theodor Ludwig Lau we find a quasi-juridical division of his persona into that of a private Christian and of a public "heathen," which was opposite to the conventional persona that distinguished the clandestine philosophical radical from the public (non-anonymous) cameralist reformer. We will examine this in chapter 3.

Chapter 5 begins a discussion of knowledge transfer but foreshadows what will be discussed more thoroughly in chapters 9–11. This earlier chapter concerns itself with the preservation of information about texts that were destroyed and therefore have not been handed down to today. In these cases the problem of the radical persona was always festering because when intellectuals collected information about burned books, they were engaging in a critical activity, especially if they intended thereby to "save" the radical texts. The "library of burned books" was actually the logical and reflexive project of the intellectual precariat, because its members were only too well aware of the endangered status of forbidden texts; they tried, therefore, to pull precarious knowledge out of its endangered condition and into the light of a broader public.

In saying this, I would not want to go as far as Leo Strauss, who understood the (real) philosopher as a radical, who always stood in opposition to his surrounding society and was therefore always endangered. That would mean that every true philosopher has been committed to a persona of dissimulation.[8] In my opinion that would erase the real situation and make perfectly sensible distinctions difficult. As we know, Strauss's conception opens the door to a "hermeneutic of suspicion," encouraging readers to look between the lines of all philosophical texts to locate a different teaching from what is clearly visible on the surface. But that is an invalid generalization from the rather rare tactics of the libertines.[9]

7. Michel de Certeau, *The Practice of Everyday Life* (Berkeley, 1984), e.g., xix, 36–37.

8. Leo Strauss, *Persecution and the Art of Writing* (Glencoe, IL, 1952).

9. See the critical contributions in Laurent Jaffro, ed., *Leo Strauss: Art d'écrire, politique, philosophie* (Paris, 2001); and Jean-Pierre Cavaillé, "Leo Strauss et l'histoire des textes en régime de persécution," *Revue Philosophique de la France et de l'Etranger* 130 (2005): 39–60.

1

The Clandestine Precariat

Precarious working conditions create a biographical problem for workers who suddenly need to recast and reinterpret their working lives.[1]

—ROBERT CASTEL AND KLAUS DÖRRE

Precarious Life Stories

In May 1719, shortly after the spring book fair in Frankfurt, Theodor Ludwig Lau slit his wrists.[2] He had come to the city because he was once again trying to get a book published. That was risky because ever since 1717 he had been

---

1. Robert Castel and Klaus Dörre, "Einleitung," in *Prekarität, Abstieg, Ausgrenzung*, ed. Dörre, 11–19, at p. 17.

2. This report of his attempted suicide comes from an anonymous pamphlet, *Nachricht von Frankfurth am Mayn vom 30. Maji 1719: Wegen des Autoris der Meditationum De Deo Mundo & Homine* (unpaginated, 4 pp.). There on p. 4: "Da er dann so bald mit Arrest beleget worden: In welcher Gefangenschafft der Teuffel sich seiner dergestalt bemächtiget / daß er verzweifelt / sich mit einer Zange die Adern an beyden Armen mit Gewalt aufgerissen / und hat man ihn kurz hernach halb todt in seinem Blut liegend gefunden: Als er nun durch Hülffe des Artztes wieder in so weit zu recht gebracht worden / daß er zur Sprache gekommen / hat er dem Pfarrherrn Starcken / welcher in christlicher Meynung sich zu ihm begeben / bekennet / wie es ihm von Grund der Seelen leyd seye / daß er durch seine Meditationes der christlichen Religion zuwider / sich in vielen vergangen / und also in grosse Irrthümer gerathen: Darauf hat er das heilige Abendmahl verlanget / so ihm aber noch nicht so augenblicklich hat zugestanden werden wollen." This passage was also included in a manuscript held by the Duke August Library in Wolfenbüttel: Ms. Extrav. 15.1, fols. 172r–173v. On Lau, see Kurt Zielenziger, *Die alten deutschen Kameralisten* (Jena, 1913); Paul Konschel, "Theodor Ludwig Lau, ein Literat der Aufklärungszeit," *Altpreußische Monatsschrift* 55 (1918): 172–92; Hanspeter Marti, "Grenzen der

31

banished from the city for secretly publishing a freethinking work, the *Meditationes philosophicae de Deo, Mundo, Homine* (*Philosophical Meditations on God, the World, and Man*). Using an aphoristic style, he had there cobbled together all the recent radical literature he could find on the market: Spinoza and Vanini, Hobbes and Locke, Beverland and Toland.[3] Lau obviously thought that it was high time to discuss such thoughts even in Germany. In 1717 the book was immediately confiscated. So in 1719 he was trying to up the ante, so to speak, by defending his right to publish freely and to hammer home his ideas once more. That meant that he had to come to Frankfurt again, traveling once more that dangerous road. He was counting on the "liberty of the trade fair," because no one visiting the fair could be prosecuted.[4] So Lau accepted the risk, but he was also arriving as a royal Prussian official. Still, something went wrong. Lau was recognized, the liberty of the trade fair was ignored, and he was arrested and thrown in jail. At that point he took up a pair of pincers that he found, or that someone had neglected to take from him, and set about to slit his wrist arteries.

His was a precarious existence on the political fringes of early modern society, in the age of "political" and "gallant" ideals for behavior in the "early Enlightenment."[5] I intend to recount several similar stories to establish a solid foundation for further questions concerning what I'm calling the "clandestine

---

Denkfreiheit in Dissertationen des frühen 18. Jahrhunderts," in *Die Praktiken der Gelehrsamkeit in der Frühen Neuzeit*, ed. Helmut Zedelmaier and Martin Mulsow (Tübingen, 2001), 295–306; Mulsow, "Libertinismus in Deutschland"; idem, "Theodor Ludwig Lau," *Aufklärung* 17 (2005): 253–55; Erich Donnert, *Theodor Ludwig Lau: Religionsphilosoph und Freidenker der Frühen Neuzeit* (Frankfurt, 2011).

3. Theodor Ludwig Lau, *Meditationes philosophicae de Deo, Mundo, Homine* (n.p., 1717), reprinted in Theodor Ludwig Lau, *Meditationes philosophicae . . . ; Dokumente. Mit einer Einleitung*, ed. Martin Pott (Stuttgart, 1992).

4. Michael Rothmann, *Die Frankfurter Messen im Spätmittelalter* (Stuttgart, 1998); Alexander Dietz, *Frankfurter Handelsgeschichte* (Frankfurt, 1910–25).

5. I have adopted the concept of the "precarious" and of the "precariat" from works in sociology. See the literature cited in the introduction, note 26. The pioneering study of radicals in the German Enlightenment was Winfried Schröder, *Spinoza in der deutschen Frühaufklärung* (Würzburg, 1987); on the "political" and "gallant" characteristics of the age, see Volker Sinemus, *Poetik und Rhetorik im frühmodernen deutschen Staat* (Göttingen, 1978); Gotthard Frühsorge, *Der politische Körper: Zum Begriff des Politischen im 17. Jahrhundert und in den Romanen Christian Weises* (Stuttgart, 1974); Dirk Niefanger, Sylvia Heudecker, and Jörg Wesche, eds., *Kulturelle Orientierung um 1700: Traditionen, Programme, konzeptionelle Vielfalt* (Tübingen, 2004).

precariat." I'll proceed in three steps. First, we need to hear about precarious lives; second about precarious speech; and third about precarious knowledge.

Who were the clandestine precariat? They were intellectuals who secretly wrote and secretly distributed their manuscripts (or left them in their desk drawers) or, if they had them printed, published them anonymously and pseudonymously.[6] The reason for all this secrecy was the content of these writings: extremist political critiques, critiques of religion, contempt for what was generally regarded as moral or decent.[7] The reason for their precarious status lay in the social insecurity that almost automatically followed from their clandestine activities. If these intellectuals were identified as the authors of their texts, they usually began a long and merciless descent into marginality. Lau, who survived his suicide attempt in 1719, attempted to regain his footing socially, trying in Erfurt and then in Königsberg to obtain access to academia, but his reputation as a Spinozist followed him, a term one could read about in works entitled *historia atheismi*.[8] In the end Lau, completely impoverished and psychologically damaged, found asylum in Altona.[9]

Here, however, we will not be mainly concerned with the end of precarious lives but rather with their beginning. But I am far from offering a socially romantic story, which might tell a whig history of how radical Enlightenment philosophers were the heroic forerunners of modernity.[10] Instead we need an adequate description of the precarious status of such so-called radical Enlightenment thinkers, one that does justice not only to their social situation but also to their intellectual situation and their manner of speech and communication. "Precarious" needs to be understood in the full breadth of its various meanings, not just as insecure and unfortunate but also—as accords well with its origins in Roman law—as revocable at any time.[11]

6. See generally Wade, *The Clandestine Organization*.

7. See Martin Mulsow, "Unanständigkeit: Mißachtung und Verteidigung der guten Sitten in der Gelehrtenrepublik der Frühen Neuzeit," in *Die unanständige Gelehrtenrepublik*, 1–26.

8. See Marti, "Grenzen der Denkfreiheit." On the "history of atheism" compendia, see Hans-Martin Barth, *Atheismus und Orthodoxie: Analysen und Modelle christlicher Apologetik im 17. Jahrhundert* (Göttingen, 1971).

9. See chapter 3.

10. See Martin Mulsow, "Mehr Licht: Wie kann die Geschichtsschreibung über die Aufklärung aufklären, ohne an einen unaufhaltsamen Fortschritt zu glauben?" *Neue Zürcher Zeitung*, October 27, 2007.

11. On "precarius" in Roman law, see Jens-Uwe Krause, *Spätantike Patronatsformen im Westen des Römischen Reiches* (Munich, 1987), 254–63, citing further literature.

In 1719 Lau was going through a phase that one could call "a time to understand," to use a phrase of Roger Chartier and Pierre Bourdieu.[12] From 1711 he was unemployed. He had studied under Christian Thomasius and had spent a long time on educational travels—six years in all—and had then begun a promising career as a privy councillor and private secretary to the young duke of Kurland, Friedrich Wilhelm, who died in 1711. Suddenly he had no new appointment, and he found work only as a freelance author, hoping to apply for positions as a cameralist but also philosophically to publicize his views. There were too many well-educated lawyers, who were all pushing for jobs in the governments of the German territories.

The surplus of students in the empire during the years between 1690 and 1710 coincided with the period we call the early Enlightenment.[13] It would be naive to claim that the German early Enlightenment was based on no more than this excess of students. But let us recall that Mark H. Curtis discovered a similar correlation between radicalization and "alienated intellectuals" in his classic work "The Alienated Intellectuals of Early Stuart England."[14] From the frustrated and estranged scholars who could find no appropriate work came the body of leaders for the later movements of Puritanism and Republicanism during the Civil Wars. And yet such a correlation is problematic. If applied to the German situation, we would have to observe that Germany had no revolution in the early or mid-eighteenth century; conditions remained reasonably

12. Roger Chartier, "Die Zeit, um zu begreifen: Die frustrierten Intellektuellen des 17. Jahrhunderts," in idem, *Die unvollendete Vergangenheit: Geschichte und die Macht der Weltauslegung* (Berlin, 1989), 120–39; Chartier takes his phrase from Pierre Bourdieu, *Distinction*, trans. Richard Nice (Cambridge, MA, 1984), 142–43.

13. For the student numbers, see Willem Frijhoff, "Surplus ou déficit? Hypothèses sur le nombre réel des étudiants en Allemagne à l'époque moderne (1576–1815)," *Francia* 7 (1979): 173–218. See also Franz Quarthal, "Öffentliche Armut, Akademikerschwemme und Massenarbeitslosigkeit im Barock," in *Barock am Oberrhein*, ed. Volker Press et al. (Karlsruhe, 1985), 153–88; Grete Klingenstein, "Akademikerüberschuß als soziales Problem im aufgeklärten Absolutismus: Bemerkungen über eine Rede Joseph von Sonnenfels aus dem Jahre 1771," in *Bildung, Politik und Gesellschaft*, ed. idem et al. (Munich, 1978): 165–204. On the German early Enlightenment in general, see Werner Schneiders, *Naturrecht und Liebesethik: Zur Geschichte der praktischen Philosophie im Hinblick auf Christian Thomasius* (Hildesheim, 1971); Martin Pott, *Aufklärung und Aberglaube: Die deutsche Frühaufklärung im Spiegel ihrer Aberglaubenskritik* (Tübingen, 1992); Mulsow, *Enlightenment Underground*; Hans-Erich Bödeker, ed., *Strukturen der deutschen Frühaufklärung 1680–1720* (Göttingen, 2008).

14. Mark H. Curtis, "The Alienated Intellectuals of Early Stuart England," *Past and Present* 23 (1962): 25–43.

quiet; radicals were few and far between despite the broad layer of liberal Enlightenment thinkers, who were mostly allied with the princely states. Just
think of all the Thomasians and Wolffians who between 1700 and 1750 were
finding their way in state service.[15]

The real problem caused by the flood of students, a problem that Curtis's
approach actually obscures, has been studied by Roger Chartier, using the
sociology of Pierre Bourdieu.[16] Instead of using a Marxist idea of the direct
ideological consequences of precarious positions, Chartier emphasizes an indirect influence: the jobs held by intellectuals and their university degrees
were devalued by the pressure of large numbers; and so their cultural capital
depreciated. This demotion was socially misunderstood for quite a while.
Young people continued to flow in masses into the universities, trying to obtain their doctoral degrees and get jobs at court. But at some point the dispro-
portion between their titles and their actual positions became evident. And
then they developed new strategies to adjust; graduates reacted to their new
situation in novel ways and, for example, tried to use their traditional educa-
tions by switching over into new professions and careers.[17] According to
Chartier, these were the strategies that made for social change rather than a
supposed "alienation" or frustration.

Remarkably, many German representatives of the early Enlightenment recognized this mechanism as early as the years around 1700. After the Thirty
Years' War, thousands of students, mainly law students, streamed into the new
bureaucratic positions available in the expanding absolutist governments of
the small states and territories of the Holy Roman Empire.[18] By 1700 a bubble

15. It's sufficient to consult Wolfgang E. Weber, *Prudentia gubernatoria: Studien zur Herrschafts-
lehre in der deutschen Politischen Wissenschaft des 17. Jahrhunderts* (Tübingen, 1992); and Hans
Martin Sieg, *Staatsdienst, Staatsdenken und Dienstgesinnung in Brandenburg-Preußen im 18. Jahrhundert (1713–1806)* (Berlin, 2003).

16. See note 12 above; for the analysis of the strategies used by members of precarious social
groups, as inspired by the sociology of Bourdieu, see also Norbert Schindler, "Jenseits des
Zwangs? Zur Ökonomie des Kulturellen inner- und außerhalb der bürgerlichen Gesellschaft,"
in idem, *Widerspenstige Leute: Studien zur Volkskultur der Frühen Neuzeit* (Frankfurt, 1992),
20–46.

17. For the adjustment strategies used in prerevolutionary France, see Robert Darnton, *The
Literary Underground of the Old Regime* (Cambridge, MA, 1985).

18. See, in general, Wilhelm Kühlmann, *Gelehrtenrepublik und Fürstenstaat: Entwicklung und
Kritik des deutschen Späthumanismus in der Literatur des Barockzeitalters* (Tübingen, 1982); Sinemus, *Poetik und Rhetorik im frühmodernen deutschen Staat.*

developed because the surge was so great. That was the view of Gabriel Wagner, an awkward soul who wanted to go beyond Thomasius on the left: "What are our high lords supposed to aim for today if they no longer value true nobles just because of the countless numbers of university graduates?"[19] He meant that the academic oversupply and the inflation of titles had devalued the worth of these titles. This depreciation also affected "genuine" academics, the academics of high quality, whom Wagner called "true nobles," referring to the debate that had gone on since the time of Dante's discussion of true nobility, the nobility of the mind (*de vera nobilitate*).[20] When the reputation of real intellectual labor fell off because of too many graduates, Wagner prophesied that nobles and princes would no longer so highly value the ideal of academic education; they would not hire or support more intellectuals at their courts. Wagner reflected on the possibly changing strategies of the nobility and their effects on bourgeois scholars and academics, who would now lack support.

Chartier has labeled the phase between the actual personal inflation of personnel on the academic market and the reaction of intellectuals to the new situation as "a time to understand." This was of course much more general than just a period of actual unemployment of the sort that Lau experienced. And yet unemployment or even the common and seemingly endless period of service as a tutor for noble or wealthy students made a lasting impression, which hastened an "understanding" of one's precarious situation.[21]

What consequences flowed from this sort of understanding? While Chartier along with Frijhoff and others have tended to look for quantitative answers, I would suggest looking qualitatively at this process using several examples. When we are studying the radical Enlightenment, we are dealing with "small

19. Realis de Vienna [= Gabriel Wagner], *Discursus et dubia in Christ: Thomasii Introductionem ad philosophiam aulicam in quibus de natura et constitutione philosophiae disseritur, et ratione studiorum judicatur, et in quo consistat vera sapientia, ostenditur* (Regensburg, 1691); I am here quoting the German translation in Gottfried Steihler, ed., *Materialisten der Leibniz-Zeit* (Berlin-Ost, 1966), 118.

20. See Klaus Garber, "Sozietät und Geistes-Adel: Von Dante zum Jakobiner-Club. Der frühneuzeitliche Diskurs *de vera nobilitate* und seine institutionelle Ausformung," in *Europäische Sozietätsbewegung und demokratische Tradition*, ed. idem (Tübingen, 1996), 1:1–39; cf. Dante, *Il Convivio*, IV, canzoni 19–28.

21. On tutoring, see Ludwig Fertig, *Die Hofmeister: Ein Beitrag zur Geschichte des Lehrerstandes und der bürgerlichen Intelligenz* (Stuttgart, 1979).

numbers,"[22] and so quantification does not really help. Even so, we must refuse the too easy conclusion of impulsively connecting "understanding" with "radicalization." What we need to do, following Chartier, is pursue the strategies that certain intellectuals displayed in their behavior.

When we do so, we quickly see that their tactics were never simple or uncomplicated. That's because the tactics for protecting a social position were never automatically the same as those for developing or expressing intellectual views. Just look at a few biographies. Peter Friedrich Arpe, a jurist from Kiel, experienced his "time to understand" in the 1720s, when he lost his position as a professor of law and could not find a new one. Ironically, in a book title he named this period "Summer Vacation" (*Feriae aestivales*).[23] He turned to collecting clandestine works, pursued hobbies, which he would otherwise never have done, such as researching magical traditions, and kept his head above water with commissioned correspondence. He reacted to his dire situation with satire and with the reflexes of a historian: he manically collected material about political intrigues and academic scandals.[24] Johann Georg Wachter, one of the most gifted historians of philosophy, whose Spinozism erected barriers to an academic career, hired himself out doing insecure work at the Prussian court producing inscriptions and later in Leipzig organizing a coin collection. Doing so kept him just barely at subsistence level, without any security and dependent on the help of a few friends.[25] When Johann Christoph Gottsched (the literary critic) and Johann Jakob Brucker (the historian of

22. Arjun Appadurai, *Fear of Small Numbers: An Essay on the Geography of Anger* (Durham, NC, 2006).

23. Peter Friedrich Arpe, *Feriae aestivales sive scriptorum suorum historia liber singularis* (Hamburg, 1726). On Arpe, see Martin Mulsow, "Freethinking in Early Eighteenth-Century Protestant Germany: Peter Friedrich Arpe and the 'Traité des trois Imposteurs,'" in *Heterodoxy, Spinozism and Free Thought in Eighteenth-Century Europe: Studies on the "Traité des trois Imposteurs,"* ed. Silvia Berti, Françoise Charles-Daubert, and Richard H. Popkin (Dordrecht, 1996), 193–239; idem, "Peter Friedrich Arpe collectionneur," *La lettre clandestine* 3 (1994): 35–36; idem, *Enlightenment Underground*, passim; and chapter 4.

24. See his manuscript collections in the University Library of Rostock. On that, see Martin Mulsow, "Eine handschriftliche Sammlung zur Geschichte Schleswig-Holsteins aus dem frühen 18. Jahrhundert," *Zeitschrift der Gesellschaft für Schleswig-Holsteinische Geschichte* 120 (1995): 201–6.

25. See Schröder, *Spinoza*; Martin Mulsow, "A German Spinozistic Reader of Spencer, Cudworth and Bull: Johann Georg Wachter and his *Theologia Martyrum*," in *History of Scholarship*, ed. Christopher Ligota and Jean-Lous Quantin (Oxford, 2006), 357–83; Detlef Döring, "Johann Georg Wachter in Leipzig und die Entstehung seines *Glossarium Etymologicum*," in *Fata*

philosophy) suggested that he should renounce his opinions, he refused. He continued to write quasi-Spinozistic books without publishing them, and he died disillusioned and embittered. Gabriel Wagner, whom we mentioned earlier, was unfit for academic employment because he was forever divulging his views bluntly, without diplomacy or courtesy; and so he led an insecure existence with occasional jobs, repeatedly supported by Leibniz, who valued his intelligence. His major philosophical works, composed while he was also working for hire, were never published.[26]

These were precarious lives of the first order, as I would call them. But there was also an entirely different form of clandestine precariat, that of the well-established. The precariat did not include only the unemployed or those dependent on wages; it also included those in the highest levels of society. They were professors, members of scholarly academies, famous members of the Republic of Letters, especially if they were leading double lives. Let's take the case of Hermann Samuel Reimarus. As a professor he had ascended into the best social groups of Hamburg: he could afford to keep servants, built up a large library, and was a leader in the cultural circles of the Hanseatic city—but he also secretly composed the most radical biblical criticism that one could imagine in the eighteenth century, his *Apology or Defense for the Rational Worshippers of God*. Hardly anyone knew about it. If it had become public knowledge, there would have been an enormous scandal; he and his family might well have been persecuted by both the theologians and the Hamburg mob; and he would have lost his position, his social status, and his scholarly prestige.[27] That was precarity—the complete withdrawal of social status, together with one's "ontological security," as Giddens calls it. Even his life might have been threatened. Consider, for example, the radical journalist Wilhelm Ludwig Wekhrlin, who was unmasked in Ansbach in 1792 and then beaten to death by a mob.[28]

There were precarious lives in other countries as well, including France. Nicolas Fréret, a member of the Académie des Inscriptions et Belles-Lettres,

Libellorum: Festschrift für Franzjosef Penzel, ed. Rudolf Bentzinger and Ulrich-Dieter Oppitz (Göppingen, 1999), 29–63; and chapter 8.

26. See Gabriel Wagner, *Ausgewählte Schriften und Dokumente*, ed. Siegfried Wollgast (Stuttgart, 1997).

27. On Reimarus, see Klein, *Hermann Samuel Reimarus*; Ulrich Groetsch, *Hermann Samuel Reimarus (1694–1768): Classicist, Hebraist, Enlightenment Radical in Disguise* (Leiden, 2015); Mulsow, *Between Philology and Radical Enlightenment*. See also chapter 10.

28. On Wekhrlin, see Jean Mondot, *Wilhelm Ludwig Wekhrlin: Un publiciste des lumières* (Bordeaux, 1986).

was a noted chronologist and classicist, but secretly he was also the author of the clandestine *Lettre de Thrasybule à Leucippe* and other works savagely critical of religion.[29] These works circulated, to be sure, only in manuscript copies, but like Reimarus Fréret was lucky to die in his bed because his duplicity did not come to light during his lifetime. The enormous tension—and also the tragedy—experienced by such people can be gauged from just one detail in the case of Reimarus. We know from his household records that he employed another radical in his house as a tutor, Johann Lorenz Schmidt, an endangered person of the first order. He had been hunted throughout the empire after the publication of his rationalist Bible translation. Like Lau he was living under a false name and in Danish exile, in Altona just outside Hamburg.[30] If we try to imagine how Reimarus and Schmidt, two of the most important German critical biblical philologists, might have behaved together if they were alone in their study, would they have spoken openly with each other, discussing their deist views? I think not. Reimarus had so much to lose that he could not have afforded to let his mask slip even with the man who most closely shared his intellectual views. Every communication was risky. What would have happened if Schmidt had been placed under pressure and had betrayed Reimarus?

In what follows we will pursue the complex and by no means consistent social and intellectual tactics used by the clandestine precariat, their ways of speaking and expressing themselves, their various kinds of knowledge, noting the differences caused by the logics of living either a marginal existence or a double life.[31]

Between Revolution and Reform

During his "time to understand," Lau responded to different circumstances. As an unemployed lawyer and financial expert he was trying to figure out how to regain a position at court. He knew that he was in competition with countless other well-educated lawyers, and he reacted to this fact by writing a series of cameralist works with proposals for reform, especially with regard to taxation policies and police regulations. At the same time, however, he had used

---

29. On Fréret, see vol. 29 of the journal *Corpus, revue de philosophie* (Paris, 1995).

30. Almut Spalding and Paul Spalding, "Der rätselhafte Tutor bei Hermann Samuel Reimarus: Begegnung zweier radikaler Aufklärer," *Zeitschrift des Vereins für Hamburgische Geschichte* 87 (2001): 49–64.

31. For more detail, see chapters 2 and 3.

his long academic excursion through Holland, France, and England to cultivate an openness and receptivity to the ideas of John Locke, Thomas Hobbes,
Jean Le Clerc, Baruch Spinoza, and others. So in this respect he could use his
"time to understand" to consider how to import such authors into a Germany
where they were generally regarded as extreme and dangerous. How might
they be introduced into public discussion? As one of the earliest students of
Thomasius, he felt confident in taking such a step and thought he could still
rely on his old Halle professor's support. After all, Thomasius had shown his
students how to confront Lutheran Orthodoxy courageously by filling old
concepts with new content and redirecting whole discussions.

So Lau logically tried to do both: he presented himself as a reformer in his writings on taxation but as an intellectual revolutionary in his philosophical works.
How did that work? Didn't he feel the paradox? Weren't his works, as products of
two different "personae," necessarily in contradiction to each other? Yes, indeed
so, and it's fascinating to see how his revolutionary writings sometimes worked
their way into the invisible background of certain innocent-sounding theses in his
reforming works. As an author, Lau naturally tried to minimize the contradictions
in his writings and to conceal them in his published works. We find the same thing
with Reimarus. His physicotheological deism, which he defended in his official
books, such as the *Most Eminent Truths*, was (strictly speaking) compatible with
his radical biblical criticism. It's just that no one suspected that behind his physicotheology there might lurk deeply anti-Christian ideas.[32]

As we will see in chapter 3, Lau composed his reforming works in such a
manner that (at least for himself) he kept open a bridge to radicalism. It's true
enough that he was recommending state policies that could be justified by the
interests of territorial princely states; but those who knew his clandestine
works would not have failed to notice the philosophical reasoning, which must
have eluded more "naive" readers.

Precarious Speaking

What did Lau do to present his radical thoughts to the German public? He
used a special interpretation of "eclecticism."[33] This was a favorite concept of
the early Enlightenment, deployed to avoid the sectarianism (or fanaticism)

---

32. Hermann Samuel Reimarus, *Abhandlungen von den vornehmsten Wahrheiten der natürlichen Religion* (Hamburg, 1754).

33. On that, see chapter 2 as well as Mulsow, *Enlightenment Underground*, 297–303.

that supported only one specific school of thought rather than the unbiased truth. In modern terms, this was a cultural technique, a way of dealing with plurality. It consisted in choosing from all the various streams of thought whatever one found convincing; and generally in using one's own head. By 1700, however, "eclecticism" was enjoying such a remarkable inflation that the term became devalued; now everyone painted this slogan on their banners while disguising their plan to further only their own school, that of the so-called eclectic Thomasians. But we also find strategies of adjustment in which skepticism was praised as a better sort of eclecticism, so to speak.[34] But that was not Lau's path. As we will see more clearly in the next chapter, his procedure used Pufendorf's distinction in natural law among the various "personae morales," or social roles (as we would say today) that one can take on. Lau assumed that he could separate his speaking role as a public person, who could eclectically formulate radical viewpoints, for example that of a "heathen" or an atheist, from his role as a private person, who could remain a loyal citizen and Christian. Lau thought that this private role had to extend far enough to be tolerable to both state and church.[35]

This quasilegal construction, however, did not really work. Even Thomasius scorned it, accusing Lau of dissimulation. It was only a cowardly denial of the fact that Lau was a Spinozist and atheist. No one showed a sympathetic ear for Lau's attempt to develop an experimental form of speech, what I would call precarious speech.

There are many different forms of precarious speech. Just think of Leo Strauss's *Persecution and the Art of Writing* concerning the techniques used by al-Fārābī, Maimonides, and Spinoza to speak between the lines.[36] Here again "precarious" also means "revocable" because a radical author does not have to declare himself in favor of a doctrine that may hide implicitly between the lines of his work, and therefore he can always retreat to the surface meaning of the text. The early modern history of the "problematic" and the "precarious" in this sense, as I already suggested in the introduction, is so diffuse and so inconspicuous because it's a history of niches; of genres and strategies for

34. Martin Mulsow, "Asophia philosophorum: Skeptizismus und Frühaufklärung in Deutschland," in *Transactions of the 9th International Congress on the Enlightenment, Studies on Voltaire and the 18th Century* (Oxford, 1997), 1:203–7; idem, "Eclecticism or Skepticism? A Problem of the Early Enlightenment," *Journal of the History of Ideas* 58 (1997): 465–77.

35. See chapter 2.

36. Strauss, *Persecution and the Art of Writing*.

expression that made possible a revocable balancing act; of institutions such as academic disputations with their formal oppositions; of literary genres ranging from discussions in dialogues, to equivocations, to joco-serious utterances that could be half joking or intentionally obscure.[37]

These forms of expression varied according to the sort of clandestine precarity one found oneself in.[38] An author living a double life could speak openly in a clandestine work because he was not publishing it; but he had to practice the art of concealment in his profession and everyday life and for his official works find a form of argumentative equivocation in which he did not completely contradict himself. A half-clandestine author like Lau, who published his *Meditationes*, even if anonymously, might use legalisms like that of having a double role; but he could also use joco-serious ways of blurring his meaning, so that the exact illocutionary status of individual ideas was left unclear. In the foreword to his *Meditationes, Theses, Dubia*, Lau said that some of the views expressed in the book were "no more than a joking intellectual game" (jocosi tantum Ingenii Lusus) and the result of rather unrestrained speculations ("liberioris Rationis Meditationes"); several were truths, brighter than the noonday sun, but others remained doubtful and disputable theses pointing in different directions ("dubiae et in utramque Partem, Theses . . . disputabiles").[39]

Precarious Knowledge

Precarious speaking was obviously not the same thing as precarious knowledge. With the latter term I mean simply the revocable existence of the written production of clandestine authors in general. Whoever did not publish, whoever had no academic position, had no disciples and no guaranteed public, could all too easily lose everything he had ever thought. Precarious knowledge in this sense was knowledge that at any time could evaporate. That was the everyday reality for intellectuals of the radical Enlightenment. If one wanted to guarantee the survival of one's papers after one's own death, then one had

37. See Mulsow, "Libertinismus in Deutschland"; Cavaillé, *Dis/simulations*; Mehtonen, *Obscure Language, Unclear Literature*.

38. For similar tactics during Soviet rule, see Jurij Malzew, *Freie russische Literatur 1955–1980: Der Samisdat in der Sowjetunion* (Berlin, 1981); Matthias Buchholz et al., eds., *Samisdat in Mitteleuropa: Prozeß—Archiv—Erinnerung* (Dresden 2007); and note 11 in the introduction to this book.

39. Theodor Ludwig Lau, *Meditationes, Theses, Dubia*, "Freystadii" (n.p., 1719), fol. 5r. See Mulsow, "Libertinismus in Deutschland," 40.

to trust the executors of one's literary estate, and many tricky maneuvers and schemes had to be invented both organizationally and financially.[40] In the case of Spinoza they worked, but for many others they did not. And then everything was lost.

I would like to emphasize that the clandestine precariat had to rely on a special kind of "care of the self." This care—for the survival of one's own thoughts, one's own insights—could determine one's whole attitude toward life itself. How could one's works be both hidden and yet preserved? How could the felt pressure to convey insights that might overturn conventional wisdom be restrained and postponed to some uncertain future that one would never directly experience? Here one really can agree with the notion of Konrad Ehlich, who speaks of an "extended" communicative situation, or even of an "extended" existence.[41] A message may reach its recipient only after the death of the sender.

We can see concretely what precarious knowledge is from a couple of facts drawn from the history of crime during the early Enlightenment. In 1693 Gabriel Wagner had turned in the manuscript of his big book, *Weltweise Geschicht* (*Philosophical History*), to a book dealer in Leipzig to be printed. But Christian Thomasius, whom Wagner had fiercely attacked in 1691, managed through his brother-in-law Adam Rechenberg to wrest the manuscript out of the hands of the book dealer and to release it to a few scholars.[42] Jakob Friedrich Reimmann, who in this way got an impression of the quasi-stolen text, undertook to cannibalize it in his *Historia literaria . . . of the Germans*.[43] There was nothing left for Wagner to do but to try laboriously and with much cursing to rewrite his whole book from memory. In 1715 he published a short summary of his newly reconstructed work, which had now probably expanded to some 3,500

40. We should speak of a "politics of memory," which becomes necessary with precarious bodies of knowledge.

41. Konrad Ehlich, "Text und sprachliches Handeln: Die Entstehung von Texten aus dem Bedürfnis nach Überlieferung," in *Schrift und Gedächtnis*, ed. Aleida Assmann, Jan Assmann, and Christof Hardmeier (Munich, 1983): 24–43. For Ehlich the text itself is a distention of a communicative situation, but I'm more interested in the communicative connection that the text makes possible years or decades later. See also the adaptation of the concept in Jan Assmann, *Das kulturelle Gedächtnis: Schrift, Erinnerung und politische Identität in frühen Hochkulturen* (Munich, 1992), 22.

42. Siegfried Wollgast, "Einleitung" to Wagner, *Ausgewählte Schriften*.

43. Jakob Friedrich Reimmann, *Versuch einer Einleitung in die Historiam Literariam so wohl insgemein als auch derer Teutschen insonderheit*, 6 vols. (Halle, 1708–13).

pages; this summary was intended as a promotional text as part of his quest to find another publisher for his huge work.[44] And yet the book never appeared, and the manuscript went missing. We do not have to imagine spectacular cases like those of the Spanish Inquisition, which had imprisoned Tommaso Campanella in Naples. His philosophical manuscripts were confiscated over and over, even though he then repeatedly wrote them out again. Works "disappeared" even in central Germany.[45] Throughout his life Theodor Ludwig Lau tried to get his many writings published. As late as 1736, shortly before his death, he published a bibliography of his unprinted works so that at least he could call attention to their existence.[46] When he died in 1740 he took his works with him into the grave. His literary estate remains missing today. Philosophically, Johann Georg Wachter continued to develop after the scandal provoked by his early publication of *Elucidarius cabbalisticus*, in which he tried to forge a synthesis of Spinoza and the Kabbalah; but he did not wish to publish his later books.[47] So these manuscripts could not influence the later course of the German Enlightenment and are today virtually unknown. All the same, some of them can still be found in archives, although some seem to have been carried off by the Soviet Union during World War II.[48]

Thus the absence of so many clandestine works has clearly distorted the Enlightenment for later historians. Just knowing that there had been a clandestine precariat and knowing the manner in which it adjusted to the processes of communication (and of non-communication) can clear up such distortions. Any history of communications during the Enlightenment certainly has to recognize the many methods of dealing with the intellectual turbulence of the early eighteenth century, methods that were part of a whole

44. *Nachricht von Realis de Vienna Prüfung des Europischen Verstandes durch die Weltweise Geschicht*, ed. Martin Disselkamp (Heidelberg, 2005).

45. On Campanella, see Luigi Amabile, *Fra Tommaso Campanella, la sua congiura, i suoi processi e la sua pazzia* (Napoli, 1882).

46. Lau, "Die Original-Rede," in idem, *Meditationes; Reprint*, 179–88.

47. On Wachter's late philosophy, see Mulsow, "A German Spinozistic Reader of Spencer, Cudworth and Bull." On the embitterment of the late Wachter, see Döring, "Johann Georg Wachter."

48. See the volumes that have been returned from the former Soviet Union to the State and University Library of Hamburg, catalogued as Cod. theol. 1876 and Cod. theol. 1842; on other manuscripts by Wachter, see the introduction by Winfried Schröder to Wachter, *De primordiis Christianae religionis* (Stuttgart, 1995), 8–11.

collection of coping strategies whose main direction was compromise rather than confrontation.[49]

To return to the beginning of this chapter: the "time to understand" was the subjective time in which the clandestine precariat became aware of its true situation. But it's unclear that this "time to understand" produced insights that could be communicated from one person to another, that it could contribute to a social learning process or to an objective "time to understand." Any chances of doing so were not cushioned by institutional supports. For the clandestine precariat, as we can see from many cases, any hope of finding readers was completely contingent on factors beyond the writer's control.[50] Papers left behind at death disappeared, manuscripts were taken away from authors, appointments and patron-client relations were ended abruptly. So someone could easily be driven to slit his wrists.

49. For the reforming and compromising character of the "moderate" German early Enlightenment, see Anthony La Vopa, *Grace, Talent, and Merit: Poor Students, Clerical Careers, and Professional Ideology in Eighteenth-Century Germany* (Cambridge, 1988).

50. On the role of contingency, see Rudolf Schlögl, "Kommunikation und Vergesellschaftung unter Anwesenden: Formen des Sozialen und ihre Transformation in der Frühen Neuzeit," *Geschichte und Gesellschaft* 24 (2008): 155–224.

2

The Libertine's Two Bodies

If he wanted to show his "I" in its natural state (*in puris naturalibus*) or only in nightshirt and nightcap, everyone would flee such triviality and worthlessness; and so he dons colorful theater costumes and holds up a mask of joy and love before his face in order to appear interesting, and with an internal speaking tube he raises his voice; so in the end he looks down on his costumes and imagines that that's his real self.[1]

Nature and Grace

In the fourteenth century, a bishop in France claimed that he was strictly obeying celibacy in his capacity as bishop, while being happily married, in his capacity as baron.[2] This may seem a somewhat frivolous example to illustrate a venerable phenomenon, namely, that one and the same person can take on several different institutional roles. In his classic *The King's Two Bodies*, Ernst Kantorowicz wrote the juridico-sacral history of this phenomenon. In the very beginning of the book he refers to the so-called *Anonymus Normannus* who speaks of the king, around the year 1100, as a "gemina persona," a double person: "Thus we have to recognize [in the king] a twin person, one descending from nature, the other from grace."[3] Later it was said that the king never dies

---

1. [August Klingemann], *Die Nachtwachen des Bonaventura* (Munich, 1960), 83. An earlier and shorter version of this chapter appeared in English as "The Libertine's Two Bodies: Moral Persona and Free Thought in Early Modern Europe," *Intellectual History Review* 18 (2008): 337–47.

2. Ernst Kantorowicz, *The King's Two Bodies: A Study in Medieval Political Theology* (Princeton, 1957), 43.

3. Quoted in ibid., 46: "Itaque in unoquoque gemina intelligitur fuisse persona, una ex natura, altera ex gratia, una in hominis proprietate, altera in spiritu et virtute."

because when the individual who holds the dignity perishes, his function, as a one-man corporation, immediately passes to his successor.

When Kantorowicz wrote his book, in Princeton, in the years before 1957, he was trying to explicate the medieval origins of the modern nation-state.[4] The book's provocative thesis was that the roots of the state are a juridical and theological fiction. The fictitious split described by Kantorowicz was still operative in the seventeenth century, which had not forgotten the construction of the king's two bodies or corporations. However, the perspective of the theory of state is not the only possible one from which to tell this story. The idea of the "gemina persona" might also raise the question of whether this model of a person doubled by nature and grace attracted intellectuals who were driven by a desire to split their own selves.

This question leads away from the sources studied in *The King's Two Bodies*, but the basic idea cannot be dismissed. Was it possible, in an age of dissimulation and Nicodemism[5]—the concealment of one's own religious beliefs—that the politico-theological model of the royal person provided a pattern for the self-fashioning of a "gemina persona" for the early modern intellectual?

One example is François La Mothe Le Vayer, one of the so-called *libertins érudits* in Richelieu's France. La Mothe adapted the models of ancient Stoicism and Pyrrhonist skepticism, and in the prologues to his works—for instance, the pseudonymous 1630 *Dialogues faits à l'imitation des anciens*—he had to convince his suspicious readers and censors that it was a mistake to infer that the *imitatio* of the pagan authors of antiquity transformed the modern Christian author into a pagan.[6] It was essential for La Mothe to establish this distinction, employing, like the *Anonymus Normannus*, a terminology that toys with the difference between nature and grace.

In his dedication, La Mothe writes that: "I would be more worried about justifying to you some purely natural moral consideration in terms of religion, if I had not already stated that I merely wrote as an ancient philosopher and

4. On Kantorowicz, see Kay Schiller, *Gelehrte Gegenwelten: Über humanistische Leitbilder im 20. Jahrhundert* (Frankfurt, 2000); Alain Boureau, *Kantorowicz: Stories of a Historian* (Baltimore, 2001).

5. See Carlo Ginzburg, *Il nicodemismo: Simulazione e dissimulazione religiosa nell' Europa del Cinquecento* (Torino, 1970); Zagorin, *Ways of Lying*.

6. [François La Mothe Le Vayer], *Quatre dialogues faits à l'imitation des anciens par Orasius Tubero*, "Francfort, 1506" [Paris, ca. 1630]. I am using this edition: *Dialogues faits à l'imitation des anciens* (Paris, 1988). On La Mothe Le Vayer, see Pintard, *Le libertinage érudit dans la première moitié du XVIIe siècle*.

pagan *in puris naturalibus,* and if you were not somewhat familiar with the submission of my spirit to the Divine Things, which I respectfully turn over to those who are entitled to touch the Ark and approach the sanctum [i.e., the theologians]."[7] Hence La Mothe was writing as a pagan although privately it was understood that he was a Christian. He split his persona into the roles of author and private person.

Of course, others had earlier referred to the use of different speech roles, in order to protect themselves. In 1519, Girolamo Benivieni contritely reassured the Church authorities that in their early work, *Commento sopra una canzone d'amore,* he and Giovanni Pico had spoken "as Platonists rather than Christians."[8] This was admittedly a structural problem that originated with the Renaissance itself.

Imitating pagan culture meant almost necessarily speaking as pagans. Nevertheless, La Mothe describes his pagan authorial role in clearly theological terms: "in puris naturalibus" (in a purely natural state). This was a technical term among contemporary Church theoreticians, particularly the Jesuits.[9] It had been widely used in connection with the debate on predestination and grace, so widely that it could find its way into a libertine's preface. The concept signifies a hypothetical natural state of man, counterfactually disregarding any relation to divine grace. A pure state of nature does not actually exist: it can only be postulated as an intellectual construct.[10]

For instance: in discussing the wisdom and the legal titles of natural man. Or: in contemplating some aspects of the human soul and the *fatum,* beyond the truth of Revelation—as the natural philosopher Pomponazzi did many

7. La Mothe Le Vayer, *Quatre dialogues,* 14: "Je serois plus en peine de vous justifier en termes de Religion quelques moralitez purement Physiques, si je ne m'estois déja fait entendre à vous que je n'ay rien écrit qu'en Philosophe ancien et Payen in puris naturalibus; et si vous ne connoissiez assez la submission de mon esprit aux choses divines, lesquelles je laisse par respect traitter à ceux qui ont droict de toucher l'Arche, et s'approcher du Sanctuaire." Carlo Ginzburg has noted this passage in *Wooden Eyes: Nine Reflections on Distance,* trans. Martin Ryle and Kate Soper (New York, 2001), 46.

8. Giovanni Pico della Mirandola, *Commento sopra una canzione d'amore* (Palermo, 1994); see Thorsten Bürklin's foreword to his German translation: *Kommentar zu einem Lied der Liebe* (Hamburg, 2002).

9. Beginning with Robert Bellarmine, "Sententiae D. M. Baii refutatae," in *Auctarium Bellarminianum: Supplement aux oeuvres de Cardinal Bellarmin,* ed. Xavier-Marie Le Bachelet (Paris, 1913), 314–38.

10. On this, see the thorough treatment of Henri de Lubac, *Surnaturel: Études historiques* (Paris, 1946; new ed., Paris, 1991).

years before this debate on grace. In these cases, it was claimed that "in puris naturalibus" the opinion of Aristotelians and Stoics was acceptable, in accordance with the dictum of Albertus Magnus and the Averroists that it was permissible and advisable to act "de naturalibus naturaliter," to treat natural things in a "natural" way.[11]

This "natura pura" was, like the "gemina persona," a juridical construction of sorts, and they both postulate a state of nature abstracted from the state of grace, whether the monarch's natural body or the philosopher's natural mental state.

But what was "nature" for La Mothe? The punch line of his artificial argument was that the hypothetical "natura pura" was prior to any effects of grace; but he equated it with the natural reason of pagan antiquity. Antiquity was, as it were, mankind's natural state. When La Mothe embellished his imitative use of Greek antiquity—which was basically the same as the Florentine Platonists'—with the theological claim that pagan antiquity represented things as they are "naturally," he was essentially arguing that antiquity thought according to the rules of reason. Theological hypothesizing was therefore reduced to the imitation of antiquity. In this reduction, supported by the various semantic traditions of speaking about "natura pura," we can find lurking—as in Pomponazzi—the Averroist idea of double truth but now applied to the personality of one person who combined them in himself rather than separating them into the philosophical and theological faculties of a medieval university.[12] That comfortable institutional distinction was erased. Here lay the genuine provocation behind Le Vayer's apparent accommodation to the Jesuit rules of the game.

Pomponazzi and Averroes

Let us try to understand this difference more clearly, using the example of Pomponazzi. We will see his true concerns best if we follow him into the lecture hall and listen to him teaching in the intimate circle of his students. As

11. Pietro Pomponazzi in Franco Graiff, "I prodigi e l'atrologia nei commenti di Pietro Pomponazzi al De coelo, alla Meteora, e la De generatione," *Medioevo* 2 (1976): 331–61.

12. On the doctrine of double truth, see Anneliese Maier, "Das Prinzip der doppelten Wahrheit," in idem, *Metaphysische Hintergründe der spätscholastischen Naturphilosophie*, vol. 4 of *Studien zur Naturphilosophie der Spätscholastik* (Rome, 1955), 1–44; Alain de Libera, *Raison et foi: Archéologie d'une crise d'Albert le Grand à Jean-Paul II* (Paris, 2003); Markus Friedrich, *Die Grenzen der Vernunft: Theologie, Philosophie und gelehrte Konflikte am Beispiel des Helmstedter Hofmannstreits und seiner Wirkungen auf das Luthertum um 1600* (Göttingen, 2004), 281ff.

Pomponazzi wrote in 1516 in his *De immortalitate animae* (*On the Immortality of the Soul*):

> Behaving in this manner [not telling the truth about the mortality of the soul] should not be held against a politician [*politicus*]. Just as a doctor invents many stories in order to help a sick person recover his health, so the politician also becomes teller of fables [*apologos format*] in order to guide citizens on the right path. As Averroes remarks in the foreword to Book III of the *Physics*, strictly speaking there is neither truth nor falsehood in his fables.[13]

Pomponazzi was appealing to Averroes, and it is indeed true that the medieval polymath, in his prologue dating from about 1180, claimed that religious utterances were neutral on questions of truth. He stated,

> Modern speakers[14] say, as we see, that he who first learns philosophy cannot later learn religion [*leges*], and whoever learns religion first, for him no other path is later darkened. And they are right. He in whom are joined both custom and the comprehension of the truth will not regularly hit an obstacle in falsehood but rather in a place where there is neither truth nor falsehood, i.e., in religious speech.[15]

For Averroes and his followers religions were "leges"—laws—which had only normative force and made no claim to truth. Whoever claimed otherwise

13. Pietro Pomponazzi, *Tractatus de immortalitate animae* (Bologna, 1516), quoted here according to the edition by Burkhard Mojsisch, *Abhandlung über die Unsterblichkeit der Seele* (Hamburg, 1990), 198: "Neque accusandus est politicus. Sicut namque medicus multa fingit, ut aegro sanitatem restituat, sic politicus apologos format, ut cives rectificet. Verum in his apologis, ut dicit Averroes in prologo tertii *Physicorum*, proprie neque est veritas neque falsitas." See Pomponazzi, "On the Immortality of the Soul," trans. W. H. Hay II, in *The Renaissance Philosophy of Man*, ed. E. Cassirer, P. O. Kristeller, and J. H. Randall Jr. (Chicago, 1948), 257–384.

14. Translator's note: Mulsow points out that the word *loquentes* was the equivalent of the Arabic *Mutakallimun*, the representative of the "Kalām," or literally the discourse, i.e., Islamic theology; thus the *loquentes* were the theologians.

15. The prologue by Averroes to the *Third Book of Aristotle's Physics* is printed in *Aristotelis opera cum Averrois commentariis*, ed. Marcantonio Zimara, vol. 4 (Venice, 1560), fol. 69r/v: "Et ideo videmus modernos loquentes dicere quod qui in principio addiscit philosophiam, non potest addiscere leges, et qui primo addiscit leges, non ei abscondentur post aliae scientiae: et bene dixerunt: in quo enim congregatur consuetudo et comprehensibilitas veritatis, ille non habet impedimentum semper a falsitate, vel saltem ab eo, in quo non est veritas, neque falsitas: ut in legibus."

(like the theologians, for Averroes the *Mutakallimun*) was making a category mistake.

It's interesting that Averroes did not distinguish philosophy from religion absolutely but drew a distinction only in connection with the sequence of a course of studies and the consequences of custom. "If someone is accustomed to hearing falsehoods he will be predisposed to ignore the truth."[16] If one is accustomed to (intellectual) fare that is indifferent to truth, as when one is accustomed to eating bread but then receives a spicier food, it is not well tolerated. Habituation varies socially, and the problem lies precisely here: that ordinary people do not have stomachs accustomed to such robust and various fare as philosophers, who are used to digesting unusual viewpoints. Philosophers can digest a lot—they learn to cope with plurality and with strange hypotheses.[17]

This brings us back to the sixteenth century with its many diverse innovations. In the summer semester of 1514 in Bologna, when Pomponazzi commented on Averroes's *Prologue to the Physics*—a commentary that survives in a manuscript found in Arezzo—he became abusive toward the "statuarii," a term he adopted from Plato; they were the people who established rules and laws: "One barrier [for philosophers] is that they are commonly despised by the citizenry. . . . The legislators are thought valuable. They have knowledge of the laws because they are robbers. And the governors [*gubernatores*] are

16. Ibid., fol. 69v: "Sed qui habet consuetudinem recipiendi falsum, aptus est ut impediatur a veritate." The argument continues: "quemadmodum in quo congregatur cum nutrimento panis, qui est cibus temperatus, consuetudo nutrimenti, rectum est ut non impediatur in aliqua hora abhoc, quia nutriatur ab eo, et quin non accidat ei nutrimentum: sed qui assuetus est ad aliquid aliud, quam panem, bene potest impediri a nutrimento illius. Et ex hoc modo, scilicet per consuetudinem estimator quod apologi propositi civitatum corrumpunt multa principia naturae, et hoc est per assuetudinem. Et ideo fides vulgi est fortior quam fides philosophorum. Quoniam vulgus non assuevit audire aliud, philosophi autem audiunt multa, et ideo, quando disputatio et consideratio consequens est omnibus, corrumpitur fides vulgi, et ideo quaedam leges prohibent disputare. Et potest bene videre quantum operatur audire res extraneas in opinione, quae est per consuetudinem in hoc tempore. Homines enim multi, cum instraverunt res speculativas, et audierunt res extraneas eis, cum fuerint assueti, statim corrumpitur opinio, quam habuerunt ex assuetudine: et non fuerint tantum assueti ad istas res extraneas, ut possint recipere, et fuit destructa apud eos maior pars legum, et multiplicati sunt homines apud eos, qui dicebantur zenodic [from Arabic *zanādiqa*, Plural of *zindiq*]. Et Algazel fuit maior causa huius cum suis compositionibus mixtis." On Averroes's polemic against al-Ghazali, see also the commentary by Frank Griffel in Ibn Rushd, *Maßgebliche Abhandlung/Faṣl al-maqāl* (Berlin, 2010).

17. See the previous quotation: "philosophi autem audiunt multa."

robbers, and robbers love one another. And they are all ignoramuses, and one ignoramus loves another. . . . [But philosophy] does not want the friendship of princes."[18]

The other barrier for philosophers was, just as Averroes said, custom. "No philosopher can study religion [*studere legibus*]. For it is all foolish nonsense [*sunt pedochiarie tot nuge*]; a true philosopher cannot listen to that."[19] He would have to give up his taste for truth. Pomponazzi's student Tiberio Russiliano, who took the same course of study four years later, drew radical conclusions from such claims.[20] But after 1516 even Pomponazzi stopped publishing his own investigations into the natural causes of miracles or the determinacy of the world.[21]

How did the philosopher regard lying? Were they lies presented to the people? Was it a lie that he, the philosopher himself, told his censors or the broader public? Was this a sort of legitimate lying? In contrast to religiously motivated lying, which was common in the sixteenth century, we are here speaking of philosophically motivated lying. We are not talking about white lies but about beneficial lies. White lies use mental reservation, so that one may inwardly distance oneself from what one says openly, and equivocation, so that one's words might be intended differently from what is most likely understood. These were the result of Nicodemism, the discretion of religious minorities who had to fear persecution. The philosophical theory of double truth did have something in common with the protection of intellectuals from ecclesiastical persecution, but the defense of the "beneficial lie" was even richer in implications. "These fables are neither true nor false," says Pomponazzi about Averroes. "Let us say that they are fantastical stories because under

18. Pomponazzi: Ms. Arezzo, Biblioteca della Fraternità de' Laici, Ms. 390 (today 389), fol. 191r. Quoted by Bruno Nardi, *Studi su Pietro Pomponazzi* (Firenze, 1965), 132: "Unum est, quia communiter spernuntur a civitate et habentur villi precio; apud rectores nihil sunt; viri statuarii sunt in precio; habent cognitionem iuris, quia sunt latrones; et gubernatores latroni [*sic*] sunt, ideo latro latronem amat; et omnes ignorantes sunt, et ignorans ignorantem amat. Non enim phylosophi existimantur esse digni secretarii. . . . Ecce ostendimus phylosophiam: ipsa non vult amicitiam principum."

19. Ibid., fol. 193r. (Nardi, p. 134): "Nullus phylosophus potest studere legibus: sunt pedochiarie tot nuge; verus phylosophus iustus non potest ista audire."

20. Tiberio Russiliano Sesto, *Apologeticus adversus cuculatores* (1519), published in Paola Zambelli, *Una reincarnazione di Pico ai tempi di Pomponazzi: Con l'edizione critica di Tiberio Russiliano Sesto Calabrese: "Apologeticus adversus cucullatos" (1519)* (Milan, 1994).

21. Paola Zambelli, "Aristotelismo eclettico' o polemiche clandestine? Immortalità dell'anima e vicissitudini della storia universale in Pomponazzi, Nifo e Tiberio Russiliano," in *Die Philosophie im 14. und 15. Jahrhundert*, ed. Olaf Pluta (Amsterdam, 1988), 535–72.

their appearance they intend the good; under cover they intend the truth. . . .
They were truly good people who made those religious laws for our welfare. . . .
It's appropriate for the physician to tell falsehoods."[22]

Here Pomponazzi was claiming that physicians and the founders of religion
were using speech in the illocutionary act of healing, so to speak, rather than
speaking propositional truth. But this also sets up a social differentiation between religious legislators on the one hand and simple people on the other.
And the philosopher stood in the middle. Was he himself a "physician"? No,
he did not lie; rather, he refused to go along with them out of a fear of impair-
ing his sense of truth. I do not therefore think that Pomponazzi simply assumed he had permission to lie and that his own public statements were nothing more than camouflage.

We can see that it is not at all a question here of the doubling of truth into
two sorts, philosophical and theological (as the memory of the Parisian prohibitions of 1277 might suggest), but a reflection on the shifting pragmatic
status of philosophical or religious statements. Religious statements were leg-
islative directives; they were political and had a complex structure with respect
to the truth. They "intend the true" only to the extent that they intend the
good. One might think here of Petrarch, who said that it was better to will
the good than to know the true.[23]

But if we now ask whether using the theorem of the double truth in the
sixteenth century undermined the concept of truth—so that in the end the
truth could be mocked—then we have to qualify our question so that we ask
whether understanding religion and politics as beneficial lies undermined the
concept of truth. Bernard Williams has spoken of the virtues of the truth,
among which he understands accuracy and sincerity.[24] Both of these virtues

22. Pomponazzi: Ms. Arezzo, fol. 193r (Nardi, pp. 134ff.): "Non sunt nec veri nec falsi ap-
pologi; dicimus quod sunt sermones fabulosi, quia illo tegumento intendant bonum, sub illo
intendant verum. . . . Erant viri boni qui fecerunt illas leges propter bonum nostrum, quia non
possemus ire per vias. Intendunt bonum, etsi sciant se <non> dicere veritatem. Decet medicum
dicere falsitatem, ut dicunt infirmo quod parum commode valet; sicut in ipsis appologis intendant bonitatem."

23. On Petrarch's moral philosophy, see Sabrina Ebbersmeyer, Homo agens: Studien zur Genese und Struktur frühhumanistischer Moralphilosophie (Berlin, 2010). On the prohibitions of 1277,
see Kurt Flasch, Aufklärung im Mittelalter? Die Verurteilung von 1277 (Mainz, 1989). In 1277 the
Bishop of Paris, Etienne Tempier, condemned 219 theses, many of which had supposedly been
taught by the "Latin Averroists."

24. Williams, Truth and Truthfulness.

can certainly suffer if we speak of beneficial political or religious lies. For religious truth the idea of double truth surely had an undermining effect, one that became evident in the seventeenth century.

The Man in a Mask

Do the origins of the theory of double truth as found in La Mothe Le Vayer go back to the Renaissance or all the way back to the Middle Ages? Some historians have given good reasons to suspect that in the Middle Ages this "theory" was no more than an artificial construction, a bogeyman invented by defenders of Orthodoxy with which to attack their opponents.[25] Medieval Aristotelians such as Boethius of Dacia (Sweden), Siger of Brabant, and Jean de Jandun were denounced in this way. Sergio Landucci took up this question again in his book *La doppia verità* and in opposition to "revisionist" historians provides a reading of the original texts that shows that these Parisian university masters may indeed have been speaking incipiently of a double truth.[26] In contrast Luca Bianchi has tried to raise this controversy to a higher level and to investigate the consequences of what he calls the "legend" of the double truth, or to find out how the concept of "duplex veritas" was used in entirely different contexts.[27] So the question remains somewhat open and has been broadened into new areas. Moreover, one always has to notice whether the separation of two spheres of truth was made explicitly or only assumed implicitly, as well as whether an opponent's empty denunciation might give rise within libertine circles to a real theory of double truth, even if it was only vaguely suggested or playfully presented.

Regardless, we should consider comparing Le Vayer's separation of roles to a painting by Salvator Rosa from the same decade, the 1640s: a painting portraying a man who is showing another man a mask, a "persona" that was used to "speak through" or, to use the Latin, *personare* (figure 1).[28] Like Le Vayer, Rosa was a courtier, who here depicted his experiences with dissimulation,

25. See also the discussion in chapter 8.

26. Sergio Landucci, *La doppia verità: Conflitti di ragione e fede tra Medioevo e prima modernità* (Milan, 2006).

27. Luca Bianchi, *Pour une histoire de la "double vérité"* (Paris, 2008).

28. The painting is often misleadingly entitled *The Lie*. See Eckhard Leuschner, *Persona, Larva, Maske: Ikonologische Studien zum 16. bis frühen 18. Jahrhundert* (Frankfurt, 1997). See also Caterina Volpi, "The Great Theatre of the World: Salvator Rosa and the Academies," in *Salvator Rosa*, ed. Helen Langdon, Xavier F. Salomon, and idem (London, 2010), 51–73, esp. 68.

FIGURE 1. Salvator Rosa, *The Lie*. Florence, Palazzo Pitti, Galerie de Palatine, Inv. No. Mif-1962.

just as Le Vayer had translated his experiences into tactics. Rosa was also shaped by ancient Stoicism just as much as Le Vayer.[29] At the same time he was also participating in debates about the sense and purpose of the theater; and so one might suggest that Rosa's two men depicted Terence and Plautus. A short time later he completely turned away from the genre of comedy, having become disgusted by it. The painting appears, however, to testify to his continuing and intensive preoccupation with the possibilities of alternating roles.

One can therefore see the painting as an illustration of the philosopher who explains to his counterpart, just as Le Vayer did to his addressee, what changing one's persona meant: the difference between the ancient pagan speaking tube and one's own identity. Underlying this image was the paradox that the mask reveals even as it conceals, and that the supposedly true face behind the mask can only be true if it wears the mask.[30]

Persona Moralis

The libertine La Mothe Le Vayer's quasi-juridical construction was restated and updated in the early eighteenth century. Successors of the French libertines were to be found in the school of "eclectic philosophers," of whom the economist, jurist, and heterodox philosopher Theodor Ludwig Lau, whom we met in chapter 1, is a striking example.[31] Let's recall that in 1717, Lau published his *Meditationes philosophicae de Deo, Mundo, Homine* and in 1719 the *Meditationes, Theses, Dubia*.[32] Both books digested philosophical ideas from Hobbes, Spinoza, Toland, Vanini, and others and were banned immediately after their publication. Lau was arrested and expelled from Frankfurt. He was quickly branded an atheist.

Yet Lau took his philosophical bearings from Samuel Pufendorf, the theoretician of natural law, who had developed the moral-philosophical notion of the "ens morale." The moral being of man extends beyond his natural being so that the human difference from mere nature, which Le Vayer described with

---

29. On Rosa as a Stoic, see Jonathan Scott, *Salvator Rosa: His Life and Times* (New Haven, 1995); Helen Langdon, *Salvator Rosa* (London, 2010).

30. Richard Weihe, *Die Paradoxie der Maske: Geschichte einer Form* (Munich, 2003).

31. See the literature cited in chapter 1.

32. Lau, *Meditationes philosophicae de Deo, Mundo, Homine* (1717); idem, *Meditationes, Theses, Dubia philosophico-theologica* (1719); idem, *Dokumente* (1992).

the theological term "grace," could now be called an "ens morale" or the "persona moralis," using a juridical term. Men were moral persons to the extent that they fulfilled certain roles in their personas as citizens, spouses, officials, and so on. This applied to groups as well.[33]

According to Lau, those who burn books and persecute heterodox authors were not only unfairly hunting for the supposed consequences of statements but also confounding distinct kinds of authorial persona: "Confundunt diversos et personas morales."[34] It was possible to speak as a theologian or as a philosopher and thereby occupy very different roles: "because of their divergent characteristics, one must not fuse and shape into one person the two *personae morales* of the theologian and the philosopher."[35] Lau adopted this point of view in his justification vis-à-vis his former preceptor, Christian Thomasius: he demanded that he not be condemned as an atheist but judged according to his various roles. In the accusation leveled against him, he claims, this was precisely what happened: readers had confounded his personae, without acknowledging that he expressed himself in his writing as a philosopher rather than a theologian. These "fallacias compositionum & divisionum"— false conclusions due to the blending of different personae—opened the floodgate to arbitrary interpretations of his writings, "easily charging me [with heresies] that my reason and my senses reject."[36] As a philosopher, Lau argued,

33. Cf. Samuel Pufendorf, *De jure naturae et gentium libri octo* (Lund, 1672), I, 1; see Theo Kobusch, *Die Entdeckung der Person: Metaphysik der Freiheit und modernes Menschenbild*, 2nd ed. (Darmstadt, 1997), 67–82.

34. Lau, *Meditationes, Theses, Dubia* § II: "Verborum et Cogitationum unicus, optimus et infallibilis Interpres: non Auditor vel Lector, sed Orator et Scriptor. Summa ergo Impietas: innoxiis ex Principiis, Praemissis et Intentionibus; falsas, erroneas et fictitias, pro lubitu elicere Conclusiones. Compositionis et Divisionis committere Fallacias. Diversos Respectus et Personas Morales: Consequenter earundem: Philosophicas, cum Theologicis confundere Notionibus; et Ethnicum, cum Christiano: Philosophum, cum Theologo: Philosophum Eclecticum, cum Philosopho Sectario: Theologum Naturalem cum Theologo Revelato: pro uno eodemque habere Subjecto." In Lau, *Meditationes philosophicae de Deo, Mundo, Homine*, 119ff.

35. "Die zwo Personae morales eines Gottesgelehrten und Weltweisen ... müssen [= dürfen] wegen ihrer gegen einander lauffenden Eigenschaften durchaus nicht zusammen geschmolzen und zu einer Person geformet werden." Lau in a letter to Christian Thomasius, published in Thomasius, "Elender Zustand eines in die Atheisterey verfallenen Gelehrten," in idem, *Ernsthaffte, aber doch Muntere und Vernünfftige Thomasische Gedancken und Erinnerungen über allerhand auserlesene Juristische Händel*, part 1 (Halle, 1720), 272, reprinted in Lau, *Meditationes*, ed. Pott (1992).

36. Thomasius, *Ernsthaffte*, 272: "weil durch dergleichen fallacias compositionum et divisionum: combinationes contrarium, uti personarum, ita proprietatum: die gröbste

he explored thoughts that he would not entertain as a Christian or "theologi-cal" person. Thus, accusations of atheism based on the imputed theological consequences of his philosophical statements were inappropriate. It should be permissible, he continues, to reconsider older heretical opinions. Doing so could mean theologically that one might strengthen one's own orthodox faith by working through heretical errors. "But just because I wrote this book, I wholeheartedly deny that one can logically conclude that the following impli-cations" necessarily follow: "That there my own basic teachings are revealed, which I affirm as orthodox truth with both lips and heart; that I am therefore a Spinozist and incarnate atheist. And that therefore I should play a role in a Vanini-like tragedy."[37] Playing a role in a Vanini-like tragedy clearly meant being burned at the stake.

These words were a new way of occupying the space of intellectual freedom that the Parisian Averroists had created in the thirteenth century through the separation of theology from philosophy.[38] To reach his goal, however, Lau used neither the terminology of Averroes nor the Jesuit legal fiction but Pufen-dorf's political idiom. Having been trained by Thomasius in Pufendorf's natu-ral law, he was well versed in the opening chapter of Pufendorf's *De jure natu-rae et gentium.*

Ironically, by employing Pufendorf's persona concept, Lau was wielding a weapon that Thomasius had forged. Twenty-five years earlier, when Thoma-sius himself was the target of attacks by Reverend Hector Masius of the Danish court, he had successfully used Pufendorf's philosophy by distinguishing the political from the private person.[39] Accordingly, as a political person the king could command obedience from his subjects, but if he wanted to take up horseback riding—as a private person—he needed to follow the instructions of the teacher, just like anybody else. Thomasius thus concluded: obedience

---

Irrthuümer / irraisonabelste Ketzereyen und solche Articuli Fidei Philosophicae et Christianae, die meine Vernufft und Sinnen mißbilligen: mir ohne Schwürigkeit / angezettelt werden könten."

37. Ibid., 278.

38. On the Averroists, see notes 12 and 25 in this chapter and especially de Libera, *Raison et foi,* chap. 4: "La philosophie des professeurs."

39. See Kasper Risbjerg Eskildsen, "Christian Thomasius: Invisible Philosophers, and Edu-cation for Enlightenment," *Intellectual History Review* 18 (2008): 319–36. On the controversy between Thomasius and Masius, see Frank Grunert, "Zur aufgeklärten Kritik am theokratischen Absolutismus: Der Streit zwischen Hector Gottfried Masius und Christian Thomasius über Ursprung und Begründung der summa potestas," in *Christian Thomasius (1655–1728): Neue Forschungen im Kontext der Frühaufklärung,* ed. F. Vollhardt (Tübingen, 1997), 51–78.

and the public interest were essential to some of the king's personae but not to all of them. So in his capacity as a writer Thomasius did not feel any obligation to obey. As an author, he needed to present arguments and everything else was irrelevant. It was therefore a mistake for the Danish court to accuse him of disrespect.

Without being explicit about it, Lau adopted this argument but in a modified form. For Lau it is no longer a matter of the distinction between the freedom of the author and the duties of the subject but of that between the public persona of the atheist-author and the private one of the Christian. What was at stake here was not the decorum or public conduct of the author but the status of personal belief.

But the terminological debt to Pufendorf does not hide the influence of another great thinker: Thomas Hobbes. Hobbes left no doubt that "Beleef, and Unbeleef never follow mens Commands," and, therefore, that every citizen can privately believe whatever he likes.[40] Other rules applied only with respect to what the Church taught. According to Hobbes, there could be no general Church above the state, to which all Christians owe obedience.[41] Rather the sovereign of any state had the authority to lay down the guidelines for the public and ritual veneration of God. From this Hobbesian doctrine, Lau claimed the right to go to church as a private citizen, thus fulfilling his "duty" to the church, but as a thinker he had the right to naturalist philosophical convictions.[42]

However, it appears that Lau's position was more far-reaching than just a split of roles, because he expressly demanded the right to publish his deist

40. Thomas Hobbes, *Leviathan*, ed. C. B. Macpherson (London, 1968), chap. 42, p. 527.

41. Ibid., chap. 39, p. 498: "It followeth also, that there is on Earth, no such universall Church as all Christians are bound to obey."

42. One should mention here that Johann Salomo Semler also wrote of "private religion," distinguishing the religious views of individuals from those of the institution of the church and its theology. In his *Lebensbeschreibung*, part II (Halle, 1782), he wrote that for him it was clear and crucial "to distinguish theology and its determination by the outward religious society from the Christian private religion for so many different, separate persons." Cited by Markus Meumann, "Hermetik als Privatreligion?" in *Atlantic Understandings*, ed. Claudia Schnurmann and Hartmut Lehmann (Münster, 2006), 185–200, at 194. Semler also differentiated between the "Word of God" on the one hand and "Scripture," which was a human product, and these two distinctions form the key to neological understandings. See Martin Laube, "Die Unterscheidung von öffentlicher und privater Religion by Johann Salomo Semler: Zur neuzeittheoretischen Relevanz einer christentumstheoretischen Reflexionsfigur," *Zeitschrift für Theologiegeschichte* 11 (2004): 1–23.

books. He clearly conceded that censorship was acceptable for reasons of state, but he claimed that a book had to be permitted if only ideological— theological—reasons could be mustered against it, that is, if a book was not directly harmful to the state. In order to see the relation between this plea for freedom of publication and a human being's various personae, it is helpful to look several decades ahead to Kant.

The Public and the Public Sphere

In *Was ist Aufklärung?* (1784), Kant says: "The public use of one's reason must always be free, and it alone can effect enlightenment among the people; the private use of the same [sc. reason] may frequently be sharply limited, without considerably impeding the progress of enlightenment."[43] At first glance, this sounds like the exact opposite of Hobbes: there, private freedom and public restriction; here, private restriction and public freedom. The truth is that there is no thoroughgoing opposition, because by "private," Kant means the use of reason in a "civil position" ("bürgerlichen Posten"). Kant is here in total agreement with Hobbes, holding that the state has an interest in keeping the "machine" running, as he puts it. Only in his demand for a free public sphere does Kant go well beyond Hobbes, claiming that persons can understand themselves as belonging to a cosmopolitan society of citizens, and these citizens have the duty to address a public. The state must not impede this duty in any way. This cosmopolitan society of the world was a kind of universal authority that Hobbes had rejected when it took the form of the church. But now it existed, and it diminished the power of the state. Freedom for the public use of reason was therefore much more than just the private freedom we find in Hobbes.

43. "Der öffentliche Gebrauch seiner Vernunft muß jederzeit frei sein, und der allein kann Aufklärung unter Menschen zu Stande bringen; der Privatgebrauch derselben aber darf öfters sehr enge eingeschränkt sein, ohne doch darum den Fortschritt der Aufklärung sonderlich zu hindern." I. Kant, "Was ist Aufklärung," in idem, *Von den Träumen der Vernunft: Kleine Schriften zur Kunst, Philosophie, Geschichte und Politik* (Wiesbaden, 1979), 227. On Kant, see Jürgen Habermas, *The Structural Transformation of the Public Sphere: An Inquiry into a Category of Bourgeois Society* (Cambridge, 1989). On the public sphere, there is now a considerable literature; see, e.g., *"Öffentlichkeit" im 18. Jahrhundert*, ed. H.-G. Weber (Göttingen, 1997); Gestrich, *Absolutismus und Öffentlichkeit*; D. Goodman, *The Republic of Letters: A Cultural History of the French Enlightenment* (Ithaca, 1994); Michael Warner, *The Letters of the Republic: Publication and the Public Sphere in Eighteenth-Century America* (Cambridge, MA, 1992); T.C.W. Blanning, *The Culture of Power and the Power of Culture: Old Regime Europe, 1660–1789* (Oxford, 2002).

Lau was on the way toward a Kantian public sphere because in his writings he was developing a sense for a target readership, whom the philosopher hoped to address. His distinction of different moral personae goes beyond merely reformulating the distinction between "nature" and "grace." Through the multiplication of moral personae, the position of the philosopher became differentiated or, more accurately, distanced from himself. This was the origin of Lau's understanding of the philosopher as an "eclectic," a term that shows that Lau was exploiting not only Pufendorf's arsenal but also that of his old teacher Thomasius. Eclectics—which was for Thomasians a key polemical term with which to combat the "sectarians"—did not think they needed to adhere to authorities; they thought they could confront the whole range of conflicting traditions and consider them using their own judgment.[44] These views about the free circulation of thought were similar to those of Anthony Collins's *Discourse of Free-Thinking* (1713), although in Germany at that time only Nikolaus Hieronymus Gundling openly accepted such an alliance between eclecticism and freethinking.[45]

In Lau's view, the eclectic philosopher is someone who tests what he finds in the theater and auditorium of the world.[46] As a *veritatis eclecticae amicus*, a "friend of eclectic truth," he submits his writing to the *magno mundi auditorio*, to "the great audience of the world."[47] He says that he is putting on a "philosophical masquerade" as if he were the prop master who hands out the

44. On eclecticism, see Michael Albrecht, *Eklektik: Eine Begriffsgeschichte mit Hinweisen auf die Philosophie- und Wissenschaftsgeschichte* (Stuttgart, 1994); Ulrich Johannes Schneider, "Eclecticism and the History of Philosophy," in *History and the Disciplines: The Reclassification of Knowledge in Early Modern Europe*, ed. D. R. Kelley (Rochester, NY, 1997), 83–102.

45. Günter Gawlick, "Die ersten deutschen Reaktionen auf A. Collins' *Discourse of Free-Thinking* von 1713," in *Eklektik, Selbstdenken, Mündigkeit* (= *Aufklärung* 1/1), ed. Norbert Hinske, 9–26.

46. Lau to Thomasius, in Thomasius, "Elender Zustand eines in die Atheisterey verfallenen Gelehrten," 283: "da mir die Masque eines Heydnischen Weltweisen angezogen / und auf dem Papiernen Theatro der Meditationum . . . raisonniret / geredet und geschrieben." On the early modern use of the theater metaphor, see Ann Blair, *The Theater of Nature: Jean Bodin and Renaissance Science* (Princeton, 1997); Markus Friedrich, "Das Buch als Theater: Überlegungen zu Signifikanz und Dimensionen der Theatrum-Metapher als frühneuzeitlichem Buchtitel," in *Wissenssicherung, Wissensordnung und Wissensverarbeitung: Das europäische Modell der Enzyklopädien*, ed. T. Stammen and W. Weber (Berlin, 2004), 205–32; Flemming Schock et al., eds., *Dimensionen der Theatrum-Metapher in der Frühen Neuzeit* (Hanover, 2008).

47. Lau, *Meditationes, Theses, Dubia*, title page; reprint in Lau, *Meditationes*, 107.

masks.[48] So in Lau's eclecticism an author has no personal "authority" when he stands before the public. The author is only an editor,[49] because his construction specifically argues against a commitment to specific authorities: he only wants to provide a *Schauplatz* (a "stage"), a *Theatrum*. This is why Lau compares himself to actors who, in the vein of Daniel Casper Lohenstein's exuberant baroque plays, perform detestable things onstage (like Nero and Agrippina): "Just as these actors and moral comedians," are not to be considered "immoral people," so he, Lau the author, should not be viewed as an atheist, merely "because I have put on the mask of the pagan sage."[50]

Here we are back at La Mothe Le Vayer. But there was, of course, a difference between Lau's metaphor of "masks" and La Mothe's. Le Vayer insisted on his right to let his hypothetical *natura pura* speak. Lau, on the other hand, insisted that he could perform another role "within" his role as a philosopher, that is, of staging a certain kind of philosophy. He wanted to submit opinions to judgment without being identified with these opinions. Without much ado, Lau introduced the distinction between an actor and the author of a play. The person who plays the tyrant's murderer cannot be accused of murder. That was Lau's argument.

Actors

Despite its fragility, Lau's argument was complex; we can get a better understanding of it from a brief excursion to England. At around that same time, similar ideas were circulating there. In 1698, the conservative theologian and

48. Lau to Thomasius, in Thomasius, "Elender Zustand eines in die Atheisterey verfallenen Gelehrten," 283: "daß dieser Philosophischen Masquerade wegen / ich ein bannissement aus dem Fürsten- und Christen-Staat d.i. ex Societate Civili & Ecclesiastica: ja gar eine Annihilationem per Ignem, sollte verdienet und mir zum Lohne zugezogen haben."

49. Ibid., 273: "wie ein Collector & Relator."

50. Ibid., 282ff: "So wenig diese Repraesentanten und moralische Comödianten aber vor untugendhaffte Leute / criminelle Bösewichter und Gotteslästerer zu benennen: ob wohl eine wieder Gott / die Tugend / Ehrbarkeit und Gerechtigkeit schnur geradelauffende Conduite sie angenommen; weil zu solcher / aus dem Vorsatz / sie verbunden gewesen: die ihnen zugefallenen Roolen [*sic*] / wohl zu agiren und Characteren=mäßig sich aufzuführen: das allgemeine Händeklopfen der Zuschauer / zum Wahrzeichen einer lauten Approbation dadurch zu gewinnen; eben so wenig kann mir . . . solches zu einer so ungemein strafbahren Ubertretung ausgedeutet warden." On Lohenstein's plays, see, e.g., R. Meyer-Kalkus, *Wollust und Grausamkeit: Affektenlehre und Affektdarstellung in Lohensteins Dramatik am Beispiel von "Agrippina"* (Göttingen, 1986).

critic of theatrical culture Jeremy Collier triggered a controversy when he attacked popular plays with the claim that the dramatic portrayal of a mean and immoral act was itself a mean and immoral act.[51] All theater performances should be rejected as potentially immoral.

Interestingly, it becomes clear that Collier's critics emphasized, as Lau did a bit later, that it was important to distinguish the author of a play from a character in it. The distinction between public and private is important here, because Collier's critics equated the private with what was actual and real, and the public with what was only rhetoric and fiction. "Nothing," William Congreve suggested, "should be imputed to the Persuasions or private Sentiments of the Author, if at any time one of these vicious Characters in any of his Plays shall behave himself foolishly, or immorally in Word or Deed."[52] Michael McKeon has highlighted the significance of this debate for what he has called the "division of knowledge"—analogous to the division of labor—between public and private sphere. According to McKeon, the arguments of Collier's critics were "aided by the understanding that the sentiments of the character exist in something like a public sphere, whereas those of the author have a private existence."[53] It is not clear if Lau followed this debate or its German equivalents, such as the theater dispute in Hamburg around 1690.[54] If he was paying attention, it could have provided him with incentives for his own arguments.

But there is more to it. Another English philosopher—Anthony Ashley Cooper, the Third Earl of Shaftesbury—had already compared the problem of separating the public from the private sphere to the problem of publishing one's own writings. Shaftesbury subtly combined an aristocratic distrust of the vulgarity of the printed word with a philosophical reflection that drew from both Stoicism and the philosophy of John Locke. Modern writing for the sake of publication, Shaftesbury pointed out, depersonalizes the author. Even if the author pretends to be "personal," in fact he creates only a fake role in order to curry favor with his readership. The author needs to counterbalance this

51. On Collier, see E. Salmon in *Oxford Dictionary of National Biography* (Oxford, 2005), sub verbo.

52. William Congreve, *Amendments of Mr. Collier's False and Imperfect Citations* (London, 1698), 9.

53. McKeon, *The Secret History of Domesticity*, 101.

54. On the Pietists' objections to the Hamburg opera in 1681–88, see Hermann Rückleben, *Die Niederwerfung der hamburgischen Ratsgewalt: Kirchliche Bewegungen und bürgerliche Unruhen im ausgehenden 17. Jahrhundert* (Hamburg, 1970), 50ff.

problem by looking back to ancient models of authorship, which incorporated particular techniques to create an inner distance between his two personae.[55] If publishing leads to depersonalization, then, according to Shaftesbury, this could be used, as was the case in the Socratic dialogues, to obtain an increase of knowledge. The author needs to "multiply himself into two Persons, and be his own Subject";[56] and another passage reads: "We must discover a certain Duplicity of the Soul, and divide ourselves into two Partys."[57]

It seems rather doubtful that Shaftesbury had either Pufendorf or even La Mothe Le Vayer in mind when making these remarks. He was thinking of the Socratic dialogues, the Socratic-Platonic "Daimon" and Stoic devices from Epictetus or Marcus Aurelius. Doubling techniques that created distance, however, were interpreted by Shaftesbury in the light of John Locke's concept of "reflection" as a "notice, which the Mind takes of its own Operations."[58] This constituted a different splitting of "personae" from that undertaken in the tradition of "Libertine-Averroism" and Pufendorfian natural law. It became popular later on in England, when it was incorporated by George Berkeley in his *Alcyphron* and by Adam Smith in his *Theory of Moral Sentiments*.[59] "As the author learns the mental reflexivity of private and public microdomains," McKeon comments, "so the private author, his character separated from the public world in the process of publication, is equipped to overcome that separation through the very same mental reflexivity."[60]

Eclecticism

Theodor Ludwig Lau did not follow this intricate theory of reflexive publishing, which results in an ironic splitting of one's own opinions and dialogical reflection. Irony was not his thing, and it was probably his confidence in the methodological power of eclecticism that enabled him—in his opinion—to

55. See Ginzburg, *Wooden Eyes*, 1–24.
56. Shaftesbury, *Characteristics of Men, Manners, Opinions, Times*, ed. L. Klein (Cambridge, 1999), 72.
57. Ibid., 77. See McKeon, *The Secret History of Domesticity*, 102–5.
58. John Locke, *An Essay Concerning Human Understanding* (London, 1690), book II, chapter 1, section 4.
59. *The Works of George Berkeley* (London, 1843; reprint, Chestnut Hill, MA, 2000), 1:427 (Alcyphron, Dialog 5); on Smith, see V. Brown, "The Dialogic Experience of Conscience: Adam Smith and the Voices of Stoicism," *Eighteenth Century Studies* 26 (1992/93): 233–60.
60. McKeon, *The Secret History of Domesticity*, 104.

do without irony or burlesque writing styles.[61] Whereas Shaftesbury rejected titles such as "Meditations" or "Solitary Thoughts" as naive forms of a pseudo-privacy, Lau consistently called his publications from 1717 and 1719 "Meditationes," by which he probably intended to emphasize less the confessional than the provisional, experimental aspect.

Looking at England, however, has shown us that it is not anachronistic to apply concepts such as the "public sphere" to periods as early as the years around 1700. Rather, a number of considerations about a separation of the private and the public were already current by that time. Therefore, in the light of the idea of the public, Lau's interpretation of eclecticism as an instrument of detachment marked a step toward the *sapere aude* (Kant's phrase: "dare to know") of enlightened public discourse. Eclectics emphasized individual judgment, inasmuch as it is the eclectic author's task to choose among the arguments of several "sects": *Selbstdenken* (think for yourself) was eclecticism's motto.[62] In Lau's eclecticism, the reader rather than the author had to make this choice. This imposed a greater responsibility on the reader than the common notion of eclecticism. Lau did not claim to support the theses he presented. In the foreword of the *Meditationes, Theses, Dubia*, he confessed that some of the statements were only a matter of a playful thought experiment and a permissive train of thought, while others were "truths, brighter than the midday sun," and the rest doubts and theses that could be discussed from several perspectives.[63] Hence the reader must decide what to do with what is offered.[64]

61. On the methodological employment of "burlesque" writing for libertine purposes, see Mulsow, "Libertinismus in Deutschland"; idem, *Die unanständige Gelehrtenrepublik*, chaps. 2 and 4.

62. See N. Hinske, "Die tragenden Grundideen der deutschen Aufklärung: Versuch einer Typologie," in *Die Philosophie der deutschen Aufklärung: Texte und Darstellung*, ed. R. Ciafardone (Stuttgart, 1990), 407–58, esp. 417–24; see also chapter 8.

63. Lau, *Meditationes, Theses, Dubia*, fol. 5r; reprinted in idem, *Meditationes*, 115; for an interpretation, see Mulsow, "Libertinismus in Deutschland," 40.

64. For this conception of eclecticism Lau relied on the Pufendorfian distinction among diverse *personae morales*. See Lau to Thomasius, in Thomasius, "Elender Zustand eines in die Atheisterey verfallenen Gelehrten": "so militieret [spricht] so wohl die Distinction inter Spinosistica & Atheistica referre & Spinosam vel Atheum esse: als auch die genaue Absonderung des . . . Philosophi Eclectici a Philosopho Sectario: ebenen maaßen vor mich und meine Schrifften." There were important differences between drawing on Spinozist and atheist materials, presenting such ideas, and actually being a Spinozist or atheist. In his view, only the last should be prosecuted.

The suspicion that all of these arguments were developed only as sham arguments, advanced just to distribute libertine ideas more effectively—a suspicion voiced by Christian Thomasius—cannot be simply dismissed out of hand. In any event Lau used them to protect himself, for he did not say which of his theses he actually believed ("truths, brighter than the midday sun") and which ones he merely thought worth discussing. In Lau's striving to use legalese to make himself invulnerable, doubtless a certain conceptual haziness crept into his thinking—as for example when he compared himself to an "editor" of a work but then to an "actor" who speaks his part: this mixed up two completely different functions. An actor is really only an innocent mouthpiece, but an editor who publishes a work on tyrannicide could surely be doing so to pursue political goals.

Still, to a certain degree I think that Lau's thought experiments should be taken seriously. The interpretation of eclecticism that he suggested is possible even if highly unusual, and the early eighteenth century saw other experiments with rudimentary notions of the public sphere. Quasi-juridical argumentation can be found, for example, in the contemporary debate on how to deal with cases of plagiarism. In this instance, too, the imaginary institution of the Republic of Letters was elevated to the status of a sort of Court of Reason.[65] A generation after Lau, Johann Lorenz Schmidt seized the opportunity presented by the prohibition of his Bible translation to appeal to the public as the authority that was entitled to decide such disputed issues. Ursula Goldenbaum goes so far as to postulate the beginnings of a German public sphere in this affair.[66]

Coping with Pluralization

In reflecting on this series of quasi-juridical ideas of double personhood from La Mothe Le Vayer to Lau—a series in which other thinkers such as the English libertine deist Charles Blount could be included[67]—we are probably

65. See H. Jaumann, "Öffentlichkeit und Verlegenheit: Frühe Spuren eines Konzepts öffentlicher Kritik in der Theorie des 'plagium extrajudiciale' von Jakob Thomasius (1673)," *Scientia Poetica: Jahrbuch für Geschichte der Literatur und der Wissenschaften* 4 (2000): 62–82; Martin Mulsow, "Practices of Unmasking: Polyhistors, Correspondence, and the Birth of Dictionaries of Pseudonymity in Seventeenth-Century Germany," *Journal of the History of Ideas* 67 (2006): 219–50.

66. Goldenbaum, *Appell an das Publikum*, 1:175–508.

67. Blount had "edited" Herbert of Cherbury and others (often without citing their names) in order to promote their ideas. See J.A.I. Champion, *The Pillars of Priestcraft Shaken: The Church of England and Its Enemies, 1660–1730* (Cambridge, 1992), 142–48.

confronting not just isolated cases and exceptions but a symptom of something bigger: the crisis of modern pluralization, of an erupting diversity of traditions, positions, and worldviews among which to choose.[68] This gives us a new perspective on the origins of the public sphere. What else did these men do but search for freedom within given theological and juridical discourses? They sought a freedom for legitimately voiced dissenting opinions, for a rational debate and circulation of arguments that could proceed without limitations arising from revelation or other sorts of authority. This connection between moral personhood and eclecticism constitutes, therefore, a keystone in the yet unwritten history of coping with pluralization: a process that had to be assimilated but also endured.[69] This history could be traced from the political compromises of the Peace of Augsburg and from humanist notions of dialogue to the Enlightenment's models of tolerance—not to mention the present-day problem of basic social consensus, cultural identity, and the toleration of diversity.

Such a history would certainly be a strange parallel to Kantorowicz's sacro-juridical constructions. While in Kantorowicz's story nation-states gradually emerged from universal Christianity, in our story a new kind of universality emerges from the constrictions of the nation-state and its religion, but now based on the pragmatic acknowledgment of equally valued worldviews. The libertine's two bodies are part and parcel of the prehistory of this modern detachment or distancing. It is an open question, however, how long these proffered models could be used, because the libertines' subtle splitting of the person probably did not survive the vogue for personal authenticity sparked by Rousseau during the mid-eighteenth century.

The later eighteenth century after Rousseau was, to use Burkhard Gladigow's expression, characterized much more by singularization than by pluralization. In the field of religion, singularization meant it was impossible, or even forbidden, to "have" more than one religion. This resulted in the state's asserted ability to order this one religion.[70] Going beyond Gladigow, I think that

68. See Martin Mulsow, "Pluralisierung," in *Oldenbourg Geschichte Lehrbuch Frühe Nuzeit,* ed. Anette Volker-Rasor (Munich, 2000), 303–7; and more generally the works of the Special Research Group in Munich (Sonderforschungsbereich), no. 573.

69. See Mulsow, *Die unanständige Gelehrtenrepublik,* 191 and passim.

70. See Burkhard Gladigow, "Polytheismus und Monotheismus: Zur historischen Dynamik einer europäischen Alternative," in *Polytheismus und Monotheismus in den Religionen des vorderen Orients,* ed. M. Krebernik and J. van Oorschot (Münster, 2002), 3–20; see also P. L. Berger, *The Heretical Imperative: Contemporary Possibilities of Religious Affirmation* (Garden City, NY, 1979).

we can observe singularization or "depluralization" in other areas as well. Although Lau relied on the most modern juridical terminology of his time—that is, Pufendorf's—his opinions were hardly accepted, and the splitting of moral man into different personae came to appear less and less possible. The many roles granted to institutions were not by any means granted to the philosopher. Perhaps the emergence of the public sphere went hand in hand with a process of singularization, by carving out the free space for discussion the quasi-juridical constructions had fought to secure, making the latter superfluous.

The idea of splitting one's own moral personality into several personae (and the ability to do so) survived only in a restricted sense. In this respect, Goethe was exceptional. In 1813, in a letter to Friedrich Heinrich Jacobi, he boasted: "As a poet I am a polytheist, as a natural scientist a pantheist, and one just as decisively as the other." But as a moral person he was a monotheist Christian.[71] However, Goethe's "moral person" was no longer Pufendorf's "persona moralis" but the subject of individual morality. Lau's deployment of the juridical notion of the person and of personae belonged to an already bygone era.

71. J. W. Goethe to F. H. Jacobi, January 6, 1813, *Sämtliche Werke, Briefe, Tagebücher und Gespräche*, sec. II, vol. 7, ed. R. Unterberger (Frankfurt, 1994), 147.

3

Portrait of the Freethinker
as a Young Man

Poems and Paints can speak sometimes bold truths,
Poets and Painters are licentious youths.
John Denham, *Directions to a Painter* (1667), from
[*Poems on Affairs of State from the Time of Oliver Cromwell
to the Abdication of K. James the Second*, 1697, p. 57]

Portraits

Portraits of freethinkers and radicals are rare. How should someone with a precarious status present himself in a portrait? As a gentrified libertine, having a good time with a mistress and smoking a pipe—like Adrian Beverland, the Dutch scholar who reinterpreted the biblical story of the Garden of Eden as a sex story?[1] Or perhaps as a blasé nobleman crowning his ape with poet's

---

1. [Attributed to] Ary de Vois: *Portrait of Adrian Beverland*, Rijksmuseum Amsterdam. Another portrait by Godfrey Kneller hangs in the Ashmolean Museum in Oxford. There is a copper plate portrait from 1686 by Isaak Beckett portraying a parody of a frontispiece by Abraham Blooteling from the year 1670 showing the Italian antiquarian Lorenzo Pignoria. Like Pignoria, Beverland is sitting amid the relics of antiquity, but he is drawing a female nude statue. See Edward Chaney, "Roma Britannica and the Cultural Memory of Egypt: Lord Arundel and the Obelisk of Domitian," in *Roma Britannica: Art, Patronage and Cultural Exchange in Eighteenth-Century Rome*, ed. D. Marshall, K. Wolfe, and S. Russell (Rome, 2011), 147–70. Concerning Beverland, see Rudolf de Smet, *Hadrianus Beverlandus (1650–1716): Non unus e multis peccator. Studie over het leven en werk van Hadriaan Beverland* (Brussels, 1988); Mulsow, *Die unanständige Gelehrtenrepublik*, 6–9, 40–43. On the portraits of scholars, see Ingeborg Schnack, *Beiträge zur*

FIGURE 2. Attributed to Ary de Vois, *Portrait of Adrian Beverland.*
Rijksmuseum Amsterdam, Inv. No. SK-A-3237.

laurels—like the Earl of Rochester, the satirist and obscene eroticist who died of syphilis and alcoholism?[2] If we can trust the attribution, Beverland had his portrait painted by Ary de Vois, a well-known Leiden artist (figure 2). The portrait therefore comes from some time before 1679 because in that year Beverland had to flee to England. The scandal provoked by his book of 1678, *De peccato originale*, was enormous because in it he applied the allegories of Latin and Greek erotic lyrics to the story of Adam and Eve. He interpreted the tree of the knowledge of good and evil as a symbol for the phallus and the apple that Eve picked as a codeword for the testicles. The grandson of the great philologist Gerrit Janszoon Vos (Vossius), Beverland was then twenty-eight years old. He was pleased to have himself portrayed with a prostitute, who sat reading a book with her blouse wide open, more or less as if she were the muse who had inspired his biblical studies. We can make out the title of her book: *De prostibulis veterum*—"On the Prostitutes of Antiquity." That was Beverland's big project, his obsession. Just in case the presence of a real prostitute in the flesh was not provocation enough in this picture, a glass of wine is also sitting on the table, and Beverland, in a chic posture, is robed in a dressing gown and holding his tobacco pipe in his fingertips. This grandson from a good family and a connoisseur of pornographic literature could obviously afford to live well. And he wanted to show posterity that he was a man of the world, a libertine.

Geschichte des Gelehrtenporträts (Hamburg, 1935); Margrit Vogt, ed., *Gelehrte Selbstinszenierung: Gelehrtenporträts in Europa und Asien zur Zeit der Aufklärung* (not yet published). For representations of atheists and heretics, see Luisa Simonutti, "*Pittura detestabile*: L'iconografia dell'eretico e dell'ateo tra rinascimento e barocco," *Rivista storica italiana* 118 (2006): 557–606. Parts of this chapter are drawn from an English-language text published in Italy: Martin Mulsow, "Radical Enlightenment, Cameralism and Traditions of Revolt: The Case of Theodor Ludwig Lau (1670–1740)," in *La centralità del dubbio: Un progetto di Antonio Rotondò*, vol. 2, ed. Camilla Hermanin and Luisa Simonutti (Firenze, 2011), 747–63. The epigraphs for this chapter come from the anonymous work *The Fifth Advice to a Painter*, from the year 1667, as quoted from Hans-Joachim Zimmermann, "Simia Laureatus: Rochester Crowning a Monkey," in *Functions of Literature: Essays Presented to Erwin Wolff on his Sixtieth Birthday*, ed. Ulrich Broich et al. (Tübingen, 1984), 147.

2. [Attributed to] Jacob Huysmans: *Portrait of the Earl of Rochester*, Warwick Castle; a copy, reprinted here, can be found in the National Portrait Gallery, London. On Rochester, see Kirk Combe, *A Martyr for Sin: Rochester's Critique of Polity, Sexuality, and Society* (Newark, 1998). See also Graham Greene, *Lord Rochester's Monkey, Being the Life of John Wilmot, Second Earl of Rochester* (New York, 1974). Concerning the portrait, see Zimmermann, "Simia Laureatus," 147–72; Don-John Dugas, "The Significance of 'Lord Rochester's Monkey,'" *Studia Neophilologica* 69 (1997): 11–20; Keith Walker, "Lord Rochester's Monkey (again)," in *That Second Bottle: Essays on John Wilmot, Earl of Rochester*, ed. Nicholas Fisher (Manchester, 2000), 81–88.

FIGURE 3. Copy of a painting attributed to Jacob Huysmans,
Portrait of the Earl of Rochester. National Portrait Gallery, London, NPG 804.

Similarly with John Wilmot, the Second Earl of Rochester. The portrait,
painted by the Flemish artist Jacob Huysmans, was even more provocative (figure 3). Huysmans was a painter at the court of Charles II, where Rochester lived
as a confidant of the king and as an enfant terrible. If the picture was done about
1675–76, it also portrays—as in the case of Beverland—a twenty-eight-year-old.
He was much better off than the Dutch scholar. He had distinguished himself in

battle and was a glittering presence at court, able to converse brilliantly. But he drank heavily, led a dissolute life, and was overly fond of dirty jokes. In 1676 he was finally banished from the court. Rochester had himself portrayed as a poet, which he was, displaying a blasé face and a shocking gesture. With a manuscript in his hand, he is crowning an ape with the laurels of a poet. The ape for his part has torn pages out of a book and offers one to Rochester.

The scene is certainly both a painted joke and a provocation. Yet what was it exactly that Rochester wanted to tell the viewer? One suspects that Rochester's portrait illustrates his satirical attack on the person and work of John Dryden, the great dramatist, critic, and poet. For a time Dryden enjoyed the patronage of the aristocratic Rochester, who brought Dryden's works to the attention of the king. This lasted only a short time, however, because their temperaments were so different, and in 1675–76 a poisonous controversy broke out between them. Rochester despised Dryden's "apish" gestures of loyal submission as false and obviously conceived the idea of a double portrait: of himself and of Dryden, whom he had depicted as an ape, who offers his empty and meaningless dedication to his patron. The deeper meaning of the portrait, of course, goes well beyond that. The fact that an ape was portrayed reveals Rochester's deep skepticism about Dryden's high ideals about inspiration and human reason. The aristocratic libertine composed a counter to such ideals, entitled "Satire against Mankind."

These portraits of Beverland and Rochester are not really the poses in which a serious intellectual would choose to present himself. Even though provocation and blasphemy adorned the exterior appearance of many dissenters, there was also nevertheless a true model of the sober freethinker. Could such a model also be depicted? How would one represent a serious freethinker?

One of the very few pictures we have of a German radical from the early Enlightenment is the portrait of Theodor Ludwig Lau, whom we find in a copperplate engraving that survives (perhaps as a unique exemplar) in the Dresden Museum of Engravings (figure 4).[3] Lau, to whom we return in this chapter, attended university in Königsberg and Halle and then went traveling for six years through western Europe, where he was exposed to a wide variety of ideas.[4] His areas of interest and knowledge ranged from applied mathematics and physics (he attended lectures by Newton), jurisprudence, philosophy, theology, and literature to politics, economy, and tax policy. To understand

3. Kupferstichkabinett Dresden, Inventory Number A 20121. I am deeply grateful to Hanspeter Marti for making me aware of this portrait some time ago and for providing me with a reproduction of it.

4. On Lau, see the references given in chapter 1.

FIGURE 4. *Portrait of Theodor Ludwig Lau.* Kupferstichkabinett Dresden, Inv. No. A 20121.

his interest in all these subjects we have to see his topics as related and view his life in the manner that Pamela Smith has applied to Johann Joachim Becher, the economist, inventor, and alchemist. Becher too was a polymath, drawn to natural science, philosophy, politics, and economics, an unstable wanderer whom we find constantly in search of a patron and new areas in which to apply his knowledge.[5] One has to look carefully for the common patterns of thought in these fields in order to draw a general profile of such intellectuals. Just a glance at the biography of Becher, who was active in the 1660s and 1670s, should warn us against too quickly throwing around terms like "baroque" or "Enlightenment"—and absolutely forbid the use of empty labels like "transitional figure." But if we study men like Becher and Lau within the currents of their day, we can learn some amazing lessons about the radical Enlightenment.

The portrait of Lau in the Dresden Museum, according to an annotation on the print, was engraved in 1737 in Hamburg by Christian Friedrich Fritzsch, and was drawn "from life." But it was finished with the help of two earlier oil paintings that had both been painted in 1734.[6] One of them was by Leonhard Schorer from Königsberg and already displays the hourglass with very little sand left that we see in the engraving. The other one was by Christian Sidau in Mittau (Jelgava in Latvia), who surrounded its subject with a series of emblems.[7] Both of these paintings have disappeared, but we know that the copper-plate engraving by Fritzsch unites the characteristics of these two pictures so that the meanings Lau wanted his painters to represent were retained.

The portrait is lively, autobiographical, emblematically encoded, and impressive. It stands in shocking contrast to the real misery of the thinker himself, who ever since 1711 had been unemployed and looking for a secure appointment. Therefore this portrait—Lau was already sixty-seven years old—was also, importantly, a promotional image of himself as a younger man. Despite his lack of money, Lau had attired himself sumptuously with coat and sword and wearing a wig. But with this portrait he was obviously also hoping to

5. Pamela H. Smith, *The Business of Alchemy: Science and Culture in the Holy Roman Empire* (Princeton, 1994).

6. Christian Friedrich Fritzsch, the son of the copper-plate engraver Christian Fritzsch, was born in 1719 and was therefore only eighteen years old when he completed the portrait.

7. Lau provides this information in his *Palingenesia honoratissimorum et post funera adhuc perdilectissimorum parentum suorum, bene natorum . . . bene denatorum . . . essentiae statum et existentiae, tandem accepit Die XV Junii, anni MDCCXXXVI ab intus nominato*; Altonaviae. The text appeared also in German translation as *Die Wiederbelebung seiner Höchstgeehrtesten . . . Eltern, im selben Büchlein*, 12–24. The description of the portrait: pp. 1ff., or in the German version, pp. 12ff.

FIGURE 5. Lau, *Portrait*, detail: "Haec mysteria."

display his legacy, his achievements and merits, and he did so in emblematic manner by appearing as someone who casually points with his right hand to an open book in which we can read "Vobis haec mysteria manent"—"for you this remains mysterious" or perhaps "for you these mysteries remain" (figure 5). Mysteries? Therefore something into which one must be initiated, if one hopes to understand. One thinks at once of Freemasonry, which had just taken shape in England and was, in 1733, attempting to obtain a foothold in Germany.[8] Or perhaps it's a reference to John Toland, one of Lau's freethinking role models, who in his *Pantheisticon* of 1720 provided a sort of confession of faith and liturgy for a "Socratic Society," his imaginary association of pantheists.[9]

Whatever exactly he was referring to, Lau presented himself as a fighter, who used the pen (on his sword was inscribed the word "penna") to order the reader of this image to decode his personal "mysteries"—the emblematic riddles of his teachings concerning God, human beings, and society, which he had painted on the columns that framed him.[10]

8. Helmut Reinalter, *Die Freimaurer* (Munich, 2000); Rolf Appel, *Schröders Erbe: 200 Jahre Vereinigte fünf Hamburgische Logen* (Hamburg, 2000).

9. John Toland, *Pantheisticon* (London, 1720). On Toland, see Champion, *Republican Learning*.

10. As early as 1725 the unemployed Lau was offering his services in providing emblems and similar designs to interested parties: "Hof-Comoedianten und Theatralisten, Medailleurs, Mahler, Kupferstecher, Architecteurs, auch galant gelehrte Satyren beliebende Virtuosi können sich frey bei ihm angeben, wo sie nach ihren Desseins, auf Lustige- und Trauer-Fälle, und so

The Piper of Frankfurt

I will begin with a few provocations. "I have piped [i.e., played my flute] loudly and melodiously enough, but they did not want to dance." This was Lau's final account of his life composed shortly before his death, after sixty-six years of life, nineteen of them as a persecuted, restless man: someone branded as an atheist for whom the path back to a bourgeois life was barred.[11] For a radical Enlightenment philosopher, a biblical reference to such an "account" was unusual. In Matthew 11:16–17 Jesus declared that John the Baptist was the greatest of prophets, "He that hath ears to hear, let him hear!" But those who did not wish to hear the prophet were "like unto children sitting in the markets, and calling unto their fellows, And saying, We have piped unto you, and ye have not danced; we have mourned unto you, and ye have not lamented." Even in the prior sentence Lau struck a religious note: "Dixi et liberavi animam" (I have spoken and delivered my soul). That was the sort of groaning sigh of confession, derived from Ezekiel 3:19, that Kierkegaard, one hundred years later, was also to utter.[12]

What sort of freethinker was this, who could give voice to such religious formulations and who also in just those years fell back on emblems and hermetic ideas concerning the transmigration of souls?[13] Posing the question more broadly, what were freethinking and the radical Enlightenment in

---

weiter, Inventiones, Erfindungen und Auszierungen de bon gusto, in gebundenen und ungebundenen Versen Stylo Lapidari, oder Inscriptionen, Symbolis, Emblematibus u.s.w. zu haben begierig." I quote this passage from a text reproduced by David Fassmann in *Der gelehrte Narr* ("Freyburg" [Berlin], 1729), 47.

11. *Die Original-Rede welche der hochwohlgebohrne Herr Tribunals- und Hof-Gerichts-Rath Wilhelm Ludwig von der Groeben, als des Königlichen Preußischen Ehrwürdigen Sambländischen Consistorii Praesident und Officials; Bey einem gewissen Actu solemni retractationis im Jahr 1729. den 6. Octobr. An den Hoch-Fürstlich-Churländischen Staats-Rath und Cabinets-Directorem Theodor Ludwig Lau, J.V.D. gehalten* (Altona, 1736). This piece is contained in Martin Pott's reprint edition: Lau, *Meditationes philosophicae de Deo, Mundo, Homine*, 157–88; it includes Lau's official recantation of his supposed atheism. I am quoting Lau's attached footnote from p. 32.

12. Søren Kierkegaard, *Entweder Oder*, ed. Hermann Diem and Walter Rest (Munich, 1975), 702.

13. On Lau's doctrine of palingenesis, see *Meditationes philosophicae de Deo, Mundo, Homine*, chap. III § XL: "Nullam propterea exhorresco Mortem: quae aliis, rerum omnium terribilissima. Interitus est nullus. Annihilatio nulla. Conceptus sunt, Ideae, Non-Entia, Somnia, Chimerae. Vita rerum aeterna. Natura Creaturarum immortalis. Migratio Animarum perpetua. Corporum Metamorphosis continua." He was using the concept of palingenesia in a metaphorical sense

Germany around 1700? Did they belong wherever possible to the tradition of radical prophecies, in a continuation of oppositions to established authority? The reference to piping provides a clue, for it could direct our attention toward the so-called "Piper of Niklashausen." This was a certain Hans Böheim, a shepherd, who appeared in 1476 at the Marian pilgrimage shrine of Niklashausen in Franconia and preached about his own private revelations. His sermons quickly revealed an anticlerical campaign against the clergy mixed with "communist" demands: "Pope and emperor, princes and counts, knights and their servants, burghers and peasants, should share with the common man, all equally with one another, abolishing all taxes and restoring community of property."[14] Over thirty thousand supporters followed Böheim, and St. Matthew's reference to "piping" and to "summoning listeners to the dance" resonated in the name they gave him.

But the days of the radical Reformation and its late medieval forerunners were long past by 1717, the two hundredth anniversary of the Reformation, when the "piper" Lau appeared in Frankfurt and published his radical *Meditationes de Deo, Mundo, Homine.*

Lau had probably never heard of Böheim. At that time men of his sort wore a coat and leggings after the French fashion along with a sword at one's belt. Millenarian revolts had evolved into cleverly calculated plans for reform. Even so, one could see Lau as a social rebel, though one who had been transformed by absolutist cameralism, a man who pursued large-scale notions ranging from philosophy to tax policy—and who failed because he came too early.[15] His philosophy appeared anonymously and clandestinely, but his financial and economic writings appeared legally at the same time and under the name of their author, as we saw in the previous chapter.

An adequate notion of the "radical Enlightenment" in Germany will need to confront or disperse many paradoxes. It's not just the fact that radical thinkers moved in circles that included moderate early Enlightenment spokesmen sometimes even at the courts of German princes—as cameralists, theorists of

---

(note 7). On the transmigration of souls, see Helmut Zander, *Geschichte der Seelenwanderung in Europa: Alternative religiöse Traditionen von der Antike bis heute* (Darmstadt, 1999).

14. Richard van Dülmen, *Reformation als Revolution: Soziale Bewegung und religiöser Radikalismus in der deutschen Reformation* (Frankfurt, 1987), 21. On other social-religious traditions of this sort, see George H. Williams, *The Radical Reformation* (Philadelphia, 1962); Antonio Rotondò, *Studi di storia ereticale italiana del Cinquecento* (Florence, 1974).

15. On the concept of social rebels, see Eric Hobsbawm, *Primitive Rebels: Studies in Archaic Forms of Social Movement in the 19th and 20th Centuries* (Manchester, 1959).

statecraft, or jurists in courts of public law—facts that apparently contradict the oppositional spirit of the radical Enlightenment.[16] We need to explain another great contradiction: the alliance between radical Enlightenment thinkers and radical spiritualists such as Johann Konrad Dippel or Johann Christian Edelmann—after all, it's not so clear how radical critiques of religion fit together with mystical motivations.[17] And finally we also see in many radical authors, from Knutzen to Gundling and Zeidler, the remnants of satirical traditions dating back to the coarse farces of the sixteenth century—these too were resources that seem far distant from the "modern" world of Locke and Spinoza.[18] To grasp these paradoxes more clearly I will undertake a double reading. I will read the "official" cameralist writings of Lau on the one hand, but then in parallel the radical philosophical works he published anonymously. What sort of picture do we get?

Cameralism

Theodor Ludwig Lau's cameralism was an economic theory that rested on ideas of social justice. The deeper motivations for these ideas may lie in his philosophical writings. His treatises on economics and taxation, however, were early examples of ideas on how a princely state might plan to intervene in commerce; they derived from recent insights into the laws of the economy.[19]

---

16. Here is a small selection of the literature: Frühsorge, *Der politische Körper*; Gestrich, *Absolutismus und Öffentlichkeit*; Horst Dreitzel, *Monarchiebegriffe in der Fürstengesellschaft: Semantik und Theorie der Einherrschaft in Deutschland von der Reformation bis zum Vormärz* (Cologne, 1991); Kühlmann, *Gelehrtenrepublik und Fürstenstaat*; Ian Hunter, *Rival Enlightenments: Civil and Metaphysical Philosophy in Early Modern Germany* (Cambridge, 2001).

17. Attempts like those of Siegfried Wollgast, *Der deutsche Pantheismus im 16. Jahrhundert* (Berlin, 1972), remain unsatisfactory.

18. On the use of burlesque style as a "niche" for libertinism, see Mulsow, "Libertinismus in Deutschland."

19. See, in general, Zielenziger, *Die alten deutschen Kameralisten*; Erhard Dittrich, *Die deutschen und österreichischen Kameralisten* (Darmstadt, 1974); Jutta Brückner, *Staatswissenschaften, Kameralismus und Naturrecht: Ein Beitrag zur Geschichte der politischen Wissenschaft im Deutschland des späten 17. und frühen 18. Jahrhunderts* (Munich, 1977); Keith Tribe, *Governing Economy: The Reformation of German Economic Discourse, 1750–1840* (Cambridge, 1988); Volker Bauer, *Hofökonomie: Der Diskurs über den Fürstenhof in Zeremonialwissenschaft, Hausväterliteratur und Kameralismus* (Cologne, 1997); Rainer Gömmel, *Die Entwicklung der Wirtschaft im Zeitalter des Merkantilismus 1620–1800* (Munich, 1998); Marcus Sandl, *Ökonomie des Raumes: Der kameralwissenschaftliche Entwurf der Staatswissenschaften im 18. Jahrhundert* (Cologne, 1999);

For Lau the underpinnings of economic and financial policy were manufacturing, flourishing trade among merchants, good management, a bank, a principality's treasury, and general frugality. He modeled his ideas on those of Johann Joachim Becher but also Veit Ludwig von Seckendorf, Wilhelm Schröter, and the English mercantilist Sir Josiah Child, the director of the East India Company.[20] Among the authors he quoted we find John Locke, with his theory of money: "The true value of money is, when it passes from one to another in buying and selling."[21] So Locke was not just the groundbreaking spokesman for a "reasonable Christianity," an expression Lau adopted for his own position,[22] but also a theorist of commerce.

Lau produced these works after he was dismissed from state service as a financial expert in Kurland (Kurzeme in Latvia), so they were also conceived as promotional brochures directed to potential princely employers.[23] In them he based his claims on the interests of princes and their lands: introducing religious freedom was good for attracting the immigration of burghers; guaranteeing justice; securing wealth and peace. All of these were preconditions for a flourishing kingdom and for the stability of a monarch's power.[24] But these

Thomas Simon, *"Gute Policy": Ordnungsleitbilder und Zielvorstellungen politischen Handelns in der Frühen Neuzeit* (Frankfurt, 2004).

20. Veit Ludwig von Seckendorff, *Teutscher Fürsten-Staat* (Jena, 1737); Wilhelm von Schröder, *Fürstliche Schatz- und Rentkammer* (Leipzig, 1686); Josiah Child, *Brief Observations concerning Trade and the Interest of Money* (London, 1668); idem, *A New Discourse of Trade* (London, 1668/1690). Lau quotes Child in his book: *Politische Gedancken, welcher Gestalt Monarchen und Könige, Republiquen und Fürsten, nebst ihren Reichen, Ländern und Unterthanen, durch eine leichte Methode mächtig und reich seyn oder werden können* (Frankfurt, 1717), § 3, pp. 7ff.

21. John Locke, *Some Considerations of the Consequences of the Lowering of Interest and the Raising the Value of Money* (London, 1691). See Lau, *Politische Gedancken*, 51ff. On Locke's theory of money, see Patrick Hyde Kelly, ed., *Locke on Money*, 2 vols. (Oxford, 1991).

22. In his list of unpublished works at the end of the *Original-Rede*, Lau lists this title: *Das vernünftige Christenthum des Hochfürstl: Churländischen Staat-Raths und Cabinet-Directors Theodor Ludwig Lau.*

23. In 1711, at the death of the duke of Kurland, Lau was dismissed from service as a Cabinet Director at the urging of the Russian royal house.

24. See Lau, *Entwurff einer Wohl-Eingerichteten Policey* (Frankfurt, 1717), chap. I, § XIX: "Sie [the citizens] werden angelocket: durch 1. Unbehindertes Zu- Durch- und Abreisen / auch sichere Verbleibung in den ländern und Städten eines Staats: 2. Die Freyheit des Gewissens: 3. Exemtiones, Freyheiten und Privilegien: 4. Die Wohlfeiligkeit der Vivres, Materialien und Waaren: 5. Einen reichen Verschleiss und Gelosung natürlicher und politischer Früchten: 6. Eine Coaequation: in regard der Würden und übrigen bürgerlichen Vorzügen: 7. Eine ungedruckte Ausübung ihrer Gewerben / Künsten und Professionen: 8. Zulängliche Assecurationes

social goods could just as easily be justified by recourse to his philosophical theories because for Lau freedom was the original condition of mankind and his highest good.[25] Even though Lau took over a great deal from Hobbes, on this point he was as much a critic of Hobbes as the roughly contemporaneous clandestine work *Symbolum Sapientiae*.[26] For him freedom of religion and conscience were essential.[27] Lau's ideas of wealth were grounded in a naturalist and hedonistic worldview, one that took its bearings from Spinoza, Toland, and Vanini. The physiology of that viewpoint depended on understanding human strivings and impulses mechanically—they were at first spontaneous but were

---

und Einladungs-Patenten." Lau profited from the experiences that the Elector of Brandenburg had with his Huguenot policy after the Revocation of the Edict of Nantes in 1685. See Gottfried Bregulla, ed., *Hugenotten in Berlin* (Berlin, 1988).

25. Lau, *Meditationes philosophicae de Deo, Mundo, Homine*, chap. IV, § XXVI and XXVII: "Durus ergo Civium & Subditorum, in toto Orbe est Status: Hodiernos attamen secundum Mores apprime necessarius. Approbo eundem, Civis ipse & subditus: cui sola Obedientiae Gloria relicta; Insimul autem deploro. Bruta siquidem, imo Brutis sumus deteriores. Regum Servi. Mancipia Magistratuum. Machinae sine Sensu, Ratione, Voluntate. Sentientes, Intelligentes & Appetentes non aliud, nec aliter: quam prout Imperantes nostri volunt & nos jubent. Status longe felicior, licet non amplius dabilis nec utilis: Homnis est: ceu Creaturae. Liberum tunc ens: Libere agens & libere cogitans. Sine Rege: Lege: Grege: Praemia non sperat: Poenas non timet. Vitia ignorat: Peccata nescit; Omnibus in Actionibus Dictamina praelucentis Rationis & ducentis Voluntatis, pro Vitae Cynosurus habens. Beata Vita talis: imo Divina! Assimilatur hoc modo Creatura Deo: Deus enim Libertate Intellectus & Appetitus gaudet. Tantum!" Lau, *Meditationes, Theses, Dubia, philosophico-theologica* (1719, ed. Pott), § III: "Primus et verus Hominis Status: est Libertinismus. Exerit is se in Vita: Ratione: Sermone: Scriptione. Ens quia Liberum: libere vivit, cogitat, loquitur, scribit. Quale Ens: tales Entis Affectiones. Sunt vero illae: ab Homine inseparabiles; Has ipsi demere velle: foret destruere Essentiam Homnis." On Lau's special style, see Mulsow, "Libertinismus in Deutschland."

26. *Symbolum Sapientiae*, Sectio IV: De origine boni et mali ex doctrina Hobbesii, ubi de origine societatum, § 10: "Sane (4) si homines hunc naturae statum conservassent, et sua sorte solisque frugibus contenti in naturali illa societate mansissent, nec ad rerum possessiones dominiaque aspirassent, non opus habuissent legibus, sed eadem tranquillitate, qua heri hodieque bruta, societatem domesticam colere potuissent." *Cymbalum mundi sive Symbolum Sapientiae*, ed. Guido Canziani, Winfried Schröder, and Francisco Socas (Milan, 2000), 272. See Mulsow, *Enlightenment Underground*, 159–60. Concerning the state of nature for humanity, see also *Theophrastus redivivus*, ed. Canziani and Paganini, 805ff., 840ff., as well as the ancient models in Lucretius, *De rerum natura* V, 932ff. and Ovid, *Metamorphoses* I, 89ff.

27. See Lau, *Meditationes, Theses, Dubia*, § VI: "Tolerantia cujusve generis Librorum, utilis & necessaria." § XXVII: "Religio videtur mihi optima . . . quae . . . Liberae est Rationis & Voluntatis; Electionis non Coactionis. Propriae Convictionis: non alienae Persuasionis. . . . Reliquas Dissidentium Opiniones: examinat, non accusat. Ponderat, non damnat."

then, later, restrained by the structures of society.[28] When we read in his *Design for a Well-Planned Policy* that the inner constitution of a state consists of a cheerful society of people, who lead a light-hearted life,[29] he means one in which religious fear and state violence are absent—but this is clear only if we look at the *Meditationes*. It seems highly ironic that concealed behind this supporter of early modern social disciplining[30] and author of state regulations stood an anarchist, who thought that the greatest happiness resided in having no regulations at all: "A much happier condition, even if it's no longer possible or expedient, is that of man as mere creature. For then he's a free being, acting and thinking freely, without king, law, and outward restraint. He does not look for rewards and fears no punishments; he knows no errors and is ignorant of sin."[31] The contradiction is only slightly reduced by his proviso, "even if it's no longer possible or expedient." This clause reveals the inner balance in Lau, the balance between the revolutionary (in his philosophical views) and the reformer (as a realist); we need to keep this tension always in mind if we are to understand his

28. See Lau, *Meditationes philosophicae de Deo, Mundo, Homine*, chap. IV § XII: "Nescit hinc talis, appetitui suo relictus Homo, in hoc Libertatis, quem a Nativitate accepit statu: Leges vetanes & permittentes." § XIII: "Cum vero pro Temperamentorum Varietate: Appetitus varius, variaeque sic actiones; Primos mox inter Homines, Jurgia, Lites, Oppositiones, Contradictiones, Resistentiae, Tumultus, Caedes, Bella exorta." On the doctrine of temperaments in the German early Enlightenment, see Pott, *Aufklärung und Aberglaube*.

29. Lau, *Entwurff einer Wohl-Eingerichteten Policey*, 3ff.: The polity ("Policey") takes care of the "inner and outer constitution of a state." The inner constitution consists in "1. . . . einer vergnügten Gesellschaft: die 2. Ein vergnügtes Leben führen. Die Gesellschaft wird starck durch den Anwachs der Einwohner und eine glückliche Bevölckerung." See Zielenziger, *Die alten deutschen Kameralisten*, 401.

30. I will provide here only a small selection of the literature: Gerhard Oestreich, *Geist und Gestalt des frühmodernen Staates: Ausgewählte Aufsätze* (Berlin, 1969); Winfried Schulze, "Gerhard Oestreichs Begriff 'Sozialdisziplinierung' in der frühen Neuzeit," *Zeitschrift für Historische Forschung* 14 (1987): 265–302; Paolo Prodi, ed., *Glaube und Eid: Treueformeln, Glaubensbekenntnisse und Sozialdisziplinierung zwischen Mittelalter und Neuzeit* (Munich, 1993); Heinz Schilling, "Disziplinierung oder 'Selbstregulierung der Untertanen'? Ein Plädoyer für die Doppelperspektive von Makro- und Mikrohistorie bei der Erforschung der frühmodernen Kirchenzucht," *Historische Zeitschrift* 264 (1997): 675–91; Wolfgang Reinhard, "Sozialdisziplinierung—Konfessionalisierung—Modernisierung: Ein historiographischer Diskurs," in *Die Frühe Neuzeit in der Geschichtswissenschaft: Forschungstendenzen und Forschungsergebnisse*, ed. Nada Boškovska Leimgruber (Paderborn, 1997), 39–55.

31. Lau, *Meditationes philosophicae de Deo, Mundo, Homine*, chap. IV, § XXVII.

work as a whole. Instead of explaining away his inner inconsistencies as logical weaknesses we can see them as symptoms of an intrinsic tension.[32]

To that extent Lau's ostensible concern for the interests of princes was not a flat contradiction of "democratic" traditions and radical Enlightenment but rather a sort of strategy for implementing radical doctrines. Viewed more carefully, the cameralist writings of Lau thus conceal a remnant of dissimulation, if we are right in taking his historical sketch of culture and power as expressing his own ideas: he wrote that monarchical rule made originally free men into "slaves" by binding them with the "fetters of religion"; and then these "new lords" invented all sorts of laws. Even the laws of nature and of nations had their origins there.[33] It was a critique of princely rule when he wrote that "even though princes forbid their subjects to do so, they themselves have only one supreme goal in all their actions: to cultivate and satisfy their desires, seeking only their own advantage and profit."[34] Lau was playing with thoroughly anarchist and seditious ideas, which if they were taken seriously would have made all his training in natural law worthless, to say nothing of his employment at a princely court.[35]

His dissimulation, however, was not perfect. At many points in his political theory Lau's naturalism shows through, for example in his reforming proposals, which went well beyond customary restraints, and nowhere better than in his feisty defense of polygamy.[36]

32. One could try to cover this tension with the complex concept of "self-fashioning," which describes a formation of identity that involves both inner attitudes and external forces. Stephen Greenblatt, *Renaissance Self-Fashioning: From More to Shakespeare* (Chicago, 1980). On prudence and cautious behavior, see Claudia Benthien, *Barockes Schweigen. Rhetorik und Performativität des Sprachlosen im 17. Jahrhundert* (Munich, 2006).

33. Lau, *Meditationes philosophicae de Deo, Mundo, Homine*, chap. IV, § XIX: "Per Leges vero, quo Hominum Cerebrum & Cor, Ratio & Voluntas, Intellectus & Appetitus domarentur, ne quid, novos contra Imperantes, primae Libertatis Usurpatores, tentare auderent: nescio quot ipsis ab Imperantibus, earundem adinventae Divisiones. Ex eorum ergo Mente, Jus Naturae & Gentium: Prohibens & Permittens: Negativum & Affirmativum: suas habuere Origines."

34. Ibid., chap. IV, § XXIV: "Iisdem interdicunt quidem subditis, Principes. Principes vero, ipsi, omnibus in actionibus: Desideriis satisfacere, & Interesse seu Utilitatem quaerere, unico & primo pro Scopo habent."

35. On this basis one could see Lau as a worthy contributor to the traditions of resistance theory. On that topic, see Winfried Schulze, *Bäuerlicher Widerstand und feudale Herrschaft in der frühen Neuzeit* (Stuttgart, 1980). On the way in which Spinozism undermined natural law, see Schröder, *Spinoza*, 162–66.

36. Lau, *Entwurff einer Wohl-Eingerichteten Policey*, chap. I, 6: "Die Populosität eines Staates zu facilitiren: wollte zwar die / in dem Orient fürnemlich / im Schwang gehende Polygamie in

Polygamy

Speculations about polygamy, which surfaced repeatedly among cameralists and students of natural law around 1700, were, as Isabel Hull rightly says, a sort of thought experiment, with which one could act out the possibility of radical social change. On this topic revelation and natural law diverged and the variety of customs among other peoples became visible.[37] Oriental morals in the West? Lau had been deeply influenced by Beverland and insisted more clearly than any other on pursuing this experiment, justifying it as a cameralist by citing the need of states for a dense population in order to secure their welfare. He stood at the very beginning phase of what Foucault called "biopower" (*biopouvoir*): the growing concern of the state for the bodies and sexuality of its subjects.[38] The naturalism of radical Enlightenment thinkers like Lau fit perfectly into this growing concentration on biopower.

Vorschlag bringen; weil aber durch selbigen / wie einer Sturm-Glock / die schreckbare Cantzeln ich wider mich zum gefährlichen Aufflauff ermuntern würde: halte vor sicherer / davon zu abstrahiren. Jedoch wann die Menge der priviligirten Bordels, Musick- und Spielhäuser: die florirende Mode der öffentlichen und heimlichen cocüages: die Winckel-Embrassaden: Mariages de Conscience: die Matrimonia ad Morganaticam: die mutuelle Expectantien auff die Todten-Fälle der Eheleute: die Unterhaltung der Maitressen entweder in eigenen Palästen / Familien oder garnirten Chambres: und mehrere unzulässige fleischliche Galanterien / die unter uns Christen / Lehrer und Zuhörer verüben / mit serieusen Reflexionen erwege; muß dieses freymüthige Urtheil fällen: Dass vor besser und excusabler ich halte / die Viel-Weiberey zu vergönnen / als die erzehlte sündliche Lebens-Manieren zu conniviren und durch publique Gesetze gar zu rechtfertigen. Denn da die Juden etliche Frauen zugleich haben heyrathen und mit ihnen nach ihrem gusto sich divertiren können: Dieser Praxis auch von den moratesten Nationen im Orient und anderswo beobachtet wird; Warumb sollte dergleichen unschädliche Licenz den Christen eben zu einer verbottenen Frucht gedeyhen? Da gleichwohl mit keinen unwidertreiblichen Beweissthümern erhärtet werden kann / daß vielen Ehefrauen beyzuwohnen / den Göttlichen und natürlichen Rechten schnur-gerade entgegen lauffe."

37. Isabel V. Hull, *Sexuality, State, and Civil Society in Germany, 1700–1815* (Ithaca, 1996), 176–79; on the debate on polygamy in natural law, see Stephan Buchholz, "Erunt tres aut quattuor in carne una: Aspekte der neuzeitlichen Polygamiediskussion," in *Zur Geschichte des Familien- und Erbrechts*, ed. Heinz Mohnhaupt (Frankfurt, 1987), 71–91; Mulsow, "Unanständigkeit," 1–26; Manuel Braun, "Tiefe oder Oberfläche? Zur Lektüre der Schriften des Christian Thomasius über Polygamie und Konkubinat," *Internationales Archiv für Sozialgeschichte der deutschen Literatur* 30 (2005): 27–53.

38. Michel Foucault, *Naissance de la biopolitique: Cours au collège de France (1978–1979)* (Paris, 2004); idem, *The History of Sexuality*, vol. 1: *The Will to Knowledge* (original French ed.,

In arguing for polygamy, Lau also advanced an argument based on "good civic order" (*gute Policey*), because polygamy would serve to curb abuses like prostitution. But he noted that the "clergy, all zealous for the honor of God," would not permit such a reform.[39] If one adds the theory of lordship advanced in clandestine fashion in his *Meditationes*, one can see what Lau thought of the power base of the clergy. There he declared that the status of religion depended on a complex interplay between the "melancholy" superstitious mentality of the dominated and the striving for power of "choleric" rulers, who exploited religious fears, introduced oracles, and mysteries and used them to install their clergy.[40]

1976; English translation, London, 1976). See Petra Gehring, *Was ist Biomacht? Vom zweifelhaften Mehrwert des Lebens* (Frankfurt, 2006).

39. Lau, *Entwurff einer Wohl-Eingerichteten Policey*, chap. I, 7: "Weil indessen / wegen der Contradiction der / vor die Ehre Gottes eiffernden Clerisey / nicht zu verhoffen: es werde die fruchtbare Polygamie, die das souverainste Mittel ist / ein Land zu peupliren / durch eine Sanctionem Publicam autorisiret werden; muss die Bevölkerung des Staats durch andere Expedientia bewerckstelligt werden."

40. Lau, *Meditationes philosophicae de Deo, Mundo, Homine*, chap. IV, § XIVff.: "Bellorum horum & discordiarum Autores: Temperamento Colerico praedominantes, principaliter fuerunt. XV. Fuerunt vero uti Bellorum, ita & Imperiorum Autores: quorum Fundamenta prima, posuerunt per Arma & Opressiones. Colerici enim sensim atque sensim, vi Complexionis, aliis imperitare volentes: Melancolicis, qui eorundem Ambitioni, maxime contrarii videbantur, vi, clam, precario devictis; Phlegmaticos, & Sanguineos: plurimi quorum, se sua sponte, Metu suadente, tradentes; Servitutis Compedes laeto exosculabantur Ore: Dominationi suae, facili subjecerunt Opera. XVI. Monarchia ergo, prima Mundi fuerunt Imperia. Colerici enim, primi Monarchae extiterunt. Uti vero Coelum duos non patitur Soles, Taedae Socium nesciunt: sic Colericus, nullum in Regno & Throno, Consortem admittit & Co-Imperantem. XVII. Imperio Monarchico sic fundato, ad illud conservandum: Religio. Leges. Praemia. Poenae: introducta. Subsidia Ambitionis. Dominatus Arcana. Omnia Colericorum Inventa. XVIII. Religionis Vinculo, Homines ex Liberis, Servi facto." For similar thoughts that do not, however, have a basis in the doctrine of temperaments, see *Theophrastus redivivus*, ed. Canziani and Paganini, 343ff.: "Primi igitur quos incessit regnandi libido, ad artes et commenta animum traduxere et leges ad societatis vinculum condidere. Deosque excogitaverunt . . . et religionem, quae est de rebus ad deos pertinentibus tractatio, instituerunt: ad quam ut pervenirent, postquam deos esse docuerunt, illos res humanas regere et gubernare finxerunt, quod providentiam dixere"; p. 345: "Religio vero, ad dei cultum et populi utilitatem primum instituta, eo tandem devenit ut omnis utilitas illius ad solos sacerdotes religionis ministros redundaverit, quorum authoritas temporis progressu tantum apud credulos et devotos invaluit crevitque, ut sacerdotes tamquam deos reputent, nec non illis honores solis diis decretos reddant." Lau could find such theories about the political origins of religion (which originated with the Sophists such as Critias) not only in libertine literature but also in Orthodox refutations, e.g., in Daniel Clasen, *De religione politica* (Magdeburg, 1655).

Fundamentally, Lau could reckon to a certain extent on the support of princes against ecclesiastical Orthodoxy, just as Thomasius could, but his proposals for polygamy certainly overstrained this alliance. And so it was characteristic for what we have called the inner division in Lau that he felt caught in a double bind, expressing his proposal but then admitting that it was not practicable. We can recognize the division also in the fact that in the discussion of polygamy collective memories of the radical Reformation also came to the surface, notably the polygamous experiment of the Anabaptists in Münster in 1534–35.[41] To that extent Lau's call for polygamy was not only a consequence of his naturalism but— purely historically—also in a long tradition of spiritualist revolts.

Emblems

We can see that with Lau we are dealing with many layers of thinking, which blended several traditions and levels. In chapter 2 it became clear that his thought borrowed from Pufendorf to describe the intellectual's different personae. Here, however, we see something different. Lau's thought was employing emblems as a form of expression, which identifies him as a man of the baroque despite his Enlightenment characteristics—at least if we take our bearings from Walter Benjamin and Albrecht Schöne.[42] But that fact places us on the shores of a forgotten continent, that of the political-moral-philosophical emblems of the sixteenth and seventeenth centuries and also of philosophical "metaphorology."[43] Like Becher, Lau turned to images when he wanted to explain his basic ideas. Becher, for example, chose as his personal symbol a cup (*Becher*), playing on the literal meaning of his name, but a cup in which as in an alchemical furnace a transformation took place. A hand from heaven trickles the juice of a grape into this cup. Becher thus intentionally mixes religious and profane connotations: the cup is the vessel of transubstantiation but also a

---

41. See Lyndal Roper, *Oedipus and the Devil: Witchcraft, Religion and Sexuality in Early Modern Europe* (London, 1994), chap. 2.

42. Walter Benjamin, *The Origin of German Tragic Drama* (original German edition, 1928, trans. John Osborne; London, 1998); Albrecht Schöne, *Emblematik und Drama im Zeitalter des Barock* (Munich, 1993).

43. Translator's note: In the thinking of Hans Blumenberg, metaphorology is the study of metaphors as essential and foundational elements of philosophical language. See Hans Blumenberg, *Paradigms for a Metaphorology*, trans. Robert Savage (Ithaca, 2010).

technical instrument; but then he adds an adage: "Bibat qui potest, lavet qui vult, turbet qui audet" (Let him drink who can, let him wash who wants to, let anyone who dares be disturbed), an adage that fuses an apparently profane, hedonist-sounding toast with the deep symbolism of the Holy Grail. This motto was also a hidden quotation from the *Chymische Hochzeit Christiani Rosen-Creutz* (*The Chemical Wedding of Christian Rosenkreutz*), one of the foundational texts of the Rosicrucians, but one recognized only by the initiated.[44]

FIGURE 6. Lau, *Portrait*, detail: "Rationis & Revelationis Objecta."

When Lau had his portrait painted in 1734, he instructed the artist to decorate the border of his portrait with seven emblems that were supposed to sum up his whole thinking in simple images.[45] In the first emblem (figure 6), at the top left, we read a superscript "Rationis & Revelationis Objecta mea" (my objects—meaning "my chief concerns"—[are those] of reason and of revelation).[46] The image shows a coastal landscape with lighthouses, and at the top a triangle in the style often used for the Trinity. The corners of the triangle are labeled D, M, and H, which can easily be deciphered as Deus, Mundus, and Homo (God, World, and Man), which refer to the three basic areas of metaphysics: rational theology, cosmology, and psychology. Thus the title of Lau's work from 1717 was *Meditationes philosophicae de Deo, Mundo, Homine* (and three years later the

44. [Johann Valentin Andreae], *Chymische Hochzeit* (Strasbourg, 1616), Fourth Day: "Bibat ex me qui potest, lavet qui vult, turbet qui audit: Bibite fratres, et vivite." This reference is not acknowledged in Smith, *Business of Alchemy*, 274.

45. The emblems are visible in the copper-plate version of the portrait produced by C. F. Fritzsch in 1737. They were described in *Wiederbelebung*, 12–14, at 13: "In Mitau bin an. 1734 von dem erfahrnen Maler Sidau / gleichfalls abgeschildert / und bestehet der Unterscheid zwischen diesem und dem ersten Portrait: daß an beyden Seiten / des Churlandischen Sinnbilder zu sehen / die mit meinem Glauben / Leben / Humeur und Genie, herausgegebenen Schrifften / Verfolgungen / Avantüren u.s.w. eine offenbahr-geheime Connexion unterhalten / und wie Spinges und Oedipi, d.i. Rätzel und ihre Auflöser zugleich seyn."

46. Ibid., 14: "Diese seyn die Vorwürffe von meiner Vernunft und geoffenbahrten Religion."

FIGURE 7. Lau, *Portrait*, detail: "Sunt mihi curae, utraque Salus."

similarly titled work by Christian Wolff: *Vernünfftige Gedancken von Gott, der Welt und der Seele des Menschen* [i.e., *Reasonable Thoughts on God, the World, and the Soul of Man*]). Inside the triangle the number "III" can be seen, another reference to this philosophical triad. But why is all of this floating over a coastal landscape? Probably because these philosophical labels depict the course of thinking itself. Anna Roemers Visscher used an emblem in her 1620 book *Zinne-Poppen* (*Meaningful Images*) with the note that it was "Intelligentibus," that is, for those who could understood. And she too depicted a beacon on a seacoast.[47]

Images of Public Spirit and the Welfare of the State

Lau's other images lead us into his ideas for cameralist reform. The second emblem (figure 7), placed directly below the first, displays two columns joined at the top by a crown, on which we find a double-faced Janus-head—and in the background the towers of some kingdom. On the left-hand column was painted "Regnorum" (of kingdoms) and on the right-hand "Regum" (of kings). Above the whole emblem stands the epigraph "Sunt mihi curae, utraque Salus," which Lau translated freely as "The welfare of kingdoms and of their kings has become dear to my heart."[48] This is a good example of the hardships reform politicians experienced at a princely court. Naturally, he had to stress that he served his monarch; but he wanted to make it clear that the "kingdom," that is, the population, was just as dear to him. He could not profess more. But what was his teaching for rulers?

That's what the third emblem shows (figure 8). It contains a crown with an interlocked sword and scepter, and below a spider in a web, a beehive with bees, and an ant heap. At the very bottom one sees a quill pen or perhaps a plow, a caduceus, and a cannon; and surmounting them all: "Vobis, Tales Eos Facere Monstro" ("I teach you world monarchs how to turn your estates, inhabitants, and subjects into just these sorts of spiders, bees, and ants"). This was another

47. Anna Roemers Visscher, *Zinne-Poppen, alle verciert met Rijmen*, 3rd ed. (ca. 1620), no. 58.
48. Lau, *Wiederbelebung*, 14.

reference to the Bible (Prov. 6:6).[49] In *Political Thoughts*, Lau had tried to teach princes and their ministers how to increase the wealth of their states and also "like busy ants and bees how to strive, produce, and collaborate."[50] The upper row of symbols depicts the ruling powers, the spider in his nest presents the ruler's dominion over his kingdom, while the lower row gives us the estates of the learned, merchants, and soldiers. We may recall such symbolism in the engraving on the title page of Hobbes's *Leviathan*.[51] Lau could have borrowed the imagery of the monarch as a spider in his web from Zincgref's *Emblemata ethico-politica*.[52]

FIGURE 8. Lau, *Portrait*, detail: "Vobis, Tales Eos Facere Monstro."

The symbolism of the spider suggests yet another echo in Lau's work, for it appears also in his *Meditationes de Deo, Mundo, Homine*, where we read that "God is the spider and the world is his web."[53] Here the metaphor appears as a theological statement, indeed as an anti-Trinitarian statement: God was only unitary (and not triune), and Lau went on to interpret him in the pantheistic sense of Spinoza's *natura naturans*.[54]

Lau's image also points us to a relativistic understanding of human reason, for in Thomas Browne's *Religio Medici*, a text that Lau knew well, the verse

49. Ibid.

50. Lau, *Politische Gedancken*, § 8, p. 15: The princes and their ministers had to "gleich fleissigen Ameisen und Bienen / anzuschaffen und zusammen zu tragen / bemühet seyn."

51. See Horst Bredekamp, *Thomas Hobbes visuelle Strategien: Der Leviathan, Urbild des modernen Staates* (Berlin, 2002).

52. Julius Wilhelm Zincgref, *Emblematum ethico-politicorum centuria* (Heidelberg, 1664), Emblem 37: "In centro / Le milieu gouverne le tout. // Un Monarque prudent doit imiter l'araigne, / Se tenir sur sa terre en gardent le milieu; / Pour pouvoir d'autant mieux secourir chasque lieu / Le vil hoste des Rois ce bel art leur enseigne. // Wie es sich gebührt. // Ein König sol mitten im Reiche sich setzen / Wie Spinnen in ihren selbsteigenen Netzen / Auff welchen sie leichtlich die Grentzen beschutzen / Der Spinnen ihr wesen kann manchem was nutzen." See in general Arthur Henkel and Albrecht Schöne, eds., *Emblemata: Handbuch zur Sinnbildkunst des XVI. und XVII. Jahrhunderts* (Stuttgart, 1967).

53. Lau, *Meditationes philosophicae de Deo, Mundo, Homine*, chap. II, § 3: "Mundus hic: in Deo, ex Deo, & per Deum est. Deus Aranea: Textura Mundus."

54. Translator's note: For Spinoza, *natura naturans* refers to the self-causing activity of nature, in contrast to *natura naturata*, which refers to nature as the passive product of an infinite causal chain.

from Proverbs was put this way: "Indeed, what reason may not goe to Schoole to the wisedome of Bees, Aunts, and Spiders? What wise hand teacheth them to doe what reason cannot teach us?"[55] Here we find that each biologically different form of life has been granted its own specific reason,[56] but Lau was also speaking in favor of physicotheology, the proof of God drawn from the perfect arrangements of Creation. He was playing off physicotheology against theological explanations drawn from revelation, but also subverting the very goal of theology inasmuch as he saw God not as transcendent but as the immanent cause of the world.[57]

And what about the dominated? The fourth emblem speaks of them (figure 9). This emblem depicts a cloud from which a hand descends—as with Becher—but here it is holding shears; and below, two sheep, one almost dead, the other with a full coat of wool. The motto on this emblem reads: "Tondereque docui non deglubere" (i.e., "I have also taught how sheep may be shorn without skinning them").[58]

55. Thomas Browne, *Religio Medici* I, 15; *The Major Works*, ed. C. A. Patrides (London, 1977), 77ff. In the Latin translation by Levinus Moltke that Lau might have used, this passage reads: "quotus et quisque est, quem non Apes, Formicae & araneae sapientiam docere possunt? Quae tandem docta manus haec illos docet, quae nos ratio ipsa docere nescit." *Religio medici, cum annotationibus* (Strasbourg, 1665), 80. Lau mentions Browne among the authors who influenced him: Thomasius, "Elender Zustand eines in die Atheistery verfallenen Gelehrten," 233–358; reprinted in Pott's edition, p. 273: Lau had "bey seinen Recreations-Stunden / zusammt dem Alten und Neuen Testament: der Theologia Christiana & Gentili: den Aristotelem, Platonem, Pythagoram, Epicurum, Cartesium, Herbertum, Hobbesium, Machiavellum, Spinosam, Beverland, Pereira, Boccalini, Ovidium, Lucanum, Lucretium, Clericum, Montagne, Vayer, Broion [this appears to have been a misprint for "Brown"], Blount, Baelium, Huygenium, Tolland, Brunum &c. &c. mit ihren op- & propugnatoribus, wie ein Philosophus Eclecticus durchgeblättert und conferiret."

56. See similarly Giordano Bruno, *De monade numero et figura* (Frankfurt, 1591); Hieronymus Rorarius, *Quod animalia bruta ratione utantur melius homine Libri duo* (Amsterdam, 1654).

57. Lau, *Meditationes philosophicae de Deo, Mundo, Homine*, chap. I, § Vff: "Existentia Dei: nulla indiget probatione; Sensus enim omnium incurrit. Oculus eum videt. Auris audit. Nasus olfacit. Lingua gustat. Manus tangit. En Testes infallibiles, & omni exceptione majores! VI. Mihi ea patet, ex mirabili, tot Mundorum, Globorum Terr-aqueorum & igneorum, ac ex Triplicis Regni, Animalis, Vegetabilis & Mineralis Creatione, Gubernatione & Conservatione: in qualibus palpabili & visibili modo, Deus sese manifestavit ac revelavit. VII. Est haec Dei, in Operibus & per Opera sua, facta Revelatio, certissimum, mathematicum & infallibile: lucidissimum quoque & sufficiens, Deum ejusque existentiae Realitatem, cognoscendi & convincendi Principium." But then see Lau's utterances concerning the immanence of God: "IV: Mihi: Deus Natura Naturans: ego Natura naturata." On physicotheology, see Wolfgang Philipp, *Das Werden der Aufklärung in theologiegeschichtlicher Sicht* (Göttingen, 1957).

58. See the description in Lau, *Wiederbelebung*, 14.

This image is directed first at Lau's theory of taxation, and indeed beneath the sheep is a book
with the initials "A. S.": an abbreviation for Lau's
book, *A Candid Proposal for the Increase of Income... through improved Regulation of the...
Tax System.*[59] Lau knew the passage in Suetonius's biography of Tiberius, in which Tiberius
orders his commanding officers not to extract
too much in taxation from his subjects.[60] And he
probably also knew how this passage had been
translated into emblems, as for example in Nicolas Reusner's *Emblem Book, Partly Ethical and
Physical, but Partly Historical and Hieroglyphic* of

FIGURE 9. Lau, *Portrait*, detail:
"Tondereque docui non deglubere."

1581 (*Emblemata partim ethica, et physica, partim
vero historica et hieroglyphica*). Wilhelm Schröter
had drawn on it for the frontispiece of his *Princely Treasury and Exchequer* (figure 10).[61] The idea that taxation should be socially tolerable, as we find among
moralists and cameralists,[62] turns out to be another indicator that Lau was smuggling his radically Enlightened convictions into his practical political proposals. As
a revolutionary who could not abolish the rule of princes, he could at least try to
ease the burden of domination. He had had to stand by too often as the governed

59. Lau, *Aufrichtiger Vorschlag von glücklicher, vorteilhafter, beständiger Einrichtung der Intraden
und Einkünften der Souverainen und ihrer Untertanen: in welchen von Policen- und Kammer-
Negocien und Steuer-Sachen gehandelt wird* (Frankfurt, 1719). Translator's note: The first word of
the title is *Aufrichtiger* and the last word is *Steuer-Sachen*, i.e., A and S.

60. "Boni pastoris est tondere pecus, non deglubere": Suetonius, *Vita Tiberii* 32.1.

61. Nicolas Reusner, *Emblemata partim ethica, et physica, partim vero historica et hieroglyphica*
(Frankfurt, 1581), vol. II, no. 26. See Henkel and Schöne, *Emblemata*, col. 1100. Wilhelm Schröter
(von Schröder), *Fürstliche Schatz- und Rentkammer* (Leipzig, 1686; Königsberg and Leipzig, 1752).

62. See generally Michael Stolleis, "Pecunia nervus rerum: Zur Diskussion um Steuerlast
und Staatsverschuldung im 17. Jahrhundert," in *Pecunia est nervus rerum: Zur Staatsfinanzierung
der frühen Neuzeit*, ed. idem (Frankfurt, 1983), 63–128; Ingomar Bog, *Der Reichsmerkantilismus:
Studien zur Wirtschaftspolitik des Heiligen Römischen Reiches im 17. und 18. Jahrhundert* (Stuttgart,
1959); Johannes Kunisch, "Staatsräson und Konfessionalisierung als Faktoren absolutistischer
Gesetzgebung: Das Beispiel Böhmen (1627)," in *Gesetz und Gesetzgebung im Europa der Frühen
Neuzeit* (= *Zeitschrift für Historische Forschung*, Beiheft 22), ed. Barbara Dölemeyer and Diethelm
Klippel (Berlin, 1998), 131–56; on the relationship between the government and its subjects, see
Winfried Schulze, "Die veränderte Bedeutung sozialer Konflikte im 16. und 17. Jahrhundert," in
Europäische Bauernrevolten der frühen Neuzeit, ed. idem (Frankfurt, 1982), 276–308.

FIGURE 10. Wilhelm Schröder, *Fürstliche Schatz- und Rentkammer* (Königsberg and Leipzig, 1752), frontispiece.

were truly fleeced in order to support the luxuries of the court. Lau's words, quoted earlier, about the self-dealing of princes spoke directly to this issue.[63]

Addressing Persecution

Emblem number 5 (figure 11) carries the slogan "Aerem feriunt Cornua vestra" (i.e., Your horns will hit only air; they will swing and miss). Lau explains, "Those of you who regard me resentfully! You will not catch me. I will mock

63. See note 34: "princes . . . have only one supreme goal in all their actions: to cultivate and satisfy their desires."

your prosecutions."[64] This encoded mystery
blatantly reflects the persecution experienced
by the radical. The emblem displays a lion
(Lau), accompanied by a fox and a lamb.
Above them stands a silver star on a black
field; three black rams oppose them, ready to
attack. The lion, the fox, and the lamb: three
figures with three political qualities. Machiavelli had told the prince that he needed to be
both a lion and a fox,[65] and later politicians
adopted the slogan: be both strong and cunning; but along with them Lau emblematically
added that the prince should be like the innocent lamb, permeated with only the purest motives. For then a lucky star will stand over you

FIGURE 11. Lau, *Portrait*, detail:
"Aerem feriunt Cornua vestra."

and the attacks of your persecutors will come to nothing. So here Lau is calling
attention to his "cunning," his art of dissimulation and his double-entry politics,
a tension-filled balancing act between reforming politician and radical philosopher of the Enlightenment.

The sixth emblem (figure 12) also serves the purpose of revealing himself, and
it shows how bitter was his opponents' campaign of constant persecution. "Pro
re nata, sum usus utroque," that is, "Yes, according to circumstances I have used
both." Lau explains it this way: "Sometimes I have heartily and reasonably
laughed as a Christian at that gang of malicious, straggling, and envious *messieurs*, but sometimes because of their myopic or even blind eyes I've had to
express a truly lively condolence."[66] Laughing and weeping—these were embodied in Democritus and Heraclitus, portrayed as two satyrs holding masks and
standing next to two trees. Behind them, a mountain—Lau explains it as Pindus
or Helikon (or Parnassus)—and Pegasus on top. A waterfall flows down; it's the
Castalian fountain of the Muses.

This emblem is a very complex picture of "self-fashioning." We sense a roller
coaster of emotions, the masking of which disguises various personae, but also
Lau's reaction to secret scheming. And yet this place of constant flux is also the

64. Lau, *Wiederbelebung*, 15.

65. Michael Stolleis, "Löwe und Fuchs: Eine politische Maxime im Frühabsolutismus," in
idem, *Staat und Staatsräson in der frühen Neuzeit* (Frankfurt, 1990), 21–36.

66. Lau, *Wiederbelebung*, 15.

FIGURE 12. Lau, *Portrait*, detail:
"Pro re nata, sum usus utroque."

place where the poet, the seer, drinks from the source of inspiration. The fact of Pegasus's presence confirms that here the emblem points to the wellspring of poetry and wisdom, for when Pegasus kicked Mount Helikon, a spring bubbled forth.[67] Iconographically it was unusual that Lau intertwined the ideas of satyrs and the Muses with the motif of Democritus and Heraclitus. The two philosophers to some extent replace the personifications of comedy and tragedy, the Muses Thalia and Melpomene, which we would more commonly expect. But because Lau saw himself as both a philosopher and a poet (and translator of poetry), he may have hit on the idea to weave the two ideas together. Democritus, who laughed at the world, and Heraclitus, who wept for the world, illustrate how Lau as a writer had reacted to attacks: with ironic satire, or with sober tragedy, according to the circumstances.[68] The fact that the philosophers appear as satyrs holding masks reflects a tradition in which satyrs, Bacchus, or cherubic forms wore masks in order to indicate the role playing found in the world of the theater.[69] Lau and his artist perhaps had Peter Aubry's title engraving for Moscherosch's satire in mind: *Philander von Sittewald*, in which a putto and a satyr sit opposite each other holding masks (figure 13).[70]

But did Lau write satires? Was he imitating Democritus? In the list of his unpublished works there are indeed a few that might fit this description. We find, for example, a work entitled *Soloecismus Adami-Evae*—in other words, "The Error of Adam and Eve" (which was probably a translation or adaptation of Adrian Beverland's obscene *Peccatum originale*).[71] Lau himself characterized the

67. See Walter F. Otto, *Die Musen und der göttliche Ursprung des Singens und Sagens* (Düsseldorf, 1954).

68. See Reinhard Brandt, *Philosophie in Bildern: Von Giorgione bis Magritte* (Cologne, 2000), 91–113; Oreste Ferrari, "L'iconografia dei filosofi antichi nella pittura del secolo XVII in Italia," in *Storia dell'Arte* 57 (1986): 103–81.

69. Leuschner, *Persona, Larva, Maske.*

70. Johann Michael Moscherosch, *Wunderliche und Wahrhafftige Gesichte Philanders von Sittewald* (Frankfurt, 1642).

71. Lau, *Vale suum respective ultimum! Famigeratissimae Academiae Lugdunensi Batavorum Gratitudinis ex Obligatione triplici, obtulit* (1736), 10; see Adriaan Beverland, *Peccatum originale* ("Eleutheropoli," 1678). On Beverland, see note 1 in this chapter.

FIGURE 13. Michael Moscherosch, *Philander von Sittewald*,
part II (Strasbourg, 1650), frontispiece.

style of this work as "Historice-Theologice- & Satyrico" but also "Reflexive-Criticus."[72] And other works were similarly "Heraclitean," at least in the sense that they complained about the accusations heaped up against him.

The picture of exchanging masks also reminds us of the basic pattern in Lau's thinking: he often referred to the double role he played as a clandestine philosopher but also as a cameralist at court. In defending himself against his teacher Thomasius, as we have seen, he used Pufendorf's doctrine of different *personae morales*, claiming that it was legitimate to slip into various roles. In this way he could in public "be" a "heathen" or atheist, even if as a private person

72. Lau, *Vale suum respective ultimum!*

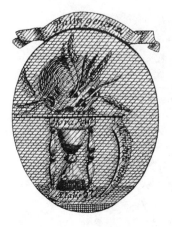

FIGURE 14. Lau, *Portrait*, detail, "Palingenesia."

he was a Christian. He had deeply internalized this sort of alternating change of roles.[73]

And this emblem possesses another dimension of a personal nature, concealed behind all the writing postures and public roles: it testifies to the emotional ups and downs that Lau experienced as a human being living under intense pressure, persecuted and unable to publish his many writings. We should recall that Lau had attempted suicide in 1719 while in jail, when he tried to slit his wrists. He was then in his Heraclitean mode of depression, of naked fear. But sometimes he may have burst out in wild laughter, a horrified laughter at the narrow-mindedness of his times.

After these six images of deep reflection about his own existence, a separate final emblem comes to our attention (figure 14)—the very one that was originally on the painting by Schorer. It stands off to the side of the others, is larger but in content also more private. It's the emblem of death, one's own death. Using the classic symbolism of vanitas, it displays an hourglass and a skull, from which four green spikes protrude. Despite that, this is not a conventional warning of "memento mori" (even though that can be read on the added scythe blade) but rather something completely idiosyncratic. It has to do with "Palingenesie," as the superscript caption says, that is, revival and resurrection, as Lau calls it. This emblem posits a connection to a peculiar late work of Lau's with the title *Palingenesia parentum meorum*, an annotated epitaph not only of his parents but also for himself.[74] In that work he spoke at length of his father, Philipp Lau, and of what he became (finance official, associate professor) but also—strangely—of what he did not become (judge and full professor): "He never rose to those heights!" In long sentences Lau brooded over a judgment that applied to his own failed career as well. "In reality he achieved all he wanted, inasmuch as he did not really want to rise higher," and then he comes to speak of himself, in an epitaph in which he composed the warning, "That . . . he cease to be a foolish sinner; and begin to be a new man and one reborn; in

73. See chapter 2.
74. Lau, *Palingenesia*.

order to live and to die truly reasonable and truly Christian, in the new zodiac of his life."[75]

"Three-quarters of the sand" has already flowed through the hourglass, and Lau was feeling the approach of death. In 1736 he was virtually obsessed with thoughts of death. He realized that "with every stroke of the clock the thought sounded constantly with the strongest basso: Consider that you are dying!"[76] Lau considered that year as the "greatest climacteric year" of his life, one that he would hardly survive. Therefore he sought to put his life in provisional order by publishing a bibliography of his many unpublished works. He had been driven out of Rödelheim near Frankfurt, where he had lived, and then out of The Hague. In both places they lit fires for him and burned some of the works that he had in manuscript; no wonder he felt persecuted and perhaps fell into paranoia.[77] His last words invoked Psalm 140: "Rescue me, Lord, from evildoers; protect me from the violent, who devise evil plans in their hearts and stir up war every day."[78]

75. Lau, *Wiederbelebung*, 18.

76. Lau's short autobiography is in *Privilegierte Hamburgische Anzeigen* no. 24, March 26, 1737, pp. 186–90, here at p. 189.

77. These biographical details have not been known before. We only knew of the notice by Nemeitz that Lau was seen in 1730 "not far from Frankfurt . . . looking by chance out of a farm house." Johann C. Nemeitz, "Von einem Plagio, und zugleich einige Particularia von dem Herrn Lau," in idem, *Vernünftige Gedancken über allerhand historische, critische und moralische Materien*, part III (Frankfurt, 1740), 72–80, at 76. But one should compare that with the remark in Lau's bibliography (the *Original-Rede*, 30): "33. Deutscher Commentarius über die zwo ersten Bücher des Telemachs: denn von weiterer Fortsetzung abstrahire; Warum? Ist nicht nöthig zu erinnern! Undanck, Verfolgungen u.s.w. würckliche Recompencen meiner Patriotischen Arbeiten, haben mir ein Edictum prohibitorium, sub Poena rigorosissima in Contraventionis Casum, insinuiren lassen: Wie sie gleichfalls Uhrstifter der Feuerwercken zu Rödelheim-Solms und im Grafenhaag [= The Hague] gewesen, die verschiedene meiner vorgehabter und in etwas auch schon entworffen gewesener Arbeiten: Z.E. Amsterdamsches Welt-Magazin, der Kauf-Handel zu Amsterdam, Entwurf eines wohl-regulirten Krieges-Etats u.s.w. nebst allen dazu gehörigen vielen Collectaneis u.s.w. in die Wesenheit der Asche verwandelt haben." On his paranoia, see the notice by Nemeitz, p. 78: "es spückte ihm im Gehirn." On Lau's Dutch intentions in The Hague, see the *Rede: Curiosis Rei Litterariae Amatoribus. Peraeque uti Bibliopolis, Hagae-Comitum habitantibus: Latino suo Stylo Philosophico-Politico-Juridico reali, iis inserviendi inclinationem, praesenti in Scheda offert et manifestat* Theodor Ludwig Lau. J.U.D. [1735].

78. This translation, from the New International Bible, is closer to that of the German (Luther's) translation that Lau knew. Lau, *Wiederbelebung*, 24: "Vergiß nimmer / was ich dir gesagt: // Ich habe durch die Warnung / meine Seel gerettet! // Mit völliger Erlaubniß gehe nun hin / wo du willst // Rechts / oder Lincks; // zu den gläubigen weisen Schafen / oder ungläubigen

Lau's *Palingenesia* was probably in part an expression of hope that he would be remembered, that he would have made some lasting impression on posterity, but in part it was also truly Christian and spiritual hope for the resurrection as the Pietist belief in being "reborn" suggested. In his *Meditationes* of 1717 Lau confessed his belief in the transmigration of souls: "Therefore I fear no death, which for others is the most horrible of all things. There is no doom, no process-of-becoming-nothing. . . . The migration of souls never ends."[79] At one time he followed Epicurus and Lucretius in holding that all things were made of tiny atoms, which were constantly being reassembled anew. But now in 1736 his thinking sounded more alchemical, recalling Johann Konrad Dippel and others, and no longer necessarily suggests any eternal transmigration of souls: "Until through the art of chemical-alchemical transformation, out of this world's burnt remnants and petrified chaos are created and formed a new earth and a new heaven."[80]

One can wonder if the idea of palingenesis and of the transmigration of souls functioned as substitute religions for Lau, an alternative consolation in the face of death. A very similar substitute religion can be found among left-wing Wolffians, who speculated voluminously about the soul's journey to the planets.[81]

A Kind of Transcendence

And so, in the end, we can ask if a deist like Lau could cultivate a public spirit without transcendence, political engagement without religion. Does the portrait of this freethinker that we've been analyzing depict a secular libertine or a baroque representative of some private religion?

---

schwartzen Böcken: // nach dem freyen Willen deiner eigenhirnichten Phantasie; // Ich werde dich / zu der Auswahl nicht zwingen. // Behte indessen von den treuen Rathgebenden Mentor von Hertzen: / daß der Innhalt des hundert und viertzigsten Psalms // wie ein Triumph-Lied // in seiner unschuldig-verhaßten Person // möge erfüllet werden!"

79. See note 13 in this chapter.

80. Lau, *Wiederbelebung*, 24. On Dippel, see Karl-Ludwig Voss, *Christianus Democritus—Das Menschenbild bei Johann Konrad Dippel: Ein Beispiel christl. Anthropologie zwischen Pietismus und Aufklärung* (Leiden, 1970); Stephan Goldschmidt, *Johann Konrad Dippel (1673–1734): Seine radikalpietistische Theologie und ihre Entstehung* (Göttingen, 2001).

81. See Martin Mulsow, "Das Planetensystem als *Civitas Dei*: Jenseitige Strafinstanzen im Wolffianismus," in *Das Jenseits: Facetten eines religiösen Begriffes in der Neuzeit*, ed. Lucian Hölscher (Göttingen, 2007), 40–62. See also generally Zander, *Geschichte der Seelenwanderung in Europa*; on "esotericism" as an alternative religion, see Monika Neugebauer-Wölk, "Aufklärung—Esoterik— Wissen: Transformationen des Religiösen im Säkularisierungsprozeß. Eine Einführung," in *Aufklärung und Esoterik: Rezeption—Integration—Konfrontation*, ed. eadem (Tübingen, 2008), 5–28.

Lau belonged to the age of the growing absolute state in Germany, with its need for jurists and economic experts, for "Polizey" (civic order) and regulation.[82] But this was also an age that saw the rise of "concrete experience"—what Erhard Weigel called "Wisdom about the Real World" (*Realweisheit*)—as opposed to purely theoretical doctrines and dogmas.[83] A reform movement took shape, which included educators such as Wolfgang Ratke and Johann Balthasar Schupp as well as natural scientists and technicians such as Joachim Jungius or linguists and economic experts like Johann Joachim Becher.[84] We can find both tendencies in Germany from the middle of the seventeenth century, so that the period around 1700—when Lau was active—did not mark a break but a kind of continuity. The biggest innovations, like those in natural law or in the thinking of Spinoza, had to fit somehow into this new framework. Lau's eclecticism seems to have been a patchwork composed of fragments from the most varied political and philosophical languages: Machiavellism, cameralism, Spinozism, libertinism, and the teachings of natural law. Even spiritualistic mysticism and occult hermeticism left their traces on his thinking. This was partly due to his role as a cultural mediator and reformer, a role Lau claimed for himself, and in which he produced a sort of eclecticism. Lau has been accused of using such fragmented or discordant languages that his arguments were inconsistent; they deployed certain metaphors polemically in specific cases but in such a way that they could not comport well with his other metaphors in any larger system.[85] To some extent these "inconsistencies" had their roots, as we have seen, in the inner tension between his anarchism and a more realistic politics, but also in part in the fact that Lau was still

82. For literature, in addition to Simon, *"Gute Policy,"* see Hans Maier, *Die ältere deutsche Staats- und Verwaltungslehre*, 2nd ed. (Munich, 1980); and Michael Stolleis, *Geschichte des öffentlichen Rechts in Deutschland*, vol. 1: *Reichspublizistik und Policeywissenschaft 1600–1800* (Munich, 1988).

83. Edmund Spieß, *Erhard Weigel: Weiland Professor der Mathematik und Astronomie zu Jena, der Lehrer von Leibnitz und Pufendorf* (Leipzig, 1881). See Lau's remarks on his style in *Original-Rede*, 26, in his list of unprinted works: "13. Scheda, qua curiosis Rei Litterariae Amatoribus peraeque uti Bibliopolis, Hagae Comitum inhabitantibus, Latino meo Stylo Philosophico Politico-Juridico reali, iis inserviendi Inclinationem offero & manifesto, 4to 1735. . . . 15. Palingenesia perdilectissimorum meorum Parentum! Seu Epitaphium Latino-Germanicum in eorum Honorem, Stylo Lapidario exaratum in 4to Altonaviae 1736."

84. See, for example, the works of Wolfgang Ratke or Johann Balthasar Schupp. And in general and especially with regard to England, see Charles Webster, *The Great Instauration: Science, Medicine and Reform, 1626–1660* (London, 1975).

85. Schröder, *Spinoza*; Pott, "Einleitung," in his reprint edition cited in note 11.

thinking in the seventeenth-century style of complex visual symbolism, one that was also steeped in biblical imagery. Despite his own theoretical emphases on reason and the critique of religion, his thinking was grounded in this historically specific mentality.

Of course one could interpret this implicit element of transcendence in his thinking either as a late Christian "reversion" or as the inevitable complement or necessary anchor for someone who saw himself as the mouthpiece for new initiatives, whether as laughing and ironic or perhaps as playful, or even perhaps full of real conviction. Philosophically speaking, the dependence on transcendental ideas in the *Meditationes* can be found in Lau's use of natural law. God is still necessary as the source of obligations of each individual to the whole of society. At the same time, however, Lau's pantheism undermined the personhood of the God whom his legal thinking presumed.

This contradiction cannot be resolved, but if we look more closely, we can at least see where certain "civil religious" sacralizations reveal themselves in Lau's eclectic balancing act, sacralizations that were evasions for what was otherwise reserved for Christian transcendence. At one point we find a certain utopianism in the idea of a free life beyond any notion of sin, at another point he assumes a basic corporeality, and at still others he depends on the transmigration of souls, as we've seen. Even at the end of his life Lau was probably still persuaded of all of them, and so one cannot really speak of any real "relapse."

With his theory that he could play the roles of different personae, however, he did reserve for himself a small inner space in which he could preserve something Christian: emotional rootedness, hopes, a deep-seated biblicism in his imagery, the Proverbs and Psalms. This, so it seems to me, is the real center of transcendence for Lau, quite apart from his inclinations toward civil religion. Publicly a heathen, privately a Christian—this paradoxical attitude, which was the precise opposite of what might make for a politically correct candidate for president. But being publicly a heathen and privately a Christian also meant that there was a limit for this man, who experimentally promoted a secular worldview, including revolutionary thoughts. The limit was that privately he allowed himself to retreat into the traditional. His portrait portrays that clearly, especially his use of the hourglass at the bottom edge. In contrast to the social and religious rebellion of the "Piper of Niklashausen," Lau was a modern "Piper of Frankfurt," thinking only inwardly of a radical Enlightenment while in his political plans he was working for "reform from above." And in contrast with the modern pluralized human being, he outwardly supported a secular worldview while inwardly seeking relief from it.

4

The Art of Deflation, or:
How to Save an Atheist

"Philosophy as the search for truth about an independent metaphysical and moral order cannot . . . provide a workable and shared basis for a political conception of justice in a democratic society." We must, therefore, "stay on the surface, philosophically speaking."[1]

DEFLATION IS NOT a well-established category in intellectual history. It takes firm shape only if we bring it into dialogue with concepts like toleration, compromise, and eclecticism. Leveling or deflation is the conscious flattening of sharp points, of extreme positions: a plea for calm. If we recall the notion of inferential explosiveness that I described in the introduction, we can understand deflation as the flattening of conclusions that worried contemporaries who were trying to preserve Christianity. We will see that this "flattening" was linked to a specific philosophical persona, that of the "wise man." In chapter 6 the figure of the wise man will become clear as the counterfigure to that of

1. Translator's note: A few passages from this chapter were published in English translation as "Practices of Unmasking," trans. Ulrich Groetsch. I have occasionally borrowed or modified this translation.

John Rawls as quoted by Richard Rorty, "The Priority of Democracy to Philosophy," in Richard Rorty, *Objectivity, Relativism, and Truth: Philosophical Papers* (Cambridge, 1991), 175–96, at 180–81; John Rawls, "Justice as Fairness: Political Not Metaphysical," *Philosophy and Public Affairs* 14 (1985): 230; reprinted in Samuel Freeman, ed., *John Rawls: Collected Papers* (Cambridge, MA), 388–414, at 395. I gave a version of this chapter as a lecture in the spring of 2005 at the Ecole des Hautes Études en Sciences Sociales. Thanks to Jean-Pierre Cavaillé, Alain Mothu, Sylvain Matton, and the other participants in this discussion for their criticisms.

academic philosophy, a wise man who knew how to guard against the ups and downs of "fortuna" and remain autonomous.

Ian Hunter has proposed that we should place the persona of the philosopher at the center of attempts to understand the thought worlds of earlier ages.[2] If we do that and then look at our findings about "problematic" forms of speech and our earlier inferences concerning the precariat, as I propose, we will find that a close reading of a specific text will allow us to see which persona the author implicitly favored and what strategies he was using. And when we do so, we will bump into an unexpected habitus: a philosophy of calm equanimity that had repercussions well beyond debates over objective truth.

Vanini and Libertinism in Germany

Giulio Cesare Vanini and the French thinkers of "libertinage érudit" never attracted much attention in Germany, in sharp contrast to France and Italy.[3] Vanini is known today as an "atheist" who was burned to death in 1619 in Toulouse, after first having his tongue torn out. His philosophy has been seen as pantheistic, subversive, and radical. So much for the stereotype. In reality, however, Vanini's books were complicated constructions full of concealed and hidden utterances, and it would be much easier to evaluate the accusations and defenses offered for and against him before and after 1700 if we could only determine clearly what Vanini actually thought. But modern researchers are not at all agreed on the matter. In an essay that makes all sorts of careful distinctions, Cesare Vasoli showed why one has to be careful even in claiming that Vanini was no more than a libertine.[4] And yet it is amazing that a text

2. Ian Hunter, "Die Geschichte der Philosophie und die Persona des Philosophen," in *Die Cambridge School der politischen Ideengeschichte*, ed. Martin Mulsow and Andreas Mahler (Berlin, 2010), 241–83.

3. On *libertinage érudit*, see the classic work by Pintard, *Le libertinage érudit dans la première moitié du XVIIe siècle*, as well as the two-volume collection of texts: Jacques Prévot, ed., *Libertins du XVIIe siècle*, vol. 1 (Paris, 1998), vol. 2 (Paris, 2004); on the problems of interpreting Vanini, see Cesare Vasoli, "Riflessioni sul 'problema' Vanini," in *Il libertinismo in Europa*, ed. Sergio Bertelli (Milan and Naples, 1980), 125–68.

4. Vasoli, "Riflessioni sul 'problema' Vanini." On the reception history of Vanini, see Giovanni Papuli, "La fortuna del Vanini," in *Le interpretazioni di G. C. Vanini*, ed. idem (Galatina, 1975), 5–52; Andrzej Nowicki, "Vanini nel Seicento e gli strumenti concettuali per studiare la sua presenza nella cultura," *Atti dell'Academia di scienze morali e politiche della Società nazionale di scienze, lettere e arti in Napoli* 82 (1971): 377–440; Francesco de Paola, *Vanini e il primo Seicento*

such as the *Amphitheatrum divinae providentiae* was allowed to pass unhindered by the censors. The book seems on its surface to be an apology for the Christian religion. The conclusion that it was really a witness to "libertinism" depends on seeing this frame as just a mask behind which stood a mocker of religion. But as early as the 1960s Antonio Corsano showed that if we take the circumstances into account under which the book was written, we can see that in a certain sense it may have been a genuine apology, one that partly for career reasons was specifically aimed at scholars and *politici*, and yet one that also sought to spread the philosophical ideas of Pomponazzi.[5] With that specific readership he could persuasively argue that religion was a factor that played an important role in politics: to be sure, it contained fables for the common people, but it was also naturally given and inescapable.[6] These were the facts on which a "defense of religion" could be mounted.

We got to know Pomponazzi's arguments in chapter 2. The tenor of Cesare Vasoli's careful, contextualizing presentation of Vanini is that he was not necessarily being deceptive just because he quoted the texts of Scaliger and inveighed against atheism. Rather, his works were polemics directed more often against occultism and the magical mixing of religion and philosophy, polemics that seem to be genuine. Fighting this illicit mixture, Vanini used all his acerbic dialectical skills to separate philosophical from theological arguments.[7] So if with Pomponazzi he emphasized the findings of natural reason, that did not in itself impugn revelation.

All the same, around 1700 Europe was full of talk about the "case" of Vanini, not least because many Huguenots, after being forced into exile from France in 1685, developed an acute sensitivity to persecution and the lack of toleration. This also expressed itself historically, and so we find a growing interest in spectacular cases from the past, such as the burning of Servetus and the execution of Vanini. Germany produced its own independent sensitivities among spiritualists who had been driven out of their churches, sensitivities that led some to historically rehabilitate the unjustly persecuted if they had at least been

---

anglo-veneto (Taurisiano, 1979); Guido Porzio, "Saggio di bibliografia vaniniana," in *Le opere di Giulio Cesare Vanini tradotte per la prima volta in italiano*, 2 vols. (Lecce, 1912), 1:135–43, 2:3–102; Lorenzo Bianchi, *Tradizione libertina e critica storica: Da Naudé a Bayle* (Milan, 1988), 177–212; Andrzej Nowicky, "Studia nad Vaninim," *Euhemer przegląd religioznawczy* 50 (1966): 23–32.

5. Antonio Corsano, "Per la storia del pensiero del tardo Rinascimento II: Giulio Cesare Vanini," *Giornale Critico della Filosofia Italiana* 27 (1968): 201–44.

6. Vasoli, "Riflessioni sul 'problema' Vanini," 141ff.

7. Ibid., 145.

upright in their inner convictions. Gottfried Arnold's *Impartial History of the Church and of Heresy* (1699–1700) became the model for this sort of history.[8] In the early Enlightenment in Halle these currents flowed together. When Christian Thomasius attacked the "manufacture of heretics" (*Ketzermacherei*), the figures of Gabriel Naudé and Pierre Bayle were in the back of his mind but so was Gottfried Arnold.

It was one thing to be outraged by persecution, but it was quite another to discuss the actual doctrines of the persecuted. This was where many writers abandoned the early Enlightenment. True, they did not want Spinozists to be executed, but they mostly repudiated Spinoza's teachings. In the case of Vanini it was the same at first; to be sure the circumstances of his trial and the obscurities of his works suggested that he may not even have been the atheist that many had assumed. That's the reason some Protestant authors even undertook to "rescue" Vanini.[9]

These rescue operations have not been much studied in Germany, any more than the whole current of so-called *libertinage érudit*, the scholarly and philosophical libertinism of authors such as Gabriel Naudé, François La Mothe Le Vayer, Pierre Gassendi, and Guy Patin. The whole phenomenon of libertinism has been too little noticed in the Holy Roman Empire, and even today the absence of German research testifies to a lack of sympathy for libertinism in a country that invested its intellectual energies more in spiritualist movements and whose classical tradition running from Kant to Hegel was attuned to idealism rather than to naturalism.[10]

There were exceptions, however, and the very few translations of libertine authors are an index of when and where and how they were received in the German lands.[11] What's the situation with Vanini? He was never translated

8. On Arnold, see Antje Mißfeldt, ed., *Gottfried Arnold: Radikaler Pietist und Gelehrter* (Cologne, 2011); Dietrich Blaufuß and Friedrich Niewöhner, eds., *Gottfried Arnold (1666–1714): Mit einer Bibliographie der Arnold-Literatur ab 1714* (Wiesbaden, 1995).

9. On the genre of "rescuing," see Michael Multhammer, "Lessings Rettungen: Geschichte und Genese eines Denkstils" (PhD diss., University of Erfurt, 2012).

10. Mulsow, "Libertinismus in Deutschland."

11. Pierre Charron's "scandalous" book *De la sagesse*, for example, was first translated into German anonymously, surprisingly by a woman from the circle around Johann Valentin Andreae. See Sabine Koloch and Martin Mulsow, "Die erste deutsche Übersetzung von Pierre Charrons *De la sagesse*: Ein unbekanntes Werk der intellektuellen Außenseiterin Margareta Maria von Bouwinghausen (1629–nach 1679)," *Wolfenbütteler Barock-Nachrichten* 33 (2006): 119–50. Gabriel Naudé was received in Germany as a political thinker early and relatively

into German, neither the *Amphitheatrum* nor *De admirandis*.[12] But at the beginning of the eighteenth century, when the "case" of Vanini was of greatest importance among the discussions of intellectuals, there was a great deal of interest in him. Johann Gottfried Olearius and Johann Moritz Schramm wrote biographies of Vanini, Arnold dedicated a chapter of his *History of Heretics* to him, and Mathurin Veyssière La Croze dealt with him in his *Entretiens*.[13] But most importantly in 1712 an anonymously published *Apologia pro Vanino* appeared.[14] Its author was Peter Friedrich Arpe, a jurist and scholar from Kiel, who later lived in Hamburg.[15] His *Apologia* was the first to undertake an extended effort not only to criticize the execution of Vanini as barbarous but also to exonerate him from the charge of atheism.

---

intensively, with his *Bibliographia politica* and his *Considérations politiques sur les coups d'Estat*, both of which were available in German by 1678. On Naudé, see Lorenzo Bianchi, *Rinascimento e libertinismo: Studi su Gabriel Naudé* (Naples, 1996). On his reception in Germany, see Martin Mulsow, "Appunti sulla fortuna di Gabriel Naudé nella Germania del primo illuminismo," *Studi filosofici* 14/15 (1991/92): 145–56. See also Annette Syndikus, "Philologie und Universalismus: Gabriel Naudés enzyklopädische Schriften und ihre Rezeption im deutschsprachigen Raum," in *Philologie als Wissensmodell*, ed. Denis Thouard, Friedrich Vollhardt, and Fosca Mariani Zini (Berlin, 2010), 309–43. The *Apologie pour tous les grands personnages qui ont esté faussement soupçonnez de magie* played a relatively large role in the early Enlightenment in the circle around Christian Thomasius, and then it also appeared in translation in 1704. Gabriel Naudé, *Apologie pour tous les grands personnages qui ont esté soupçonnez de magie* (Paris, 1625); the translation: Christian Thomasius, *Kurtze Lehr-Sätze von dem Laster der Zauberey . . . und aus des berühmten Theologi D. Meyfarti, Naudaei, und anderer gelehrter Männer Schrifften erleutert* (Halle, 1704). On Naudé's *Apologie*, see also chapter 12. On the other hand, François La Mothe Le Vayer was hardly translated. Only his *Discours* on uncertainty in history was published anonymously in a small edition in 1704, in a German translation by Jakob Friedrich Reimmann; and in the 1730s the satirist Christian Ludwig Liscow contributed another small anonymous translation of one essay. On Reimmann's translation, see Martin Mulsow, "Die Paradoxien der Vernunft: Rekonstruktion einer verleugneten Phase in Reimmanns Denken," in *Skepsis, Providenz und Polyhistorie: Jakob Friedrich Reimmann 1668–1743*, ed. idem and Helmut Zedelmaier (Tübingen, 1998), 15–59, at 31; on Liscow's translation, see Friedrich Hagedorn, *Briefe*, ed. Horst Gronemeyer (Berlin, 1997), 1:117. It is clear that authors rejected by Lutheran Orthodoxy did not have an easy time getting published.

12. See the most recent edition of his work, ed. Francesco Paolo Raimondi and Mario Carparelli: Giulio Cesare Vanini, *Tutte le opere* (Milan, 2010).

13. On these works, see Francesco Paolo Raimondi, "L'apologia arpiana tra le prime letture illuministiche del Vanini," in *Giulio Cesare Vanini dal testo all'interpretazione*, ed. Giovanni Papuli (Taurisano, 1996), 59–94.

14. [Peter Friedrich Arpe], *Apologia pro Vanino* ("Cosmopoli" [Rotterdam]), 1712.

15. On Arpe (1682–1740), see Mulsow, "Freethinking"; idem, "Arpe collectionneur"; idem, *Enlightenment Underground*, 165–70.

Admittedly, Arpe's apology for Vanini is as many-layered and difficult to interpret as the man and his works themselves. We do have to understand it, however, if we are to grasp the assimilation and transformation of libertine thinking in the Germany of that time. I'd like to approach this task by taking three steps, following these questions. First, what was the external and internal context for the reception of Vanini and other freethinking writings of the seventeenth century? How was collecting or exchanging exotic works connected to the intellectual currents and beliefs in Germany around 1700? What was the exact relationship between collecting forbidden and anonymous works—an activity that was central for scholars pursuing the "history of scholarship" (*historia literaria*)—and the evaluation of such works in current discussions? Next, I will take a second step and look more closely at Arpe's *Apologia pro Vanino*, pointedly asking: Was Arpe himself a libertine? Was he using the literary techniques of dissimulation to disguise (or to signal to initiates) the fact that he himself sympathized with atheism? Or are there other ways of describing his attitude toward Vanini and his ideas? Then, in a third step I will try to solve this interpretive dilemma by comparing it with Richard Rorty's provocative assertion that democracy should have priority over philosophy. This solution could then lead in the future to posing the right questions about the reception and circulation of forbidden works in the Germany of the eighteenth century—and in this case, especially in Hamburg. As truth, it is not yet clear whether libertine and clandestine writings made any decisive contribution to the Enlightenment or whether they were only marginal phenomena and curiosities of interest to collectors but not the source of new ideas for theorists.[16]

The Context in Hamburg

Let us begin with the practice of collecting forbidden books. It is striking that Hamburg and really the whole Republic of Letters throughout the region of the North Sea and the Baltic were a special center of collecting and scholarly research into clandestine books.[17] How did this happen? To understand this, we need to go back to the 1670s.

16. See Friedrich Niewöhner's review of my book *Enlightenment Underground* in *Frankfurter Allgemeine Zeitung*, July 8, 2002, p. 39.
17. Martin Mulsow, "Johann Christoph Wolf (1683–1739) und die verbotenen Bücher von Hamburg," in *500 Jahre Theologie in Hamburg: Hamburg als Zentrum christlicher Theologie und Kultur zwischen Tradition und Zukunft*, ed. Johann Anselm Steiger (Berlin, 2005), 81–112; idem,

At that time the "polyhistor" Vincent Placcius published a work with the title *De scriptis et scriptoribus anonymis atque pseudonymis syntagma* (*A Dictionary of anonymous and pseudonymous Authors and Writings*). It was a set of documents comprising reprints of two catalogs of anonymous works and two long lists, compiled by Placcius himself, in which "scriptores occulti" (hidden writers) were unmasked.[18] In this book Placcius borrowed from scholarly friends such as Gerhard Mastricht, Gottfried Melm, and Martin Fogel. But it was only the publication of this *Dictionary* that unleashed a whole wave of activities— some in letter form, others in short printed essays—that expanded the number of unmasked "cryptonyms," which was the collective term for anonymous and pseudonymous works. The time was ripe for such a topic because the Republic of Letters was in its essence an institution that functioned through such exchanges. Placcius then explicitly strengthened this dynamic by issuing a printed "invitatio amica" (friendly invitation), which, as if it was a competition, set a goal of obtaining more than four thousand such exposures.[19] This stimulus was effective and the goal was attained. In 1708, nine years after Placcius's death, his *Theatrum anonymorum et pseudonymorum* appeared, with information about 2,777 anonymous works, 2,930 pseudonymous works, and an additional 519 Hebrew cryptonyms.[20] The publication of the *Theatrum* did not stem the flood of revelations. To the contrary, as a supplement to Placcius's collective unmasking enterprise, the creation of catalogues of pseudonymous and anonymous works even became a fad among scholars in northern Germany

---

"Die Transmission verbotenen Wissens"; idem, "Entwicklung einer Tatsachenkultur: Die Hamburger Gelehrten und ihre Praktiken 1650–1750," in *Hamburg: Eine Metropolregion zwischen Früher Neuzeit und Aufklärung*, ed. Johann Anselm Steiger and Sandra Richter (Berlin, 2012), 45–63. The following section is a shortened version of my conclusions in my book *Die unanständige Gelehrtenrepublik*, 217–45.

18. Vincentius Placcius, *De scriptis et scriptoribus anonymis atque pseudonymis syntagma* (Hamburg, 1674). Placcius's own contribution uncovered 617 anonymous works und 909 pseudonymous works: "De scriptoribus occultis detectis tractatus duo, quorum prior anonymos detectos in capita, pro argumentorum varietate distinctos, posterior pseudonymos detectos catalogo alphabetico exhibet."

19. Placcius, *Invitatio amica ad Antonium Magliabecchi aliosque Illustres et Clarissimos Reip. Litterariae atque librariae Proceres, Fautores, Peritos, super Symbolis promissis partim et destinatis ad Anonymos et Pseudonymos Detectos et Detegendos Vincentii Placcii Hamburgensis. Accedit Delineatio praesentis status et consilium atque votum, absolvendi D.V. ac edendi Operis Totius, ultra 4000 Autores detectos exhibituri. Cum indicibus adjunctis necessariis* (Hamburg 1689).

20. For the following, see Mulsow, *Die unanständige Gelehrtenrepublik*, 217–45.

and beyond.[21] The most obvious sign of this fashionable way of dealing with precarious knowledge was the considerable number of publications proclaiming new discoveries, often in special and limited areas of scholarship such as Hebrew literature.[22] Most of these works, however, remained hidden. They consisted of a tremendous mass of private handwritten catalogues and lists, the extent of which still needs to be determined. One could even call this phenomenon a whole separate culture of scholarly unmasking.

It was a fashion that needs to be viewed in connection with other trends: most of all, the collecting of books and manuscripts, and mainly the forbidden, suppressed, and therefore rare. The possession of "rarissima" (extremely rare books and manuscripts) satisfied more than the "curiosity" of the learned; it also increased their social prestige within the *Res publica literaria*, and it became a precondition for learned correspondence and the exchange of texts.[23] On this basis and in cooperation with the authors of popular histories of atheism, these connoisseurs effectively assured the transmission of knowledge about the clandestine underground of the early Enlightenment, and even its very existence as a coherent group. They guaranteed its transmission because the exchange of clandestine works was a favored practice of scholarly collectors, and this was how these texts sometimes found their way to other radical authors.[24] Without the presence of such texts in the huge libraries of collectors, their transmission would in most cases have been impossible because the clandestine underground was so fragmented. It had no coherent social space, not in France but even less in Germany.[25] These authors may have known

21. To name just a few of these authors: Caspar Heinrich Starck, Johann Friedrich Mayer, Johann Diecmann, Georg Serpel, Christoph August Heumann, Polycarp Lyser, Theodor Crusius, Johann Christoph Nemeitz, Gottfried Ludwig, Johann Christoph Wolf.

22. This development reached a sort of conclusion in Johann Christoph Mylius, *Bibliotheca anonymorum et pseudonymorum detectorum, ultra 4000 scriptores, quorum nomina vera latebant antea, omnium facultatum scientiarum et linguarum complectens, ad supplendum et continuandum Vincentii Placii Theatrum anonymorum et pseudonymorum et Christoph August Heumanni Schediasma de anonymis et pseudonymis* (Hamburg, 1740).

23. On the pursuit of social prestige, see Anne Goldgar, *Impolite Learning: Conduct and Community in the Republic of Letters, 1680–1750* (New Haven, 1995).

24. See the early observations of Wade, *The Clandestine Organization*; Mulsow, *Enlightenment Underground*. Take as an example the provocative crowing by Johann Christian Edelmann in his *Moses mit aufgedecktem Angesicht* (n.p., 1740), 33ff., concerning books "supposedly containing the seeds of hellish weeks," which God "through his unsearchable wisdom has allowed to be purchased for much money and . . . to be preserved carefully by their own enemies."

25. See Mulsow, *Enlightenment Underground*.

some of the writings of other radicals, but generally they did not know one another personally—that was a consequence of the anonymity their works required.

Indeed, as a result of their marginalization and their public ineffectiveness, they could hardly ever develop a sense of themselves, over time, as direct disciples of significant forerunners. This explains why the literary underground did not exist as a dense network of personal relationships, in which an immediate reproduction of intellectual radicalism would have been possible. Rather, the underground became an object of perception mainly through the activities of classification and identification practiced by the Orthodox Placcius and his Lutheran successors. When they exposed the authors of anonymous texts, when theologians such as Valentin Ernst Löscher and Siegmund Jakob Baumgarten described heterodox texts in their journals and warned against them, when a scholar like Jakob Friedrich Reimmann composed his *Historia atheismi*, or when Johann Anton Trinius assembled his *Dictionary of Freethinkers*, they were actually constituting freethought as an object of perception and conveying the false impression that a coherent clandestine underground existed.[26] The group of connoisseurs who put together their catalogs of cryptonyms also collected these cryptonymous writings and made their transmission to others possible. Thus the group of polyhistors, who classified and condemned these precarious writings, generated through their compendia and lexica a virtual space for heterodox persons and writings, one not accessible to the authors themselves, but now given an apparently visible and unified body.

Arpe's Socialization

That was the situation into which the young Peter Friedrich Arpe was intellectually socialized during the years around 1705 in Copenhagen and Kiel, the world of the polyhistor Daniel Georg Morhof. It was in the private libraries of connoisseurs such as Otto Sperling, Christian Reitzer, Gustav Schrödter, and Gerhard Ernst Franck von Frankenau—who all belonged at least in part to the collectors' and correspondents' network of Placcius—that Arpe got to know

26. Valentin Ernst Löscher, ed., *Unschuldige Nachrichten* (Leipzig and Wittenberg, 1701ff.); Siegmund Jakob Baumgarten, ed., *Nachrichten aus einer Hallischen Bibliothek* (Halle, 1748–58); Jakob Friedrich Reimmann, *Historia universalis atheismi* (Hildesheim, 1725); Johann Anton Trinius, *Freydencker-Lexikon* (Leipzig, 1765).

his first forbidden writings and developed his appetite for them. Frankenau's library, for example, had Vanini's volumes on its shelves and provided a space for discussing them.[27] Frankenau himself expressed the conventional view that Vanini had been an atheist, but Arpe, who had gotten into these volumes, dissented. He said that he could find nothing truly atheistical and claimed that the entire structure of accusations rested only on slanders and false attributions.

The intellectual world of Copenhagen during the years when Vanini was being discussed was shaped by the currents of discussion surrounding names such as Pierre Bayle, Gottfried Arnold, Christian Thomasius, and Gabriel Naudé. Bayle had launched the problem of the "virtuous atheist" and had led the movement in favor of a historical and critical revision of the whole Western intellectual tradition.[28] Gottfried Arnold had composed a history in which heretics were the genuine and authentic seekers after God—in shocking contrast to standard church history.[29] And Christian Thomasius was the central figure of the new and fresh philosophy in Germany of that day, a philosophy that was both sensationalist and antimetaphysical, inspired by both natural law and historical criticism.[30] In the wake of Bayle, Arnold, and Thomasius, the earlier work of Gabriel Naudé seemed once again timely; indeed it was only now that his full message could be understood—that all the old charges leveled at supposed magicians and sorcerers should be reexamined because they often disguised merely popular prejudices against free spirits in science, mathematics, and philosophy.[31]

27. See Arpe's dedication to Frankenau in his *Apologia*. See also the autobiographical letter from Arpe to Johann Fabricius, July 19, 1723, Det Kongelige Bibliotek Kopenhagen (KBK), Ms. Thott 1218, 4° fo. 3: "Imprimis FRANCKI DE FRANCKENAU qui jam Viennae publica Regia Majestatis Daniae negotia curat, jucunda subit recordatio / Cui felle nullo, melle multo mens madens / Avum per omne nil amarum miscuit / tam seriorum quam jecorum particeps. / Hic mihi Dux et autor extitit apologiae VANINI, cum lectissimum Parentis optimi apparatum literarium perlustrarem, quique sub literis initialibus primae editionis hujus apologiae, cum ipse apparere nollem, securis delituit." On the library, see also the letter from Franck von Franckenau to Johann Albert Fabricius, Copenhagen, March 15, 1711, KBK, Ms. Fabr. 104–23.

28. See Michael Czelinski-Uesbeck, *Der tugendhafte Atheist: Studien zur Vorgeschichte der Spinoza-Renaissance in Deutschland* (Würzburg, 2007).

29. Gottfried Arnold, *Unpartheyische Kirchen- und Ketzer-Historie* (Frankfurt, 1699/1700).

30. The fundamental work is still Schneiders, *Naturrecht und Liebesethik*.

31. Mulsow, *Enlightenment Underground*, 201–3, as well as chapter 12 in this book.

Critical reappraisals of the whole intellectual tradition were, therefore, the order of the day. To accomplish that task collecting books and manuscripts was just as necessary as it had been for Placcius's task of unmasking cryptonyms. They both shared the recognition that scholars now needed to focus their attention on anonymous and forbidden texts. It was thought that only those scholars who built themselves library holdings of libertine and clandestine works, collections of forbidden and burned writings, would be equipped to carry out Naudé's program of rehabilitating freethinkers from "erreurs populaires."

On the surface this activity was the same as the bibliographical project of the conservative offshoot of the north German collecting movement. Johann Albert Fabricius and Johann Christoph Wolf had assembled tremendous private libraries, intending to use them for their editorial and bibliographical enterprises. They too hoped to base their work on the whole corpus of inherited knowledge. So Arpe never tired of referring over and over to Fabricius and his contributions. But Fabricius's project was different: it was apologetic in intent and used historical criticism ultimately to rescue the truth of Christianity once again from its enemies.[32] This rescue mission had one of its foundations in physicotheology, and this formed the common basis for the project of Arpe (inspired by Naudé) and the project of Fabricius and Wolf (aiming at apology).[33] This resulted in a sometimes confusing overlap between "radical" and "conservative" positions within the German early Enlightenment, especially in the interpretation and reinterpretation of libertinism. Everything depended on the correct interpretation of physicotheological "naturalism." We will come back to that topic.

Sublimated Philosophy

The historical-critical projects of the generation after Placcius and Morhof were something that I'd like to call "sublimated philosophy." Scholars were not exactly philosophizing but editing, commenting, defending, and, above all else, making bibliographies. This form of philosophy was a result of the connection between collecting books and building libraries. But it also enabled a

32. See Ralph Häfner, *Götter im Exil: Frühneuzeitliches Dichtungsverständnis im Spannungsfeld christlicher Apologetik und philologischer Kritik (ca. 1590–1736)* (Tübingen, 2003); Erik Petersen, *Intellectum Liberare: Johann Albert Fabricius—en humanist i Europa* (Copenhagen, 1998).

33. Philipp, *Das Werden der Aufklärung in theologiegeschichtlicher Sicht.*

peculiarly "elegant" sort of learning, one that might avoid the much-maligned "pedantry" of academics by appealing to connoisseurs and putting on a brilliant display of "delectable" quotations, choice footnotes, and unusual topics.[34] For the radical variant of these projects—Arpe provides our example here—there was also the opportunity to avoid stating a personal position, so that no one could decide whether someone here was actually sympathizing with the libertines. To the outside world it seemed that he was only listing the titles of works and historically refuting old denunciations.

Thus Arpe never wrote a book on fate or on divination but only compiled bibliographies on those topics.[35] Nevertheless, these bibliographies revealed an editor who was both a connoisseur and an enthusiast, so that they at least were open to an "esoteric" interpretation, one that actually approved what the compiler had apparently only reported. Arpe's *Apologia pro Vanino* was of course different: it was not a bibliography and it presented itself as a dedicated defense of the Italian philosopher, and yet it deployed numerous elements of indirectness and refined elegance. Arpe's means of distancing himself was historical reconstruction. And so he left the question open: what did the author himself think of Vanini's philosophy?[36] Was he really trying to prove Vanini's innocence or only using the discussion of his case to stimulate discussions of controversial topics such as miracles, the veneration of saints, astrology, or the prohibition of books, topics that could be discussed using bibliographical and literary-historical methods in a proven manner and with connoisseurship to describe heretical ideas?

Ever since its appearance, therefore, the *Apology* was read in extremely different ways. Some saw it as a thinly disguised defense of the libertine and atheist Vanini, but others could not and simply did not want to believe that the book was intended seriously. Its author was surely joking, according to Vanini's biographer David Durand, writing about Arpe in 1717.[37] Even recent scholars cannot agree on how one should read the book. Thus Francesco Paolo Raimondi has shown convincingly that many of Arpe's replies to religiously

34. For the critique of pedantry, see Kühlmann, *Gelehrtenrepublik und Fürstenstaat*, 285–454; Gunter E. Grimm, *Literatur und Gelehrtentum in Deutschland: Untersuchungen zum Wandel ihres Verhältnisses vom Humanismus bis zur Frühaufklärung* (Tübingen, 1983).

35. [Arpe:] P. F. RP. *Epistolarum Decas, Sive Brevis Delineatio Musaei Scriptorum De Divinatione* (n.p., 1711); idem, *Theatrum fati sive Notitiae scriptorum de providentia* (Rotterdam, 1712).

36. On this question, see Raimondi, "L'apologia arpiana."

37. David Durand, *La vie et les sentiments de Lucilio Vanini* (Rotterdam, 1717).

critical objections were strikingly (perhaps intentionally) weak.[38] And so it seems likely that he was writing deceptively and that the author therefore was disguising libertine convictions.[39] On the other hand, however, Giovanni Papuli has pointed to the emphasis on integrity in the *Apologia*, which he regards as a sign of Arpe's proximity to the radical Pietism of Arnold.[40] And that, too, cannot be denied. How can we resolve this dilemma?

It seems certain that the solution is to be found in the specific style of the *Apologia*, which Raimondi had also placed squarely in the center of his investigation. The book was written in a complex rhetorical style of address to the reader, partly in the form of a fictional legal trial of Vanini, a sort of dialogue with the dead, interlarded with frequent quotations and references to ancient classical authors such as Horace, Seneca, Juvenal, Lucian, Claudian, and many others. I'd like to suggest, therefore, that we approach Arpe's text through an analysis of his artful arrangement of arguments, quotations, references, and allusions.[41]

In doing this I will rely heavily on the manuscript amendments that Arpe added to his *Apologia*, which are roughly double the size of the printed text and provide many more indications of his views (figure 15).[42] I will choose a section that illuminates the accusations aimed at Arpe as refracted through Arpe's discussion of accusations leveled at Vanini that Vanini was reporting the statements of atheists. Arpe concedes: "Whoever reports godless things appears godless himself."[43] But then he begins a series of considerations that serve to weaken this appearance. First Arpe points out that a doctor must know a poison if he's to heal a patient. Theologians often used this simile, too, when they were refuting heresies. A second parallel cites the mariner who has to see the rocks if he is to steer safely through them. "So even if rocks, cliffs,

38. Raimondi, "L'apologia arpiana."

39. On deceptive techniques of writing, see Cavaillé, *Dis/simulations*; Jon R. Snyder, *Dissimulation and the Culture of Secrecy in Early Modern Europe* (Los Angeles, 2009). And in general, see the still controversial book by Strauss, *Persecution and the Art of Writing*.

40. Papuli, "La fortuna del Vanini."

41. My approach here is similar to that of Markus Völkel, who followed the "textual logic" of one article from Bayle's *Dictionnaire*: "Zur 'Text-Logik' im Dictionnaire von Pierre Bayle: Eine historisch-kritische Untersuchung des Artikels Lipsius (Lipse, Juste)," *Lias* 20 (1993): 193–226.

42. State and University Library of Hamburg, Cod. theol. 1222. I am grateful to Susanna Reger for help with the transcriptions and translations.

43. [Arpe], *Apologia*, 44: "Non nego; profani speciem habet, qui profana referat."

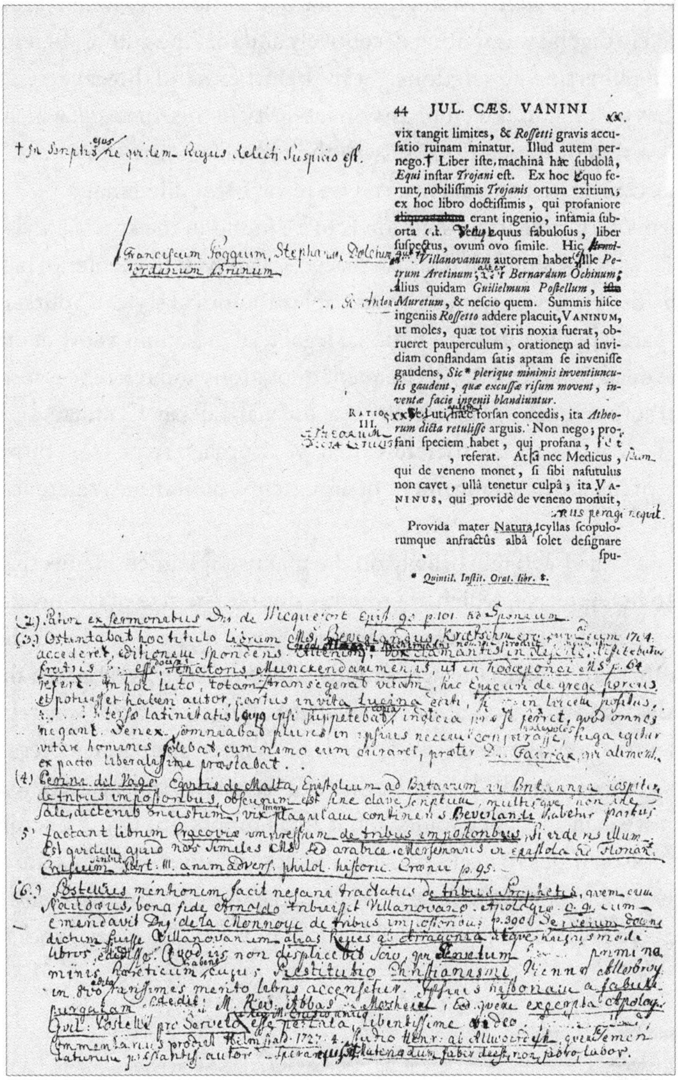

vix tangit limites, & *Roffetti* gravis accu-
fatio ruinam minatur. Illud autem per-
nego.† Liber iste, machinâ hâc fubdolâ,
Equi inftar *Trojani* eft.   Ex hoc Equo ferunt, nobiliffimis *Trojanis* ortum exitium,
ex hoc libro doctiffimis, qui profaniore
~~thiquoratium~~ erant ingenio, infamia fub-
orta c.t.   Vellis equus fabulofus, liber
fufpectus, ovum ovo fimile.   Hic, ~~Herrni-~~
~~ai~~ *Villanovanum* autorem habet; ille *Pe-*
trum Aretinum; ii ? *Bernardum Ochinum*;
Alius quidam *Guilielmum Poftellum*, ~~alii~~
. . . , íi *Ant. Muretum*, & nefcio quem.   Summis hifce
ingeniis *Roffetto* addere placuit, VANINUM,
ut moles, quæ tot viris noxia fuerat, ob-
rueret pauperculum, orationem ad invidiam conflandam fatis aptam fe invenifle
gaudens, *Sic* plerique minimis inventiuncu-
lis gaudent, quæ excuffæ rifum movent, in-
ventæ facie ingenii blandiuntur.

RATIO XX Bell uti, hæc forfan concedis, ita *Atheo-*
III.   *rum dicta retuliffe* arguis. Non nego; pro-
fani fpeciem habet, qui profana, Est et
, referat. At fa nec Medicus , *Rom.*
qui de veneno monet, fi fibi nafutulus
non cavet, ullâ tenetur culpâ ; ita VA-
NINUS, qui providè de veneno monuit,
. . . ius perag. requir.

Provida mater Naturæ fcyllas fcopulo-
rumque anfractûs albâ folet defignare
fpu-

* *Quintil. Inftit. Orat. libr. 8.*

[handwritten marginal and footnote annotations, largely illegible]

and sandbars appear in Vanini's books, one should not blame him for carefully describing them and warning the reader."[44] The cliffs of atheism appear in Vanini's books only because that way he can avoid them. Arpe then shifts the attention of the reader to a footnote in which the image of the mariner is switched over to that of a gladiator. Vanini "armed himself to fight the [atheists]," and this battle would have proceeded like that of the *andabatae*, those gladiatorial fighters who stumbled around, wearing a helmet without even eye slits, "if he had not wanted to combat their godless statements."[45] The defender of Christianity, in a role Arpe depicted himself as filling—like Vanini—must proceed with open eyes and in full knowledge of his opponents' arguments. Arpe adds, "To wish to know nothing of one's opponents' arguments would be a symptom of a mind gone awry and turned to evil. And even if such [atheistic] words provoke nausea or fear, one must recall that Hercules, too, was nauseated when he was cleaning out the Augean stables. Against fear you need to protect your head with a helmet."[46]

Yet, further on in the footnote Arpe criticizes Vanini's accusers for raising objections to Vanini just because they wanted to blame him for something. "They do not know what they want; he just has to be an atheist. He reports the words of the [atheists], but so what? Jerome says in volume III of his works, in the letter to Minervius and Alexander: 'If anyone grumbles, wondering why I am reading depictions of the opposing side, with whose doctrines I disagree, he should know that I have gladly heard the words of the apostle, "Prove all things; hold fast that which is good."' "[47] These words of St. Paul were a

44. Ibid., 44ff.: "Provida mater *Natura*, scyllas scopulorumque anfractus alba solet designare spuma; attamen saepe improvidus nauta naufragium patitur, an quis arguet eam? Profecto nemo. Si quis noctu flammis e pharo, ligneisque structuris de Syrtibus interdiu navigantem monuit, cùm tamen nauclerus iniquum littus amans perit, non caedis arguitur. Ita nec VANINUM, si scyllae, scopuli, Syrtesque in ejus libris sunt, qui diligenter notavit eas, monuitque Lectorem, arguere decet."

45. Ibid., 45, note: "*Atheorum dicta* retulit, quia iis pugnam parabat, illa autem fuisset *Andabatarum in more* instituta et, *clausis oculis*, nisi improba ipsorum effata agerentur."

46. Ibid.: "Adversariorum argumenta ignorare velle, animi praevaricantis et mala sibi conscii . . . est. Aut taedium tibi parium dicta, aut matum. Taedium ferre oportebat *Hercules*, cum *Augiae stabulum purgaret*. Contra *metum* galea muniendum caput est."

47. Ibid.: "Nesciunt quid velint, modo fiat *Atheus*. Dicta eorum retulit; *quid tum?* Hieronymus *opp. tom. III. in epist. ad Min. et Alex.*: si quis *contrariae factionis* immurmurcit, quare eorum *explanationes* legam, quorum *dogmatibus* non acquiesco. Sciat me illud *Apostoli* libenter audire. *Omnia probat quod bonum est, retinete.* Haec, si valerent, nec ipse *Salomon* Rex sapientissimus culpa cureret ob *ecclesiastes* verba *c. III. v.19. seqq.*"

standard reference for often-mentioned "eclectic" early Enlightenment in Germany, words that urged the use of one's own judgment after carefully listening to all points of view.[48] If one criticized this attitude, Arpe continues in his footnote, then "the most wise King Solomon himself would not be blameless because of what he said in Ecclesiastes 3:19ff."[49] Solomon had indeed been dragged into these debates over eclecticism during the early Enlightenment, especially by Jakob Friedrich Reimmann in a controversial, anonymous essay.[50]

The main body of the text in contrast proceeds with a different defensive strategy. There Arpe argued that Vanini merely lined up several trivial items. So now it's not the dangers of poison, the threatening rocks, but just trifles. "Carneades, that most astute of all thinkers, says (as Pliny relates) that one cannot easily see what the mark of truth is. . . . Just as it could not be day if there were no night, so, by Jupiter, virtue would be sought in vain if there were no flaws innate in the nature of things. Thus trees are strengthened by resisting the wind; roses smell all the sweeter when garlic is planted nearby; the palm grows under stress; it's from vice that virtue is recognized; and the erroneous arguments of the atheists serve to fortify the teachings of Christianity."[51] We can call this the argument by contrast. It was a venerable argument, ranging

48. Albrecht, *Eklektik*.

49. Ecclesiastes 3:19: For that which befalleth the sons of men befalleth beasts; even one thing befalleth them: as the one dieth, so dieth the other; yea, they have all one breath; so that a man hath no preeminence above a beast: for all is vanity.

20: All go unto one place; all are of the dust, and all turn to dust again.

21: Who knoweth the spirit of man that goeth upward, and the spirit of the beast that goeth downward to the earth?

22: Wherefore I perceive that there is nothing better, than that a man should rejoice in his own works; for that is his portion: for who shall bring him to see what shall be after him?

50. Mulsow, "Eclecticism or Skepticism?"; Ralph Häfner, "Das Erkenntnisproblem in der Philologie um 1700: Zum Verhältnis von Polymathie und Aporetik bei Jacob Friedrich Reimmann, Christian Thomasius und Johann Albert Fabricius," in *Philologie und Erkenntnis*, ed. idem (Tübingen, 2001), 95–128.

51. [Arpe], *Apologia*, 45: "*Carneades*, ille omnium argutissimus, quo dissertante, *quid veri esset, haud facilè discerni poterat*, memorante *Plinio*, cùm olim *pro vitio* summa cum hominum admiratione verba faceret. *Quemadmodum*, inquit, *nisi nox esset, dies non esset; ita per Jovem, nisi vitium innatum esset rerum naturae, virtus frustra quaereretur*. Sic vento roborantur arbores; allio apposito gratius spirant rosae; palma sub onore crescit; ex vitio noscitur virtus, & vitiosis *Atheorum* dictis, confirmata Christi floret doctrina."

from natural philosophy to rhetoric: only the contrast distinguishes the spice. So because atheism was only the spice in Vanini's books, one could see it as trivial.

Then the argument runs toward the thought pattern of eclecticism again. Arpe reports that Vanini had free access to all the books in Roberto Ubaldino's library.[52] He was told that he could use anything he wanted. And Arpe mouthed the familiar saying: "Choose those that please; reject whatever is discordant, and with certain books, if it's necessary, separate the good from the bad. Perhaps in what seems to you a dung heap, you will find some pearl. Pliny, the glory of the Roman nation, used to say that no book is so bad that it is not useful in some way."[53] Here again was the appeal to eclecticism with its trust in the individual's powers of judgment. It was strengthened by the view that every book, no matter how bad (e.g., even in an atheist work), has something good. Arpe embellished his reference to Pliny with a quotation from Vergil: "Non omnis fert omnia tellus" (Not every piece of land yields every kind of fruit).[54] And so one simply must help oneself to a multitude of sources because a monoculture (e.g., exclusively Christian books) will not produce the greatest harvest. "So let us pick out the roses from the leftover thorns," as Arpe expressed it.[55]

Then comes another twist in Arpe's line of defense. One should not follow Vanini's accusers in becoming furious before one has really understood, but exercise judgment. Christian Thomasius called this problem the "prejudice of overhaste" ("das Vorurteil der Praezipitanz").[56] The attentive reader will connect this with the previous appeal to eclectic thinking and conclude that

52. Ibid., 46: "*Nam* Lutetiae *cum essem, et* Apologiam pro Concilio Tridentino *conscribendam, suscepissem ab illustrissimo reverendissimoque Domino* Roberto Ubaldino, *Episcopo Politiano, ad Christianissimum Regem Apostolicae Sedis Nuncio amplissimo, quosvis libros pervolutandi facultatem impetravi.*"

53. Ibid.: "Elige quae placent; rejice absona & si quod in quibuslibet libris necessum est feceris, ut bonum a malo segreges; in sterquilinio hoc, ut tibi videtur, margaritam forsan invenies. *Plinius* sane, Romanae gentis decus, dicere solebat, *Nullum librum esse tam malum, ut non aliqua ex parte prodesset.*"

54. Ibid.: "*omnis fert omnia tellus.*" See Vergil, *Ecloga* 4, 39; but also Georgica II:109: "Nec vero terrae ferre omnes omnia possunt."

55. Ibid.: "Decerpamus spinis relictis rosas, seligamus abjectis testis margaritas; ut dispulsis mentis nubibus lux clara appareat."

56. Werner Schneiders, *Aufklärung und Vorurteilskritik: Studien zur Geschichte der Vorurteilstheorie* (Stuttgart, 1983).

whoever does not know all the sources cannot truly understand, and then he may react too quickly and lose his temper. Arpe expresses the consequence with another quotation (from Seneca): "We shall acquit many if we begin with discernment instead of with anger."[57] The result of eclectic thinking, of judging only after a comprehensive review, was usually toleration. Here was Naudé's project again, shining through. In a footnote Arpe expands the thought with a quotation from Claudian: "He is closest to the gods whom reason, and not passion, impels."[58] This would prevent the notorious *odium theologicum* (theological hatred). Arpe then reveals that it was indeed Naudé's and Charron's ideal of the freethinker that provides the foundation for this eclecticism: "Those who do not get stuck on externals and mere husks will not be touched by any basic claim. One does not have to fly into a rage over just any old word."[59] So one has to have the capacity to endure difficult and problematic things. Not everyone has this capacity; only those who accustom themselves to getting to the bottom of things develop it. This—unspoken—ideal of the *esprit fort*, the strong-minded freethinker, seems to me to be an essential assumption in Arpe's thinking and one of the points on which he agreed with the French libertines, even if his idea of eclecticism bound him rather to Thomasius. The combination produces what one might call a philosophy of equanimity or serenity: a philosopher with a strong spirit could take even heretical books in stride; they would not make his blood boil.

Arpe tells an anecdote to illustrate this frame of mind. A young man had once visited, offering him nothing but forbidden writings and openly voicing radical thoughts. Arpe managed to remain completely composed during their encounter and did not reprove him even once. Surely the youth's maturity and healthy reason would develop with age.[60] Of course this anecdote, to which we will return later, could cut both ways if one considers that Arpe was himself

57. [Arpe], *Apologia*, 46: "*Multos absolvemus, si coeperimus ante judicare quam irasci.*" Seneca, *De ira* III, 29.

58. [Arpe], *Apologia*, 46, note: "*Diis proximus ille est / Quem* ratio, *non* ira *movet.*" Claudian, *De Consulatu Malii Theodori Panegyris*, CCXXVII.

59. [Arpe], *Apologia*, 46, note: "Quinon in cortina aut putaminibus haererent, ferre poterunt, quaecunque nucleum, non tangunt[ur]. Nec, ad quodvis verbum excandescere oportet." On the freethinker, see Pintard, *Le libertinage érudit dans la prèmiere moitié du XVIIe siècle.*

60. [Arpe], *Apologia*, 46, note: "Memini ad me venisse juvenem aliquando, qui thesauri instar integros titulos *librorum* vulgo *damnatorum* offerret sed rariorum. M Serveti *restitutionis Christianismi.* Bruni *Spaccio della Bestia trionfante*, Bodini *de rerum sublimium arcanis* Godofredi Vallae *artis nihil credendi.* Cymbali *mundi.* Caroli Blount *oraculum rationis.* Curiositatem

a collector of forbidden writings. If he was himself thinking radically, then that would have been the reason he did not reprove the young man. But Arpe wanted to present the story differently. He distanced himself mildly from the Spinozist or libertine "fanatic" and retreated into the aloof attitude of the mature connoisseur, for whom even radicalism required too much emotion.

To understand this stoic-skeptical attitude better it will make sense to take a look at an enigmatic footnote that will also occupy us later in this book: a note in which by his standards Arpe clearly distances himself from Spinozism. "Of the various conflicting opinions among philosophers concerning the existence of God," he says, "the most pious seems to me to distinguish rightly between the Creator and Creation, between the cause and the effect, and does not dare to invent one unique substance, which was the fabrication of Spinoza and his disciples. After the fate of Vanini this exalted question was pushed to extremes, and there is no lack of wicked treatises that attribute eternity to created things. To particles of matter they attribute movement (with Epicurus and Toland), or life (with Democritus and Campanella), or qualities of all kinds (with Anaximander), or plastic force (with the Pseudo-Stoics), or admirable harmony (with Leibniz and Wolff), or finally the power of thought (with Spinoza)."[61] And why does Arpe reject this? Perhaps for the same reasons that Jakob Thomasius or Johann Franz Budde gave, that is, that such ideas did not agree with Holy Scripture? No, he had a different reason: "With these [notions] the human understanding cannot come to rest because the efficient cause (*causa efficiens*) has been removed."[62] The understanding cannot come to rest? The understanding can evidently come to rest only when it arrives at a point beyond this world—at some sort of meditative standstill. That is exactly how Arpe interpreted Vanini's controversial rejection of arguments about a first mover, adding: "Vanini appears to have treated this correctly, for he did

---

corripuit, quae erat nimia atrociter damnare eam non poteram, Ad frugem et sanae rationis usum conducit aetas."

61. Ibid., 58, note: "Inter varias *de Dei existentia* opiniones, in *Philosophorum dissensu*, illa mihi videtur maxime pia, quae *Creatorem* a *creatura*, *causam* ab *effectu* recte distinguit, nec unam sibi inde substantiam [fingere?] audet quod *Spinosa* et *discipulorum* commentum est. Sublimis haec post *Vanini* fata, acerrimi agitata est quaestio, nec desunt *dissertationes infidiosae* rebus creatis *aeternitatem* tribuentes et *materiae particulis motum* cum Epicuro & Tolando; *vitam*, cum Democrito et Campanella; *omnis generis qualitates*, cum Anaximandro, *vim plasticam* cum pseudo Stoicis; *harmoniam praestabilitam* cum Leibnitio et Wolfio: denique *rationem* et *sensum* cum Spinosa."

62. Ibid.: "In his mens humana acquiescere nequit, causa efficiente remota."

not wish to confuse the eternal Godhead with the first mover."[63] Arpe interpreted Vanini as if he supported a mysticism of the Overbeing, which he had adopted through his reading of the Kabbalah. And yet it seems here, according to Arpe, that he was less concerned with any specific metaphysics than with the art of living with peace of mind.

It is tempting to interpret Arpe's skeptical-stoical mentality (which assimilated Vanini's apparent mysticism along with Thomasius's eclecticism and Naudé's "rescues") within the context of the contemporary revival of Anacreontics in Germany. After all these writers too retreated into privacy and abandoned the feuding of university, church, society, and politics; they too displayed "areligiosity" and anticlericalism but refused to draw any active political consequences.[64]

Naturally we must consider the conditions of that time, when such a mixture of radicalism and quietism took shape. A radicalism combined with political conservatism can also be found in many of the thinkers connected with *libertinage érudit* in the France of Richelieu, in the circles of Naudé or La Mothe Le Vayer. But the situation in Germany in the early eighteenth century was different. Arpe belonged to a generation of unemployed academics, who worked for years as private tutors and rarely found positions at the university; recall the discussion of the clandestine precariat from chapter 1. After a brief "academic adventure"[65] as a professor in Kiel in 1723–24, he quickly fell back into life as a private person. Despite the fact that the early Enlightenment is most often seen as the dawn of a new era, his generation was often sunk in resignation over an Enlightenment that seemed to have gotten stuck.[66] Just as Barthold Hinrich Brockes recommended a life at home in one's garden, so Arpe lived among his books, even if they included the radical books from Giordano Bruno to Baruch Spinoza. His generation came too early to have the organizational form provided by a secret society, which later intellectuals maintained before they too retreated into a purely private world. I will treat this topic in more detail in chapter 7.

63. Ibid.: "et recte egisse videtur *Vaninus*, qui *aeternum Numen* cum *primi mobilis motorem* confundere noluit."

64. Ernst Fischer, "Er spielt mit seinen Göttern: Kirchen- und religionskritische Aspekte der anakreontischen Dichtung in Deutschland im 18. Jahrhundert," in *Les Lumières et leur combat/ Der Kampf der Aufklärung*, ed. Jean Mondot (Berlin, 2004), 71–86.

65. *Akademische Abenteuer* is the title of his sketches, preserved as Mss. hist. part. K[iel] 2° "Historie der Academie Kiel 1720–1725," university library of Rostock. See Mulsow, "Eine handschriftliche Sammlung zur Geschichte Schleswig-Holsteins aus dem frühen 18. Jahrhundert."

66. See chapter 7.

Let us proceed, however, with our reading of Arpe's *Apologia* to try to understand its inner logic. In the main text the author next pointed to the polemical writings of other religions, obviously as an example of antichristian literature, in order to expand the idea that the "wicked" works that an eclectic thinker acquires are only trivia. "Often you walk dryshod past the evil in blasphemous books of the pagans, the rabbis, the Arabs and the Turks; so just walk past and do not trample the poor man under foot, whom his enemies long ago reduced to ashes."[67] The other religions have not been a threat to Christianity for a long time—this seems to be Arpe's argument—so therefore one can permit a generous toleration to rule. In a footnote Arpe pulls in Wagenseil's *Tela ignea satanae* (*The Fiery Missiles of Satan*) for reinforcement. That book was permitted to be printed in 1681 even though it contained antichristian texts like the infamous *Chizzuk Emunah* (*Faith Strengthened*) by Isaac of Troki.[68] Arpe took this permission to publish as evidence that such polemics presented no real danger. In reality, Wagenseil's edition, which included a refutation, was hotly contested, and not without reason. A sharp critic of Christianity like Hermann Samuel Reimarus—whom Arpe probably knew—later characterized the *Chizzuk Emunah* as one of the most persuasive books, one that had provided him with many an argument for his own *Apologie*.[69] Even the Koran, Arpe continued, which was a "quagmire of deceits," had been translated into many languages and recently even explained (and the reader is expected to add: without harming) Christianity.[70] And then his footnote makes an odd leap; Arpe adds this reflection: "Even so, one cannot deny that people can more easily deceive and seduce if they wear the appearance of truth than those who cannot rid themselves of the blemish of a small stain or who are completely blackened with coal. With the latter, we see an immediate sign, 'Beware

67. [Arpe], *Apologia*, 46: "Pejora saepius in *Gentilium* & blasphemis *Rabbinorum, Arabum, Turcarumque* libris sicco pede praeteris, praeteri ergo & hunc, nec miserum conculca, quem jam in cineres jam dudum hostes redegerunt."

68. Ibid., note: "Nostram sententiam Wagenseilii *Tela ignea Satanae* et *Eisenmengeri* scripta probant." See Johann Christoph Wagenseil, *Tela ignea Satanae, hoc est: Arcani, et horribiles Judaeorum adversus Christum Deum, et Christianam religionem libri* (Altdorf, 1681). See Richard H. Popkin, *Disputing Christianity: The 400-Year-Old Debate over Rabbi Isaac Ben Abraham Troki's Classic Arguments* (Amherst, 2007).

69. Reimarus, *Apologie oder Schutzschrift für die vernünftigen Verehrer Gottes*, 2:268.

70. [Arpe], *Apologia*, 46, note: "Quid aliud *Alcoranus*, quam imposturarum ... colluvies. Habemus tamen et in alias linguas translatum et non solum legimus, sed nuper *quidam* certo modo *explicare ausus est. 1713.*"

of the Dog!'"[71] This remark seems totally counter to the preceding argument, for it implied that openly polemical and antichristian works such as the Koran or Jewish clandestine writings were less dangerous than those that were apparently true. This latter group could only mean works that on the surface do not argue polemically, and even pretend to be Christian and orthodox. But what could Arpe be getting at? Simply those works of subtle criticism or those that dissimulate? This is a passage in Arpe's book where a Straussian reader, one constantly on the lookout for double meanings, would see Arpe hinting about his own writings, as if to say: "See here, dear reader, this work of mine pretends to be quite harmless, completely conformable to Christianity, but just for that reason it's all the more subversive." But I won't belabor this line of reading because I'm treating Arpe mainly as a philosopher of serenity, and so I'm only suggesting that this other interpretation is possible.

However that may be, the somewhat bewildered reader returns to the main text, where he's just been told not to trample on the "poor" followers of other religions. The text then adds, "If just one nasty word carelessly slips out, it spreads until everyone repeats it; indeed the petty precision of opponents exaggerates it."[72] Notice that this is now a different argument from the previous one that held the words of pagans, Jews, and Muslims to be innocuous because they had been conquered. Now we are told that one should not artificially exaggerate the importance of some passing remark because in refuting it, one might make it so precise and cutting that it spreads and becomes truly dangerous. Of course the antichristian polemics of Jews and Muslims were not unthinking or careless.[73] Moreover, Arpe had just referred to Wagenseil's edition of the *Chizzuk Emunah*, which had been published with a refutation. But now he recommends not responding to antichristian allegations, and not writing refutations at all. Of course he was right in thinking that rebuttals could easily broadcast many of the arguments of one's opponents for the first time. It was in just this way in fact that many radical philosophers of the Enlightenment,

71. Ibid.: "Neque dissitendum illos et facilius et blandius fallere, qui speciem veritatis supra se ferunt, quam qui levis notae maculam non effugerunt aut plane atro carbone notantur. *Occurrit subito. CAVE CANEM*."

72. Ibid., 46: "Si improvidum maleeante verbum excidit spretum viliferet qua nunc in ore omnium fertur, adversariorum intempestiva diligentia."

73. On these polemics, see Richard H. Popkin, "Some Unresolved Questions in the History of Scepticism: The Role of Jewish Anti-Christian Arguments in the Rise of Scepticism in Regard to Religion," in idem, *The Third Force in Seventeenth-Century-Thought* (Leiden, 1992), 222–35; Silvia Berti, "At the Roots of Unbelief," *Journal of the History of Ideas* 56 (1995): 555–75.

such as Abbé Meslier, did find out about the arsenal of religiously critical arguments.[74] But here, and in this context, this recommendation was counterproductive, because Arpe had just claimed that the opponents of Christianity had been conquered—with stiff refutations. Indeed, if one read them in the light of what Arpe had just written in his footnote, that it was precisely inconspicuous assertions and not openly polemical arguments that were especially subversive, then Arpe's argument turns into its opposite.

The very next sentence should obviously have illustrated the futility or vanity of antichristian polemics. He says, "In considering the winds, we especially despise the one that . . . ruffles our clothing, that's just like especially disapproving those people who write the most unimportant and mostly false things, making them appear to have written something much more important than others."[75] Thus the critics of religion were just "hot-air merchants" who spread their blasphemies abroad in order to inflate their own importance. A serene and sober person should ignore them. Here we find the added insinuation that criticism of religion was in the end no more than posturing for effect. Admittedly, that is not very persuasive if one considers that the original point was the poison that a doctor had to understand, that is, genuinely serious objections to Christianity to which one simply had to respond. Arpe moves again to a footnote, in which he cites Lucian's *De scribenda historia* (*On Writing History*) to highlight the problems of those who get obsessed with pointless inanities rather than dealing with matters of substance: "Those who concentrate on speculations of this sort recognize neither how inappropriately they themselves are behaving nor do they really know the subject they are discussing; for history usually discusses only high affairs and does not inquire into the humble causes of unimportant matters." These people do not "notice what's happening but only what ought to happen," because their prejudices steer their thinking.[76]

74. Alan Charles Kors, *Atheism in France, 1650–1729*, vol. 1: *The Orthodox Sources of Disbelief* (Princeton, 1990).

75. [Arpe], *Apologia*, 46: "Quodsi *inter ventos* illum praecipue *aversamur*, ut *triste* dicebat, *qui vestes nostras tollit*, sic et illi displicent homines, qui minutissima et plerumque falsa conscribunt, ut videantur aliquid quam alii retulisse argutius."

76. Ibid., note: "Qui hujusmodi *conjecturis* nituntur, hi nec se norunt, quam inepti sint, nec rem quam tractant, novunt, cum historia assueta sit discurrere per negotiorum celsitudines, non humilium minutias indagare causarum. *Lucian de Scribend. historia*. Observo non quod fiat, sed quod fieri debeat."

So here again was an appeal to the art of living, to self-awareness, which Arpe held to be necessary if one was to avoid straying into intolerance. The critic of religion should not behave like a fanatic, but just as surely the historian or theologian should not take their blasphemies seriously. In the background we can sense again the ideal of the wise man in the sense of Charron's *preud'hommie*—the learned man, who does not allow himself to be provoked by superficialities.

Let me break off from our tour through Arpe's chapter, which keeps going on and on with shifting arguments, quotations, and allusions. After reading this chapter, and it's only one of many, the reader may be confused. We've gone on a roller coaster of arguments, some of them additive but others self-contradictory. How should we understand them? Was Arpe the author of a rather bumbling line of argument, in which a somewhat naive apologist, aiming only at rhetorical effects, piles up all the possible exonerations, all in the service of his client? That's a real possibility because after all the *Apologia pro Vanini* in its first version was a youthful work, the book of a man in his midtwenties. This was the way that Johann Lorenz von Mosheim also defended the harmlessness of this work when he wrote to La Croze, probably at the request of Arpe, when Arpe fell under suspicion of having been connected with the production of the *Traité des trois imposteurs*.[77] And yet the expanded manuscript copy we have before us was no longer a merely youthful work. Indeed, it even strengthens and reinforces our original concern. Arpe certainly proved in his other works that he was neither naive nor stupid; so our problem must lie more in his line of argument. I have tried to describe a philosophy of serenity, which, despite all the obfuscations, continues to be visible between the lines and whose "gestus" was that of appeasement: no, Vanini's philosophy is not dangerous; it is harmless; all the so-called radical writings are ultimately harmless, at least for those who can stay calm. One could tell that Vanini's equation of nature with God (or the goddess) was harmless by taking something from the custom of apotheosis as understood in political theology, in which the Roman emperor was deified everywhere.[78] If that was fairly

77. Johann Lorenz Mosheim to Mathurin Veyssière La Croze, March 10, 1718, in *Thesaurus epistolicus Lacrozianus*, ed. Ludwig Uhl (Leipzig, 1742–46), 1:276. See Mulsow, "Freethinking," 200ff.

78. [Arpe], *Apologia*, 66, note: "Latini promiscue utuntur his vocibus *Dominus* et *Deus*, ut se vocari voluit Domitianus *Sueton. in vit. c.12* De hinc et titulum *Domini* abnuit *Augustus* vitandae invidiae causa, non quod christiani *Christus Dominus natus esset* ut putat *Orosius*, neque quod Judaei appellationem *Domini* et *Dei* aversarentur, ut *Philo* censuit. *Clerici histor. eccles. p.223.* appellationem *divinitati honorum P.1. c.4. 5.8.10.70.* De Apotheosi nos *de jure Pontificali Romae*

harmless, why not a divinized nature? And strictly speaking, atheism hardly existed. In the end, didn't all people know God?

Physicotheology and Deism

In his denial of atheism, because nature itself was divine, Arpe held a position that was almost identical to that of Theodor Ludwig Lau.[79] At the very beginning of his *Meditationes philosophicae de Deo, Mundo, Homine* Lau had written that it was a foregone conclusion that God existed. There were no atheists, and there were no atheist nations.[80] This was a well-known position in the current debate that had been going on at least since Jakob Thomasius (the father of Christian Thomasius), concerning which authors and traditions from classical antiquity and later should be regarded as implicitly or explicitly atheist, so that they could provide no foundation for Christian philosophy.[81] In this debate it was assumed that atheism certainly could exist. But Lau, in contrast, relied on authorities such as Herbert of Cherbury, Ralph Cudworth, or Michel Mourgues, who postulated an original knowledge of God in every person, and who therefore denied that genuine atheists could exist. That Lau was influenced in this view by Arpe can be seen from his letters to Christian Thomasius in which he referred to the meaning of the *Apologia pro Vanino* for his convictions.[82] Lau's conclusion that atheism did not exist, however, has to be regarded in its tactical relationship with two other elements of his thinking: to the sort of "physicotheology" that he used for support; and to his demand for freedom of thought and for toleration with respect to forbidden books.

Veteris et Novae. De divino in disciplinis Morhofius Polyhist. libr.1.c.12 contranitente F.G.H.I.K. Joanne Friderico Kaisero. Gusta Hasso Halae 1715. 8. De eo quod *theion* est in disciplinis, De reliquis *Morhofi* commentariis, *Möllerus, in vita Polyhistori* praemissa. De divinis honoribus *Imperatori* et *Magistratibus Romanorum* et *Tulliola* a *Cicerone* patre praestiss. *Abb. Mongault."* On political theology in this context, see Mulsow, *Enlightenment Underground,* 165ff.

79. On Lau, see chapter 1, notes 2 and 3, as well as chapters 2 and 3.

80. Lau, *Meditationes philosophicae de Deo, Mundo, Homine,* chap. I, § I and II: "Deus est: Deus existit. Utrumque me & omnes, Sensus docent & Ratio. Atheismus hinc nullus. Atheae Nationes nullae. Athei Homines nulli." See idem, *Meditationes, Theses, Dubia,* § VIII: "Atheismus nullus datur."

81. Jakob Thomasius, *Schediasma historicum* (Leipzig, 1665).

82. Lau to Thomasius, in Thomasius, "Elender Zustand eines in die Atheisterey verfallenen Gelehrten," 279ff.

Let's begin with the first element. Lau derived his idea that God was experienced by every person not from inborn ideas but from sensory experience.[83] On the surface, therefore, he seemed to agree with the popular movement of that time called physicotheology, which exploited the latest discoveries of natural science to provide ever new proofs of an intelligent Creator who was responsible for creation. Arpe too regarded this as the best manner of apologetics: "The strongest argument for the existence of God is drawn from nature, which appeals to those who know more than others."[84] He refers not only to Cicero in this regard but also to his fellow Hamburg citizens, Johann Albert Fabricius and Barthold Hinrich Brockes, who had promoted physicotheology in Hamburg. But then he undermines this view by remarking in passing that God could be experienced everywhere, with every sense, with one's eyes, ears, and senses of smell and taste.[85] Could a physicotheologian taste God? No, he could only conclude from his understanding and from observing nature that God is. One could taste God only if God was nature. That was the subversive element in Lau's "physicotheology." So with this suspicion of possible subversion in mind, we should also read Arpe's assertions about God and nature. Thus he says: "If one sees the spear point of God's Word brought to a sharp enough point, we can see reason joined to nature, and then we can slaughter the atheists and the enemies of God, so to speak, with their own sword."[86] Surely Arpe here had in mind a natural theology like that of Cicero more than the barely disguised materialism of Lau. But Arpe too was deflating physicotheology in a way as well—as had Vanini—by rejecting the idea of God as a

83. Lau, *Meditationes philosophicae de Deo, Mundo, Homine*, chap. I, § V: "Existentia Dei: nulla indiget probatione; Sensus enim omnium incurrit."

84. [Arpe], *Apologia*, 31, note: "Firmissimum *existentiae divinae argumentum ex natura* petitur quod illis placet, qui prae reliquis sapiunt. Hinc provenit tanta commentariorum copia, quantam vix modica bibliotheca capet, inter quos merito primi nominis *Rudolphus Cudworth, God. Whiston, J. Ray, John Derham, Wollaston, Nieuentijdt, Fenelon de Salignac* et gravissimus nostrorum Poetarum, *Barthold Henr. Brockes.* de quibus 9.XX *Fabritius libro scripsit* laudato *de relig. christ.scriptorib.c.20.* Sic ipsius . . . , mundi qui omnia complexu suo coercet et continet, non artificiose solum, sed plane arripit consultoque et providus utilitatum opportunitatumque omnium agnoscitur. . . . praecipue autor *libro II. de natura Deorum* magna argumenta tractat elegantia."

85. Lau, *Meditationes philosophicae de Deo, Mundo, Homine*, chap. I, § V: "Oculus enim videt. Auris audit. Nasus olfacit. Lingua gustat. Manus tangit. En Testes infallibiles, & omni exceptione majores."

86. [Arpe], *Apologia*, 31: "Qui tela sacra Verbi Divini satis acuminata cernens, *naturae* rationem junxit, & *Atheos* hostesque *Dei*, proprio, ut ajunt, gladio jugulare aggressus est."

first mover and accepting God only as a vague Overbeing. Like Lau he had derived his own concept of God from the pseudo-Hermetic *Book of the Twenty-four Philosophers*: God was an infinite sphere, whose center was everywhere and whose circumference was nowhere.[87] Should one interpret this as with Lau as *natura naturans*? Arpe did not wish to be confined in this manner. He saw "logomachy" lurking in all such concepts, the potential for conflicts that could leave one vulnerable and could lead to being convicted of heresy when the wise man should try, instead, to withdraw from all such fixed positions.[88] Logomachies were the result of inferences from incendiary statements.

This refusal to make himself explicit was connected to the second fundamental element of Lau's thinking: the demand for toleration and freedom of thought. Just as the *Meditationes* of 1717 had begun with the denial of the very possibility of atheism, so the *Meditationes, Theses, Dubia* of 1719 began with the demand that forbidden writings should be permitted, and even that a book like the *De tribus impostoribus* should be printed.[89]

A Philosophy of Serenity

How do these three theses relate to each other: that there can be no true atheism; that God can be grasped through the senses; and that radical writings should be tolerated? Can they be reconciled? Or is this an instance of unforgivable theoretical carelessness owing to their fudging or evasion of controversial positions? Was this the purely deceptive strategy of a convinced deist or

87. Ibid., 42: "Neque omnino mihi *Hermetici* displicent, qui Deum *Sphaeram* vocarunt, *cujus centrum ubique, circumferentia nullibi*." See Martin Mulsow, "Ignorabat Deum: Scetticismo, libertinsmo ed ermetismo nell'interpretazione arpiana del concetto vaniniano di Dio," in *Giulio Cesare Vanini e il libertinismo: Atti del convegno di studi Taurisano 28–30 ottobre 1999*, ed. Francesco Paolo Raimondi (Galatina [Lecce], 2000), 171–82; Kurt Flasch, *Was ist Gott? Das Buch der vierundzwanzig Philosophen* (Munich, 2011), 29.

88. [Arpe], *Apologia*, 10, 51, 66, 74, 79. See above all Samuel Werenfels, *Dissertatio de logomachiis eruditorum* (Basel, 1702).

89. Lau, *Mediationes, Theses, Dubia*, in *Meditationes philosophicae de Deo, Mundo, Homine*, § I: "Confiscatio et Combustio Librorum: ex Ratione Status pernecessaria saepe est et utilis. Ast ubi solo ex Odio Theologico, Politico, Philosophico, profecta; Tyrannidem sapit Litterariam. Ignorantiam promovet et Errores. Solidam impedit Eruditionem. Rationi adversatur et Veritati. Autoribus interim: tales qui patiuntur quasi-Poenas: nullam Ignomiae vel Infamiae inurunt Notam. Libri: gloriosum sustinent Martyrium. Autores: illustres pro Veritate et Ratione, Martyres sunt." § VI: "Optandum hinc: ut ille, de Tribus Mundi Impostoribus, Liber: veram cujus Existentiam, Eruditus tuetur Orbis; in Lucem denuo prodeat."

atheist, or was it something else? In order to understand the relationship of these theses to one another, I propose taking a little detour into the present.

About thirty years ago Richard Rorty advanced the provocative thesis that democracy should take priority over philosophy.[90] He was combining the claim of John Rawls that a theory of justice could be erected without some prior agreement on human nature with the opinion (following the pragmatism of John Dewey) that philosophy is only a means of perfecting ourselves, or striving for the good, but not something that ultimately is grounded in "the truth." If you take Rawls's proposal that "philosophically speaking" we should "remain on the surface" and read it through the eyes of Dewey, one can arrive at a commitment to "antiphilosophy," to the priority of democratic solidarity over against any claim to objectivity. In making these connections, Rorty was drawing a line that stretches from Rawls back to Thomas Jefferson and the Enlightenment: the father of American Independence thought that one ought to practice toleration for all men, regardless of their religious persuasions, so long as they prove themselves to be reliable citizens in the political life of the community.[91]

Keeping in mind this notion that philosophical claims may need to be restricted by the claims of toleration and solidarity, we can now try to reconstruct the argument that stands behind Arpe's (and to some extent Lau's) philosophy of Serenity. It would have to look something like this: Freedom of thought is essential as an attitude of the informed judgment that avoids making premature enemies. The necessity of informing oneself comprehensively is so great that all substantial philosophical controversies pale in comparison. Indeed, because substantial controversies run the risk of driving their participants into states of high emotion, which then turn disputes into logomachies, merely verbal battles, the first demand for a tolerant and responsible scholar is, therefore, to downplay substantial controversies.

In this sense we can see Arpe's thinking as politically "conservative" and comparable to the political actions of Brockes as a Hamburg city councillor, who tried to damp down the explosiveness of the civil disturbances between church and citizenry.[92] In the end, this is probably where we will find the

---

90. Rorty, "The Priority of Democracy to Philosophy."

91. Ibid.

92. On Brockes, see Hans-Dieter Loose, ed., *Berthold Heinrich Brockes: Dichter und Ratsherr in Hamburg. Neue Forschungen zu Persönlichkeit und Wirkung* (Hamburg, 1980); Ernst Fischer, "Patrioten und Ketzermacher: Zum Verhältnis von Aufklärung und lutherischer Orthodoxie in

roots of the otherwise bewildering commonalities between Arpe and the conservative Hamburg Enlightenment centered on Fabricius, a movement that also cultivated a skeptical-stoic disposition along with the eclectic practice of book collecting, even if its members intended to foster Christian apologetics. In any event these commonalities were a precondition for the culture of exchanging books and ideas among the scholars of Hamburg, and so Arpe could trade clandestine writings with both Fabricius and Wolf.[93]

The "deflation" that we can see everywhere in Arpe's *Apologia pro Vanino*, therefore, was not the tactical dissimulation of a disguised deist or atheist but first and foremost the intentional deescalation of an eclectic "wise man." This wise one might harbor certain sympathies for atheism, but they did not cohere in him as a fixed worldview and certainly not as part of a political program. Instead, he skillfully insisted on an indifferentist and minimalist view of matters, one that reminds us of Spinoza's minimalist religious program in his *Tractatus theologico-politicus*, in which the whole of biblical teaching was reduced to love of neighbor. In a footnote Arpe says, "In my view the basis of Christian doctrine is knowledge of oneself and love of one's neighbor. I call out to the 'wrestlers' of literature: *How much futility there is in things!* Above all we should avoid two errors: one, that we regard the unknown as known; and second, spending too much time and effort on dark and difficult matters."[94] Even if Arpe here or there said what he considered to be "Christian" or "pious," he regularly avoided saying that he himself accepted such ideas. Instead he stoically or skeptically pointed to the emptiness of theological disputes in general. We can see how light-footed (or thoughtless) Arpe was in the fact that he thought the ancient pagans had accepted a sort of Christianity: "even in that cultural darkness and general benightedness of spirit long ago, they came close to touching the truth." They sensed the divine nature of Christ but had no

---

Hamburg am Beginn des 18. Jahrhunderts," in *Zwischen Aufklärung und Restauration: Festschrift für Wolfgang Martens*, ed. Wolfgang Frühwald and Alberto Martino (Tübingen, 1989), 17–47.

93. See Mulsow, "Entwicklung einer Tatsachenkultur."

94. [Arpe], *Apologia*, 98, note: "Meo animo fundamentum Sanctae Christi doctrinae est *cognitio sui* et CHARITAS. Et reliquis literarum palaestribus magna voce acclamo. *Quantum est in rebus inane. Dua* nobis *vitia* praecipue vitanda sunt: *unum* ne incognita pro cognitis habeamus, hisque temere assentiamus. *Alterum* quidque nimis magnum studium, multamque operam in res obscuras atque difficiles conferunt, easdemque non necessarias. Quibus vitiis declinatis, quid in rebus honestis et cognitione dignis, operae curaeque ponetur, ut jure laudabitur." See Spinoza, *Theologisch-politischer Traktat* (Hamburg, 1994), esp. chaps. 4, 5, 12, 13, and 14.

concept with which to grasp his role as the Messiah.[95] Here he tactically deploys the theological pattern of thought implicit in the "immanent trinity," the unity of Father, Son, and Holy Spirit, in order to draw the (logically alarming) conclusion that whoever worshiped God was therefore worshiping Christ as well. But hadn't Arpe just rejected such subtle Christian dogmatics?

We find something similar in Lau. Recent interpreters have accused him of thinking superficially, as if he collected arguments, caring only if they could be used against Christian dogma.[96] He supposedly was not concerned that they should fit together. But if we read Lau in the light of the "priority of toleration over philosophy," then this sort of "negative" eclecticism makes more sense. Lau too, one could say, cared more about deflation and less about formulating coherent truths. So a tactical deployment of certain propositions was always possible and legitimate.

Comparing the two, Arpe was surely the one who retired more readily into quietist skepticism. He went so far in that direction that because of the almost universal rejection of Spinoza's *Tractatus* and Collins's *Discourse of Free Thinking*, both of which were called politically dangerous, he did not dare anything more than the defensive demand: "that I may be granted freedom to comment without punishment on a matter that provokes not so much danger as distrust."[97] By deflating the claims of philosophy, he was also denying its actual dangers.

95. [Arpe], *Apologia*, 32, note: First it states: "*Nullam* extra Christum *salutem esse* divinum *Aposteli* effatum est. Quod tamen *Gentium Doctores in religione duntaxat sua* pueris stolidiora ... docuerint fabulisque anilibus totum negotium peregerint, vana est persuasio." But then comes the quoted sentence: "In illa rerum caligine et mentis nebulis parum abfuit, quin attingerent verum."

96. Schröder, *Spinoza*, 129–31; Martin Pott, "Einleitung," in Lau, *Meditationes*, ed. Pott, 36ff.

97. Gawlick, "Die ersten deutschen Reaktionen auf A. Collins' *Discourse of Free-Thinking* von 1713." See also Kay Zenker, *Denkfreiheit: Libertas philosophandi in der deutschen Aufklärung* (Hamburg, 2021). [Arpe], *Apologia*, 29, note: "Velitis jubeatis me *libero ore et animo* causam hanc agere, quam defendendum suscepi. *Libertate* enim *sentiendi* et *loquendi* anima consiliorum habenda est et veritatis pedisequa. Non me fugit quidem, quam gravi Reip. malo, hac libertate multi fabulantur, quo nomine male audiunt. *Benedictus Spinosa* in tractatu Theologico-Politico. Nec non *Antonius Collins* celebris *de libertate sentiendi*, et *de religionis christianae fundamentis* hoc saeculo *in Anglia* promulgatis. Nec ipse prudentissimus autor *liberarum cogitationum de religionis ecclesiae et Reip.* negotiis Hag. Com. 1722. 8. omnibus placet. Ipse tantum, ut sine noxa mihi libertas concedatur potestate ac causa non tam periculosa quam invidiosa disserendi. Quod si lectores eodem erunt in me animo, quam ipse in illis sum, optime spero nobis conveniet tam

But writing to Thomasius, Lau too had called himself an "indifferentist"; and in his books Lau (like Arpe) was more concerned to raise ideas for discussion, to be a "broker," to present a "theater" of radical views, so that the reader, exercising a well-considered eclecticism, would use his powers of judgment to choose the true from the false.[98] Seen this way, Arpe's freethinker was the ideal reader of Lau's *Meditationes*.

The Clandestine Black Market

I have stressed that it was precisely this sublimated radicalism, the bracketed or deflated sense of danger, that made possible a continuum of thinking from Arpe's position to that of the Christian-apologist-bibliophiles, a continuum that enabled him to exchange books with them, despite all his differences with Wolf and Fabricius on specific issues.

Let's use a handwritten note by Arpe on his copy of *Apologia pro Vanino* to penetrate a little into this milieu of clandestine black markets in northern Germany and determine the connection between their ideas and practices. I am returning to the episode, mentioned earlier, when someone offered Arpe forbidden writings. Arpe wrote, "I remember that once a young man came to me and showed me, as if they were treasures, complete copies of rare forbidden books. Michael Servetus's *Christianismi restitutio*, Bruno's *Spaccio della bestia trionfante*, Bodin's *De rerum sublimium arcanis*, Geoffroy Vallée's *Ars nihil credendi*, the *Cymbalum mundi*, Charles Blount's *Oracles of Reason*, etc. I can't blame him for bubbling over in his lust for novelty. [But] with age comes moral capacity [*frugem*] and the use of healthy reason."[99] Arpe acted with detachment and serenity, as if he was an experienced connoisseur of forbidden writings, a man who could dismiss worries that the excited hunt for clandestine works among curious young intellectuals might cause damage. Arpe used the Latin word "offere," and so it's not entirely clear if the young man was only showing him these writings or if he was also offering them for Arpe to copy. Of course, usually one went hand in hand with the other. This choice of clandestine works was in any event outstanding, especially if the title *Ars nihil credendi* was the work by the so-called Pseudo-Valée and that the *Cymbalum*

---

sua aetate *Athanasius* dissertationem in illos edidit *qui dijudicant veritatem ex multitudine Magistrorum.*"

98. See chapter 2.

99. See note 60 in this chapter.

mundi was the *Symbolum Sapientiae*.[100] Who could this young man have been, who was offering such an assortment? Probably not Conrad Zacharias von Uffenbach, the Frankfurt patrician and bibliophile, with whom Arpe was in correspondence in the 1720s concerning these sorts of writings, because Uffenbach was about the same age as Arpe.[101] I would consider Charles Etienne Jordan a good candidate. In the years around 1725 Jordan, then in his mid-twenties, was intensively involved in the clandestine book trade; he was one of the few at that time who could have offered the *Cristianismi restitutio*.[102] Anne Goldgar has described him as a typical eager young man hoping to rise in the Republic of Letters, one who collected rare texts and information in the hopes of gaining access to scholars and of making a name for himself in the world.[103] Because Jordan was a member of the Huguenot colony in Berlin and a former student of the librarian there, Mathurin Veyssière La Croze, he had had the opportunity to copy out various rare works; and this allowed him to seek out connoisseurs and collectors, offering to sell or trade *clandestina*—and in the process calling attention to himself. In 1725 he tempted Uffenbach with the *Cristianismi restitutio*, and after he took the bait, a lucrative trade developed, mostly by barter but also sometimes for cash, transactions in which Jordan acted as a broker. Jordan, who later served as the private tutor and friend of Crown Prince Frederick of Prussia, later Frederick the Great, provided Uffenbach with Stosch's *Concordia rationis et fidei*, complete with marginalia by the author (figure 16), Servetus, and the *De tribus impostoribus*, in return for which he received Italian works by Giordano Bruno, Lau's *Meditationes*, and Jean Bodin's *Six livres de la République*. By 1726 Jordan had made connections with England in order to approach the clandestine market there.[104] These may have been the years when he also showed up at Arpe's

100. On the *Ars nihil credendi*, see Alain Mothu, "La beatitude des Chrétiens et son double clandestin," in *La Philosophie clandestine a l'Age classique*, ed. Anthony McKenna and idem (Oxford, 1997), 79–117. On the *Symbolum*, see *Cymbalum mundi sive Symbolum Sapientiae*, ed. Canziani, Schröder, and Socas.

101. See the correspondence between Arpe and Uffenbach in Uffenbach, *Commercii epistolaris Uffenbachiani selecta*, ed. Johann Georg Schelhorn (Ulm and Memmingen, 1753).

102. Jens Häseler, *Ein Wanderer zwischen den Welten, Charles Etienne Jordan (1700–1745)* (Sigmaringen, 1993).

103. Goldgar, *Impolite Learning*.

104. Häseler, *Wanderer*, 40–47; Martin Mulsow, *Die drei Ringe: Toleranz und clandestine Gelehrsamkeit bei Matthurin Veyssière La Croze 1660–1739* (Tübingen, 2001), 88ff.

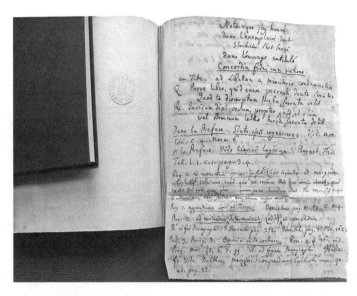

FIGURE 16. Friedrich Wilhelm Stosch, marginal additions to his *Concordia rationis et fidei*. State and University Library of Hamburg, Cod. theol. 2152.

house in Hamburg, because Arpe was known by then as an expert with such materials through his *Apologia pro Vanino* and in 1726 his *Feriae aestivales.*[105]

The fact that Arpe reacted calmly to Jordan's probably passionate offering may have been an echo of Arpe's own youth. When he had been a young man in his mid-twenties he had also been rather hot-headed. Johann Christoph Wolf, who knew him then, described him as someone who was attracted, "who knew why," by forbidden texts and who was abusing his talents with wicked things.[106] But taking Arpe's *Apologia pro Vanino* into account, however, we can understand his serene reaction as part of his complex habitus, one that combined *preud'hommie*, eclecticism, and ideas of toleration.

105. Arpe, *Feriae aestivales.*

106. Wolf to La Croze, May 1, 1716, in *Thesaurus epistolicus Lacrozianus*, 2:107: "Equidem Arpii illius, hominis docti et elegantis, vices aliquoties miseratus sum, qui et opera et ingenio suo abuti mihi videatur. Relatum enim mihi est, eundem in societate quadam erudita, quae Kilonii certis per hebdomadem diebus cogi solet ad recensendos libros recens editos, plerumque ea in medium afferre, quae animum eiusmodi rerum percupidum et studiosum ostentent, quarum notitiam alius ne titivillitio quidem emerit. Ita famosum illud Jo. Bodini colloquium Heptaplomeres sibi lectum praesenti mihi ipse ante decennium circiter referebat, in quo aliquot post annis nihil eorum inveniebam, quae nescio quam doctrinae ingeniique praestantiam spirare ipsi videbantur."

To understand the circulation of forbidden books in Protestant Germany during the 1720s, we need to start with a triangle of cities: Berlin-Frankfurt-Hamburg.[107] As we've seen, Arpe, Johann Albert Fabricius, and Johann Christoph Wolf were living in Hamburg; in Berlin we find both Jordan and La Croze; and in Frankfurt, Uffenbach. There were of course other collectors of clandestine works, such as the Hildesheim church superintendent Jakob Friedrich Reimmann, but they were not usually swept up in active trading to the extent that Jordan and Uffenbach were.[108] In many cases it is possible, using variant manuscripts or their proven provenance, to show how a manuscript made its way from Berlin to Frankfurt, and then as a loan to Hamburg, where it was transcribed. There it could be compared with other copies and then make its way back, along with other texts. When Jordan laid out his offerings, Arpe too would have compared one text with another, hoping to detect variations or other information about its origins.

It gets harder to follow the German trade in clandestine books during the 1730s and 1740s. Many of the trading nodes are still unknown, the places where professional or semiprofessional transcripts were produced and sold. We do get a glimpse of changing conditions from the relations between the radical Pietist and freethinker Johann Christian Edelmann and his supplier of *clandestina*, Georg Christoph Kreyssig.[109] Officially, Kreyssig was a local historian and auctioneer in Dresden, but secretly he was a follower of Edelmann. As auctioneer and friend of the wealthy book collector Johann August von Ponickau, he was in a position to fulfill almost all of Edelmann's desires for rare books. Just in 1744 alone copies of *De imposturis religionum*, the *Symbolum Sapientiae*, the *L'Esprit de Spinoza*, the text by "Mutianus de Bath," and the biblical interpretation of Hermann von der Hardt were sent from Dresden to Neuwied, where Edelmann was living.

Did other cities also have such apparently respectable auctioneers, who were really acting as black marketeers? There must have been at least a few. In Berlin, for example, we know of a Jewish merchant named Pinell, who performed similar services to those of Kreyssig.[110] But in Hamburg we

---

107. See also Mulsow, "Transmission."

108. On Reimmann, see Mulsow and Zedelmaier, *Reimmann*.

109. Johann Christian Edelmann, *Sechs Briefe an Georg Christoph Kreyssig*, ed. Philipp Strauch (Halle, 1918). See Strauch's introduction to the letters, pp. 5ff., concerning the contacts between Edelmann and Ponickau on the one hand, but also the fact that the letters to Kreyssig landed in Ponickau's library.

110. Many thanks to Hermann Stockinger for information on Pinell.

cannot yet see how the market for clandestine books worked. It seems probable, however, that Arpe was involved in it. Let's look at what sorts of *clandestina* a Hamburg collector's library around 1750 might contain. At that time the Hanseatic city was the home of the physician Christian Joachim Lossau.[111] Anyone entering Lossau's library would have noticed a glass case in which about a thousand *libri rari prohibiti* (rare, forbidden books) could be found, some of them in manuscript form, others printed. This was the largest cache of clandestine works in Hamburg and maybe in all of Germany. Next to that case was another containing an even more specialized collection: *libri publice combusti*, books that had been publicly burned. In the early Enlightenment such books had awakened a lively interest among many liberal scholars, first Andreas Westphal; then Johann Lorenz Mosheim, who as a young man had intended to write a book called *Bibliotheca Vulcani* to recount the history of burned books; and finally Arpe's friend Johann Heinrich Heubel, who intended to complete Mosheim's stillborn enterprise, elegantly and with the aid of French connoisseurs like Bernard de la Monnoye and Antoine Lancelot. The project never was completed, and all we have of it is the simple list of titles that Heubel sent to Arpe. But perhaps something called "Volume XX" of the "Sententiae librorum combustorum," which Lossau had in his library, was actually a mixed lot from Heubel's collection of materials. In the next chapter I will discuss it in detail.

Among the clandestine works that Lossau possessed we find, in addition to several copies of *De tribus impostoribus* in both the French and Latin versions, and along with Stosch and Lau, such rare works as the *Symbolum Sapientiae*, the *Ineptus religiosus*, the so-called *Judaeus Lusitanus*,[112] the work of "Mutianus de Bath," Hatzfeld's *Découverte de la verité*, the Pseudo-Vallée, Wachter's *De origine rerum humanorum*, the *Examen de la Religion*, a commentary on Horace by Beverland, texts by Postel, Radicati, Bury, Collins, Cuffeler, Koerbagh, Toland, Dippel, Servetus, Blount, and La Mettrie, dozens of titles

---

111. See the anonymous sales catalog: *Catalogus einer auserlesenen Bibliothek aus allen Teilen der Wissenschaften insbesondere der medicinischen Gelehrsamkeit, worunter sich zugleich die mehresten der sogenannten raren Bücher aus der Theologie theils gedruckt, theils im Manuskript, wie auch eine vortreffliche Sammlung von medicinischen Disputationen, und Landcharten befinden, welche 1761 den 1. März und folgende Tage im Hartmannschen Hause bey der Börse durch den Auktionarium, Johann Diederich Klefeker, öffentlich sollen verhauft werden* (Hamburg, 1760; preserved in the State and University Library of Hamburg).

112. Translator's note: The anonymous work of a Portuguese Jew.

by and about Edelmann, and much more. Many of these texts have survived only because the Orthodox pastor and later opponent of Lessing, Johann Melchior Goeze, had them bought up after Lossau's death in order to keep them out of circulation.[113]

I suspect that many books from Arpe's private collection had found their way into Lossau's library. One hint of that is the so-called Bourboniana-manuscript, which Arpe used and which can be found among Lossau's books.[114] Arpe, who never had permanent employment, had speculated with money in Hamburg and had thus been able—along with his trade in manuscripts—to assemble a serious collection of "rare and especially of paradoxical writings," whose content we can partially reconstruct from his footnotes and letters.[115] Of Giordano Bruno alone, for example, he owned seven or eight printed works along with others in manuscript copies. But we also know that Arpe's collection was dispersed well before his death in 1740, bringing it into

113. On this, see Martin Mulsow, *Monadenlehre, Hermetik und Deismus: Georg Schades geheime Aufklärungsgesellschaft 1747–1760* (Hamburg, 1998), 238ff. On Goeze, see Ernst-Peter Wieckenberg, *Johann Melchior Goeze* (Hamburg, 2007).

114. The *Bourboniana* contained remembered sayings related to Nicolas Bourbon, an old professor of Greek at the Collège Royal in Paris and a canon of Langres, as well as the friendly father figure to Guy Patin. The book belonged to a separate genre called "ana-literature" because they added "ana" to the name of the beloved persons whose sayings were commemorated. In the 1630s he often received scholarly visitors in his room in the Oratory in the Rue Saint-Honoré, and indeed he sometimes gathered around himself a regular small "academy" of Parisian intellectuals. Concerning his conversations with Patin, or more precisely the utterances of Patin to Bourbon, there were memoirs, and in a complicated way the largest volume of these written memories (725 pages) found its way into Arni Magnusson's hands. The manuscript had already had a long history before it reached Magnusson. During his Paris sojourn Matthias Worm, a Danish scholar, had lived in Patin's house and gained possession of the volume. Back in Denmark he gave it to Peder Schumacher, the Count of Griffenfeld, who was arrested for high treason in 1676; and so the text came to Oluf Rosenkrantz, privy councillor and treasury official. One can thus see in what high political circles manuscripts like this circulated. After Rosenkrantz's death Arni Magnusson came into possession of the *Bourboniana*; but Magnusson was unable to make much of the work (which today is listed as Ms. 77 in the Hessian State Library in Wiesbaden) and traded it for others belonging to Christian Reitzer, one of Arpe's professor friends in Copenhagen, who was extremely interested in the latest intellectual currents such as Cartesianism and natural law. Finally it was Reitzer who allowed Arpe to make copies from this unique source for French intellectual life in the first half of the seventeenth century.

115. See also Mulsow, "Arpe collectionneur."

the hands of others.[116] Obviously he had had to sell off his books and manu-scripts because he had landed in financial difficulties. Lossau may well have bought a part of that collection, but other items, like the transcripts of Vanini, found their way into the library of Rudolph Johann Friedrich Schmid, a col-lector of alchemical works.[117]

Effects?

One final question we have to ask in view of the large amount of clandestine material available in Hamburg (and in other German cities to a lesser extent) is this: Was Arpe's "serenity"—a serenity that was partially just tactical—justified? Was it really true that the presence of radical writings critical of religion did not justify fears of their social or political impact? Or were the Orthodox right to worry as they screamed warnings about the effects of such works? Maybe their moral panic was not totally unjustified. The jury is still out on the question. No one has yet really investigated what impact reading clandestine works had on the radicalization of Reimarus or other philoso-phers of the Enlightenment. So long as the transmission of clandestine ideas has not been adequately tracked in detail, the question must remain unset-tled. How much was an effect of these *clandestina* and what was really only defiance of a dominant Orthodoxy, a dismay at the predominance of strict Protestantism? Alan Charles Kors has shown for France that many cases of "radicalization" cannot be explained by the "influence" of dangerous ideas; they were instead the independent consequence of recognizing internal con-tradictions in orthodox Christian arguments.[118] We should therefore proceed cautiously if we want to judge the impact of these *clandestina*. We also have to distinguish between the effects of texts on the radicalization of individual thinkers and the politically and "morally" destabilizing effects on broader layers of society, on people who recognized that Orthodox theologians were worried.

116. See the report in the *Hamburger Berichten* for 1740 (No. 100), 874–76. Arpe's collection of rare and paradoxical writings was scattered during his own lifetime and came into other hands.

117. On Schmid, see Martin Mulsow, "You Only Live Twice: Charlatanism, Alchemy, and Critique of Religion in Hamburg (1747–1761)," *Cultural and Social History* 3 (2006): 273–86. See also idem, "Transmission."

118. Kors, *Atheism in France*.

How and why did the Enlightenment prevail? This broad question has several aspects, one of which is the question we've been asking here, the problem of estimating the impacts of these clandestine works. Even so, with a better understanding of the situations and arguments of Peter Friedrich Arpe and Theodor Ludwig Lau, we can now see more clearly why questions concerning the effect of underground writings deserve an answer. They affect not only our retrospective view from the present, the reconstructions made by historians, but also the prospective view of the actors themselves, their evaluation of their own actions, their habitus, their attitude, and how they dealt with the explosive knowledge they possessed.

5

A Library of Burned Books

A Satirical Stove?

There are satirical poems, satirical epitaphs, satirical coins—and there's even a satirical stove. It stands today in the Salzburg Carolino Augusteum Museum, but it was originally most likely from the archiepiscopal abbey of St. Peter's in Salzburg. The convent had a stove installed in the eighteenth century that looked like a library bookcase (figure 17).[1] Skillfully constructed backs of books in its lower structure look like real books on real shelves. On the backs of these apparent folio volumes are prominently displayed the names of heretics, beginning with Arius and Nestorius down to the early modern Protestant heretics. And above the shelves stands a banner with the inscription "Bibliotheca Vulcano Consecrata," that is, "A Library Dedicated to the God Vulcan"—the god of fire. In view of the function of a stove, the title was mocking, as if the writings given over to it would be incinerated even as their authors landed in hell. At that time all of Salzburg's Protestants were being expelled from the archbishopric (1684–1731). Such a "Bibliotheca Vulcani" did not exist only in the fantasies of Catholic priests, however, for such a paper library had been designed just a few years earlier, albeit in another manner and for quite different purposes.

This paper "library" was a reconstitution of lost knowledge. One effect of the plurality of claims to truth made by different world interpretations during the early modern period was the "precarization" of various fields of knowledge.

---

1. The rococo stove in the Museum Carolino-Augusteum can be found in the "Reformation room." See Hans Tietze, *Die Kunstsammlungen der Stadt Salzburg* (Vienna, 1919), figure 350. Following that source, in the first edition of this book I originally stated that the stove had come from the Abbey of Mattsee, but Dieter Wölfel has kindly informed me that the stove originally stood in the room of "libri prohibiti" in St. Peter's in Salzburg.

FIGURE 17. Satirical stove, Stift Mattsee. Hans Tietze, *Die Kunstsammlungen der Stadt Salzburg,* Vienna, 1919, ill. 350.

As we've seen, knowledge can become precarious when it's insecure, problematic, revocable. If whole epistemic regions were challenged as having no truth—as happened, for example, when Protestants rejected Catholic claims, and vice versa—these appeals amounted to a huge revocation of legions of authors and their writings. Who could be surprised then that the early modern period saw numerous prohibitions of books and even book burnings. Of course that had happened during the Middle Ages, too, as Thomas Werner has strikingly shown.[2] In this regard, however, the early modern period with its increasingly consolidated forms of rule was an age of extremes. Just think of the Index of Prohibited Books or the regular series of autos-da-fé in certain regions.[3]

My chief interest at this point is the connection between pluralization and radicalization, on the one hand, and radicalization and precarization, on the other. Pluralization and radicalization were mainly connected because the

2. Thomas Werner, *Den Irrtum liquidieren: Bücherverbrennungen im Mittelalter* (Göttingen, 2007).

3. See, e.g., Hermann Rafetseder, *Bücherverbrennungen: Die öffentliche Hinrichtung von Schriften im historischen Wandel* (Vienna, 1988); Volker Weidermann, *Das Buch der verbrannten Bücher* (Cologne, 2008); Mona Körte and Cornelia Ortlieb, eds., *Verbergen—Überschreiben—Zerreißen: Formen der Bücherzerstörung in Literatur, Kunst und Religion* (Berlin, 2007).

growth of plural claims to truth led in an altogether unintended manner to a relativization of them all. Plurality made itself felt as people made ever stronger statements of belief, truth, and certainty, which happened during the sixteenth and seventeenth centuries as part of what Benjamin Nelson called a process of "anti-probabilistic" modernization.[4] Obviously none of these pretenders to certainty intended that truth—for example theological truth—should be undermined. But that's just what happened when two equally certain antagonists were observed by a third party, who might draw the conclusion from their contest that the whole foundation of their discourse, for example the belief in the Bible as God's revelation, needed revision. As Christianity was compared with other religions, similarities and dependencies on earlier traditions were discovered, and all at once Christianity was no longer the simple and absolute measure of truth.[5]

Martin Gierl has pointed to such a structure, the abandonment of direct contrapositions, in the Pietist and then in the early Enlightenment reforms of communication around 1700 in Germany. First Philipp Jakob Spener challenged the traditional Orthodox Lutheran *elenchus* (their policy of finding, refuting, and expelling heresy), which had led them to define heresies as fundamental doctrinal errors; then Christian Thomasius picked a fight over the very process by which the Orthodox "manufactured" heresies.[6] Instead of fearing becoming infected with heresy, a new trust arose from the possible reconciliation of errant positions, along with an assumed immunity against errors and a new social and historical understanding of why some people were declared (and were still being declared) heretics. That was a big step in the achievement of mechanisms by which plurality could be accommodated; and if one sees early modern Europe as extremely polarized, this was a process of leaving the early modern period behind. Let us now turn our attention to this intersection. It connects plurality with the rise of "eclectic philosophy," which we've already treated, but also with "Historia literaria"; these two developments considered a whole panoply of available positions, before rendering any final judgment.[7]

4. Benjamin Nelson, *On the Roads to Modernity: Conscience, Science, and Civilizations: Selected Writings*, ed. Toby E. Huff (Totowa, NJ, 2011).

5. See Martin Mulsow, "Die Thematisierung paganer Religionen in der Frühen Neuzeit," in *Religionen in Nachbarschaft*, ed. Christoph Bultmann et al. (Münster, 2012), 109–23.

6. Martin Gierl, *Pietismus und Aufklärung: Theologische Polemik und die Kommunikationsreform der Wissenschaft am Ende des 17. Jahrhunderts* (Göttingen, 1997).

7. See Horst Dreitzel, "Entwicklung und Eigenart der 'eklektischen Philosophie,'" *Zeitschrift für Historische Forschung* 18 (1991): 281–343; Frank Grunert and Friedrich Vollhardt, eds., *Historia literaria: Neuordnungen des Wissens im 17. und 18. Jahrhundert* (Berlin, 2007).

This period saw a reform of communications that took varying forms, for example, in the codes of behavior of French *galanterie* and the code of civility for English gentlemen, but in Germany the Pietist-Thomasian reform in communications came with philosophical and religiously critical radicalizations that were certainly not shared by all the Thomasians. Radical philosophers of the Enlightenment rejected the path of moderate reform and practiced instead a radical form of eclecticism by abandoning belief in revelation, and with it the very essence of Protestantism, an essence that continued to nourish the Pietists of Halle. With their anarchic plea against all forms of lordship such radicals called into question the basis of all realistic politics, which was the very starting point for the moderates.[8]

This brings us to my second concern, the possible connection between radicalization and precarization. The thinking of radical philosophers of the Enlightenment was actually much more precarious than the views of conflicting religious parties of the sixteenth and seventeenth centuries, when the general religious and ideological lines of conflict also provided a way to reject what one disagreed with from a viewpoint on the other side. Radicals, however, stood outside the basic consensus of both sides and beyond the norms of the established version of eclectic philosophy. The consequence was a precarization of the social status of radical authors, so that we can speak of a knowledge precariat throughout the whole clandestine scene. While moderate reformers were not generally made precarious, inasmuch as they could still publish and teach at universities, radicals lost their jobs and had to retreat into the underground.

I will concentrate on the point where pluralization, radicalization, and precarization intersected: the project to "save" forbidden books. The attempt to do so began as early as the sixteenth century and reached a high point in the late seventeenth and early eighteenth centuries. The general context was the huge debate over toleration that erupted after the fiery execution of Michael Servetus (1553) and more specifically the debate over freedom of thought and publication.[9] Most Thomasians in Germany favored permitting the publication of radical works (although they were divided on the issue and wanted restrictions on publication), while the partisans of *Historia literaria* were deeply interested in previously banned works. The decisive authors here were

---

8. See chapters 2 and 3.

9. See Joseph Leclerc, *Histoire de la tolerance au siècle de la Reforme*, 2 vols. (Paris, 1955); Perez Zagorin, *How the Idea of Religious Toleration Came to the West* (Princeton, 2005). On freedom of thought, see Zenker, "Libertas philosophandi."

Gabriel Naudé and Pierre Bayle, as I said earlier. And yet the enterprise of writing a history of banned and burned books was risky because it spelled the retrieval of precarious knowledge, the retrospective tolerance for plurality among various points of view, and the revival of radical thinking. That was especially so if official judgments and the exercise of governmental authority were suspended, for then the reconstruction of specific cases of prohibition easily became criticism of the authorities and implicitly a retrieval of forbidden knowledge. In such cases the suspicion lingered—as we saw in the previous chapter—that anyone who "rescued" Servetus, or Vanini, or Spinoza must be eo ipso someone who sympathized with them. That pushed the whole venture in the direction of what radical Pietists such as Gottfried Arnold and Friedrich Breckling were doing by listing the "witnesses to truth," persons who were sanctified only because they found themselves in opposition to authority. For radical philosophers of the Enlightenment, when they rescued *auctores et libri combusti* (books and authors who had been burned), they seemed to be sanctifying them in a secular manner.[10]

A comprehensive *Dictionnaire critique . . . des principaux livres condamnés* was finally published in 1806, compiled by Gabriel Peignot.[11] There had been earlier efforts, however, as part of the project of *Historia literaria* and the Thomasians at the beginning of the Enlightenment. The most important of these projects was the compiling of a *Bibliotheca Vulcani*, which was supposed to list and investigate all the books that had been burned. In the end, the project came to nothing, a fact that was connected to the suspicion that it was itself a radical gesture. The precariat of radical thinkers were caught up in their own evaluation, for very little survives of their project. While in Hamburg the great *bibliothecae*, the encyclopedias of the knowledge bourgeoisie, continued to expand, especially the *Bibliotheca graeca* of Fabricius and the *Bibliotheca hebraea* of Wolf; their radical counterpart, the *Bibliotheca Vulcani*, although conceived in their immediate vicinity, never appeared.[12]

10. On the topos of "witnesses to truth," see Mißfeldt, *Gottfried Arnold*; Brigitte Klosterberg and Guido Naschert, eds., *Friedrich Breckling (1629–1711): Prediger, "Wahrheitszeuge" und Vermittler des Pietismus im niederländischen Exil* (Halle, 2011).

11. Gabriel Peignot, *Dictionnaire critique, littéraire et bibliographique des principaux livres condamnés au feu, supprimés ou censures* (Paris, 1806).

12. Johann Albert Fabricius, *Bibliotheca graeca* (Hamburg, 1705–28); idem, *Bibliotheca Latina* (Hamburg, 1697); idem, *Bibliotheca Latina mediae et infimae Aetatis* (Hamburg, 1734–36); Johann Christoph Wolf, *Bibliotheca hebraea* (Hamburg, 1715–33). On the context, see Mulsow, "Entwicklung einer Tatsachenkultur."

The Production of Knowledge at Court

The author of the intended *Bibliotheca Vulcani* was Johann Heinrich Heubel, who had been born in 1694 and died in 1758, which places him in the same generation as Mosheim and Reimarus.[13] If he has to be ranked among the "quixotic projectors" because his work was never completed, there are two specific reasons for this.[14] For one thing, his project was incendiary; but Heubel also stood mostly outside the academy and was active in the milieu of the court. Anyone working at court was forced to cultivate scholarly studies as a sideline, and that meant they were often left unfinished. And the enterprise of constructing a *Bibliotheca Vulcani* was itself precarious. On the other hand, the diplomatic and courtly ambience also offered real opportunities for such a project. It seems sensible, therefore, to take a closer look at this ambience and to watch Heubel on his travels in the entourage of official ambassadors, hoping to see how his particular interests (and his role in the history of information) were dependent on a structure that allowed him mobility, permitted his activities as a book collector, and exploited the circulation of texts—advantages that were by no means available to mere professors.

After studying law in Wittenberg, Heubel obtained a post in 1717 as a private tutor in the palace at Eutin in Holstein for the children of the Protestant prince bishop of Lübeck, Christian August, who was at that juncture still serving as custodian for the young duke of Schleswig, Karl Friedrich. Through his activities at the palace Heubel was drawn into the circle of leading north German politicians, especially Count Henning von Bassewitz, who, near the end of the Great Northern War (1700–1721) and after the execution of Baron Georg Heinrich von Goertz in 1719, was able to establish himself as a strong new leader.[15] Little Schleswig-Holstein had placed all its bets on Sweden in

13. For Heubel there are scattered biographical details in Hans Schröder, *Lexikon der Hamburgischen Schriftsteller* (Hamburg, 1857), 3:241, and in Henning Ratjen, "Johann Heinrich Heubel," in *Schriften der Universität zu Kiel aus dem Jahre 1858* (Kiel, 1859), 62–67. I am grateful to Detlef Heubel for informing me of his date of death. The following study continues a project that I first worked on long ago: "Bibliotheca Vulcani: Das Projekt einer Geschichte der verbrannten Bücher bei Johann Lorenz Mosheim und Johann Heinrich Heubel," *Das achtzehnte Jahrhundert* 18 (1994): 56–71.

14. On "quixotic projectors," see Markus Krajewski, ed., *Projektemacher: Zur Produktion von Wissen in der Vorform des Scheiterns* (Berlin, 2006).

15. On Bassewitz, see Hubertus Neuschäffer, *Henning Friedrich Graf von Bassewitz 1680–1749* (Schwerin, 1999). See the information provided in [P. F. Arpe], *Das verwirrte Cimbrien in der*

the war and was therefore hostile to Denmark. But now Charles XII was dead, and Sweden was about to negotiate a peace with Russia. And because Karl Friedrich was the nephew of the slain Swedish king, he was drawn into all the negotiations; a period of frenzied travel for the court ensued. That's probably why we see Heubel in Berlin in 1720–21 and then between April and June 1721 in Stockholm, in the vicinity of Adolf Friedrich von Bassewitz, the cousin of Count Henning.[16] At this time Heubel was an enthusiastic student of medieval documents, so that his patrons Fabricius and Wolf harbored the hope that he might someday be a major figure in this field. In Berlin he was accepted as a member of the newly founded Academy and associated with its linguists, La Croze, Johann Leonard Frisch, and Johann Georg Wachter. In Sweden, when his duties did not require his presence at court, he buried himself in the book treasuries of Stockholm and Uppsala. He discovered a manuscript by Benzo (bishop of Albi) and unpublished materials concerning Olof Rudbeck's *Atlantica*.[17] Meanwhile the duke set out for St. Petersburg

merkwürdigen Lebensbeschreibung Herrn Henning Friedrich Grafen von Bassewitz, vornehmen Staatsbedienten, zu Erläuterung der Geschichte unserer Zeiten, University Library of Kiel, Ms. S. H. 74.

16. See the biographical notice concerning Johann Georg Wachter by Heubel, Bibliothèque Nationale Paris, which was cordially given to me by Ralph Häfner (see Mulsow, *Die drei Ringe*, 92): "Dissertationem *De Lingua Codicis Argentei Upsalensis* concinnandi ansam praebuit ingeniosa Arnae Magnui Islandi de eodem argumento Epistola ad Bassewitium Electoris Brunswicensis in Sueca Ablegatum inedita, Wachtero ex septentrione a me allata, in qua post Hickelium aliosque viros doctos Gothicam originem pretiosi istius voluminis impugnare, et illud lingua veteri Germanica potius quam Gothica certe non ab Ulfila Episcopo conscriptum esse ostendere, ac illud Germaniae postlimini jure vindicare voluit."

17. See the letters from Erik Benzel to Wolf published in *Erik Benzelius' Letters to His Learned Friends*, ed. Alvar Erikson and Eva Nielsson Nylander (Göteborg, 1984). On Rudbeck, see David King, *Finding Atlantis* (New York, 2005). Concerning Benzo, Johann Burkhard Mencke published the text in his *Scriptores rerum germanicarum praecipue Saxonicarum*, 3 vols. (Leipzig, 1728–30). See Mencke to Benzel, May 15, 1722: "Cl. Heubelius nuper ad nos venit e Russia redux, et secum attulit Benzonis vitam Henrici III, quam Cl. Eccardo ad Scriptorum medii aevi hactenus ineditorum Syntagma, quod mox typis hic subjicietur complendum communicabit. . . . Accepit et Eccardus a Fontanino collationes ab Adami factas, quas cum aliis, longe etiam majoris momenti, edere parat. De Heubelii Bibl. hist. Germaniae nihil certi habeo, nisi quod vix ante annum prelum subituram existimem: et jam ipse, quid statuat, in ancipiti est, postquam et Cl. Struvium similem Bibliothecam promittere comperit." *Letters to Erik Benzelius the Younger from Learned Foreigners*, ed. Alvar Erikson, 2 vols. (Göteborg, 1984). In 1722 when he was back in Hamburg, Heubel wrote at once to Eccard and Toustain: Heubel to Eccard, Nieidersächsische Staats- und Universitäts-Bibliothek Göttingen, 8 Cod. Ms. philos. 135; Heubel to Dom Toustain, October 29, 1722, Royal Library of Copenhagen, Ms. Böll. Brevs. D. 4° 378.

from his castle in Gottorf with Henning Friedrich von Bassewitz and a hand-picked entourage.[18] Bassewitz prepared the way like a reckless gambler: he had the Swedish state secretary von Höpken travel to Stockholm carrying a secret message, pretending that the letters he carried had been stolen—papers that wound up with the Swedish privy council, hoping to persuade the Swedes that Holstein was again taking a specifically pro-Swedish position. It's possible that Heubel was in Stockholm as part of this mission, but this episode shows how important travel was for the circulation of texts and ideas. For most academics, however, traveling in grand style was only possible as part of the entourage of diplomats and politicians. Daniel Roche has pointed to these connections in his *Humeurs vagabondes*.[19] Bassewitz let his cousin Adolf Friedrich in on his secret diplomatic game—he was the very man with whom Heubel in Stockholm was communicating. Adolf Friedrich was by then in the service of Hanover, working from 1719 onward as an envoy in the Swedish capital, in order to arrange a peace between England and Sweden. As a scholarly politician and soldier, he got to know Heubel and gave him a transcript of an unpublished treatise by Arni Magnusson, the Icelandic librarian in Copenhagen, concerning the Wulfila Bible, the Gothic *Codex argenteus*. On his return journey Heubel then passed this manuscript on to his friend Wachter.[20]

In June 1721 Heubel was staying in St. Petersburg where he obviously met up with the remainder of the court and where the Peace of Nystad was negotiated on September 10. He was still there in December, drinking with the two German professors Bayer and Strimesius.[21] The ducal court of Holstein was to remain there in the vicinity of Peter the Great—until Duke Karl Friedrich had married his daughter—and people told stories of the legendary feasts and

18. Neuschäffer, *Bassewitz*, 124.

19. Daniel Roche, *Humeurs vagabondes: De la circulation des hommes et de l'utilité des voyages* (Paris, 2003). On mobility, see chapter 13.

20. See note 16 in this chapter.

21. See Siegfried Theophil Bayer to Mathurin Veyssière La Croze, in *Thesaurus epistolicus Lacrozianus*, 1:47ff.: "Transiit hac Heuselius [*sic*], Holsato duci a consiliis aulicis, tui studiosissimus. Cum eo apud Strimesium [probably J. S. Strimesius, Prof. eloqu. in Königsberg] nomen tuum Lusitanico vino inter multa vota bibebam." La Croze to Bayer, ibid., 3:55: "Hoebelius [*sic*], quem Heufelium perperam appellas, hic iam degit et quotidie fere apud me est. Iam narraverat, se a te et Strimesio acceptum fuisse perbenigne. Vir est sane cultissimus et elegantis litteraturae valde studiosus." Both letters were from December 1721; Uhl (the editor), however, obviously got the exact dates wrong.

burlesque spectacles that took place there among Peter's "Faithful Society."[22] In 1723, for example, Peter the Great in the presence of the duke of Holstein staged some buffoonery parodying the clergy and then had a model of his favorite summer residence burned down, as if in this way the spectacular fireworks should be transformed into an allegory of war.[23]

We have to understand this exalted parodic and blasphemous background in order to understand how risky the appearance of Heubel was when, in 1723, he was installed as a professor of law in Kiel—under the auspices of the trustee of the university, Henning von Bassewitz. Immediately, right at his inauguration in April, he celebrated with arias by Weichmann and music by Telemann, and then with a lecture that attacked the "pedantry" of the jurists: *Oratio de pedantismo juridico*.[24] Ten years earlier, in February 1713 during Carneval in Leipzig, Heubel's friend Johann Burkhard Mencke had given a talk entitled *De charlataneria eruditorum* (*On the Fraudulence of the Learned*); Heubel drew inspiration from it and hoped to publish his talk, like the one on the hypocrisy of the learned with pleasant copper-plate engravings.[25] They sang a song

22. See Robert K. Massie, *Peter the Great: His Life and World* (New York, 1980).

23. Ernest A. Zitser, *The Transfigured Kingdom: Sacred Parody and Charismatic Authority at the Court of Peter the Great* (Ithaca, 2004), 174–76. I am grateful to Victoria Frede for informing me of this book.

24. The *Oratio* was printed *Stats- und Gelehrte Zeitung des hollsteinischen unpartheyischen Correspondenten*, 128th Stück, August 11, 1723. The aria was printed in Christian F. Weichmann, ed., *Poesie der Nieder-Sachsen, 1721–1738*, vol. 2 (reprint, Munich, 1980), 326–31: "Als Herr Johann Heinrich Heubel / . . . / Seine Professionem Juris Ordin. zum Kiel, durch eine Antritts-Rede von der Juristische Pedanterey, übernam," 328ff. For example: "Wie vielen Gecken hat das Wissen / Dermaßen ihr Gehirn verrückt / Daß man von ihrer Gaukeley / Von ihrem tummen Stolz / und närr'schen Phantasey / Viel Unruh / Zwiespalt / Ketzerey / Und harten Zwang / erleben müssen? / Die thörigten Gelehrten / Sind recht diejenigen Verkehrten / Auf welche sich das alte Sprichwort schickt / Und weil sich / bey den stärksten Gründen / Zugleich so viele Probe finden: / So will ich auch bey meinem Schluß beharren: / Gelehrte Narren sind die allergrößten Narren." "Ihr Falsch-Gelehrte, / Ihr Grund-Verkehrte, / Fort, packet euch! / Auf Holsteins Musen-Sitze / Wird kein Pedant was nütze; / Hier herrscht Vernunft und Wissenschaft zugleich. / Ihr Falsch-Gelehrte, / Ihr Grund-Verkehrte, / Fort, packet euch!" On Weichmann, see Elger Blühm, "Christian F. Weichmann: Redakteur des Schiffbeker Correspondenten," *Zeitschrift des Vereins für Hamburgische Geschichte* 53 (1967): 69–78. Telemann seems to have written music for this aria. On the context of the lecture, see Erich Döhring, *Geschichte der juristischen Fakultät 1665–1965* (Neumünster, 1965), 37–43.

25. Johann Burkhard Mencke, *De charlataneria eruditorum declamationes duae* (Leipzig, 1715). The lecture of 1713 was printed along with another on the topic. Heubel had returned from Russia in May 1722, passing through Leipzig, where he surely met with Mencke.

asking: "How many dandies has knowledge driven so crazy in their brains that we have to endure their deceits, their stupid pride, and their foolish fancies, that lead to unrest, division, heresy and harsh coercion?" Heubel's friends nearly fell off their benches with laughter. The background of his lecture was the perennial conflict between German law and Roman law; Heubel sided with his colleagues Peter Friedrich Arpe and Johann Vogt in backing German law.[26] The university itself was in a phase of adapting to a new constitution after the Great Northern War, and some academics were ready for reforms and a fresh start. But only some parts of the university. So his destiny was foreordained: Heubel had grossly miscalculated and gone too far. Despite feeling protected by the court, he was dismissed in the summer of 1724. He had made a complete mess of his relations with the duke.[27]

After this defeat, Heubel took up a project that was developing among the Thomasians: he would write a history of burned books. In Kiel the young Johann Lorenz Mosheim—a man who was about the same age as Heubel—had already begun work on such a project when he got wrapped up in the case of Servetus.[28] But the fighting that broke out between Heubel and his colleagues at the university repelled Mosheim as they degenerated into full-scale student battles.[29] That may be the reason why he did not go further than the part on Servetus, so that Heubel could now take up the idea for himself.

26. The conflict took shape as a late humanist university struggle with libelous assaults, dramatized fighting, and parodies. On such a culture, see Ingrid de Smet, *Menippean Satire and the Republic of Letters, 1581–1655* (Geneva, 1996); Marian Füssel, *Gelehrtenkultur als symbolische Praxis: Rang, Ritual und Konflikt an der Universität der Frühen Neuzeit* (Darmstadt, 2006); Kai Bremer and Carlos Spoerhase, eds., *Gelehrte Polemik. Intellektuelle Konfliktverschärfungen um 1700* (Frankfurt, 2011) (= *Zeitsprünge* vol. 15).

27. Wolf to La Croze, May 3, 1724, in *Thesaurus*, 2:197ff.: "Fuit vero hic nuper quidam ministrorum principis Holsatiae, qui omni gratia domini sui illum excidisse mihi confirmabat. Vereor itaque, ut recuperet, quod tam imprudenter amisit."

28. Johann Lorenz Mosheim (praes.)/Heinrich von Allwoerden (resp.), *Historia Michaelis Serveti* (Helmstedt, 1727). See Martin Mulsow, "Eine 'Rettung' des Michael Servet? Der junge Mosheim und die heterodoxe Tradition," in *Johann Lorenz Mosheim 1693–1755*, ed. idem et al. (Wiesbaden, 1997), 45–92.

29. Mosheim to Lorenz Hertel, Kiel, December 2, 1722: "Daher entstehen täglich Unordnungen, die ich mich zu melden schäme, und die zu nichts als zum Verderben der guten Academie ausschlagen können." Quoted in Karl Heussi, *Johann Lorenz Mosheim: Ein Beitrag zur Kirchengeschichte des achtzehnten Jahrhunderts* (Tübingen, 1906), 66.

Investigations at the Peace Conference

According to Reinhart Koselleck, the conquered actually have a stronger mo-
tivation to write history than conquerors. In any event, it's true that Heubel
was highly motivated. After ruining his academic career he appears to have
taken up his old duties as a tutor for Christian August, the prince bishop of
Lübeck. Among others, he taught Adolf Friedrich, the later king of Sweden,
and Friedrich August, the later duke of Oldenburg. It seems that he also accompanied them on their travels. For example, in April 1727 Johann Burkhard Mencke reported that Heubel was traveling outside Germany.[30] This was
a journey to Paris where, as in Sweden and Russia, Heubel exploited the
chance to plunge into libraries and archives at any opportunity. As luck would
have it, this journey too was overtaken by international politics. From
June 1728 on, a large peace congress was meeting in Soissons where the European powers were trying to preserve and fortify the balance of power. Bassewitz traveled there as the envoy of the duke of Holstein, but the situation
was difficult for him because Sweden and Denmark had drawn closer to each
other, to the disadvantage of the little duchy.[31] All the same, Bassewitz lived
like a lord in Soissons. We don't know if Heubel was part of his entourage or
was rather more concerned to keep an eye on the sons of the prince bishop
in nearby Paris.[32] In any event, he exploited his time there. He was once again
on the track of medieval sources, among others the *glossarium* of the Gothic
bishop Ansileubus, which he discovered in the library of the Maurist abbey
of Saint-Germain-des-Prés.[33] At the same time his friend Arpe had given him

30. Reinhart Koselleck, "Erfahrungswandel und Methodenwechsel," in *Theorie der Geschichte*, ed. Christian Meier and Jörn Rüsen (Munich, 1988), 13–61. Johann Burkhard Mencke
to Erik Benzel d.J., April 2, 1727, in *Letters to Erik Benzelius*, 306: "qui jam pridem peregre abest
extra Germaniam."

31. Neuschäffer, *Bassewitz*, 142ff.

32. To be sure, we have the reports of correspondence that Arpe in Hamburg wrote to
the court in Wolfenbüttel, where he held a position at the time. Every four days he filed a
report. And in these reports information crops up occasionally that Heubel had sent from
Soissons. Afterward, Heubel seems to have followed the activities of Bassewitz from
nearby. Lower Saxony State Archives, Wolfenbüttel, 2 Alt 2103, for example, fol. 2r: "Aus
Frankreich meldet ein guter Freund wie der Herr v. Bassewitz daselbst am Podagra danie-
der liege."

33. Today: Bibliothèque Nationale Paris, fonds latin, ms. 11529 and 11530 du fonds latin; previously: S. Germain latin 12.

the task of looking for the trial documents concerning the case of Vanini, which we learned a good deal about in the previous chapter. Thus it appears that he really was working on the *Bibliotheca Vulcani*, for Vanini had after all been incinerated along with his books. Antoine Lancelot, a member of the Académie des Inscriptions et Belles-Lettres and a guardian of the tradition of *libertinage érudit*, contributed to his cause by giving him an *Extrait des Registres de la maison de Ville de Toulouse*.[34] Moreover, Heubel also got to know Bernard de la Monnoye, who was the one man in Paris besides Lancelot to whom one would turn if one was looking for information on rare and forbidden books. Among other things, in 1712 La Monnoye had written a *Lettre au président Bouhier sur le prétendu livre des trois imposteurs*, in which he doubted the existence of the legendary treatise on the three great impostors.[35] The eighty-seven-year-old man, who was to die shortly thereafter, appears to have actually received Heubel and discussed his project with him; one of his epigrams has survived, a "Prognostication for the Author of the *Bibliotheca Vulcani*," in which he skeptically says: "As you rummage through the famous writings of men / who were consumed by the fierce flames of public execution, / I worry that your library, containing the books consecrated to Vulcan, / may suffer the same demise as they."[36] La Monnoye could hardly imagine that Heubel's *Bibliotheca Vulcani* could be published without it also ending at the stake. It must have been clear to Heubel as well that he was taking a big risk. What publisher would back such an enterprise, one that extended Thomasius's debate over the manufacture of heresies into a revival of those infamous ghosts?

34. Thus in Arpe's manuscript expansion of his *Apologia pro Vanino*, State and University Library of Hamburg, Cod. theol. 1222, before this text we find fol. 78v: "Ex benevola communicatione cariss. Antonii Lancelotti opera et studio Jo. Henrici Heubelii principis Holsatiae et episcopi Lubecensis cancellari." Probably Heubel through Lancelot put Arpe in touch with the procurator of Toulouse, de la Forcade, who is listed in the *Bibliotheque raisonnée*, vol. 1, p. 461. On Lancelot, see P. Gasnault, "*Antoine Lancelot* et la bibliothèque *Mazarine*," *Bibliothèque de l'École des Chartes* 146 (1988): 383–84.

35. Bernard de la Monnoye, "Lettre au président Bouhier sur le prétendu livre des *Trois imposteurs*," in *Menagiana* (Paris, 1715), 4:283–312 or in the Amsterdam edition (1716), 4:374–418; see Miguel Benitez, "La coterie hollandaise et la reponse a m. de la Monnoye sur *Le Traité de Tribus Impostoribus*," *Lias* 21 (1994): 71–94.

36. "Bibliothecae Vulcani Auctori Prognosticon. / Quam vereor famosa virum dum scripta recenses, / Quae rapido absumsit publicus igne rogus; / Ne tua Vulcano libros complexa dicatos / Exitio pereat bibliotheca pari." *Bibliothèque raisonnée* 1 (1728), 463.

Heubel's Lists

In August 1729 at the conclusion of the Congress of Soissons, Heubel returned to Hamburg.[37] He had already sent Arpe from France a long list of precarious authors and works, and now he made several additions and showed his list to Johann Christoph Wolf, who copied it out for himself.[38] The list contained the names of 67 authors who had been burned at the stake and more than 160 titles of burned books (figure 18). When one examines it, one is reminded of Friedrich Breckling's list of "witnesses to truth" (*testes veritatis*), mentioned earlier, and of a tradition of thinkers who suffered for their convictions and thus joined the ranks of true seekers and heroes.

Heubel's list of authors included such illustrious names as Urbain Grandier (d. 1634), who had been accused of witchcraft because of his connections with the nuns of Loudun; Claude Le Petit, the satirical poet (d. 1662); Giordano Bruno, who was burned to death in 1600 at the Campo dei Fiori in Rome; Michael Servetus, the antitrinitarian (d. 1553); Jerome of Prague (d. 1416) and Jan Hus (d. 1415), who were both victims of the Council of Constance; the author Quirinus Kuhlmann, who ended his life at the stake in Moscow in 1689; Girolamo Savonarola, the religious prophet (d. 1498); and of course Lucilio Vanini (d. 1619); but also a host of lesser-known victims who had been burned to death. The long list of incinerated books begins with the letter A, including Abelard's *De trinitate*, and goes through to Z, with works such as Johann Ehrenfried Zschackwitz's *Examen juris publici imperii germanici*, which had appeared in 1716 in Coburg and had displeased the emperor in Vienna. Thereupon Zschackwitz fled from Coburg to Halle in Prussian territory. But Heubel's list also included anonymous works or whole areas of knowledge, such as *Sibyllini & vaticini libri item Magici, Chymiae artis volumina* (*A Volume of Sibyllene and Prophetic Books of Magic and the Art of Chemistry*) and *Manichaeorum scripta* (*Writings of the Manichaeans*). This was so vague that it almost reminds one of the sweeping labels on the mock books displayed on the satirical stove at the abbey of St. Peter's. The value of Heubel's list does not lie

37. Wolf to Benzel, August 5, 1729, *Letters to Erik Benzelius*, 320: "Cl. Heubelius nuper admodum Parisiis, ubi per biennium fere moram duxit, redux ad nos factus est feliciter."

38. See State and University Library of Hamburg, Cod. Hist litt. 4° 76, fols. 107–16: "Scriptores ad rogum damnati," "Alia scripta, igni addicta." On this, see Mulsow, "Johann Christoph Wolf," 104ff. I published the list sent to Arpe, which is today in the University Library of Rostock (Mss. hist. part. S[chlesw.-Holst.] 2°: "Cimbria illustrata," vol. II: "Propylaei Continuatio," following fol. 464, unpaginated); see Mulsow, "Bibliotheca Vulcani."

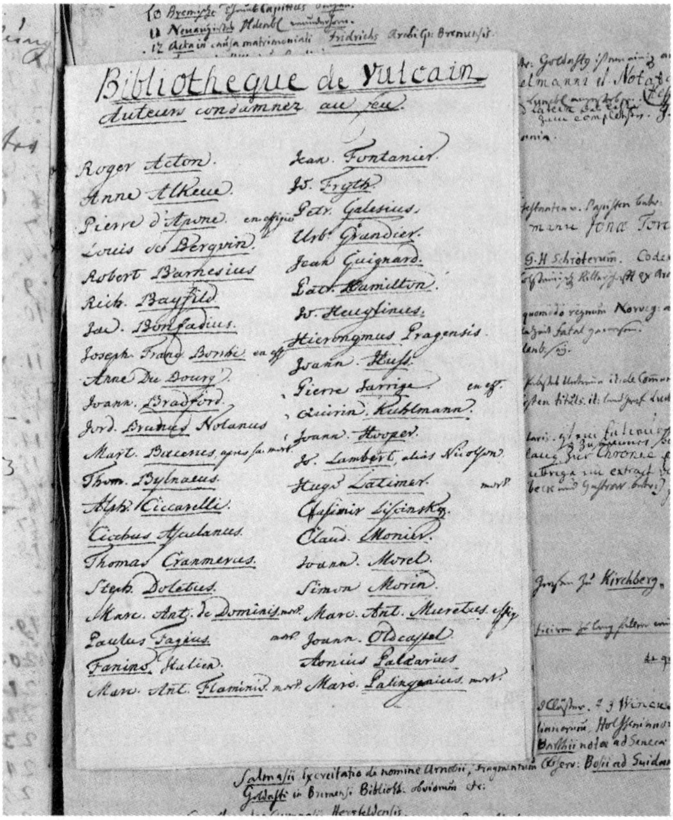
Bibliotheque de Vulcain
Auteurs condamnez au feu

Roger Acton.	Jean Fontanier.
Anne Alkew.	Jo. Fryth.
Pierre d'Apone. en effigie	Petr. Galesius.
Louis de Berquin.	Urb. Grandier.
Robert Barnesius	Jean Guignard.
Rich. Bayfild.	Patr. Hamilton.
Jac. Bonfadius.	Jo. Heuglinus.
Joseph Franc Borrhi en eff	Hieronymus Pragensis.
Anne Du Bourg.	Joann. Huss.
Joann. Bradford.	Pierre Jarrige en eff.
Jord. Brunus Nolanus	Quirin. Kuhlmann.
Mart. Bucenes, apres sa mort	Joann. Hooper.
Thom. Bylnaeus.	Jo. Lambert, alias Nicolson.
Alph. Ciccarelli.	Hugo Latimer. mort
Ciccus Asculanus.	Casimir Lisinsky.
Thomas Cranmerus.	Claud. Monier.
Steph. Doletus.	Joann. Morel.
Marc. Ant. de Dominis mort	Simon Morin.
Paulus Fagius. mort	Marc. Ant. Muretus. eff.
Fanins Italien.	Joann. Oldcastel.
Marc. Ant. Flaminius mort	Aonius Paldarius
	Marc. Palingenius. mort

FIGURE 18. Heubel's list. University Library of Rostock, Mss. hist. part. S(chlesw.-Holst.) 2°: "Cimbria illustrata," vol. II, "Propylaei Continuatio," after fol. 464.

in these general references, however, but in the many exact titles of works that it contained: for example, *Pompe funebre Charles VIII, Roi de France*; *Aletophili veratitis lacrymae*; *Mysteria politica*; *La Morale des Jesuites*; *Le cabinet Satyrique*; *L'ecole des filles*; and many others. From the numerous French titles we can see that Heubel did most of his research during his stay in France.

The list can therefore be read as a sort of table of contents for his never-completed book. Heubel filled up folders with the information he'd gathered about these authors. In the library of Christian Joachim Lossau, which I described in chapter 4, one finds today a collection that could possibly be one of these folders, because it is especially full of French cases from the years before 1729, as was typical for Heubel's list. Maybe it arrived in Lossau's library as part of the literary estate of Heubel or Arpe.[39] This folder contains just under two dozen mostly ten-page-long dossiers about several book burnings. In several cases, like the one that occurred in Hamburg on September 12, 1729, right after Heubel's return, he could have been there personally to experience what actually happened at such a book burning. In this case it concerned libels by Professor Edzardi: "The deputy (*Frohn*) came with his two servants," a contemporary source relates in the copy Heubel made of it, "who carried an iron shovel or kettle (*Schopen*) filled with glowing coals and placed it on the dishonorable [execution] block. . . . The soldiers closed up in a half-circle, and two judges walked from the city hall into the lower court house. Then the bell of disgrace (*Schandglocke*) was rung for the first time, and the deputy read off the following notice."[40]

Heubel immediately included this case in his collection. Other cases—if we use the surviving dossier as evidence—included Johann Bissendorf, a theologian who had been executed in Hildesheim in 1629;[41] the Jew Chazzim from the Bohemian Engelsberg (Andělská Hora) who converted to Christianity and lived in Vienna as Ferdinand Franz Engelberger, whose trial in the year 1642 was described by Johann Christoph Wagenseil in his *Tela ignea Satanae*; and a chiliastic pastor from Schönfeld, who was forced to watch his books being burned in Kiel in 1702.[42] The dossier contains only excerpts of judgments or reports, which were assembled partly from official records, partly from publications. This relic, if it really does come from Heubel, could be nothing more than a minuscule part of his whole project, a simple file folder as opposed to the projected grand body of documents.

In a report that Peter Friedrich Arpe added in handwriting on the margin of a manuscript, he stated with regard to the condemnation of Vanini: "He was

39. State and University Library of Hamburg, Ms. Hist. Litt. 4° 67. See Elke Matthes, *Die Codices historiae litterariae der Staats- und Universitätsbibliothek Hamburg* (Stuttgart, 2009), 87–89.

40. State and University Library of Hamburg, Cod. Hist. Litt 4° 67, fol. 165r. On Edzardi, see Fischer, "Patrioten und Ketzermacher."

41. State and University Library of Hamburg, Cod. Hist. Litt 4° 67, fols. 73r ff. The dossier includes an excerpt from Jakob Friedrich Reimmann. On this case, see Johann Andreas Gottfried Schetelig, *Historische Abhandlung von einigen höchstseltenen und wegen des unglücklichen Schicksals ihres Verfassers merkwürdigen Schriften Johann Bissendorfs, eines Zeugen der evangelischen Wahrheit im siebzehnten Jahrhunderte* (Hamburg, 1770).

42. See Cod. Hist. Litt 4° 67, fols. 79r ff. (Engelberger) and 145r ff. (Siegfried Bentzen, Pastor zu Schönfeld). On Ferdinand Franz Engelberger, see Maria Diemling, "Grenzgängertum: Übertritte vom Judentum zum Christentum in Wien 1500–2000," *Wiener Zeitschrift zur Geschichte der Neuzeit* 7 (2007): 40–64, at 45ff.

condemned, I admit, like many innocent men. And no one has dared assert that he has ever killed someone without reason. Let us be judged by our inclination to rule rightly and according to the laws—but of course a judge may be poorly informed. To inform him better an appeal process (provocatio) exists, which the highly learned author of the *Bibliotheca Vulcani*, Brenno Vulcanus Heiseishe, will illustrate with many examples—if the stars decree that the work should ever appear."[43] Who was "Brenno Vulcanus Heiseishe"? That was the name Heubel chose, with its double reference to fire and burning, and then to the hot iron he was grabbing.[44] This pseudonym recalls the wordplay that Heubel obviously loved, the humor and joy in provocation that had also marked his inaugural lecture in 1723 in Kiel.

Talking about a "Bibliotheca Vulcani" as a term for burned books was not completely exceptional in the eighteenth century. We began this chapter with the satirical stove from the abbey of St. Peter's. And yet Heubel and Arpe had something totally different in mind. They did not wish to add fuel to the fire but rather to rescue the truths expressed by disgraced authors, if they were truly worth preserving, and to render justice to them posthumously. In doing so, were they not approaching radical thoughts themselves? Was there not some danger of getting "infected" by heretical thoughts?

In the Vicinity of the Spinozist Underground

It would seem so because in 1735 Heubel's list of burned books suddenly popped up in a completely unexpected place. It appeared in the French language, printed as an appendix to an edition of the anonymous *La vie de Spinosa*, supposedly printed in "Hambourg" "chez Henry Kunrath" (figure 19).[45] That appears more amazing than it really was. *La vie de Spinosa* was not one of

---

43. State and University Library of Hamburg, Cod. theol. 1222, p. 105, note: "Damnatus est; concedo, ut multi innocentissimi viri, neque enim quisquam asserere ausit, neminem sine noxa cecidisse. Pro judice militat favor, recte et secundum leges pronuntiasse sed a male informato, ad melius informandum datur provocatio quae pluribus exemplis illustrabit Bibliothecae Vulcani eruditissimus autor Brenno Vulcanius Heiseishe, si in fatis est eam prodire. Joannes Henricus Heubelius, sive per Anagramma J.H.H."

44. Translator's note: "Brenno" was a play on the name Benno but also on "brennen," the German for "burn." "Vulcanus" referred to Vulcan, and the German for "hot" is "heiß" while "iron" is "eisen."

45. *La vie de Spinosa, par un de ses disciples: Nouvelle edition non tronquée, augmentée de quelques Notes et du Catalogue de ses ecrits, par un autre de ses Disciples. &c.* (A Hambourg, chez Henry Kunrath, 1735).

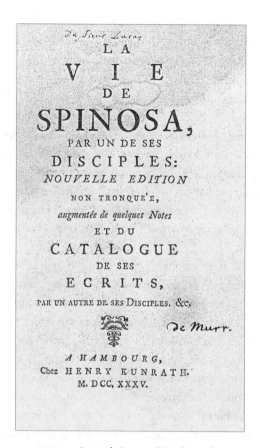

FIGURE 19. *La vie de Spinosa*, "Hambourg," 1735.

those disparaging biographies of Spinoza that were common in the eighteenth century. Indeed, it was perhaps the most authentic biographical description of the philosopher, probably written by Jean-Maximilien Lucas, a doctor and close friend of Spinoza.[46] This biography circulated for a long time only in

46. See Jakob Freudenthal, *Die Lebensgeschichte Spinozas: Quellenschriften, Urkunden und nichtamtliche Nachrichten* (Leipzig, 1899), 1–25, 239–45 (edition of *La vie de Spinosa*); Stanislaus von Dunin-Borkowski, "Zur Textgeschichte und Textkritik der Ältesten Lebensbeschreibung Benedikt Despinozas," *Archiv für Geschichte der Philosophie* 18 (1905): 1–34; Abraham Wolf, *The Oldest Biography of Spinoza* (Port Washington, NY, 1927); *Die Lebensgeschichte Spinozas: Mit einer Bibliographie*, ed. Manfred Walther with the collaboration of Michael Czelinski, 2nd expanded ed. with commentary by Jakob Freudenthal (1899; Stuttgart, 2006).

manuscript but was finally published in 1719 in one of the most infamous episodes in the history of printing. In the years just after 1700 the freethinking Huguenot publisher Charles Levier of The Hague was using the library of the Quaker Benjamin Furly in Rotterdam; there he found the atheist treatise on the three "impostors," Moses, Jesus, and Mohammed, entitled *Traité des trois imposteurs*, whose author is still unknown. Levier copied it out and then, with the help of the scholarly thief Jean Aymon, jiggered it into shape for a publication that now included *La vie de Spinosa*. The new book was entitled *La vie et l'Esprit de Spinosa*, and the *Traité* was now given the title *Esprit de Spinosa*.[47] Only a very small number of copies of this edition circulated, and only a few of those have surfaced. The printing remained a spectacular exception—after that, for another half century, the *Traité des trois imposteurs* circulated only in manuscript.[48]

The printing did, however, have repercussions that involved the *Bibliotheca Vulcani*. Levier died in 1734, and among his belongings was found a cache of about three hundred copies of the infamous edition from 1719, which Levier had evidently withheld—not only out of fear of the police but probably also to boost the black market price of the circulating manuscripts. Prosper Marchand (1678–1756), Levier's friend and former accomplice in similar printing adventures, now took over this legacy. But what was he supposed to do with three hundred copies? He destroyed them.[49] Or, more precisely, he destroyed a part of them, the part that contained the *Esprit de Spinosa* (the *Traité*). He separated the other part, the part containing *La vie de Spinosa*, and thus was able to reuse at least several copies of it. He did want to complete the remnant he saved, however, so that it would not go forth "naked" into the world.

Marchand was just then writing a lexicon article entitled "Impostoribus, de tribus" for his planned *Historical Dictionary*, a large folio volume in the style of Bayle's *Dictionary*, filled with all he knew about rare and secret texts, a work that finally appeared in 1758–59, after his death.[50] For his essay he pulled together the information necessary to reconstruct how the published *Esprit de*

---

47. This is the reconstruction of the publication history that is now widely accepted. See Jacob, *The Radical Enlightenment*, 235ff.; Benitez, "La coterie hollandaise."

48. For its circulation, see the listings of locations in Benitez, *La face cachée des lumières*.

49. On Marchand, see Christane Berkvens-Stevelinck, *Prosper Marchand: La vie et l'oeuvre (1678–1756)* (Leiden, 1987).

50. Prosper Marchand, *Dictionnaire historique ou Mémoires critiques et littéraires concernant la vie et les ouvrages de divers personnages distingués, particulièrement dans la république des lettres* (Den Haag, 1758–59).

Spinosa had been fabricated, a story he already knew pretty well because it involved his closest companions. Even so, he had not known all the details. And so at the end of 1735 he renewed his long-dormant relations with Kaspar Fritsch, an old publishing colleague, who was working in Rotterdam at the time; but he obviously also contacted Arpe, whom he'd met in 1712 during a trip to Holstein.[51] This was probably the point at which Marchand decided to expand his new edition of *La vie de Spinosa* by adding the list of books in the *Bibliotheca Vulcani* to replace the destroyed *L'esprit de Spinosa*. Marchand placed the list under the subtitle: "A collection alphabetically arranged of authors and books condemned to the fire, or worthy of being burned." That last phrase, "books . . . worthy of being burned," was, of course, only a self-protective deceit.[52] It is entirely possible that Arpe sent Marchand his list, with more than a little pride, when the latter resumed correspondence with him after so many years. And Marchand may have thought that the list would make a good addition to his text, which already had a bibliographical supplement to the works of Spinoza. With this list from Hamburg added to the biography of Spinoza and published in 1735, connoisseurs of Spinoza may also have seen a hidden reference to Spinoza's friends in Hamburg, linking them to the fictitious place of publication ("Hambourg") listed for 1670 edition of the *Tractatus theologico-politicus*—but it may be that only Marchand, Arpe, and Heubel

51. See Miguel Benitez, "La diffusion du *Traité des trois Imposteurs* au XVIIIe siècle," *Revue d'histoire moderne et contemporaine* 40 (1993): 137–51. That letter from Fritsch in which he told his friend in Holland that Levier had copied the text of *L'esprit de Spinosa* from Furly's library reports: "Levier le copia fort précipitament." Marchand thereupon gave him a copy of the printed version of *La vie et l'esprit de Spinosa* from 1719, and Fritsch compared it with the copy by Levier that he had in his possession. On November 7, 1737, Fritsch informed Marchand that Rousset had probably written the *Réponse* (University Library Leiden, Ms. March. 2). That was a relief to Arpe, who had been suspected as the author of the pamphlet.

52. We can further assume that in this contact in 1735 and in the following years Arpe received the information from Marchand that he inscribed along the lower margin of the page of his copy of the *Esprit*: "P. M. [Prosper Marchand] gab die Nachricht Mr. Rousset im Haag hatte die Fabel de tribus Impostoribus, gegen Mr. de la Monnoye zu behaupten sich gefallen laßen. Ea occasione hätte der H. Vroese conseiller de la cour de Braband daselbst folgende Schrift aufgesetzt, welche unter jetzt erwähntem Titel weiter ausgeführet, da ihr sogar einige Capittel aus Charron de la sagesse und Naudee coup d'Etat inseriret, worden" (State Library of Berlin, Ms. Diez C. Quart 37, fol. 42v). In exchange, Arpe conveyed to Marchand some of his knowledge concerning the book on the impostors, and not least his insistence that he had not written the *Réponse*—as Marchand then reported in his lexicon article: "on attribue cette pièce à M. Arpe; et on lui fait tort." Marchand, *Dictionnaire historique*, 323n71.

would have understood this inside joke.[53] But what sort of strange authorization was this for combining Heubel's list with this Spinoza-*Traité* venture? Did this make Spinoza into another "witness to the truth" on the list? Did Heubel's and Arpe's activities bring them into the orbit of Spinozism and atheism? However we answer those questions, we must not overlook the fact that the title page described the additions to the biography of Spinoza as the work "of another of his disciples."

Medieval Studies, Jurisprudence, and Anticlericalism

To answer these questions I will connect what we now know about the *Bibliotheca Vulcani* project to the beginnings of German studies. By German studies I mean the field that joined German legal studies, medieval historiography, and German philology, a combination that was characteristic of the early modern period. These elements of German studies had not yet been separated into discrete departments and were enjoying a new sense of excitement about the future because of the scholarly initiatives of Gottfried Wilhelm Leibniz and Johann Georg Eckhard, Burkhard Gotthelf Struve and Johann Burkhard Mencke, along with Wilhelm Ernst Tentzel and Johann Peter Ludewig.[54]

One might consider the connection between the nascent field of Old German philology and radical literary history as purely accidental, but there's a parallel case: Heubel's acquaintance, the philosopher Johann Georg Wachter, who after several daring publications was denounced as a Spinozist and had to give up his academic career; he then transferred his interests to the history of the German language and took up studies of the Gothic Bible translated by Wulfila in the fourth century, work that resulted in a fat volume entitled *Glossarium Germanicum*.[55] Usually the history of the language was driven by a

53. [Baruch de Spinoza], *Tractatus theologico-politicus* ("Hamburg," 1670).

54. See Siegfried von Lempicki, *Geschichte der deutschen Literaturwissenschaft bis zum Ende des 18. Jahrhunderts* (1920; Göttingen, 1968); Wolfgang Stammler, *Deutsche Philologie im Aufriß* (Berlin, 1966), 1:108ff.; on Eckhard, see Hermann Leskien, "Johann Georg von Eckhart: Das Werk eines Vorläufers der Germanistik" (PhD diss., Würzburg, 1965).

55. Johann Georg Wachter, *Glossarium Germanicum: Continens Origines et Antiquitates Linguae Germanicae Hodiernae* (Leipzig, 1727). On Wachter, see Döring, "Johann Georg Wachter"; Schröder, *Spinoza*, 59–123; Mulsow, "A German Spinozistic Reader of Spencer, Cudworth and Bull." On early German studies, see also Konrad Burdach, "Die nationale Aneignung der Bibel und die Anfänge der germanischen Philologie," in *Festschrift Eugen Mogk* (Halle, 1924), 1–14, 231–34, esp. 313–34.

desire to understand medieval culture in general; similarly the history of medieval German law enabled scholars to draw inferences about German history
from the Middle Ages or early modern period because German legal traditions, as they blended together with Roman law, allowed conclusions about
the oldest Germanic customs and institutions.

Seen up close, the lawyer's *Usus modernus*, the Renaissance humanists'
amalgamation of Roman and native law, and the sustained emphasis on German law were symptoms of the burgeoning plurality of the early modern period, for it asserted the rights of particular localities against the universalism
of Roman law.[56] Around 1700 scholars used this sort of legal particularism to
support various local patriotisms—in the case of Heubel and Arpe in defense
of the "Cimbrian" tradition of Holstein—and they could also deploy it as a
weapon in religious struggles. Johann Georg von Kulpis charged that "Roman
law was being touted as a remedy for the splintered state of German law, but
it could easily make the German empire into a mere vassal of the pope,"[57] and
Christian Thomasius extended these accusations, giving what had begun as a
quarrel among jurists an anti-Catholic twist. That twist and the project of defending "German liberty" supported a "liberal" attitude toward tradition and
a general critique of the clergy—it was part of the extended Protestant critique
of the Catholic hierarchy.[58]

We can see the consequences in Heubel's friend Arpe. On the occasion of
the two hundredth anniversary of the Reformation, celebrated in 1717, Arpe
reacted with an oration at the University of Kiel on papal law and with a book
entitled *Laicus veritatis vindex* (*The Layman Is the Defender of Truth*), in which
he treated secular law and especially the German laws.[59] Arpe saw laymen,
those not bound by the laws of the church, as the defenders and guarantors of
truth. A few years earlier, the University of Halle canon lawyer Justus Henning
Böhmer had tried to employ Tertullian's views, but Arpe was less concerned

56. See Frank Ludwig Schäfer, *Juristische Germanistik: Eine Geschichte der Wissenschaft vom
einheimischen Privatrecht* (Frankfurt, 2008).

57. Ibid., 63.

58. On "German liberty" ("teutschen Libertät"), see Heinz Duchhardt and Matthias
Schnettger, eds., *Reichsständische Libertät und habsburgisches Kaisertum* (Mainz, 1999). On the
connection between anticlericalism and "liberty," see Silvia Berti, *Anticristianesimo e libertà:
Studi sul primo illuminismo europeo* (Bologna, 2012).

59. Peter Friedrich Arpe, *De iure pontificiali Romae veteris, et novae* (Kiel, 1717); idem, *Laicus
veritatis vindex sive de iure laicorum praecipue Germanorum in promovendo religionis negotio commentarius* (Kiel, 1717).

with that church father and was more dedicated to combining a specifically "German" secular law with the Reformation's critique of the Catholic Church in a manner that could quote anticlerical literature generally.[60] This is most visible in the footnotes to his book, into which Arpe poured his large and discriminating knowledge of precarious authors and clandestine works. Jean Bodin's *Colloquium heptaplomeres*, Guy Patin's *Reflections* in the *Bourbonia* manuscript, Antonius van Dale, Hobbes, and Vanini—works hardly ever cited or quoted in Germany at that time—they all peek out of the underbrush of Arpe's notes, almost as if that was where revival efforts associated with a library of burned books had to occur in order to make such authors socially acceptable. This was Arpe's own personal *Tractatus theologico-politicus*. A friend of his, who hid his identity with the initials J.A.R.D., contributed a poem to Arpe's treatise appealing to *libertas philosophandi*, to freedom of thought—which Spinoza, who of course was not mentioned, had also voiced—but also advocating the ideal of eclecticism; these two ideals were the very same combination we find in Arpe. First he presents a negative view of the present day: "Honored friend / I have often wondered / What makes people so crazy? / Finally I have found the truth / The reason is / That we think ourselves obliged / To think as we think; to speak / As we speak / To live / As we live. And so without reservations / If we lack some sort of knowledge or wisdom / We may borrow from our neighbor's house the oil [we need] for our lamp."[61] In the present this "borrowing from the neighbor" had become just as thoughtless and foolish as in Jesus' parable of the wise and foolish virgins. In Jesus' day, the poem continues, one could still exercise an eclectic freedom to borrow from a "neighbor" the needed intellectual oil because such borrowing happened with discernment: "Everyone used to select the best." The author regarded the life lived through thinking for oneself as connected directly with the original Christian moral ideal. This was the same link that Theodor Ludwig Lau also produced in his radical, deist understanding of eclecticism, as we saw in chapter 2. Like Lau, Arpe chose this quotation from Tacitus as a motto for his book: "Rara temporum felicitas, ubi sentire, quae velis, et quae sentias, dicere licet" (Rare are the happy times when one may think what one wants and say what one thinks).

---

60. See Justus Henning Böhmer, *Dissertationes iuris ecclesiastici antiqui ad Plinium Secundum et Tertullianum genuinas origines praecipuarum materiarum iuris ecclesiastici demonstrantes* (Leipzig, 1711), 316ff. (Dissertatio VI). On Böhmer, see Renate Schulze, *Justus Henning Böhmer und die Dissertationen seiner Schüler: Bausteine des Ius Ecclesiasticum Protestantium* (Tübingen, 2009).

61. Arpe, *Laicus veritatis vindex*, 110.

The original ideal condition had become corrupted: "There was one God, one faith, one undivided spirit, until superstition, envy, greed, pride, and self-love (along with whatever other names we give those smooth beggars) shamelessly drove truth out of the temple."[62] This was a Lutheran version of the notion of corruption that resounded among the deists: "Natural Religion was easy first, and plain; / Tales made it Mystery, Offerings made it Gain; / Sacrifices and Showes were at length prepar'd, / The Priests ate roast-Meat, and the People star'd."[63] It made almost no difference if one was speaking of original Christianity or of natural religion. For Christian freethinkers like Matthew Tindal, they were identical.[64]

This allows us to glimpse the radical potential bound up in the movement for German law. Let us return to Heubel and to the convergence of juridical, German-philological, and literary-historical disciplines. One key point needs to be underlined if we are to understand Heubel's plan for a *Bibliotheca Vulcani*: the sharp edge of historical critique. The juridical German studies pursued by the Thomasian school differed from the older legal studies in the tradition of "usus modernus" in that it did not grant direct authority to native, medieval German law but rather observed its development from its origins and then cautiously adapted it; but the Thomasians also took up Hermann Conring's thinking and subjected medieval legal sources themselves to historical criticism.[65]

The means were now at hand for that task. The Maurist Jean Mabillon was the shining example of scholarly authenticity for Heubel. The field of diplomatics developed by Mabillon had made it possible to detect forgeries and arrive at exact datings for old documents.[66] Thus after the scandal of his

---

62. Ibid., 111.

63. The verses were quoted, for example, in Matthew Tindal, *Christianity as Old as the Creation* (London, 1730), 1:92. Translator's note: In 1692 Charles Gildon published *The Deist's Plea* with the line as quoted: "The Priests ate roast-Meat, and the People star'd," but when this verse was used by Toland in his *Letter to Serena* (1704), it was sometimes later quoted as "and the people starv'd."

64. Tindal, *Christianity*.

65. Hermann Conring, *De origine juris germanici* (Helmstedt, 1643); in German: *Der Ursprung des deutschen Rechts* (Frankfurt, 1994). On Hermann Conring, see Alberto Jori, *Hermann Conring (1606–1681): Der Begründer der deutschen Rechtsgeschichte* (Tübingen, 2006); Constantin Fasolt, *The Limits of History* (Chicago, 2004).

66. See Heubel's letter in the *Nova literaria*, ed. Johann Gottlieb Krause, April 1719, pp. 85–90: "Hamburgi. Excerpta ex litteris I. H. H. ad I. G. K.," at p. 88: "Cum itaque doctissimum &

inaugural lecture in Kiel, Heubel said in his published "Juridical Statement of Faith": I am "firmly convinced that without knowledge of the history and relics of the church and without comparing the laws that regulate both the church and criminal procedures, no one can properly say what should still be valid today."[67] Concerning Roman law he said: "I believe that in those places where Roman law lives by being received into common usage, or where it shines because of its equity and reason, studying it will be necessary for everyone and should not be neglected; but I am also firmly convinced that they will make no progress if they come [to such studies] with unclean hands, that is, in ignorance of ancient history and universal jurisprudence, but also those who dispense with the other necessary auxiliary tools, and [therefore] treat this noble science with a distorted method."[68]

What he aimed at was legal scholarship that depended heavily on historical and critical studies of the Middle Ages, using the most recent philological advances and discrimination. Unclean hands here were no longer permissible. We may suspect that Heubel applied these standards to his literary-historical studies of burned books as well. If documents dealing with book burnings were to be treated in the same manner as the medieval *Sachsenspiegel*, that would require, first, a rational inspection of the contents of these books, applying "equity and reason," the Thomasian description of Roman and canon law that Heubel had cited; but second, each individual case would need to be

---

nunquam laudandum satis Mabillioni de Re diplomatica volumen in nostris terris non adeo frequenter appareat, certe non toties, quam ejus praestantia & dignitas postulabat, auctor fui bibliopolis nostris atque suasor, velint nitidissimum & pretiosissimum opus una cum supplemento in lucem veluti retrahere, &, nisi turgescat nimis volumen, supra enarrationem opusculorum delectum quendam adjungere; nec dubito quin omnem sint daturi operam, ut libro jam ante gratissimo ex elegantia typorum & accuratissima figurarum in aes incisarum imitatione aliqua super accedat commendatio." On Mabillon, see Blandine Barret-Kriegel, *Jean Mabillon* (Paris, 1988).

67. Heubel, *Oratio de pedantismo juridico*: "II: . . . Sed firmiter quoque persuasum habeo, absque Historiae atque Antiquitatum Eccles. ope, & absque collatione Constitutionum, quae ad ordinationem tum Ecclesiae tum Processus forensis spectant, neminem, quid in ipsis hodie obtineat rerum argumentis, recte definire posse."

68. Ibid.: "I. Credo in illis locis, ubi jus Romanum usu receptum viget, aut quatenus aequitate atque ratione naturali nititur, ejus studium omnibus necessarium esse, nec quenquam eodem carere posse. Sed firmiter persuasum simul habeo, illotis manibus accedentem, id est, historiae veteris ac antiquitatum item jurisprudentiae universalis ignarum, aliisque huc spectantibus subsidiis destitutum perversaque methodo nobilissimam hanc scientiam pertractantem parum in eadem promoturum esse."

reconstructed historically and critically. As with legal documents that could be proven to be forgeries, so with trials of books, one might prove that justice had been distorted by secret denunciations, the influence of powerful figures, or other perversions of justice; but it was also possible that legal procedures had been observed and that a certain level of fairness had prevailed.[69] This double manner of proceeding seems to have formed the ideal that justified Heubel's enterprise, if he really did want to live up to standards that he praised so highly. If we look at the *Apologia pro Vanino* by Heubel's friend Arpe, a book that was published in 1712 and in a certain sense represented the model case for the early Enlightenment's efforts to "rescue" a burned author and his forbidden books, we can see the application of these two criteria clearly.

They gave Heubel's scholarly enterprise a weighty burden when it might otherwise have been undertaken in a more rhapsodic or essayistic manner. It may even be that Heubel set such high standards that he could not finish his project. If someone in Hamburg wanted to compose a *Bibliotheca* in the 1720s or 1730s, he would have to measure his efforts against the awesome *Bibliothecae* composed by Fabricius and Wolf—to put it rather casually, one would have to compile a gigantic work with at least one thousand pages containing highly learned, historically critical, and philological investigations.[70] Hadn't Heubel cried out to his listeners during his scandalous oration, "You falsely learned, / you fundamentally perverse, / Begone! Get out!"?[71] It's no wonder that Heubel's project came to grief because he set standards for collecting materials and fully researching them that he himself could not meet.

Transforming Research on the Enlightenment

What does Heubel's story tell us about the Enlightenment? Should we rank Heubel among the typical radical Enlightenment thinkers that Jonathan Israel has often described? For Israel, radicals, especially those associated with the *Traité des trois imposteurs,* were fully modern thinkers, who by 1700 had

69. In this context, cf. the historical method used by a French counterpart to Heubel, the freethinking historian Nicolas Lenglet du Fresnoy, *Méthode pour étudier l'histoire: Où après avoir établi les principes & l'ordre qu'on doit tenir la lire utilement, on fait les remarques nécessaires pour ne se pas laisser tromper dans sa lecture: avec un catalogue des principaux historiens, & des remarques critiques sur la bonté de leurs ouvrages, & sur le choix des meilleures éditions* (Brussels, 1714). There were many later expanded editions.

70. See note 12 in this chapter.

71. See note 24 in this chapter.

become uncompromisingly committed to such fundamental ideals as equality, secular reason, freedom, democracy, equality of the sexes, and human rights, all undergirded by a monistic metaphysics.[72] Everything else in his view was a "modernity cut in half," if we use the description invented for the twentieth century by Ulrich Beck; if it was not radical, it was perhaps only a "moderate Enlightenment," one that carries the distinct flavor of being all too eager to compromise.

I would not deny that there were individual examples of ruthless or even fanatic radicals in the sense that Israel has described. But the picture we obtain from the case histories like those of the *Apologia pro Vanino* (chapter 4) and the *Bibliotheca Vulcani* (in this chapter) is different. It's the picture of a skeptical generation that put a lot of effort into constructing a scholarly persona that could successfully maintain neutrality when buffeted by the waves of pluralization and could evaluate all sorts of information for their historical and rational validity. Such a person could not a priori exclude any possibility. But such scholarship was also undertaking a comprehensive new attack on the understanding of the past, especially with research that uncovered delicate issues or inconvenient truths. We have seen (as early as chapter 1) that for this generation the problem of the precarious and of one's own precarity—whether because one was dependent on a princely court or because one had been kicked out of a university—was far more urgent that any fidelity to some specific philosophy that we might designate "radical." I would therefore propose that we transform Israel's division between radical and moderate Enlightenments, not rejecting it entirely but making it capable of dealing more sensitively with the risky epistemic situations of our protagonists.

The transformation I have in mind (as I suggested in the introduction) would be to distinguish the knowledge precariat from the knowledge bourgeoisie. On the side of the precariat are not only the radicals and heretics but also those who only dreamed up wild projects and others who were insecure fence-sitters. Even if they were committed to change, as Heubel had been when he scolded the pedants, such persons could also be ideologically open and skeptical at the same time. Their scolding was more a habitus (an acquired attitude) than a set of beliefs. Therefore the knowledge precariat was characterized more by its habitus, its practiced habits of emotional serenity and impartiality and its ability to cope with plurality, than by commitments to specific

---

72. Israel, *Radical Enlightenment*; idem, *Enlightenment Contested*; idem, *Democratic Enlightenment*.

philosophies. Over on the side of the knowledge bourgeoisie we find both the Orthodox, who enjoyed secure access to the organs of publication and of intellectual reproduction (with disciples), and those reformers who had succeeded in making alliances—for example, with the absolutist territorial state—and in securing safe employment. One could describe both of these sides, the precariat and the bourgeoisie, through their varying attitudes toward plurality and through their varying modes of legitimation or delegitimation.[73]

To be sure, "moderate philosophers of the Enlightenment" in established positions possessed similar conceptual tools to those of the radicals, ranging from eclecticism, the critique of prejudice, and the ideas of different human temperaments; but they agreed on placing limits on the freedom of thought and on the validity of their principles. For the established, some conclusions were flatly intolerable. Their habitus was directed toward social and intellectual reproduction, toward successful reforms and polemics directed against their Orthodox opponents. Sometimes their theoretical preferences were less important to them than the achievement of practical results.

In many ways I think that this dividing line between the knowledge precariat and the knowledge bourgeoisie portrays the actual circumstances of the seventeenth and eighteenth centuries better than some line between "halfway" and supposedly "full-scale" modernization, because it is more sensitive to the real-life conditions, hostilities, and insecurities. Thus the phenomenon of "indifferentism," which was so vigorously discussed in Germany around 1700, now looks a little different.[74] According to Israel's criteria, indifferentism would be uninteresting because such thinkers were stuck between opposing parties. Look at Gottfried Arnold, who was like Heubel in some ways but far more religiously serious and vastly more productive and influential in rescuing "witnesses to truth" from oblivion; in his day Arnold was denounced as an indifferentist because he defended the ostracized only because they opposed authority and searched for truth; he did not seem to care about the actual truth or falsity of their teachings. This was exactly the shift in mentality that we've

73. It must be emphasized that in an analogous manner to the sociology of work, from which these concepts are taken, we are not dealing with fixed social classes but with social formations that can be found throughout most social classes to make up what can be called "zones."

74. See Martin Mulsow, "Mehrfachkonversion, politische Religion und Opportunismus im 17. Jahrhundert. Plädoyer für eine Indifferentismusforschung," in *Interkonfessionalität-Transkonfessionalität-binnenkonfessionelle Pluralität: Neue Forschungen zur Konfessionalisierungsthese*, ed. Kaspar von Greyerz et al. (Gütersloh, 2003), 132–50.

seen in this chapter: it was a direct reaction to the crisis of pluralization in the early modern period. Any author of an "impartial church history" or an author of a *Bibliotheca Vulcani* was clearly an indifferentist. But such a thinker was not necessarily a radical in Israel's sense even if he was most likely a member of the knowledge precariat. He was a custodian of precarious knowledge, practicing an attitude that combined commitment with serenity. And that was precisely the attitude that placed him in a precarious social situation.

Trust, Mistrust, Courage: Epistemic Perceptions, Virtues, and Gestures

The times have changed from when we could hope to distinguish almost mechanically between the external and the internal conditions of knowledge. Too much was concealed under that distinction; it was too obviously a defensive reflex of philosophers who did not wish to consider the contexts surrounding knowledge. If we accept the division, for example, then all the historically variable circumstances among knowledge cultures become merely external, including even the semantics of the theories, the habitus of the theoreticians, and the forms of argument typical of one age or another. One of the scholars who most effectively broke down the dichotomy in the theory of knowledge and the history of science was—after Thomas S. Kuhn of course—Stephen Shapin. Together with the sociologist of science Simon Schaffer he showed, using the example of Thomas Hobbes and Robert Boyle, just how complicated the conditions for verification were in a specific case and that these conditions required tacit technical knowledge as well as a specific context in which observations of experiments could be accepted.[1] In his *Social History of Truth*, Shapin broadened these conclusions and placed trust at the very center, the trust that in seventeenth-century England was conferred only on an observer from secure social circumstances, in short, a gentleman. He argued that trust depended on social situations and therefore belonged to the conditions for

---

1. Stephen Shapin and Simon Schaffer, *Leviathan and the Air Pump: Hobbes, Boyle, and the Experimental Life* (Princeton, 1985).

verifying knowledge.[2] But if we are aiming not so much at a social history and more at a cultural history of truth and knowledge, then other aspects come into play as well. The question of trust can then be studied in other media, and distinguishing among various knowledge cultures expands these contexts to include even situations of distrust. That's especially true for the case of libertines and radicals, who needed to stay alert and constantly needed to employ evasive tactics—as we saw in chapter 1. In chapter 6, I will highlight the special case of a particular social context and will using images show, in the case of libertine circles in seventeenth-century Venice, that threats and distrust affected the sense of trust even among close acquaintances.

Trust as an almost transcendent social condition is not just a hot topic in research; it's also one of the specific virtues needed for convictions to be proven true. Thus Bernard Williams has described accuracy and sincerity as the two primary virtues of truth.[3] Linda Zagzebski has even asserted that a theory of knowledge could be grounded in the possible behaviors of epistemically virtuous persons.[4] I do not wish to pursue these theories here, but I think it's valuable to follow historical references to such epistemic virtues over the centuries of the early modern period. Chapter 8 examines therefore the appeals for intellectual courage that were issued under the slogan "sapere aude" (dare to know), investigating this partly as the history of a concept and partly as the history of ideas and their reception. Under what circumstances and with what goal were people urged to have the courage to know? What should this courage be directed toward? The question reminds us of Michel Foucault's project of studying how "truth telling," governmentality, and the "practices of the self" were related in the ancient world; he emphasized the importance of *parrhesia*—the courage needed to speak openly.[5] We can see the modern history of "sapere aude" as related to the ancient ideas of frankness and of wisdom (chapter 8). But before we get to that sort of courage, chapters 6 and 7

2. Stephen Shapin, *A Social History of Truth: Civility and Science in Seventeenth-Century England* (Chicago, 1994).

3. Bernard Williams, *Truth and Truthfulness* (Princeton, 2002); Lorraine Daston and Peter Gallison also speak of epistemic virtues in their book, *Objectivity* (New York, 2007), 41ff.

4. Linda T. Zagzebski, *Virtues of the Mind: An Inquiry into the Nature of Virtue and the Ethical Foundations of Knowledge* (Cambridge, 1996).

5. I'm referring especially to his late lectures from 1982 to 1984: Michel Foucault, *The Government of Self and Others: Lectures at the Collège de France 1982–1983*, trans. Graham Burchell (New York, 2010); idem, *The Courage of Truth: Lectures at the Collège de France 1983–1984*, trans. Graham Burchell (New York, 2011).

consider the strategy of retreating from dangers. Until recently, gestures have been more closely studied by medievalists than by early modernists. But gestures appear not only in early modern allegorical images of knowledge (as we will see in chapter 6) but also in early modern texts, and they allow us to describe the habitus of their authors. So reconstructing the gestures of the scholarly persona will depend on visual as well as written (and paratextual) sources but also on reports of symbolic actions, such as the refusal to publish certain texts, or protests achieved by quitting certain official positions or by ridiculing the authorities. Sometimes we find that persons expressing precarious knowledge might feel forced by their surroundings to assume defiant postures or gestures. But many drew back or adopted a double identity, like Dr. Jekyll and Mr. Hyde. Although Hegel thought that absolute knowledge was the "Spirit (Mind) that knows itself in the shape of Spirit (Mind)," this book presents an idea of knowledge that is the exact opposite: a mind that knows itself in the form of a body.[6] This suggests not only the material fragility and scarcity of knowledge, and not only the instability of knowledge because of its precarious status, but also and especially the tacit and praxeological dimension of this knowledge.

6. Translator's note: Translation modified from G.W.F. Hegel, *Phenomenology of Spirit*, trans. A. V. Miller, ed. J. N. Findlay (Oxford, 1977), para. 798, p. 1155.

6

Threatened Knowledge

PROLEGOMENA TO A CULTURAL
HISTORY OF TRUTH

Metaphorology seeks to burrow down to the substructure of thought, the
underground, the nutrient solution of systematic crystallizations; but it also
aims to show with what "courage" the mind preempts itself in its images, and
how its history is projected in the courage of its conjectures.

—HANS BLUMENBERG

An Allegory

As a close associate of Pietro Aretino (the notorious author of erotica and
scourge of the powerful), the Venetian Marcolino da Forli called his publishing
house a Bottega della Verità, a "shop of truth."[1] As a printer's emblem for his
books Marcolino chose an allegorical image in which the truth is being pulled up

1. See Fritz Saxl, "Veritas filia temporis," in *Philosophy and History: Essays Presented to Ernst
Cassirer*, ed. Raymond Klibansky and H. J. Paton (New York, 1963), 197–222; on Aretino, see
also Klaus Thiele-Dohrmann, *Kurtisanenfreund und Fürstenplage: Pietro Aretino und die Kunst
der Enthüllung* (Düsseldorf and Zürich, 1998). Because I am not a trained art historian and am
here treading the ground of art history, I am most grateful for the help I've received from David
Stone, Irving Lavin, Gabriele Wimböck, Frank Büttner, and Frank Betzner. This study was first
part of a project financed by the Deutsche Forschungsgemeinschaft, which I directed within
the Munich Sonderforschungsbereich (Special Research Project) no. 573 on "Pluralization and
Authority in the Early Modern Period"; an earlier and shorter version was printed in the report
of the SFB 573 in April 2006. The epigraph comes from Blumenberg, *Paradigms for a Metaphorology*, 5.

FIGURE 20. Marcolino's printer's emblem,
woodcut by Adrien Willaert, *Cinque Messe*,
Venice, 1536. Fritz Saxl, "Veritas filia temporis," in
*Philosophy and History: Essays Presented to Ernst
Cassirer*, ed. Raymond Klibansky and H. J. Paton
(New York, 1963), ill. 2.

from the earth into the light by Chronos, time, which is rescuing truth from the
attacks of Calumnia, slander (figure 20). This image is framed by the ancient
epigram, "Veritas filia temporis" (Truth is the daughter of time). The emblem
was an expression of the intellectual and political struggles that Aretino and
Marcolino fought in Venice during the 1530s and 1540s. It located claims to truth
within the welter of false assertions, flattery, fakery, and fraud, charges that were
commonplace in the sophisticated world of the early modern court. But it also
kicked off a new round of emblematic representations of truth that came to
decorate walls, title pages, and paintings. In this chapter we will examine such
representations, looking for a key to understanding the connections among

different sorts of interpretation, libertinism, and the problem of truth.[2] By stepping off the well-trodden paths of traditional intellectual history, I'm hoping to follow emblems and allegories into a kind of cultural history of truth, one that does not try to create a new theory but an understanding of intellectual adaptations, attitudes, and perceptions—and especially the perception of threats. Looking at the emblems in Theodor Ludwig Lau's portrait, as we did in chapter 3, pointed us in this direction. In later chapters this approach will be further applied to the epistemology of virtue and to the theory of "emotional communities."

Let us begin in the middle of the seventeenth century, a time of advancing pluralization, a hundred years after the appearance of Aretino but still under the spell of his influence. The Accademia Carrara in Bergamo possesses a puzzling painting by the Venetian painter Pietro della Vecchia from the year 1654 (figure 21).[3] It obviously displays an allegory of truth: a barely clad woman holding a pair of compasses is being grasped by an old man, while next to her another person crouches, looking at her. What's unusual about the picture is that the old man and the person to the side—a figure who might represent envy, calumny, or fortune—are exchanging obscene gestures: the man is making the sign of the horns with his outstretched little finger and index finger; the other person is making the fig sign with a thumb sticking out between the fingers. Is the truth being held up to mockery? Is this the result of some intellectual contortions of truth?

It almost seems so. In this painting della Vecchia was violating several iconographic conventions all at once. The personification of truth, signified by the sun that floats like a diadem over her brow, is not abstract and untouchable as would have been customary but has been put into an intimate and erotic situation by a lustful old man. This man, who has the position in this painting usually taken by Chronos unveiling "truth as the daughter of time," is here more likely a philosopher who lusts after truth.[4] And obscene gestures (taken from Giovanni Bonifacio's book *L'arte dei cenni*, on signs and gestures)[5] normally have no place in philosophical allegories.

2. On this set of questions, see Mulsow, *Die unanständige Gelehrtenrepublik*.

3. On della Vecchia, see Bernard Aikema, *Pietro della Vecchia and the Heritage of the Renaissance in Venice* (Florence, 1990).

4. On this topos, see Erwin Panofsky, "Vater Chronos," in idem, *Studien zur Ikonologie: Humanistische Themen in der Kunst der Renaissance* (Cologne, 1980), 109–52.

5. See Giovanni Bonifacio, *L'arte dei cenni con la quale formandosi favelle visibile si tratta della muta eloquenza, che non è altro che un facondo silentio* (Vicenza, 1616), 335: "Fare il fico." See also

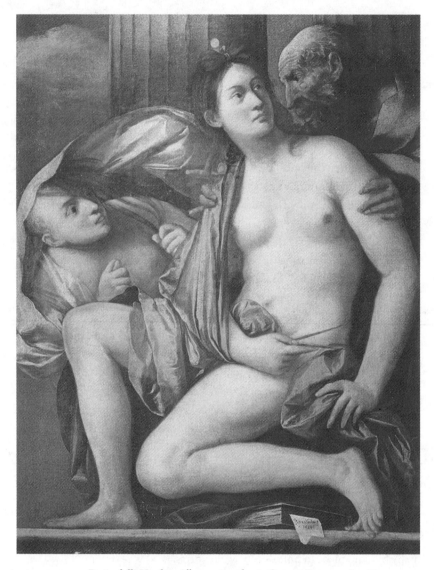

FIGURE 21. Pietro della Vecchia, *Allegory*. Accademia Carrara, Bergamo, Inv. No. 143.

But there's more. Della Vecchia was obviously close to the Venetian Accademia degli Incogniti (Academy of the Unknowns), which had been thoroughly infiltrated by disciples of Cesare Cremonini, an intellectual descendant

Tintoretto's painting *Krönung Christi mit Dornenkrone* (private collection, London); and Aikema, *Della Vecchia*, 107.

of Pietro Pomponazzi.[6] It was rumored that Pomponazzi and Cremonini were both guilty of maintaining the infamous doctrine of double truth: the assertion that something could be true in philosophy while it was false in theology, and vice versa.[7] We learned something about that in chapter 2. The head of the Accademia was Giovan Francesco Loredano, a rich nobleman, whose stance was so ambiguous that one could not easily tell if he was merely "gallant" intellectually or if he was fundamentally subversive as well. Under an illustration included in two editions of Loredano's letters della Vecchia's name appears, which proves that along with Francesco Ruschi and Daniel van den Dyck he was one of those artists whom the Incogniti trusted when they wanted illustrations for their books. Moreover, della Vecchia was van den Dyck's brother-in-law and thus already a member of Loredano's circle.[8]

So one might wonder if the libertine spirit of the Accademia found expression in della Vecchia's pictures and if such thinkers were fed up with the search for "truth." According to a common understanding, libertines were people who cared only about the enjoyment of this world and the moral relativity of all situations. That's the direction taken by Bernard Aikema regarding della Vecchia's allegory. He even suggests that the allegory could have hung on

6. See Aikema, Della Vecchia, 57–92. On the Accademia, see Giorgio Spini, Ricerca dei libertini: La teoria dell' impostura delle religioni nel seicento italiano, 2nd ed. (Florence, 1983). See also the bibliographical research of Tiziana Menegatti, Ex ignoto notus: Bibliografia delle opere a stampa del principe degli incogniti: Giovan Francesco Loredano (Padua, 2000), and Monica Miato, L'Accademia degli Incogniti di Giovan Francesco Loredan a Venezia (1630–1661) (Florence, 1998). Paolo Marangon, "Aristotelismo e cartesianesimo: Filosofia accademica e libertini," in Storia della cultura veneta, vol. 4: Il Seicento, ed. Girolamo Arnaldi and Manlio Pastore Stocchi, part 2 (Vicenza, 1984), 95–114.

7. On Cremonini, see Heinrich Kuhn, Venetischer Aristotelismus im Ende der aristotelischen Welt: Aspekte der Welt und des Denkens des Cesare Cremonini (1550–1631) (Bern and Frankfurt, 1996). On the complicated problem of double truth, see, e.g., Martin Pine, "Pomponazzi and the Problem of 'Double Truth,'" Journal of the History of Ideas 29 (1968): 163–76; Friedrich, Die Grenzen der Vernunft, esp. 281ff.

8. Lionello Puppi, "Ignoto Deo," Arte Veneta 23 (1969): 169–80; see Aikema, Della Vecchia. Della Vecchia was married to Clorinda, a daughter of the painter Niccolò Renieri. Another daughter of Renieri's had married Daniel van den Dyck, so that van den Dyck, who also worked for the Accademia degli Incogniti, was della Vecchia's brother-in-law; and probably the art critic and connoisseur of della Vecchia's works, Marco Boschini, belongs in this family web as well. See P. L. Fantelli, "Nicolò Renieri 'pittor fiamengo,'" Saggi e memorie di storia dell'arte 9 (1974): 77–115; idem, "Le figlie di Nicolò Renieri: Un saggio attributivo," Arte Veneta 28 (1974): 267–72; Venezia! Kunst aus venezianischen Palästen (Ostfildern-Ruit, 2002), 201.

display in the meeting room of the Incogniti, as did Titian's allegory of wisdom on the ceiling of the old Library of St. Mark's, where the Accademia della Fama had met in the sixteenth century.[9]

I would like to question and correct part of Aikema's interpretation, but in other respects I gratefully follow his collection of evidence. I do not believe that truth in this painting was being mocked. Rather, it was a comprehensive treatment of the relationship of the philosopher to truth, or more precisely to precarious truth.

This relationship becomes more understandable if we consider two similar allegories by della Vecchia: a painting (probably from 1666) from a private collection in Moscow and a painting owned by the Civic Museum of Vicenza. If we line up these three pictures for comparison, we can draw the following conclusions. In the first of these paintings, the Moscow allegory, an old man with a beard, probably a philosopher, is fleeing from a woman with a wheel, the image of Fortuna, and toward the arms of a young woman wearing a coat. In the second, the Vicenza allegory, the philosopher embraces the young woman, who now represents either wisdom (sapientia) or truth (veritas), with her left arm posed as in the previous picture but with her right hand placed not self-protectively so much as expressing desire (figure 22). Her coat is now open, revealing her breast while she looks at him. She is holding a rolled-up paper, on which we can read "Saepe sub sordido pallio magna latet Sapientia" (Often great wisdom is hidden under a filthy garment).[10] Thus the philosopher has turned toward wisdom and is seeking to fathom her secrets (the Vicenza allegory).[11] Now look at the third allegory, the one from Bergamo. We can understand the image this way: here the philosopher is standing behind wisdom or truth but still grasps her and is essentially barricaded behind her. He now confronts the unhappy fate that he has escaped, a fate that mocks him with his fig sign, while he for his part responds to fate with his own obscene gesture, the sign of the horns, but the figure of truth is also shielding the philosopher.

9. Aikema, *Della Vecchia*, 111.

10. This epigram comes from Caecilius Statius; on the contexts, see also chapter 9.

11. *Allegory* from the Civic Museum of Vicenza published in Aikema, *Della Vecchia*, cat. 151, ill. 112. There is a variant of this picture in an Italian private collection, in which the old man has wings and can thus be interpreted as Chronos (time). But his gesture is still one of desire. See figure 22 in Bernard Aikema, "Marvellous Imitations and Outrageous Parodies: Pietro della Vecchia Revisited," in *Continuity, Innovation and Connoisseurship* (University Park, PA, 2003), 111–33, at 122.

FIGURE 22. Pietro della Vecchia, *Allegory*, Vicenza,
Museo Civico. Bernard Aikema, *Pietro della Vecchia
and the Heritage of the Renaissance in Venice*
(Florence, 1990), cat. 151, ill. 112.

Magical Foundation

If we look closely at the central gestures of the Bergamo allegory, we can see a
more nuanced picture. These gestures were not simple obscenities, in my view,
because they possessed a magical foundation. In late sixteenth- and early
seventeenth-century Italy, magic and protective spells were still alive, and that
was certainly true for southern Italy, for example in Naples and Calabria, but
even for northern regions like Venice too. One well-known defensive gesture
was the so-called *manu cornuta*, which was used against anyone from whom
one expected a magical attack or the evil eye: one held out one's hand with the
index finger and the little finger spread out, like an amulet made with one's
own hands.[12] This is exactly the gesture made by the philosopher in della
Vecchia's painting. Andrea de Jorio, the Neapolitan specialist on gestures from

12. On the "evil eye," see Thomas Hauschild, *Magie und Macht in Italien* (Gifkendorf, 2002).

FIGURE 23. Abraxas gem. Bernard de
Montfaucon, *L'antiquité expliquée et
representée en figures, supplement*, vol. 2
(Paris, 1724), plate LV.

the 1830s, claimed to have found this
specific gesture as far back as in ancient
images, for example, on an engraved
bronze Silenus figure from Herculaneum or on a gem from Montfaucon
with an image of Abraxas (figure 23).[13]
One can suppose that Pietro della Vecchia, who was often involved in magic,
was using this gesture in a complex manner in his allegory.[14] And only if we understand this gesture can we really decode the picture. For then it would read:
An old man, probably a wise man or philosopher, has unveiled the naked truth
(*nuda veritas*), portrayed as a nude woman
with a solar diadem, and is protecting
her against attacks and profanations
from without. This external threat is
presented as another person, probably
representing Fortuna, who also de-
ploys a magical gesture, the *mano in fica*. This gesture could also possess an
apotropaic force, but here della Vecchia is playing more aggressively and
with an obscene meaning.[15] However, it could also insultingly mean "Get
lost!" as well as suggesting an obscene, sexual "Come hither!" With an understanding of gestures, we can glimpse just how endangered and precarious the truth is, if it is exposed to the outside world, the simple people, or
to "fate." Truth needs to hide under a proverbial "filthy garment" (*saepe sub*

13. Andrea de Jorio, *La mimica degli antichi investigata nel gestire napoletano* (Naples, 1832); I
am using the new English edition, *Gesture in Naples and Gesture in Classical Antiquity* (Bloomington, 2000), 171; Bernard de Montfaucon, *L'antiquité expliquée et representée en figures, supplement*, vol. 2 (Paris, 1724), plate LV.

14. Pietro della Vecchia, *Allegory*, Accademia Carrara, Bergamo. Inv. No. 143.

15. De Jorio, *Gestures*, 215. On the interpretation of the picture, see Aikema, *Della Vecchia*,
57–60. The gesture can also be seen in a painting by della Vecchia in the Lakeview Museum in
Peoria, Illinois. There an old woman, probably an allegorical representation of envy, is crouching
before a young, beautiful woman with wings, who has feathers in her hand. The old woman is
making the *mano in fica* gesture.

sordido pallio magna latet sapientia), and her lover (literally the *philosophus*), while revealing her, must also conceal and protect her.[16]

Such an interpretation would also agree with the topos found in contemporary books of emblems in various forms: "sapiens supra fortuna" (The wise man is superior to fate). That was the Roman Stoic view of Seneca and the Neo-Stoic view revived by Justus Lipsius (d. 1606).[17] Influenced by that movement, in 1618 the Dutch inventor of emblems Florentius Schoonhoven (whom we will meet again in chapter 8) published a work, *Emblemata partim moralia partim etiam civilia*, in which the fourth emblem portrays an old man who is kneeling over and binding a naked woman lying on a wheel and a cloth that could be used as a sail (figure 24).[18] Over them stands the motto: "Sapiens supra Fortunam" (The wise man is superior to fortune). In the image the man is the wise one, the woman whom he's binding is Fortuna. But now della Vecchia, who may have borrowed from Schoonhoven's ideologically neutral book, translated this "binding" into a gesture from his own culture, using a magical sort of "binding."[19]

Naked Truth

So one can think of della Vecchia's image as an allegory about truth, both threatened and protected. Now we can understand the wider contexts of the painting, and implicitly the epistemic situation of the painter or his patron. Why should truth feel threatened? At the outset it's important to note that truth is again caught up in the dialectic of veiling and unveiling. When she is veiled, she cannot be recognized as truth. Such a notion of truth is reminiscent of esoteric ideas and occult philosophy. And indeed the notion of truth as "occultatio" (concealment)

16. See the allegory in the Civic Museum of Vicenza, reprinted in Aikema, *Della Vecchia*, Illustration 112.

17. See Gerda Busch, "Fortunae resistere in der Moral des Philosophen Seneca," *Antike und Abendland* (1961): 131–54.

18. Florentius Schoonhovius, *Emblemata partim moralia, partim etiam civilia* (Gouda, 1618), 4. On Schoonhoven, see Arnoud Visser, "Escaping the Reformation in the Republic of Letters: Confessional Silence in Latin Emblem Books," *Church History and Religious Culture* 88 (2008): 139–67. Translator's note: although the cloth in the illustration does not look much like a sail, Fortuna was conventionally portrayed with a sail.

19. The metaphor of "binding" is one of the oldest characteristics of ancient Greek magic; see Fritz Graf, *Gottesnähe und Schadenzauber: Die Magie in der griechisch-römischen Antike* (Munich, 1996).

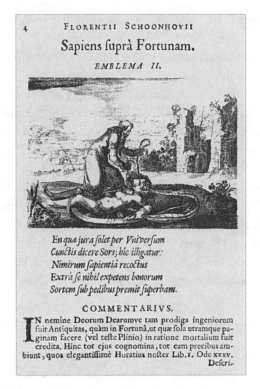

FIGURE 24. "Sapiens supra Fortunam." From
Florentius Schoonhovius, *Emblemata partim moralia,
partim etiam civilia* (Gouda, 1618), 4.

can be found not only in the Kabbalist and neo-Platonic traditions[20] but also in Paracelsism. And sometimes thinkers in the Paracelsist-alchemical tradition admitted that they wanted to see the truth unveiled and naked. Thus Gerhard Dorn wrote in 1583, "I do not regard the golden mantle of Pallas [Athena] as a replacement for Pallas herself; for I would rather behold Pallas under her woolen dress than just her dress; it would not be proper to look at her naked . . . except perhaps for such a Pallas who may offer herself to the view of intellects when she grants them her favor."[21] We know that della Vecchia was in contact with such circles.

20. See, e.g., Leone Ebreo, *Dialoghi d'Amore*, ed. S. Aramella (Bari, 1929), 98–102. According to Ebreo, the wise always disguised the truth.

21. Gerhard Dorn, *In Theophrasti Paracelsi Auroram Philosophorum Thesaurum et mineralem oeconomiam commentaria* (Frankfurt, 1583), foreword: "Pallium aureum non accipiam Palladis pro Pallade ipsa, imò potiùs sub lanea veste Palladem, et non vestem eius, intueri cupio.

One of his portraits shows a young man holding a pansophic chart with instructions about techniques "inaccessibilem veritatem apprehendere," of "grasping an inaccessible truth." We will examine this portrait more closely in chapter 9.

Truth was fundamentally hidden, but the investigator desperately wanted to reveal it. Francis Bacon stood with Montaigne in a growing fascination with the "naked truth."[22] "Truth is naked," Bacon wrote, and in good Platonic tradition he compared investigation with "love-making and wooing."[23] This did not mean, however, that the nakedness of truth simply revealed its sensuousness. Most notably, for della Vecchia it seems clear that the external world was only appearance. Some of his other paintings thus ruthlessly caricatured the five human senses as grotesque and unreliable, so that for the viewer only one conclusion remains: that truth must be sought beyond the senses (figure 25).[24] In the Accademia degli Incogniti, moreover, the idea that one needed to distinguish between appearance and reality, between surface and invisible depths, between elite knowledge and popular errors, was widespread. In the *Academic Discourses* of the members we find constant emphasis on the need to see through the "dissimulations" and "falsity" of superficial beauty in order to know and learn to love true beauty.[25]

Quanquam eam videre nudam aequum non est, nisi fortassis talem se contemplandam praebuerit gratia sua dignatis ingenijs." Also printed in Wilhelm Kühlmann and Joachim Telle, *Corpus Paracelsisticum*, vol. 1, part 2 (Tübingen, 2004), 907, with comment on 913.

22. Ralf Konersmann, "Wahrheit, nackte," in *Historisches Wörterbuch der Philosophie*, vol. 12 (Basel, 2004), cols. 148–51, at 149; Montaigne, *Essais* III, 11. See Blumenberg, *Paradigms for a Metaphorology*.

23. Francis Bacon, "Essays or councels, civil and moral" (1625), in idem, *Works*, ed. von J. Spedding et al. (London, 1857–74): *Of Truth*: "But howsoever these things are thus in men's depraved judgments and affections, yet truth, which only doth judge itself, teacheth that the inquiry of truth, which is the love-making or wooing of it, the knowledge of truth, which is the presence of it, and the belief of truth, which is the enjoying of it, is the sovereign good of human nature" (6:378). For the relation between earthly and "heavenly" love in connection with "nuda veritas," see also Erwin Panofsky, "Die neoplatonische Bewegung in Florenz und Oberitalien (Bandinelli und Tizian)," in idem, *Studien zur Ikonologie*, 203–50, esp. 220ff.

24. Aikema, *Della Vecchia*, 69, recognizes here only the comic and grotesque genre. For the tradition of illustrating the five senses, see Carl Nordenfalk, "The Five Senses in Late Medieval and Renaissance Art," *Journal of the Warburg and Courtauld Institutes* 48 (1985): 1–22; idem, *Sèvres et les cinq sens* (Stockholm, 1984). On the grotesques, see N. Ivanoff, "Il grottesco nella pittura del Seicento: Pietro il Vecchia," *Emporium* 99 (1944): 85–94.

25. Giambattista Doglioni, "Della bellezza," in *Discorsi academici de' Signori Incogniti, havuti in Venezia nell 'Accademia dell' Illustrissimo Signor Gio. Francesco Loredano* (Venice, 1635). See Iain Fenlon and Peter N. Miller, *The Song of the Soul: Understanding Poppea* (London, 1992), 35ff.

AVDITVS.

FIGURE 25. Pietro della Vecchia, grotesque of the sense of hearing, Venice, art dealer
P. Scarpa (1975). Bernard Aikema, *Pietro della Vecchia and the Heritage of the Renaissance
in Venice* (Florence, 1990), cat. 148, ill. 121.

This was at least the official and exoteric doctrine of the Incogniti; we need
to take it seriously and beware of too quickly concluding that Venetian "libertinism" was "Aristotelian" or "proto-materialistic." Even so, under this surface
of exoteric doctrine, there are other connotations, and for libertine members
of the Incogniti the charm was to be found in savoring these broader connotations, especially if they pointed toward eroticism and sexuality, as in the poems
of Giambattista Marino.[26] Such connotations were visible if one paid attention
to the smallest, most inconspicuous modifications of conventional iconography. Thus the direct model for della Vecchia's Bergamo allegory was obviously
a frontispiece to a book by Loredano, in which certain changes could be noted,
as Aikema has shown. I'm speaking of Francesco Ruschi's copper-plate engraving for the title page of *Dianea* from 1653, which was published one year before
della Vecchia's painting (figure 26). In this engraving one can also find a column in the background, and the position of Fortuna in della Vecchia was obviously modeled on the position of Veritas in Ruschi; in the images by della
Vecchia and Ruschi, Fortuna's robe has been pulled completely to one side,
and for the same reason: that Chronos unveils the truth, *Veritas filia temporis.*
I suspect that Ruschi borrowed his image of Veritas from a painting by Palma

26. On Marino one should still consult James V. Mirollo, *The Poet of the Marvelous: Giambattista Marino* (New York, 1963).

FIGURE 26. Francesco Ruschi, title engraving
for Giovan Francesco Loredano, *Dianea*
(Venice, 1653). Bernard Aikema, *Pietro della
Vecchia and the Heritage of the Renaissance in Venice*
(Florence, 1990), ill. 108.

Giovine, which was on display in the Doge's Palace.[27] But there it was truth as
in Psalm 85:11, striving upward from the earth ("veritas de terra orta est" [Truth
is sprung out of the earth]).[28] In Ruschi it is truth that is unveiled by time, but
he consciously modified the traditional image for the Incogniti; here he

27. See Saxl, "Veritas," 216 (Fig. 10).
28. Translator's note: This is the reading of the Douai translation, but the KJV reads: "Truth
shall spring out of the earth."

FIGURE 27. Successor of Frans Floris, *Truth Protected by Time*. Wrocław Art Museum (before 1945).

portrayed time not as an old man, as the iconography demanded, but as a youth. This lends the unveiling an erotic note. Undoubtedly Ruschi's desire to eroticize the nude was stronger than his desire to remain iconographically correct.

Della Vecchia made another change. The man is old again, but he's no winged figure of time. The eroticism has been preserved but it now takes place weirdly between an old man and a young woman. The posture of the woman has been moved to upright, while her old recumbent form has now been adopted by Fortuna. Instead of a group of two, there are now three figures, a fact that associates the subject more closely with other allegories of truth, that is, those that place truth in the midst of a struggle between Chronos and Invidia, time and envy or ill will (figure 27). We are dealing here with a hybrid imagery, inspired by the two phrases *veritas filia temporis* and *veritas de terra orta est*. Through this association della Vecchia's allegory of the threatening fate with its obscene gesture is now imbued with envy and ill will. Indeed, the gesture confirms another slogan about truth: *Veritas odium parit* (Truth gives birth to hatred).

Let us dwell a bit longer on the extraordinary eroticism arising from the old man and the young woman, a theme that connects iconographically with the episode of Susanna and the elders.[29] And in fact if one blends the biblical story of Susanna with the allegory of truth, one sees that here, too, there's a story of unveiling. Two elders had secretly watched Susanna and lusted after her as she bathed, but despite their threats she refused to have sex with them. When the elders were brought before the court, the text states: "As she was veiled, the scoundrels ordered her to be unveiled, so that they might feast their eyes on her beauty."[30] If applied allegorically as a story of truth, these two philosophers

29. Aikema saw this (*Della Vecchia*, 59). The story is told in the apocryphal Daniel 13.

30. Daniel 13:32 (also known as Susanna 1:32), using the translation of *The New Oxford Annotated Bible*, 3rd ed., ed. Michael Coogan et al. (Oxford, 2007).

wanted to remove the veil covering truth in order to become intoxicated with her beauty.

At this level of meaning the issue was the outrage of denying one's desire for the divine and innocent truth. The elements of the story tarnish the image of della Vecchia's philosopher, who has barricaded himself behind the truth but is also defending her against fate. So if we read the Bergamo allegory through the story of Susanna, the old man is making the sign of the horns as if to say, "She has cuckolded her husband by lying with another man." And the woman crouching next to the truth is making a fig sign to the truth, as if reacting to the old man's accusation and saying: "Yes, you have slept with another man!" But actually Susanna/Dea/Truth is innocent.

Della Vecchia's painting *The Kingdom of Love* (figure 28) also invokes the theme of profanation: a crowd is standing around a statue of the naked goddess of love in her temple.[31] It's a parody of the well-known theme of "the toilet of Venus," because here the "toilet" is interpreted in a drastically realistic manner—many of the surrounding spectators are holding their noses at the stink arising from the basin at the foot of the Venus. To the right in the picture the "old men" appear again, as if they had been transported directly from a painting of Susanna at her bath into the temple of Venus.[32] The elders who were ogling Susanna are here profaning the goddess.

There's no doubt: these old men, these philosophers of della Vecchia, are lustful.[33] And yet the image does not necessarily imply criticism. Depending

31. Baldassare Bonificio, who was close to the Accademia degli Incogniti, wrote on the veneration of Venus statues in his *Historia ludicra*. I quote from the third edition (Brussels, 1656), 417ff.: "Venerem, commune hominum, Deorumque gaudium et delicium. Buti Siculo, Priamidi Alexandro, Anchisae Dardanio, Cynarejo Adonidi, Vulcano, Marti, Mercurio, Neptuno, aliisque adamatam, nihil profecto mirum: his enim omnibus vivam sese, atque adeo nudam ostendit: imo vero Diis etiam cunctis id de se spectaculum praebuit, juxta Poetam, tametsi repugnans et coacta; cum videlicet egregiis ille faber cassibus adamantinis implicitam cum adultero deprehendit,—*Valvas patefecit eburnas, / Admisitque Deos: Ambo jacuere ligati / Turpiter: Atque aliquis de Diis non tristibus optat / Sic fieri turpis.*" Bonifacio was interested in those cases in which a Venus statue was so realistically formed that men fell in love with her. And it appears that elsewhere too Bonifacio was interested in the motif of "consecrating" women. See his work, which he called a *Tractatus de consecratione virginum*, which he appended to his book, p. 590.

32. On this, see Aikema, *Della Vecchia*, 58ff. As a contrast, see, e.g., Titian's *Young Woman at Her Toilet* or Rubens's *The Toilet of Venus*.

33. Those emphasizing the forcible profanation of truth should also recall the nightmare that the late antique neo-Platonist Macrobius handed down from his predecessor Numenius, who (because he worried that his philosophical interpretations of the Eleusinian mysteries had

FIGURE 28. Pietro della Vecchia, *The Kingdom of Love*, Venice, private collection. Bernard Aikema, *Pietro della Vecchia and the Heritage of the Renaissance in Venice* (Florence, 1990), cat. 152, ill. 110.

on the patron, this motif could also have been intended as sexy and affirmative, if for example the request for the painting actually came from the gentlemen members of the Incogniti. There is a series of other paintings by the same artist that all portray a philosopher or teacher and his disciple in a relationship charged with erotic intimacy (figure 29). We find the same motif in the libertine Antonio Rocco's clandestine book, the satirical homosexual dialogue entitled *L'Alcibiade, fanciullo a scola* (*Alcibiades the Schoolboy*).[34] In his version, della Vecchia employed a painterly quotation—the specific gesture of the

profaned them) dreamed that he saw the Eleusinian goddesses standing like whores at the entrance to a brothel. Numenius believed that the divine *numen* had thereby showed him how seriously he had insulted it through his excessive desire for knowledge. From such experiences the neo-Platonist drew the conclusion that in the future religious things had to be treated in the veiled form of fables, in a "theologia poetiké." In the eighteenth century the scenario of outrageously unveiling one of the mystery goddesses was revived in the image of Isis, "whose veil no mortal had ever lifted."

34. Antonio Rocco, *L'Alcibiade fanciulla a scola*, D.P.A. ("Oranges," 1652); German translation: *Der Schüler Alkibiades: Ein philosophisch-erotischer Dialog*, ed. Wolfram Setz (Hamburg,

FIGURE 29. Pietro della Vecchia, *Socrates and Two Pupils*, Milan, art trade.
Bernard Aikema, *Pietro della Vecchia and the Heritage of the Renaissance in Venice*
(Florence, 1990), cat. 132, ill. 113.

teacher was possibly based on the figure of the protecting angel in Achille
Bocchi's *Symbolicae quaestiones* (figure 30).[35] For initiates this would open up
a deeper level of meaning, in this case the relationship of teacher and student.
This allusion may suggest a connection to the Socratic *genius* or *daemon*, and
the idea of depicting Chronos as a young, winged figure may point to another

2002). On Rocco, see Spini, *Ricerca*, 164ff. See also Graham Turner, *Schooling Sex: Libertine
Literature and Erotic Education in Italy, France, and England, 1534–1685* (Oxford, 2003).

35. Achille Bocchi, *Symbolicae questiones* (Bologna, 1574), Lib. I, p. VIII, with the epigram:
"Pictura gravium ostenduntur pondera rerum. Quaeque latent magis, haec per mage aperta
patent." In the attached verses dedicated to Alexander Farnese, Bocchi developed a poetics of
wisdom painting. On Bocchi and his friends Lelio Giraldi and Pietro Valeriano, see Elisabeth S.
Watson, *Achille Bocchi and the Emblem Book as Symbolic Form* (Cambridge, 1993). Of course the
figure of an angel bending over a writing man is also present in paintings of the evangelists to
indicate that the evangelists were inspired by God.

FIGURE 30. Achille Bocchi, *Symbolicae quaestiones* (Bologna, 1574), p. VIII.

aspect of the teacher-student relationship. So here again: iconographic hybridity.

The "esoteric" and "Platonizing" aspects of a search for deeper truth were not fundamentally opposed to erotic playing around. As we have seen, della Vecchia's allegory of truth was dramatically multilayered. It depicted a philosopher, who has fled into the arms of truth from an envious and mocking fate, and from that defensive position deploys a magical defensive gesture; but admittedly it also depicts a philosopher, who feels an erotic or even obscene lust for uncovering the truth. In chapter 9 we will see more clearly why della Vecchia understood this sort of intimacy so well and perhaps even felt it himself; in 1649 he painted a portrait of a man who was preaching a hermetic-Kabbalistic method for discovering the universal and fundamental structures of the world. The method appears in the guise of mathematics as Pythagorean and geometrical. And so the man had himself depicted holding a pair of compasses.

These are just the sort of compasses we find in the Bergamo allegory too. For that reason in the Accademia Carrara it is registered as an "Allegory of Architecture." It seems to me, however, that the architecture in question here is of the inner structure of the world, not some professional discipline. The poster that the subject of the 1649 portrait is holding does not refer to architecture at all. Instead it has a lot to do with philosophy. Della Vecchia was here imaging the intimate connection between the philosophical and geometrical search for truth, but that connection was accompanied by an ambivalent feeling of profanation. The quest for geometric and esoteric insights was combined with a defiling mockery of the outer circumstances—or even of the external world—which generated a serious tension between such "higher" quests and the "lower" realm of everyday life. And yet precisely those groups that were esoterically seeking to discover hidden truths also cultivated the topos of playing seriously (*serio ludere*), of disguising the deepest mysteries in foolish and grotesque stories. Edgar Wind called this stylistic method "elliptical vulgarization."[36] Bocchi's *Symbolicae quaestiones* (*Symbolic Questions*) was a book of just this sort; but Bonifacio's *Historia ludicra* (*Playful History*) also tells the "fables" of gods and mythological secrets in an amusing and sometimes erotic manner. That fact suggests that the members of the Accademia degli Incogniti, despite their well-known skepticism regarding the dogmas and institutions of the Catholic religion, provided an opportunity to be "pious" if one were prepared to think of combining obscenity with esotericism, sexual desire with a philosophical inclination, jocular quotations from the Bible with deep seriousness.

Trust and Distrust

Our analysis of della Vecchia's pictures has shown how complex the forms of representing the truth were in the early modern period and how difficult they are for us to decode. Starting there, in the rest of this chapter I'd like to suggest several perspectives that can contribute to a "cultural history of truth," with special attention to Venice in the seventeenth century. But perhaps before that we should ask if a cultural history of truth is even possible or reasonable. It would be so only if among the various representations and discussions of truth—literary, artistic, philosophical—some consistency can be found. But that's just what seems to be lacking. The motto "veritas filia temporis" was used in philosophy by those such as Giordano Bruno and Francis Bacon to illustrate the way in which one knowledge suppresses another so that hypotheses can only be provisional; but that seems to have little to do with the same motto when we find it in emblematics and art from the time of Pietro Aretino onward, in which the victory of truth over slander is illustrated.[37] The philosophical adoption of the idea was not translated into pictorial forms, as Fritz Saxl warned, and he added, "Abstract theories are the last to be illustrated."[38]

If a cultural history of truth, however, aims at more than just a list of parallel usages of topics dealing with truth, and tries rather to create an integrative discipline, how should it be conceived? To answer that question I fall back on the excellent project that Stephen Shapin launched in 1994: a social history of

36. For this model of thinking, developed in the Platonizing Second Sophistic, see Edgar Wind, *Pagan Mysteries in the Renaissance* (Baltimore, 1967), 11, 36.

37. On Bruno and Bacon, see Giovanni Gentile, "Veritas filia temporis," in idem, *Giordano Bruno e il pensiero del Rinascimento* (Florence, 1975), 225–48.

38. Saxl, "Veritas," 218.

truth. Shapin focused his social history on seventeenth-century England and the concept of trust. Trust is (in the terms also of Luhmann and Giddens) the crucial medium without which social action and truth-oriented communications are impossible.[39] Today's highly differentiated society with its many abstract institutions and systems of expertise demands trust among actors that these institutions will function, so that they will participate in them. That is true and in even greater measure for cultures of knowledge. In the early modern period, however, and this was Shapin's thesis, the relationship between trust (including credibility and *fides*) and truth and perception was structured differently. It was a basic element of a face-to-face communication between the scientist and those who had intercourse with him; and as a necessary background for learning, such communication included the workplace (e.g., the laboratory), the assistant technicians, and any materials that were put to use.[40] The key concept of the early modern culture of truth, as Shapin shows with the example of Robert Boyle and the English science of his day, was "civility," the social recognition of the gentleman as a virtuous citizen. It was only as a gentleman that a scholar or scientist was credible; his status proved that he was not a charlatan but one whose statements were reliable.

Shapin has acknowledged that his social history of truth was designed with the England of the Scientific Revolution in mind. Therefore there's something attractive in presenting my intended cultural history of truth, to some extent, as an alternative to Shapin. How was it different in Venice? My thesis is that in Venice one could present a history of truth not as focused on trust but on distrust—distrust at least to the extent that there a society formed in which masquerade and dissimulation were fundamental social dispositions, and not just superficially but structurally.[41] The "shop of truth" that I mentioned at the

39. Shapin, *A Social History of Truth*; Niklas Luhmann, *Vertrauen* (Stuttgart, 1973); Anthony Giddens, *The Consequences of Modernity* (Stanford, 1989).

40. See also the further development within the history of the body and material culture by Pamela H. Smith, *The Body of the Artisan: Art and Experience in the Scientific Revolution* (Chicago, 2004).

41. See, e.g., Arnaldo Momo, *La Carriera delle Maschere nel teatro di Goldoni Chiari Gozzi* (Venice, 1992); Gaetano Cozzi, "Della riscoperta della pace all' inestinguibile sogno di dominio," in *Storia della Venezia dalle origini alla caduta dalla Serenissima*, vol. 7: *La Venezia barocca*, ed. Gino Benzoni and idem (Rome, 1997). On the cultural atmosphere of Venice, see especially the definitive volumes: *Storia della cultura veneta*, vol. 4: *Il Seicento*, parts 1 and 2 (Vicenza, 1983–84); see generally Paolo Procaccioli and Angelo Romano, eds., *Cinquecento irregolare e capricciosa:*

start of this chapter was established to oppose the mighty and the slanderous; it pursued its goals with sophisticated, cleverly devised tactics against the mocking and malicious force of fortune—just what della Vecchia was depicting. Where knowledge is precarious, those who know must be careful and distrustful.

Distrust of claims to truth was one of the causes of the rise of skepticism in the seventeenth century, as Brendan Dooley has argued with specific reference to Venice.[42] If the facts reported in the privately financed "newsletters" (*Avvisi*) were not reliable, one simply could not trust information anymore, not even historical accounts. So it was no wonder that skepticism arose to oppose *fides*, whether it was actual religious faith or faith in history (*fides historica*). That formed the social-historical side of the story. In contrast, the intellectual history of skepticism starts with the revival of ancient Pyrrhonism and with a countermovement directed against a nascent and all-too-self-confident modern rationalism.[43]

So the problem is to find a way to help social and intellectual histories—not just of skepticism but also of truth—to collaborate. Surely that is possible only in a sort of thick description, by which I mean focusing narrowly on a specific social setting, that is, on a microhistorical or mesohistorical level, but also analyzing this culture as an ensemble of social relations and symbolic practices, so that we see the practices as an expression of specific social relations.[44] With this in mind I will examine Venetian society in the mid-seventeenth century, or more precisely the culture of libertines in that society. I propose that Venetian libertinism as cultivated by the Incogniti can become a crucial key to and focal point for understanding the way contemporary Venetians dealt with truth. In doing so we will treat libertinism the way Jean-Pierre Cavaillé does, as a philosophical culture, a composite of discourses and practices that set up

---

Eresie letterarie nell'Italia del classicismo (Rome, 1999); Patricia Eichel-Lojkine, *Excentricité et Humanisme: Parodie et détournement des codes à la Renaissance* (Paris, 2002).

42. Brendan Dooley, *The Social History of Skepticism* (Baltimore, 1999).

43. See Richard H. Popkin, *The History of Scepticism from Erasmus to Spinoza* (Berkeley, 1979).

44. See also "Zum Methodenprofil der Konstellationsforschung," in *Konstellationsforschung*, ed. Martin Mulsow and Marcelo Stamm (Frankfurt, 2005), 74–97. For an excellent example of the analysis of symbolic practices, see Peter Burke, *Städtische Kultur in Italien zwischen Hochrenaissance und Barock* (Berlin, 1986). For the concept of "thick description," see the well-known book by Clifford Geertz, *The Interpretation of Cultures: Selected Essays* (New York, 1973).

the model philosopher over against the model Christian.[45] Our survey of della Vecchia's allegories has confirmed the usefulness of this approach.

The culture of Venetian libertines as a culture of distrust? A distrust that combined both external and internal, real and symbolic elements? What could that mean? A culture of distrust developed new forms of communication that opened up different ways of understanding for members of the inner circle from those available to mere outsiders. It developed and favored ambivalent and ambiguous forms of expression. I don't mean that negatively, as if they lacked courage, but as a neutral description: simulation and dissimulation were the order of the day; equivocation and an ambiguous style of writing were cultivated along with a preference for paradoxical encomia, eulogies for repulsive things.[46] For example, Antonio Rocco impudently asserted in his academic lecture *Della Brutezza* (*On Brutality*) that both Venice and religion itself were founded on vice. He explained his provocative paradox by pointing out that if people were not immoral, neither laws nor religion would be necessary.[47] He was playing with the topos of the "happy fault," the *felix culpa*, and entertained his listeners with a witty but also highly charged lecture on the transvaluation of values.

In general the specific libertinism of this academy seems to have emerged from the distinction between appearance and reality[48] and from the then-common contempt shown for earthly things. If all the things learned from sensory experience are vain, if—as in the mock epitaphs composed by Loredano—it makes no difference whether Alexander the Great, Socrates, or some mere

45. Cavaillé, *Dis/simulations*; idem, ed., *Stratégies de l'équivoque =Cahiers du centre de recherches historiques* 33 (April 2004).

46. For a stylistic analysis of libertinism, see my "Libertinismus in Deutschland." On the paradoxical style, see Patrick Dandrey, *L'Éloge paradoxal de Gorgias à Molière* (Paris, 1997); Adolf Hauffen, "Zur Litteratur der ironischen Enkomien," *Vierteljahresschrift für Litteraturgeschichte* 6 (1893): 161–85; Jon R. Snyder, *Writing the Scene of Speaking: Theories of Dialogue in the Late Italian Renaissance* (Stanford, 1989); Letizia Panizza, "The Semantic Field of 'Paradox' in 16th and 17th Century Italy: From Truth in Appearance False to Falsehood in Appearance True. A Preliminary Investigation," in *Il vocabolario della République des Lettres*, ed. Marta Fattori (Florence, 1997), 197–220.

47. Antonio Rocco, "Della bruttezza," in *Discorsi academici*, 161.

48. Depth in place of mere appearance was emphasized in the *Discorsi academici*, 104; there the academy was also called the school of shamefacedness, arguing against fortuna and nature, and recommending not the wide, golden path but the narrow, thorny path; see Fenlon and Miller, *Song of the Soul*, 35ff. Of course the reconciliation attempted there of these Platonizing ideas with Neo-Stoicism is not persuasive.

criminal is buried in a cemetery because all fame and wisdom are transient, then an unprecedented contempt and indifference toward all secular and religious authority was warranted.[49] That would make the insulting fig fist sign admissible in allegories. Markus Völkel has shown that the Roman historian Paolo Giovio also used imitative and fictive embellishments in his historical portraits in order to carve out a space for his critiques;[50] similarly the unconventional Venetian scribblers Nicolò Franco and Antonfrancesco Doni, both of whom like Giovio had taken Lucian to heart, brilliantly deployed their rhetorical and imitative tools.[51] Simulation and dissimulation in a society like theirs, suffused with distrust and inequalities of power, served them (and later the libertines of Venice) in creating a space for polemical and blasphemous shake-ups but also for the use of comedy, jokes, and capriccios.[52] The powerful well understood the potential danger of such whimsies, as we see in Giovanni Gilio's theological critique of Michelangelo or in the case brought against Paolo Veronese because of the scurrilous ideas in his painting of the Last Supper.[53] Donatella Riposio has even called the polyvalent novels of the Incogniti "labyrinths of truth."[54] So these examples provide ways in which diverse findings in literature, art, and philosophy can be brought together: as practices that

49. Giovanfrancesco Loredano, *Il cimiterio* (Tivoli, 1646). On that, cf. Michele Battafarano, "Epitaphia ioco-seria. Loredano und Hallmann," in *Beiträge zur Aufnahme der italienischen und spanischen Literatur im Deutschland im 16. und 17. Jahrhundert*, ed. Alberto Martino (Amsterdam, 1990), 133–50.

50. Markus Völkel, *Die Wahrheit zeigt viele Gesichter: Der Historiker, Sammler und Satiriker Paolo Giovio (1486–1552) und sein Porträt Roms in der Hochrenaissance* (Basel, 1999). On the decorative practices of Vasari, see Paul Barolsky, *Why Mona Lisa Smiles and Other Tales by Vasari* (University Park, PA, 2004).

51. See Paul Grendler, *Critics of the Italian Renaissance: Anton Francesco Doni, Nicolò Franco and Ortensio Lando* (Madison, 1969); on the reception of Lucian, see Letizia Panizza, "La ricezione di Luciano da Samosata nel Rinascimento italiano: Coripheus atheorum o filosofo morale?" in *Sources antiques de l'irréligion moderne: Le relais italien (XVe–XVIIe siècles)*, ed. Jean-Pierre Cavaillé (Toulouse, 2001), 119–37.

52. See Puppi, "Ignoto Deo," 172ff.

53. Giovanni Andrea Gilio, *Dialogo nel quale si ragiona degli errori e degli abusi de' pittori circa l'istorie* (Camerino, 1564); cf. Roland Kanz, *Die Kunst des Capriccio: Kreativer Eigensinn in Renaissance und Barock* (Munich, 2002), 152–61; on Veronese, see Philipp Fehl, "Veronese and the Inquisition: A Study of the Subject Matter of the So-called 'Feast in the House of Levi,'" *Gazette des Beaux-Arts* 58 (1961): 325–54.

54. Donatella Riposio, *Il laberinto della verità: Aspetti del romanzo libertino del seicento* (Alessandria, 1995).

were not separate from politics, religion, and society but rather were operating actively in those areas.

A Complex Habitus

However: no culture of distrust can survive without elements of trust. Jan Philipp Reemtsma has shown how thoroughly trust is part of how we constitute ourselves: "The practices of social trust thus undergird the mutual assurance of 'who and what we are,' to the extent that we live under heteronomy (domination by others) and become comfortable with the status of heteronomy."[55] One could argue that inside the circle of libertines the levels of mutual trust had to be ever higher the more one wished to express immoral and blasphemous thoughts.[56] In view of our efforts to understand della Vecchia's paintings, it seemed important to contextualize them so that the social and symbolic space of both trust and distrust might become visible. In this sense describing the erotic attractions of truth—attractions that della Vecchia and the Incogniti so eagerly relished in obscenity and that became allegorically visible as the bodily contact between the philosopher and the truth—required a kind of trust. Trust was part of both a naturalistic and a platonizing utopia in which the spiritual and the corporeal did not conflict in any way.[57] Thus Baldassare Bonifacio—another member of the Incogniti—ended his *Historia ludicra* with an ambiguous eulogy for fertility. He was being only apparently conventional when he valued the "conceptions" of the spirit over those of the body, for in the same sentence he relishes a comparison with the *conceptiones inguinis* (the conceptions in the loins): "To the extent that the spirit is more sublime and more excellent than the body, to that extent are the productions of the spirit nobler than those of the loins; and so too the procreations of the

55. Jan Philipp Reemtsma, *Vertrauen und Gewalt: Versuch über eine besondere Konstellation der Moderne* (Hamburg, 2009), 63.

56. This idea could be combined with Reinhart Koselleck's argument on the development of the modern state through the "social inner space" of such societies (*Kritik und Krise* [Frankfurt, 1973]), or with Klaus Garber's emphatic theses on the democratizing role of these societies ("Sozietät und Geistes-Adel," 1:1–39).

57. Along these lines, cf. Thomas More's epicureanizing *Utopia*. And generally: Wind, *Pagan Mysteries in the Renaissance*, 86ff.

mind and intelligence are more divine than those of libidinous lusts and obscene pleasures."[58]

On the negative side, however, the aggressive and obscene gestures and the
defensive magical signs that appear in della Vecchia's allegory seem to belong
to the sphere of distrust—*veritas odium parit* (truth gives birth to hatred). The
philosopher sets himself apart from fate, from the outer world, from the ill will
of the crowd, in order to preserve his space of freedom and intimacy. Therefore
truth must always be cloaked.[59] The naturalistic utopia cannot be realized
explicitly for two reasons. First, erotic desire would lose its essential charm,
for the eros at which Loredano, Bonifacio, or Pallavicino was aiming was constituted first and foremost by transgression of the forbidden and by the unveiling of the hidden. Second, members of these circles knew very well that as
libertines they were risking arrest and the loss of honor and reputation.[60] So
a cultural history of truth in Venice has to reconstruct the contexts of censorship, reason of state, and the moral public that forced a differentiation between
secret actions and public appearances.[61]

In this way the tensions that must have dominated the Accademia degli
Incogniti become more understandable. When Loredano discussed the design
of a frontispiece in total secrecy in the backrooms of the print shop of Francesco Valvasense or handed over a text to be published that would not mention either the place or the publisher, that required circumstances of the

58. Bonifacio, *Historia ludicra*, 589: "Quanto enim animus corpori sublimior atque prae-
stantior; tanto nobiliores ingenii, quam inguinis conceptiones; tantoque diviniores mentis atque
intelligentiae, quam Venereae lubedinis [*sic*], obscoenaeque voluptatis procreationes."

59. On this topic generally, see Aleida Assmann and Jan Assmann, eds., *Schleier und Schwelle:
Geheimnis und Offenbarung* (Munich, 1998); Hans G. Kippenberg and Guy G. Sroumsa, eds.,
Secrecy and Concealment (Leiden, 1995).

60. For the comparable risk taken by those who dealt with magical writings, see the examination of police records in Federico Barbierato, "Il libro impossibile: La Clavicula Salomonis a
Venezia (sec. XVII–XVIII)," *Annali della Fondazione Luigi Einaudi* 32 (1998): 235–84; idem, *The
Inquisitor in the Hat-Shop: Inquisition, Forbidden Books and Unbelief in Early Modern Venice* (Al-
dershot, 2012).

61. See, e.g., Rosario Villari, *Elogio della dissimulazione: La lotta politica nel Seicento* (Rome,
1987); Gino Benzoni, *Gli affanni della cultura: Intelletuali e potere nell' Italia della controriforma
e barocca* (Milan, 1978); A. Enzo Baldini, ed., *Botero e la "ragion di Stato"* (Florence, 1992);
Cristina Stango, ed., *Censura ecclesiastica e cultura politica in Italia tra Cinquecento e Seicento*
(Florence, 2001). For a complex concept of cultural history, see Peter Burke, *What Is Cultural
History?* (Cambridge, 2004).

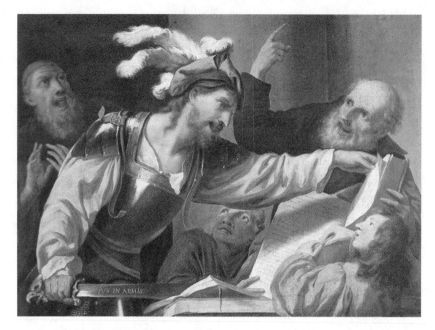

FIGURE 31. Pietro della Vecchia, *Ius in Armis*. Bernard Aikema, *Pietro della Vecchia and the Heritage of the Renaissance in Venice* (Florence, 1990), cat. 156, ill. 115.

highest mutual confidence.[62] Antonio Rocco, whose libertine views and homosexual practices had become notorious, had to be freed repeatedly from the jaws of justice by his patrons.[63] It's possible, moreover, that della Vecchia's picture of *Ius in armis* (Might makes right) reflects the forceful seizure of writings by the authorities (figure 31). We see a soldier on whose sword is inscribed the motto "Ius in armis" (a quotation from Seneca's *Hercules furens*), as he bursts into a room in which a master is teaching a student. The soldier threatens the scholar and is about to rip a page from an open book. Perhaps he wants to destroy the whole book, which, being handwritten, is still unpublished.[64]

62. See Spini, *Ricerca*, passim.

63. See ibid., 167ff.

64. *Jus in armis*: Palatinate Museum Heidelberg, No. G 702. Aikema, *Della Vecchia*, 68, interprets the picture as comic on the basis of a passage in Cicero that I do not think was the intended reference. The image is reproduced by Aikema as fig. 115 and catalogued as no. 156 (p. 139). See Seneca, *Hercules furens* 253: "ius est in armis, opprimit leges timor."

The tension, the dialectic of trust and distrust, however, also had a positive effect. Spaces were opened up for speculation by developing an innovative pictorial language open to insider allusions and latent eroticism; the masking customary at Carnival time allowed the Incogniti to experiment with new forms of stage drama; they assisted with their patronage in creating the first operas in all of Europe.[65]

We have to imagine a complex habitus, therefore, with which the Venetian libertines were operating: they cultivated a heightened sensibility for the differences between appearance and reality, surface and depth, esoteric and exoteric, spirituality and corporeality, just as we find in della Vecchia's allegory of truth. I think this habitus resulted from dealing with widely different roles, claims to truth, and forms of argumentation. In the end the multiplication of interpretive options also came in to play, caused partly by the many cultural influences in this major trading center.[66] Venice also had its own historically contingent ensemble of practices and attitudes toward authorities and traditions. For example, Venice had long distanced itself from the authority of the pope in Rome.[67] For economic reasons Venetians made special commercial and social accommodations with Jews and even Muslims.[68] When as a result of the interdict crisis (1605–7) the Jesuits were banished from Venice, the

65. See Edward Muir, "Why Venice? Venetian Society and the Success of Early Opera," *Journal of Interdisciplinary History* 26 (2005): 331–53. Muir emphasizes the paradoxical connection between spaces of distrust and spaces of trust: "Opera—despite its claims to 'serious,' as opposed to comic, theater—was from the beginning completely implicated in the Bacchanalian behaviour of Venetian carnival. The irony is that the public nature of the opera houses made true privacy possible, especially in contrast to princely courts in which the prince was the ultimate person, acknowledged by everyone. In public theaters, patrons could disguise their true identities or at least avoid full responsibility for what appeared on stage" (pp. 332ff.). On the creation of play spaces through risky maneuvering within the orbit of Aretino or Giovio, see Völkel, *Wahrheit*.

66. On the concept of pluralization, see Winfried Schulze, "Kanon und Pluralisierung in der Frühen Neuzeit," in *Kanon und Zensur*, ed. Aleida Assmann und Jan Assmann (Munich, 1987), 317–25; as well as the project of the Special Research Group in Munich (SFB), no. 573. On the aspect of trade, see Peter Burke, *Venice and Amsterdam: A Study of Seventeenth-Century Elites* (London, 1974); Brian Pullan, ed., *Crisis and Change in the Venetian Economy in the Sixteenth and Seventeenth Centuries* (London, 1968).

67. On the interdict crisis, see especially William Bouwsma, *Venice and the Defense of Republican Liberty: Renaissance Values in the Age of the Counter Reformation* (Berkeley 1968).

68. See, e.g., Pier Cesare Ioly Zorattini, "Gli ebrei nel Veneto," in *Storia della cultura veneta*, vol. 4: *Il Seicento*, part 2 (Vicenza, 1984), 281–312; and Paolo Preto, "I Turchi e la cultura veneziana del seicento," in ibid., 313–41.

anticlerical elites of Italy began to gather there.[69] Aristotelian doctrines so often favored in Padua were diminished by the Platonic preferences of the Venetian patricians.[70] And overall they developed eclectic and syncretistic practices and a certain laxness and liberality that allowed them to live on different levels at the same time. The free flow of exempla and rhetorical arguments, which were aimed more at influencing the play of forces rather than at fidelity to one historical tradition, also had a pluralizing effect. Völkel called his little book on Giovio *The Truth Has Many Faces*, and one can indeed justify many different interpretations of the portraits that Giovio drew. And as we've seen, the pictures of Pietro della Vecchia did not just reflect a complex multiplicity, for they also created new interpretations and added exponentially to this multiplicity. Here too the free and eroticized use of a pictorial language expanded at the cost of "historical accuracy," understood as iconographic adequacy. Libertinism and its techniques stood counter to the efforts of others to establish clear and authoritative conclusions. But libertinism was a parasite: it cuddled up to multiplicity and operated with and inside it.

To that extent these libertines were examples of what the French sociologist Bernard Lahire has called the "plural actor."[71] That's a person whose simultaneous actions on several levels need to be interpreted, one who operates with a variety of roles without forfeiting his identity. Of course, Lahire has in mind the (post)modern person in a pluralized society, but that should not hinder us from recognizing this type in a few intellectuals from the early modern period. Stephen Shapin's gentlemen, members of the English scientific culture of the seventeenth century, were training themselves to enact reliability and thus to reduce diversity. Their roles as members of society and as producers of scientific truth overlapped in their aim. But the freethinking intellectuals of

69. Muir, "Why Venice," 331ff. Muir speaks of the "conjunction between Venetian carnival festivity and the intellectual politics of Venetian republicanism during the two generations after the lifting of the papal interdict against Venice in 1607. This extraordinary period of relatively free speech, compared to what was possible elsewhere at the same time, might be termed the Sarpian moment, in honor of the Servite Friar Paolo Sarpi, the famous Venetian martyr to the antipapal cause. During those two generations, Venice was the one place in Italy open to criticisms of Counter-Reformation papal politics. That moment brought libertines and religious skeptics to Venice from all over Italy."

70. See Sandra Plastina, "Concordia discors: Aristotelismus und Platonismus in der Philosophie des Francesco Piccolomini," in *Das Ende des Hermetismus: Historische Kritik und neue Naturphilosophie in der Spätrenaissance*, ed. Martin Mulsow (Tübingen, 2002), 213–34.

71. Bernard Lahire, *L'homme pluriel: Les ressorts de l'action* (Paris, 1998).

Venice were different. They had to keep their roles carefully separate: Aristotelian at the university, Platonist in private; courtly in public but obscene in
intimate circles; by profession a moral philosopher but in the boudoir a champion of free love. Truth in this situation had two faces. More precisely a "pluralized" truth in this context was the effect of a constant duality; it was a self-
contradictory, witty conceitist figure, hardly understandable, full of obscene
gestures, self-denigrating as in the self-mockery of the Incogniti, creeping
toward truth like the elders toward Susanna in her bath. But at the same time,
if my interpretation of della Vecchia is right, there were certain patterns of
thought that served to hold the duality together and made diversity "livable"
and identity possible. One of them was the idea of disguising serious and high
intentions in fabulous and erotic stories; another was an imagined utopia in
which corporeal pleasure was the beginning of spiritual pleasure. A cultural
history of truth in Venice would have to trace these movements of thought in
all their diversity and in their connections to real history; it would have to scan
all the represented forms of truth, looking for the tracks left behind by the
multiplication of options and interpretations.

7

Harpocratism

GESTURES OF RETREAT

A Defensive Culture

Precarious knowledge can have defensive consequences. In this chapter we will consider a special sort of precarity: outdatedness. How does an author react if his writing does not suit the spirit of his times? If his convictions are "misplaced ideas"[1] that simply no longer fit in where he or she lives and works? Should they simply plow ahead in the face of failure, facing their readership with self-confidence? Or should they beat a retreat? Retreat does not necessarily mean abandoning one's opinions; on the contrary, it can be an indicator that one feels misunderstood and believes one's audience to be unprepared, or not yet prepared, to grasp the truth. Then one draws a line between oneself and the majority of intellectuals of one's day, a protective line that places one above the "vulgar" or run-of-the-mill world. Michel Foucault referred to Heraclitus as the type of wise man who did not find it necessary to speak; in contrast there was the type of the "parrhesiast," who speaks his mind to the public.[2] But the withdrawn author remains silent; he stays in his little groups, he merely suggests: *Sapienti sat* (A word to the wise is sufficient).[3] I will call this habitus harpocratism for reasons that will soon emerge.

---

1. Translator's note: I have profited from Pamela Selwyn's translation of an early form of this chapter, but I have modified it in places: "Harpocratism: Gestures of Retreat in Early Modern Germany," in *Common Knowledge* 16 (2010): 110–27. See Roberto Schwarz, *Misplaced Ideas: Essays on Brazilian Culture* (New York, 1992); Elías José Palti, "'The Problem of Misplaced Ideas' Revisited: Beyond the 'History of Ideas' in Latin America," *Journal of the History of Ideas* 67 (2006): 149–79.

2. Foucault, *The Courage of Truth*, 18ff.

3. Plautus, *Persa* IV, 7.

The question of whether to retreat or to take the offensive became particularly acute in Germany in the heyday of rationalism, an era marked by the great success of the philosophy of Christian Wolff. Wolff represented a philosophical style that virtually worshiped the intellect, along with a mode of argumentation based on definitions and syllogisms. During this phase, from approximately 1720 to 1760, Wolffian rationalism became the first philosophical tendency in German history to reach a broad segment of the educated public.[4] Hence people who were so old-fashioned as to refuse Wolffian rationalism were put all the more on the defensive. In the case at hand, old-fashioned is a way of labeling speculative thinkers who had the bad luck to live in the period between the Baroque and Romanticism, after the appreciation of Baroque theosophical speculations had faded out but before the appreciation of Idealist speculations had arisen. The mid-eighteenth century had no taste for speculation. If we wish to understand the prehistory of Sturm und Drang and Romanticism, however—which means the transmission of ideas between the early eighteenth and early nineteenth centuries—we cannot afford to ignore the "harpocratic" authors in between. Schelling, Baader, and Herder all profited from reading them.

But which German authors were thinking against the grain in this period? In the 1720s, one of them was a professor of Oriental languages, Hermann von der Hardt, whom the Helmstedt University authorities had forbidden in 1712 to give exegetical lectures on the Bible. In 1727 he was relieved of all academic duties except for library business. Hardt's inconvenient notion was that the Bible consists of a series of coded historical documents, and he believed that he was gradually finding the key to the interpretation of these texts by carefully studying the history, geography, and language of the ancient Israelites. Myths such as that of Adam and Eve or the Flood could, according to Hardt, be interpreted as messages about city foundings, crusades, or conquests. Demystification of the Bible was not to the liking of contemporary orthodox Lutheranism; hence Hardt's sovereign, the duke of Brunswick-Wolfenbüttel, forbade him to publish anything further in that vein. At that point Hardt burned his book manuscripts and presented the ashes to his duke.[5]

<hr />

4. See Cornelia Buschmann, "Philosophische Preisfragen und Preisschriften der Berliner Akademie 1747–1768: Ein Beitrag zur Leibniz-Rezeption im 18. Jahrhundert," *Deutsche Zeitschrift für Philosophie* 35 (1987): 779–89, especially regarding the 1747 prize question on monadology. On Wolffianism in general, see Hunter, *Rival Enlightenments*.

5. On Hardt, see Hans Möller, *Hermann von der Hardt (1660–1746) als Alttestamentler*, ed. Albrecht Möller (Norderstedt, 2021); Mulsow, *Die unanständige Gelehrtenrepublik*, chap. 1. An

Then there was the Wassertrüdingen pastor and philosopher Siegmund Ferdinand Weißmüller, who had the nerve in the 1730s to offer Pythagorean speculations on the nature of the world and to ponder how to square the circle. He enjoyed a degree of protection at the Ansbach court and so could afford to publish, in small print runs, his writings on the Zoroastrian "world of light" as composed of straight and crooked lines of force. He was ridiculed, denounced as an alchemist, and so he withdrew from normal scholarly life. The rest of his works remained in manuscript.[6]

Finally, in the 1740s, a Celle philosopher, Andreas Clavius, claimed to have solved the problems of Leibnizian monadology and of their application to physics. Clavius limited himself to hints couched in obscure allegories but also took out a newspaper advertisement enjoining the public to buy subscriptions to his book, whereupon he would divulge his solution bit by bit. He too was mocked, accused of promoting a "ducat monadology"—selling purported knowledge for money—and therefore of being a charlatan.[7]

It is easy from our present vantage point to overlook Hardt, Weißmüller, Clavius, and others like them. That's because of their harpocratism: they declined to make themselves heard and, historically speaking, they were on the losing side. History gets written by the victors, of course; but even when at some later date attempts are made to rehabilitate the victors' defeated opponents, it can be extremely difficult to find out anything about them. It is impossible to assess what roles they might have played in intellectual history if their work had been recognized and encouraged in their own time. Clavius's monadology never appeared in print, any more than Weißmüller's final system or Hardt's complete biblical commentaries did. That makes the study of the intellectual potential of such authors difficult.

Their harpocratism seems to have been quite a complex syndrome, composed of various elements the origins of which we need to understand in the double contexts of history and the sociology of knowledge. Viewed from the

English translation is planned under the title "Decorum and Disorder: The Republic of Letters, 1550–1750" with Johns Hopkins University Press.

6. See Martin Mulsow, "Pythagoreer und Wolffianer: Zu den Formationsbedingungen vernünftiger Hermetik und gelehrter 'Esoterik' im Deutschland des 18. Jahrhunderts," in *Antike Weisheit und kulturelle Praxis: Hermetismus in der Frühen Neuzeit*, ed. Anne-Charlott Trepp and Hartmut Lehmann (Göttingen, 2001), 337–96.

7. Mulsow, *Monadenlehre*, 13–20. On Clavius, see Hanns-Peter Neumann, *Monaden im Diskurs, Monas, Monaden, Monadologien (1600 bis 1770)*, Studia Leibnitiana Supplementa, no. 37 (Stuttgart, 2013).

latter perspective, the harpocratism of such authors seems a direct response to the mockery and derision they experienced. Hardt was quickly stamped an exegetical "crank," Clavius was derided in journals, and Weißmüller was satirized by Adelgunde Luise Gottsched.[8] Understood sociologically, the pattern is one of reaction rather than action. When viewed historically, however, the pattern of reaction gains in depth: we can see motives, concepts, and behaviors that point to models from the past.

The label of quietism was occasionally employed in such circles. Thus in 1721, Johann Christoph Colerus, then thirty years old and an assistant professor (an insecure "Adjunkt") in Wittenberg, informed his friend Christoph August Heumann that he was cultivating a "Quietismus literarius."[9] Colerus apparently modeled the term on such contemporary phrases as "Machiavellismus literarius."[10] We can see what he meant from the context of the letter: Colerus was maintaining peace of mind by not reading current academic journals. He felt isolated and uncomfortable in Wittenberg. He no longer trusted the protection (*patrocinium*) of his patrons Gottlieb Wernsdorf and Valentin Ernst Löscher, and he found Lutheran Orthodoxy hollow and hypocritical. For these reasons, he had pulled back: "As soon as I gave up thinking of any public position, I scarcely hesitated to choose a private life decently spent."[11] Heumann had no trouble understanding the sentiment: at the time he was working on a treatise concerning *docta ignorantia*, which he defined as abstention from the exaggerated claim that it was possible to know everything, especially in dogmatic matters.[12] In 1746 Heinrich Theodor Wagner, at the University of Gießen, wrote a dissertation entitled *De quietismo philosophico*, in which he, like Colerus, took up Miguel de Molinos's term but imbued it with a

8. Martin Mulsow, "Aufklärung versus Esoterik? Vermessung des intellektuellen Feldes anhand einer Kabale zwischen Weißmüller, Ludovici und den Gottscheds," in *Aufklärung und Esoterik: Rezeption—Integration—Konfrontation*, ed. Monika Neugebauer-Wölk (Tübingen, 2008), 331–76.

9. Johann Christoph Colerus to Christoph August Heumann, June 13, 1721, Gottfried-Wilhelm-Leibniz-Bibliothek Hannover, MS. XLII, 1915, 24.

10. Michael Lilienthal, *De machiavellismo literario sive de perversis quorundam in Republica Literaria inclarescendi artibus dissertatio historico-moralis* (Königsberg, 1713).

11. Colerus to Heumann: "Vix dubitavi, abjecta omni muneris publici cura vitam eligere privatam honestissime transigendam."

12. Christoph August Heumann, *Disputatio logica atque theologica de ignorantia docta* (Göttingen, 1721). See also Johannes C. Colerus, *De pyrrhonismo in historia ecclesiastica* (Wittenberg, 1719).

meaning that suited his own purposes. In Wagner's case, quietism meant peace of mind and freedom from emotion, attained by Stoic adherence to the principles of reason.[13]

"Harpocratism," as I am calling it, was at once broader and more specific than this *quietismus literarius* and *philosophicus*. Harpocratism involved a combination of intellectual withdrawal, political savvy, and the awareness of an "esoteric" tradition. The relationship I am seeking to understand did not arise all of a sudden but developed gradually, beginning with the late phase of humanism near the end of the sixteenth century.

Initially harpocratism was just a gesture, but we should not underestimate the role of gestures in the history of philosophy.[14] They include, for example, the gestures of the provocateur, who roundly rejects tradition and boldly suggests a new thesis; the gestures of the purist, who scorns the slightest admixture of foreign elements in a treasured doctrine; the gestures of the tolerant traditionalist, who incorporates new and divergent opinions into his or her doctrine, arguing (with a superior smile) that these views have always existed and have long since proved themselves part of the great tradition. Considered in this sense, a gesture is the expression of a philosophical or scholarly persona.[15] Sometimes personae of this sort are learned and practiced during one's education, when modes of argument, various convictions, behavioral ideals, and cultural rules are passed on. But sometimes these personae develop in reaction to specific challenges or situations. Gestures serve to 'assert and strengthen identity.

First and foremost this applies to individuals. In making a gesture, the individual does not relate just to others for he is also describing himself. He stages himself dramatically with specific actions. If we examine more closely the imagery and language that such a person uses along with the cultural patterns of his or her conflicts, we can recognize that these gestures and vocabularies can become superindividual and then generic, as some observers may

13. Andreas Boehm (praes.)/Heinrich Theodor Wagner (resp. et auctor), *De quietismo philosophico* (Gießen, 1746); Wagner republished the text in 1750. See § 7: "Ea itaque animi affectio, quae oritur ex principiis rationis tantum, et ad quietem animi perducit, quietismus philosophicus a nobis appellatur."

14. See especially Jean-Claude Schmitt, *La raison des gestes dans l'occident médiéval* (Paris, 1990).

15. See especially Hunter, "The History of Philosophy and the Persona of the Philosopher"; Condren, Gaukroger, and Hunter, *The Philosopher in Early Modern Europe*; Daston and Galison, *Objectivity*, 191–252. See also the introduction to this book, part 1.

come to recognize themselves in others' gestures. Gestures help to constitute something akin to emotional communities.[16] It would be wrong to deny philosophers and scholars—despite their image as dispassionately rational people—a grounding in emotional states capable of creating group identities. Indeed, the very sources of intellectual morality and rationality, to use the terms of Charles Taylor, may well lie in social practices and emotional structures that provide all abstract activities with meaning.[17] Those structures may well play an even greater role for authors who operate outside the intellectual mainstream than for those who need no stronger identity because they follow the crowd and thus are under no pressure to justify themselves.

Gestures may thus provide a key to locating intellectual groupings or currents in the "intellectual field."[18] The descriptive labels that we use—for example, "early Enlightenment," "Pietism," "esotericism"—tend to be adopted on the basis of "content" (whether theoretical or doctrinal). But there are intellectual conflicts that cannot be understood solely in terms of differences of content. On the contrary, differences between groups often develop over the course of a conflict that began for other reasons. If we regard intellectual groups as comprising not just theories and doctrines but also personae and cultural patterns, and moreover as existing only in their dynamic relationships to other such groups or currents, we will understand their identities much better. The gestures of a philosopher comprise his or her symbolic positioning in the field—a communication to opponents and allies alike—and at the same time a reassurance of membership in an emotional community.

In this context, we may understand harpocratism as the gesture par excellence of early modern esotericism. The harpocratic gesture does not presuppose a particular body of hermetic or cultic lore; rather it defensively creates an exclusive elite culture of silence for an initiated few. The great mass of academics had to remain, at least apparently, ignorant of such higher insights.

16. See Barbara H. Rosenwein, *Emotional Communities in the Early Middle Ages* (Ithaca, NY), 2006.

17. Charles Taylor, *Sources of the Self: The Making of the Modern Identity* (Cambridge, 1989).

18. For an application of the notion of "intellectual field" to the early modern period, see Martin Mulsow, "Literarisches und Philosophisches Feld im Thomasius-Kreis: Einsätze, Umbesetzungen, Strategien," in *Thomasius im literarischen Feld*, ed. Manfred Beetz and Herbert Jaumann (Tübingen, 2003), 103–16; Füssel, *Gelehrtenkultur als symbolische Praxis*.

Harpocrates

But why call this attitude harpocratism? As the Egyptian sun god Horus, Harpocrates represented the god as a child. There are numerous images showing him placing his index finger to his lips—a symbol, according to Plutarch, of insight into divine matters. But Plutarch misinterpreted the finger gesture as a profound gesture of secrecy, even though in Egypt it had alluded merely to the god's childhood.[19] Nevertheless, Harpocrates became a touchstone among authors who venerated esoteric secrecy and silence.[20] One could even write a history of academic silence in the early modern period by tracing the allusions to Harpocrates.[21] Interest in ancient portrayals of him emerged with the rise of antiquarianism in the sixteenth century and peaked in the later seventeenth century. When Athanasius Kircher dealt with Harpocrates in his 1652 *Oedipus aegyptiacus*, it was as part of a dispute with Goropius Becanus and Lorenzo Pignoria over canopic jars in which the entrails of mummified corpses were separately stored.[22] Some of these canopic jars featured depictions of Harpocrates.[23] Gnostic engraved gems also portray the god, as do some terra-cottas and bronze statuettes.[24] Kircher believed that these representations confirmed the god as an emblem of silence.

19. Plutarch, *De Iside et Osiride*; see also Iamblichus, *De mysteriis Aegyptiorum* VII.2. On Harpocrates, see Hans Bonnet, *Lexikon der ägyptischen Religionsgeschichte*, 3rd ed. (Berlin, 2000), 273–75; Benjamin Hederich, *Gründliches mythologisches Lexikon* (Leipzig, 1770; Darmstadt, 1996), cols. 1191–95.

20. See, e.g., the title page engraving in Hermann von der Hardt, *Aenigmata prisci orbis: Jonas in luce in historia Manassis et Josiae* (Helmstedt, 1723); von der Hardt transferred Harpocrates to the Homeric garden of Alcinous with its apples. In 1603 the Calvinist politician Hippolytus a Collibus composed a work, *Harpocrates sive de recta silendi ratione*; in 1617 Remacle de Vaulx wrote *Harpocrates divinus seu altissimum de fine mundi silentium*; in 1665 Michael Schirmer produced *Christlichen Harpocrates*; and in 1676 the ancient historian from the Netherlands, Gisbert Cuper, published a learned antiquarian treatise entitled *Harpocrates*. See note 28 in this chapter.

21. Benthien, *Barockes Schweigen*.

22. Goropius Becanus (Jan van Gorp), *Hieroglyphica*, lib. VIII, in *Opera* (Antwerpen, 1580); Lorenzo Pignoria, *Mensa Isaica, qua sacrorum apud Aegyptios ratio et simulacra subiectis tabulis aeneis simul exhibentur et explicantur* (1605; Amsterdam, 1670).

23. Athanasius Kircher, *Oedipus aegyptiacus*, 3 vols. (Rome, 1652), 1:212–14. For a recent discussion of such vessels depicting Harpocrates, see Sandra Sandri, *Har Pa-Chered (Harpokrates): Die Genese eines ägyptischen Götterkindes* (Louvain, 2006).

24. Kircher, *Oedipus aegyptiacus*, vol. 3 (Rome, 1654).

FIGURE 32. Harpocrates images. Jacques Spon, *Miscellanea eruditae antiquitatis* (Leiden, 1685), 18 (Mulsow's copy).

Not long after that dispute, a brief scholarly piece by Jacques Spon, a learned physician in Lyons, used materials gathered by Nicolas-Claude Fabri de Peiresc to describe ancient portrayals of Harpocrates (figure 32).[25] In a mode of studying antiquity that he termed "archaeography," Spon drew upon eight genres of source for mutual illumination: coins, inscriptions, architectural remains, pictorial representations, engraved stones, marble tablets,

25. Jacques Spon, *Miscellanea eruditae antiquitatis* (Leiden, 1685), 16–20, at 17: "a me inter Peireskii schedas repertis." On Peiresc as antiquarian, see Peter N. Miller, "The Antiquary's Art of Comparison: Peiresc and Abraxas," in *Philologie und Erkenntnis*, ed. Ralph Häfner (Tübingen, 2001), 57–94.

manuscripts, and objects of everyday use.[26] The items Spon examined regarding Harpocrates were mostly engraved stones, as they had been also for Kircher, but they included statues as well. Spon was particularly interested in the "pantheist" attributes of many such statues: his interest was in the typically late antique "henotheist" composition of a divine figure who had the characteristics of all other gods.[27] As early as 1676 the Dutch scholar Gisbert Cuper wrote an entire monograph on Harpocrates inspired by a small silver portrait depicting him as the sun.[28]

This "antiquarianization" of the image of Harpocrates did not prevent Plutarch's interpretation of the god from continuing on its own path.[29] Antiquarianism ran parallel but not counter to this path, which was first and foremost political. It was in the political understanding of late humanist Tacitism (the milder version of Machiavellianism) that secrecy assumed a new meaning (figure 33). What interested people now was no longer some mystical arcanum but rather the secular practice of distinguishing between communication and noncommunication in the modern state.[30] Hence it was a jurist and politician, Ippolito de' Colli (of the Electoral Palatinate), who first adopted the harpocratic motif of silence as a representation of prudent conduct.[31] Sometime

26. Spon, *Miscellanea*, praefatio.

27. Ibid., 16: "Hic divinitatis radios diversimode creatis rebus impressos, aut potius Divinitatis participatione divina effecta rerum simulacra, Deorum quoque nominibus insigniri voluerunt. Nec absque ratione et energia Sacrae eorum Theologiae Antistites Diis per ipsos vocatis, quaedam propria dedicata et consecrata fuere, uti Vulcano Pyramides, Mercurio Hermae, Apollini sacri Obelisci, ut de reliquis taceam, ea marmoreis, metallicisque formis aut aliis sculptilibus vel etiam portalibus annulis gemmisve, affabre non minus quam mystice imprimentes." On henotheism, see F. Max Müller, *Lectures on the Origin and Growth of Religion: As Illustrated by the Religions of India* (London, 1878).

28. Gisbert Cuper, *Harpocrates, sive explicatio imagunculae argenteae antiquissimae, sub Harpocratis figura ex Aegyptiorum instituto Solem repraesentantis* (Amsterdam, 1676). This work went unnoticed by Spon, who may have already completed his research by that time.

29. Translator's note: Mulsow uses the term "antiquarianization" to describe giving a picture or some other theme a learned perspective that sets it in the cultural history of the ancient world, thus removing it from immediate relevance to the contemporary world.

30. On dissimulation and "political" behavior in the context of the early modern state, see Peter Burke, "Tacitism, Scepticism, and Reason of State," in *The Cambridge History of Political Thought*, ed. James H. Burns and Mark Goldie (Cambridge, 1991), 479–98; Frühsorge, *Der politische Körper*.

31. On Colli, see Klaus Conermann, "Hippolytus a Collibus: Zur Ars politica et aulica im Heidelberger Gelehrtenkreis," in *Europäische Hofkultur im 16. und 17. Jahrhundert*, 3 vols., ed. August Buck (Hamburg, 1981), 3:693–700; Cornel A. Zwierlein, "Heidelberg und 'Der Westen'

FIGURE 33. Political Harpocrates. Athanasius Kircher, *Principis Christiani Archetypon politicum* (Amsterdam, 1672), from Claudia Benthien, *Barockes Schweigen: Rhetorik und Performativität des Sprachlosen im 17. Jahrhundert* (Munich, 2006), 51.

after 1593, Colli must have seen the picture by Jan Müller entitled *Harpokrates Philosophus, Silentii Deus* (*Harpocrates the Philosopher, the God of Silence*), showing the head of a scholar with a finger pressed against his lips (figure 34). Colli chose this image as the model for the frontispiece engraving in his book *Harpocrates sive de recte silendi ratione* (*Harpocrates, or the Right Reason for Remaining Silent*).[32] As in his earlier work on the ideal courtier and politician, Colli sought to demonstrate in this text, written in the Senecan style popularized by Lipsius, the uses of silence in social and political action. A colleague of Colli's, Bartholomäus Keckermann, wrote a comparable work in 1608.[33]

Some decades later, in the work of Athanasius Kircher, Harpocrates became a symbol not only for "politicians" but also for devotees of hermetic knowledge. Kircher explained canopic vessels and statues but also used his learning to achieve a more precise description of the Harpocrates symbol for prudent

---

um 1600," in *Späthumanismus und reformierte Konfession*, ed. Christoph Strohm et al. (Tübingen, 2006), 27–92, esp. 76–86.

32. De' Colli, *Harpocrates sive de recta silendi ratione* (Leiden, 1603). See the illustration in Benthien, *Barockes Schweigen*, 67.

33. Kühlmann, *Gelehrtenrepublik und Fürstenstaat*, 243–55.

FIGURE 34. Jan Müller, *Harpocrates*. Claudia
Benthien, *Barockes Schweigen: Rhetorik und
Performativität des Sprachlosen im 17. Jahrhundert*
(Munich, 2006), 67.

behavior: "He presses his finger to his lips because wisdom is acquired not
amidst noise and clamor, but in silence, solitude, isolation and with a contempt for all earthly matters, which is also splendidly expressed by the night
owl, the nocturnal and solitary animal."[34]

Kircher was also the author in whom another historical meaning of harpocratism surfaced: the "esoteric." The Egyptian god became a symbol not just
for "politicians" but also for the adherents of higher and sacred knowledge.
This interpretation of Harpocrates was also particularly evident in the *Symbolicae quaestiones* of Achille Bocchi, in which Harpocrates is identified with
Hermes. Many gods were associated with Harpocrates, as we have seen, in

34. Athanasius Kircher, *Principis Christiani Archetypon politicum sive Sapientia Regina-
trix* . . . (Amsterdam, 1672), 79: "Digito labra premit, quia sapientia non inter strepitus et tumultus, sed silentio, solitudine, secessu, et omnium rerum terrenarum comtemptu comparatur;
quae per noctuam nocturnum et solitarium animal pulchre indicantur."

many ancient "pantheistic" depictions, but there is a good deal more to Bocchi's deliberately obscure emblem book. Here the Hermes of mythology is also Hermes Trismegistos, and Bocchi's insistence on silence aimed at all who were privy to the secrets of Creation.[35] "The mind," Bocchi writes, "is the ornament of Man, the likeness of the divine mind, which is never exposed to the sensual world. Whosoever desires to know this mind must [first] know himself, . . . and above all consult the Egyptian Harpocrates. *He who has partaken of the divine mind must keep his mind far removed from the senses.*"[36]

Carlo Ginzburg, in his essay "High and Low," shows how complicated the relationships were between "higher" knowledge and the common folk, scholarly innovation and religious transgression, self-empowerment and prohibition, during this era. Invoking such mottoes as *Noli altum sapere, sed time* (Do not wish to know; instead thou shalt fear) and *Altum sapere periculosum* (Knowledge of high things is dangerous), Ginzburg shows that the "political language" of emblems was central to marking the limits and possibilities in this bewildering field.[37]

This insight can also be applied to the case of harpocratism. The Harpocrates figures of Bocchi and Kircher belong to a language of exclusiveness through citation and imagery, whose motto of silence was also evidence of membership in a knowledge elite. Such emblems, whether hermetic and esoteric or "merely" ethical and political, had an impact in many fields and often in unexpected contexts. In a pioneering monograph of 1964, Albrecht Schöne showed the extent to which emblems—perhaps the most important pictorial medium of the early modern era—influenced Baroque thought, demonstrating also that many passages of seventeenth-century drama cannot be understood unless one recognizes them as paraphrases of emblems.[38] The same might be said of the early modern habitus I am calling harpocratism.

35. Achille Bocchi, *Symbolicae quaestiones de universo genere, quas serio ludebat* (Bologna, 1555). On Bocchi, see Watson, *Achille Bocchi*.

36. Bocchi, *Symbolicae quaestiones*, CXXXIII: "Mens decus est hominis, divinae mentis imago, Non ullis unquam sentibus exposita. Noscere qui cupit hanc ipsum se noscat oportet. In primis, Paharium, & consultat Harpocratem. Revocanda mens a sensibus, divina cui mens obtigit."

37. Carlo Ginzburg, "High and Low: The Theme of Forbidden Knowledge in the Sixteenth and Seventeenth Centuries," *Past and Present* 73 (1976): 28–41.

38. Schöne, *Emblematik und Drama im Zeitalter des Barock*.

Hardt, Weißmüller, Clavius

If we look for the concrete forms of this habitus—which, as I suggested, comprised "political" thought, esotericism, and antiquarian learning—we encounter a number of people in the eighteenth century who did retreat from the busy field of academe. The scholars to whom I refer ceased publishing altogether or announced that henceforth they would print their works only for selected readers or on request. This circumstance introduces a peculiar phenomenon in the history of publishing. It runs counter, on the one hand, to the development of the early modern "public sphere" as described by Jürgen Habermas.[39] Instead of increasing publicity, here is a process of exclusion by deliberate nonpublicity. On the other hand, the phenomenon represents a hybrid of aristocratic behavior and market orientation. The early modern nobility were proud of not making common cause with common folk by means of the printing press: aristocrats who wrote poetry, for instance, felt no need to publish it (indeed, doing so was very much frowned upon).[40] This insistence on exclusivity is very different from another development in the book market, which in the mid-eighteenth century made it commonplace to solicit subscriptions before venturing to print books.[41] Thus when harpocratic authors announced in newspapers that they would publish their works only in small editions for paying subscribers, the procedure seemed a hybrid of pseudoaristocratic superiority and shifty business. People accordingly suspected charlatanry and warned against such practices.[42]

The accusation of charlatanry, however, offers little help when we are trying to understand the motives and complex habitus of the protagonists. Only by looking at the precise circumstances of a given case can we break through the stereotype. We can begin with Hermann von der Hardt. He loved riddles, oracles, and all manner of arcana. From experience of the Pietists, he was familiar with the game of drawing lots from a box, slips of paper inscribed with biblical verses as mottoes for the day or for a life situation.[43] By 1709 his patron

39. Habermas, *The Structural Transformation of the Public Sphere.*

40. On early modern nobility and its customs, see Otto Brunner, *Adeliges Landleben und europäischer Geist* (Salzburg, 1949); Ronald Asch, *Der europäische Adel im Ancien Regime* (Cologne, 2001).

41. On subscriptions, see Robert Darnton, *The Business of Enlightenment: A Publishing History of the Encyclopédie, 1775–1800* (Cambridge, MA, 1979).

42. See the reference in note 7 in this chapter.

43. I am grateful to Shirley Brückner, who is working on these Pietist oracle practices, for this reference. See Shirley Brückner, "Losen, Däumeln, Nadeln, Würfeln: Praktiken der Kontingenz

FIGURE 35. Hermann von der Hardt, *Justitia* and
Silentium. Herzog August Library Wolfenbüttel,
Ms. Extrav. 119, fol. 30r.

Duke Rudolf August of Wolfenbüttel had been dead for five years, and since
then Hardt had become increasingly distrustful of the political world. In that
year he showed the two traveling students his cabinet of harpocratic mottoes
and emblems, initiating them into what he called his "oracle." One of these
students, Conrad Zacharias Uffenbach, wrote that he "led . . . us to a table
upon which stood a square chest, about a cubit wide, painted all over, whose
exterior he showed us with great pomp, after removing a leather covering from
it; thereupon we were supposed to perceive on the outer lid all the depths of
sapientia and *politica*, indeed of everything in the world. And this consisted of
two emblems." The first emblem showed a landscape as a symbol of *Justitia*,
while the second showed "nothing but the night, with the stars visible in the
sky, and the moon shining on the water, and bore this motto: *Silentium*" (figure 35.)[44] *Justitia* and *Silentium*—these two concepts encompassed Hardt's

als Offenbarung im Pietismus," in *Spiele der Bürgerlichkeit*, ed. Ulrich Schädler and Ernst Strouhal
(Vienna, 2011), 247–72; eadem, "Die Providenz im Zettelkasten: Divinatorische Praktiken in der
pietistischen Frömmigkeit," in *Geschichtsbewusstsein und Zukunftserwartung in Pietismus und Er-
weckungsbewegung*, ed. Wolfgang Breul and Jan Carsten Schnurr (Göttingen, 2013), 351–66.

    44. Conrad Zacharias von Uffenbach, *Merkwürdige Reisen durch Niedersachsen, Holland und
England*, 3 vols. (Ulm, 1753), 1:192.

worldview, as even the inscription on his gravestone testifies.[45] In a utopia, Hardt would say, a community is ruled by justice and all is right with the world; but in reality there is no justice and all is night. In the consequent darkness, one "must be silent and dissimulate."[46] At which point, the hermeneutics of indirect speech, or of "political" tactics, took effect, along with symbolic historical narratives. It was in this way that Hardt's *Aenigmata prisci orbis* (1723) came into being. It consists of riddles from early times, when the "custom . . . was to relate in emblems the stories of great lords, and most gracefully leave them behind for the memory of mindful descendants."[47]

As early as 1706, right after the death of his patron Duke Rudolph August, on the occasion of a party for Duke Anton Ulrich, von der Hardt handed his new duke a little handwritten "comedy," an emblem book full of allusions and enigmas. The messages that he wanted to convey through such many-layered, polysemic means were ambivalent. They congratulate the duke but also revealed that von der Hardt was inevitably behaving with the calm that he had probably been advised to maintain in audiences. Indeed, his very first emblem shows Harpocrates while later emblems developed other figures of silence (figure 36).[48]

In the following years Professor von der Hardt came under increasing pressure. Because of his rationalistic biblical exegesis, in 1712 the university board of trustees forbade him to give exegetical lectures anymore. By 1727, as I mentioned earlier, he was stripped of all academic duties except for work in the library and was then sent into retirement. Hardt's book from 1723, with its explicit title *Aenigmata prisci orbis* (*Mysteries of the First Sphere*), begins with an emblematic image of Harpocrates in the garden of the Hesperides (figure 37). He stands before a baroque garden with a classical villa in the background and statues along the edges. Behind him, geometrically ordered rows of delicate plants grow upward, supported by stakes. Four of the rows of plants are marked Orpheus, Homer, Hesiod, and Nonnus. Harpocrates, depicted as a boy with a cornucopia overflowing with flowers, stands in the foreground making the gesture of

45. "Hic jacet homo ex terra et terra ex homine pro justitia et silentio ex fide et caritate ut resurgat homo ex terra ad vitam aeternam pro Dei potentia et gratia ex verbo et promissione." See Möller, *Hermann von der Hardt*, 99.

46. Ibid.

47. Hardt, *Aenigmata prisci orbis*, 761.

48. Lower Saxony State Archives, Wolfenbüttel, 37 Alt 378, fol. 225r.

FIGURE 36. Hermann von der Hardt, *Harpocrates.*
Herzog August Library Wolfenbüttel,
Ms. Extrav. 119, fol. 5r.

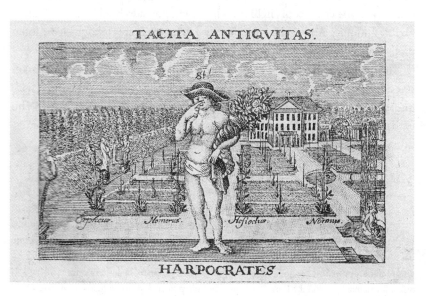

FIGURE 37. Hermann von der Hardt, *Aenigmata prisci orbis* (Helmstedt, 1723),
title page (Mulsow's copy).

silence.[49] The onomatopoeic "St!" (Shh!) is written above him. The boy is wearing only a loincloth and hat. The caption over the image in Hardt's book reads *Tacita antiquitas* (mute antiquity). The reverse side takes up the harpocratic theme, listing several quotations from classical authors about Alcinous and the garden of the Hesperides, under the heading "Harpocrates in Alcinoi horto."[50] The Hesperides were nymphs who tended a garden of the gods; in the *Odyssey*, Alcinous, king of the Phaeacians, offers hospitality to Odysseus, in a palace with a wonderful garden like that of the Hesperides. The words under the list refer again to classical antiquity: "Most fecund antiquity, knowing, golden."

What was Hardt trying to say by associating Harpocrates with the garden of the Hesperides, and why did he bring the god together with Alcinous? In the allegorical tradition, the garden of the Hesperides with its golden apples was considered a coded reference to sublime matters (such as eternal youth and fertility). Alcinous and his garden were also prominent in the allegories of Homer among the Stoics and neo-Platonists.[51] Since Hardt writes of "most fecund antiquity," the garden must symbolize antiquity itself. The garden of antiquity contains fruitful pearls of wisdom, if one can only "pick" (i.e., decipher) them. In Hardt's mysterious little image, Harpocrates succeeds, like another Hercules, in picking these fruits. With the cornucopia in his hand, this Harpocrates holds the key to interpreting antiquity. And yet he is prudent and does not simply relinquish the interpretive key. Instead his gesture signals that he knows how to be discreet.

The image is playful, but Hardt ends his *Aenigmata prisci orbis* with a darker one. Placing himself in the role of Moses in Egypt, he bitterly complains (with quotations from Acts and Exodus), "But they understood not" and "Who made thee . . . a judge over us?"[52] We could easily imagine that this last question was intended for the duke of Brunswick-Wolfenbüttel.

49. The cornucopia and hat show that Hardt modeled this figure on the "pantheist" Harpocrates depictions that one could find, for example, in Spon's antiquarian work, *Miscellanea*, 18.

50. "Virgilius: Pomaque & Alcinoi sylvae [Georgica II 87]. Ovidius: Praebeat Alcinoi poma benignus ager [Amores I, X 56]. Plinius: Antiquitas nihil prius mirata est, quam hesperidum hortos & regum Adonidis & Alcinoi [Naturalis historia XXVII 19]; Papinius: Quid bifera Alcinoi referam pomaria? vosque, / Qui nunquam vacui prodistis in aethera rami? [Silvae I, II 81ff.]; Juvenalis: Illa jubebit / Poma dari, quorum solo pascaris odore, / Qualia perpetuus Phaeacum autumnus habebat [Sat. V. Parasiti]."

51. See, in general, Robert Lamberton, *Homer the Theologian: Neoplatonist Allegorical Reading and the Growth of the Epic Tradition* (Berkeley, 1986).

52. Hardt, *Aenigmata prisci orbis*, 792: "At illi non intellexerunt [Acts 7:25] / Quis te nobis constituit iudicem? [Exod. 2:14; Acts 7:27]."

Hardt's use of emblems, riddles, and harpocratic gestures was not really esotericism in the hermetic sense but rather a consequence of his rationalist biblical exegesis. Because he was seeking the origins of holy writ in completely earthly conditions, he had to encrypt his interpretations so that only he could decrypt them. Hardt was also a devotee of rabbinical hermeneutics, according to which the object of interpretation and the circumstances of the interpreter are mutually illuminating. This reciprocal relationship virtually generates riddles and masquerades, much as in the Baroque roman à clef.[53]

Do these generalizations apply also to Weißmüller? Sigmund Ferdinand Weißmüller loved not just the symbols and gestures of esotericism but also its themes and contents (but not uninterruptedly). He had been a student of the great Christian Wolff and had thoroughly studied Leibniz and Newton. The Pythagoreanism he developed was conceived as a solution to current problems in monadology and the natural philosophy of light, space, gravitation, and cohesion. Thus we should not speak here simply of esotericism or hermeticism but perhaps of "rational esotericism."[54]

On the other hand, Weißmüller's participation in the latest philosophical discourse did not prevent him from rummaging deeply among the resources of self-important symbolism when, in 1736, he undertook to summarize his system in just a few pages, using insinuation more than explicit argumentation. He claimed to have solved the old mystery of the tetractys. At the end of his *Analyse des êtres simples et réels*, in a polemic intended to modify or transcend Leibniz's theory of monads, Weißmüller cites the riddle "Aelia Laelia Crispis," taken from the inscription on a tombstone in Bologna.[55] This was an epitaph

53. On the Baroque roman à clef in Germany, see Elida Maria Szarota, *Lohensteins Arminius als Zeitroman: Sichtweisen des Spätbarock* (Bern, 1970).

54. On this term ("vernünftige Esoterik," "vernünftige Hermetik"), see Mulsow, *Monadenlehre*, 148–62; Monika Neugebauer-Wölk, ed., *Aufklärung und Esoterik* (Hamburg, 1999); Monika Neugebauer-Wölk, ed., *Aufklärung und Esoterik. Rezeption-Integration-Konfrontation* (Tübingen, 2008).

55. Weißmüller, *Analyse des êtres simples et réels* (Nuremberg, 1736), 27. For an alchemical interpretation of the inscription, see, e.g., Nicolas Barnaud, *Commentariolum in aenigmaticum quoddam epigraphum Bononiae studiorum, ante multa secula marmoreo lapidi inscuptum* (Leiden, 1597); Athanasius Kircher, *Oedipus Aegyptiacus*, pars altera, pp. 418–20: "Primum aenigma chimicum eiusque explicatio." In general, see Nicola Muschitiello, ed., *Aelia laelia crispis: La pietra di Bologna* (Bologna, 1989). The alchemical context may also explain the reports concerning Weißmüller that he claimed that one might use six hundred dog souls to synthesize one human soul.

that intrigued alchemists and hermeticists, and so it "marks" Weißmüller's intellectual position. To be sure, he preferred to call himself not a "hermeticist" or an "alchemist" but a "Platonic-Pythagorean philosopher."

Weißmüller deployed esoteric imagery and gestures again in a work of 1742: "After the veil of Isis has been lifted, and after nearly seven years of reflection, the geometrical Platonic system now radiates in the light."[56] All these concepts and motifs became for him modes of exclusiveness: Weißmüller used them to set himself apart from the industrious Wolffians and their desire for publicity. At the same time, Weißmüller's uses indicate the caution he needed to exercise given the unorthodox content of his philosophy. The result was perhaps typical of the courtly culture of allusion he was familiar with in Ansbach. "This is sufficient for the wise, but much too much for others," he writes in his brief *Specimen definitionum philosophiae pythagoricae*.[57] And he let Leipzig know that he was "suppressing" his virtually complete *Systema Platonicum*. Weißmüller moreover did not send his *Salomoneis* to press. Clearly, he was in no hurry to publish.[58]

56. Weißmüller, *Speculum Dei fabricantis in septenario* (n.p., 1742), 4: "Post Isidis peplum revelatum, et septem paene annorum meditationes, geometrica jam luce radiat Systema Platonicum."

57. Weißmüller, *Specimen definitionum philosophiae pythagoricae* (Frankfurt, 1736), fol. B2v: "Sapientibus satis, aliis forte nimium!"

58. Weißmüller to Johann Heinrich Wolff, March 6, 1740, ed. in Mulsow, "Aufklärung versus Esoterik," 374–76: "Meanwhile I am suppressing my almost finished *Systema Platonicum* until the time is right, and instead I am amusing myself with a German heroic poem called *Salomonäes*." By 1742 Weißmüller appears to have pulled back to holding that he would communicate his system to those who specifically asked to see it, in other words to avoid publishing it broadly and instead to prefer a halfway publication among sympathizers. Cf. *Speculum Dei*, 4: "Our famous Wolff has himself tacitly suggested the most important men of Britannia were extremely keen judges of matters having to do with ancient philosophy. Those men would have very much liked the meditations presented here, as he openly testified. Now that the veil of Isis has been lifted, and after nearly seven years of reflection, the geometrical Platonic system now radiates in the light, which anyone who wants and does not regret the desire can request from me. The shadow of true wisdom pays no attention to jeering and envy, so live well and please send [your] support, corrections, additions, and criticisms [to me] in Ansbach." The original read: "Summos Britanniae viros rerum, quae antiquam Philosophiam spectant, judices acutissimos praecipue tacite suggessit ipsemet illustris noster WOLFIUS, quorum ad palatum ejusmodi maxime meditationes fore, coram nobis et ingenue testatus est. Post Isidis peplum revelatum, et septem paene annorum meditationes, geometrica jam luce radiat Systema Platonicum, quod a me, qui volet, nutu non poenitendo, petat. Cavillationes atque invidiam cum ignoret verae vel umbra

Even though Weißmüller may have needed to portray himself this way in order to dissociate himself from other scholars, his peculiar habitus served to irritate others, who thought he was being self-congratulatory and self-important. "With this he is handing over to all the geometers, physicians, and great minds of Europe the key to a cabinet stuffed with mind-boggling curiosities," said one reviewer, caricaturing Weißmüller: "But he withdraws at last, the modest satisfaction of having infinitely improved and expanded music, metaphysics, and theology, and of foreseeing the new sciences that he has thereby brought to light."[59] His withdrawal inevitably provoked mockery, and in 1739 Luise Gottsched wrote a satire in the style of Christian Ludwig Liscow, portraying Weißmüller as a backward and naive preacher.[60] Her satire was inspired by a venomous polemical exchange between Weißmüller and the Wolffian Carl Günther Ludovici, a friend of the Gottscheds. Alchemical obscurantism was only one of the accusations raised against Weißmüller.

When one considers the errors he made in his use of contemporary scholarship and mathematics, the negative response was at least partially justified. But this scorn for scholarly hubris was just part of the fashionable derision of pedants and charlatans, as we see in the satires of Christian Ludwig Liscow, which took off from Swift, Mencke, and Saint-Hyacinthe. Luise Gottsched adapted Liscow's schema for her satire on Weißmüller. His response was to stop publishing altogether. "Matters of the spirit must be judged only by the spirit," Weißmüller wrote to Johann Heinrich Wolff with regard to Ludovici, "for which reason Harpocrates is silent until it pleases divine wisdom to shine a brighter light upon vanished knowledge."[61] Wounded, Weißmüller withdrew, writing only "for the drawer," or occasionally sending his findings to the academies of Europe in epistolary form. He promised to provide the elaborated system of his special Pythagoreanism to those who specifically wrote requesting it, making it available to "anyone who wants [it] and does not regret his desire." "The shadow of true wisdom pays no attention to jeering and envy,

---

sapientiae; valete, favete, corrigite, pergite, et monenda, si placet, Onoldum mittite!" We find similar behavior in Clavius and Schade; see Mulsow, *Monadenlehre*.

59. Review of Weißmüller's *Analyse* in the *Leipziger Zeitungen* (1756), 75th Stück, pp. 665–72.

60. *Horatii als eines wohlerfahrenen Schiffers treu-meynender Zuruf an alle Wolfianer, über die Worte der XIV. Ode des 1.Buchs Horatii betrachtet. Wobey zugleich die neuere Wolfische Philosophie gründlich wiederlegt wird, von X.Y.Z. dem Jüngeren*, 1739. On this anonymous piece, see Mulsow, "Aufklärung versus Esoterik?"

61. Weißmüller to Wolff, 375.

so live well and please send [your] support, corrections, additions, and criticisms [to me] in Ansbach."[62]

Weißmüller was not the only one to wrestle with the physical problem of Leibniz's monads. In 1747, Andreas Clavius also took up the problem in a response to the Royal Academy of Berlin's prize question on monadology.[63] But Clavius's two contributions to the competition were unusual—written in code and presented under the "emblem" of Odysseus's return home after twenty years of wandering. Thus had philosophy also returned, after two thousand years, to its home: the court of Alcinous (standing for the Brandenburg court of Frederick William I in Berlin, where Leibniz had established the Prussian Academy of Sciences). Thus Clavius explained his main point about modern philosophy in the same cryptic terms of antique mythology that von der Hardt had used.

Clavius had emphasized the heroic stance of intellectuals pushed onto the defensive in his *Philosophiae antiquissimae et recentissimae prodromus* of 1741: "Truth may be kept down but cannot be crushed; abuse makes it stronger, or else there would be nothing but lies."[64] Here he clearly had in mind the emblematic motto *Veritas premitur non opprimitur* (Truth can be kept down but not crushed) (figure 38).[65] To which he added another motto, *premendo virescit* (under pressure it grows stronger), alluding to a doctrine of ancient natural philosophy known as "antiperistasis."[66] According to Aristotle and others, when heat is surrounded by cold it draws together and intensifies. The motto *Virtus laesa magis lucet* (When wounded, virtue shines all the more brightly) made a similar point.[67]

Like Hardt and Weißmüller (and also Theodor Ludwig Lau, whom we met in earlier chapters), Clavius was clearly influenced by emblematic thinking, which pretended to argue that a defensive position was actually better. Such

62. Weißmüller, *Speculum Dei.*

63. On the question, see Buschmann, "Philosophische Preisfragen."

64. Andreas Clavius, *Philosophiae antiquissimae et recentissimae prodromus* (Celle, 1741), § 210, p. 213: "Veritas se premi, verum non opprimi sinit, & premendo virescit, alias esset nihil, mendacium."

65. An emblem with this motto is in Gabriel Rollenhagen, *Selectorum emblematum centuria secunda* (Utrecht, 1608), no. 38.

66. On antiperistasis, see Martin Mulsow, *Frühneuzeitliche Selbsterhaltung: Telesio und die Naturphilosophie der Renaissance* (Tübingen, 1998), 47–103.

67. An emblem with this motto can be found, e.g., in Mathias Holtzwart, *Emblematum tyrocinia: Sive picta poesis latinogermanica* (Strasbourg, 1581), no. 40.

FIGURE 38. "Veritas premitur non
opprimitur." Gabriel Rollenhagen,
Selectorum emblematum centuria secunda
(Utrecht, 1608), no. 38.

modes of argument or pseudo-argument are highly illuminating for any cultural history of truth.[68] In his book, Clavius mentions two bulwarks against the enemies of truth, the first of these being: "Truth—unlike untruth—forces itself upon no one, but prefers to withdraw; from enemies its flight is all the quicker." This *inimicis fuga est celerior* is also based on vitalist imagery and on emblems of natural philosophy. "The truth," Clavius continues, "is aware of being a boon to mankind. For that reason, truth responds to the objections of its opponents with silence, in order to avoid destroying an opponent unworthy of its benefactions."[69] Once again, harpocratism was a last resort: only silence could maintain a scholar's dignity and honor.[70] Aristocratic aloofness also

68. See in addition chapter 6.

69. Clavius, *Prodromus*, 214: "Veritas sese nemini obtrudit, uti mendacium, sed potius cedit, & inimicis fuga est celerior. . . . Veritas sibi suimet est conscia, se esse hominibus beneficio. Hinc veritas ad inimicorum objectiones respondet silentio, ne inimicos beneficiis indignos obruat."

70. For emblems that depict Harpocrates and have the motto *Fuge, tace, quiesce* (which combines withdrawal with remaining silent), see Hadrianus Junius (Adriaan de Jonge),

marked this gesture of withdrawal and defined Clavius's second defense: "Truth has erected the second bulwark prudently, sagaciously, and wisely. For truth is prudence, sagacity, and wisdom itself."[71] For the first, harpocratism was an honor-based defensive habitus, but for the second bulwark it represented an offensive *prudentia*. As Colli realized, these two naturally went together.

Emotional Communities

Like islands in an ocean, the emotional-intellectual communities of eighteenth-century Germany were weakly connected with one another only by their origins and feeble means of communication. Each one cultivated its own individual gestures and its own pictorial language. The gestures and pictorial language of harpocratism were characteristic of rational esotericism, though harpocratism itself was without specific doctrines. Its self-descriptions, such as "Pythagorean" or "theosophist," were nothing more than communicative acts—self-interpretations offered to specific recipients. Such offers, made during a struggle over the interpretation of scientific data and methods, existed in a tension of distinctions between various communicative stances, and they were part of larger research programs—in Weißmüller's case, for example, his supposedly "realistic program" as opposed to the "idealist program" of Leibniz. Harpocratism had deep and traceable roots in the history of philosophy, extending back to the Renaissance and from there back to late antiquity—an atypical origin for German scholars of the early eighteenth century. These scholars might enjoy special free zones for communication, such as princely courts, but they also met opposition in places like the publishing center of Leipzig. All these actors were hemmed in by specific constraints.

All of these coordinates need to be considered when we discuss instances of Enlightenment quietism, esotericism, or harpocratism, for to do otherwise would be to establish fictitious fixed positions that never existed.[72] We must

---

Emblemata, ad D. Arnoldum Coebelium: Eiusdem Aenigmatum libellus, ad D. Arnoldum Rosenbergum (Antwerp, 1565), no. 61; also *Audi, tace, fuge*, in ibid., no. 63.

71. Clavius, *Prodromus*, 214: "Posterius propugnaculum veritas circumspecte, prudenter, & sapienter extruit. Est enim veritas circumspectio, prudentia, & sapientia ipsa." For a modern account of the "virtues" of truth, see Williams, *Truth and Truthfulness*.

72. The situation is as complicated as we found with efforts to define the "radical Enlightenment," examined in chapters 3, 4, and 5.

avoid being fooled by contemporary polemics, in which the Ludovicis and Liscows used their journalistic and literary prowess to assume the upper hand. As a corrective to such distortions—and as a part of our current effort to understand "reasonable esotericism"—it would make sense to look for those with positions comparable to Weißmüller's in intellectual fields where such "disruptive factors" were once visible even if they no longer survive.

Later in the eighteenth century, these dissident communities were increasingly absorbed, I suspect, in emergent Freemasonry. Thus assimilated, they would participate in the process that Reinhart Koselleck has described as the formation of an interior space in society.[73] It could be fruitful to understand this process—to the extent that it was influenced by harpocratism—as a reaction to oppression and ridicule. Clavius was unsurprisingly among the losers in the 1747 competition for work on monadology, and he dealt with his failure by helping to found a secret society.[74] Harpocratism, we could say, flourished within a culture of defeat.[75]

73. Reinhart Koselleck, *Critique and Crisis: Enlightenment and the Pathogenesis of Modern Society* (Cambridge, MA, 1998).

74. Mulsow, "Pythagoreer und Wolffianer," 345–55.

75. See Wolfgang Schivelbusch, *Die Kultur der Niederlage: Der amerikanische Süden 1865. Frankreich 1871. Deutschland 1918* (Berlin, 2001), translated as *The Culture of Defeat: On National Trauma, Mourning, and Recovery*, trans. Jefferson Chase (New York, 2003).

8

Dare to Know

EPISTEMIC VIRTUE IN
HISTORICAL PERSPECTIVE

Virtue Epistemology

For some years now there has been an intensive discussion among philosophers of the so-called "epistemic virtues." In 1980 Ernest Sosa introduced
the idea of "intellectual virtue" into discussion of theories of cognition in
order to clear away an insoluble debate between "foundationalists" and "co-
herentists" by showing that it was superfluous.[1] Instead, he proposed that
we should concentrate on the virtues of persons rather than on the characteristics of various dispositions to accept this or that as true. Since then,
Sosa has expanded his virtue epistemology into a complex performance
theory of knowledge, and especially of "knowing full well." Someone with
a specific conviction is like an archer who executes the tasks of aiming and
shooting. Epistemic normativity consists first and foremost of procedures
performed competently. So it concentrates exclusively on certain characteristics of the person. But on a higher level it also emphasizes the fact that
an archer knows how to judge the risks and estimate when and whether he
will shoot at all.[2]

---

1. As an introduction to these debates, see Ernst, *Das Problem des Wissens*; idem, "Der Wissensbegriff in der Diskussion," *Information Philosophie* 3 (2007): 38–48. This chapter builds on
an article I published: "Erkühne dich, vernünftig zu sein: Auf den Spuren der Leipziger *Alethophilen*: Zur Herkunft des Wahlspruchs der Aufklärung," in *Frankfurter Allgemeine Zeitung*,
April 11, 2001, p. N6.
    2. Ernest Sosa, *Knowing Full Well* (Princeton, 2011).

Strictly speaking, the notion of virtue for Sosa and his followers[3] is intentionally not very well elaborated. It consists of nothing more than certain personal abilities, including reliability and the estimation of risk. But the spirits summoned by Sosa are alive. Encouraged by his proposal, some have tried to connect epistemology explicitly to more recent discussions of virtue ethics. Authors indebted to Aristotle such as Alasdair MacIntyre have criticized a purely normative approach to ethics by situating ethical behavior firmly in social communities.[4] Then in an extension of these efforts, Linda Zagzebski in *Virtues of the Mind* has presented a "virtue epistemology" that actually deserves this description.[5] Here again the characteristics of persons make up the foundation for knowing, but Zagzebski argues for a concentration on the whole person and his or her social situation, just as virtue ethicists place the virtues into the context of all the characteristics of the person. On this view, correct cognitive acts are whatever persons possessing the requisite intellectual virtues would do in certain circumstances. James Montmarquet has claimed that an epistemically virtuous person has to do justice to his or her "epistemic responsibility";[6] so too Zagzebski makes moral duty parallel to epistemic duty: "a belief is an epistemic duty (strong sense) in certain circumstances if and only if it is unjustified not to believe it."[7] According to the Aristotelian view, virtue includes not only motivational components but also an element of reliability. Thus, someone who acts from false reasons—from an internalistic point of view—cannot be regarded as virtuous. And someone who is not successful in his or her actions cannot be called virtuous either. Zagzebski analyzes the notion of knowledge in neither purely externalistic nor internalistic terms.[8]

Intellectual Courage

In view of these epistemological considerations, the historical efforts connecting knowledge to a specific kind of courage now appear in a new light. In particular the most famous Enlightenment slogan, "Sapere aude!" takes on a new significance. In 1784 Kant used this exhortation in his epoch-making answer to the question, "What is Enlightenment?" He added that "the motto of the Enlightenment is

---

3. See, e.g., John Greco, *Putting Skeptics in Their Place* (Cambridge, 2000).
4. Alasdair MacIntyre, *After Virtue: A Study in Moral Theory* (Notre Dame, 1981).
5. Zagzebski, *Virtues of the Mind*.
6. James Montmarquet, *Epistemic Virtue and Doxastic Responsibility* (Lanham, MD, 1993).
7. Zagzebski, *Virtues of the Mind*, 242.
8. Ernst, "Der Wissensbegriff."

therefore 'Have the courage to use your own understanding.'"[9] It is well known that the words "sapere aude" were taken from Horace, who in a letter to Lollius said,

> "Come now, have courage to be wise [or: Dare to know]: begin:
> You're halfway over when you once plunge in:
> He who puts off the time for mending, stands
> A clodpoll by the stream with folded hands,
> Waiting till all the water be gone past;
> But it runs on, and will, while time shall last."[10]

In Horace the advice is just a harmless practical encouragement about how to live—there was no talk about philosophical knowledge or of enlightenment. But Kant challenges the reader to have courage and to think his or her own thoughts. In the language of virtue ethics, Kant was appealing here to an epistemic duty and responsibility, to develop one's own beliefs and to test them rationally.

Perhaps a survey of the uses to which the Horatian quotation was put during the early modern period can illuminate how this motto came to have such an epistemologically loaded meaning. What contexts help explain this history? How was epistemic responsibility understood? And where did Kant get the charged meaning of the words: "Have the courage to use your own understanding"? What was the source for his quotation?

In Italy modern scholars paid close attention to the slogans used by the German Enlightenment much earlier than in Germany itself. And so in 1959–60 two Italian historians, Franco Venturi and Luigi Firpo, staged a little mock battle to track these famous words. Venturi was a professor of history in Turin, who traced the prehistory of the Kantian motto in the eighteenth century and discovered a winding path that reflected the various meanings of "Enlightenment."[11]

9. Immanuel Kant: "Beantwortung der Frage: Was ist Aufklärung?" in idem, *Schriften zur Anthropologie, Geschichtsphilosophie, Politik und Pädagogik* 1 (= *Werkausgabe* vol. XI), ed. Wilhelm Weischedel (Frankfurt, 1993), 53–61. On the context, see the collection of texts in Norbert Hinske, ed., *Was ist Aufklärung? Beiträge aus der Berlinischen Monatsschrift* (Darmstadt, 1981), and especially the afterword by Hinske, pp. 519–58. For an English translation of Kant's treatise, see the online edition, trans. Lewis White Beck: https://en.wikisource.org/wiki/What_is_Enlightenment%3F.

10. Project Gutenberg: Release Date: April 2004 [EBook #5419], trans. John Conington, Ep. I, 2: "Dimidium facti, qui coepit, habet; sapere aude, / incipe. vivendi qui recte prorogat horam, / rusticus expectat dum defluat amnis; at ille / labitur et labetur in omne volubilis aevum."

11. Franco Venturi, "Contributi ad un dizionario storico 1: Was ist Aufklärung? Sapere aude!" *Rivista storica italiana* 71 (1959): 119–28.

He did not, however, mention Melanchthon's programmatic inaugural lecture when he arrived in Wittenberg in 1518: *De corrigendis adolescentium studiis* (*On Improving the Studies of Young People*). Melanchthon ended his lecture with the challenge that students should dare to acquire knowledge ("sapere audete"), that they should honor the ancient Latins and treasure Greek as the foundation of Latin.[12] He was of course using Horace's words to encourage students to study, but obviously only in the humanist context of learning from the ancient authors. It was not yet functioning as a plea for the autonomous use of reason. Venturi's search for the traces of this slogan led him to an entirely different century: to the "Alethophiles," a small learned society founded around 1736 by Count Ernst Christoph von Manteuffel with the purpose of spreading the philosophy of Christian Wolff and of protecting it from the attacks coming from conservative churchmen.[13] Gottsched in Leipzig was a member, and so was Provost Johann Gustav Reinbeck in Berlin. There they hit on the idea of following the custom among Italian societies of having a medal struck with an emblem including the superscript, "Sapere aude" (figure 39). Starting with this medal, according to Venturi, the Horatian slogan can be found on numerous frontispieces of Enlightenment works. They range from the 1767 work of the Viennese opponent of witchcraft trials, Constantin Franz von Cauz, to Christian August Wichmann's translation of Shaftesbury's *Characteristics* (1768).[14]

One year later Firpo did Venturi one better with his discovery that one can find the slogan as early as with the freethinking skeptical philosopher Pierre Gassendi.[15] According to Firpo, the freethinker Samuel Sorbière in his biography of Grotius described a family album from the 1640s in which Sorbière's teachers wrote down mottoes for how to live. One of these teachers was Gassendi, who had roused a furor as an atomist and opponent of Descartes.[16] In that day it was common for students to collect entries in their albums—they

12. Philipp Melanchthon, "De corrigendis adolescentium studiis," in *Corpus Reformatorum* XI, 15–25: "sapere audete, veteres Latinos colite, Graeca amplexamini, sine quibus Latina tractari recte nequeunt." See Asaph Ben-Tov, *Lutheran Humanists and Greek Antiquity: Melanchthonian Scholarship between Universal History and Pedagogy* (Leiden, 2009), 139.

13. On Manteuffel and the Alethophiles, see Johannes Bronisch, *Der Mäzen der Aufklärung: Ernst Christoph von Manteuffel und das Netzwerk des Wolffianismus* (Berlin, 2010).

14. Venturi, "Contributi," 123ff.

15. Luigi Firpo, "Ancora a proposito di 'sapere aude!' *Rivista storica italiana* 72 (1960): 114–17.

16. On Sorbière, see Albert G. A. Bal, "Samuel Sorbière (1615–1670)," *Philosophical Review* 39 (1930): 573–86; Lisa T. Sarasohn, "Who Was Then the Gentleman?: Samuel Sorbière, Thomas Hobbes, and the Royal Society," *History of Science* 42 (2004): 211–32. On Gassendi, see

FIGURE 39. Medal of the Alethophiles, from "Nachricht von der zu Berlin auf die
Gesellschafft der Alethophilorum oder Liebhaber der Wahrheit geschlagene Müntze."
Johannes Bronisch, *Der Mäzen der Aufklärung* (Berlin, 2010), 159.

were a side branch of the fashion for emblem books and *impresas*—and so the
young Sorbière got Gassendi to inscribe his album. Gassendi wrote down the
motto "Sapere aude" and thus appeared to declare himself in favor of freedom
of thought and impartiality. Firpo emphasized, however, that this freedom
should not be misunderstood as unbelief; in contrast to many of the learned
libertines in his circle, Gassendi thought that Christianity and free scholarship
could be peacefully combined. But now we know that the Horatian dictum
was current in certain private circles as a motto for freedom of thought.

The Alethophile Medal

The Leipzig historian Detlef Döring came even closer to solving the riddle of
the prehistory of the Enlightenment's most famous catchphrase.[17] With the
help of Gottsched's correspondence, he discovered that it was the philosopher
Johann Georg Wachter who designed the medal for the Alethophile Society.
Wachter is no longer an unknown in the history of philosophy. Ever since
Winfried Schröder's editions and reprints of Wachter's works criticizing

Olivier Bloch, *La philosophie de Gassendi: Nominalisme, matérialisme et métaphysique* (Den Haag,
1971); Tullio Gregory, *Scetticismo ed empirismo: Studio su Gassendi* (Bari, 1961).

17. Detlef Döring, "Beiträge zur Geschichte der Gesellschaft der Alethophilen in Leipzig,"
in *Gelehrte Gesellschaften im mitteldeutschen Raum, 1650–1820*, part 1, ed. idem und Kurt Nowak
(Stuttgart and Leipzig, 2000), 95–150.

religion, he has been rehabilitated as one of the most prominent radical thinkers of the German early Enlightenment.[18] He anticipated Gershom Sholem's
thesis concerning the Kabbalist influence on Spinoza (Sholem himself picked
up on this), as well as the fierce discussion generated by the discoveries at
Qumran showing that the sect of Essenes may have influenced early Christianity. If it now turns out that Wachter was also a forefather of Kant's Enlightenment motto, it would serve to underscore his extraordinary status.

Döring suspects that there were mutual sympathies between Wachter and
the Leipzig circle around Gottsched. Of course Wachter was a persona non grata
in Leipzig, having committed the error of declaring himself a Spinozist, which
was roughly equivalent to a social death sentence. But Gottsched and his wife
cautiously attempted to carve out a little space of toleration for the embittered
and impoverished philosopher.[19] Part of that effort was asking Wachter for his
advice in designing a memorial coin for the Society of Alethophiles.

Wachter immediately came up with four proposals for the emblematic lay-
out of the coin for the "Friends of Truth": (1) truth holding a torch in her hand;
(2) a globe surrounded by a chain; (3) the Copernican solar system; and
(4) the head of Minerva with relief images of Socrates and Plato on her helmet. While the first proposal used a current "Enlightenment" image, it is
important to consider the other suggestions, especially in the context of the
motto "sapere aude," which Wachter proposed for these emblems.

The globe with a chain and the depiction of the Copernican solar system
can be found on Matthias Merian's title page engraving of a famous and elabo-
rately illustrated book: Robert Fludd's hermetic *Utriusque cosmi maioris scilicet
et minoris Metaphysica, physica atque technica historia* (*The Metaphysical, Physical, and Technical History of the Large and Small Worlds*), dating from 1617.[20]
Horst Bredekamp has highlighted the implications of Merian's engraving for
Thomas Hobbes's *Leviathan* (1650).[21] But for Wachter, too, the book appears
to have had a certain importance. His Spinozistic thinking, which also

18. Johann Georg Wachter, *Der Spinozismus im Jüdenthumb* (1699), ed. Winfried Schröder
(Stuttgart, 1994); idem, *De primordiis Christianae religionis, Elucidarius Cabalisticus* (1706), ed.
Winfried Schröder (Stuttgart, 1995). On him, see Martin Mulsow, "Den 'Heydnischen Saurteig'
mit den 'Israelitischen Süßteig' vermengt: Kabbala, Hellenisierungsthese und Pietismusstreit
bei Abraham Hinckelmann und Johann Peter Späth," *Scientia Poetica* 11 (2007): 1–50.

19. Döring, "Alethophilen," 127ff.

20. Robert Fludd, *Utriusque cosmi maioris scilicet et minoris Metaphysica, physica atque technica historia*, 2 vols. (Oppenheim, 1617).

21. Bredekamp, *Thomas Hobbes visuelles Strategien*.

included elements of Kabbalah and hermeticism, was fully attuned to the motif of the great chain of being, as depicted on Fludd's frontispiece. The hermetic *Asclepius* speaks of "a connected chain, whose first link is held by the hand of God."[22] In that image the Spinozist Wachter could recover Spinoza's doctrine of the seamless linkage of all things (and all ideas), which has its immanent foundation in God. And from there he could mark his own proximity to the Wolffianism of the Alethophiles. Indeed, the Alethophiles, as disciples of Leibniz and Wolff, had made the idea of the seamless nexus of causes and foundations into a tenet of their creed. "Hold nothing to be true, hold nothing to be false, unless you are persuaded by a sufficient reason."[23]

Because of this principle of sufficient reason Wolff was suspected of being a determinist and hence a Spinozist: he therefore lost his professorship in Halle.[24] Wachter's proposed emblem with the chain motif and the device "Sapere aude" would have been a titillating reference to this context and would moreover have given Wachter the chance to smuggle his Kabbalist-hermetic Spinozism into Enlightenment propaganda. But it turned out differently. Count Manteuffel chose the fourth motif, Minerva (as the goddess of wisdom) with her helmet. And it was agreed that instead of the heads of Socrates and Plato, the heads of Leibniz and Wolff should be depicted.

Johannes Bronisch has pointed out that Manteuffel himself—and with him the whole Alethophile Society—was not at all sympathetic to Spinoza or his critique of religion.[25] Manteuffel discussed the designs for the medal thoroughly with Johann Christoph Gottsched and his wife;[26] they decided that the "sapere aude" should not be presented as a challenge to the reader but solely as a description of the heroic intellectual efforts of Leibniz and Wolff: "Sapere audent" (They dare to know). So the Alethophiles did not intend to

22. "Asclepius," in *Das Corpus Hermeticum: Übersetzung, Darstellung und Kommentierung*, ed. Jens Holzhausen and Carsten Colpe, vol. 1 (Stuttgart, 1997). The chain was depicted on the title page of the first translation of the Corpus into German (Hamburg, 1706).

23. On the "Hexalogus" or the six "laws" of the Alethophiles, see Döring, "Alethophilen."

24. See Bruno Bianco, "Freiheit gegen Fatalismus: Zu Joachim Langes Kritik an Wolff," in *Zentren der Aufklärung I: Halle, Aufklärung und Pietismus*, ed. Norbert Hinske (Heidelberg, 1989), 111–55.

25. Bronisch, *Der Mäzen der Aufklärung*, 158–66.

26. See University Library of Leipzig, from Ms. 0342 V, 334r–335v (Manteuffel to Luise Gottsched, 30.11.1739) to Ms. 0342 Via, 301r–v (Manteuffel to Luise Gottsched, August 31, 1740); see also the designs for a medal in the University and State Library of Halle, Ms. Geneal. 2° 8, 268r–270r, cited in Bronisch *Der Mäzen der Aufklärung*, 163.

preach the autonomous use of reason; rather they were concerned to prove the importance (and orthodoxy) of Wolffianism. Manteuffel was a connoisseur of Horace and years before the medal had founded an "Order of Sans Souci" as a tribute to Horace (and well before Frederick the Great). He was therefore, but only for that reason, in favor of Wachter's design proposal.[27]

When the medal was struck, it was sent to the members of the Alethophile Society in recognition of their participation in the association of Wolffians. These shipments—a sort of indirect publication—had surprisingly large effects, for the image pointed to something like epistemic virtue, especially if members put it together with one of the basic rules of the society: if another member, "whose insight is more correct that your own," should draw a conclusion that is proven true, one must not stoop to contradicting it for unworthy reasons, "from arrogance, obstinacy, or other unreasonable motives."[28] Over the next decades the knowledge of the motto "sapere aude" can be easily documented on the basis of the spread of these coins. Venturi gives the example of the Polish reformer Stanislaw Konarski, for whom a coin was minted with the inscription "Sapere auso" (To him who dared to know): the Horatian motto now designated a specific person, which marked him as a philosopher of the Enlightenment.

There was, however, still a long way to go from here to Kant. One is surprised to find that shortly after its publication on the coin in 1740, the motto was emblazoned on a translation of Shaftesbury. This was his book entitled *The Moralists: A Philosophical Rhapsody a Recital of Certain Conversations on Natural and Moral Subjects* (1709), which appeared in German in 1745.[29] The anonymous translator was the theologian Johann Joseph Spalding, who was then just thirty years old, and who would soon thereafter ignite a frenzy with his *Reflections on the Destination of Man* (1748). It seems probable that Spalding, who was then working in Berlin as secretary to the Swedish ambassador von Rudenskjöld, had come into contact with projects of the Alethophiles. He had, after all, been a friend for several years of Alethophile member Johann

27. Bronisch, *Der Mäzen der Aufklärung*, 164; see University Library of Leipzig, Ms. 0345, 216r–217v, Manteuffel to Wolff, July 23, 1740.

28. Bronisch, *Der Mäzen der Aufklärung*, 160; Zedlers Universal-Lexikon, s.v. "Wahrheitsliebende Gesellschaft," vol. 52, col. 952.

29. Anthony Ashley Cooper, Third Earl of Shaftesbury, *Die Sitten-Lehrer oder Erzehlung philosophischer Gespräche, welche die Natur und die Tugend betreffen* (Berlin, 1745); a translation of *The Moralists: A Philosophical Rhapsody* (London, 1709). See Reinhard Brandt, *Die Bestimmung des Menschen bei Kant* (Hamburg, 2007), 61ff.

Joachim Schwabe, but he had also chosen as his publisher Ambrosius Haude, who was himself a friend of Manteuffel and an Alethophile. And so the device for his translation with its invocation of "Sapere aude" can be seen as using it to align Shaftesbury's philosophy with the Alethophile Wolffian program.[30] Venturi's and Firpo's instincts failed them in this regard; they did not notice the comparable works published by Haude (although admittedly they were less influential), for example, his edition of Horace with the Minerva of the Alethophile medal on its title page or the weekly journal entitled *Der Freygeist* (*The Freethinker*), written by Lessing's cousin Christlob Mylius, who used the Horatian slogan as its motto.[31]

The Italians also overlooked a work in which the Horatian motto was placed front and center, and without the window dressing of philology. This was Johann Philipp Murray's Göttingen dissertation (presented in August 1754), which provided a philosophical commentary on the motto "sapere aude." The twenty-eight-year-old Murray was at the time the secretary of the Royal German Society in Göttingen,[32] a society that saw itself as an offshoot of Gottsched's German Society. Murray did not disguise his sympathies for Wolffianism and refers at the beginning of his dissertation to the motto, which he claimed had always meant a great deal to him. He noted that it was stamped on the coin of the Alethophiles, a society, he noted, "that is still in existence"—it was almost as if he was recruiting for the society.[33]

When Kant adopted the motto in 1784, there were therefore many ways by which he could have come upon it. The best candidate is probably Spalding's translation of Shaftesbury because the reception of Shaftesbury and then of the *Destination of Man* had prompted a powerful move away from speculative metaphysics and had placed the question of self-determination according to reason in the very center of the Enlightenment—almost as an axiom by which

30. This is also the suggestion of Mark-Georg Dehrmann, *Das "Orakel der Deisten": Shaftesbury und die deutsche Aufklärung* (Göttingen, 2008), 219ff.

31. *Der Freygeist*, 8 Stücke, Berlin, 1742. On Mylius, see Martin Mulsow, *Freigeister aus dem Gottsched-Kreis. Wolffianismus, studentische Aktivitäten und Religionskritik in Leipzig 1740–1745* (Göttingen, 2007).

32. Translator's note: The Königliche Teutsche Gesellschaft (Göttingen) was a learned society founded in 1738 under the leadership of Johann Matthias Gesner to cultivate scholarship especially on German topics and especially the German language. Later it became prominent in the natural sciences as well.

33. Johann Philipp Murray, *Horatianus ille sapere aude succincta commentatione illustratus* (Göttingen, 1754).

theoretical philosophy might even be defined.[34] However that may be, the various possibilities open to Kant mostly lead back to Wachter's medal of 1740.

That is remarkable: How amazing that the freethinker Wachter occupied the key position from which Kant could make "sapere aude" into the battle cry of the German Enlightenment. The history of that motto casts a new light on the "subhistory" of the German Enlightenment, the history of its precarious knowledge, even though the Alethophile Society itself favored a conservative Enlightenment.[35] So we could now ask the question—which Döring did not: What sort of radical ideas did this motto smuggle into the Enlightenment? Let us recall that Wachter was probably advancing a hidden agenda with his hermetic-Spinozistic chain of being. Indeed, many radical ideas within the mostly moderate German Enlightenment survived only as disguised contraband. So can we find Wachter's critique of Christianity hiding within his proposed image for a medal? Absolutely yes. The modern career of our Horatian quotation can only be understood if we also recognize that it stood in tension with a very common piece of advice: St. Paul's admonition, *Non altum sapere, sed time* (Be not highminded, but fear) (Rom. 11:20). Firpo had earlier noticed this as well. But in the early modern period this injunction was often misunderstood (or was even intentionally distorted) as if it meant "You should not know high things that are not permitted for you," even though originally the "altum" of highmindedness and the "sapere" did not refer at all to intellectual knowledge.

The Anti-Orthodox Attack

A third Italian historian, Carlo Ginzburg, has also taken an interest in our motto because he was working on the prohibitions that served to block the access of popular culture to the resources of established elite culture.[36] The words of St. Paul (as misunderstood) were such a prohibition. Following Firpo's hint about emblematic sources, Ginzburg also discovered something about "sapere aude": the Dutch scholar Florentius Schoonhoven, whom we already know from his device, "Sapiens supra Fortunam," which gave us access to the allegory of Pietro della Vecchia.[37] In 1618 Schoonhoven used just

34. Brandt, *Die Bestimmung des Menschen bei Kant.*
35. On the "moderate enlightenment," see Israel, *Radical Enlightenment.*
36. Ginzburg, "High and Low."
37. See chapter 6.

FIGURE 40. Florentius Schoonhovius, *Emblemata partim moralia, partim etiam civilia* (Gouda, 1618). Frontispiece with portrait of the author (Mulsow's copy).

this motto in his Emblemata; he proudly placed it over his portrait at the beginning of the book (figure 40).[38] With this discovery Ginzburg probably uncovered the source for Gassendi's entry into Sorbière's album. Like many other scholars Gassendi had consulted an emblem book in search of a suitable device for his student. Obviously Schoonhoven's book fell into his hands and inspired him to place Horace's words into the context of his own liberated views.

For Schoonhoven himself the motto still had an ambiguous meaning. Schoonhoven was a Neo-Stoic follower of the recent revival of the Stoic philosophy of moderation, or political prudence, and of self-restraint, which

38. Florentius Schoonhoven, *Emblemata partim moralia, partim etiam civilia* (Gouda, 1618).

Justus Lipsius had initiated in the late sixteenth century.[39] This sort of Stoicism marks the precise point from which the philosophy of self-determination as expressed by Shaftesbury and Spalding took off in the second half of the eighteenth century. Whatever his intentions, Schoonhoven placed the "sapere aude" over his portrait in the context of the first three emblems of his book. "Nosce te ipsum" (Know thyself) stands under the first emblem; under the second we read "Sapiens supra fortunam" (The wise man is superior to the changes of fortune); and then follows finally "Altum sapere periculosum" (It is dangerous to know high things), which was a variant of St. Paul's dictum. That was the one that interested Ginzburg. For a cultural history of truth this context is significant. With "high things" Schoonhoven clearly meant the confessional and theological disputes that he hated. This was no wonder during the years of the Synod of Dort (1618–19) and the bitter divisions among Dutch Calvinists. He was clearly trying to find a balance between his allegiance to independent knowledge and his devout Christian rejection of intellectual hubris. And he found this balance by interpreting knowledge as self-restriction and as renunciation of speculative ventures.

It now appears therefore that the modern idea of "sapere aude"—despite Melanchthon's earlier use of the dictum—unfolded as a movement of withdrawal from theology, whether as the habitus of Stoic self-restraint or in the more aggressive variant of the independent new science. It is not difficult now to pull these threads together. Ever since his work on emblems at the Berlin court, Wachter was thoroughly familiar with emblem books. Because his Spinozism had closed off any academic career for him, he tried to keep his head above water financially in Berlin from 1705 onward by taking occasional jobs designing mottoes and inscriptions for emblematic books. In 1723, however, he lost his Berlin position and moved to Leipzig, where he continued to practice his craft: he oversaw the coin and medal collection of the Leipzig town hall library. Wachter would surely have known Schoonhoven's widely circulated emblem book, and therefore also the motto "sapere aude" prominently displayed in that work. He could not have known, however, that Gassendi had adopted the motto and had understood it in an avant-garde manner because Sorbière's report had not yet been published. And yet Wachter interpreted the motto almost exactly as did the French scholar: as a device favoring autonomous reason and freedom of thought independent of ecclesiastical dogmas.

39. On Neo-Stoicism, see Oestreich, *Geist und Gestalt des frühmodernen Staates*; Mark Morford, *Stoics and Neostoics: Rubens and the Circle of Lipsius* (Princeton, 1991).

The Alethophiles of Leipzig and Berlin could not have been aware of his intentions. They were not mainly opposed to Lutheran Orthodoxy; instead they were more concerned to make Wolffianism tolerable for that Orthodoxy. But Manteuffel's enthusiasm for Horace had led him to swallow Wachter's proposal, whose latent bias toward autonomy became clear only in the reception of the coins. The contradiction between Manteuffel's intentions and Wachter's "submarine" attack did, however, become readily apparent to every close observer: Could this gesture in favor of freedom fit with a partisan devotion to Christian Wolff? Early on some contemporaries recognized and criticized the inherent paradox within the Alethophile medal. Wachter himself had argued for the profiles of Socrates and Plato, but his advice was not taken. And so from the end of 1740 onward an anonymous author published several letters in the journal *Historical Amusement with Coins* (*Historische Münz-Belustigung*) condemning the "almost blind applause" the medal offered to Wolff.[40] With clear irony he proposed that one might also choose another Horatian motto: *Sapiens uno minor est Iove*, which he translated as "Only God alone is superior to the philosopher." To those who esteemed Wolff simply as "the philosopher," with the implication that "the other bumblers may always guard the doors," these words of Horace might be needed. Of course Horace himself had already joked about his saying when he wrote that "the wise man is king, except when he suffers from the sniffles."[41]

Probably, as Döring rightly suspects, the anonymous writer came from the circle of Adolph Friedrich Hoffmann and Christian August Crusius.[42] They were Leipzig philosophers who opposed the dominance of the Wolffians and followed the teachings of the early Enlightenment philosopher Christian Thomasius, who had consistently condemned the overestimation of intellectual endeavors and the participation in academic "sects." Later, Crusius exercised a strong influence on Kant and from there it's only logical that in his anonymous criticism one might hear adumbrated the ways in which Kant's "sapere aude" differed from that of the Alethophile medal. The crucial point was Kant's departure from that sectarian spirit; the subject of the Enlightenment was the individual person himself, not some orientation to this or that structure or doctrine, no matter how progressive it claimed to be. Have the courage to use your *own* reason, Kant said. Have the courage to assume epistemic responsibility.

40. *Der Wöchentlichen Historischen Münz-Belustigung* 47th Stück, 49th Stück, and 52nd Stück (1740); see Döring, "Alethophilen," 144ff.

41. *Der Wöchentlichen Historischen Münz-Belustigung* 49th Stück (1740), 386.

42. Döring, "Alethophilen," 144–50.

PART II

Fragility and Engagement in the Knowledge Bourgeoisie

SECTION III

Problematic Transfers

Historical scholarship has produced many sorts of theories of transfer. In recent years theories of "cultural transfer" have proliferated.[1] They have attempted to analyze what happens exactly when literature, pictures, motifs, concepts, and theories move from one national culture to another; often they undergo what look like processes of decomposition and recomposition. More recently some scholars have moved on to complex studies of what they call "histoire croisée" (multiperspectival, reflexive, comparative history), in which multiple intertwinings and changes of perspective are crucial.[2] During the early modern period Europe was not yet sharply divided by national cultures, although this was the period when the territorial state was establishing itself as dominant in Europe but before the creation of "national" cultures.[3] And yet the early modern transfer of knowledge under the sign of precarious knowledge has much more specific problems than just those of recontextualizing such transfers in changed cultural surroundings. This is of course also true in other areas—for example the transfer of heresy when socially marginal and persecuted religious movements from other religions find new areas of resonance[4]—but problems of transfer usually begin well before anything

1. See, e.g., Espagne and Werner, *Transfers*; Wolfgang Schmale, *Historische Komparatistik und Kulturtransfer: Europageschichtliche Perspektiven für die Landesgeschichte: Eine Einführung unter besonderer Berücksichtigung der sächsischen Landesgeschichte* (Bochum, 1998); Hans-Jürgen Lüsebrink and Rolf Reichardt, eds., *Kulturtransfer im Epochenumbruch: Frankreich-Deutschland 1770–1815* (Leipzig, 1997).

2. Michael Werner and Benedicte Zimmermann, eds., *De la comparaison à l'histoire croisée* (Paris, 2004).

3. See, therefore, the adaptations in Schmale, *Kulturtransfer*.

4. Martin Mulsow, "Socinianism, Islam and the Radical Uses of Scholarship," *Al-Qantara: Revista de estudios árabes* 31 (2010): 549–86.

moves to another culture. In chapter 1, I gave examples of this: one can see how isolated German freethinkers were, how hard it was for them to have their texts printed or to make disciples. If we want to study the circulation and diachronic spread of radical ideas, we have to look for "constellations over time," as I have called them; that is, we have to follow the trail of radical ideas as evidenced by the purchase of manuscripts in auctions or through the black market for clandestine works.[5] Freethinkers appropriated the ideas of earlier freethinkers partly by intervening in the texts and updating them at the same time.[6] We need to follow the paths of these manuscripts over decades or even centuries. And here too we find the processes of contextualization and recontextualization, as the specific uses of Vanini by the early Enlightenment philosopher Arpe showed in chapter 4. Most importantly, however, the literary "rescue" missions that I described in chapter 5 testify to the specific problems associated with the transfer of rare and materially fragile knowledge.

Chapter 9, with which this section begins, highlights a most unusual case in which rare knowledge was transmitted, namely the case of a "publication" of this knowledge not in a book but on a written chart included in a painting. It will be necessary to trace very carefully the circumstances and authorship of this form of publication in order to recognize why this sort of tabular knowledge could not be printed and why it found its way into an oil painting that hung in some anteroom or backroom in Venice. Obviously many contingencies influenced this process, but an analysis of the writing in this picture permits a retrospective reconstruction of knowledge that actually did get lost.

The problems in the area of the knowledge bourgeoisie are rather different; they will be the focus of Section Three. In general here the transfers were much more secure, both from place to place and over time as well as those from one discipline to another. Intellectual reproduction was guaranteed by the universities and by a publishing industry that operated under censorship. But even here there were risks. One underestimated form of risk applied to the "inner circle," transfers within one's own family. It was almost axiomatic that scholars

5. Mulsow, "Transmission."

6. As an example, see the copy of Christian Tobias Damm, *Vom historischen Glauben* (Berlin, 1772/73) in the Streitsche Stiftung collection in Berlin (GKI A 384 1/2), in which a kindred spirit entered additions. On this, see Klein, *Hermann Samuel Reimarus*, 192–96. Or also the adaptation of the clandestine manuscript "Symbolum Sapientiae" by the freethinker Johann Georg Wachter. See Winfried Schröder, "Il contesto storico, la datazione, gli autori e l'influenza sul pensiero dell'epoca," in *Cymbalum mundi sive Symbolum Sapientiae*, ed. Canziani, Schröder, and Socas, 9–35, at 33ff.; Mulsow, *Enlightenment Underground*, 160–65.

often came from "family dynasties" of scholars, that a son would become a professor if the father was a professor.

In such cases family dynamics could lead to distortions. Chapter 10 tries to bring in the insights of family systems therapy in order to study the behavior of established scholars when a blot marred the "family history of knowledge." Had one's own grandfather really been a radical, who passed his manuscripts down to a grandson? How did an heir react? For him precarious knowledge burst in on the secure relations within a family. What forms of appropriation or denial were possible in such cases?

Chapter 11 shows that even among the knowledge bourgeoisie transfers could go terribly wrong; it deals with a lost package that contained advisory notes for a history of philosophy. Chapter 14 will give an impression of what such notes could look like. But why did the package get lost? Were the contents so incendiary (or so good) that competitors saw to it that the text disappeared after they had made use of them? In chapter 1 we saw from the case of Gabriel Wagner that at least in the milieu of the knowledge precariat such things definitely occurred. In the case of the lost package, it is now possible to provide a different version of the beginnings of the history of philosophy. Until now we knew only the history of philosophical historiography through a dry succession of works and their authors. But it looks rather different if we view it from the perspective of the history of communications.

9

A Table in One's Hand

HISTORICAL ICONOGRAPHY

Implicit Textuality

Can we take a picture and reconstruct a philosophy from it? What if it's the teacher of Leibniz? I am speaking here not of using illustrations and deducing theories from them, and not of finding the philosophical content of certain pictorial contents.[1] Instead, I'm concerned here with a perspectival turn in some recent developments in art history. The shift in art history that has led it toward "historical image studies" (*historische Bildwissenschaft*) is now well advanced. Many works now investigate pictures and illustrations in their relations to the sciences;[2] the history of science and the history of the book have moved closer together.[3] Historical image studies have taken on an incredibly wide range of objects, including artisanal works that represent and communicate information; they are no longer restricted to "high art." So these studies can detect fascinating visual communications from distant areas and pursue "pictorial memory" into the past following its own nonverbal logic.[4]

---

1. On that project, see Brandt, *Philosophie in Bildern*.

2. See, e.g., Claus Zittel, *Theatrum philosophicum: Descartes und die Rolle ästhetischer Formen in der Wissenschaft* (Berlin, 2009); Horst Bredekamp, *Die Fenster der Monade: Gottfried Wilhelm Leibniz' Theater der Natur und Kunst* (Berlin, 2004); idem, *Thomas Hobbes visuelle Strategien*.

3. See, e.g., Sachiko Kusukawa and Ian Maclean, eds., *Transmitting Knowledge: Words, Images, and Instruments in Early Modern Europe* (Oxford, 2006); Marina Frasca-Spada and Nick Jardine, eds., *Books and Sciences in History* (Cambridge, 2000).

4. I will mention here only a few titles (see also the introduction to this book): the essential author is Horst Bredekamp with many contributions; see "Bildwissenschaft." For an overview,

The reverse, however, is also true. In textual scholarship and historical philology it is no longer necessary to restrict our attention to books, manuscripts, journals, and pamphlets as the vehicles of writing. For here as well there are more distant fields where written messages appear that have been all too easily ignored. That can happen in pictures, for example. And so "historical textual studies," as an analogy to "historical image studies," should work to discover just such unexpected vehicles for texts that had their own logic. And then these studies would have to investigate why such texts appear in oil paintings instead of in "normal" printed form. Were there reasons for the change in medium? Was there a knowledge that avoided and evaded the official media because it was precarious?

Of course painted pictures are hardly encrypted or secret cipher messages. After all, they hang in full sight on the walls and cannot be tucked into a coat pocket when the police approach. To be sure, there were "cabinet" pictures that were mostly withheld from public view and often contained private, erotic, or even obscene material. But in general one can assume that many chance circumstances had to come together if a page full of risky, unwelcome ideas or confidential inventions were to find their way into an oil painting. It could be that someone entrusted a page to a friend or student, with the understanding that it would not be made public, and after many wanderings and maybe after changes in ownership the page might suddenly emerge as the pattern for a painting, even if only as a detail.

That's the sort of case we will be dealing with here. And because it concerns the discovery of contingencies, a microhistory will be necessary; and because the page in question contains notes of a philosophical record, this will require a philosophical microhistory. In the introduction I introduced the concept of "inferential explosiveness," which is present when the implications of statements, once they are made explicit, threaten larger or well-established bodies of knowledge. In the seventeenth century, for example, many "occult" and hermetic-Kabbalistic texts contained such "dangerous" statements. These texts were commonplace throughout the Holy Roman Empire and indeed in other countries, but after the decade 1610–20, as confessional orthodoxies solidified their power, they and their authors were increasingly forced to the margins. Anyone hoping to become a university teacher needed to consider carefully whether to declare himself openly for Paracelsus, Böhme, Hermes, or the

see also Martin Schulz, *Ordnungen der Bilder: Eine Einführung in die Bildwissenschaft* (Munich, 2008).

Zohar.[5] It was safer to continue teaching Aristotle and to practice Galenic medicine. Therefore, much remained unpublished and confined to a small circle, especially if it concerned expansive speculations about the coherence of the microcosm and macrocosm, and particularly if they originated with true innovators and inventors. Such an inventor was the teacher of Leibniz.

Erhard Weigel

One day before his seventeenth birthday, on June 20, 1663, Gottfried Wilhelm Leibniz enrolled at the University of Jena.[6] There he was soon listening to the lectures of the mathematician and philosopher Erhard Weigel, who became one of his most important teachers.[7] So here we find ourselves from the outset in the middle of the knowledge bourgeoisie. Weigel had recently moved more conspicuously into the history of philosophy. Gradually historians are coming to see him not just as a predecessor of Leibniz but as very much his own figure, with his own characteristic combination of mathematics and moral philosophy, astronomy and technology, calendar reform and pedagogy, natural science and the art of engineering. Indeed, Weigel was for his contemporaries a sort of miracle man. His house in Jena was full of technical inventions that astonished his fellow citizens. There was a special pipe for wine that led from the cellar up to the ground floor; he had a sort of elevator that connected the different floors; up under the roof he installed an apparatus so that he could view the stars even in the broad light of day.

Weigel had become a professor in 1653, ten years before the arrival of Leibniz. He had received his postdoctoral teaching qualification (*Habilitation*) in Leipzig with two *Dissertationes metaphysicae* that dealt with existence and duration, both in the tradition of Aristotelian school philosophy.[8] This was the

5. See, e.g., Howard Hotson, *Johann Heinrich Alsted: Between Renaissance, Reformation, and Universal Reform* (Oxford, 2000). More generally: Siegfried Wollgast, *Philosophie in Deutschland zwischen Reformation und Aufklärung 1550–1650* (Berlin, 1988).

6. On the biography of Leibniz, see Kurt Müller and Gisela Krönert, eds., *Leben und Werk von G. W. Leibniz: Eine Chronik* (Frankfurt, 1969); Eike Christian Hirsch, *Der berühmte Herr Leibniz: Eine Biographie* (Munich, 2000); Maria Rosa Antognazza, *Leibniz: An Intellectual Biography* (Cambridge, 2008).

7. On the relationship between Leibniz and Weigel, see Konrad Moll, *Der junge Leibniz*, vol. 1 (Stuttgart, 1978).

8. *Dissertatio metaphysica prior de existentia* (Leipzig, 1652); *Dissertatio metaphysica posterior de modo existentiae* (Leipzig, 1652).

only open path to an academic career. Weigel's inaugural lecture at Jena, *De Cometa Nova* (*On the New Comet*), and the writings associated with it still moved within the realm of natural science and logic.[9] It only gradually became clear that this man also had "pansophic" interests, that is, interests that today one might call interdisciplinary but that in that day were embodied in systems, or in aspirations one could find most easily in hermetic or theosophic speculations.[10] There were only weak hints of that in his *Analysis aristotelica ex Euclide restituta* of 1658,[11] but they became more visible in the early 1670s when Weigel was already well established in Jena.[12]

When did the young Erhard Weigel begin to develop the pansophic ideas that he perhaps kept under wraps for a long time out of concern for his career? What were his thoughts at the end of the 1640s, when he had just finished his bachelor's degree? Did Weigel move slowly from Peripatetic school philosophy to the Pythagorean-pansophic world of ideas, or were the later ideas just waiting to come to the surface in the 1670s after slumbering for years under wraps?

We know very little of his early years, and yet it is known that during his student years at gymnasium in Halle he had such a good reputation as a teacher that students of mathematics in Leipzig journeyed to Halle to receive instruction from him.[13] From the fall of 1647 onward Weigel was himself

9. See, e.g., *Geoscopiae selenitarum*, 2 parts (Jena, 1654); *Exercitationum philosophicarum prima, de natura logicae* (Jena, 1655); *Astronomiae pars sphaerica methodo Euclidea conscripta*, 3 parts (Jena, 1657); *Speculum Uranium Aquilae Romanae Sacrum, das ist: Himmels Spiegel* (Jena, 1661); *Cometologia* (Jena, 1665).

10. On hermetic, lullist, kabbalist, and ramist encyclopedism, see Wilhelm Schmidt-Biggemann, *Topica universalis: Eine Modellgeschichte humanistischer und barocker Wissenschaft* (Hamburg, 1983); idem, *Philosophia perennis: Historische Umrisse abendländischer Spiritualität in Antike, Mittelalter und Früher Neuzeit* (Frankfurt, 1998); Andreas Kilcher, ed., *Die Enzyklopädik der Esoterik* (Paderborn, 2010).

11. Erhard Weigel, *Analysis aristotelica ex Euclide restituta* (Jena, 1658).

12. Above all: Weigel, *Universi corporis pansophici caput summum, a rebus naturalibus, moralibus & notionalibus, denominativo simul & aestimativo gradu cognoscendis, abstractum, exhibens artis magnae sciendi specimen tri-uno-combinatorium . . .* (Jena, 1673), reprint ed. and introduced by Thomas Behme (Stuttgart, 2003). The title refers (along with a general play on the Lullist *ars magna*) to Athanasius Kircher, *Ars magna sciendi* (Amsterdam, 1669). Weigel's *Caput summum* contains the *Pantognosia* and the *Pantologia*, but the planned *Pantometria* and the *Logica pansophica* were not carried out; see also *Physica pansophica* (Jena, 1673); *Arithmetische Beschreibung der Moralweisheit von Personen und Sachen* (Jena, 1674).

13. See Johann Caspar Zeumer, *Vitae Professorum . . . qui in Illustri Academia Ienensi ab ipsius fundatione ad nostra usque tempora vixerunt et adhuc vivunt* (Jena, 1711), 106ff. On Weigel, see

studying in Leipzig; to finance his studies he may well have continued for a time to give private lessons in mathematics.[14] But what sort of mathematics instruction was this? Was he merely conveying the classic ideas, or was the secret of his success the weaving together of pansophy and metaphysics with his mathematics? Or that he was supporting his mathematics instruction with new and astounding instruments?

In November 1649, after two years of study, the twenty-three-year-old Weigel received his bachelor of arts degree. The Chrysler Museum of Art in Norfolk, Virginia, possesses a painting by the Venetian painter Pietro della Vecchia from that very year, 1649 (figure 41).[15] Della Vecchia was the "index fossil" that led us in chapter 6 into the labyrinthine treatments of truth, and he will serve again here as our guide into unknown regions. The painting in the Chrysler Museum depicts a young man with a mustache, sitting at a table and pointing at a chart or table, a large carefully written page.[16] The man is holding a pair of compasses in his left hand, while with his right hand he points upward.

On the written page, at the end of the chart depicted there, we can read in tiny writing the name "Erhardus Weigelius." Art historians have known about this (in principle) since 1914, when a catalog listed the name for the first time.[17] Ever since then the painting has been regarded as a portrait of Erhard Weigel. But historians of philosophy have obviously been unaware of this fact. To be sure, Bernard Aikema in his 1990 monograph on Pietro della Vecchia showed

---

also Spieß, *Erhard Weigel*; Wilhelm Hestermeyer, *Paedagigia Mathematica: Idee einer universellen Mathematik als Grundlage der Menschenbildung in der Didaktik Erhard Weigels, zugleich ein Beitrag zur Geschichte des pädagogischen Realismus im 17. Jahrhundert* (Paderborn, 1969); Ulrich G. Leinsle, *Reformversuche protestantischer Metaphysik im 17. Jahrhundert* (Augsburg, 1988), 63–87.

14. Detlef Döring, "Erhard Weigels Zeit an der Universität Leipzig (1647 bis 1653)," in *Erhard Weigel, 1625 bis 1699: Barocker Erzvater der deutschen Frühaufklärung*, ed. Reinhard E. Schielcke, Klaus-Dieter Herbst, and Stefan Kratochwil (Thun and Frankfurt, 1999), 69–90.

15. Oil on canvas, 90 × 70 cm, Chrysler Museum of Art, Norfolk, Virginia. Provenance: Coll. H. Bendixon. Any earlier owner is not listed. A request placed with the Getty Provenance Project in Los Angeles did not yield any further information.

16. Illustration: see Pietro Zampetti, ed., *La pittura del Seicento a Venezia* (Venice, 1959), 64, no. 100.

17. Official catalog of the centenary exhibition of German art 1650–1800, the "Jahrhundert-Ausstellung deutscher Kunst 1650–1800" (Darmstadt, 1914). Doubts that Weigel was the person depicted were first expressed in B. Frederiksen and F. Zeri, *Census of Pre-Nineteenth-Century Italian Paintings in North American Public Collections* (Cambridge, MA, 1972).

FIGURE 41. Pietro della Vecchia, *Portrait of a Young Man*. Chrysler Museum
of Art, Norfolk, Virginia, Inv. No. 71.614.

convincingly that the person depicted cannot be Weigel.[18] There is no resemblance to the other known portraits of Weigel,[19] nor are there any hints to suggest that the impecunious student Weigel had visited Venice in 1649 or that the painter della Vecchia had visited Leipzig in that year.

But even if the young man with the mustache was not Erhard Weigel, the painting may be of great interest all the same—if it can be shown that the content of the chart originated even partially from Weigel. For that would be the earliest evidence of his philosophy. We would then possess the remarkable opportunity to reconstruct from this painting the hitherto unknown early philosophy of Leibniz's teacher. The content of the chart is mostly legible. It contains a sketch of a pansophic-Kabbalistic system with the intimation of a "mechanical" method of analogy.[20]

Additionally, the question I posed earlier would also find an answer: what Weigel as a student was privately teaching his fellow students. The transfer of this chart from Leipzig to Venice could only mean that a student or interested scholar had copied out the page during his private lesson or had acquired it and then taken it along to Italy, where it came into the hands of della Vecchia.

The depicted person could then be this carrier, or it could be della Vecchia himself, even though in 1649 he was already forty-six years old; but so far as the depicted person is concerned, he may have wished to present a more youthful appearance. The painting does have a few other hints that it's a self-portrait, not the least of which are the blatantly obvious words at the bottom of the page: "Petrus Vechia Pic[tor] 1649." Della Vecchia did not sign any of his other paintings so distinctly.[21] The man depicted is gesturing to the chart,

18. Aikema, *Della Vecchia*, 63–65. See also idem, "Pietro della Vecchia: A Profile," *Saggi e Memorie di Storia dell' Arte* 14 (1984): 77–100; idem, "Marvellous Imitations and Outrageous Parodies."

19. Aikema adduces the portrait by Elias Nessenthaler from 1668, but a better example is the comparison with the portrait of Weigel by Christian Richter from 1655 (reproduced in Schielcke, Herbst, and Kratochwil, *Weigel*), which also shows no similarity.

20. See the transcribed text in the framed transcription provided on page 254f (on pp. 248–49 in the original book). Aikema offers a transcription on p. 117, but it is incomplete and filled with errors.

21. Aikema does not go so far as to assert that it could be a self-portrait, but he too suspects an unusual level of involvement of the painter (*Della Vecchia*, 65): "It is as though Vecchia felt a personal involvement with the young scholar and the intellectual climate in which he worked, for this is the only portrait that he signed as 'Petrus Vechia Pic.' I have not been able to establish

making it clear that he identifies with its doctrine, and as noted he is holding a pair of compasses in his left hand, indicating that he was perhaps also a painter or architect or more generally someone who followed the "geometric-mathematical" ideal in philosophy (as we saw in chapter 6).

Philosophy at a Glance

Let us examine the chart more carefully. It belongs to the genre of broadsheets or single-page woodcuts, with which one could show students or others philosophy "at a glance": an overview of the complex connections between first principles and deductions derived from them.[22] Sometimes such representations could be bought in printed form, but often they were only written by hand. One well-known broadsheet of this sort is Johann Baptist Großschedel's *Calendarium naturale* of 1614 (figure 42). On this one page Großschedel illustrated doctrines concerning *res secretissimae* (very secret matters) that he had drawn mainly from Agrippa von Nettesheim's *Occulta philosophia*; he displayed a series of diagrams, images, and charts arranged over, under, and next to the others. And above all the categories of elements, angels, planets, and temperaments floats as a fixed point in the middle *Deus*, represented as the sun surrounded by a cloud.[23]

In della Vecchia's painted depiction of a chart, God was also present at the top as the fixed anchor of the whole. There it is called *Ensoph seu Veritas* (The Infinite or Truth) shown as a square with a dot in the center. The chart, which is not much less "occult" than the one by Großschedel, thus makes an impact

---

the exact meaning of this unusual signature, but the deliberate contrast between the artist or 'pictor,' and the subject of the portrait, the 'philosophus,' is very striking and could well mean that this work was more than a routine commission."

22. Barbara Bauer, "Die Philosophie auf einen Blick: Zu den graphischen Darstellungen der aristotelischen und neuplatonisch-hermetischen Philosophie vor und nach 1600," in *Seelenmaschinen: Gattungstraditionen, Funktionen und Leistungsgrenzen der Mnemotechniken vom späten Mittelalter bis zum Beginn der Moderne*, ed. Jörg Jochen Berns and Wolfgang Neuber (Vienna, 2000), 481–519, esp. 504ff.

23. Johann Baptist Großschedel, *Calendarium naturale magicum perpetuum profundissimam rerum secretissimarum contemplationem totiusque philosophiae cognitionem complectens* (ca. 1582/83, published by Johann Theodor de Bry in Oppenheim); see Bauer, "Die Philosophie auf einen Blick"; Carlos Gilly, "Il ritrovamento dell'originale del Calendarium naturale magicum perpetuum di Großschedel," in *Magia, alchimia, scienza dal 400 al 700: L'influsso di Ermete Trismegisto/Magic, Alchemy and Science 15th–18th Centuries: The Influence of Hermes Trismegistus*, ed. idem and Cis van Heertum (Venice, 2002), 295–309 (English on 310–15).

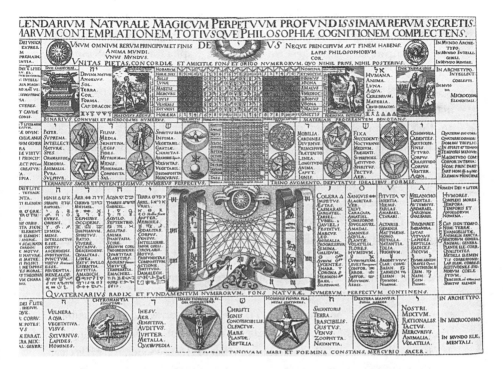

FIGURE 42. Johann Baptist Großschedel, detail from *Calendarium naturale magicum perpetuum profundissimam rerum secretissimarum contemplationem totiusque philosophiae cognitionem complectens* (ca. 1582/83), printed by Johann Theodor de Bry, Oppenheim.

that is both Kabbalistic and philosophical. "Ensoph," the infinite God of the Kabbalah, is equated with the truth as the originating principle. And according to the title at the top the whole chart presents "the most ancient principles of things" (*Antiquissima rerum principia*). This invocation of the most ancient, of *prisca sapientia* (the oldest wisdom), evokes a Renaissance motif that was still powerful in 1649, one that was regularly used by hermetic philosophers, neo-Platonists, Paracelsists, and Rosicrucians—regardless of the fact that individual elements of this intellectual structure had been subjected to a blistering historical critique starting in the late sixteenth century.[24] We can recognize

24. See Charles B. Schmitt, "Prisca theologia e philosophia perennis: Due temi del Rinascimento italiano," in *Atti del convegno internazionale di studi sul Rinascimento e sull' umanesimo italiano* (1970), 211–35; Daniel P. Walker, *The Ancient Theology: Studies in Christian Platonism from the Fifteenth to the Eighteenth Century* (London, 1972); on the contemporary critique of this

this affiliation also in the gesture of the man holding the chart, for his right hand is pointing to the central dot of "Ensoph." This gesture—his finger is extended upward—is the gesture of Plato in Raphael's famous School of Athens.[25]

But let us pursue what the chart is depicting. It promises to specify "how many and which principles" there are and above all how they relate to one another. All of that should be proved using a "Kabbalistic or an analogous mechanism" (CABALISTICA SEU ANALOGICA MECHANICA).[26] Later we will try to discover what this strange "analogous mechanism" was supposed to be, but first we must note that the block of text directly under the title lines makes it clear how the ideas of principles and proof will be displayed here. The text begins, "To grasp the inaccessible truth and to prove it with mathematical method is an operation of the intellect; for that the [best] minds exert themselves in order to prove it manually through experience as well as with the senses. The truth, which is completely unique, counts many suitors but few adepts, who are either mathematicians—and therefore rationalists—or natural scientists—and therefore mechanists [mechanici]. The former know their subject through the cause, the latter investigate the cause from its effects in things."[27]

Here is a language totally different from that of Großschedel. Here it is clear that the text connects mathematics and philosophy while showing an interest in Aristotelian proofs.[28] I consider this the most substantial indication that the text of the chart derives definitively from Erhard Weigel, because it was precisely the connection of mathematics, mechanics, the idea of proof, and pansophical philosophy that constituted a chief characteristic of his thinking. And

---

conceptual model, see Mulsow, *Das Ende des Hermetismus*; idem, "Ambiguities of the *Prisca Sapientia* in Late Renaissance Humanism," *Journal of the History of Ideas* 65 (2004): 1–13.

25. On the language of gesture at that time, see the handbook by Giovanni Bonifacio, which della Vecchia used: *L'arte dei cenni*.

26. "ANTIQUISSIMA RERUM PRINCIPIA QUOT ET QUAENAM SINT EORUMQUE ORDO HAC CABALISTICA SEU ANALOGICA MECHANICA DEMONSTRATUR." See the text of the whole chart in the framed transcription provided.

27. "Inaccessibilem Veritatem apprehendere, eamque ratione mathematica probare operatio intellectus est; eadem vero per experientiam [?] sensibus perceptibilis ut praebeatur manualiter desudant ingenia. Veritas quae unica tantum est, procos multos, adeptos tamen paucos enumerat, qui, aut sunt Mathematici, seu rationales, aut Naturales, seu Mechanici, quorum alteri rem per causam cognoscunt, alteri ab effectibus rerum causam investigant."

28. For the early history of such thinking, see Giovanni Crapulli, *Mathesis Universalis: Genesi du un' idea nel XVI secoli* (Rome, 1969); for its further development, see Paolo Rossi, *Clavis universalis* (Milan, 1960).

if this attribution is plausible, then we can see as early as 1649 the clear outlines of Weigel's future development. In the *Analysis aristotelica* published nine years later, Weigel was still concerned with the different sorts of proof in scholarship because the truth "lies concealed as if in a deep well."[29] Here too, the method "of the ancients" provides the paradigm, and so one reads at the end of the book from 1658 a declaration of allegiance to teaching oriented to "the ancients": "Here—where else?—the ancients were able to arrive at great wisdom, whose shadows we today can hardly follow even with the greatest effort; even though they [the ancients] knew neither grammatical science nor artificial logic (the torture of our students), they advanced the empirical sciences [*disciplinis reali-bus*]. And they did that despite their lack of all our newly discovered information and developments . . . while many of us in contrast, despite being outfitted with all of these things, spend our whole lives expending the greatest efforts but remain mere grammarians or mere logicians, that is, as we can see, mere assistants. I will say it this way: If we do not return to using the same method of instruction that the ancients used (Oh, if only the divine Plato would rise again!), we will never experience the highest good of the philosophers that we pursue."[30]

Proof

It was characteristic of the chart as depicted in 1649 that we find a sharp contrast between "Mathematici" and "Mechanici": the intellectually oriented mathematicians used a deductive method of deriving conclusions from a first cause; the experimentally oriented natural scientists and technicians "sought" inductively the causes for the effects that they observed or tried to produce. According to the Aristotelian understanding of causes, there were different types of proof that could be called analytic and synthetic or resolutive and compositive. Although these proofs were not identical, they were related to

29. Weigel, *Analysis aristotelica*, 2: "Verum enim vero, cum in profundo quasi puteo lateat rerum plerarumque Veritas."

30. Ibid., 288: "Hic, uti minor, (scilicet) quei Veteres ad tantam aspirare potuerint Sapientiam, cujus nos umbram hodie vix maximo labore consequimur, qui tamen nec Grammaticam Scientiam didicerunt . . . nec Logicam artificialem (puerorum crucem) disciplinis realibus praemiserunt, omnibus insuper destituta mediis & expedimentis noviter inventis . . . cum e contrario multi nostrum omnibus his instructi summaque diligentia progressi per totam vitam maneant *Puri Grammatici, Puri Logici*, h.e. quos nostis, puri socii; ita dico: *Nisi revertamur, ut eadem, qua Veteres* (o utinam divinus nunc reviviceret Plato) *usi sunt, in docendo progrediamur methodo, Summum Philosophorum Bonum nos assecutos esse non experiamur unquam.*"

ANTIQUISSIMA RERUM PRINCIPIA QUOT ET QUAENAM SINT EORUMQUE ORDO HAC CABALISTICA SEU ANALOGICA MECHANICA DEMONSTRATUR

Inaccessibilem Veritatem apprehendere, eamque ratione mathematica probare operatio intellectus est; eadem vero per experientiam [?] sensibus perceptibilis ut praebeatur manualiter desudant ingenia. Veritas quae unica tantum est, procos multos, adeptos tamen paucos enumerat, qui, aut sunt Mathematici, seu rationales, aut Naturales, seu Mechanici, quorum alteri rem per causam cognoscunt, alteri ab effectibus rerum causam investigant, utrique sane confiteri conati sunt in nua.. [?] proportionis finem obiectivam ab aliquo triuno principio conditore exorant, ut palam appositum schema]aucis omnia complectens tamquam totius Hermeticae Ortodoxaeque Philosophiae fundamentum Veritatis amatoribus aperit.

ENSOPH SEU VERITAS

Philosophice M.....[?] ל	Ens צ [?]	Verum א [?]	Bonum	&Unum &Universum[...] [...]כ[?]
Physice	**Ignis**	**Aqua**	**Aer**	**&Terra**
Mathematice	Numerus	Pondus	Mensura	& Omnia mixta [?]
Hermetice	Anima	Corpus	Spiritus	& Viv.. [?]
Chimice-physice	Sulphur	Mercurius		& Mon ... ? [...]
Mosaice	Adam	Ham	S[..]nen [?]	& Ho.. [?] per[?] Deum [?]
Logice	Subiectum	Praedica- tum [?]	Copula	& Conclusio
Aristotelice [?]	Causa efficiens	Materialis	Formalis	& Finalis
Otto Tachenius	Acidum	Alcali	Rector [?]	& Omnes res [?] in (?) [...]
Erhardus Weigelius	Scincte ... [?]	Quatuor	Quadriquatuor & Cubi quatuor	Erhardus

Ex relictis alijs quam plurimis; quot enim capita tot sententiae supra enarrata sufficiant.

Vocet igitur unus quisque sua principia [....] quae licet multa, et duo milia apparerunt; revera tamen secundum istum Cabalisticae figurae ordinem eadem sunt: ita ut si tria principia in quacunque Scientia, aut Arte aut viva aut mortua intelliguntur [?], his addito quarto ex ipsis exorto et vitam ab eis accipiente, via brevi et finita [...] bili methodo ab una ad aliam Scientiam in Artes facilius [?] emergit transitus [...] omnes Scientiae, ac Artes sic inter se analogice respondentes; exempli gratia, unitas [?] apud Arithmeticos idem sonat [?] ac punctum apud Geometros [...] et sic de singulis.

Quid sit scire rem per causam: in hoc habetur Analogismo.

Canens Caecus canens organo motum [...] abanicum, quem non videt intelligit: scit enim profecto choreas fidium modulationibus accommodari debere siquidem tastatores [?] tenent obedire sonans [?] tamquam [?] effectus luce [?] causae [?] [....] materia formae &c.

Quid sit ab effectibus cognoscere causas in hoc Epilogismo adiectitur [?]

Surdus, videns ludentes in numerum iucundum [?] ex illorum saltationibus cernit quod ex pulsato orga[nis ?] audire non potest, profecto enim prospicit pulsationes Cithariste, saltationes manibus, pedibus, totisque corporis areabus [?] secundare, et sic respondet [?] ultima primis, et e contra illud Hermetis quod est superius idem quod est inferius et utrumque probat hac

MECHANICA

---

the ones named on the chart. Weigel hit on the idea of showing the unity of the two opposed sorts of proof in their common foundation. "Both of course have undertaken to confess . . . that they are asking some triune creator principle for the objective goal of an analogy, that he should reveal a striking diagram to the lovers of truth for all the world to see: a diagram that contains everything in a few points—as the foundation of the whole hermetic and orthodox philosophy."[31] Mathematicians and mechanists both require a "striking diagram," some operable doctrine of categories, which finds a common basis in the "triune principle." The *Analysis aristotelica* also concluded with an expression of thanks to the "triune God."[32]

By describing the basic trinitarian principle as the foundation of both "hermetic" and "orthodox" philosophy—he was referring to the hermetic tripartite structure (or "ternary") as well as to the Christian Trinity—Weigel was forcing a unity that by 1650 had come to seem deeply problematic to the confessionally Orthodox.[33] That would have been one of the main reasons why Weigel, at the very beginning of his academic career, carefully suppressed all hermetic-Kabbalistic traces from his vocabulary.

---

31. "utrique sane confiteri conati sunt in nua . . . [?] proportionis finem obiectivam ab aliquo triuno principio conditore exorant, ut palam appositum schema paucis omnia complectens tamquam totius Hermeticae Ortodoxaeque Philosophiae fundamentum Veritatis amatoribus aperit."

32. Weigel, *Analysis aristotelica*, 288.

33. On the relationship between hermeticism and Lutheran Orthodoxy, see Robin B. Barnes, *Prophecy and Gnosis: Apocalypticism in the Wake of the Lutheran Reformation* (Stanford, 1988); Anne-Charlott Trepp, "Hermetismus oder zur Pluralisierung von Religiositäts- und Wissensformen in der Frühen Neuzeit," in *Antike Weisheit und kulturelle Praxis: Hermetismus in der Frühen Neuzeit*, ed. eadem and Hartmut Lehmann (Göttingen, 2001), 8–16; on the decisive rejection of hermeticism around 1700, see Sicco Lehmann-Braun, *Weisheit in der Weltgeschichte: Philosophiegeschichte zwischen Barock und Aufklärung* (Tübingen, 2004).

Why had he thought that those using deductive and inductive proofs needed such a schema of categories? We might think here of the traditions to which the young Weigel felt connected. As a student in the gymnasium in Halle he had become acquainted with the reforming doctrines of Wolfgang Ratke and Jan Amos Comenius oriented to "realia," to the real world;[34] but he may also have learned of the efforts of Johann Valentin Andreae to base these reforms on a universal mathematics. Georg Wagner suspected that Andreae's *Collectaneorum mathematicorum decades XI* of 1614 made a strong impression on Weigel[35] with its claim that mathematics should have a key role in reforming learning. At the same time this tradition, especially in Comenius, was concerned to emphasize the fundamental principles that expressed the ternary (tripartite) form of all reality because it was the image of the trinitarian God. By using these fundamental principles a person trying to prove something indirectly invokes the Trinity as the formal reason for the deduction of categories.

Ternaries

The trinitarian principles express themselves on the chart in ternaries of categories that appear convergently in all possible aspects of reality and from the perspective of the most various traditions. Thus there are philosophical and proto-linguistic aspects, physical and mathematical aspects, chemical and Mosaic aspects, the logical aspect and beyond that still other aspects. The chart depicting these conceptual ternaries comprises eleven orders of being or tradition.

There is, however, one great peculiarity. These ternaries also generate a quaternity for a fourth concept always accompanies the first three. The inventor of this chart has here bumped into the problem that despite his dedication to explanation by terneries (because of his Christian and theoretical definition

34. Uwe Kordes, *Wolfgang Ratke (Ratichius, 1571–1635): Gesellschaft, Religiosität und Gelehrsamkeit im frühen 17. Jahrhundert* (Heidelberg, 1999); Klaus Schaller, *Die Pädagogik des Johann Amos Comenius und die Anfänge des pädagogischen Realismus im 17. Jahrhundert* (Heidelberg, 1962).

35. See Georg Wagner, *Erhard Weigel, ein Erzieher aus dem XVII. Jahrhunderte* (Leipzig, 1903), 132–35; Johann Valentin Andreae, *Collectaneorum mathematicorum decades XI* (Tübingen, 1614). Wagner's hypotheses are not, however, always very reliable. See further: Johann Amos Comenius, *Pansophiae diatyposis* (Danzig, 1643). On Comenius, see also Schmidt-Biggemann, *Topica universalis*, 139–54.

of a triune basic principle), many of his groups of categories actually came in groups of four. They were quaternaries, just as Weigel was later deeply invested in the Pythagorean tetractys.[36] The author solved the problem by giving them what Reinhard Brandt has called a 1, 2, 3/4 structure: to the three ternary elements of each group a fourth was added in each case, one that did not strictly belong to the structure but that formed a concluding element that expanded and reflexively completed it.[37] In the words of the chart, "a fourth has been added that proceeds from them and that draws its life from them."[38]

The unity that lay at the basis of the ternaries or quaternaries of the diagram stood on the page over them and was entitled "Ensoph or the Truth," with a symbol: but then also as a ring or a crown (perhaps with a further reference to the uppermost Kabbalistic *sefira* known as "Keter").[39] The symbol for Truth-God is a square with a dot in the middle.[40] Whatever that is supposed to mean, we can be sure that the square with a dot is an expression of a geometrical symbolism. This is confirmed in the lower ring in which the Tetragrammaton is inscribed (הוהי), but also as if symbolizing the concept of the Tetragrammaton: the geometrical succession of point, line, plane, and cube. The cube, so to speak, completes the succession of dimensions of 0, 1, 2, in the number 3. The idea of combining the Tetragrammaton and the Pythagorean series of numbers goes back to Johannes Reuchlin. In his works *De verbo mirifico* from 1494 and *De arte cabalistica* from 1517 he developed a Christian Kabbalah with strongly Pythagorean features.[41] In Reuchlin we find just the understanding of "Cabala" that forms the basis for the "Kabbalistic mechanism"

36. See Weigel, *Tetraktys, Summum tum Arithmeticae tum Philosophiae discursivae Compendium* (Jena, 1673).

37. Reinhard Brandt, *D'Artagnan und die Urteilstafel: Über ein Ordnungsprinzip der europäischen Kulturgeschichte (1,2,3/4)* (Stuttgart, 1991).

38. "his addito quarto ex ipsis exorto et vitam ab eis accipiente."

39. On Keter, see Gerschom Scholem, *Zur Kabbala und ihrer Symbolik* (Darmstadt, 1965).

40. In alchemy this was only very rarely the sign for "sal" or salt. Normally the symbol for salt was a circle bisected by a line. Remarkably, further down in the scheme of chemical reality, where "sal" should be found, we find an empty space. On the alchemical meaning of salt, see Claus Priesner and Karin Figala, *Alchemie: Lexikon einer hermetischen Wissenschaft* (Munich, 1998), 319–21.

41. Johannes Reuchlin, *De verbo mirifico* (n.p., 1494); idem, *De arte cabalistica* (n.p., 1517). On Reuchlin, see Charles Zika, *Reuchlin und die okkulte Tradition der Renaissance* (Stuttgart, 1998); Daniela Hacke, *Die Welt im Augenspiegel: Johannes Reuchlin und seine Zeit* (Stuttgart, 2002). But now also see Wilhelm Schmidt-Biggemann, *Geschichte der christlichen Kabbala*, part 1, *15. und 16. Jahrhundert* (Stuttgart, 2012).

on the chart; and that's the first clear source of the chart, whether delivered directly or as mediated to the inventor of the diagram.

It was an old notion in numerological philosophy that the ternaries or quaternaries could be declined through various kinds of reality. Agrippa von Nettesheim spoke of *scalae*, that is, "ladders" or "steps" of reality; and Giordano Bruno too had used this terminology in his *De monade*.[42] The inventor of our diagram began with the "philosophical" order. This was the order of transcendentals: *ens*, *verum*, and *bonum* (being, the true, the good). The final category was *unum* (the one), and indeed one could say that the mutually convertible transcendentals could be seen numerologically as One. (We should recall scholastic maxims such as "ens et bonum convertuntur," that "Being and the Good are interchangeable," that they coincide and are to an extent one and the same.) There follow now a series of Hebrew letters that obviously represent the sacred language, understood as the original language. One recognizes a lameth (ל), then perhaps a zade (צ), then—but very hard to recognize— perhaps an aleph (א), and finally most likely beth (ב) or kaph (כ). It may be that for the inventor the numerical values of these letters was of some importance and that his source was the Sefer Yetzirah.[43]

In the next series, the row for natural philosophy, we find fire, water, air, and earth. Here it seems striking that not fire but the earth holds the fourth place; if an element from the traditional four was singled out, it was usually fire. In the mathematical row it's the common quotation from the book of Wisdom 11:20 that organizes things: God has "arranged all things by measure and number and weight."[44] The hermetic series lists as ternary: soul, body, and spirit. One cannot tell what the fourth category is called.

Next follows the "chemical" or rather the alchemical series. Here sulfur and mercury are named, but where the reader expects salt in the third position, to complete the Paracelsian list of principles, we find an empty space instead.[45]

---

42. Agrippa von Nettesheim, *De occulta philosophia libri tres*, ed. Vittoria Perrone Compagni (Leiden, 1992); Bruno, *De monade numero et figura*. See also Martin Mulsow, "Sachkommentar," in Giordano Bruno, *Über die Monas, die Zahl und die Figur*, ed. and trans. Elisabeth von Samsonow (Hamburg, 1991), 181–269, at 187.

43. See, in general, Moshe Idel, *Kabbalah: New Perspectives* (New Haven, 1988).

44. In connection with the doctrine of the Trinity, this expression was treated philosophically, e.g., by Augustine in *De trinitate* XI.

45. On the alchemical principles of sulfur and mercury, see Priesner and Figala, *Alchemie*, s.v.; on the Paracelsian trinity, see Walter Pagel, *Paracelsus: An Introduction to Philosophical Medicine in the Era of the Renaissance*, 2nd ed. (Basel, 1982).

One cannot determine whether the painter simply forgot an entry—which would be strange—or intentionally left a blank. This row also leaves it unclear what the author thought should go in the fourth category.

After the alchemical series, the author moved to a "Mosaic" row, following the idea of a *Philosophia Mosaica*, as propounded by Alsted, Fludd, Comenius, and other theoreticians who thought they could reconstruct a Christian *Philosophia perennis* (*Perennial Philosophy*).[46] The chart lists the names of Adam, Ham, and one beginning with the letter S. It is doubtful that that name should be read as "Shem." And the fourth name is illegible.

The last four rows give us even less that one can recognize. The first appears to contain a row of logical concepts, such as *subjectum*, *copula*, and *conclusio* (subject, link, conclusion), and then a row of Aristotelian causes: efficient, material, formal, and final. Then follows a completely indecipherable row followed finally by a row that seems to take up the Pythagorean references within the ring with the Tetragrammaton and appears to contain mathematical concepts. "Quatuor" (four) and "Quadriquatuor" (the square of four) are legible, along with "Cubi quatuor" (the cube of four) as the last category. This last row has no heading as did the rows called "philosophic" or "chemical" but instead bears the name "Erhardus Weigelius." The fact that his name appears just here could mean that the inventor—whether Weigel or not—credited Weigel with being especially original in this last row.

Much in this diagram is hard to understand. One can easily see that the ternaries and quaternaries do not designate the common conceptual rows that were then current everywhere but that they undertake transpositions and represent highly deliberate alterations. This was no simple chart extracted from just one source; and if we take the context of the introductory section into account, we also see that the text presents a combination of occult, hermetic-neo-Platonic tradition, on the one hand, and Aristotelian scholastic philosophy on the other, a combination that was common in German philosophy of the late Renaissance.[47] This chart displays these combinations by showing the concordance of various four-part groups (philosophical, hermetic, Mosaic, etc.) with the two fundamental sorts of knowledge presented in Aristotle's *Posterior Analytics*. Johann Heinrich Bisterfeld (d. 1655) was another philosopher

---

46. See Ann Blair, "Mosaic Physics and the Search for a Pious Natural Philosophy in the Late Renaissance," *Isis* 91 (2000): 32–58; Schmidt-Biggemann, *Philosophia perennis*.

47. On these connections, see Martin Mulsow, ed., *Spätrenaissance-Philosophie in Deutschland 1570–1650* (Tübingen, 2009); Hotson, *Alsted*.

who spoke of his "Kabbalah" in referring to his theory of the last or ultimate categories of reality.[48]

Syncretism and the Method of Analogy

Let us turn to the portions of text at the bottom of the chart. Perhaps they will disclose to us *how* the understanding of proofs is connected to the rows of coordinated concepts. To be sure, these passages are very hard to read because of the tiny script. The first parts still refer to the diagram and explain that it could be continued as desired: "From the many other [traditions]—*there are as many opinions as there are persons*[49]—the list presented above is sufficient."[50] *Quot capita tot sententiae* (literally: "as many heads, just that many opinions") indicates that the most various traditions and thinkers expressed their basic principles in the most diverse vocabularies, but they all meant the same thing and had the same structure. This was the belief in philosophical syncretism that had flourished in late antiquity and was revived in the Renaissance syncretism of Giovanni Pico della Mirandola.[51]

Further down we read: "Each one therefore should invoke his own principles . . . even if they are numerous or quite possibly two thousand; but actually they are all the same according to this array of Kabbalistic figures: so that in each kind of knowledge or art, whether living or dead, are found principles, with which . . . from one science to the other, all the sciences and arts are analogically related to one another, as [can be] easily discovered with a [conclusive . . .] method."[52] Thus the function of the concordance of conceptual rows

48. See Martin Mulsow, "Bisterfelds 'Cabala': Zur Bedeutung des Antisozinianismus für die Renaissancephilosophie," in idem, *Spätrenaissance-Philosophie in Deutschland*, 13–42. The combination of Kabbalistics and Pythagorean numerology with the beginnings of modern science can be seen not just in Weigel and Bisterfeld but in a whole series of authors. See, e.g., Johann Faulhaber, *Mysterium Arithmeticum sive cabalistica et philosophica inventio, nova, admiranda et ardua, qua numeri ratione et methodo computentur* (n.p., 1615); on him, see Ivo Schneider, *Johann Faulhaber (1580–1635): Rechenmeister in einer Welt des Umbruchs* (Basel, 1993); Johann Ludwig Remmelin, *Arithmos-O-Sophos* (Cologne, 1628). I am grateful to Jean-Pierre Brach for this reference.

49. Terence, *Phormio* 454: "Quot homines, tot sententiae"; Horace, *Sat.* 2,1,27: "Quot capita, tot sensus."

50. "Ex relictis alijs quam plurimis; quot enim capita tot sententiae supra enarrata sufficiant."

51. See, e.g., Stephen A. Farmer, *Syncretism in the West: Pico's 900 Theses (1486): The Evolution of Traditional, Religious and Philosophical Systems* (Tempe, AZ, 1998).

52. "Vocet igitur unus quisque sua principia . . . quae licet multa, et duo milia apparerunt; revera tamen secundum istum Cabalisticae figurae ordinem eadem sunt: ita ut si sua principia

consists of showing that the diverse arts and sciences such as philosophy, physics, chemistry, and mathematics all rest on just a few fundamental principles,
which can be displayed as such in separate rows and traditions. The author
underlines this point with an example: thus "the unit for the arithmeticians is
the same as the point for the geometricians, and so on for all the others."[53]

The passages after that each contain a title and a paragraph in which the
question posed in the title is answered with an example. The questions lead us
back to the Aristotelian understanding of proofs and seek to demonstrate in
real terms the analogy between the different areas of knowledge and the two
sorts of proof, inductive and deductive. The first of these questions corresponds to the above-mentioned resolutive procedure of understanding an
object through its cause.[54] "What is it to know a thing through its cause? We
see it in this analogy (*analogismo*). "The "analogy" itself uses the example of a
singing blind man, who cannot see the reactions that he provokes but can
grasp them intellectually: he knows that the round dance he starts with his
singing is conveyed by the modulations of his voice.[55] It would be interesting
to know to what extent the current researches into acoustics, as conducted for
example by Mersenne and Kircher, influenced the choice of examples here.[56]

---

in quacunque Scientia, aut Arte aut viva aut mortua intelliguntur [?], his addito quarto ex ipsis
exorto et vitam ab eis accipiente, via brevi et finita . . . bili methodo ab una ad aliam Scientiam
in Artes facilius [?] emergit transitus . . . omnes Scientiae, ac Artes sic inter se analogice
respondentes."

53. "unitas [?] apud Aritmeticos idem sonat [?] ac punctum apud Geometros . . . et sic de
singulis."

54. On the resolutive procedure, see Aristotle, *Posterior Analytics*; on that, see J. Barnes,
"Aristotle's Theory of Demonstration," *Phronesis* 14 (1969): 123–52; Ludger Oeing-Hanhoff,
"Analyse/Synthese," in *Historisches Wörterbuch der Philosophie*, vol. 1 (Basel, 1971), cols. 232–48.
For its reception, see Neil W. Gilbert, *Renaissance Concepts of Method* (New York, 1963).

55. "Quid sit scire rem per causam: in hoc habetur Analogismo. / Canens Caecus canens
organo motum . . . abanicum, quem non videt intelligit: scit enim profecto choreas fidium
modulationibus accommodari debere siquidem tastatores [?] tenent obedire sonans [?]
tamquam [?] effectus luce [?] causae [?] . . . materia formae &c." The terminology of "analo-
gism" was not very widespread in the early modern period; it was most common in medicine:
e.g., Johann Crato, *Cui post indicem consiliorum, analogismus, sive artificiosus transitus a generalis
methodo, . . . praefigitur* (Frankfurt, 1671). It appears here in close connection with methodical
considerations. This was also the sense that the physician and theorist of method Cornelius
Gemma used in his book *De arte cyclognomica* (Antwerp, 1569), when he coined neologisms
such as "aetiologismus."

56. Marin Mersenne, *Traité de l'Harmonie Universelle ou est contenu la Musique Theorique et
Pratique des Anciens et des Modernes, avec les causes de ses effets: Enrichie de Raisons prises de la*

A contrary example prompts the second question, which asks, "What is it to know the cause from the effects?"[57] The answer to this is not given in an analogy but in an *epilogismus*: in a conclusion "from behind." The example imagines a deaf man who sees people playing an instrument. He cannot hear but he uses his sense of sight to see the oscillations produced by the guitar, and he feels with his sense of touch "the vibrations with his skin, his feet, and his whole body." In this way he can infer the cause from the effects of the music on his senses of sight and touch: he can infer the sound.[58] Here again the logical conclusion is combined with the diverse sorts of reality (seen, heard, felt). This exemplifies (in an ad hominem argument) how someone using the recommended "Kabbalistic mechanics" could bring his scientific procedures to a conclusion by following a detour through other areas of reality. That means that if a cause is sought in the physics of earth, air, fire, and water, the seeker can resort to his knowledge from alchemy of sulfur and mercury or from the logic of subject and linkage. It must become clear to him that fire corresponds to sulfur and the subject and that all of these may be considered as similar to a geometrical point. The example of the deaf man, who only sees and feels the music, concludes with the remark that with his art of reasoning he is enacting that sentence from Hermes: "that the superior is the same as the inferior."[59]

That was an homage to the hermetic *Tabula smaragdina* (*The Emerald Tablet*), one of the foundational texts of alchemy.[60] This "tabula" contained the sentence, "What is above is like that which is down here; and what is down here is like that which is up there."[61] Here the higher world of the

Philosophie, et des Mathematiques (Paris, 1627); Athanasius Kircher, *Musurgia universalis sive Ars magna Consoni et Dissoni in X libros digesta* (Rome, 1650). The book was published one year after the chart was depicted.

57. "Quid sit ab effectibus cognoscere causas in hoc Epilogismo adiectitur [?]." The term "epilogismus" was most widespread in astronomy and chronology. See, e.g., *Eclipseos lunaris anno MDLXXIII mense decembri futurae Epilogismus et typus* (Erfurt, 1573); but see also note 55 in this chapter.

58. "Surdus, videns ludentes in numerum iucundum [?] ex illorum saltationibus cernit quod ex pulsato orga[nis ?] audire non potest, profecto enim prospicit pulsationes Cithariste, saltationes manibus, pedibus, totisque corporis areabus [?] secundare."

59. "et sic respondet (?) ultima primis, et e contra illud Hermetis quod est superius idem quod est inferius."

60. See Julius Ruska, *Tabula smaragdina: Ein Beitrag zur Geschichte der hermetischen Literatur* (Heidelberg, 1926).

61. "Quod est inferius, est sicut (id) quod est superius, et quod est superius, est sicut (id) quod est inferius, ad perpetranda miracula rei unius."

stars and principles is connected to the lower world of the elements and matter and they are declared analogous to each other. In the example given on the chart as depicted by della Vecchia the hierarchy of the senses has become interchangeable. Since the homage of the last sentence on the page is built in, the whole page could be seen as a commentary on the *Tabula smaragdina*. The newly conceived system itself was only a reflection and confirmation of the mysterious Emerald Tablet containing the most ancient wisdom.

Mechanism

The greatest mystery in this newly created system, however, doubtless resides in its reference to mechanism. The title itself spoke of a "Kabbalist or analogous mechanism," and the final word (and hence the key to the whole chart) is also "Mechanica." It ends with a quotation from Hermes, "and he proves both through this mechanism."[62]

What lies hidden here? It probably cannot be completely determined, for tables and charts like this one were intended not just as instruction but also as the sort of mystification that aimed to attract purchasers. *Mechanica* in the current terminology often meant some technical instrument.[63] Inventions or mechanical or geometrical instruments—like recipes—could not yet rely on any patent protections; the inventor had to try instead to suggest his invention without also revealing it. Only the purchaser of the instrument (or the initiated adept of an alchemist) received the whole set of instructions, and then in part only personally.[64] The set of "proportional compasses" invented by Fabrizio Mordente in 1585, for example, was presented in its directions for use as a form

---

62. "et utrumque probat hac / MECHANICA."

63. See as one example out of many, Andreas Albrecht, *Eigentlicher Abriß und Beschreibung eines sehr nützlich und nothwendigen Instruments zur Mechanica/so auf eine Schreib-Taffel gerichtet und zum Feldmessen/Vestung-außstecken/Hoch und Tieff messen/Land und Wasser abwegen: Ingleichen auch zur Perspectiv und andern gar füglich zu gebrauchen* (Nuremberg, 1673).

64. On keeping secrets in the hermetic tradition, see Florian Ebeling, "'Geheimnis' und 'Geheimhaltung' in den Hermetica der Frühen Neuzeit," in *Antike Weisheit und kulturelle Praxis*, ed. Trepp and Lehmann, 63–80; generally: Eamon, *Science and the Secrets of Nature*. On the lack of patent protection, see Pamela O. Long, *Openness, Secrecy, Authorship: Technical Arts and the Culture of Knowledge from Antiquity to the Renaissance* (Baltimore, 2001). On the economy of secrecy, see Jütte, *Das Zeitalter des Geheimnisses*.

of secret knowledge.[65] We are dealing with an "economy of secrets," a topic to which I will return. Only the handwritten additions to the printed broadsheets and instructions from the seller explained in detail how it was to be used.

This made such knowledge so precarious that it often got lost entirely; this would also have been true of the knowledge that the inventor recorded on our pansophic chart if it had not by chance been immortalized in a portrait. Even so, something got lost forever, that is, whatever the inventor communicated orally to make it possible to understand his chart. The page refers to an invention that is not explained. We can only say that it used some method of analogy, some manner of creating a chain of reasoning that took detours through concepts from other areas of reality. It is not clear if it was an early example of the "conceptual arithmetic" that one finds in Weigel's later writings. And yet the series with "four," "four squared," and "four cubed" can be identified as a series of the first significant values in the tetractic number system that Weigel later deployed, as we will see. It was a numerical system based on four, so that the given values of 4^1, 4^2 (16, or "Secht" in Weigel's language), and 4^3 (64, or "Schock" in Weigel's language) can be read.[66] The author intends that whatever this means for arithmetic should be true for other categories as well, and from there he seems to have hit upon the thought that one should be able to "calculate" with the categories too—an idea that we otherwise associate with Leibniz's notion of a "lingua characteristica universalis."[67]

We may gain a little more understanding of the character of this "analogy mechanism" in the drawing that is placed at the bottom edge of our chart. The drawing appears roughly where Großschedel's broadsheet of 1614 had placed the magical *horologium* (clock), a sort of astrological sundial with numerous diagonal lines from one area of the sky to another. Weigel's drawing also has diagonals, but they are organized more as a sort of construction in perspective. What does this strange drawing represent? It depicts a die, but one shown in

65. See Mulsow, "Sachkommentar," 198ff.; Filippo Camerota, *Il compasso di Fabrizio Mordente: Per la storia del compasso di proporzione* (Florence, 2000).

66. See, e.g., Weigel, *Caput summum*, 141ff.; see the commentary by Thomas Behme on pp. 294ff.; see further Weigel, *Arithmetische Beschreibung der Moral-Weißheit worauf das gemeine Wesen bestehet: Nach der Pythagorischen CreutzZahl in lauter tetractysche Glieder eingetheilet* (Jena, 1674). On Weigel's tetractic thinking, in addition to his *Tetraktys, summum . . . compendium* (Jena, 1973), cf. the works by his student, Georg Arnold Burger, *Tetractys trigonometrica* (n.p., n.d.), as well as Johann Schultze, *Tetractys Pythagorica* (Jena, 1672).

67. Cf. Heinrich Schepers, "Scientia generalis," in *Leibniz—Tradition und Aktualität* (Hannover, 1988), 350–59.

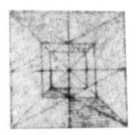

FIGURE 43. Dice, detail from della Vecchia, *Portrait of a Young Man.*

extreme foreshortening, like the perspective we recall from Holbein's famous painting *The Ambassadors*.[68] The die is cut in half on each side by a midline, so that we get the impression that it is made up of eight smaller dice that are all the same size (figure 43).

Now we understand why at the top of the chart God is shown as a die with a dot in the middle: the midpoint is the exact middle of the eight dice, the center of gravity so to speak, its pivot and fulcrum. The symbol for God is, however, also an instruction for producing the "Kabbalistic mechanism." But how could this instrument have functioned? And what's the connection to Weigel's tetractic system? If it really did refer to some movable mechanism, then this die (whose form was already only halfway understandable) must have been a sort of encoded instruction, according to which an instrument could be made using the rotating axes, with which one could then "reckon" with the categorial quaternary units: a sort of Lullian combination generator in the shape of a die. It is reminiscent of the first calculating machines, which also originated at just this time—for example, those of Wilhelm Schickhardt or Kaspar Schott—and which used little rods that could be slid over and back against each other.[69] In any case, the mechanism was the operationalized conversion of Weigel's idea of the tetractys into a philosophical combination machine.

The actual technical details cannot be reconstructed using only the meager suggestions shown on the chart. To understand more clearly, however, what this combination machine had to do with the depicted table of categories, it is helpful to resort to the pansophic system that Weigel produced twenty years later. There we read that Weigel was imagining a sort of conceptual cube, in which he interpreted categorial ideas (*prädikamentale Ideen*) (or "Typus," as Weigel called his diagram) as numerical, as "ideae numericae." So he writes,

68. On geometric constructions of perspective in the seventeenth century, see Martin Kemp, *The Science of Art: Optical Themes in Western Art from Brunelleschi to Seurat* (New Haven, 1990); John David North, *The Ambassadors' Secret, Holbein and the World of the Renaissance* (London, 2002).

69. On these calculating machines, see, e.g., Wilfried de Beauclair, *Rechnen mit Maschinen— Eine Bildgeschichte der Rechentechnik* (Braunschweig, 1968); Bruno von Freitag-Löringhoff, "Über die erste Rechenmaschine," *Physikalische Blätter* 14 (1958): 361–65; Ernst Martin, *Rechenmaschinen mit automatischer Zehnerübertragung* (Pappenheim, 1925).

"And thus the abstract conceivables (called species and genus) of these general-special formalities are quasi categorial ideas, according to which the *quiddities* [*"quidditates,"* the "whatnesses" or essences] themselves (seen as anything at all, speaking formally) can be conceived and treated well by the intellect. The abstract conceivables of the digital-articular-formalities [*digito-articularum ... formalitatum*] of this sort, named for the nouns 'finger' and 'joint,' are not different, being somewhat like numerical ideas, according to which numbers (any at all, speaking materially) are usually conceived and treated distinctively, as we have said above. Therefore, it can be clearly seen that the essences of things are like numbers, which the wisest ancients of yore used to teach."[70] Each row of categories proceeds in this sense from one numerical operation of the mind. The concept "substance," for example, if it is compared with itself evokes the second concept of measure (*modus*), and these two together evoke two more: "act" and "quality," until in this way a completed categorial quaternity has been reached (which at the same time amounts to ten, if one considers how it was generated,[71] just as the Pythagorean tetractys teaches).[72]

From these more precise details from the later years, we can now vaguely discern how the author (Weigel or his disciple) imagined his encyclopedic "cube" in 1649, one that was supposed to contain the fundamental principles

70. Weigel, *Caput summum*, 146ff.: "§ 11. Sunt adeo communi-propriarum harum formalitatum abstractae conceptibilitates (*Species* & *Genera* dictae) quasi *Praedicamentales Ideae*, juxta quas ipsae Quidditates (tanquam Unumquodque formaliter spectatum) ab intellectu commode concipi tractarique possunt: non secus ac digito-articularum ejusmodi formalitatum abstractae conceptibilitates, substantivo nomine *Digiti & Articuli* dictae, quaedam velut *Ideae Numericae* sunt, juxta quas Numeri (tanquam Unumquodque materialiter spectatum) distincte concipi tractarique solent, ut Supra diximus. ADEO RERUM ESSENTIAS SICUT NUMEROS ESSE, QUOD SCIENTISSIMI VETERUM OLIM MONUERUNT, HINC CLARE PERSPICERE LICET." On this, see Thomas Behme's introduction in his edition of Weigel, *Caput summum*, ix–xxxi, esp. xviii ff.

71. Translator's note: $4+3+2+1=10$.

72. Weigel, *Caput summum*, 189: "Quapropter ut intellectus unum cum uno sumit, & binarum illico constituit, cumque cum uno sumens ternarium conflat, quem iterum cum uno sumens quaternarium absolvit, in quo commodissimum articulum nectit, *unitatem* quasi *multitudinariam* sibique clariorem & divisioni, (ad quam in aestimando propendet, quam tamen in unitate vera non invenit) aptam constituens; ita Substantiam cum seipsa conferens illico duplicem ejus rationem saltem sibi cognoscibilem advertit, & sic inter Substantiam & Modos distinguit, quos pro duplici tum cognitionis gradu, tum propriae constitutionis ratione, duplicando, illic ternarium adhuc imperfectum; sed hic, quaternarium, ceu perfectum Summorum generum numerum, constituit, & sic Tetractyn realem, Tetracty numericae correspondentem, exprimit."

of all areas of knowledge and that allowed them to build on each other. To understand the historical background of this cube, let us recall that during the years around 1649 Weigel was a close friend of the military officer and private scholar Basilius Titel.[73] He took over the motto "Theoria cum praxi" from Titel and presumably was welcome to use his book collection as he worked on the teachings of the Pythagorean, Kabbalist, alchemical, and hermetic traditions. Even as early as 1645/1646, when Weigel was serving as secretary to the astrologer Bartholomäus Schimpfer in Halle, he was certainly reading around in such subjects.[74] We also know that Titel was active as an instrument maker, primarily optical instruments. Did Weigel adopt an apparatus from Titel and turn it to other uses? Perhaps turning it into a machine for making philosophical analogies?

The idea is not completely absurd. In the sixteenth century Cornelius Gemma, for example, transformed a "planeto-sphere" into a three-dimensional Lullian instrument for making "cyclognomic" combinations.[75] Giordano Bruno, too, had praised Mordente's proportional compasses to the skies because he found there the prototype of a tool for making philosophical analogies.[76] His *Lampas triginta statuarum* (*Lantern of the Thirty Statues*), indeed, was intended to be a sort of machine for making proofs.[77] Weigel's idea was possibly similar.

73. See Döring, "Weigel," 88ff.

74. On Schimpfer, see *Deutsches Biographisches Archiv*; Johann Dorschner, "Johann Weigel in seiner Zeit," in *Erhard Weigel—1625 bis 1699: Barocker Erzvater*, ed. Reinhard E. Schielicke, Klaus-Dieter Herbst, and Stefan Kratochwil (Acta Historica Astronomiae, vol. 7) (Frankfurt a.M., 1999), 11–38, here at 12 and 14.

75. Gemma, *De arte cyclognomica*. On this, see Martin Mulsow, "Seelenwagen und Ähnlichkeitsmaschine: Zur Reichweite der praktischen Geometrie in der Ars Cyclognomica von Cornelius Gemma," in *Seelenmaschinen*, ed. Berns and Neuber, 249–78; idem, "Arcana naturae: Verborgene Ursachen und universelle Methode von Fernel bis zu Gemma und Bodin," in *Der Naturbegriff in der Frühen Neuzeit*, ed. Thomas Leinkauf (Tübingen, 2005), 31–68.

76. Giordano Bruno, "Mordentius," in idem, *Due dialoghi sconosciuti e due dialoghi noti*, ed. Giovanni Aquilecchia (Rome, 1957).

77. See Martin Mulsow, "Figuration und philosophische Findungskunst: Giordano Brunos Lampas Triginta Statuarum," in *Giordano Bruno in Wittenberg 1586–1588: Aristoteles, Raimundus Lullus, Astronomie*, ed. Thomas Leinkauf (Rome, 2004), 83–94. Bruno was probably using the type of "demonstratio per aequiparentiam," which he found in Lullist logic and addressed in his own Lullist writings. This sort of proof was specially formulated for correlatives and meant that something was proven by what was given with it and assumed if the other was assumed too.

The Painter

But let us return again to Pietro della Vecchia. What might have fascinated him in the chart that contained so many clues to Weigel's early pansophy? What might have so fascinated him that he proudly added his name as *Pictor* (painter) at the bottom of his portrait, or even possibly depicted himself as the man holding the chart? It seems obvious that the answer lies in the connection portrayed between mathematics and philosophy. Significantly, there is another painting by della Vecchia, the earlier allegory containing a "pansophic" page, on which one can also see the sequence of point, line, square, and cube (see figure 22).[78] It was shown rolled up, and so only the upper left-hand corner can be deciphered. There we find the words, "Saepe sub sordido pallio magna latet Sapientia" (Often great wisdom is hidden under a filthy garment). Here the filthy garment is the coat of the old man, probably a philosopher. Wisdom or Truth that lies hidden with him is portrayed as a naked woman, who, as in the portrait in Norfolk, Virginia, is holding a pair of compasses in her hand, the symbol of mathematics or of the geometric approach to philosophy. Presenting the old man in a lustful and intimate proximity to the embodiment of wisdom was very different from other allegories of this sort, but that was della Vecchia's specialty, as we saw in chapter 6.[79] What fascinated della Vecchia in the pansophy of the rolled-up page was surely the claim that geometry was the key to a higher wisdom. The draftsman, the painter, and architect all possessed in their abilities and instruments the means that enabled someone, according to Weigel, to establish the coherence of the whole universe. They could draw the connections between "upper" and "lower."

Let us, however, lift our gaze beyond della Vecchia himself to whoever it was that commissioned his painting. It is by no means sure that this was a self-portrait. It could as easily have been a commission from someone with whose worldview the artist earnestly sympathized. One genre that della Vecchia liked to paint and often sold—perhaps to professors in nearby Padua—was "The Mathematics Lesson." In these pictures there was always a wise teacher, who was intimately initiating boys into the secrets of the world of numbers. On a table full of books we find a poster on which a chart or diagram is depicted that a teacher and his student are looking at. Depending on his commission,

78. Vicenza, Museo Civico. See Aikema, *Della Vecchia*, 59, cat. 151, fig. 112.
79. Besides Aikema, *Della Vecchia*, see also chapter 6.

FIGURE 44. Pietro della Vecchia: *Mathematics Lesson,* Thiene (Vicenza), private collection.
Bernard Aikema, *Pietro della Vecchia and the Heritage of the Renaissance in Venice*
(Florence, 1990), cat. 157, ill. 116.

della Vecchia could paint exoteric or esoteric versions of this scene. In the exoteric variant the chart contains only rows of numbers.[80] But in the esoteric
variant we find a pansophic design like that from Weigel or the one from
Großschedel (figure 44).[81] There the fingers of the teacher are pointing toward
the upper part of the chart where "En soph" or "Deus triunus" would be
placed; with three outstretched fingers the teacher is making the sign of the
Trinity. Here we find not just mathematics but a higher wisdom.

This bit of research tells us something about the intellectual atmosphere in
Venice and Padua around 1650, something that fits well with what else we
know about the "exoteric" and "esoteric" circles there. In Padua they obviously
taught more than merely standard mathematics, while in Venice some intellectuals were deeply immersed in Hermetic philosophy, neo-Platonism, and
Kabbalah. That at least is true for the sixteenth century and for the proclivities
of the Accademia Veneziana at the time of Giulio Camillo (d. 1544) and

80. Della Vecchia, *Mathematikunterricht*, Modena, Galleria Estense. Illustration: Aikema,
Della Vecchia, cat. 157A, ill. 114.

81. Della Vecchia, *Mathematikunterricht*, Thiene (Vicenza), private collection. Illustration:
Aikema, *Della Vecchia*, cat. 157, ill. 116.

Francesco Patrizi (d. 1597).[82] So it may well also have been true for the early and mid-seventeenth century, but the history of Venetian philosophy for this period is still rather poorly understood. The spectrum running from a geometrizing pansophy to the dominant form of subversive Aristotelianism found in the circle of the Accademia degli Incogniti is broad and presents many riddles.

Moreover, the case we're looking at involves a cultural transfer from German pansophy to Italy. That situation needs every bit as much clarification as the isolated reception of Johann Heinrich Alsted's works in the Naples of Giacinto Gimma in the 1690s: Alsted's *Hexalogia, Archeologia*, and *Technologia*. Other such sporadic phenomena exist.[83] Certainly we know that German students, artisans, and artists came over the Alps to Venice, and some of them may have been carrying "occult" teachings in their baggage with which to enrich the colorful intellectual milieu of Venice. If they were the ones who commissioned paintings—if they were so well established that they could afford a portrait—then della Vecchia probably chose the "esoteric" version of his "Mathematics Lesson."

Otto Tachenius

More and more riddles. We come closer to a solution by taking a look at the penultimate line on the diagram in Weigel's chart. If one looks closely, one sees there the name of Otto Tachenius. That was a clear reference to the iatrochemist Otto Tachenius (Otto Taken), who published a book entitled *Hippocrates Chimicus* in 1666, a work that played a role in the alchemy (and nascent chemistry) of the late seventeenth century. The most interesting aspect of the book for us is its place of publication: Venice. Born in 1610, Tachenius was a north German scientist who worked as a servant in various pharmacies—in Herford,

82. On the Accademia Veneziana, see Lina Bolzoni, "L'Accademia Veneziana: Splendore e decadenza in una utopia enciclopedica," in *Università, accademie e società scientifiche in Italia e Germania del 500 al 700*, ed. Laetitia Boehm and E. Raimondi (Bologna, 1981), 117–67. On Camillo, see Frances Yates, *Giordano Bruno and the Hermetic Tradition* (London, 1966); on Patrizi, see Cesare Vasoli, *Francesco Patrizi da Cherso* (Rome, 1989). On the separation of esoteric from exoteric between Venice and Padua, see Plastina, "Concordia discors." On the milieu in Venice, see Jütte, *Das Zeitalter des Geheimnisses*.

83. See Cesare Vasoli, "L'abbate Gimma e la *Nova Enyclopaedia* (Cabbalismo, lullismo, magia e 'nuova scienza' in un testo della fine del Seicento)," in idem, *Profezia e ragione: Studi sulla cultura dei Cinquecento e Seicento* (Naples, 1974), 821–912.

Bremen, Kiel, Danzig, Vilnius, and Vienna—before he enrolled as a medical student in Padua in 1645. In 1647 he obtained his medical doctorate and then settled in Venice.[84] With such a background Tachenius fits perfectly the profile expected of someone who could have transported Weigel's teachings to Italy. It is conceivable, indeed, that during one of his visits to his hometown of Leipzig he even met with Weigel and adopted from him the pansophic theory of tetractic propositional ideas.[85] So he could have been the one who carried the chart with him, had his name inscribed onto it, and then had della Vecchia paint his portrait with it.

But if there was no direct contact between Tachenius and Weigel, there could have been a middleman who brought Tachenius into contact with the teachings from Leipzig. Or maybe there was a third person in this drama, who could have known Weigel's unwritten teachings and also those of Tachenius and could have spliced them together into a coherent structure. It seems obvious that some of the more chemical-hermetic elements of the chart were additions from Tachenius or some other person who had become familiar with his ideas. That allows us to decipher the hitherto illegible penultimate line of the table of categories, or at least the first two entries, "Acidum" and "Alcali," because according to Tachenius acids and alkalis were the two fundamental chemical principles, whose discovery went back to Hippocrates.[86] One then has to interpret the two Hippocratic principles of fire and water in similarly chemical fashion; in this way one could claim that Hippocrates, as a representative of the earliest wisdom, had been a "chemist."[87] The conviction that principles from one tradition of knowledge correspond to those from another was the basic assumption of the whole chart, which we could therefore in a sense call the Weigel-Tachenius Table.

84. See the biography by Heinz-Herbert Take, *Otto Tachenius (1610–1680): Ein Wegbereiter der Chemie zwischen Herford und Venedig* (Bielefeld, 2002).

85. After he moved to Italy, we know of Tachenius's German sojourns in 1659, 1660, 1667, and 1678 (see ibid., 102ff.), but it is of course possible that Tachenius was intermittently in Leipzig in the years before 1649.

86. Otto Tachenius, *Hippocrates Chimicus, qui novissimi viperini salis antiquissima fundamenta ostendit* (Venice, 1666). On the two principles, see Take, *Tachenius*, 91ff.

87. Tachenius appeals first and foremost to the Hippocratic work *De diaeta* (also known as *De victu*, or as *Regimen*), chap. III (CH VI 473ff.). See also Ingo W. Müller, "Untersuchungen zum Hippokratesverständnis von Otto Tachenius und Michael Ettmüller," *Medizinhistorisches Journal* 22 (1987): 327–41.

If Tachenius was in fact the man who commissioned the painting and the man portrayed in it, he must have met Pietro della Vecchia in Venice no later than 1649. He was then thirty-nine years old.[88] If the picture went to him, he probably hung it in his house in Calle de Morte in the parish of Saints John and Paul in Venice, possibly where it could be admired by both patients and visitors.[89] In Tachenius's works we do find occasional references to a special secret method. If it was identical with the one depicted on the chart, it must have made those who examined it more closely curious to learn how the "Kabbalistic mechanism" worked. In his 1669 book, *Antiquissimae Hippocraticae Medicinae Clavis* (*Key to the Most Ancient Hippocratic Medicine*), Tachenius alluded in several passages to a method, which he calls "this private, clear, and absolutely secure method of ours" (*hac nostra privata, explanata, atque tutissima via*), and which he apparently passed on as a sort of secret only to his students and colleagues.[90] He became vehemently angry when his critics failed to recognize its success.[91] His students, however, "through the method we taught," had "grasped the Pythagorean dictum that Nature is similar in every thing, that it manifests not some simulated or painted truth, but the genuine and infallible truth."[92] At the end of his book Tachenius speaks literally of the method of "mechanically" proving the connections among causes in the order of nature.[93] "And just as I have mechanically shown that the

88. We do not know of a picture that would allow comparisons. It is possible that the man portrayed was only a student of Tachenius, but the fact that the portrait presents an imposing or prestigious man suggests this was not the case.

89. On the address, see Take, *Tachenius*, 39ff.

90. *Antiquissimae Hippocraticae Medicinae Clavis, manuali experientia in naturae fontibus elaborata, qua per ignem et aquam inaudita methodo, occulta naturae, et artis, compendiosa operandi ratione manifesta fiunt et dilucide aperiuntur* (Frankfurt 1669), 21ff. (Ad lectorem candidum): "Ab hac nostra privata, explanata, atque tutissima via plurimi viri literati (quos decanorum sociorumque ridiculae censurae exponere ratio dissuadet) antiquissimae hujus philosophiae studiis dediti non parum fructus, et emolumenti exinde esse assecutos, confessi sunt: deprehenderunt enim hac nostra tradita via Pythagoricum illud: naturam in omni re similem: non simulatam, et fucatam, sed sinceram, et infallibilem veritatem prae se ferre."

91. See, e.g., the criticism in Helvig Dieterich, *Vindiciae adversus Otto Tachenium* (Hamburg, 1655); Johann Zwelfer, *Animadversiones in Pharmacopoeiam Augustanam* (Vienna, 1652).

92. See Cicero, *De amicitia* 95 for the opposition of simulatus/fucatus vs. sincerus/verus.

93. Tachenius, *Clavis*, 283ff.: "Ponderet itaque incontaminatus lector aequa lance, & moderato animo antiquissimam hanc veritatis doctrinam, & veterum nostrorum firmissima fundamenta, quae in Hipp. Chim. & in hoc commentariolo, juxta eorum sententiam jacta & stabilita sunt, & justam quin ferat sententiam, non dubito: ex iisdem enim fontibus omnia experimenta

macrocosm behaves unfailingly this way, so too have I concluded with good reason from the views of the ancients that the microcosm must behave in the same way in all the ways we can experience it." Microcosm and macrocosm were interactively related to each other. The "secrets of nature,"[94] the hidden forces of nature, could be deciphered in this manner: by comparing the fundamental principles of nature (which can be validated as the most ancient wisdom) with the evidence that chemical experiments provide.[95] Tachenius writes in the margin of the passage describing the entanglement of microcosm and macrocosm: "Hermes in his little sheet of paper." It's clear that by "little sheet" he meant Hermes's *Tabula smaragdina*. This echoed exactly what it said on the chart in della Vecchia's portrait, that "the upper is the same as the lower." At the same time Tachenius refers to the Hippocratic work *De diaeta* (*On Regimen*), which formulates a virtually Heraclitean dialectic of fire and water: "And destruction comes to all things mutually, to the greater from the less, and to the less from the greater, and the greater increases from the smaller, and the smaller from the greater."[96] If one has understood the entanglement of macrocosm and microcosm, according to Tachenius, then one could

---

deprompta intelliget, ex quibus veneranda antiquitas, & recentiores abditorum naturae interpretes ea duxerunt, minimeque fallacia esse deprehendet: imo reperiet causarum inter se necessarias connexiones, alias ex aliis, ultima a primis, infima a supremis, majora a minoribus, minora a majoribus, debilia a potentibus doctissimo naturae ordine invicem dependentia, & mutua commutatione, digestione, & fermentatione augeri, conservari, interire, & rursus coram oculis nostris in entia nova resurgere, ut Hipp. de diaeta. Et sicut in macrocosmo talia infallibiliter esse mechanice ostendi: sic quoque in microcosmo ejusmodi esse debere omnibus experimentorum indiciis justa ratione ex veterum sententia conclusi. Ideoque hac methodo fieri morbos, & eadem methodo depelli, cum ars imitetur naturam, & haec rursus artem Hippoc. nos docuit: cujus antiquissimam doctrinam IGNE & AQUA firmissimis principiis suffultam contra omnem iniquam invasionem, dum spiro solus defendere confido, eo quod pro hac re obtinenda non indigeo sicut Nobilissimae Medicinae destructores meretricum more multis blandientibus procis."

94. On the "secrets of nature" (*abdita naturae*), see Mulsow, "Arcana naturae."

95. The Hippocratic basis of this method is the procedure of concluding from analogies that the author of *De diaeta* was preaching, with the obvious reliance on Anaxagoras ("The knowledge of the invisible lies in visible phenomena").

96. Hippocrates, *Regimen*, I, v: Loeb ed., trans. W.H.S. Jones, *Hippocrates*, vol. 4 (Cambridge, MA, 1959), 237–39; Hippocrates, *De diaeta* CH VI, 478. See Hippokrates, *Schriften*, ed. Hans Diller (Hamburg, 1962), 233. On this work, see Jacques Jouanna, *Hippocrates* (Baltimore, 1999), 408ff. See generally G.E.R. Lloyd, *Polarity and Analogy: Two Types of Argumentation in Early Greek Thought* (Cambridge, 1966).

recognize, by proceeding methodically and geometrically from the smallest bits of evidence "as if in a mirror" (*quasi in speculo*), the unseen forces of nature.[97]

These agreements between the teachings of the chart as painted by della Vecchia and the secret method of Tachenius must remain matters of historical speculation because the quotations come from Tachenius and were clearly written after 1649. The parallels could therefore be merely accidental. All the same, Tachenius with his empirical interest in the discovery of chemical processes had a motive for adopting the ideas of the early Weigel for turning the Aristotelian doctrine of causes into geometry. He could then have merely expanded Weigel's teachings with his own natural-scientific convictions. But in that case, where could the changes have come from that Tachenius introduced into Weigel's chart, even if we ignore for a moment the penultimate line where his name appears? How or why would he have gone beyond Weigel? Certainly it would be going too far to speculate that the symbol for God in the cube, with its dot in the middle, was adapted by Tachenius simply because it was so close to the chemical symbol for salt (and because salt was the synthetic product of acid and alkali). Admittedly a peculiar salt was the basis of Tachenius's success as a doctor and pharmacist. He had produced a certain "viperine salt"—the product of incinerating poisonous snakes—which he used successfully with patients and marketed throughout all of Europe. According to Tachenius, the alkali in this salt was empty and sought acids with which to saturate itself, something of its own kind. His remedy could help with coagulations, with illnesses caused by acid, such as asthma, kidney stones, and epilepsy.[98] If we

97. Tachenius, *Clavis*, 21: "In demonstrandis autem rebus observavi Geometricorum ordinem, qui a minimo puncto, et a facilimis fundamentis ad maxima difficilimaque gradatim assurgit, quibus mens ingeniosa super aethera scandit: quoque antiquissima Hippocratica medicina et nostra scientia ordine convenienti primum ostendit minus rara imo praeclariora educit; sic Hermes ab ovo: Hippocrates ab artibus: Morienus a veste: Basilius a cerevisa: Cosmopolita a coloribus etc. et tandem admirabili modo, tam in macro, quam microcosmo (eadem enim ratio) naturae arcana, et abdita reserarunt, ut eorum principia, rationes, et causae, quasi in speculo agnoscerentur." The cited alchemical authorities: Morienus, *De re metallica, metallorum transmutatione, et occulta summaque antiquorum medicina libellus* (Paris, 1564); Basilius Valentinus, *Fratris Basilii Valentini Benedictiner Ordens/Geheime Bücher oder letztes Testament. Vom grossen Stein der Uralten Weisen und andern verborgenen Geheimnussen der Natur* (Strasbourg, 1645); Cosmopolita [= Michael Sendivogius], *Novum lumen chymicum* (Cologne, 1610); see generally *Theatrum Chymicum*, 6 vols. (Strasbourg, 1659–61).

98. See Tachenius, *Hippocrates Chimicus*; Take, *Tachenius*, 86ff.

consult again the series of elements listed on the table under "physice," the first two mentioned are fire and water, which were the basic elements according to the Hippocratic *Regimen* and which corresponded to acid and alkali according to the series of Tachenius. Because the various scientific "languages" listed interchangeable entities, they could be represented above one another. Here again there was agreement and correspondence.

The Economy of Secrecy

As I have said, all of this is merely speculation and cannot really be proved. We must always reckon with the possibility that there was another person, unknown to us, who immortalized the ideas of Weigel and Tachenius on the chart as depicted. And yet we now have gained a vague impression of the intellectual atmosphere cultivated in some social circles in Venice around 1650, circles to which even painters such as della Vecchia belonged. These were the social groups with their unorthodox, occult-hermetic interests that finally help us to understand the many pictures by this artist. We can now see that this milieu cultivated an "economy of secrecy," where medical methods, chemical products, or even scientific "universal machines" (ones that produced the "method of analogy" depicted on the chart) could be offered to potential purchasers. This environment even supported a "professorship of secrets," for those who dealt in secret knowledge.[99] In chapter 6 we learned through della Vecchia about precarious knowledge because he had close connections with libertines, who kept their freethinking attitudes a secret; but now we have discovered another aspect of precarity: that of buying and selling secrets. Speculation about the coherence of the whole universe, economic interests, keeping secrets, and the fragility of knowledge were all facets of a single, complex whole.

By following Tachenius, we have found a trail that allows us to glimpse the further contacts that surrounded Marco Aurelio Severino, a famous physician in Naples.[100] Severino was a member of the Accademia degli Investiganti,

99. Jütte, *Das Zeitalter des Geheimnisses.*

100. Take, *Tachenius*, 40ff. On Severino, see Nicola Badaloni, *Introduzione a Vico* (Milan, 1961), 25–37; Luigi de Franco, "La medicina come 'ultimo complemento della scienza': Un discepolo di Campanella: Marco Aurelio Severino," in idem, *Filosofia e scienza in Calabria nei secoli XVI e XVII* (Cosenza, 1988), 237–57, 364–67; Mario Agrimi, "Telesio nel Seicento napoletano," in *Bernardino Telesio e la cultura napoletana*, ed. Raffaele Sirri und Maurizio Torrini (Naples, 1992), 331–72, esp. 353–60. On the alchemical-scientific ambience in Naples, see in addition

which dedicated itself to the latest scientific advances. He was close to the philosophy of Bernardino Telesio, for whom—as for Tachenius—there were two fundamental natural principles, which clashed and in their conflict generated all the phenomena of nature. For Telesio they had been fire and earth (heat and cold), not fire and water; and yet here was clearly a framework within which the two scholars could approach each other, especially since Telesio conceived of his philosophy as the revival of the most ancient teachings.[101] Had Tachenius learned from Severino to find inspiration in Telesio?

It is also fascinating to learn that the young Franciscus Mercurius van Helmont paid a visit to Tachenius in the years right around 1650, just when the portrait was being painted.[102] Tachenius had the reputation of someone who had adopted and elaborated the doctrines of Franciscus's father, Jan Baptist van Helmont, and so Franciscus Mercurius turned to the German doctor in Venice, who took him on as his guest for several months.[103] While there, the younger van Helmont worked on preparing the second edition of his father's works, which were published in 1651 by Juntas and Hertz in Venice.[104] In the preparation of this edition there was much to discuss, and contacts with the publisher had to be established.

Franciscus Mercurius was an extremely unusual young man, four years younger than Tachenius. He intentionally wore very simple clothing and abstained from all conventional courtesies. He was often found in the company of odd and "ill-mannered" people.[105] In that sense he fit well with della Vecchia's discourse about the *sordidum pallium*, the "filthy garment" under which wisdom might be hiding. Could he have been the "third man," who provided the Kabbalistic synthesis of the

Massimo Marra, *Il Pulcinella filosofo chimico di Severino Scipione (1681): Uomini ed idee dell' alchimia a Napoli nel periodo del Viceregno con una scelta di testi originali* (Milan, 2000).

101. Bernardino Telesio, *De rerum natura juxta propria principia* (Rome, 1586). See Mulsow, *Frühneuzeitliche Selbsterhaltung*.

102. Take, *Tachenius*, 43ff.

103. Tachenius tells about this in his *Epistola de famoso liquore Alcahest*, printed in Dieterich, *Vindiciae*, Lit. B.

104. Johann Baptist van Helmont, *Ortus Medicinae id est, initia physicae inaudita, progressus medicinae novus, in morborum ultionem ad vitam longam, nostra autem haec editio, emendatius multo & auctio . . . prodit* (Venice, 1651). In a later edition F. M. van Helmont even included a letter of 1652 from Tachenius to a friend in Nuremberg: *Aufgang der Artzney-Kunst*, trans. Knorr von Rosenroth (Sulzbach, 1683), 56ff.

105. See the foreword by Franciscus Mercurius van Helmont in J. B. van Helmont, *Oriatrike* (London, 1662), 3.

FIGURE 45. Double portrait of father and son
van Helmont. Johann Baptist van Helmont,
Ortus Medicinae (Amsterdam, 1648).

ideas of Weigel and Tachenius? There is only one formal portrait of him from much later (1671), an oil painting by the painter Peter Lely. But there is also an engraving from 1648, a double portrait of the van Helmonts, father and son, that testifies to the fact that the younger man was assuming the mantle of the elder (figure 45). This engraving is found in the first edition of Jan Baptist van Helmont's *Ortus Medicinae* (*The Origin of Medicine*) of 1648. In this image van Helmont is beardless and is wearing his hair longer than that of the man depicted in della Vecchia's portrait, and yet such details could have changed over the course of the next year. The frontispiece of Franciscus Mercurius van Helmont's *Alphabetum naturae* from the year 1667 shows a man with a mustache and goatee like that of the man holding the chart in della Vecchia's painting. Moreover, the figure in the frontispiece is holding a pair of compasses in his left hand.[106]

At the end of 1661 van Helmont was arrested by the Roman Inquisition in Mainz and brought to Rome.[107] Why? He had gained the reputation of being

106. Franciscus Mercurius van Helmont, *Alphabeti vere naturalis Hebraici brevissima delineatio* (Sulzbach, 1667).

107. See Allison P. Coudert, *The Impact of the Kabbalah in the Seventeenth Century: The Life and Thought of Francis Mercury van Helmont (1614–1698)* (Leiden, 1999), 43–57. Coudert says nothing about Helmont's stay in Venice with Tachenius.

someone who was using his chemistry to construct a new worldview—and
therefore he was dangerous, especially because he was exercising unusual influence over the Prince of Palatinate-Sulzbach. He was also a "vagabond," who
placed himself above all the known religions, scoffed at them, and with the
help of his "inner light" had assembled various elements into his own religion.[108] In our terms, he belonged to the knowledge precariat. One wonders
whether during his stay in Venice and through his contact with Tachenius the
younger van Helmont had met della Vecchia and the groups connected to the
Accademia degli Incogniti. For them, such a "chameleon in religion" would
have fit in rather well. But even suspicion must remain speculation—like so
much concerning the connections between libertinism and iatrochemistry in
seventeenth-century Venice. All the same, there are a series of possible connections that could be investigated. The ground for iatrochemistry in Venice
had been prepared by Angelo Sala, who died in 1637, that is, long before Tachenius showed up in Venice.[109] Then in the 1650s and 1660s in addition to Tachenius there were a few other doctors who pursued chemical methods: Giorgio
Torre, who had been born in 1607, and Johann Wepfer, born in 1620—another
immigrant from the north—and Francesco Pona, born in 1594.[110] And Pona
was one of the secretly heterodox members of the Accademia degli Incogniti.[111]
He was a physician, historian, and literary figure from Verona, but he was often
to be found in Venice, where he met up with his friends from the Accademia.

108. See the "Informatio de Helmontio" from 1662 printed in ibid., 363ff.: "Franciscus Mercurius van Helmont, medicus et alchimista, ex variis religionibus (cum sit censor omnium et
irrisor) videtur secundum lumen suum internum quintam aliquam essentiam novae fidei aliqua
re, homo vagabundus, vanorum principum in aulas sectator, inter illos simulat legationes et
fingit, catholicum se dixit, confiteri etiam visus et communicare, quia si aliam religionem palam
profiteretur, multorum principum aulas subire non posset, et simul catholicam ecclesiam er-
rorum accusat, et ita gratus est et acceptus acatholicis, et chamaeleon varios religionis colores,
quando vult, induit."
109. See Giulio Cesare Provenzal, "Angelo Sala (1576–1637)," in Profili di chimici italiani
(Rome, [1938]), 11–16. Sala had grown up in Germany.
110. See Loris Premuda, La medicina e l'organizzazione sanitaria, in Storia della cultura veneta,
vol. 4: Il seicento, part 2 (Vicenza, 1984), 115–50, esp. p. 142.
111. See Giorgio Spini, Richerca dei libertini: La teoria dell' impostura delle religioni nel seicento
italiano, 2nd ed. (Florence, 1983), 51ff. and passim; see, in addition, Pietro Rossi, F. Pona nella
vita e nelle opere, in Memorie dell' Accademia di Agricoltura, Arti e Commercio di Verona, series III,
73 (1897): 67ff.; Francesco Pona was the author of the novel La Lucerna, which was placed on
the Catholic Index of Prohibited Books. See Francesco Pona, La Lucerna, ed. G. Fulco (Rome,
1973).

Did he know Tachenius? We do not know. There certainly were places in Venice where the two of them could have met, for example, at book dealers who specialized in selling forbidden books under the counter. One such book dealer was Salvatore de' Negri, who had a bookstore in the neighborhood of the Church of San Rocco. If della Vecchia, Tachenius, van Helmont, or Pona needed some sort of precarious knowledge, say, Agrippa von Nettesheim's *De occulta philosophia* or Pietro d'Abano's astrological writings, or the *Clavicula Salomonis*, or even some piece of clandestine philosophical literature, they were well advised to go to de' Negri's shop.[112] And Salvatore de' Negri was only one of several.

Hidden Occult Philosophy

Let me attempt a conclusion. We have investigated a fascinating portrait containing a chart that presents clues to the hitherto unknown early philosophy of Erhard Weigel from the time when he was himself still a student. These clues point so clearly to Weigel's later published works that we cannot regard the similarities as merely accidental. That is our first discovery: that the young Weigel was an adherent of occult philosophy to a much greater extent than we had previously known. Obviously stimulated by Bartholomäus Schimpfer and Basilius Titel and through using their libraries, he assembled a remarkable knowledge of occult, alchemical, and hermetic texts and tried to construct his own, original pansophic system and to provide it with a mechanism for inventing and proving new conclusions. Even if we can no longer reconstruct this mechanism, his achievement can be measured, for it consisted in extricating himself from these occult origins from 1649 to 1658. The idea of combining an Aristotelian understanding of causes with Euclidean geometry, as Weigel tried to do in 1658, was foreshadowed in those early years, just like his interest in the Pythagorean tetractys. We can see, moreover, that surprisingly many of his basic ideas, which we only knew from Weigel's much later *Caput summum* of 1673, and especially the combinatorics that wove together concepts as if they were spatially related, were fully present a quarter century earlier. Weigel had kept these ideas to himself for a long time and at most handed them on in handwritten form. We can interpret this situation as proof that either he found it necessary first to jettison the Kabbalist-hermetic conceptual structure in

112. See the studies by Francesco Barbierato, especially *"La rovina di Venetia in material de' libri prohibiti"*: *Il libraio Salvatore de' Negri e l'Inquisizione veneziana (1628–1661)* (Venice, 2007).

order to arrive at the conceptual clarity that characterizes his later works or he failed to publish his ideas in order to protect his career as a university teacher, because by 1650 occult philosophy was not tolerated at a Lutheran university. But if we know Weigel's early sketches, it is perfectly clear how structurally important his repudiated early hermetic-occult philosophy was: structurally important for all of Weigel's later continuing efforts to design a mathematical metaphysics and an encyclopedic science.[113]

Weigel never published his early excursions into pansophy. But in unforeseen ways this sort of precarious knowledge was preserved anyway for it popped up in a Venetian painting. We cannot tell exactly how della Vecchia learned of this theory, but the fact is that Weigel's ideas on the chart that the man portrayed in the painting is holding were expanded by Otto Tachenius's ideas. That suggests that Tachenius could have been the one who carried Weigel's ideas from Leipzig to Venice, but it could have been someone else—most likely someone from north of the Alps—who took up Weigel's and Tachenius's theories and developed them further. It seems possible that this person (and therefore the man portrayed in the painting) was the famous Franciscus Mercurius van Helmont, but that is also not certain. But if so, would we not expect that any chart held by the young van Helmont would more prominently display the influences of his father's natural philosophy? Finally, there's also the possibility that della Vecchia himself gathered together these ideas from his surroundings and recorded them in paint.

No matter what the case may be, the intellectual climate from which this picture arose piques our curiosity. It was a milieu characterized by an "economy of secrecy" and it appears to have been much more precarious than bourgeois—a restless milieu bubbling with fermenting ideas about the nature of the universe but also self-confident, trusting in mathematical methods and often well connected to the wealthy nobles of the Venetian patriciate.

113. This was exactly analogous to the case of Alsted: see Hotson, *Alsted*, 95–181.

10

Family Secrets

PRECARIOUS TRANSFERS WITHIN INTIMATE CIRCLES

HOW WAS precarious knowledge carried forward down the generations? Or more precisely, how was such knowledge passed on within the interior social space of the family? I would like to answer this in two steps, following two different approaches. The first step concentrates on the relationship of theorists around 1700 with their grandfathers, who lived around 1600. The second step, in contrast, takes us to the middle of the eighteenth century. There I will investigate the inner dynamics of a family who belonged to the knowledge bourgeoisie but who could easily have fallen into the precariat—but not all the family members were aware of that fact. This is a story from the scholarly culture of Hamburg, a topic we touched on in chapters 4 and 5, but now we will follow their peculiar history over several generations.[1]

Secret Germany

Every family has its own secrets. The father's brother who was a drunk; the grandmother who had had a child out of wedlock; the parents who ran up debts—but also the concealed former Nazi or covert homosexual. If an entire country upholds secret traditions, strange and unexpected connections can

---

1. See Mulsow, "Entwicklung einer Tatsachenkultur." This chapter is a further development of two newspaper articles: "Die Aufklärung und ihre Enkel: Familiendynamik und Ideengeschichte—Drei Fallbeispiele," *Neue Zürcher Zeitung*, no. 170, July 23, 2011, p. 26, and "Von der Ironisierung zur Kritik der Bibel. Deutsche Aufklärung als Familiengeschichte: Die Korrespondenz von Reimarus," *Frankfurter Allgemeine Zeitung*, December 1, 2010, p. N3.

develop. In an impressive book, Ulrich Raulff has unveiled the "secret Germany" of the followers of Stefan George, the German poet (d. 1933).[2] Raulff's story begins with the death of George in Ticino, touches on the intended assassin of Adolf Hitler, Claus Schenk Count von Stauffenberg, and follows the trail down to Richard von Weizsäcker and the neo-humanists of the 1950s and 1960s. As secret histories are preserved, memories, rumors, and significant objects get handed down. Treasured packages of letters can become icons of membership; Stauffenberg's saber comes to represent unexpected relationships.

So what was the "secret Germany" of the early modern period, say, from the period before the Thirty Years' War down to the beginning of the Enlightenment in the early eighteenth century?[3] Scholars have studied this important period from many points of view—from its economic crises, from the development of education, from the changes in population—but hardly ever as the personal succession of three generations.[4] Anyone whose career was getting started around 1700 had usually been born between 1650 and 1675, in the third quarter of the seventeenth century. This generation had grandfathers who had been born before the catastrophic war, having been conceived as early as the late sixteenth century. At that time in the Holy Roman Empire intellectual and religious currents emerged from which the grandchildren would have preferred to distance themselves, as we may recall from the example of Erhard Weigel. There had been so-called "enthusiasts" or spiritualists, who believed in personal revelations, viewed Christianity as an inward path of salvation, and expected an imminent end to all of history;[5] there had been

2. Ulrich Raulff, *Kreis ohne Meister: Stefan Georges Nachleben* (Munich, 2009).

3. On Germany in this period, see Volker Press, *Kriege und Krisen: Deutschland 1600–1715* (Munich, 1991); Paul Münch, *Das Jahrhundert des Zwiespalts: Deutschland 1600–1700* (Stuttgart, 1999); Heinz Dieter Kittsteiner, *Die Stabilisierungsmoderne: Deutschland und Europa 1618–1715* (Munich, 2010).

4. On the theory of generations, see Karl Mannheim, "Das Problem der Generationen," in idem, *Wissenssoziologie: Auswahl aus dem Werk*, ed. von Kurt H. Wolff (Neuwied/Berlin, 1964), 509–65; Sigrid Weigel et al., eds., *Generation: Zur Genealogie des Konzepts—Konzepte von Genealogie* (Munich, 2005); Christian Kuhn, *Generation als Grundbegriff einer historischen Geschichtskultur: Die Nürnberger Tucher im langen 16. Jahrhundert* (Göttingen, 2010).

5. See, e.g., Martin Brecht, "Die deutschen Spiritualisten des 17. Jahrhunderts," in *Geschichte des Pietismus*, ed. idem, vol. 1: *Das 17. und frühe 18. Jahrhundert* (Göttingen, 1993), 205–40; Hans Schneider, "Der radikale Pietismus im 17. Jahrhundert," in ibid., 391–437.

Socinians or "Photinians," who rejected the holy Trinity.[6] We could ask about the "secret Germany" of that time, looking for the continuation of these sectarian traditions during a period of persecution. And yet that may be less revealing than uncovering the behavior of later descendants, who silently distanced themselves from their ancestors.

By 1700 most Germans felt rather removed from the excitements of earlier periods. Respectable members of German postwar society (after 1648) had taken on the airs of French gallantry and abandoned the blind alleys of fanatical sectarianism, developing models of openness and nonchalance, and calling themselves "eclectic"—a movement that soon led to the Enlightenment.[7] How did such a gallant, modern intellectual deal with the discovery that an ancestor had been a black sheep, one of those fanatics or uninhibited truth seekers? Historians have not usually sought insight from family systems therapy as that field has developed over the past few decades, but family therapists do offer a few concepts that could help us to describe the embarrassments that "enlightened" grandchildren had with their grandfathers. With the necessary use of a "many generations perspective," therapists speak of a "family ledger" containing quantities of shame, debt, and merit that are unconsciously tallied and inherited by family members.[8] Children and grandchildren often act as if bound by invisible debts and loyalties that derive from these ledgers; the conflicts that arise from them can influence the whole course of a life. Such family systems of duty are "healthy," so say the therapists Boszormenyi-Nagy

6. See Zbignew Ogonowski, "Der Sozinianismus," in *Die Philosophie des 17. Jahrhunderts,* vol. 4: *Das Heilige Römische Reich Deutscher Nation, Nord- und Ostmitteleuropa,* 2 vols., ed. Helmut Holzhey and Wilhelm Schmidt-Biggemann (Basel, 2001), 871–81 (with additional literature); Wollgast, *Philosophie in Deutschland.*

7. On gallantry, see Jörn Steigerwald, *Galanterie: Die Fabrikation einer natürlichen Ethik der höfischen Gesellschaft 1650–1710* (Heidelberg, 2011); Florian Gelzer, *Konversation, Galanterie und Abenteuer: Romaneskes Erzählen zwischen Thomasius und Wieland* (Tübingen, 2007). On eclecticism, see Albrecht, *Eklektik.*

8. See, e.g., Günter Reich, Almut Massing, and Manfred Cierpka, "Die Mehrgenerationen-perspektive und das Genogramm," in *Handbuch der Familiendiagnostik,* ed. Manfred Cierpka, 2nd ed. (Heidelberg, 2003), 289–326; John Bradshaw, *Familiengeheimnisse: Warum es sich lohnt, ihnen auf die Spur zu kommen* (Munich, 1999), first published in English as *Family Secrets: The Path from Shame to Healing* (1995); Evan Imber-Black, ed., *Geheimnisse und Tabus in Familie und Familientherapie* (Freiburg 1995), first published in English as *Secrets in Families and Family Therapy* (1993); Monica McGoldrick, Randy Gerson, and Suell Petry, *Genogramme in der Familienberatung,* trans. Irmela Erckenbrecht, 2nd ed. (Bern, 2000), first published in English as *Genograms in Family Assessment* (1985).

and Spark, if there's an opportunity to spread out obligations to children and to bring them into harmony with "the eventual emotional individuation of the members."[9] But that is especially difficult if the parents' or grandparents' legacy is dark and burdened, hidden in secretiveness and taboo subjects. Such precarious relations of obligations also afflicted grandchildren around 1700. They too had to cope with specific family secrets. Let us take three of them in order to see several different sorts of reactions.

Chiliasts and Socinians

In the house of the Brandenburg Prussian court preacher Daniel Ernst Jablonski hung a two-meter-tall painting.[10] It depicted Jan Amos Comenius, the famous Bohemian theologian and pedagogue, the last bishop of the Bohemian Brethren (Unitas Fratrum), and tireless advocate for toleration, reconciliation, and educational reforms; but he had also believed in prophecies and in the imminent end of the world.[11] Jablonski was his grandson. Interestingly, however, he never published anything about his grandfather and never even referred to him in his writings. He did not deny his kinship: friends and acquaintances knew about his relationship, but it seemed important to him that he not be directly identified with his grandfather's program. Jablonski was a politician, and it was clear to him that times had changed and that many a grand vision was now obsolete. Therefore he presented a double image: to intimates

9. Ivan Boszormenyi-Nagy and Geraldine M. Spark, *Unsichtbare Bindungen—Die Dynamik familiärer Systeme*, 7th ed. (Stuttgart, 2001), 78. I am grateful to Daniela Braungart for the reference to this book. The book was first published in English as *Invisible Loyalties: Reciprocity in Intergenerational Family Therapy* (Hagerstown, MD, 1973); the quotation is on p. 47.

10. Joseph Müller, "Die Bilder des Comenius," *Monatshefte der Comenius-Gesellschaft* 1 (1892): 205–9, cited in Werner Korthase, "Johann Amos Comenius und Daniel Ernst Jablonski: Einflüsse, Kontinuitäten, Fortentwicklungen," in *Daniel Ernst Jablonski: Religion, Wissenschaft und Politik um 1700*, ed. Joachim Bahlcke and idem (Stuttgart, 2008), 385–408, at 398. See also Joachim Bahlcke, Boguslaw Dybas, and Hartmut Rudolph, eds., *Brückenschläge: Daniel Ernst Jablonski im Europa der Frühaufklärung* (Dößel, 2010), and in that book esp. Joachim Bahlcke, "Comenius—Figulus—Jablonski: Eine mitteleuropäische Familie zwischen Heimat und Exil," 35–51.

11. On Comenius one must still consult the biography by Milada Blekastad, *Comenius: Versuch eines Umrisses von Leben, Werk, und Schicksal des Jan Amos Komenský* (Oslo and Prague, 1969).

the portrait was open evidence of his loyalty to his grandfather; but in public he was concerned to attract no attention.[12]

It was different for the Prussian law professor in Halle Nikolaus Hieronymus Gundling.[13] His brother, Jacob Paul von Gundling, was famous or infamous for being the fool and figure of ridicule in the "Tobacco Cabinet" of the soldier king Frederick William I.[14] Nikolaus was, however, one of the most liberal disciples and followers of the early Enlightenment professor Christian Thomasius. His skeleton in the closet was a crypto-Socinian grandfather. As a young man of around twenty (before 1615), Johann Vogel was a student and disciple of Ernst Soner, a professor at Altdorf, who secretly promoted antitrinitarian ideas, according to which Jesus Christ could not be called God. Soner's most brilliant student was Martin Ruar, who converted Vogel to these ideas.[15] Two generations later Gundling dealt decisively with this awkward fact. The second essay he ever published in his journal, *Gundlingiana*—a journal he published for many years—treated the case; it was as if Gundling wanted to make a family confession quickly to rid himself of a burden. He begins with an excerpt from a letter by a Lutheran who spoke of a "highly learned man" (*vir doctimissimus*) who had cultivated contacts with Judaizing groups. "This highly learned man," Gundling confessed, "was my late grandfather, Johannes

12. This statement should be qualified by recognizing that around 1700 Comenius was not someone whom one had to reject absolutely; his work for the reform of pedagogy was still acknowledged while many of his views on prophecy and chiliasm could seem antiquated. Jablonski did not distance himself at all from his grandfather; indeed, he was concerned to prevent his unpublished writings from falling into oblivion. Even so, he refrained from invoking him directly.

13. On Gundling, see Martin Mulsow, "Gundling," in *Die Philosophie des 18. Jahrhunderts: Heiliges Römisches Reich deutscher Nation*, ed. Helmut Holzhey and Vilem Mudroch (Grundriss der Geschichte der Philosophie vol. 5/1) (Basel, 2014), 67–71; Notker Hammerstein, *Jus und Historie: Ein Beitrag zur Geschichte des historischen Denkens an deutschen Universitäten im späten 17. und im 18. Jahrhundert* (Göttingen, 1972).

14. Martin Sabrow, *Herr und Hanswurst: Das tragische Schicksal des Hofgelehrten Jacob Paul von Gundling* (Stuttgart, 2001).

15. On this affair, see Gustav Georg Zeltner, *Historia Crypto-Socinismi Altorfinae Quondam Academiae Infesti Arcana* (Leipzig, 1744); Wollgast, *Philosophie in Deutschland*, 378ff.; Wolfgang Mährle, "Eine Hochburg des 'Kryptocalvinismus' und des 'Kryptosozinianismus'? Heterodoxie an der Nürnberger Hochschule in Altdorf um 1600," *Mitteilungen des Vereins für Geschichte der Stadt Nürnberg* 97 (2010): 195–234; Martin Schmeisser and Klaus Birnstiel, "Gelehrtenkultur und antitrinitarische Häresie an der Nürnberger Akademie zu Altdorf," *Daphnis* 39 (2010): 221–85.

Vogel."[16] He quotes from the papers of his grandfather to illuminate his life and contacts. And at the end he emphasizes that in his later years Johann Vogel renounced the errors of his youth in a recantation that Gundling declared that he would publish. Grandfather Vogel had died "peacefully and blessedly" in 1663. "My father Wolfgang Gundling bore him solemnly to the grave on the ninth of June and delivered the funeral sermon."[17] Gundling intended to publish such details, for in those days the manner of one's death was still taken as a clear sign of whether a person would be eternally damned or saved.

The energy and zeal with which Gundling made such announcements reveal his strong desire to erase this stain on his origins. When later he himself was accused of having Socinian tendencies, he was able to dismiss these charges and did not have to worry about supposed family secrets anymore. That heritage had been openly ventilated earlier: the curse associated with not dying "peacefully and blessedly" had been lifted.

In the Midst of the Dispute over Pietism

In contrast, the chief pastor of Hamburg Abraham Hinckelmann reacted allergically to the tension between his family's past and the present, a stress that wounded him so badly that in February 1695 he died of a "hemorrhage" (possibly a ruptured stomach ulcer).[18] Hinckelmann had to keep his family secret hidden as if it had been a severe crime because he was living in a Hamburg that had been engulfed in a virtual civil war. The Pietists and the Orthodox had been fighting each other with everything short of knives and swords; pulpits resounded with death threats.[19] And Hinckelmann was in the middle of it. He belonged to the small group of pastors who had refused to take the oath

16. "Einige besondere Nachrichten von Jacobo Martino, Joanne Vogelio, Martino Ruaro, Martino Seidelio, Sebastiano Hainlino, und andern," in *Gundlingiana, Darinnen allerhand zur Jurisprudenz, Philosophie, Historie/Critic/Litteratur und übrigen Gelehrsamkeit gehörige Sachen abgehandelt worden*, Erstes Stück (Halle, 1715), 27–51, at 31.

17. Ibid., 49.

18. On Hinckelmann, see Mulsow, "Den 'Heydnischen Saurteig' mit den 'Israelitischen Süßteig' vermengt"; idem, "Abraham Hinckelmann und die Genealogie von Böhmes 'Grund-Irrtum,'" in *Offenbarung und Episteme: Zur europäischen Wirkung Jakob Böhmes im 17. und 18. Jahrhundert*, ed. Friedrich Vollhardt and Wilhelm Kühlmann (Berlin, 2012).

19. Rückleben, *Die Niederwerfung der Hamburgischen Ratsgewalt*; Gierl, *Pietismus und Aufklärung*; Daniel Bellingradt, *Flugpublizistik und Öffentlichkeit um 1700: Dynamiken, Akteure und Strukturen im urbanen Raum des Alten Reiches* (Stuttgart, 2011).

demanded by the Orthodox, and therefore they were regarded as "Pietists." Among other things the oath required condemnation of the writings of the "enthusiastic" philosopher Jakob Böhme, the shoemaker and dark mystic who had lived in Görlitz around 1600 and had composed Kabbalistically and al- chemically inspired works.[20] Hinckelmann was torn. Intellectually, he repudi- ated the mysticism of Böhme, but as a liberal citizen he rejected prejudice and hoped instead that the public might reach a balanced judgment. But what no one knew was that Hinckelmann himself was ensnared in the legacy of Böhme. His grandfather Benedikt Hinckelmann had been a close personal friend and disciple of Böhme. More than that: the Hamburg pastor had done some re- search into his forefathers and had drawn the conclusion that his grandfather had originally been named Balthasar Walther.[21] And this Walther was known as an even closer friend of Böhme's and had—or at least so Abraham Hinckel- mann suspected—written the greater part of Böhme's works, for he was much more learned than the shoemaker.[22] To disguise himself he had supposedly attributed the authorship to the shoemaker of Görlitz, and when he later fell under official scrutiny, he had changed his identity and switched to calling himself Benedikt Hinckelmann.

Modern research does not support this hypothesis, even though much of the life of Jakob Böhme remains a mystery. And yet that is not the decisive fact at all. The only important matter is how things seemed to Abraham Hinckel- mann, who was living in the midst of the Hamburg hurricane over Pietism

20. On Böhme and his reception, see Alexandre Koyré, *La Philosophie de Jacob Boehme* (Paris, 1929); Wollgast, *Philosophie in Deutschland*, 677–740; Vollhardt and Kühlmann, *Offen- barung und Episteme*.

21. See the report in Vincentius Placcius, *Theatrum anonymorum et pseudonymorum* (Ham- burg, 1708), Part II: *De scriptis pseudonymis*, p. 582. I am grateful to Carlos Gilly for alerting me to the family connections between Walther and Hinckelmann. See also Carlos Gilly, "Zur Ge- schichte und Überlieferung der Handschriften Jacob Böhmes," in *Jacob Böhmes Weg in die Welt: Zur Geschichte der Handschriftensammlung, Übersetzungen und Editionen von Abraham Willemsz van Beyerland*, ed. Theodor Harmsen (Amsterdam, 2007), 39–54; idem, "Zur Geschichte der Böhme-Biographien des Abraham von Franckenberg," in ibid., 329–64 (and the notes on pp. 440–45, esp. 42 on p. 444).

22. On Walther, see Leigh Penman, "A Second Christian Rosencreutz? Jakob Böhme's Dis- ciple Balthasar Walther (1558–c. 1630) and the Kabbalah, with a Bibliography of Walther's Printed Works," in *Western Esotericism*, ed. Tore Ahlbäck (Turku, 2008), 154–72; idem, "'Ein Liebhaber des Mysterii, und ein großer Verwandter deßselben': Toward the Life of Balthasar Walther: Kabbalist, Alchemist and Wandering Paracelsian Physician," *Sudhoffs Archiv* 94 (2010): 73–99.

when he came to the conviction that he was himself the grandson of the author of the offensive works that had ignited the violent tumults in Hamburg. There was no way he could admit that, or he would have been either lynched or pilloried as a "Behmenist," guilty of having strong family ties to Böhme himself. So between 1691 and 1694 Hinckelmann painfully cut himself off from his own family history. In the course of his scholarly struggle with Böhme's philosophy, he arrived at an informed critique, arguing with the tools of religious history that Böhme's teachings derived from age-old errors going back to gnosticism and the time of the ancient Persians.[23] He resumed his contacts with the leading spokesmen of Lutheran Orthodoxy, Johann Friedrich Mayer and Johann Benedikt Carpzov. He probably saw to it that his grandfather's library containing many Böhme treasures, a legacy owned by his aunt, was rejected by the family and sold off.[24] There could hardly be a more symbolic gesture to eradicate a debt than this move to clean up his family's "multigenerational ledger."

In doing so Hinckelmann must have been of two minds. He held onto the valuable hoard of orientalist and Kabbalistic manuscripts that he had inherited personally from his grandfather and expanded the collection with new manuscripts. Following his family tradition, he proved himself a connoisseur of Kabbalah and in his marginal comments he sometimes showed how highly he valued Jewish mysticism. Hinckelmann was, therefore, practicing an inner balancing act, for he was repudiating Böhme's Kabbalism and increasingly repositioning himself on the side of Lutheran Orthodoxy. It was only when the Orthodox spokesman Mayer went beyond all socially decent norms in slamming Hinckelmann's friend Johann Heinrich Horb for refusing the anti-Pietist oath, and when Horb then proved too weak for this level of stress and died—only then did Hinckelmann out of solidarity waver again and move back to the Pietists. But then he too was attacked, this time by radical Pietists, who repudiated him as lukewarm, causing Hinckelmann himself to die of a hemorrhage.

These three cases reveal the difficulties grandsons had around 1700 with their family "burdens." Jablonski held himself back elegantly and cautiously;

23. Abraham Hinckelmann, *J. N. J. C. Detectio fundamenti Böhmiani, Untersuchung und Widerlegung Der/Grund-Lehre/Die/In Jacob Böhmens Schrifften verhanden: Worinnen unter andern der Recht-gläubige Sinn der alten Jüdischen Cabalae, wie auch der Ursprung alles Fanaticismi und Abgötterey der Welt entdecket wird* (Hamburg, 1693).

24. See the list in Wilhelm Ernst Tentzel, *Monathlichen Unterredungen einiger guten Freunde von allerhand Büchern und andern annehmlichen Geschichten* (Leipzig, 1692), 258–74; and see Gilly, "Zur Geschichte und Überlieferung," 48, 53.

Gundling went on the offensive; and Hinckelmann cast his family legacy aside but hid his connections as well. In all of these cases they had to cope with the bonds of family and the conflict of loyalties but also with the problems of family possessions and especially manuscripts and other sorts of exclusive information handed down by ancestors. Here the precarious transfer of texts created problems if they were to become public knowledge: Jablonski knew about the existence of Comenius's unpublished magnum opus in Halle; Gundling intended to publish Vogel's recantation; and Hinckelmann owned manuscripts of Böhme's writings. For the historian of today who does "Enlightenment research" into what I'm calling "secret Germany," it is harder than for the modern family systems therapist to reconstruct the emotional climate into which a protagonist was born. And yet even we can draw—tentatively— the rudiments of the "genograms" of different family dynamics, sketches that could then be expanded with the "genograms" of manuscript transfers.[25] Jablonski's private library, for example, was studded with rare Comenius works; Hinckelmann's was overflowing with Kabbalistica from the circle around Böhme. The Enlightenment of the eighteenth century, which began with their generation, perpetuated within itself the old holdings of works by sectarians and religious deviants. The varying patterns of adoption, repression, and transmission make up the deep layers of the "Age of Reason and Sentiment"; they caused more than mere ripples on its surface.

The Sacred and the Profane

Let us now push deeper into the "Age of Reason and Sentiment." The second step I mentioned earlier changes the question. Now we will be looking not at precarious adaptations or rejections within the legacy of a family but at ways of circumventing or omitting individual family members from communicating between one generation and the next. But here we will mainly be dealing with the means chosen for such communications: an internal language that thrived on parody and allusions.

Transgressing the border between the sacred and profane always entailed hidden and incalculable risks. It might suffice just to change one's tone of voice. If one spoke in the tones of the Bible, one risked provoking the suspicion that one did not take the Bible seriously enough. Karl Marx loved this

---

25. On genograms, see note 8 in this chapter. On research into the passing on of manuscripts as a kind of "natural history of discourse," see Mulsow, "Transmission," and chapter 4.

impudent tone of voice. In his and Friedrich Engels's book *The Holy Family* (1844), for example, they laughed at their opponent "Herr Hirzel":

> And I saw and heard a mighty angel, Herr *Hirzel*, flying from Zurich across the heavens. And he had in his hand a little book open like the fifth number of the *Allgemeine Literatur-Zeitung*, and he set his right foot upon the mass and his left foot upon Charlottenburg; and he cried with a loud voice as when a lion roareth.[26]

Such imitations of the unctuous words of Scripture had of course been happily deployed by others before Marx. Exactly one hundred years earlier, in 1744 and 1745 a series of war reports from the War of the Austrian Succession appeared that adopted the tone of Old Testament chronicles, supposedly written by a certain "Abraham Ben Saddi" or by his brothers and cousins.[27] So we read:

> And it came to pass at that time that the king in Germany, who was named Emperor Charles the Sixth, died and was gathered to his fathers. But because he had no son who could sit after him upon the throne in Germany, lo, he wrote a letter and sealed it, using the largest seal that he had, and then he died.[28]

The author of most of these pseudo-chronicles was the jurist and journalist Christoph Gottlieb Richter of Altdorf and Erlangen. He had taken inspiration from the English writer Robert Dodsley (d. 1764), a friend of Alexander Pope.[29] It was Dodsley who unleashed the fashionable flood of biblical imitations.

26. Karl Marx und Friedrich Engels, *Die heilige Familie, oder Kritik der kritischen Kritik. Gegen Bruno Bauer und Consorten* (Frankfurt, 1845), 222; MEGA 1/3, p. 387, trans. Richard Dixon into English as *The Holy Family*, chapter 9: "The Critical Last Judgement" at the beginning of that chapter. See Reinhard Buchbinder, *Bibelzitate, Bibelanspielungen, Bibelparodien, theologische Vergleiche und Analogien bei Marx und Engels* (Berlin, 1976).

27. See Ivo Cerman, "Maria Theresia in the Mirror of Contemporary Mock Jewish Chronicles," *Judaica Bohemiae* 38 (2002): 5–47. On parodies of biblical language in England, see Michael Suarez, "The Mock Biblical" (PhD diss., Oxford, 1999); idem, "Mock Biblical Satire from Medieval to Modern," in *A Companion to Satire: Ancient and Modern*, ed. Ruben Quintero (London, 2007), 525–45.

28. Jeckof Ben Saddi [Christoph Gottlieb Richter], *Die Bücher der Chronicka von den Kriegen welche die Frantzosen mit Theresia, der Königin zu Ungarn feführet haben in Oesterreich, und im Reich, Böhmen und in Bayerland und an einem Fluß, der genannt wird der Rhein, beschrieben in Jüdischer Schreibart* (Prague, 1744), 1.

29. On Dodsley, see Harry M. Solomon, *The Rise of Robert Dodsley: Creating the New Age of Print* (Carbondale, 1996); James E. Tierney, ed., *The Correspondence of Robert Dodsley, 1733–1764* (Cambridge, 2004).

The Reimarus Family

In Germany these biblical parodies in chronicle form were best sellers, but "decent burghers" had to handle them like a hot potato. That was certainly true in Hamburg, where the Reimarus family owned several of these books. The father, Hermann Samuel Reimarus, is famous today as one of the leaders of the German Enlightenment and as the sharpest critic of Christianity.[30] And yet during his lifetime that was known to only a few initiates. The manuscript of Reimarus's *Apology*, his biting analysis of the Bible, lay hidden under lock and key in his cabinet for decades before Lessing published parts of it and ignited the "Fragments Controversy."[31] Reimarus did not even entrust his own wife with knowledge of his double life. But his children Albert Hinrich and Elise were much closer to their father's liberal spirit.[32] We know that from a letter that the Reimarus researcher Almut Spalding transcribed, written by the twenty-five-year-old Johann Albert Hinrich on April 8, 1755. At that time he had been studying medicine for a year in Edinburgh. Good-humoredly he asked his little sister Elise, "Aren't you frightened of anatomy?"[33] And then he added, "But now you should regard me as a person (like Maupertuis) who

30. On Reimarus, see note 27 in chapter 1, as well as *Hermann Samuel Reimarus (1694–1768): Ein bekannter Unbekannter der Aufklärung in Hamburg* (Göttingen, 1973); Peter Stemmer, *Weissagung und Kritik: Eine Studie zur Hermeneutik bei Hermann Samuel Reimarus* (Göttingen, 1983); Wilhelm Schmidt-Biggemann, "Einleitung," in *Reimarus: Kleine gelehrte Schriften*, ed. idem (Göttingen, 1994).

31. See William Boehart, *Politik und Religion: Studien zum Fragmentenstreit (Reimarus, Goeze, Lessing)* (Schwarzenbek, 1988); Gerhard Freund, *Theologie im Widerspruch: Die Lessing-Goeze-Kontroverse* (Stuttgart, 1989); Klaus Bohnen, "Leidens-Bewältigungen: Der Lessing-Goeze-Disput im Horizont der Hermeneutik von 'Geist' und 'Buchstabe,'" in *Verspätete Orthodoxie: Über D. Johann Melchior Goeze (1717–1786)*, ed. Heimo Reinitzer and Walter Sparn (Wiesbaden, 1989), 179–96.

32. We still need a monograph on Albert Hinrich Reimarus. But see Franklin Kopitzsch, *Grundzüge einer Sozialgeschichte der Aufklärung in Hamburg und Altona*, 2nd ed. (Hamburg, 1990), 528ff. and passim. On Elise Reimarus, see Almut Spalding, *Elise Reimarus (1735–1805), the Muse of Hamburg: A Woman of the German Enlightenment* (Würzburg, 2005). On the Reimarus household, see Almut Spalding and Paul Spalding, "Living in the Enlightenment: The Reimarus Household Accounts of 1728–1780," in *Between Philology and Radical Enlightenment*, ed. Mulsow, 201–30.

33. Johann Albert Hinrich Reimarus to Elise Reimarus, Edinburgh, April 8, 1755, State Archive of Hamburg, not yet catalogued. Transcription by Almut Spalding, to whom I am most thankful for providing me with the text.

always carries a knife with which to slice up people."³⁴ He describes the difficulty in Scotland of obtaining cadavers for anatomical dissections. And then he suddenly fell into a parody of biblical language as he described how they had almost obtained the corpse of a deceased madman: "Before we could avail ourselves of it, behold, his friends arrived and bore it off to the grave, and so you see that makes it hard for us to dissect a dead body here; but more of this later. Yet careth heaven not always for His own, as is written in the Chronicle of the Kings of England?"³⁵ That was the title of Dodsley's book, as translated by Richter.³⁶ By referring to the title and by adopting its biblical tone, Reimarus was signaling in code to his sister so that she would understand. And then he added, "a work which you do not have to admit we have in our house, because it is hated for its outward appearance."

And then something unusual follows. Reimarus added a *Nota bene* and directed his sister: "Read this at leisure; afterwards you can show it to Papa."³⁷ Clearly it was customary in the Reimarus household that the daughter read her brother's letters aloud, mainly to their mother. Meanwhile the father was lecturing at Hamburg's academic gymnasium or burying himself in his study with his books.³⁸ Young Reimarus determined that he would, not "later" as he had said, but immediately describe the dangerous business of joining other young doctors at night secretly to dig up corpses. Mother was not supposed to learn about that. "Now at that time there went out four mighty men of valor," he began, using the tone of Dodsley and Richter, "along with the man who had need of them," that is, the young doctor who arranged for the help of four sturdy helpers at the graveside. "Then he spake unto them, 'You know, dear brethren, we need the dead for the sake of the living and seek instruction from those who have died. But now is an evil time and so we look about us to see if someone has been gathered to his fathers, perhaps a member of the king's

34. The text continues: "Ja, letzt hatte mich mein Doctor gar bestellt gleich jenem die Beschaffenheit der Seele zu untersuchen in dem Gehirne nämlich eines Menschen der rasend geworden war."

35. Albert Hinrich Reimarus to Elise, April 8, 1755.

36. *Die Bücher der Chronick derer Könige von Engelland: Beschrieben in jüdischer Schreibart durch Nathan ben Saddi. Nach dem Original verdollmetscht und fortgeführt bis auf den heutigen Tag [von Christoph Gottlieb Richter]*, 2nd ed. (Frankfurt and Leipzig, 1744). The original: [Robert Dodsley], *The Chronicle of the Kings of England* (London, 1740). Sometimes Lord Chesterfield was also regarded as the author of this chronicle.

37. Albert Hinrich Reimarus to Elise, April 8, 1755.

38. On Reimarus's lectures, see chapter 14.

bodyguards [literally "Crethi und Plethi"] or one who was languishing in jail, or perhaps one who was hanged in the sun; behold, there was no one on the right side or on the left. Therefore there came to me a physician [literally: one who was serving Aesculapius] who said "Let us go up even unto the grave [literally: to Hell (Hölle)—i.e., the hole ('Höhle') in the ground] to bring out someone who has been gathered [to his fathers]."' . . . And they came unto the place where a dead man had been laid, and dug him up, and brought out his coffin, and there was a big bang. And there were in the houses round about people who were awake, here a light and there a light. But all the people were stricken with blindness, so that they saw not the men as they went forth nor as they went in."[39]

For young Reimarus this artificially alienated language was clearly a means of masking his discussion of a risky event. The fact that they had become grave robbers was probably easier to tolerate, for himself as well as for his sister and father, because he did not describe the situation in colloquial language. His parodic distancing from the Bible despite all the joshing was a basic presupposition of the story; the effect was similar to what we find in comparable stories of alienation from the early eighteenth century, such as Giovanni Paolo Marana's *Turkish Spy* (1684–86), in which a fictitious "Arabian" wrote letters describing his impressions of the European courts, or Montesquieu's more famous *Persian Letters* (1721), which proceeded on a similar basis.[40]

Biblical Criticism

One should not foolishly leap to the conclusion that Hermann Samuel Reimarus based his biblical criticism on nothing more than the distance caused by the pseudo-biblical chronicles in his library. But there was probably some kind of kinship between the parodic imitation of sacred texts and the self-confident freedom to imagine the background of the sacred texts as all-too-human dirty tricks. For the younger Reimarus, stealing corpses could be described in biblical language; in the father's *Apology* after Jesus' death, the

39. Albert Hinrich Reimarus to Elise, April 8, 1755.

40. [Giovanni Paolo Marana], *L'espion dans les cours des princes chrétiens, ou Lettres et mémoires d'un envoyé secret de la Porte dans les cours de l'Europe* ("Cologne," 1684); see Salvatore Rotta, "Gian Paolo Marana," in idem, *La letteratura ligure: La repubblica aristocratica (1528–1797)* (Genoa, 1992), 2:153–87; Montesquieu, *Persische Briefe* (Stuttgart, 1991). Cf. Randolph Paul Runyon, *The Art of the Persian Letters: Unlocking Montesquieu's "Secret Chain"* (Newark, 2005).

Apostles snatched his corpse in order to fake his resurrection.[41] One of the fellow students with whom young Reimarus went looking for corpses in Scotland was probably Erasmus Darwin, who was Reimarus's closest friend from his student days.[42] Darwin too was scientifically "modern" and skeptical about the doctrines of the church. He was well versed in literary matters and would have appreciated the poetic manner of expression chosen by his German friend. This generation completed the step from philology to practical Enlightenment; fully two generations before Erasmus Darwin's grandson Charles, they were considering the likelihood that human beings had arisen from lower forms of life; they were also preaching the usefulness of electricity.[43] It was Albert Hinrich Reimarus who introduced the lightning rod to Hamburg in 1768. To adopt the phrase of Heinz Dieter Kittsteiner—who himself was borrowing the concept from Jean Delumeau—this lightning rod signaled the end of the age of "guilt culture" (French: "culpabilisation"): the thunderstorm, understood as the wrath of God, lost its supernatural power; the shifting of guilt onto the sinner was now lifted—and that was also true for those who had committed a sin by stealing a corpse for medical dissection.[44] In 1755 parodying the language of the Bible was already a bit like a lightning rod for this young man.

41. Reimarus, *Apologie oder Schutzschrift für die vernünftigen Verehrer Gottes*, 2:188ff.

42. On Erasmus Darwin, see Desmond King-Hele, *Erasmus Darwin: A Life of Unequalled Achievement* (London, 1999); Jennifer Uglow, *Lunar Men: The Friends Who Made the Future, 1730–1810* (London, 2003).

43. Johann Albert Hinrich Reimarus, *Die Ursache des Einschlagens vom Blitze, nebst dessen natürlichen Abwendung von unseren Gebäuden* (Langensalza, 1769). Cf. Cornel Zwierlein, *Der gezähmte Prometheus: Feuer und Sicherheit zwischen Früher Neuzeit und Moderne* (Göttingen, 2011), 131, 191.

44. Heinz Dieter Kittsteiner, *Die Entstehung des modernen Gewissens* (Frankfurt, 1991); Jean Delumeau, *Le peché et la peur: La culpibilisation en Occident, XIIIe–XVIIIe siècles* (Paris, 1983).

11

The Lost Package

THE ROLE OF COMMUNICATIONS IN THE HISTORY OF PHILOSOPHY IN GERMANY

Knowledge is a collective good. In securing our knowledge, we rely upon others, and we cannot dispense with that reliance.

—STEPHEN SHAPIN[1]

An Alternative Version of the History of Philosophy

In the past couple of decades a great deal of solid research has been dedicated to the study of the "heroic phase" of writing the history of philosophy.[2] Only if we comprehend how our modern conception of intellectual history came

---

1. Shapin, *A Social History of Truth*, xxv. I am grateful to Detlef Döring for providing me with a transcription of the Brucker letters to Gottsched before their publication in vol. 4 of his edition. Wiebke Hemmerling kindly showed me her then still unpublished essay "Heumann contra Türck, Gundling und Gottsched—Ausschnitte früher öffentlicher Streitkultur in Rezensionszeitschriften," now published in *Christoph August Heumann (1681–1764): Gelehrte Praxis zwischen christlichem Humanismus und Aufklärung*, ed. Martin Mulsow, Kasper Eskildsen, and Helmut Zedelmaier (Stuttgart, 2017), 25–37. Wolfgang Behringer helped me with his knowledge of postal routes; Silke Wagener-Fimpel of the State Archive in Wolfenbüttel kindly informed me of the records for the "Küchenpost," i.e., the princely provisions coach; Asaph Ben-Tov showed me the document catalogued as Akte 2 Alt. No. 10329.

2. Lucien Braun, *Geschichte der Philosophiegeschichte* (Darmstadt, 1990); Mario Longo, "The General Histories of Philosophy in Germany," in *Models of the History of Philosophy*, vol. 2: *From the Cartesian Age to Brucker*, ed. Gregorio Piaia and Giovanni Santinello (Dordrecht, 2011), 301–578 (Longo wrote pp. 301–86 with Francesco Bottin); Ralph Häfner, "Jacob Thomasius und

into being—for example, the notion that philosophy begins with the Greeks—
can we also hope to grasp what this conception includes and excludes along
with the very understanding of "rationality" that it assumes. Modernity is defined in many ways, but not least by what it excludes. And yet research into
such matters needs to be expanded in two directions. First, the historians of
philosophy and literature from the early eighteenth century need to be understood not just as holding isolated positions but as a network of intellectuals.[3]
They were in contact with one another, supporting but also criticizing, and they
wrote their studies in response to those of others. We need to ask what the
networks and constellations (if they were close-knit) looked like. Second,
we need to look at more than just the finished, published works on the history
of philosophy; we should examine also the designs, student handbooks, and
reading notes. In chapter 14 we will see, using Johann Christoph Wolf's notes,
what a difference the integration of such manuscript material makes.[4] We
obtain a new and dynamic picture of the origins of the history of philosophy,
one in dialogue and response with others.[5]

In this chapter I intend to sketch what such a "new" history of the history
of philosophy might look like by using the case of Christoph August Heumann, a philosopher, philologist, theologian, and historian.[6] We will see that
the constellation he belonged to was far from collaborative and peaceful—
sometimes it could look more like a crime scene. In this story the risky transfer
of texts played a crucial role.

For scholars who worked on the history of philosophy and literature the
first essential prerequisite was procuring as many relevant books and if possible manuscripts as well. The task was hardly imaginable without the right

die Geschichte der Häresien," in *Christian Thomasius: Neue Forschungen im Kontext der Frühaufklärung*, ed. Friedrich Vollhardt (Tübingen, 1997), 142–64; Helmut Zedelmaier, *Der Anfang
der Geschichte: Zur Ursprungsdebatte im 18. Jahrhundert* (Hamburg, 2003); Ulrich Johannes
Schneider, *Die Vergangenheit des Geistes: Eine Archäologie der Philosophiegeschichte* (Frankfurt,
1990); Lehmann-Brauns, *Weisheit in der Weltgeschichte*.

3. On research into constellations or networks, see Martin Mulsow and Marcelo Stamm,
eds., *Konstellationsforschung* (Frankfurt, 2005).

4. See also Elisabeth Decultot, *Untersuchungen zu Winckelmanns Exzerptheften: Ein Beitrag
zur Genealogie der Kunstgeschichte im 18. Jahrhundert* (Ruhpolding, 2004).

5. For reflections on books and their origins, see Dieter Henrich, *Werke im Werden: Über die
Genesis philosophischer Einsichten* (Munich, 2001).

6. On Heumann in addition to Longo, "General Histories" and Lehmann-Brauns, *Weisheit*,
see Mulsow, Eskildsen, and Zedelmaier, *Christoph August Heumann*.

materials. But how did scholars use to obtain their texts? Not everyone was in a position financially to build up a huge library. To be sure, Johann Albert Fabricius, Johann Christoph Wolf, and Jakob Friedrich Reimmann did accomplish that goal, using various strategies, and we will see how they did it.[7] But Heumann never succeeded in putting together anything like their libraries, the largest of which held 20,000 to 30,000 volumes. He did, however, know how to get the help he needed. Frequently he described Conrad Zacharias von Uffenbach as the "Pinellus and Peirescus" of his age.[8] What he meant is clear enough: Gianvincenzo Pinelli was renowned as the center of communications and of book lending throughout northern Italy; Nicolas-Claude de Peiresc performed the same function in even more lavish fashion in southern France.[9] In point of fact, the rich and learned Frankfurt patrician Uffenbach— the same man we mentioned in chapter 7 as he expressed his astonishment at Hermann von der Hardt's oracle chest—helped more than one German historian of philosophy and literature through his brisk private lending practice. Uffenbach often allowed access to his private collection, which was fairly bursting with the rarest materials. He would be the worthy subject of a whole book that could describe his importance for the upsurge in the study of intellectual history in the 1720s and 1730s—lending and trading books with Fabricius, Wolf, Mathurin Veyssière La Croze, Johann Lorenz Mosheim, Gottlieb Stolle, and many others, including Heumann.[10] The Lower Saxon Library in

7. See generally Paul Raabe, ed., *Öffentliche und private Bibliotheken im 17. und 18. Jahrhundert* (Bremen, 1977). On Reimmann, see Martin Mulsow and Helmut Zedelmaier, eds., *Skepsis, Providenz, Polyhistorie. Jakob Friedrich Reimmann (1668–1743)* (Rübingen, 1998); on Fabricius, see Petersen, *Intellectum Liberare*; on Wolf, see chapter 14.

8. *Acta philosophorum* 1 (1715), 504. On Uffenbach, see Konrad Franke, "Zacharias Conrad von Uffenbach als Handschriftensammler," *Börsenblatt für den deutschen Buchhandel*, Frankfurt edition, 21 (1965): 1235–1338 (= Archiv für Geschichte des Buchwesens 45); *Zacharias Conrad von Uffenbach (1683–1734): Ein Blick auf ausgewählte Stücke aus seinen Sammlungen; eine Ausstellung d. Universitätsbibliothek der Helmut-Schmidt-Universität* (Hamburg, 2007). We still need a comprehensive monograph on him.

9. On Pinelli, see Angela Nuovo, "The Creation and Dispersal of the Library of Gian Vincenzo Pinelli," in *Books on the Move: Tracking Copies through Collections and the Book Trade*, ed. Giles Mandelbrote et al. (New Castle, DE, and London, 2007), 39–68; Anna Maria Raugei, ed., *Gianvincenzo Pinelli et Claude Dupuy: Une correspondence entre deux humanistes* (Florence, 2001). On Peiresc, see Peter N. Miller, *Peiresc's Europe: Learning and Virtue in the Seventeenth Century* (New Haven, 2000).

10. See the exhibition in Monika Estermann, *Verzeichnis der gedruckten Briefe deutscher Autoren des 17. Jahrhunderts/Drucke zwischen 1600 und 1750* (Wiesbaden, 1993).

Hanover holds sixty-seven letters from Uffenbach to Heumann from the years between 1715 and 1735.[11] Through men like him precarious knowledge was kept alive.

For simplicity's sake let us first take two slices of time in order to see how the constellations of actors changed from the years around 1715 to those around 1730. By 1715, when the first volume of Heumann's *Acta philosophorum* appeared, the history of philosophy in Germany was already highly complicated. The scholars connected with the early Enlightenment in Halle had devoted themselves to eclectic philosophy, an idea of philosophy, that tried to avoid the ossification of intellectual currents in the various philosophical "sects" (as we've seen in earlier chapters). That had been a typical reaction during the confessional age. To rule out the construction of sects and prejudices, they wanted to view all available materials first, before choosing a selection of the best.[12] At least that was the ideal. The result was the adoption of a literary-historical orientation for all scholarship, one that connected with the latest developments in historical and philological criticism.[13] Theology provided the model for understanding the critical survey as an estimate of risks and consequences, that is, of weighing philosophical currents according to how they might threaten (or historically had already threatened) Christianity and what the dangerous consequences might be. That process allowed for different conclusions: Johann Franz Budde warned against Greek materialists and Stoics, because Spinoza had supposedly arisen from them; others warned against Platonists and "enthusiasts," who served as forerunners for contemporary spiritualists, radical Pietists, and occultists. Pursuing such questions generated many specialized studies from Jakob Thomasius, Budde, Gundling, and other scholars.[14] Most of them knew each other well and were in constant communication.

11. Leibniz-Bibliothek Hannover, Ms. XLII, 1915. See also Heumann's editions of volumes of letters drawn from Uffenbach's collected volumes, *Poecile sive epistolae miscellanae ad literatissimos sevi nostri viros*, vol. 1, Halle, 1722–vol. 3, Halle 1732.

12. See Dreitzel, "Entwicklung und Eigenart der 'eklektischen Philosophie'"; Albrecht, *Eklektik*.

13. Jean Jehasse, *La renaissance de la critique: L'essor de l'humanisme érudit de 1560 à 1614* (Saint-Etienne, 1976); Herbert Jaumann, *Critica: Untersuchungen zur Geschichte der Literaturkritik zwischen Quintilian und Thomasius* (Leiden, 1995).

14. On the differences, see Martin Mulsow, "Gundling versus Buddeus: Competing Models for the History of Philosophy," in *History and the Disciplines: The Reclassification of Knowledge in Early Modern Europe*, ed. Donald Kelley (Rochester, 1997), 103–25.

There was also the broader circle of persons who were interested in the history of philosophy even though they were not in direct personal communication, and they contributed to the accumulation of historical knowledge. Here is one small example of how information circulated in 1715 among the historians of philosophy. It began with a query in 1715 about a coin or medal with the portrait of the early Greek philosopher Thales.[15] A scholar in the Margravate of Ansbach obtained such a coin, but his linguistic abilities did not permit him to read the circumscribed words around the portrait on the obverse, and perhaps the condition of the coin presented its own difficulties.[16] On the reverse of the coin was a female form with a cornucopia and sword, and before her a rooster on a small altar, but also with an almost illegible circumscription. He sent a drawing of his coin to his friend Johann Heinrich May Jr., a young professor of Greek and Oriental languages at the University of Giessen, who was much interested in coins and already had a sizable collection of them.[17] May deciphered the Greek letters as ΘΑΛΗΤΟΣ ΜΙΛΗΣΙΟΥ (Thales of Miletus) and interpreted the woman with the cornucopia as the personification of luck, the rooster as the symbol of intelligence, and the sword as the symbol of the fortunes of war. Moreover he interpreted the difficult writing on the reverse as ΟΥΤΩΣ ΑΠΟΛΛΥΕΙΝ ΔΥΝΑΜΕΘΑ (Thus can we lose).

Then May sent the sketch of the coin together with his interpretation to his friend Uffenbach in Frankfurt along with the request that he should look it up to see if it had been mentioned or even reproduced anywhere in antiquarian works.[18] Uffenbach responded that he was astonished at the skill with which May had explained the coin's meaning. "If it's genuine (which only a personal viewing could determine), it would be very rare and valuable. I myself own various coins that show the visage of ancient philosophers and poets, but almost all of them are forgeries." Uffenbach went to his bookshelves and paged

15. Heumann, "Nachricht von einer dem Thaleti zu Ehren geschlagenen Müntze," in *Acta philosophorum* vol. 1, 3. Stück, pp. 520–22. This medal was probably a contorniate medal pressed in the fourth or fifth century CE, or else a forgery.

16. It is not entirely clear who this scholar was. He may have been the director of the Ansbach gymnasium, Georg Nikolaus Köhler, or the prorector Johann Georg Christoph Feuerlein, the young Georg Ludwig Oeder, Johann Andreas Uhl, or someone else interested in numismatics.

17. See Erich Schmidt, "Johann Heinrich May der Jüngere und die Gießener Münzsammlung," *Mitteilungen des oberhessischen Geschichtsvereins* 48 (1964): 93–119.

18. Reported by Heumann; the original letters from May to Uffenbach are now in the University Library of Frankfurt am Main, catalogued as Ms. Ff. Uffenbach, vol. 1.

through the volumes of Spanheim and Wilde, consulted the history of philosophy by Thomas Stanley, but all to no avail.[19]

Then Uffenbach informed his friend Heumann in Eisenach of his thoughts because he knew that he was a historian of philosophy and would be very interested in a Thales coin for that reason. Heumann promptly printed this correspondence in his *Acta philosophorum*. In this way he offered the learned public a chance to join in the discussion of this problem but also possibly to obtain information he wanted. This was how the Republic of Letters worked: first one discussed questions in private letters, then turned the matter over to the editors of learned journals and compendia such as Heumann, Johann Burkhard Mencke, Wilhelm Ernst Tentzel, or Vinzent Placcius, who set these questions before the public. In his *Monthly Conversations*, for example, Tentzel published his doubts about alchemical coins and then the opinions about them that had been sent to him.[20] In a similar fashion back in the 1670s (as we saw in chapter 4) Vinzent Placcius appealed to scholars to help him in identifying the actual authors hiding behind pseudonymous works.[21]

The concerns about the authenticity of an image of Thales provide a fleeting glimpse of such collective and cumulative efforts in early eighteenth-century Germany. Heumann's journal, the *Acta philosophorum*, which was published in Halle, whose title imitated that of the well-established *Acta eruditorum* (published in Leipzig), was an important organ for the distribution of learned queries and discussions. There were other communication hubs as well, such as Leipzig, the major publishing center. Thus from 1710 onward the Leipzig

19. Uffenbach to Heumann, in Heumann, *Nachricht*, 522: "Sed ad dulcissimas Tuas redeo, tuamque in *Thaletis* numo explicando dexteritatem miror. Quod si genuinus foret, (quod inspectio docere potest,) rarissimus praestantissimusque esset. Varios sane ipsius possideo numos, veterum philosophorum ac poetarum vultus referentes, sed omnes fere spurii sunt. Sed cum neque ipsum, de quo quaestio est, numum neque ectypum viderim, nil definire audio. Excusi vero omnem meam antiquariorum sat locupletem, praefiscine dico, suppelectilem, sed frustra illum quaesivi. Illustrem *Spanhemium* vel *Wildium* illum erto producturos, quippe qui non Impp. Familiarumque nummos solum, sed et alios recensent, vel etiam *Stanleium in Historia philosophiae* eius mentionem facturam, sperabam; sed fefellit opinio. *Stanleius* equidem ex Cicerone, Herodoto, atque Diogene Laertio eius in rebus civilibus gerendaque rep. prudentiam singulari capite (decimo scilicet) laudat exemplisque comprobat, et *Cap. XIII.* statuam ei positam cum inscriptione Laertio refert. Quae eruditam Tuam opinionem non modo confirmant, sed probabile etiam faciunt, numum hunc in eius honorem cusum fuisse, quippe cui statua etiam erecta fuerit."

20. Tentzel, *Monatliche Unterredungen*, 423ff.

21. Placcius, *Invitatio amica*.

professor Johann Burkhard Mencke was a centrally important contact for Heumann, along with Uffenbach in Frankfurt.[22] Before the age of Gottsched (ca. 1725–45) , Mencke was the central figure in the intellectual life of Leipzig; his horizon was Europe-wide, and he hastily penned short, busy letters to his many friends. In his two lectures entitled *De charlataneria eruditorum* (*On the Fraudulence of the Learned*), which greatly pleased Johann Heinrich Heubel, Mencke made fun of the pedantry and pomposity of many scholars; and following the tradition laid down by his father, he continued the publication of the *Acta eruditorum*, a journal of reviews that was read throughout Europe in which Heumann was allowed to contribute along with Leibniz, Seckendorff, and other greats of the day.[23]

Despite all this activity one thing was lacking: a synthesis of the new scholarship concerning the history of philosophy. But who could undertake such a huge task? In the years around 1730 that was the question as the scene began to shift. A few big names had joined the scholarly conversation, including several from southern Germany such as Johann Georg Schelhorn from Memmingen (1694–1773) and Johann Jakob Zimmermann from Zurich (1695–1756). Schelhorn, the editor of *Amoenitates literariae* (*Literary Delights*), had been in contact with Heumann from 1723 onward.[24] Even more important, however, was Johann Jakob Brucker, a pastor and headmaster of the Latin school in Kaufbeuren, near Augsburg.[25] As a thirty-four-year-old in 1730, Jakob Brucker took on the actual task of providing the much-needed synthesis. The result looked like a schoolbook, with the modest title *Short Questions from the History of Philosophy*, but the project grew into a huge and comprehensive

22. Concerning Mencke, see Agnes-Hermine Hermes, *Johann Burkhard Mencke in seiner Zeit* (PhD diss., Frankfurt, 1934); Werner Fläschendräger, "Johann Burkhard Mencke (1674–1732)," in *Bedeutende Gelehrte in Leipzig*, ed. Max Steinmetz (Leipzig, 1965), 1:15–24. We need a new and comprehensive monograph on him.

23. Mencke, *De charlataneria eruditorum*; on the *Acta*, see Augustinus Hubertus Laeven, *The "Acta Eruditorum" under the Editorship of Otto Mencke (1644–1707): The History of an International Learned Journal between 1682 and 1707* (Amsterdam and Maarssen, 1990).

24. Johann Georg Schelhorn, *Amoenitates literariae, quibus variae observationes, scripta item quaedam anecdota et rariora opuscula exhibentur*, 14 vols. (Ulm, 1724–31).

25. On Brucker, see, in addition to Longo, "General Histories," Wilhelm Schmidt-Biggemann and Theo Stammen, eds., *Jacob Brucker (1696–1770): Philosoph und Historiker der europäischen Aufklärung* (Berlin, 1998); Christine Lüdke, "'Ich bitte mir Euer Hochedelgebohren Gedancken aus!': Beiträge zur Erschließung und Analyse von Jakob Bruckers Korrespondenz" (PhD diss., Augsburg 2006).

work comprising seven fat volumes that appeared between 1731 and 1737. It was the German-language forerunner of Brucker's own *Historia critica philosophiae* (*Critical History of Philosophy*, originally 5 vols., 1742–44, expanded to 6 vols., 1766–67), the largest and most important history of philosophy in the eighteenth century.[26] Without Heumann, this remarkable synthesis would not have been possible—and that's the subject of the following story.

First Contact

In 1730 in a letter that does not survive, Brucker turned to Heumann, asking politely and deferentially for information and advice. He probably included with his letter several of his already published essays, perhaps his *Otium Vindelicum* (*Augsburg Leisure*) from 1729 or some of the studies he had published in Schelhorn's *Amoenitates*. How did Heumann react? He must have recognized Brucker's great talent at once because he appears to have answered him in a manner that left Brucker speechless. Not only did he offer him friendship and continued correspondence but, perhaps impulsively, access to many of his scholarly treasures.[27]

In any event Brucker was so astonished and delighted at Heumann's reaction that he could only reply with a stammering letter, sent off on April 16, 1730.

> Great sir, what I hardly expected from you, and dared even less to request, you have now so freely offered me, that it could have no other effect than to release in me the highest joy in my soul. For you answer my letter at full length and most learnedly and generously offer your affection; you have stored up the treasures of your learning in so many areas of interest to me that there is not much there that could not usefully be poured out on me. Although I am conscious of my extreme debt to you, I am racked by this one doubt, that I am not who you think I am, or whom your humanity imagines, or whom a learned correspondence should demand, but you have generously granted it all the same. Even though I hoped only to benefit from all your hard-won learning, you have added your benevolence to me,

26. Jacob Brucker, *Historia critica philosophiae a mundi incunabulis ad nostram usque aetatem deducta*, 5 vols. (Leipzig, 1742–44, new edition, 1766, with an appendix from 1767).

27. For the following, I am referring to the letters from Brucker to Heumann in the State Library of Hanover, Ms. XLII, 1915.

supporting me as I stumble, assuring me though I waver, pulling me up when I was sinking! Please accept my most profound feelings of gratitude for your many services to humanity.[28]

Rhetorical excess was then normal, but this letter of reply is so over-the-top that one has to wonder what Heumann had actually sent him that made Brucker so "indebted" to him. We can only speculate, but it would appear that Heumann even at this early stage of their relationship had indicated that he could send him portions of his collected personal notes on the history of philosophy. These were three thick volumes of notes entitled "Collectanea historiae philosophiae" (Gatherings for the history of philosophy). As was customary at that time, throughout his life Heumann made notes and copied excerpts from everything he read and then organized them according to subjects or topics (*loci*). In the more than thirty years that had passed since the beginning of his studies in Jena, an infinite amount of material had piled up, recorded in a tiny script. In these sorts of surviving notebooks, such as those of Johann Christoph Wolf, whom we will get to know in chapter 14, we can easily see what riches were stored up. That would explain Brucker's astonished and boundless gratitude.

Writers regularly consulted notebooks like these when they wrote their essays, lectures, and books. Sometimes they had only to write out in full what such notebooks had already stored up in embryo. But why should a scholar like Heumann, who was not yet fifty years old, give something like that away— something that other scholars guarded jealously? The answer may be found perhaps in the foreword to the first volume of the *Short Questions from the History of Philosophy*, which Brucker composed in the roughly nine months after receiving Heumann's letter.[29] Perhaps he really had been stumbling

---

28. Brucker to Heumann, April 16, 1730: "Quod a Te, Vir Summe, expectare, imo petere quoque ausus vix eram, tam liberaliter praestas, ut non possit non summa inde a mihi exoriri animi laetitia: scilicet et ad literas meas copiose et eruditissime respondes, et amorem Tuum liberalissime offers, et ad qualiacunque mea ita eruditionis Tuae thesauros recondis, ut non multum non inde in me possit redundare commodum: quo nomine uti me Tibi habes longe obstrictissimum, ita hoc unum me mordet, illum me non esse, quem vel credis et depingit Tua humanitas vel postulat literarum, quod mihi tam liberaliter concedis, commercium: quicquid tamen illud est, addes hoc benevolentiae Tuae, et qui non nisi a Te consummata eruditione discere cupio, feres cespitantem, confirmabis nutantem, eriges labentem, et pro tot humanitatis officiis observantissimum semper Tui accipies animum."

29. Brucker, *Kurtze Fragen aus der philosophischen Historie*, vol. 1 (Leipzig, 1731).

when Heumann's support provided the boost he needed to write his book speedily and thus finish, as mentioned, the first of seven volumes. The questions in the *Short Questions* really were short, but the answers—that was the joke in the title—were so much longer that every volume contained about one thousand octavo pages.

By December 18, 1730, Brucker said in his foreword to volume one about Heumann:

> The beginning of his *Acta Philosophorum*, written with so much judgment and erudition, is constructed in a way that could lead one to expect something both perfect and incomparable, if he had only wished to pursue his intentions; but more important and greater matters and tasks required his skills; bad luck did not favor this blessing for the learned world and hindered [the completion of this project], and so our young people still lack a complete introduction to the history of philosophy.[30]

That would appear to be an echo of Heumann's letter to Brucker, which no longer survives. Heumann had obviously complained about the many matters he had to manage as the inspector of the gymnasium in Göttingen, and perhaps with the words "more important and greater matters" he was referring to the theological topics to which he devoted himself after obtaining his degree in theology in 1728. He appears to have cast as "bad luck" the fact that he had been denied a professorship, requiring him to pour all his energy into school-teaching for over twenty years. In 1726 he stopped editing his *Acta philosophorum*. Therefore it may have seemed like a solution when four years later an obviously very talented young man wrote to him about his plans for writing a comprehensive history of philosophy. It may have been a sort of impulsive emotional response that led him to pull his thick folders of notes off the shelf and offer to send them to a young man whom he really did not know at all.

In his late autobiographical memoir, it was also 1730 that Heumann seemed to recall as the year when Brucker returned his folders of notes (which of course had been only loaned) after having them for a year.[31] In reality, as we'll

30. Ibid., foreword, unpaginated.

31. Heumann himself was not a reliable witness because he no longer remembered the actual years when he wrote his memoirs just before his death in 1764. See the autobiographical text printed in Georg A. Cassius, *Ausführliche Lebensbeschreibung . . . D. Chr. Aug. Heumanns* (Kassel, 1768), 386ff.: "A. 1730. roganti Bruckero misi Omnia mea collectanea historiae philosophicae, postquam sancte is promisisset, se ea intra annum esse ad me remissurum. Exacto anno

see, things were more complicated than that. At first Heumann hesitated, then sent one volume, and later a second, and then finally the third folder of his notes. The whole process took more than four years. Let us see when and how Heumann sent each of these excerpts and what was actually in these folders.

Organizing the History of Philosophy

We can tell what the first issues were for Brucker's project from the letter to Heumann because he immediately turned to the fundamental question of how to organize the history of philosophy. "Please permit me to ask you one thing: For the history of philosophy I have followed the divisions and distinctions you set out in your sketch, which divides the course of philosophy into the two periods of before and after the birth of Christ."[32] This was indeed the organization that Heumann, in the third issue of the *Acta philosophorum*, had

---

scribebat, se ea Lipsam misisse ad M. Stübnerum, nec dubitasse, esse ea iam mihi reddita. Scribebam ad Stübnerum. At is petulanter mihi rescribebat, significans, se ea veredario dedisse Brunsvicensi, nec amplius hanc curam ad se pertinere. Scripsi ad postam Brunsvicensem, sed accepi responsum, a Stübnero id falso iactari. Postea multum et opere et sumptum frustra impendi. Bruckerus ita se mihi excusavit, ut credam, ipsius culpam hic esse nullam, sed Stübnerum ea retinuisse, gavisumque esse, me privatum esse magno aliquo bono. Certe ne mille quidem imperialibus venales fuissent mihi illae collectiones annorum plurium."

32. Brucker to Heumann, April 16, 1730: "Unum tamen te rogare permittes: Secutus sum in distinguenda et distribuenda Histor. Philos. quam molior tuum delineationem quae ante et post C.N. fata philosophiae distribuit: ad primam partem praeter barbaricam, Greacianam philosophiam omnem ante te referri puto: Verum de Judaica philosophia (quo sensu gentis post capitiv. Babylonica et Alexandri M. imprimis expeditionem Asiaticam sumo) quid strahendum [?] sit, ambigo? Certas quidem Graecianicorum sectas inter Judaeos ingruisse [?], non credo, quod eorum institutis admodum repugnant; gentis tamen ex religionis suae sectas Pharisaeos, Sadducaeos, Essaeos etc. et philosophiae historiam pertinere, imo Graecanicarum sectarum placita inter eos tacite irrepsisse sum persuasissimus, ex ipsius Josephi non tantum auctoritate sed exemplo confirmor; vero de eo obitu: Id unum quod an ad tempora N.C. ubi de philosophia Judaica agendum monuisti, etiam superior Paulo tempora referri queant; quod ego quidem puto: et in philosophia Romanorum explicanda itidem usu venit, apud quos Caesari et Augusti potissimum tempore Philosophia quidam involuit post susceptam tamen Carneadi, Critolai et Antiochi legationem fundamenta jam jacisse censenda est: Qua in re ut tenebras meas dispellas, enixe rogo: Vix enim separare posse puto initia ista Judaica et Romanae philosophiae ab augmentis [?] et incrementis sub ipsius nati Christi tempora conspicuis. Pro transmissis egregiis Heumannianae eruditionis speciminibus habes me longe devinctissimum quibus omnes par quicquam reperire possum: accipe tamen . . . praesentem libellum."

proposed for any future history of philosophy: "We choose therefore the method of chronology and geography and make the first division in philosophy into the pre-Christian and the post-Christian. These are the two main periods in this subject, just as they are in church history."[33] We can see that for Heumann as well as for Brucker it was church history—and with it the Christian perspective—that provided direction for the history of philosophy. The birth of the Savior was not a fact that any realm of scholarship could afford to ignore. Wilhelm Schmidt-Biggemann has described Heumann's organizing principle this way:

> He first divided pre-Christian philosophy into *Philosophia empirica sive simplex* (Empirical or Simple Philosophy) and *Philosophia scientifica sive theoretica* (Scientific or Theoretical Philosophy). His section on "Empirical or Simple Philosophy" was divided in turn into *Philosophia Graeciana* (Greek Philosophy) and *Philosophia extra Graeciam* (Philosophy outside Greece); these in turn included the subdivisions of *Philosophia barbarica* (Barbaric Philosophy) of Hebrew philosophy and *Philosophia simplex* of the Greeks. This introductory part was to include histories of philosophy to which Heumann attached little value: the wisdom of the Jewish, Chaldean, Indian, Phoenician, Egyptian, and Ethiopian priests as well as the wisdom of the Greek poets, orators, historians, and politicians.

All of this was just the prelude.

> Philosophy in the true sense, *quae in Graecia orta est et maxime floruit* (which arose in Greece and which flourished there in the highest degree) remained categorically separate from these forms of general wisdom.... Heumann subdivided post-Christian philosophy again according to criteria taken from religious history: *ante reformatam religionem, post reformatam religionem* (before and after the Reformation). In dealing with the pre-Reformation period, Heumann was most interested in the pagan schools of philosophy.... Philosophy after the Reformation was also determined by Christian categories, and here the subdivisions included eclectic philosophy and that of the various "sects." The post-Reformation sects were the Aristotelians, the gnesio-Aristotelians [i.e., those following the "original" Aristotle], the Platonists, the Kabbalists, and the Theosophists. Among the Eclectics, he thought that the Ramists and the Cartesians had

33. Heumann, *Acta philosophorum*, vol. 1, 3. Stück (Halle, 1715), 463.

constructed their own sects, while Telesio, Hobbes, and Thomasius counted as independent eclectics.[34]

Summarizing this principle of organization, Brucker continued in his letter as follows:

In the first part, I believe that, apart from barbaric philosophy, you cover the whole of pre-Christian Greek philosophy. But with Jewish philosophy (under which I understand the name of the people after the Babylonian Captivity and especially after the Asian military campaigns of Alexander the Great) I am not sure how it should be subdivided.

By that Brucker meant that he had examined Jewish thought more closely:

In any event I do not believe that specific Greek sects were received among the Jews because they fiercely resisted those traditions; in contrast I am firmly convinced that the religious sects of the [Jewish] nation, the Pharisees, Sadducees, Essenes, etc., also belong to the history of philosophy, and indeed that the doctrines of the Greek sects silently took root within them. I find that view supported by Josephus—not just by the authority of his words but by his example.

Thus it appears that Brucker was aiming for a kind of history that would consider the implicit and hidden implications of philosophy within religious currents. And he had problems therefore with dividing up ancient philosophy, and especially that of the Jews and Romans, according to the supposed pivot point of the birth of Christ. "I believe that one can hardly separate these beginnings of Jewish and Roman philosophy from the striking growth and subsequent developments after the time of Christ."

Here we see a young historian wrestling with the organization of his future work. Despite all his doubts, however, over the coming years Brucker actually did arrange his whole history of philosophy according to Heumann's model, with only a few modifications.

Correspondence to the Rhythm of Trade Fairs

Next, it's interesting to see how this exchange of letters developed, not just in terms of their contents but also with regard to the postal system. It appears that Heumann and Brucker wrote to each other following the rhythm of the

34. On these philosophical subdivisions, see Wilhelm Schmidt-Biggemann, "Jacob Bruckers philosophiegeschichtliches Konzept," in *Jacob Brucker*, ed. idem and Stammen, 113–34, at 128ff.

trade fairs. That made sense because it was much less expensive to send letters with friendly tradesmen traveling between Augsburg and Göttingen than it would have been to use the postal service, especially if heavy book packages were involved. These trade routes followed the old road through Nuremberg and almost always through Leipzig, where they might then branch off toward Halle, Magdeburg, and the territories of the old Welf (Guelph) dynasty.

In April or May 1730 Brucker clearly sent off a package, for on July 11 he wrote to Heumann, "Doubtless you have received what I recently sent you from the Leipzig trade fair through Herr Lotter, in which I responded somewhat more copiously to your great kindnesses."[35] By "copiously" he probably meant not just the length of his letter but also the size of the book package. The messenger Johann Georg Lotter was originally from Augsburg but from 1726 onward he had been active in Leipzig, associating with people connected to Gottsched's journals, while also maintaining contact with his home town.[36] He was also passionately interested in the history of philosophy. Brucker claimed that there was no speedier or more secure connection than getting something from Göttingen to Lotter (in Leipzig) and then, using merchants from Augsburg, to carry it south to the Swabian trading center.[37] Brucker added, "Because the opportunity presents itself of using an Augsburg merchant traveling to the city of Brunswick, I am appending the homage which I offer to you, great sir, . . . and add my thanks for news."[38]

This was the way it went over the next years. In May 1731 Brucker wrote again, "If you have anything you'd like to send me, that could surely be arranged after the end of the trade fair in Brunswick using Herr Apinus, even though the malicious Augsburgers call him a [mere] merchant."[39] Indeed, Sigmund Jakob

35. Brucker to Heumann, July 11, 1730: "Nullus dubito redditas Tibi fuisse meas, quas nuperis in nundinis Lipsiensibus mediante Cl. Lottero ad te misi, et in quibus copiosius ad amantissimas Tuas respondi—Quibus has incitante occasione, dum Brunswigam . . . Mercator quidam Augustana addo, observantiam, qua Te, Vir summe prosequor, summam testaturas [?], addned[as] [?] simul novitatis gratia."

36. On Lotter (1699–1737), see *Allgemeine deutsche Biographie* 19 (1884): 272.

37. See the letter dated May 24, 1731, quoted in note 39 below.

38. See note 35 in this chapter.

39. Brucker to Heumann, May 24, 1731: "poteritque fas circulus tuto tradi Cl. Lottero Lipsiae jam degenti, qui singulis fere septimanis ad me eum mittendi . . . poterit occasionem, certe Epistolae non citius vel tutius, quam ad eum mittantur, per quem intercedentibus Mercatoribus Augustanis, quibus Lipsiae semper commercium est; ad me satis mature curabuntur plura ne tibi melioribus et majoribus occupato gravis sim, non addo, sed Te omnis voti damnatum . . .

Apinus was only a merchant on the side; in reality he was a highly learned teacher at the Egidius Gymnasium (in Nuremberg) and a good friend of Brucker's. The trade fair in Brunswick took place twice a year. In the eighteenth century it reached its high point and achieved an importance similar to that of the fairs in Leipzig and Frankfurt.[40] The summer fair was scheduled for August and so Heumann still would have had some time to see if he had anything more to send to the intellectually hungry Brucker, who had almost finished his second volume of the *Short Questions*. Had Heumann already lived up to his promise and sent something? In this letter from May 1731 Brucker is pressing Heumann to deliver: "I would especially ask you again and again, in view of your generosity, to send me right away the folder that concerns Jewish history; for then Herr Lotter could surely see to its delivery as he is already waiting in Leipzig."[41] In the meantime Brucker had taken up Jewish philosophy in the first volume of *Short Questions*, but as he said, he wanted to deal with it comprehensively only later, in the section on the epoch after the birth of Christ. He could thus make use of Heumann's folder for his planned fourth volume.

On March 19, 1732, the package obviously arrived at long last. Brucker said that Heumann had dipped into the reserves of his "consummate erudition" and sent him his "aid" in "richest measure."[42] He used the word "aid" (*subsidia*), which can mean support and aid, but also specific resources, and therefore a concrete description of the notebooks. He did regret, however, that the shipment arrived only after he had published his history of Pythagorean philosophy, for which he could well have used it. From that detail we can tell that this folder contained notes on Greek philosophy. For the folder on Jewish philosophy, however, he would have to wait longer. It was September 18 of the same year that he finally wrote, "My sincere thanks to you for sending such extensive excerpts from your reading on the philosophy of the Hebrews."[43]

P.S. Si quae ad me mittenda habes, finitis nundinis Brunswicensibus per Cl. Apinum mechante dicto mercatus augustano certe curare poterunt."

40. On the trade fair in Brunswick, see Richard Moderhack, *Braunschweiger Stadtgeschichte* (Braunschweig, 1997).

41. Brucker to Heumann, May 24, 1731: "Imprimis vero iterum iterumque oro, ut quae Judaeorum historiam concernunt, Tuae liberalitatis memor [?], mature submittas poteritque fasciculus tuto tradi [?] Cl. Lottero Lipsiae jam degenti."

42. Brucker to Heumann, March 19, 1732: "ex consummatae eruditionis Tuae pessu [?] largiter subsidia subministrans."

43. Brucker to Heumann, September 18, 1732: "Tibi devinctissimum pro communicatis meum excerptis literariis Tuis amplissimis ad Hist. Phil. Ebraeorum."

Up to then, therefore, two of the three fat volumes of excerpts had found their way from Göttingen to Kaufbeuren. And the third was already on the way. In a letter dated December 20, 1732, we read that a package had again arrived from Heumann: "And you are above all measure generous, most famous Sir, that you, from the overflowing treasures of your care and erudition, should again supply my poverty with the most extensive resources."[44] This third packet may have contained excerpts from Arabic philosophy, the philosophy of the church fathers and of the Middle Ages, because those are the topics mentioned in the correspondence.

The semi-annual rhythm of letters kept on going, although sometimes letters went back and forth more frequently. Lotter's vacations at the end of semester and the trade fairs in Brunswick and Leipzig provided opportunities for exchanges, and they were regularly used. On September 18, 1731, Brucker asked Heumann if the materials he had sent off the previous summer with Sigmund Jakob Apinus to the fair in Brunswick had arrived.[45] Today one might wonder why in every letter the writer asked if a previous mailing had arrived and why they showed so much concern about finding the fastest and most secure connections. But that just shows how slow and insecure postal connections were. Things could get hung up all too easily, or even lose their way entirely, as we shall soon see. Leipzig was the regular place where letters and packages were transferred from one courier to another, or from one postal servant to another, a fact that will play a crucial role in this story.

During March 1732 the two scholars exchanged letters about the innocence of Giordano Bruno, and Brucker sent Heumann a picture of himself; in April the third volume of *Short Questions* was sent off to Göttingen with

44. Brucker to Heumann, December 20, 1732: "et ultra modum liberalis es, Vir celeberrime, qui ex abundantissimis eruditionis et diligentiae thesauris Tuis iterum amplissimas pauperitati meae submittis suppetias."

45. Brucker to Heumann, September 18, 1731: "Nullus dubito, quin meae, quas hac praeterita aestate ad Te dedi, Vir Celeberrime, et in quibus literaria, quae mihi promisisti, subsidia ex petii precibus, recte Tibi sint, proxeneta Cl. Lottero Lipsiae degente tradita: submisissem citius per Mercatorem Brunswicenses nundinas adeuntem H[istoriam] Ph[ilosophiae] Tomum 1 nisi tum temporis, cum literae parandae essent, me in vehementissimum luctum conjicisset divina providentiaque mihi praematuro fato uxorem longe desideratissimam Viri Doctissimi Cl. Großii Reiteris in Augustano Lyceo filiam abstulit: quo dolore ut Musae meae vehementer turbatae sunt, ita vehementer confusae rationes meae literariae, ut vix cum iis ingratiam redire valeam."

the help of Lotter;[46] in December the topic was Arabic philosophy; and in April 1733 a biography of John Owens stood at the center of their correspondence.[47] During all this time in Brucker's house the pile of papers from Heumann's *Collectanea* just grew and grew. It was only in January 1734, shortly before finishing the last volume of his *Short Questions*, that Brucker decided to return the three thick volumes. But that is the beginning of our crime story.

Difficulties with the Package

The usual address in Leipzig would have been Lotter again, but he was no longer available. He had received a call to St. Petersburg and was now busy getting ready for that journey. So maybe the problem was that Brucker could not use him again as his transfer agent. Instead he chose as his agent Lotter's good friend Friedrich Wilhelm Stübner; Lotter may even have recommended him.[48] Like Lotter, Stübner belonged to the circle of friends around Gottsched. He was a Franconian from Bayreuth and a mathematician by training. In January 1734 he was exactly twenty-four years old and had obtained his master's degree in philosophy five years earlier in Leipzig. From 1732 on he was working as a certified teacher (*Assessor*) in the faculty of philosophy. That year he also translated a book by Brucker's friend Schelhorn from Memmingen—which doubtless made him seem trustworthy to Brucker. Stübner was open-minded and liberal. In 1736 he became one of those Leipzig intellectuals who helped the rationalist Bible translator Johann Lorenz Schmidt escape from Wertheim to Altona when he was being hunted for violating imperial law.[49]

46. "Nullus dubitans, quin nuperae meae curante Cl. Lottero Lipsia recte ad manus Tuas pervenerit, bis subjungo Tomum tertium Philosophiae historiae." On the reception of Bruno in Germany of the early eighteenth century, see Saverio Ricci, *La fortuna del pensiero di Giordano Bruno 1600–1750* (Florence, 1990).

47. Brucker to Heumann, April 12, 1733: "P.S. In eo eram, ut has sigillo clauderem, cum ecce ad Te nuperi Decembris medio a me datas Lipsia redirent, quod editionem ovenianae biographiae hactenus impeditari post nundinas demum . . . significabat Cl. Lotterus. Nolui te ibi eam supprimere, sed cum his potius mittere."

48. On Stübner, see *Allgemeine Deutsche Biographie* 36 (1893): 712ff.

49. See Paul Spalding, "Im Untergrund der Aufklärung: Johann Lorenz Schmidt auf der Flucht," in *Europa in der Frühen Neuzeit*, ed. Erich Donnert (Weimar, 1997), 4:135–54; Döring, "Beiträge zur Geschichte der Gesellschaft der Alethophilen in Leipzig."

So at the beginning of January 1734 Brucker sent off the heavy package to the young man in Leipzig.[50] He would have again entrusted it to the care of a merchant. If that man took the postal coach, it would have been about thirty hours to Nuremberg and another seventy to Leipzig.[51] Without any lengthy pauses the journey would have taken about five days. In Leipzig the package was turned over to Stübner, and Stübner, according to his later assurances, went straight to the postal forwarding department in the house of Carpzov in the marketplace. There, on January 16, he gave the package to the postal company, addressed to Brunswick, using the so-called "kitchen postal wagon,"[52] that is, the heavy-duty postal carts that carried provisions and heavy packages. Brunswick was the central station from which shipments were distributed to all the Welfian territories, such as Göttingen in the principality of Electoral Hanover. But the package did not arrive.

At first no one noticed because shipments were always getting delayed. But on April 23 Brucker wrote to Heumann with a first inquiry, stating that "by the way" he had sent off the whole *Collectanea* to Stübner at the beginning of the year.[53] "I am sure it was taken care of properly." In August Brucker received a letter that Heumann had sent on May 6, wondering about the sluggishness of the Leipzig friends. Was the connection not working as smoothly as it had in the past? "I did certainly send off your collection of excerpts on the history of philosophy to Herr Stübner at the beginning of the year, and he confirms that he received the package and would send it on to you as regular mail [*ordinarium tabellarium*]."[54] Stübner had the additional task of sending Heumann the new, fifth volume of the *Short Questions*, and Brucker imagined that surely in the meantime both shipments

50. See Spalding, "Im Untergrund der Aufklärung"; Döring, "Beiträge zur Geschichte der Gesellschaft der Alethophilen in Leipzig."

51. See Jochen Seidel, "Abenteuer Reisen—Postkutschenfahrten in Franken," www.heinlenews.de/geschl07.htm.

52. See Brucker to Gottsched, February 20, 1737, printed in Johann Christoph Gottsched, *Briefwechsel*, ed. Detlef Döring, Rüdiger Otto, and Michael Schlott (Berlin, 2010), 4:275–80.

53. Brucker to Heumann, April 23, 1734: "Tu vero, Maxime Reverende atque Celeberrime Tuam mihi amicitiam atque benevolentiam porro conserva integrum. Ceterum Msc. Tua collectanea Cl. Steubnerum, ad quem Lipsiam ineunte anno tuto transmisi. Recte curavisse nullus dubito, pro quibus iterative mille Tibi gratias solvo: avessit sine dubio Historia vitae Occonum, Tibi destinata, de qua ut ex hoc Tomo cum his literis recte acceptis, ut, s. vacat, me edocas, Te honesto rogo."

54. Brucker to Heumann, August 11, 1734: "Certe Collectanea Tua H. Ph. Jam cum initio hujus anni ad Cl. Stubnerum misi, qui se recte accipisse, et per ordinarium tabellarium missurus ad Te pollicitus est."

would have arrived long ago in Göttingen. "If only I could have used your other pages previously, but I must accept the loss because now it is unavoidable. The opportunity to exploit so much digested material for the last volume [the sixth and seventh volumes of the *Short Questions*] was so great that I did not see how to find a satisfactory place for it all even in one volume divided into two parts; because recent history demands its light in so many places."[55] In this way Brucker regretted that he had to send back the collection of excerpts before he was entirely through with the gigantic work, but clearly Heumann had been pressing him to return the folders. Perhaps he had decided, after a lengthy pause, to write something himself about the history of philosophy.

But why did the package not arrive? When Heumann wrote in September to say that he had still not received it, Brucker gradually became uneasy. He complained to Stübner. "May the gods forfend that some accident occurred!" However it slowly became clear: something was fishy. Brucker heard nothing from Leipzig and still believed that Stübner had done the right thing.[56] Meanwhile it was now April 1735 and more than a year had passed since Stübner had supposedly sent on the package from Leipzig. Heumann himself had also written to Stübner, but he answered, as Heumann put it, "petulanter," that is, frivolously or impudently, that he had turned the package over to the Brunswick postal courier and that the matter did not concern him anymore. So then Heumann wrote to the Brunswick postal officials, who replied that Stübner's information was false. Heumann therefore became suspicious that Stübner had kept the package and, as he said, "rejoiced in depriving me of such a great good."[57] And indeed it was a great good. Heumann protested, "I would never have sold these excerpts collected over many years for even a thousand Reichstaler."[58] Meanwhile legal measures were being considered, and Heumann was making

55. Ibid.: "Utinam vero liceret et reliquis chartis Tuis uti, sed ferenda jactura, cum aliter jam id evenire nequeat. Tantum quoque materiam in Tomo ultimo apparatum obtulit occasio ut vix vidam, quomodo, in uno Tomo, etsi in duas partes diviso, possit satis digesti, cum recentior historia suam . . . lucem multis in locis poscat."

56. Brucker to Heumann, September 15, 1734: "Superi prohibeant, ne detrimenti . . . sunt." Brucker to Heumann, April 12, 1735: "Nescio quo fato fiat, ut nec ad eas, quas circa exeuntem nuperum annum, ad Te dedi, nec ad eas, quas in festo Purificationis scripsi, responsum tulerim, incertus hodiernum, quid de fasciculo a me Stubnero recte curato et Brunswigam sine dubio delato factum sit, nisi quod silentium hoc mihi persuadeat eum recte tandem ad Dominum suum pervenisse, quod ferventissimus desideriis precor et scire aveo."

57. Heumann in Cassius, *Ausführliche Lebensbeschreibung*.

58. Ibid.

efforts to start a careful investigation. For Brucker this was all deeply embarrassing, and he wished that this accident had never happened. Postmaster Heinsius in Leipzig was asked, and on December 14, 1735, he sent a document to Brucker in which one could see that the package had been sent off in due order as shipment number 14. The report from the postmaster in Brunswick, however, told a different story. Just before Christmas, on December 21, 1735, it arrived with the news that in the shipment in question there weren't fourteen packages but only twelve.[59]

59. Brucker to Gottsched, February 20, 1737; here is the full text: "Daß Ew[er]. HochWohlgeb[oren]. mir soviel Liebe zuerweisen und unter den Stübnerischen Papieren nach dem Heumannischen Paquet nachsehen zulaßen sich erbieten, nehme als eine besondere probe Dero Gütigkeit gegen mich an, die ich mit allen möglichen Diensten zuerwiedern nicht mangeln werde. Ich diene aber dabey noch zur Nachricht, daß schon vor einem Jahr der Post-Secretarium im fürstl. Posthauße bey Mad. Henneberg H. Bernhard Heinsium, wo die Braunschweigische Küchenpost abgehet, und das Paquet H. Stübner aufgegeben zuhaben, mir versichert, angegangen, unter deßen Hand auch vom 14. 8br. 1735 einen Schein bekommen, dieses Inhalts: daß ein Päckel C.A.H. an H. D. Heumann in Göttingen d. 16. Jan. 1734. laut postbuch sub N. 14 nach Braunschweig abgegangen: welchen Original-Schein an H. D. Heumann, und dieser an das Hochfurstl. Küchenpost Ammt in Braunschweig gesandt, worauf ich einen Schein von selbiger, unterschrieben Henneberg, vom 21. Xbr. 1735. bekommen, daß laut Postbuch dieses Packet nicht angekommen, selbigen Tag auch die Num[m]er nicht 14. sondern nur 12. gewesen. Diesen OriginalSchein habe in der Jubilate Meße gedachten H. Heinsio vorlegen laßen, weil dadurch seine bücher der unrichtigkeit überführet werden, er hat aber mit Ungestüm keine andere Antwort gegeben, als er seye nicht schuldig weiter darüber sich einzulaßen, seine Bücher seyen richtig. Ew. HochEdelgeb. ersehen aus dieser kleinen specie facti, daß zur Rettung der Ehre des seel. H. Stübners (von dem ich nicht glaube, daß er zu hinterhaltung des msc. wie H. D. Heumann anfangs geglaubet, mit gedachtem H. Heinsio unter der Decke gelegen), ingleichen mich von der begehrten Schadloshaltung loszumachen, kein ander Mittel übrig, als diesen H. Heinsium entweder gütlich, oder wo er nicht will, gerichtlich dahin zubringen, daß er auf den Posten zwischen Leipzig und Braunschweig untersuchen laße, wo das zimlich starke Päckel stecke. Ich habe zwar seinen Originalschein nicht beyhanden, sondern H. D. Heumann, habe aber eine copiam vidimatam davon, es kan auch jener leicht hergeschafft werden. Bey diesen Umständen ersuche nun Ew. HochEdelge. recht inständig, wann nach geschehener Nachforschung, ob nicht unter den Stübnerischen papieren nichts vorhanden, und nicht etwa ein Irrthum oder Verwechslung von dem seel. Stübner vorgegangen, dermalen nocheinmal gütlich H. Heinsium befragen zulaßen, und ihn zuersuchen, Sorge zutragen, daß das Paket auff den Zwischenposten aufgetrieben werde (worzu der brschw. Postmeister das seinige beyzutragen H. D. Heumann versprochen) maßen sonst durch weitere instanz unfehlbar die Satisfaction in Leipzig an den Principal der Brschw. Küchenpost und deßen Verwaltern würde gefordert werden. Sollte er aber gütlich nicht zu dieser ihm obligenden Pflicht bewogen werden können, so will die Scheine überschicken, und bitte alsdann Ew. HochWEdelgeb. gar inständigen Rath und Hülfe, wie durch

Who Had a Motive?

It almost looks as if Postmaster Heinsius was lying. But why would he lie? Who would have had a motive to cheat Heumann out of his notes? If we can answer these questions, then a mere accident could become a criminal case; an episode in the history of communications could become a story of corruption. And that can be done. There really was someone who, we can presume, had a motive to harm Heumann. That person was none other than Johann Christoph Gottsched.[60]

Gottsched was well acquainted with Stübner, for he had accepted the young man into the tight circle of his *Societas conferentium* and in the winter of 1733–34 had arranged a few journalistic jobs for him: as the temporary editor of the *New Reports on Scholarly Matters* (*Neue Zeitungen für Gelehrte Sachen*), which was published in Leipzig, and also a similar position with the satirical journal *Neofranconian Newspaper for Scholarly Matters* (*Neufränkische Zeitung für Gelehrte Sachen*), which bore Gottsched's stamp and in which Christina Mariana von Ziegler and her husband, Wolf Balthasar von Steinwehr, were also involved.[61] Indeed, when men such as Johann Lorenz Mosheim or Johann Friedrich May sent their best regards to Stübner, they tended to mention Steinwehr and Lotter in the same breath. It appeared to be a very tight circle of friends.[62]

gerichtliche Beschwehrung, dieser mir viel Unruhe erregenden Sache abgeholfen werde, und ich meines Orts die letzte Hand an dem, was ich in dieser Sache thun kan, anlegen könne. Ich erkühne mich zwar vieles Denenselbigen, soviele Unruhe zumachen, da aber Ew. HochWEdelgeb. selbst so gütig sind, mich Dero Dienste hierinnen zuversichern, mich auch die höchste Noth zwingt, da ich in Leipzig sonst niemand habe, den ich deswegen angehen kan, so hoffe Ew[er]. HochW[ohl]Edelgeb[oren]. werden meine Dreistigkeit nicht ungütig nehmen, in versicherung, daß ich zu allen nur möglichen Gegendiensten mich schuldigst u. willigst finden laßen werde."

60. On Gottsched it is sufficient to consult Eugen Wolff, *Gottscheds Stellung im deutschen Bildungsleben*, 2 vols. (Kiel, 1895–97); Manfred Rudersdorf, ed., *Johann Christoph Gottsched in seiner Zeit: Neue Beiträge zu Leben, Werk und Wirkung* (Berlin, 2007).

61. On Gottsched as newspaper editor, see Gabriele Ball, *Moralische Küsse: Gottsched als Zeitschriftenherausgeber und literarischer Vermittler* (Göttingen, 2000).

62. On this circle, see Döring, "Zur Geschichte"; Günter Gawlick, "Johann Christoph Gottsched als Vermittler der französischen Aufklärung," in *Zentren der Aufklärung III: Leipzig*, ed. Wolfgang Martens (Heidelberg, 1990), 179–204; Spalding, "Untergrund der Aufklärung"; Martin Mulsow, *Freigeister im Gottsched-Kreis: Wolffianismus, studentische Aktivitäten und Religionskritik in Leipzig 1740–1745* (Göttingen, 2007).

Ever since 1733 there had been some hard feelings between Gottsched and Heumann. In that year one of Gottsched's main publications, *Contributions to the Critical History of the German Language, Poetry, and Eloquence*, published an anonymous but negative review of Heumann's translation of Cicero's *Pro Milone* (*A Speech in Defense of Titus Annius Milo*). "Dr. Heumann corrupts the whole beauty [of the original]."[63] The anonymous author of this piece was Wolf Balthasar von Steinwehr, but Heumann believed that it was Gottsched himself. So he could not restrain himself from launching a reply, published in April 1734 in the *Hamburg Reports on Scholarly Matters* (*Hamburgische Berichten von Gelehrten Sachen*), in which he openly expressed his thoughts about why Gottsched was acting with bias against him. He thought it was probably because in his lectures on rhetoric he had treated Gottsched's *German Rhetoric* (*Deutsche Rhetorik*) and in doing so had alerted his students to Gottsched's many errors in translation.[64] That was a nasty dig, so it's not surprising that Gottsched replied again and that serious factions developed within the Gottsched circle, for and against Heumann.[65]

The worst provocation, however, had perhaps occurred earlier, in the late summer or fall of 1733. At that point Gottsched was hoping to obtain a professorship in German language studies at the University of Göttingen that was just being founded. Officially the university had already been inaugurated and it was set to open its doors for students in 1737.[66] Gottsched was worried that because his recently published review in the *Contributions*, Heumann, who was involved in founding the new university, might cause trouble for him. So

63. *Beyträge zur Critischen Historie der deutschen Sprache, Poesie und Beredsamkeit* (Leipzig, 1733), 7. Stück, pp. 534ff. Heumann's reply appeared in the *Hamburgische Berichten* 1734 (no. 29 of April 4), 241–44. Gottsched then replied in the *Nieder-Sächsische Nachrichten von Gelehrten Neuen Sachen* 1734 (no. 40 of May 24), 338–40.

64. Hemmerling, "Heumann contra Türck."

65. A letter from Joachim Friedrich Liscow, the editor of scholarly articles in the *Hamburger unpartheyische Correspondenten*, makes it clear that within Gottsched's inner circle, some supported while others opposed Heumann: "Der Herr Prof. Kohl ist gar zu sehr dem H. Heumann zugethan, als dass ich von ihm hoffen können, den Aufsatz durch ihn bekand gemacht zu sehen." Liscow to Gottsched, May 26, 1734, in Gottsched, *Briefwechsel* (Berlin, 2009), 3:101. And also (in the same letter): "Den Aufsatz gegen Heumann würde ich nicht ermangelt haben meinen Blättern einrücken zu lassen; wenn er nicht für den Raum, der zu gelehrten Sachen gewidmet ist, zu lang gewesen wäre." The essay was then printed in the *Niedersächs. Nachrichten* with the assistance of Liscow.

66. On the founding of the University of Göttingen, see Emil Franz Rössler, *Die Gründung der Universität Göttingen* (Göttingen, 1855).

he asked Johann Lorenz Mosheim, who replied soothingly on August 26, 1733: "Herr Heumann is not so important that he could thwart such appointments. He's not appropriate as an adviser and so he is not being employed in that way. Moreover he is not so angry and envious as you, Sir, imagine. He is an honest man who would not willingly harm anyone. Verbally he may be witty and biting, but if one can put up with this small weakness, one can always cope with him. I do not believe that he malignantly intends to claim that you, most esteemed Sir, are more able in German than in Latin."[67]

Mosheim may have misjudged Heumann. Wiebke Hemmerling has pointed to an anonymous evaluation that clearly cost Gottsched his call to the professorship in Göttingen, one that may have come from Heumann. In it the author claimed that Gottsched would not pay adequate attention to the historical aspects of the German language and that his *Contributions* were so full of laughable mistakes that one simply had to wonder. That does sound a lot like the reference to the translation mistakes in Gottsched's *German Rhetoric* that Heumann mentioned later in a reply to Gottsched. Heumann could certainly be patronizing.[68]

There are more questions here than answers. We cannot be completely sure that the fatal evaluation was written by Heumann, and we do not know if academic gossip transmitted rumors concerning the content and authorship of this evaluation all the way back to Leipzig. But we also should not underestimate such gossip. It would explain why some academics in Leipzig, especially in 1734, became so decidedly hostile to Heumann.

But would this hypothesis also explain how Gottsched got involved in the disappearance of Heumann's collection of excerpts? Let us try to imagine such a scenario. In January 1734 Stübner receives the package intended for Heumann and tells his friends about it: a circle that includes Steinwehr (the critic of Heumann's translation of Cicero), Lotter, May, and Gottsched. Did anyone restrain him from immediately sending the package on to Heumann? Did someone first open the package, out of either curiosity or evil intent, to examine the

67. Mosheim to Gottsched, August 26, 1733, in Gottsched, *Briefwechsel*, vol. 2 (Berlin, 2008), 499.

68. Hemmerling, "Heumann contra Türck." See the anecdotes recorded in Cassius, *Ausführliche Lebensbeschreibung*, 22ff. When Heumann would not stop trying to get him to change his religion, a Catholic workman in Zeitz tried to stab him; and as a student in Jena, Heumann once lectured a relative so extensively about his immoral life that he, too, very nearly stabbed him to death.

notes of an opponent who had spoiled things for Gottsched in Göttingen? I can hardly imagine that Gottsched himself would have behaved so criminally as to prevent the reshipment of the package to Brunswick and on to Göttingen. But what if several eager young people from his circle, Steinwehr or Stübner himself, wanted to show an overzealous loyalty by doing a favor for their teacher? That does not seem entirely implausible. Didn't Stübner's tight-lipped answer to Heumann's inquiry show some contempt for this "opponent"? These young men might have bribed Postmaster Heinsius to record a fictitious "Package Number 14." That is what Heumann himself must have thought. He suspected that Stübner "was in cahoots with the afore-mentioned Herr Heinsius."[69]

A Confiscation at the Prussian Border

Or had Heumann strayed into a hopeless dead end with his suspicions? Amazingly, one can sometimes check out old delivery receipts and postal lists. For the route in question, we know that the postal coach connection between Hamburg, Brunswick, and Leipzig was established in 1722 and that in 1732 the postal-union agreement had been renewed for the stretch between Brunswick and Leipzig. The starting point for this route was the electoral Saxon Superior Post Office in Leipzig, which then ran through Merseburg, Eisleben, Stolberg, and on to Brunswick (figure 46). After Stolberg, at the border (with Hanover) the postal coach had to change its coat of arms.[70] Until 1737 this route was also used by messengers from Nuremberg and wagons with provisions, but they were so unreliable that people were discontented both in Brunswick and in Leipzig. So in 1738 a new regulation was agreed to, and the postal coach route was extended to Nuremberg. The "Princely Brunswick Postal Wagon" for provisions and baggage had been founded in 1706 and in 1732 it became part of the principality's (regular) postal service.[71] So this was the situation at the time when Brucker's package was supposed to be shipped. Fortunately the state archive in Wolfenbüttel contains "Reports of the imperial and

69. Brucker to Gottsched, February 20, 1737.

70. See Heinrich Gaus, "Geschichte der Braunschweigischen Staatspost bis 1806," *Jahrbuch des Geschichtsvereins für das Herzogtum Braunschweig* 13 (1914): 84–129.

71. Günter Weinhold, "Die 'Fürstlich Braunschweigische Küchenpost,'" *Postgeschichtliche Blätter Hannover* 3 (1979). The official in 1734 was August Jacob Ulrich Henneberg (1711–63); Henri Bade, *333 Jahre Braunschweigische Post* (Braunschweig 1960), 16–19.

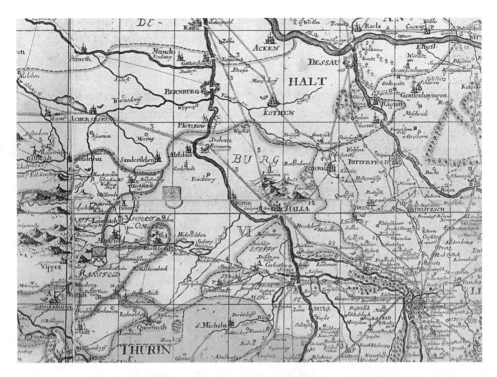

FIGURE 46. Postal route to the northwest of Leipzig; detail from *Neue Chur-Saechsische Post Charte*, 1736; revised in 1753 (Mulsow's copy).

princely Postmaster Westphal in Blankenburg (and later Postmaster in Brunswick) to the Prime Minister von Münchhausen concerning the princely provisions coach, the courier from Nuremberg, the route from Leipzig and Nuremberg, the postal duties demanded at the border with Prussia, and the seizures occasioned by refusing to pay them . . . along with other conditions and events."[72] Is that a crucial clue? Had there really been seizures? Yes indeed: precisely in the period around 1734 it is reported that during the search of the postal wagons certain shipments loaded on them had been confiscated. One wonders if Heumann's volumes of notes could have been the completely accidental victim of aggressive Prussian officials. Just beyond Stolberg one had to pass through a stretch of Prussian territory.

72. State Archive Wolfenbüttel, Archive call number 2 Alt No. 10329. The time period for these documents is 1729–52.

Let's look at this report. From the year 1734 there are four letters from Post-master Westphal to the Baron Gerlach Adolph von Münchhausen, the first one from August. And indeed in September someone shows up in these letters complaining about a "matter concerning books." "This man demands of me," said Westphal, "that I write back to him with my opinion regarding the matter of the books, in order to be able to keep the Count informed about the case." Clearly a packet of books had not arrived or had been confiscated. The trouble is that the man in question was not Heumann but an academic named Vilthat with a master's degree (*Lizentiat*).[73]

We have discovered a genuine difficulty on the route from Leipzig to Bruns-wick, but it did not involve Heumann's notes. That does not mean that we can rule out the possibility of a postal failure, but at least we can say that there is no evidence that Heumann's materials were confiscated. So we go back to our suspicions concerning Leipzig.

Repercussions

Meanwhile Brucker was not aware of the animosity of Gottsched toward Heu-mann. Indeed, he consulted Gottsched in the hopes of clearing up the prob-lem.[74] First, however, he took Postmaster Heinsius to task. At the time of the Jubilate trade fair, that is, the Leipzig spring fair in 1736, he gave a courier—probably a friendly Augsburg merchant or book dealer—the task of presenting the original certificate from the Brunswick postal authorities to Herr Heinsius in Leipzig, the certificate showing that there had been only twelve packages, and demanding an explanation: "because this was how his books came to be mistreated" (figure 47). His success was limited. "He, however, abruptly gave me no other answer than that he was under no obligation to pursue this matter further and that his records were accurate."[75] Heinsius was reacting with the same irritation as shown earlier by Stübner when Heumann had checked with him. Brucker considered, therefore, that Heinsius should be brought, "either peaceably or, if he refuses, then under legal pressure," to investigate whether the package in question had come to grief at one of the postal coaching stops

73. Ibid., fol. 20r: Westphal to Münchhausen, September 24, 1734.
74. "Da ich in Leipzig sonst niemand habe, den ich deswegen angehen kann," thus Brucker to Gottsched, February 20, 1737.
75. Brucker to Gottsched, February 20, 1737.

FIGURE 47. Certificate from the Brunswick postal
authorities from 1751. Sammlung Zinecker.

along the route between Leipzig and Brunswick.[76] But as we have seen, there
is no surviving evidence of any such hang-up.

Meanwhile young Stübner died in the course of 1736 after an accidental fall
that seems to have given rise to a fatal infection. Brucker wrote to Gottsched
and asked him to go through his literary estate to see if perhaps—as Heumann
suspected—the three volumes of excerpts might still be there. On December 19 he repeated this request and then again on February 20, 1737. Gottsched
did not respond. In April it was once again time for the trade fair, and Brucker
asked his friend, the Augsburg book dealer Merz who was traveling to the fair,
to ask Gottsched personally if the sealed papers of the deceased Stübner might
not finally be opened so that one might look for the package.[77] When August
came and there was still no response, Brucker felt compelled, reluctantly, to

76. Ibid.

77. Brucker to Gottsched, December 19, 1736, in *Briefwechsel*, 4:232ff.: "Ubrigens widerhole
ich meine in letzten schon abgelaßene inständige Bitte, unter den Stübnerischen Nachgelaßenen
Papieren nachsehen zulaßen, ob nicht drey bänd'gen Collectanea Hr. Phl. wie sie betitult sind,
darunter zufinden; welche ich vor 3. Jahren an den seel. H. Stübnern übermacht, um sie an H. D.
Heumann zubesorgen, der sie aber nicht bekommen hat, und nun erschröcklich darüber lermt.
Ich bitte umsomehr auf das allerinständigste Ew. HochEdelgeb. darum, mir in diesem sehr
verdrießlichen Falle an die Hand zu gehen, da ich förchte, bey so scharfen treiben H. D. Heumanns
dürffte unser gemeinschafftl. Freund unter dem Boden noch beunruhiget werden. Sie werden
mich dadurch mit der größten Gutthat von der Welt verbinden, und damit antreiben auf alle
mir mögliche Weise Denenselbigen zudienen. Ich förchte, wo sich nicht sonst ein Ausgang zeigt
und dieser verlohrne Pact hervorkomt, von dem H. D. Heumann glaubt, er seye noch in Leipzig,
daß es zu einer Gerichtlichen Klage und Untersuchung kommen werde, wo ich das An-
dencken H. Stübners gerne schonen möchte: So, wann sich es noch fände, wären Mittel und
Wege auf allen Seiten mit Ehren aus dem Gedränge zukommen, weswegen die Sache nochmalen
Ew. HochEdelgeb. auf das nachdrücklichste empfohlen haben will." See also Brucker to Heumann,
April 24, 1737: "De fasciculo deperdito a Cl. Gottschedio nondum responsum, quod expectabam,
tuli, rogavi Dn. Bibliopolam Augustanam Merzium."

threaten Gottsched with legal proceedings on behalf of Heumann, "and thus legally require a reckoning from Heinsius, who clearly does not want to render an account, but also from Stübner's estate and its administrators—the latter action being one I am deeply reluctant to take inasmuch as I am eager to protect the blessed memory of good friends."[78] For Brucker the situation was awkward because under no circumstances did he wish to offend the powerful Gottsched, who was still important for him. He hastened to assure him repeatedly of his willingness to perform "all possible favors." But by November 20, despite this threat, nothing had happened. Brucker now sounded somewhat more subdued: "Over several months I have not received any word from Herr Dr. Heumann about his package, and I cannot understand why."[79] Indeed, Heumann was about to break off his correspondence with Brucker; the incident had badly damaged their relationship. "I hope, however," Brucker added, "to have the opportunity to inquire of the Leipzig post office and to confront them with the stamped postal documents from Heinsius and Brunswick, who will now have to take on responsibility. I cordially wish I could be freed once and for all from this irksome case."[80] But these pleas got him no further. Finally in the spring of 1738 he received a report from Leipzig that nothing had been found among Stübner's books and papers. The report was an official document, signed by Georg Wilhelm Zähinger, who was probably a notary.

Why was this report so late in coming? Why had Gottsched failed to react for more than two years to Brucker's understandable requests? Why did the whole case stretch out over four long years? Were the officials simply that slow? Or was there something to hide? If the package really had been held back by overzealous friends of Gottsched—even if at first only on a whim or as a prank—what had then happened to it? Had they simply set it aside and allowed it to disappear into some bookcase? None of this can be decided today—unless the manuscript were to surface suddenly somewhere—and for the stubborn Heumann and Brucker, their researches had provided no clarity. Of course they were far removed from Leipzig and could only manage the matter by using intermediaries. But the whole episode leaves a bad taste in one's mouth. Because the Brunswick post office seems to have kept exact and accurate records, some residual suspicion continues to hang over Postmaster Heinsius and his accomplices.

78. Brucker to Gottsched, August 14, 1737, in *Briefwechsel*, 4:396.
79. Brucker to Gottsched, November 20, 1737, in *Briefwechsel*, 4:518.
80. Ibid.

Conclusion

This case of the missing package might appear to be nothing more than a tiny episode from the margins of the history of scholarship in the eighteenth century, and one that we cannot completely explain. But that is not the case. It had, I think, important consequences in at least three different ways.

First: Without the package from Göttingen, Brucker could never have written his momentous history of philosophy in the way he did, and that would have deprived the world of the eighteenth century of the largest and most influential philosophical-historical work of his time. Indeed, when Heumann's folders unexpectedly fell into Brucker's lap they seem to have emboldened the previously "stumbling" and "wavering" young scholar. In a work identified by Ursula Behler as his autobiography, Brucker reported that his intention in publishing his *Short Questions* was "not to write a comprehensive work, for which he believed he lacked the mental and the physical strength, to say nothing of the requisite scholarly learning."[81] At his home in Kaufbeuren, as I mentioned at the beginning of this chapter, Brucker did not have the gigantic library of Johann Albrecht Fabricius or Johann Christoph Wolf, and there were no large public libraries near him. He had to rely on the information provided by his circle of correspondents, and especially on Heumann's collection of materials. Brucker depended on Heumann even for his organizing principles, as we have seen, and so it seemed obvious that he would fill in the separate topics with information from the folders of excerpts.[82]

Second: Because the package of papers went missing on its journey back to Göttingen, Heumann was never again able to write anything substantial in the history of philosophy. Even if sending his collection to Kaufbeuren had been a spontaneous act of generosity to a young and gifted scholar who was ready to summarize these materials, a task for which Heumann did not then have the time, things may well have looked different a few years later. Heumann surely would have wanted to publish something on the history of philosophy during the thirty years he still had to live. But under the circumstances he was forced to reorient himself and turn to philology and biblical exegesis. Heumann still had his notes from his lectures at Eisenach on the books of the New Testament. They provided the basis for his many-volume *Explanation of the*

81. Brucker, *Autobiographie*, printed in Ursula Behler, "Eine unbeachtete Biographie Jacob Bruckers," in *Jacob Brucker*, ed. Schmidt-Biggemann and Stammen, 43.
82. Schmidt-Biggemann, "Bruckers philosophiegeschichtliches Konzept."

New Testament, which he published in the 1750s.[83] But Heumann never wrote his *Historia critica philosophiae.*

Third and finally: This episode also allows us to glimpse the common practices and the hassles for communication in the Republic of Letters. Trade routes and trade fairs, friends who were traveling and postal coaches—these were all parts of the social knowledge possessed by every scholar. Even if scholars themselves were not very mobile, their texts needed to circulate. As we have seen from his letters, the scholarly life of a man like Heumann was attuned to the rhythm of the book fairs. That was true of much more than his correspondence with Brucker. Even his most important borrowings from the private libraries of Uffenbach and Mencke were coordinated with the fairs because that made them so much cheaper than the postal system: in his *Memoirs* he wrote, "And for many years during almost every Frankfurt or Leipzig book fair heavy bundles were sent to him from there, which he then sent back, after he had made use of them."[84] A detailed study of the ebb and flow of the structured exchanges within the Republic of Letters according to the tides of the fairs and the fees charged by postal couriers could fill an entire book.

Precarious knowledge—or the precarity of knowing—was a constant worry. Even if we find ourselves here, in this chapter, among the knowledge bourgeoisie, among secure pastors, teachers, and university professors, knowledge could always be lost. That accounts for the constant refrain of queries about whether some earlier message or packet had arrived safely. The precariat grew, as we have seen, with the conflicts that broke out when scholars fought with each other, and it grew even faster when scholars, because of their opinions, slowly isolated themselves from one another within the Republic of Letters. That could create "zones of vulnerability," as the sociologists of labor call them, in which the social lubrication of relations and connections dried up that ordinarily helped packages to arrive as they should, reviews to get written, and positions to be properly filled. In such zones accidents could have a more devastating impact than elsewhere. But often enough, packages simply did not arrive.

83. Cassius, *Ausführliche Lebensbeschreibung,* 142.
84. Ibid., 218.

Communities of Fascination and the Information History of Scholarly Knowledge

In chapter 7 we modified Barbara Rosenwein's concept of "emotional communities" and cautiously applied it to "intellectual-emotional communities."[1] This describes textual communities[2] whose members share a similar feeling of being outsiders and who recognize one another through their common gestures. We have recently recognized that we should not ignore emotional components if we intend to reconstruct historical situations even within intellectual history. That has become clear from works as different as those of William Reddy and Ute Frevert.[3] And especially for anyone trying to detect the precarious and fragile elements of knowledge cultures, even if those cultures

---

1. Rosenwein, *Emotional Communities in the Early Middle Ages*.

2. Brian Stock, *The Implications of Literacy: Written Language and Models of Interpretation in the Eleventh and Twelfth Centuries* (Princeton, 1983). In just the way that Stock has described the social practice of dealing with texts in monastic communities as "textual communities," one can also describe the scholars of early modern Europe as textual communities—with some limitations, because of course communities that interact face-to-face present certain differences.

3. William M. Reddy, *The Navigation of Feeling: A Framework for the History of Emotions* (Cambridge, 2001); Ute Frevert, "Was haben Gefühle in der Geschichte zu suchen?" *Geschichte und Gesellschaft* 35 (2009): 183–208; eadem et al., eds., *Gefühlswissen* (Frankfurt, 2011). See also Barbara Rosenwein, "Worrying about Emotions in History," *American Historical Review* 107 (2002): 821–45; in addition: Jan Plamper, "The History of Emotions: An Interview with William Reddy, Barbara Rosenwein, and Peter Stearns," *History and Theory* 49 (2010): 237–65. Martha C. Nussbaum develops a cognitivist theory of feelings in *Upheavals of Thought: The Intelligence of the Emotions* (Cambridge, 2001).

were generally secure, the emotional components of intellectual enterprises are interesting because they can point to ambivalences, strong attractions, and revulsions concerning certain texts and objects.

For that reason I'd like to group the next three chapters under the concept of "communities of fascination," which would describe intellectuals who showed an especially strong attraction to the ancient Near East, or magic, or ancient numismatics. We all know that collecting coins can become a passion and that the hunt for the oldest possible documents has often led to forgeries or to a susceptibility to fraud.[4] We need to avoid the mistake of regarding early modern scholars as merely detached producers and recipients of texts. That would not explain the fervor with which they often dedicated their entire lives—even foolishly[5]—to collecting books and manuscripts and reading them through the night.

The idea of fascination helps connect the passions of certain scholars with the means by which communities are created. Scholars have used the term "communities of laughter" to describe the performative and socially constitutive components that laughter can possess.[6] Fascination can also have a socially constitutive function, even if a weaker one, if it is shared within intellectual circles and contributes to the cohesion of the group. These can be face-to-face constellations but also communities bound together by correspondence.

I also regard this as an opportunity to study the history of emotions and thus avoid the idea of "esotericism," which has never been an entirely satisfactory object of research.[7] The idea of "esoteric knowledge" is crippled, in my view, by the fact that it postulates continuities that never really existed; after all, until the seventeenth century astrological, hermetic, or magical topics were still acceptable for scholarly elites, while from the eighteenth century onward,

4. It is sufficient to cite Anthony Grafton, *Forgers and Critics: Creativity and Duplicity in Western Scholarship* (Princeton, 1990); Ingrid Rowland, *The Scarith of Scornello: A Tale of Renaissance Forgery* (Chicago 2004); and Rüdiger Schaper, *Die Odyssee des Fälschers* (Munich, 2011).

5. See the examples in Mencke, *De charlataneria eruditorum*; Fassmann, *Der gelehrte Narr*; as well as Alexander Kosenina, *Der gelehrte Narr: Gelehrtensatire seit der Aufklärung* (Göttingen, 2009).

6. Werner Röcke and Hans Rudolf Velten, eds., *Lachgemeinschaften: Kulturelle Inszenierungen und soziale Wirkungen von Gelächter im Mittelalter und in der Frühen Neuzeit* (Berlin, 2005).

7. In Germany Monika Neugebauer-Wölk has made a strong argument for the importance of esotericism: "Esoterik im 18. Jahrhundert—Aufklärung und Esoterik. Eine Einleitung," in *Aufklärung und Esoterik*, ed. idem (Hamburg, 1999), 1–37.

the rise of Copernicanism and the natural sciences as well as the philological discrediting of pseudepigrapha (i.e., texts with fraudulent or false claims to antiquity) pushed these traditions to the margins of knowledge and scholarship.[8] So whatever esotericism was (in terms of its content) between about 1580 and 1780 completely changed its socially validated status as knowledge. But affective communities of fascination, in contrast, may properly be termed "esoterics"—a term that can be adjusted according to time period and social context, just as the groups I discussed in chapter 7 could be said to share certain gestures.

The fascination with the most ancient of documents, with coins from the East, and with magic all share something "orientalizing" in the sense of being attracted to the exotic.[9] But orientalizing need not necessarily be understood in Edward Said's sense as a critique of colonialism,[10] because at least for Germany in the early modern period that sense does not really work.[11] As I'm using it the category applies much more to a sort of compensatory and escapist attitude among European intellectuals: they ascribed to the ancient world and especially to the East mysterious and "deep" insights that pointed to something that was the opposite of their own experience of the world—even if superficially an obsession with the sources of the ancient East could be made

8. The "flagship" of academic research into esotericism is Wouter J. Hanegraaff, ed., *Dictionary of Gnosis and Western Esotericism*, 2 vols. (Leiden, 2005); also idem, *Esotericism and the Academy: Rejected Knowledge in Western Culture* (Cambridge, 2012), a book that reformulates the concept of the esoteric in terms of making a certain kind of knowledge precarious. On the history of philological destruction, see Wilhelm Schmidt-Biggemann, "Die philologische Zersetzung des christlichen Platonismus am Beispiel der Trinitätstheologie," in *Philologie und Erkenntnis: Beiträge zu Begriff und Problem frühneuzeitlicher Philologie*, ed. Ralf Häfner (Tübingen, 2001), 265–301. On the abandonment of hermeticism and astrology in scholarship, see Park and Daston, eds., *The Cambridge History of Science*, vol. 3: *Early Modern Science*, 497–561.

9. See, e.g., Gereon Sievernich and Hendrik Budde, eds., *Europa und der Orient 800–1900* (Berlin, 1989).

10. Translator's note: In his book *Orientalism* (New York, 1978), Edward Said argued that patronizing representations of "the East" were complicit in the policies of Western powers who extended their cultural, political, and economic control over their colonies in Asia, Africa, and the Middle East. These representations, mostly from the nineteenth and twentieth centuries, usually portrayed "the Orient" as violent, superstitious, despotic, fanatic, primitive, and irrational. Such claims, Said argued, buttressed the colonial powers' sense of superiority and their right to rule over and control their Eastern dominions.

11. Said, *Orientalism*. See carefully nuanced observations of Suzanne Marchand, *German Orientalism in the Age of Empire: Religion, Race and Scholarship* (Cambridge, 2009).

to seem completely rational. Indeed, Hermeticists, Behmanists, and Kabbalists all sometimes shared this fascination with their critics, as we saw in the case of Abraham Hinckelmann in chapter 10 and as we will see in chapters 12 and 14 with scholars such as Valentin Ernst Löscher and Johann Christoph Wolf.

In the following three chapters I will connect a reconstruction of these orientalizing communities of fascination with scholarly approaches originating in the history of information in order to find out just where precarious moments and zones opened up within an otherwise well-secured culture of knowledge. The history of information and communication is proving itself to be a crucial discipline for any critical historiography, because it describes real events and concrete practices instead of chasing after phantasms of ideal knowledge, claims to power, and fantasies of surveillance.[12] In chapter 11, I tried to clear away the doxographic style of investigating Enlightenment histories of philosophy by employing an approach from the history of communications. The case histories in this section are an extension of that project. First in chapter 12 the topic is the ambivalent engagement of Western scholars with magic. It will become apparent that magic could be criticized both from the "Enlightened" side and from the Orthodox ecclesiastical side, and also that magic could be defended both by those called "esoterics" and by intellectual "radicals." To that extent the interest in magic cuts obliquely through the zones separating the knowledge precariat from the knowledge bourgeoisie and blurs the lines between them.

In chapter 13 questions from the history of communications regarding mobility and surveillance turn into something useful for the history of numismatics, a topic that has usually been treated in a totally traditional manner. Not long ago Daniel Roche and Stéphane Van Damme linked political space, scholarly mobility, and local identity together.[13] They show that knowledge could become precarious through mobility, either through the dangers of travel or

12. Here the pathbreaking book is the collection by Brendecke, Friedrich, and Friedrich, *Information in der Frühen Neuzeit*; see also Arndt Brendecke, *Imperium und Empirie: Funktionen des Wissens in der spanischen Kolonialherrschaft* (Cologne, 2009); Cornel Zwierlein, *Discorso und Lex Dei: Die Entstehung neuer Denkrahmen im 16. Jahrhundert und die Wahrnehmung der französischen Religionskriege in Italien und Deutschland* (Göttingen, 2006); Markus Friedrich, *Der lange Arm Roms? Globale Verwaltung und Kommunikation im Jesuitenorden 1540–1773* (Frankfurt, 2011); Jacob Soll, *The Information Master: Jean-Baptiste Colbert's Secret State Intelligence System* (Ann Arbor, 2009).

13. See the references in chapter 13, note 1.

through the change of one's city or country into a confessionally hostile one. In his important book *Empire and Empiricism* (*Imperium und Empirie*), Arndt Brendecke has raised the question of surveillance to a crucial position: If communicative circumstances were difficult (e.g., if information from across the ocean was compromised by surveillance), how could one test the veracity of reports?[14] This question throws a new light onto Oriental antiquarian and numismatic investigations.

In chapter 14, in contrast to the geographically wide-ranging investigations into mobility, I have devised a microhistory of information processing: I will follow the way a Hamburg scholar obsessively recorded his fascinated "knowledge of the Orient" in his notebooks and used these notes as a basis for his lectures and his published books. Such processes also reveal moments of fragility. Does knowledge have to be suppressed in the process of moving from reading one book to writing another book? Does knowledge become subversive if it is combined with other sorts of knowledge? What knowledge then gets lost?

14. Brendecke, *Imperium und Empirie*, 177–216.

12

Protection of Knowledge and Knowledge of Protection

DEFENSIVE MAGIC, ANTIQUARIANISM, AND MAGICAL OBJECTS

The standard work on "The Bondage of Superstitious Modern Man" remains to be written. It would have to be preceded by a study—also as yet unwritten—*The Renaissance of The Spirit World of Antiquity in the Age of the German Reformation.*

—ABY WARBURG

The Snake Ritual

In April 1923, when Aby Warburg gave a lecture on the snake ritual of the Hopi Indians in the Sanatorium Bellevue in Kreuzlingen, it became clear just how much psychic power—of fascination, dread, alienness, and force—he was studying here and trying to banish.[1] After his lecture, which he had prepared

1. Aby Warburg and W. F. Mainland, trans., "A Lecture on Serpent Ritual," in *Visual Culture: Histories, Archaeologies and Genealogies of Visual Culture,* vol. 2, ed. Joanne Morra and Marquard Smith (London, 2006), 156–72. On this topic, see Erhard Schüttpelz, *Die Moderne im Spiegel des Primitiven* (Munich, 2005), 137–70; Cora Bender, Thomas Hensel, and idem, eds., *Schlangenritual: Der Transfer der Wissensformen vom Tsu'ti'kive der Hopi bis zu Aby Warburgs Kreuzlinger Vortrag* (Berlin, 2007). An earlier version of this chapter appeared as "Talismane und Astralmagie: Zum Übergang von involviertem zu distanziertem Wissen in der Frühen Neuzeit," in *Magie und Religion,* ed. Jan Assmann and Harald Strohm (Munich, 2010), 135–57. The epigraph to this chapter is from Aby Warburg, *The Renewal of Pagan Antiquity: Contributions to the Cultural*

with Fritz Saxl, Warburg felt better. His examination of the magical world of
"the primitive," which he had gotten to know on his trip to America in 1895–96,
helped him exorcize his own demons. Indeed, Warburg knew such demons
only too well, and they made his life difficult right down to the crisis he experienced in the years after World War I. Much has been written about the extent
to which Warburg's involvement with Renaissance astrology and magic was a
reflection of his own psychic instability. All the same this scholar, who showed
such contempt for conventionally aestheticizing histories of art, was so driven
to study "demonic" topics that he discovered a new and deeper dimension
within the Italian Renaissance that previous scholars had all too gladly ignored. *Pagan Mysteries in the Renaissance,* a book by Warburg and Panofsky's
student Edgar Wind, described not just learned mind games and subterranean
traditions that transported psychic forces from antiquity into early modern
Europe.[2] That much is certainly true for specific mythical contents, for magical objects, for astrological formulas, and generally for the image magic found
in visual media during certain critical periods.[3]

In 1900 Warburg's studies of astrology and magic were distinctly odd. But
this was not the first time that European scholars, with a mixture of revulsion
and obsession, had found themselves intrigued with the surviving remnants
of ancient or "primitive" magic. The ambivalence displayed in Warburg's lecture in Kreuzlingen had a long prehistory—it was a precarious subject for
otherwise comfortably established scholars filled with the excitement of armchair travelers. Even Warburg, of course, had watched the Hopi dancers through
eyes that had been schooled by long humanist acquaintance with classical
antiquity. When in Oraibi, Arizona, he saw the clowns acting, it occurred to
him that "anyone acquainted with ancient tragedy will recognize the dual nature of the tragic chorus and the satyr play—'both grafted on to one stem.'"[4]
This was the sort of transverse association—from a distant location into the
deep time of antiquity—that other humanistically educated travelers to America had often experienced. A good example was the Jesuit Jean-François

History of the European Renaissance, ed. Kurt W. Forster, trans. David Britt (Los Angeles, 1999),
598 (original German published in 1920).

2. Wind, *Pagan Mysteries in the Renaissance.*

3. See the works by Horst Bredekamp, *Repräsentation und Bildmagie der Renaissance als Form-
problem* (Munich, 1995); idem, *Theorie des Bildakts* (Berlin, 2010).

4. Warburg, "A Lecture on Serpent Ritual," 165. See Schüttpelz, *Die Moderne im Spiegel des
Primitiven,* 142ff.

Lafitau, one of the forerunners of comparative cultural history, who lived in America between 1711 and 1717.[5] Lafitau saw in the Hurons, with whom he was staying, a reappearance of what he had read of the Spartans, Lycians, and other peoples from the world of ancient Greece.

Thus Warburg and Lafitau sensed that an archaic mentality had an uncanny similarity with modern examples of the magical; but the same was true for many scholars of the sixteenth and seventeenth centuries. This sense of vital similarity was by no means a marginal phenomenon, for it was especially pronounced among the more elite elements of the knowledge bourgeoisie. For them, apotropaic magic (defensive magic), the knowledge of how to protect oneself against bewitching, became an intellectual object of research, but it still carried remnants of a supercharged emotionality. Knowledge of how to protect oneself became protection of knowledge if it was used in order to ward off opponents, alternative thinkers, and persecutors. And who did not need protection?

Involvement and Distance

A cultural history of knowledge and of scholarly attention must always remain aware of what kind of knowledge is under discussion. Was a certain knowledge only distanced and interested in describing and explaining some situation, or could it enable those involved to appropriate the subject and to deal with it? Or more simply, did the person concerned with a matter believe in it or was he or she only approaching it from the outside? This distinction is especially important for those dealing with magic. Was knowledge of magical practices, the making of talismans, or prophecy a kind of insider knowledge possessed only by "religious specialists," or was it carried on by persons who did not share the premises of magic?[6]

---

5. On Lafitau, see Martin Mulsow, "Jean-François Lafitau und die Entdeckung der Religions- und Kulturvergleiche," in Götterbilder und Götzendiener in der Frühen Neuzeit: Europas Blick auf fremde Religionen, ed. Maria Effinger, Cornelia Logemann, and Ulrich Pfisterer (Heidelberg, 2012), 36–47; Lucas Marco Gisi, Einbildungskraft und Mythologie: Die Verschränkung von Anthropologie und Geschichte im 18. Jahrhundert (Berlin, 2007).

6. On the history of scholarly attention, see Daston and Park, Wonders and the Order of Nature; Lorraine Daston, Eine kurze Geschichte der wissenschaftlichen Aufmerksamkeit (Munich, 2001). On differentiating different sorts of knowledge, one must still consult Michael Polanyi, The Tacit Dimension (Chicago, 1966); Alvin Goldman, Knowledge in a Social World (Oxford 1999). On religious specialists, see Jörg Rüpke, Historische Religionswissenschaft: Eine Einführung

This distinction may seem simple, but it is not. That's especially clear if one is interested in transitions. When does belief in magic shift over into a distanced, antiquarian, or scholarly preoccupation with magic? The answer naturally depends on which regions and which social classes one is looking at. Among the European lower classes or outside Europe one finds belief in magic well into the nineteenth century, or indeed down to today. But how did things look for elite European intellectuals? When did they make a transition? One criterion for that might be the point in time when magical implements, statuettes, stones, rings, and seals began to be collected, described, compared, and catalogued.[7] Or when the origins and history of the concept of magic began to be critically investigated.[8] That would seem to have been the decades around 1600. That is when we find the first investigations into the origins, for example, of the word "talisman."

And yet a second look shows how inadequately this answers the question about transitions. For one thing, an antiquarian concern for talismans need not mean that one regards them as lacking all power. Thus in 1693 an author said this about talismans at the end of his *Disquisitio antiquaria*: "This is not the place to argue over the use of talismans and whether they are permitted. We would only remark that certain highly learned persons of our age attribute much to them."[9] But second, it also mattered what sort of effect one ascribed

---

(Stuttgart, 2007), 128–37. On the general problem, see also Georges Devereux, *From Anxiety to Method in the Behavioral Sciences* (The Hague, 1967), who points out that data in the behavioral sciences (but here also academic knowledge of magical facts) arouse anxiety, which is often countered by "method," in the sense of an unconscious countertransference, in which method is a means of subduing anxiety. In the interests of a well-balanced knowledge, Devereux recommended becoming fully conscious of this countertransference.

7. On collections, see generally Krysztof Pomian, *Collections and Curiosities: Origins of the Museum* (Cambridge, 1991); Dominik Collet, *Die Welt in der Stube: Begegnungen mit Außereuropa in Kunstkammern der Frühen Neuzeit* (Göttingen, 2007), 11–22 on the state of research. See, in addition, Mamoun Fansa, ed., *Zierde, Zauber, Zeremonien: Amulette zum Schutz von Körper, Hab und Seele. Begeitschrift zur Sonderausstellung vom 10.6.–26.8.2007* (Sigmaringen, 2007). See also *Zeitschrift für Kulturwissenschaften 1/2007: Fremde Dinge*.

8. On the concept of magic, see Hans G. Kippenberg and Brigitte Luchesi, eds., *Magie: Die sozialwissenschaftliche Kontroverse über das Verstehen fremden Denkens* (Frankfurt, 1987); Wouter J. Hanegraaff, "Magic I: Introduction," in *Dictionary of Gnosis and Western Esotericism*, ed. idem and Antoine Faivre (Leiden, 2005), 2:716–19, and now, with the recommendation that historians discontinue speaking of "magic" in their analyses; Bernd-Christian Otto, *Magie: Rezeptions- und diskursgeschichtliche Analysen von der Antike bis zur Neuzeit* (Berlin, 2011).

9. Valentin Ernst Löscher (praes.)/Johann Sigismund Koblig (resp. et auctor), *Disquisitio antiquaria de talismanibus* (Wittenberg, 1693), fol. B4v: "De usu Talismanum disputare, & an

to talismans: supernatural, natural—for example, using "sympathy" or "antipathy" or some astrophysical force—or none at all. It is difficult to determine whether scholars attributed natural effects to magic or simply held that "natural magic" was possible. Were they already on the road from belief in magic to science, to adopt the terms of modern teleology? Or were they on a dead-end street, one that unnecessarily kept the belief in magic and witchcraft alive for another hundred and fifty years, roughly from the late sixteenth century to the early eighteenth?[10]

Third, we should not confuse the strict rejection of magic and a distanced relationship to magic with "scholarly neutrality." After all, magic had long been a thorn in the side of Christian theology because it was often regarded as a remnant of pagan theology. So magic could seem like a form of idolatry, as is obvious in this book title from 1609: *De idololatria magica*, in which the author quotes church fathers like Tertullian.[11] So we have to be careful not to think that an opinion was distanced, in the sense of impartial, when in fact it was distanced because it was hostile.

Fourth, the very people who were clearly and emphatically "engaged" with magic may have been using the best philological, antiquarian, and collecting-comparative methods. One prominent example was Heinrich Cornelius Agrippa von Nettesheim with his work *De occulta philosophia* of 1510, which was published in 1530. Agrippa used a collection of Kabbalist manuscripts, employed evidence from coins, and worried as a humanist about the meanings of words, but he did all of this in order to make magic more accessible and systematic in neo-Platonic terms. Was he still a magician in the medieval sense? Or was he an example of someone taking the first steps toward antiquarianism?[12]

---

licitus sit, disquirire, hujus fori non est: istud solum notamus, quosdam nostrae aetatis pereruditos homines multum illis tribuere."

10. On natural magic, see Daniel P. Walker, *Spiritual and Demonic Magic from Ficino to Campanella* (London, 1958); *Studia leibnitiana* Sonderheft 7, *Magia naturalis und die Entstehung der modernen Naturwissenschaften* (Wiesbaden, 1978); and generally Lynn Thorndike, *A History of Magic and Experimental Science*, 8 vols. (New York, 1923–58).

11. Jean Filesac, *De idololatria magica* (Paris, 1609).

12. Agrippa von Nettesheim, *De occulta philosophia libri tres* (Antwerp, 1530; Cologne, 1533). Cf. the critical edition by Vitoria Perrone Compagni (Leiden, 1992); Charles G. Nauert Jr., *Agrippa and the Crisis of Renaissance Thought* (Urbana, 1965). See generally Paola Zambelli, *L'ambigua natura della magia: Filosofi, streghe, riti nel Rinascimento* (Milan, 1991); eadem, *Magia bianca, magia nera nel Rinascimento* (Ravenna, 2004).

And finally, was it possible to be "involved" in reading magical texts without being interested in the magic? That was more clearly the case with Giordano Bruno than with Agrippa, for Bruno was using the magical tradition to produce philosophical sparks. That's a point to which I will return.

To prevent the manifest complications bound up in this problem from plunging us even more deeply into an ocean of magical phenomena, I will concentrate on apotropaic magic and on the implements that were used for such purposes: amulets, talismans, rituals—but also just simple gestures.[13] From the point of view of an antiquarian the amulet and the talisman were the objects they were studying; but behind these material relics stood the ephemeral and commonplace background of rituals, songs, and movements, which are now mostly lost and can only occasionally be reconstructed from descriptions, such as those in the Greek Magical Papyri held by the Bibliothèque Nationale in Paris.[14] Of course, in the period we are concerned with, in the late sixteenth and early seventeenth centuries, magic and protective spells were still very much alive, especially in Italy. I would refer just to southern Italy, to Naples and Calabria, but one could cite Venice as well. A well-known defensive gesture, the *manu cornuta*, constituted a sort of amulet made by one's own hands, in which one forms a fist with outstretched index finger and little finger and holds it out toward the person from whom one fears some spell or perhaps the evil eye. As we saw in chapter 6, Andrea de Jorio, the specialist who studied gestures in the 1830s, found this gesture depicted in classical antiquity, for example, on a bronze engraved Silenus from Herculaneum and on an Abraxas gem depicted by Montfaucon.[15] As we've seen, the Venetian painter Pietro della Vecchia, who was much involved in magic, used this gesture in a complicated way in his allegorical painting of truth from 1654.[16]

13. On the history of amulets and talismans, see Roy Kotansky, "Amulets," in *Dictionary of Gnosis and Western Esotericism*, ed. Wouter Hanegraaff (Leiden, 2005), 1:60–71; outdated but still full of material: E. A. Wallis Budge, *Amulets and Superstitions* (Oxford, 1930).

14. See Fritz Graf, *Magic in the Ancient World*, trans. Franklin Phillip (Cambridge, MA, 1999), 95ff., 134ff. See generally the material in *Papyri Graecae Magici*, ed. Karl Preisendanz (Leipzig, 1928–31).

15. Andrea de Jorio, *La mimica degli antichi investigata nel gestire napoletano* (Naples, 1832); I have used the new English edition, *Gesture in Naples and Gesture in Classical Antiquity* (Bloomington, 2000), 171; Bernard de Montfaucon, *L'antiquité expliquée et représentée en figures*, supplement, vol. 2 (Paris, 1724), plate LV.

16. Pietro della Vecchia, *Allegoria dell' Architettura*; Accademia Carrara, Bergamo.

Another example would be the widespread presence in southern Italy of fears of being magically "bound." In Lucania, according to Ernesto de Martino, people are afraid of being bound and of *affascino*, the enchantment that stops the blood in its circulation, or of the "evil eye" that brings calamity.[17] We can see them at work in the ancient *defixiones* (enchantments): "I bind down Theagenes, his tongue and his soul and the words he uses," to quote a lead tablet from the fourth century BCE; and it goes on, "I also bind down the hands and feet of Pyrrhias the cook, his tongue, his soul, his words," and so forth.[18] The word used in Greek was *katadeîn*, "to tie down," to bind down in the depths. In his unpublished magical studies, such as *De vinculis in genere* (*On Chains in General*), Giordano Bruno argued that the forces mobilized in binding and exorcizing were examples of what might more generally be called "active relationality" in which relations could exercise magical effects.[19] In his published work *De monade, numero et figura* (*On the Monad, Number, and Figure*) he attempted to construct, for example, "rings" like the "Ring of Apollo," which looked like magical rings but for Bruno were most importantly geometric constructs that built out from the simplest units (starting with the monad) to arrive at more complex "deductions"; and imitating Cecco d'Ascoli (d. 1327) he wanted to ascribe forces to the intersections of such "ring lines," not in a sense that implied necromancy anymore but something more ontological.[20] So one could describe this as a philosophical purification of magic. In an entirely different manner but roughly at the same time Giambattista della Porta (d. 1615) "purified" magic and physiognomy through physics;[21] and in his *De sensu rerum et magia* (*On the Sense of Things and on Magic*), Tommaso Campanella (d. 1639), who had been strongly influenced by della Porta, set natural magic upon the foundation of the new physics of Bernardino

17. Ernesto de Martino, *Katholizismus, Magie, Aufklärung: Religionswissenschaftliche Studie am Beispiel Süd-Italiens* (Munich, 1982), 18ff.; see also Hauschild, *Magie und Macht in Italien*.

18. Graf, *Magic in the Ancient World*, 122.

19. Giordano Bruno, *Opere magiche*, ed. Michele Ciliberto, Simonetta Bassi, Elisabetta Scapparone, and Nicoletta Tirinnanzi (Milan, 2000).

20. Bruno, *De monade, numero et figura*; German edition: *Von der Monas, der Zahl und der Figur*, ed. Elisabeth von Samsonow, commentary by Martin Mulsow (Hamburg, 1991), 41; on Cecco: p. 152 and passim. On Cecco, see Richard Kiekhefer, *Magic in the Middle Ages* (Cambridge, 1989), 168–70.

21. Nicola Badaloni, "I fratelli della Porta e la cultura magica e astrologica a Napoli," *Studi storici* 1 (1960): 677–715.

Telesio (d. 1588).[22] This all illustrates the presence of a magical "mentality" as the substructure of Renaissance philosophical systems. To the north, in Protestant lands, and especially in Calvinist areas, it was somewhat easier to subject the phenomena of magic to a cool, philological examination.

Talismans and Teraphim: Philological Inquiry

In those very decades around 1600 when Bruno and Campanella were constructing their philosophical versions of magic, a massive antiquarian movement got under way to study the artifacts of the ancient world and the Orient. This was the pioneer generation of antiquarians and early Orientalists, who for the first time posed philological and critical questions of these materials. They included men such as Joseph Justus Scaliger (b. 1540) of Leiden, Isaac Casaubon (b. 1559) of Paris and London, Lorenzo Pignoria (b. 1571) of Padua, Nicolas-Claude Fabri de Peiresc (b. 1580) in Provence, and John Selden (b. 1584) of Oxford and London. With their expanding knowledge of languages that included Hebrew, Syriac, and especially Arabic, they could now investigate texts that had previously been inaccessible and raise their sights beyond the narrow horizon of Greek and Roman antiquity. In the 1580s Isaac Casaubon asked his teacher Joseph Scaliger to explain the origin of the word "talisman" and received an answer that pointed to Arabic origins.[23] The Swiss Orientalist Johann Heinrich Hottinger, however, drew a different conclusion, which depended on his knowledge of rabbinic sources and pointed to a "Chaldean" and therefore a Syrian-Babylonian origin for talismans. Scholars now argued that actually one should be speaking of talismae or tilsemae, based on the Chaldean talismoth or the Arabic tilsam, meaning "picture." In a chapter on the ancient Sabaeans and their religion, Hottinger identified their tilsemae as "dii averrunci," that is, "protective gods."[24] And he reminded readers of Moses

22. Tommaso Campanella, De sensu rerum et magia (Frankfurt, 1620); on that, see Germana Ernst, Tommaso Campanella: Il libro e il corpo della natura (Bari, 2002).

23. Joseph Justus Scaliger, Epistolae (Leiden, 1600), letters CXIX and CLXXX. On Scaliger, see Anthony Grafton, Joseph Scaliger: A Study in the History of Classical Scholarship, 2 vols. (Oxford 1983, 1993). On Casaubon, see Mark Pattison, Isaac Casaubon (London, 1875).

24. Johann Heinrich Hottinger, Historia orientalis (Zurich, 1660), 297. On Hottinger, see Jan Loop, "Johann Heinrich Hottinger (1620–1667) and the Historia Orientalis," Church History and Religious Culture 88, no. 2 (2008): 169–203.

Maimonides, who had explicated the Hebrew ceremonial laws as directed against the star-worshiping Sabaeans.[25]

In 1617 in his *De diis Syris* (*On the Syrian Gods*) John Selden discussed talismans in connection with *teraphim*, the mysterious objects mentioned in the Old Testament.[26] Were these small items, which Rachel stole from her father, something like talismans?[27] Selden found extensive discussions of them in rabbinic literature. So of course one had to study the Jewish tradition too.

In this way the philologists slowly developed a consciousness of what the historical lineage of talisman magic may have looked like. Early on the antiquarians focused on talismans as relics of Basilidian gnosticism. In 1597 in the second volume of his *Annales ecclesiastici*, Cesare Baronio (d. 1607) reproduced several gems on which the Abraxas figure was depicted, one with a rooster head and snake legs, and another with a human form on whose body the names of gods were inscribed.[28] Peiresc then showed Baronio his own collection of gnostic gems and discussed with him how they could illuminate the doctrinal systems of the Basilidians and the Valentinians, revealing much more than what one could learn from the Christian heresiologists. Peiresc also exchanged notes with another gem collector, Natalitio Benedetti, discussing a figure with the names of gods among other things (figure 48).[29] Today we know better perhaps how inscriptions of such names on statues and on actual bodies were embedded in ritual contexts; but for antiquarians of the seventeenth century, the first question worth answering was what the names of the gods were and what they meant, decoding either the numerical values of the letters or the mythical and astrological

25. Hottinger, *Historia orientalis*, 199ff.

26. John Selden, *De diis Syris* (Leipzig, 1668), 116ff. See Gerald J. Toomer, *John Selden: A Life in Scholarship*, 2 vols. (Oxford, 2009), 1:211–56; Martin Mulsow, "John Seldens De Diis Syris: Idolatriekritik und vergleichende Religionsgeschichte im 17. Jahrhundert," *Archiv für Religionsgeschichte* 3 (2001), ed. Jan Assmann and Guy Stroumsa, 1–24.

27. See the biblically antiquarian treatises on the teraphim collected in Biagio Ugolino, *Thesaurus antiquitatum sacrarum* (Venice, 1744–69), vol. 23. On this work, see A. Vivian, "Biagio Ugolini et son *Thesaurus Antiquitatum Sacrarum*: Bilan des études juives au milieu du XVIIIe siècle," in *La Republique des lettres et l'histoire du judaisme antique XVIe–XVIIIe siècles*, ed. Chantal Grell et al. (Paris, 1992), 115–47.

28. Cesare Baronio, *Annales ecclesiastici*, vol. 2 (Rome, 1597), Annus Christi 120. I have used the edition published in Lucca (1738), 92ff.

29. For the following: Miller, "The Antiquary's Art of Comparison"; on Peiresc, see generally Miller, *Peiresc's Europe*.

FIGURE 48. Natalitio Benedetti, drawing of a gnostic Mercury.
Peter N. Miller, "The Antiquary's Art of Comparison: Peiresc
and Abraxas," in *Philologie und Erkenntnis*, ed. Ralph Häfner
(Tübingen, 2001), 72.

references. Mind you, these investigations undertaken by antiquarian pio-
neers took place at a time when all over Europe witches were being burned.
Scholarly authors such as the Belgian Jesuit Martin Delrio (d. 1608) detected
the scent of witchcraft everywhere and in all times.[30] At that time people

30. Martin Delrio, *Disquisitiones magicae* (Louvain, 1599). On magic and witchcraft generally,
see Christoph Daxelmüller, *Aberglaube, Hexenzauber, Höllenängste: Eine Geschichte der Magie*
(Munich, 1996); Lyndal Roper, *Witch Craze: Terror and Fantasy in Baroque Germany* (New
Haven, 2004); Wolfgang Behringer, *Hexen: Glaube, Verfolgung, Vermarktung*, 5th ed. (Munich,
2009).

were very quick to accuse others of practicing magic, and anyone denounced as a magician might have a real struggle on his hands.

The Critique of Historical Memory

The early seventeenth century also saw the first critiques of the widespread literature attacking magic. These came not simply from people who believed in magic but from a historical-critical perspective. This movement had two important forerunners: first, the new spirit of philological criticism;[31] and second the naturalistic thinking developed in Renaissance philosophy under the influence of Pietro Pomponazzi. According to Pomponazzi's *De incanta-tionibus* (*On Enchantments*) of 1525, all supposed supernatural miracles and acts of magic could be explained naturally and scientifically, meaning without the assumption of "spiritual" or immaterial causation.[32] Earlier I called this critique "physical purification." But in addition Pomponazzi cultivated the Averroist idea that certain philosophical and scholarly insights should be accessible only to an elite of intellectuals and politicians; simple people continued to need religious fables that would impress them and keep them obedient. We considered that view in chapter 2. One hundred years later, for the young Gabriel Naudé (d. 1653) the result was a research program to "rescue" the intellectuals and politicians of earlier ages. He just had to invert the basic idea: in his view the history of supposed "magicians" was in reality a history of persons who used their scientific knowledge of nature politically to lead or direct the common people (in a positive sense); but later they were denounced as magicians. In his book *Apologie pour tous les grands personnages qui ont esté fausse-ment soupçonnéz de magie* (*Apology for all the Great Persons who have been Falsely Suspected of Magic*), published in 1625, Naudé carried out this sort of critique.[33] He "rescued" mathematicians like Pythagoras, natural philosophers

31. Jehasse, *La renaissance de la critique*; see also Martin Mulsow, "Libertinismus, Cartesian-ismus und historische Kritik: Neuere Forschungen zur Formation der Moderne um 1700," *Philosophische Rundschau* 42 (1995): 297–314.

32. Pietro Pomponazzi, *De naturalium effectuum causis sive de incantationibus* (1525; Basel, 1567). On the early reception of Pomponazzi, see Giancarlo Zanier, *Ricerche sulla diffusione e fortune del "De incantationibus" di Pomponazzi* (Florence, 1975). See Eckhard Kessler, "Pietro Pomponazzi: Zur Einheit seines philosophischen Lebenswerkes," in *Verum et factum*, ed. Tamara Albertini (Frankfurt, 1993), 397–419.

33. Naudé, *Apologie pour tous les grands personnages qui ont esté faussement soupçonnez de magie*. An English translation was published: *The History of Magick: by way of apology, for all the*

like Aristotle, and "politicians" like Numa. Chapter 8 concerned itself with
Zoroaster, because according to received opinion he was the inventor of
magic—something one could see in the concept of *mágos* (*magush*), which
the ancient Greeks had taken over from the Persians.[34]

What Naudé was doing can be described in modern terms as a critique of the
historical memory of magic. Collective memory bore the distorting imprint of
personal denunciations, political accusations, and superstitious behavior, as
well as a fear and distrust of theorists whose ideas were not understood.

Adding to this critique of historical memory, four years later Jacques Gaffarel, a friend of Naudé's, published his best seller and scandalous exposé,
*Curiositez inouyes sur la sculpture talismanique des Persans, Horoscope des Patri-
arches, et lecture des Estoilles* (*Unheard-of Curiosities concerning Talismanical
Sculpture of the Persians, the Horoscope of the Patriarchs, and the Reading of the
Stars*).[35] These audience-grabbing reports, sold as "unheard of curiosities,"
dealt with magical and astrological theories and really did offer something
unusual. Gaffarel's book was based on his competence in the field of Jewish
manuscripts, especially the Kabbalah. Gaffarel was one of the most scholarly
connoisseurs of such manuscripts and had long traveled all over Italy collecting them for Richelieu's library.[36] Like Naudé, Gaffarel was a devotee of
Giovanni Pico della Mirandola, and Pico's natural magic could be read with
Pomponazzi in the background, so that physical reasons could regularly explain apparently supernatural events.[37] Pico's and Reuchlin's conception of a
Christian Kabbalah had led many scholars to pay close attention to Jewish

---

wise men who have unjustly been reputed magicians, from the Creation, to the present age, trans.
J[ohn] Davies, s.l. ([London], 1657). See generally Bianchi, *Tradizione libertina e critica storica*.

34. Naudé, *Apologie pour tous les grands personnages qui ont esté faussement soupçonnéz de
magie*, quoted here from the new edition in *Libertins du XVIIe siècle*, ed. Jacques Prevot, vol. 1
(Paris, 1998), 139–380. On the concept of the "magus," see Walter Burkert, *Die Griechen und der
Orient: Von Homer bis zu den Magiern* (Munich, 2003), 107–33. On Naudé's chapter, see Michael
Stausberg, *Faszination Zarathushtra: Zoroaster und die europäische Religionsgeschichte*, 2 vols.
(Berlin, 1998), 535–40.

35. Jacques Gaffarel, *Curiositez inouyes sur la sculpture talismanique des Persans, Horoscope des
Patriarches, et lecture des Estoilles* (Paris, 1629); quoted here from the Paris edition (1637). See—also
for its later influence—Häfner, *Götter im Exil*, 214–217, 434–53.

36. Saverio Campanini, "Eine späte Apologie der Kabbala: Die Abdita divinae Cabalae Mysteria des Jacques Gaffarel," in *Topik and Tradition: Prozesse der Neuordnung von Wissensüberlie-
ferungen des 13. bis 17. Jahrhunderts*, ed. T. Frank, U. Kocher, and U. Tarnow (Göttingen, 2007),
325–51.

37. See also Zambelli, *Una reincarnazione di Pico ai tempi di Pomponazzi*.

texts as legitimate products of proto-Christian teachings. As a virtually official French expert on such matters, Gaffarel had to be taken seriously when he reported his discovery of a manuscript in Cremona by a certain Rabbi Elcha ben David: a manuscript which, after he had excerpted the content, was later unfortunately destroyed by a fire in the city. This work was called *De lectura per stellas* (*On Reading the Heavens*), and it presented a sort of heavenly alphabet made up of something like Hebraic letters. In *De occulta philosophia*, Agrippa von Nettesheim had spoken of a "heavenly writing," and Guillaume Postel had as well.[38] Now this manuscript discovery seemed to confirm these ideas and to make them concrete.

A further "curiosity" that Gaffarel reported from his rummaging in Italian archives concerned the discovery of a Persian text by an author named Hamahalzel in a Hebrew version by a certain Rabbi Khomer.[39] Soon, however, doubts were voiced about whether this manuscript, so frequently and gladly quoted by Gaffarel, had in fact ever existed.[40] Indeed, down to today no rabbi named Khomer and no Persian author named Hamahalzel has ever come to light. If Gaffarel's reported witness were authentic, it would surely be a Persian text from the Islamic era, but one that harked back to pre-Islamic ideas. One might think of the translations of Abū-Maʿshar into Hebrew (in reality, Pseudo-Abū Maʿshar) and of similar works.[41] Gaffarel summarized the chapter he devoted to this text with words that deliberately echoed Naudé: "That the

---

38. Agrippa von Nettesheim, *De occulta philosophia libri tres*, book III, chap. 30. I am using the German translation (Nördlingen, 1987); but see also *Three Books of Occult Philosophy*, trans. "J. F." (London, 1651), book 1, chap. 74.

39. Gaffarel, *Curiositez*, 48ff.: "Ie la tire de la Preface d'une Astrologie Persanne, traduicte en Hebreu par Rabbi Chomer, Autheur moderne, & ie ioint ses rasons avec celles que nous pouvons tirer des Latins, & des Grecs, pour les rendre plus fortes."

40. In the nineteenth century, however, A.J.H. Vincent argued that the question of authenticity should remain open: "Note relativ à l'alphabeth céleste et à R. Chomer," *Revue archeologique* 2 (1845): 619–21. Of course if the "lectura per stellas" and/or the work of Hamahalzel should prove to be spurious, that would not necessarily mean that Gaffarel was himself a fraud. When he was in Venice he came in contact with persons who provided him with manuscripts, but who might also have offered him forgeries (thanks to Saverio Campanini for this suggestion). And even forgeries could have been compiled from partially authentic materials.

41. Reimund Leicht, *Astrologumena Judaica: Untersuchungen zur Geschichte der astrologischen Literatur der Juden* (Tübingen, 2006). See, e.g., pp. 162ff. on the Sefer ha-Mazzalot by Pseudo Abu Mashar. But unlike Halmahalzel's work, this book was printed and distributed.

Persians and the curiosities of their magic, their sculpture, and their astrology have been falsely condemned."[42]

The Persians were wrongly condemned for their magic and astrology, according to Gaffarel, because their thought and practice were in conformity with those of the Jews at that time—for example, their use of teraphim statuettes—and indeed were adopted from them. It is not insignificant that at this point Gaffarel referred to a book by François de Monçeau, which also undertook an "unheard of" defense and was hardly less controversial than his own was to be: *Aaron purgatus sive de vitelo aureo* (*Aaron Purified, or, The Golden Calf*).[43] In that book Monçeau tried to show that in making the golden calf Aaron had acted righteously and had not committed idolatry.[44] "If the first Persians like Zoroaster made efforts to pray to some of these figures (statuettes such as the teraphim), in imitation of the first fathers who settled their land," Gaffarel asked, "should one conclude that they were magicians? That's no better than accusing people of witchcraft for thinking that some evil occurs just because of the swinging bell of Avila or some other wonder."[45] In other words, the Persians were orthodox or merely engaged in some popular but venial by-product of true religion. Zoroaster was thought of—by Naudé too—as Abraham's contemporary, who adopted from Abraham ideas for a religion of his own.

---

42. Gaffarel, *Curiositez*, 46: "Qu'à tort on a blasmé les Persans et les curiositez de leur Magie, Sculpture, et Astrologie." See also the mention of Naudé on p. 50.

43. François de Monçeau, *Aaron purgatus sive de vitelo aureo* (Arras, 1606). See Jonathan Sheehan, "The Altars of the Idols: Religion, Sacrifice, and the Early Modern Polity," *Journal of the History of Ideas* 67 (2006): 648–74. On Monçeau as someone who also described talismans and their effects, see C. F. Menestrier, *Le philosophe des images enigmatiques* (Lyon, 1694), 258ff.; Thorndike, *History of Magic*, 491ff. See Monçeau, *Disquisitio de magia divinatrice et operatrice* (Frankfurt and Leipzig, 1683). However, the true author of this work was Johannes Praetorius.

44. Monçeau, *Aaron purgatus*, 56.

45. Gaffarel, *Curiositez*, 61: "si les premiers Persans, comme Zoroastre, ont tasché d'observer quelqu'une de ces figures, à l'imitation des premiers Peres, qui ont habité leur pays, veut on conclurre par là qu'ils sont Magiciens? C'est tout de mesme que si on accusoit de sorcellerie ceux qui par le bransle de la cloche d'Avila ou de quelque autre prodige, concluent quelque malheur à venir."

Translator's note: The supposedly miraculous bells at Ávila are apparently unknown to modern scholars. But Prof. Alison Weber informs me that a town called Velilla de Ebro was reputed to have miraculous bells: "Perhaps Jacques Gaffarel substituted Ávila for Velilla de Ebro." See http://www.reman.es/campanas-milagrosas-velilla-ebro-zaragoza/.

Today we see the situation as paradoxically just the opposite: a Jewish magical culture thrived within the context of the Persian-Babylonian belief in magic, at the time of the Sassanids, when the Jews were living in Babylonian exile and compiling the Talmud. Research by Shaul Shaked and Peter Schäfer has proved that clearly. And the Aramaic magic bowls inscribed with magical names—including even Jesus—are proof of that.[46] Gaffarel indeed quotes his Persian author Hamahalzel again: "I am not denying, he says, that our old astrologers under specific constellations prepared images made of gold, silver, wood, wax, earth, or stone, to which they ascribed some actual use, but no one can confirm that they used enchantment or sorcery to do so."[47] That was because, Gaffarel continued, "any effect of these images could be natural."[48]

Talismans in Protestant Confessional Culture

We have seen that in the seventeenth century antiquarianism and humanist philology could definitely be a form of "engaged knowledge." Gaffarel was a proponent of natural magic, supposedly treating it in historical-critical fashion—in reality he was basing his magic on spurious or supposedly ancient Jewish-Persian texts. Fraud cannot be ruled out where Enlightenment was being pursued. That does not make our predicament any easier if we are hoping for an answer to the question about the transition from engaged to more impartial knowledge.

Now let's look at the inverse: How did scholars handle talismanic magic when they were obligated by their profession to assume a distanced or even hostile attitude toward the topic? This was the situation for Christian theologians and authors working within the context of Christian apologetics. For them naturally the prohibition of images and idolatry cast a dark shadow over all magical actions. Even much earlier, in Old Testament times, the prophets

46. Peter Schäfer, *Jesus in the Talmud* (Princeton, 2007), 38ff.; Shaul Shaked, "Jesus in the Magic Bowls," *Jewish Studies Quarterly* 6 (1999): 309–19; cf. generally Jacob Neusner, *A History of the Jews in Babylonia*, 5 vols. (Leiden, 1966–70); Michael G. Morony, *Iraq after the Muslim Conquest* (Princeton, 1984), 384–430.

47. Gaffarel, *Curiositez*, 61ff.: "Ie ne nie point, dit-il, que nos Anciens Astrologues, ne dressassent des images sous certaines constellations, soit en or, en argent, bois, cire, terre, ou pierre, desquelles ils retiroient quelque utilité, mais que ce fust par enchantemens et sortileges, il n'y a personne qui le puisse asseurer."

48. Ibid., 62: "la vertu de ces images pouvoit estre naturelle."

sometimes parodied the production of cult images.[49] So the later attacks on amulets and magical statuettes were naturally baked into both Jewish and Christian traditions from the beginning.

And yet that attitude could not always be maintained. The Judaism of the Babylonian Talmud that emerged in Sassanid Persia was, as I've already said, immersed in magic, absorbing and transforming it into its own Jewish traditions. Similarly gnostic Christianity in Egypt was full of magic. Medieval Judaism in cultural spaces dominated by Islam was suffused with magical practices, which were taught in the handbook called *Picatrix*, for example.[50] Of course in the Jewish astral magic of the Middle Ages a fine but sharp line was drawn between worshiping idols and using figures to draw the power of heaven down to earth.[51] In this regard the most important thinkers were Judah Halevi and Abraham Ibn Ezra, who undertook in the twelfth century, under the massive impact of Arabic astrology, to establish this boundary line. They interpreted the Golden Calf as an astral-magical statue, created under the sign of a specific constellation; for them the sin of the Jewish people simply consisted in using these means high-handedly without waiting for God to show them the way to draw down the power of heaven.[52] Ibn Ezra also interpreted the teraphim as a form of astral magic, even though he did not directly call them astronomical instruments for (magically) calculating the hours but regarded them instead as human statuettes that were meant to be used astrologically. Admittedly he kept this interpretation secret, as a kind of esoteric knowledge, because the simple people should see only the several ostentatious rejections of astral magic he issued in his biblical commentaries.[53] So according to him Rachel stole Laban's teraphim because Laban was an astrologer and Rachel was afraid that he could (magically) calculate the heavens in order to discover her escape route.[54]

Thus, many magical seals on Jewish manuscripts from this period should be seen as one or another form of astral magic. This is the context that helps

49. Michael B. Dick, "Prophetic Parodies of Making the Cult Image," in *Born in Heaven, Made on Earth: The Making of the Cult Image in the Ancient Near East*, ed. idem (Winona Lake, IN, 1999), 1–54.

50. *Picatrix: Das Ziel des Weisen von Pseudo-Magriti*, trans. Hellmut Ritter and Martin Plessner (London, 1962).

51. Dov Schwartz, *Studies on Astral Magic in Medieval Jewish Thought* (Leiden, 2005).

52. Monçeau drew on this tradition when he defended Aaron.

53. On esoteric writing, see also Halbertal, *Concealment and Revelation*.

54. Schwartz, *Studies on Astral Magic*, 20.

explain Maimonides's understanding of Sabaean texts and his massive backward projection of magical veneration of the stars into the most ancient times as part of a supposedly universal "Sabaean" paganism.[55]

From the seventeenth century onward Christian authors were deeply impressed by Maimonides. His thesis concerning the Sabaean character of paganism and the astral cult as the primary form of "false" religion was widespread, from Selden and Vossius down to Hinckelmann.[56] When authors like Athanasius Kircher concerned themselves in an antiquarian manner with the production of amulets, they embedded them into such grand historical-theological framing narratives.[57]

In addition there were authors of what we could call medical antiquarianism such as Fortunio Liceti, who in 1645 published a book on magical rings entitled *De anulis antiquis*.[58] Such works vacillated between a Christian reflex of flat rejection and a natural scientific curiosity regarding the effect of talismans. In 1676 the Strasbourg mathematician Julius Reichelt took up the topic.[59] He chose the safe approach and condemned amulets as signs of superstition and as a tool of the devil. In 1692 Reichelt's book was republished by Jacob Wolff, a professor in Jena, under the title *Curiosus amuletorum scrutator* (*The Curious Examiner of Amulets*), and indeed a certain scholarly passion was growing for the collection of amulets along with gems or coins.[60] Even Reichelt

---

55. Moses Maimonides, *The Guide for the Perplexed*, trans. M. Friedländer (London, 1910), book III, chap. 29. On Maimonides, see Sarah Stroumsa, *Maimonides in His World: Portrait of a Mediterranean Thinker* (Princeton, 2009).

56. See Aaron Katchen, *Christian Hebraists and Dutch Rabbis: Seventeenth Century Apologetics and the Study of Maimonides' Mishneh Torah* (Cambridge, MA, 1985); Jan Assmann, *Moses the Egyptian: The Memory of Egypt in Western Monotheism* (Cambridge, MA, 1998), 91–143; Mulsow, "Den 'Heydnischen Saurteig' mit den 'Israelitischen Süßteig' vermengt"; Guy G. Stroumsa, *A New Science: The Discovery of Religion in an Age of Reason* (Cambridge, MA, 2010).

57. Kircher, *Arithmetologia, sive de abditis numerorum mysterijs: Qua origo, antiquitas et fabrica numerorum exponitur* (Rome, 1665); idem, *Oedipus aegyptiacus* (Rome, 1652–54), vol. II,1, pp. 385–91: Fabrica et usus telesmatum, pp. 397–400: De telesmatis magnis, vol. II,2, pp. 55ff. on planet seals; pp. 461ff. on gnostic gems; p. 475 on talismans.

58. Fortunio Liceti, *De anulis antiquis* (Udine, 1645); on medical antiquarianism, see Nancy G. Siraisi, *History, Medicine, and the Traditions of Renaissance Learning* (Ann Arbor, 2008).

59. Julius Reichelt, *De amuletis* (Strasbourg, 1676). Cf. Thorndike, *History of Magic*, 569ff. See also Johann Christoph Vulpius, *De amuletis* (Königsberg, 1688).

60. Jacob Wolff, *Curiosus amuletorum scrutator* (Jena, 1692). See also August Nathanael Hübler (praes.)/Martin Friedrich Blümler (resp.), *Amuletorum historiam, earumque censuram... submittit* (Halle, 1710).

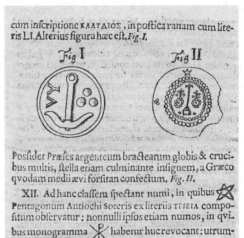

cùm inſcriptione ΚΛΑΤΑΙΟΣ , in poſtica ranam cum literis LI. Alterius figura hæc eſt, *Fig. I.*

Poſſidet Præſes argenteum bracteatum globis & cruci-
bus multis, ſtella etiam culminante inſignem, a Græco
qvodam medii ævi forſitan confectum, *Fig. II.*

XII. Ad hanc claſſem ſpectant numi, in quibus ✗
Pentagonum Antiochi Soteris ex literiis ΤΓΙΕΙΑ compo-
ſitum obſervatur : nonnulli ipſos etiam numos, in qvibus monogramma ✗ habetur huc revocant : utrumque enim ad Talismanum rationes reducit *H. C. Agrippa Lib III. Phil. Occ. p. 394.* Numos chemicos, ſignis che-
micis ornatos huc referentibus refragari nollem , de
qvibus *Cl. Reyherus* pererudite egit. Ultro autem huic
clasſi accedunt recentiores qvidam numi Mansfeldici

FIGURE 49. Valentin Ernst Löscher (praes.)/Johann
Sigismund Koblig (resp. et auctor), *Disquisitio
antiquaria de talismanibus* (Wittenberg, 1693).

himself had probably built the foundations for his book on a collection that the Strasbourg senator Elias Brackenhoffer had assembled. It included thousands of stones and minerals but also crocodiles, lions' heads, and three-legged sparrows along with ancient rings and coins.[61] But professors themselves could sometimes assemble smaller collections. Even Valentin Ernst Löscher, when still a young teacher in Wittenberg, and then later as the dean of Lutheran Orthodoxy in Germany, owned a small collection of talismans and coins (figure 49). Löscher showed the collection to his student Johann Sigismund Koblig and encouraged him to write his dissertation on it. In 1697 that work appeared as *Disquisitio antiquaria de talismanibus* (*Antiquarian Disquisition on Talismans*), in which Koblig discussed Christian magic as exemplified by silver bracteates—that is, thin coins and medals from the late ancient and

61. *Musaeum Brackenhofferianum/Das ist/Ordentliche Beschreibung Aller/so wohl natürlicher als Kunstreicher Sachen/Welche sich in Weyland Hrn. Eliae Brackenhoffers/gewesenen Dreyzehners bey hiesiger Statt Straßburg/Hinterlassenem Cabinet befinden* (Strasbourg, 1683), 79: crocodiles; p. 80: lion's head; p. 82: sparrow with three feet; p. 112: ancient rings.

medieval periods—that bore symbols of the cross.[62] He compared them with famous early Christian magical symbols of the sort that Agrippa of Nettesheim had depicted in *De occulta philosophia*, such as the sign of the cross with the inscription *In hoc vince* (In this [sign], conquer), which had supposedly been revealed to Emperor Constantine in 312 CE.[63] These were images, according to Agrippa, "that had been received only through revelation and that could never have been discovered in any other way."[64] The theologian Thomas Zacharias Nolte picked up on Agrippa's idea in a letter he wrote on March 15, 1709, to the Helmstedt professor Hermann von der Hardt, whom we met back in chapter 7. Nolte had received from merchants several coins of Jewish provenance that apparently displayed magical symbols and squares. Nolte had no idea what to make of them and requested information from the learned Orientalist, von der Hardt, who within a few weeks composed an expert opinion in a manuscript of over two hundred pages, in which he applied his knowledge of Jewish astral magic to the coins.[65] When he later published his expert opinion as a book, he instructed the bookbinder to make small secret compartments in the wooden, leather-bound inner cover of the volume, into which he laid lead and wax casts of the medals under discussion, designating them "sun," "moon," "Mars," and "Venus" (figure 50).

He was able to compose this expert opinion so quickly because magical amulets had been his burning interest for a long time. In 1705 he had spent the whole summer semester lecturing on the "secrets" of Jewish amulets, which he then turned into a book shortly thereafter.[66] He examined the attempts of the rabbis to apply complicated hermeneutic methods to the problem of

62. Löscher (praes.)/Koblig (resp. et auctor), *Disquisitio antiquaria de talismanibus.*

63. Ibid., § XI.f.

64. Agrippa von Nettesheim, *De occulta philosophia*, book III, chap. 31.

65. Baden State Library Karlsruhe, Ms. 394, fol. 36ff.: *Epistolae Zachariae Noltenii de magicis inter Judaeos et Christianos Planetarum nummis*, Scriptae A. 1709 mense Martio et Aprili. The volume extends to fol. 247. On planetary amulets and texts, in which their production is described, like the Sefer ha-Kasdim, see Leicht, *Astrologumena Judaica*, 325–31; magical planetary squares were clearly first received among the Jews in the fifteenth century. On Arabic models, see W. Ahrens, "Studien über die magischen Quadrate der Araber," *Der Islam* 7 (1917): 186–250; idem, "Magische Quadrate *und* Planetenamulette," *Naturwissenschaftliche Wochenschrift* 35 (1920): 465–75. In 1710 Nolte became a pastor in Wackersleben.

66. They were published under the title *Aenigmata Judaeorum religiosissima maxime recondita* (Helmstedt, 1705). I am grateful to Asaph Ben-Tov for alerting me to this text. He also provided me insight into Hardt's use of rabbinic traditions.

FIGURE 50. Hermann von der Hardt to Zacharias Nolte concerning magical coins.
Badische Landesbibliothek Karlsruhe, Ms. 394, inlaid secret compartment.

drawing out some religiously correct meaning from the unintelligible magical names, for example, by switching around the letters of the words, in order then to receive some "correct" monotheist message. But von der Hardt thought that such efforts were all a pious fraud on the part of the rabbis. He considered the magical names to be apotropaic signs, unintelligible charms that used words that were, for example, distortions of late ancient emperors' names.

However that may be, the cases of Nolte and Löscher show that "engaged knowledge" here unexpectedly appeared among opponents as opposed to enthusiasts. Obviously there could also be a Christian interest in favor of magic, for example if Christian symbols were involved. And that does not make our quest for the course from involvement to unprejudiced disinterest any easier. Koblig and Löscher found that they could combine a cautious interest in natural, sympathetic magic with a careful antiquarian approach to Christian semi-magical traditions. And that Constantinian symbol "In hoc signo vince" was therefore also the copper-plate title engraving of a book about talismans and amulets that appeared in 1717 (figure 51).[67] There we can

67. Peter Friedrich Arpe, *De prodigiosis naturae et artis operibus Talismanes et Amuleta dictis* (Hamburg, 1717).

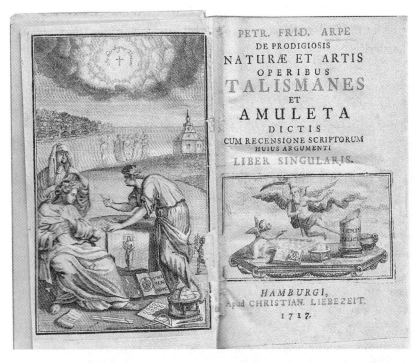

FIGURE 51. Peter Friedrich Arpe, *De prodigiosis naturae et artis operibus Talismanes et Amuleta dictis* (Hamburg, 1717), title page.

see the magical sign of victory shining down on pagan ritual objects: magical coins, statues, handbooks, and astrological instruments. Here was one way Christianity went beyond paganism but also—amazingly—stood in a sort of continuity, as a continuous line from magic to revelation (understood as Christian magic).

Was this claim of continuity explosive? Surely yes. This becomes clear if we investigate the history of a little book published in 1717. Its author, Peter Friedrich Arpe, was the collector of clandestine religiously critical manuscripts, whom we got to know in chapter 4. It appears that he truly sympathized with these works, at least within limits.[68] He had discovered the material for his book by accident. After his studies, in the years around 1705, he was working in Copenhagen, where he was permitted to use the library of the recently deceased late humanist physician Georg Franck von Franckenau.

68. On Arpe (1682–1740), see Mulsow, "Freethinking"; idem, *Enlightenment Underground*.

Like Fortunio Liceti and Julius Reichelt, Franckenau was interested in talismans for medical-antiquarian reasons and had assembled a rich collection of materials on them. As Arpe was using Franckenau's books he came upon these papers and obviously used them as the starting point for his own monograph.[69] From his writings we can tell that Arpe had deep sympathies for the naturalizing tradition, the tradition of natural magic, and for the historical criticism of thinkers like Pomponazzi, Naudé, and Gaffarel. These three currents composed an amalgam that he immediately connected with what we today call the "early Enlightenment," a movement closely connected to the "radical Enlightenment." From such a standpoint it was only a short step to seeing the continuity between pagan magic and Christianity in a subversive light: even Christianity might now appear as nothing more than a purified form of superstition, magic, and political control by the law givers. But the reverse was also true: even ancient "magicians" like Apollonius of Tyana should now be taken seriously as great thinkers who had an impact in scientific, moral, and political spheres and were comparable to Jesus.[70] Arpe did not say all of this directly in his book, but we can draw that conclusion if we examine his other writings, his collections of books and manuscripts, and his correspondence. For example, his boyhood friend Johann Lorenz Mosheim, who had examined the *Apotelesmata Apollonii* (*The Astrological Effects of Apollonius*) from a philological and critical perspective, declared that the work was spurious; but he claimed that Arpe did not see any of the works ascribed to Apollonius as fictitious. "But when I asked him about that, he could not give any satisfactory reason for thinking so—or at least he did not do so."[71] Even today the controversy is not entirely settled, and the question whether the *Apotelesmata* with its directions for making talismans and

---

69. See Arpe, *De prodigiosis*, 135: "Quod si nec ineditorum numerum inire displicet, GEORGII FRANCI de FRANCKENAU dulcis recurrit memoria, qui Medicinae Doctor, & diversis temporibus ejus Professor Argentinae Heidelbergae et Wittebergae, nec non multorum Regum Principumque Archiater fuit. Is aliquando Caroli Ludovici Principis Palatini jussu, qui talia summo studio inquirebat, integrum opus *de amuletis* tentabat, sed ob miserrima illius regionis tempora et negotium, quibus urgebatur, molem, nondum ad umbilicum perduxerat, cum Hafniae 1704. rebus humanis diceret valere et plaudere, suis vero familiaribus dolere et plaugere."

70. Cf. Maria Dzielska, *Apollonius of Tyana in Legend and History* (Rome, 1986).

71. Mosheim to La Croze, March 10, 1718, in *Thesaurus epistolicus Lacrozianus*, 1:275: "Rationem cum vero ex eo quaererem, dare non potuit sufficientem; saltim non dedit." Mulsow, "Eine 'Rettung' des Michael Servet," 71ff.

much of what was handed down in the Arabic "Balinas" tradition actually came from the historical Apollonius is as unsettled today as it ever was.[72] For understanding the situation of the early eighteenth century in Germany, however, the disagreement between Arpe and Mosheim was significant. One hundred years had gone by since the beginnings of historical-critical and antiquarian work on magic, and there were still no clear battle fronts from which we could comfortably discern the origins of modernity. It was Arpe of all people, the sympathizer with radical Enlightenment philosophers, who was flirting with natural magic, even if only because of its negative implications for Christianity. And Mosheim, the supposedly "moderate" Enlightenment thinker and representative of Lutheran "transitional" theology, was using a sharp historical criticism against every form of superstition, but especially against belief in the authenticity of ancient myths that were hostile to Christianity.[73]

Conclusion

All the way down to the Enlightenment, therefore, there was no direct path leading "from magic to the scholarly investigation of magic," at least not if we look only at the views of individuals. If we examine whole genres, however, a clearer picture emerges. Around 1600 a philological and antiquarian discourse was developing in which questions about the reality and effects of magic were suspended. To quote Koblig again: "This is not the place to dispute about the use of talismans and whether they are permitted."[74] But outside this scholarly niche any involvement with magic was precarious: witches were being burned and scholars denounced, rituals were being performed in secret, princes were being advised (on the basis of occult or magical knowledge), and magical formulas were being composed and deciphered. Emotionally speaking, the region between fascination and revulsion was highly charged. It was all the more important and astonishing that in the midst of all the interest-driven controversies concerning Christianity and paganism, natural magic and idolatry, astrology and astronomy, a free space was opening up in which

72. See F. Nau, "Apotelesmata Apollonii Tyanensis," in *Patrologia Syriaca*, ed. R. Graffin (Paris, 1907), 2:1363–85; on the Arabic transmission, see Ursula Weisser, *Das "Buch über die Geheimnisse der Schöpfung" von Pseudo-Apollonios von Tyana* (Berlin, 1980).

73. See Mulsow, "Eine 'Rettung,'" 69ff.

74. See note 4 in this chapter.

historia[75] could deal with religion in a scholarly manner. Scholars began to describe and historically contextualize their disconnected findings, the fragments and relics of ancient practices, manuscript passages and inscriptions. Here was a zone of sublimated and ambivalent fascination. That's not much, perhaps, but it was also a lot. It was the reservoir from which the scholarly study of religion emerged.

75. See Martin Mulsow, "Antiquarianism and Idolatry: The 'Historia' of Religions in the Seventeenth Century," in *Historia: Empiricism and Erudition in Early Modern Europe*, ed. Gianna Pomata and Nancy G. Siraisi (Cambridge, MA, 2005), 181–210; idem, "Die Thematisierung paganer Religionen in der Frühen Neuzeit."

13

Mobility and Surveillance

THE INFORMATION HISTORY OF
NUMISMATICS AND JOURNEYS TO THE
EAST UNDER LOUIS XIV

Mobility

The mobility of scholars in the early modern period was definitely precarious. Was it befitting for a philosopher to discover the world not just mentally but bodily as well? Did a philologist have to move beyond his texts and into foreign lands? Wasn't it precisely the mobility of books and ideas that made physical travel unnecessary? It is clear, however, that ideas move and are transferred especially when people move about, regardless of whether they are relocating, emigrating, or just traveling. The grand tour was an essential part of the education of wealthy students, just like the educational journeys of painters and writers. Recent studies in spatial sociology allow us now to approach this paradox in much more refined form. Thus the research of Daniel Roche and his student Stéphane Van Damme raises new questions: How did the geopolitical spaces in which people traveled affect their travel reports? How did the ruling authorities affect the "circulation of people" and hence the formation of identities? To what extent did changing philosophical practices help reconfigure political culture and relations with urban culture? How were cosmopolitanism and localism related to each other? How did philosophical practices and approaches change with an altered philosophical attitude toward mobility?[1] Such questions, within

---

1. Roche, *Humeurs vagabondes*; Stéphane van Damme, "'The World Is Too Large': Philosophical Mobility and Urban Space in Seventeenth and Eighteenth-Century Paris," *French Historical Studies* 29 (2006): 379–406.

a framework of the social and cultural history of travel and mobility and aimed not at philosophical problems but at general scholarly activities, develop their own specific accents. But these kinds of questions have not, I think, been applied to the history of numismatics and antiquarianism.

It is precisely numismatics, however, that has every reason to pay attention to mobility. Jean Foy Vaillant, the royal numismatist of King Louis XIV, defined coins as portable monuments.[2] These monuments circulate in many regions during the first period of their active use and then experience much later a second circulation as antiquarian objects. That means that they leave behind a double, complex trail in time and space. A history of mobility and of information regarding numismatics and antiquarianism should, therefore, also ask how the circulation of such objects were affected by the practices and networks of scholars. For my range of questions, it is especially interesting to find moments of fragility and precarity in this circulation. An internalist form of this history of information would try to discover how references to coins were used within scholarly arguments, how collections were referred to, and how the descriptions of coins by others were involved.[3] How was the meaning contained in antique objects reconstructed within groups of European experts, how were they misunderstood, how were they deployed? On the other hand, an externalist form of such a history would ask such questions as: Where did the objects of study come from? How were they traded and how much did they cost? Where did such supplemental information come from, especially when comparisons were made? What sort of network of consultants existed? But also: What social spaces supported the comparison of coins? What hierarchies were there and what restrictions?

Within this matrix of questions we should add those that ask about the use of travel reports. In what way did armchair travelers, that is, the scholars of Europe, participate in the "social circulation of the past," to use Daniel Woolf's phrase?[4] Had they sometimes traveled to the place of primary circulation? Had they read travel accounts that mentioned coin discoveries? Had they incorporated images of coins with travel reports and other sources? We need

2. On Vaillant, see note 50 in this chapter.

3. Following the suggestion of Ann Blair, "Note-Taking as an Art of Transmission," *Critical Inquiry* 31 (2004): 85–107. See also eadem, *Too Much to Know: Managing Scholarly Information before the Modern Age* (New Haven, 2010).

4. Daniel Woolf, *The Social Circulation of the Past: English Historical Culture, 1500–1730* (Oxford, 2003).

both the internalist and externalist approaches to the history of information when we are studying the disclosure of fraudulent travel reports, erroneous copies of inscriptions, or misleading images of coins; how was such deceit eliminated? How could information be confirmed through methodical surveillance?[5]

To answer these questions it is necessary to clarify a few matters at the start. First, one should never examine early modern numismatics in isolation from the broader area of antiquarianism, in which it had a place. Along with statues, inscriptions, reliefs, gems, and other archeological finds, coins were only one kind of object among others by means of which one might retrospectively acquire knowledge of antiquity.[6] Second, one must remember that coin collecting was never a socially isolated practice. In the late seventeenth century it became a more and more prestigious science.[7] Especially for princes and noblemen a stately coin collection also added a measure of symbolic capital. Louis XIV was only the most prominent coin enthusiast and owner of a numismatic cabinet; hundreds of other wealthy collectors did the same. And all of this collecting and research was backed up by enormous sums of money, without which such demanding activities were not even imaginable. The rise of such pursuits also brought changes to the scholarly landscape. Ezechiel Spanheim, a diplomat, scholar, and one of the founders of numismatics, expressed it this way: "Scholars are beginning to become connoisseurs of coins, and connoisseurs of coins are beginning to become scholars."[8] So we now have to deal with scholarly numismatists and with numismatically learned scholars.

5. See the theoretical discussion of reports from Latin America to Spain in Brendecke, *Imperium und Empirie*; see in addition Christopher Bayly, *Empire and Information: Intelligence Gathering and Social Communication in India, 1780–1870* (Cambridge, 1997).

6. One must still consult Arnaldo Momigliano, "Ancient History and the Antiquarian," *Journal of the Warburg and Courtauld Institutes* 13 (1950): 285–315; and Alain Schnapp, *Die Entdeckung der Vergangenheit* (Stuttgart, 2009). For contemporary discussions in this connection, see Peter N. Miller, ed., *Momigliano and Antiquarianism: Foundation of the Modern Cultural Sciences* (Toronto, 2007).

7. See Francis Haskell, *History and Its Images: Art and the Interpretation of the Past* (New Haven, 1993); Antoine Schnapper, *Curieux du Grand Siècle: Collections et collectionneurs dans la France du XVIIe siècle* (Paris, 1994); Krzysztof Pomian, *Collectionneurs, amateurs et curieux, Paris, Venise: XVIe–XVIIIe siècle* (Paris, 1987).

8. Ezechiel Spanheim, *Les Césars de l'empereur Julien* (Amsterdam, 1728), xli: "Les Savans commencent à devenir Médaillistes, et les Médaillistes à devenir Savans."

Third, we have to ask how any knowledge of the Orient got incorporated into Western knowledge, Western perceptions, and Western traditions. Travel accounts could be read with specific questions in mind. When Pierre Bayle, for example, went looking for forerunners of Spinozistic naturalism outside Europe, he discovered the travel report of Pietro della Valle, who had traveled through the East all the way to India between 1614 and 1626. Writing about the Persian city of Lar, he described a sect called *ahl-i-tahqiq* (men of truth), who claimed that there was nothing beyond the four elements and that there was no life after death.[9] That had nothing at all to do with Spinozism but probably represented a Persian adaptation of an ancient Greek materialism that had been handed down through the Islamic period.[10] Was numismatics something that might similarly place a misleading interpretive grid over Oriental material? That was certainly possible, especially if one recalls the case—still controversial today—of Ottavio Falconieri, who recognized *historia sacra* (sacred, i.e., biblical, history) in the history of coins and thought he saw Noah's ark represented on a coin from the Phrygian town of Apamea dating from the second century CE (figure 52).[11] But it was unclear whether any Jewish or Christian traditions were actually depicted on the coinage, or whether a Christian scholar had merely projected his own ideas onto antique pagan material.

Parisian Numismatists, Antiquarians, and Orientalists under Louis XIV

Let us look for an appropriate social context for the questions we are posing. The most prominent and densest collection of scholars studying the newly prestigious science of numismatics was the Paris of Louis XIV. Nicholas Dew has provided useful insights into the Orientalists of this group of antiquarians

9. Pierre Bayle, *Ècrits sur Spinoza*, ed. Françoise Charles-Daubert and Pierre-François Moreau (Paris, 1983), 114; Joy Charnley, *Pierre Bayle: Reader of Travel Literature* (Bern, 1998), 76ff.; Israel, *Enlightenment Contested*, 635. See Pietro della Valle, *Viagi in Turchia, Persia et India descritti da lui medesimo in 54 lettere famigliari*, 2 vols. (Rome, 1650–58).

10. Patricia Crone, "Post-Colonialism in Tenth-Century Islam," *Der Islam* 83 (2006): 2–38.

11. Ottavio Falconieri, *De nummo Apamensi Deucalionei diluvii typum exhibente dissertatio* (Rome, 1667). See J. B. Selbst, "Zu den NΩE-Münzen aus Apamea," *Zeitschrift für die Alttestamentliche Wissenschaft* 27 (1907): 73–74; on the modern state of research, see Paul Trebilco, *Jewish Communities in Asia Minor* (Cambridge, 1991), 86–95; Martin Hengel, *Paulus zwischen Damaskus und Antiochien* (Tübingen, 2000), 254.

FIGURE 52. Ottavio Falconieri, *De nummo Apamensi Deu-calionei diluvii typum exhibente dissertatio* (Rome, 1667). Ralph Häfner, *Götter im Exil* (Tübingen, 2003), 273.

and numismatists;[12] Marie Veillon has provided a short survey of the numismatists in the narrower sense; and Thierry Sarmant devoted several chapters to them in his monograph published in 2003.[13] This social group took shape in the 1660s, reached its high point in the 1680s and 1690s, and was institutionalized in 1701 with the founding of the Académie des Inscriptions.[14] Let me just mention a few names: Pierre Seguin, coin collector and scholar as early as the 1660s, dean of a church in Paris, traveler to Italy, friend of Jacques Spon in Lyons; Charles Patin, who had to flee from Paris because he had revealed the love affairs of a princess and lived first in Basel and then in Padua; Jean Foy Vaillant, physician, a traveler to the East, and numismatist; Charles-César

---

12. Nicholas Dew, *Orientalism in Louis XIV's France* (Oxford, 2009).

13. Marie Veillon, "La science des Médailles antiques sous le régne de Louis XIV," *Revue numismatique* 152, no. 6 (1997): 359–77; Thierry Sarmant, *La République des médailles: Numismates et collections numismatiques à Paris du Grand Siècle au Siècle des Lumières* (Paris, 2003).

14. See Blandine Kriegel, *L'histoire à l'Age classique*, vol. 3: *Les académies de l'histoire* (Paris, 1988), 169–321: L'Académie royale des Inscriptions et Belles-Lettres.

Baudelot de Dairval, jurist and antiquarian; Antoine Galland, Orientalist and translator of *The Arabian Nights* (*The Book of the Thousand and One Nights*); the Swiss Andreas Morell from Bern who had dedicated himself to coins; Ezechiel Spanheim, who was from 1680 an ambassador of the court of Brandenburg in Paris, a first-class philologist, and author of the standard work on numismatics as part of general classical studies, *De praestantia et usu numismatum antiquorum* (*On the Excellence and Use of Ancient Coins*), which had been published in 1664 but then was republished in expanded editions in 1671 and 1706–17; François Dron, a canon in St. Thomas du Louvre; Pierre Rainssant, superintendent of the royal coin collection; Claude Nicaise, antiquarian and canon in Dijon; Barthelmy d'Herbelot, royal translator of Arabic and author of the *Bibliothèque orientale*; Louis Jobert, Jesuit and professor of rhetoric; Pierre de Carcavy, mathematician and royal librarian, appointed by Colbert; Jean Hardouin, Jesuit philologist, chronologist, and numismatist; Nicolas Toinard, a numismatist from Orleans and an antiquarian, a friend of John Locke.

It is important to recognize that this whole social grouping was bound up in the great transformation from urban late humanism into a managed part of the bureaucratic state apparatus.[15] It was preeminently Colbert, the "information master" as Jacob Soll calls him, who systematized the flood of information into a "centralized system of information for international relations and political legitimacy."[16] The influx of manuscripts and coins from the East was not left to the chance arrival of gifts brought by merchants returning from the East but was controlled centrally by the state. Colbert sent scholars, sometimes more than once, off on journeys to the East lasting many years, with specific instructions to collect antiquarian objects and send them back to Paris: Monceaux and Laisné (1667–75), Vaillant (1670–84), Galland (1670–89), and Wansleben (1671–75). When Abbé Bignon revived this policy, further travels were organized, such as the journeys of Paul Lucas (1701–17).[17]

These expeditions resulted in published travel accounts as well as a great treasury of material objects, ranging from coins and manuscripts to statues and scientific instruments. Inscriptions were either copied or simply seized

15. Soll, *The Information Master*.

16. Ibid., 107. For Louis XIV's propaganda machine, see also Peter Burke, *The Fabrication of Louis XIV* (New Haven, 1992).

17. See Henri Omont, *Missions archéologiques en Orient aus XVIIe et XVIIIe siècles* (Paris, 1902). On connections to the Levant, see Alastair Hamilton et al., eds., *The Republic of Letters and the Levant* (= *Intersections* 5 ([2005]).

unceremoniously. From the start, the moving of antiquarian objects was mixed up with publications about their mobility.

The scholars involved in these activities were generally not professional antiquarians but had been trained in other areas. One amazingly common figure was the physician-antiquarian (such as Patin, Spon, Vaillant, Rainssant), whom Nancy Siraisi has studied in the sixteenth century.[18] These scholars were focused especially on individual specimens, which paralleled the medical case histories they were familiar with and which led to a particular kind of "historia."[19] The scientific art of describing an object was also transferred to ancient objects.[20] But in addition there were lawyers and diplomats who mutated into antiquarians (such as Baudelot or Spanheim), who proved their savoir faire by exchanging coins.

This was truly a pioneering age. Of course, Renaissance humanists had already showed an early interest in ancient coins, with figures such as Antonio Agustin, Enea Vico, and Hubert Goltzius.[21] But now numismatics flourished on a grand scale and with a much broader social base; the center of attention was no longer merely Roman coins of the imperial period but provincial Roman coins, Greek, Eastern; the feverish hunt for coins fostered an atmosphere of competitive deciphering, discovery, and classification.[22]

In view of these overlapping forms of perception and mobility among diplomats, Orientalists, physicians, and antiquarians, let us examine the different kinds of numismatic mobility. Even armchair antiquarians played an important role here, for they knew how to use the travels and publish the travel reports of others; but mobile antiquarians who settled down and on the basis of coin findings plunged into chronological scholarship mattered too, and so did

---

18. Siraisi, *History, Medicine, and the Traditions of Renaissance Learning.* Leopold Joseph Renauldin, *Études historiques et critiques sur les médicins numismatists, contenant leur biographie et l'analyse de leurs écrits* (Paris, 1851).

19. Nancy G. Siraisi and Gianna Pomata, eds., *Historia: Empiricism and Erudition in Early Modern Europe* (Cambridge, MA, 2005).

20. Brian Ogilvie, *The Science of Describing: Natural History in Renaissance Europe* (Chicago, 2006).

21. John Cunnally, *Images of the Illustrious: The Numismatic Presence in the Renaissance* (Princeton, 1999); Ulrich Pfisterer, *Lysippus und seine Freunde: Liebesgaben und Gedächtnis im Rom der Renaissance, oder: Das erste Jahrhundert der Medaille* (Berlin, 2008).

22. Something similar played itself out (although on a smaller scale) with manuscripts, with the widespread and feverish search to identify pseudonymous and anonymous authors. See Mulsow, *Die unanständige Gelehrtenrepublik,* 217–45.

involuntarily immobile antiquarians, whose only "mobility" was their correspondence with colleagues and their descriptions of the primary circulation of coinage.

Along with the "long-range" mobility of travels to distant lands, there was always the small-scale mobility of moving about within a city and its environs. Thus between 1680 and 1683 Spanheim, Vaillant, Morell, Jobert, Rainssant, Dron, Nicaise, and Galland met weekly in the house of the Duke d'Aumont to talk about coins. How did such social forms of association comport with the bureaucratic surveillance of Colbert's state? Were there tensions between free scholarship and the managerial or "finalized" Orientalism that Edward Said described?[23] Even though it's too early to speak of a French colonial empire, Oriental studies may already have been deployed as a means of rule.

Baudelot and Travel

Charles-César Baudelot de Dairval was an odd traveler.[24] He was the author of an authoritative and highly successful guide book, *De l'utilité des voyages* (figure 53), although he never undertook any large-scale journey. And yet he loved travel and knew how to turn it to his own advantage. That began early, when he intentionally bought up collections that travelers had brought back to France as plunder. The long-term French ambassador to Constantinople Charles Ollier de Nointel, for example, had been able to obtain two huge marble blocks with two-thousand-year-old inscriptions concerning Athenian soldiers. When he was dying they came into the possession of Melchisédech Thévenot, the superintendent of the French royal library. And when Thévenot died in 1692, Baudelot managed to buy the blocks. Of course that meant having to transport these heavy monsters from Issy in the Seine valley to his house in Paris, but Baudelot spared no effort to accomplish the task. These marble tablets were not exactly the sort of "portable monuments" that Vaillant had spoken of. It was of course easier to deal with paper and to publish the travel reports of others. That's what Baudelot did in 1704 when he published the *Voyage*

23. Translator's note: Scholars have referred to "finalized" science as science that is put to social or political purposes by those who fund, organize, or control the scientific enterprise. In his book *Orientalism*, after discussing academic and imaginative Orientalism, Edward Said described a third type of Orientalism as an ideology of political repression.

24. On Baudelot (1648–1722), see *Dictionnaire de biographie française*, vol. 5 (Paris, 1951), col. 840; see also Roche, *Humeurs vagabondes*, 62ff.

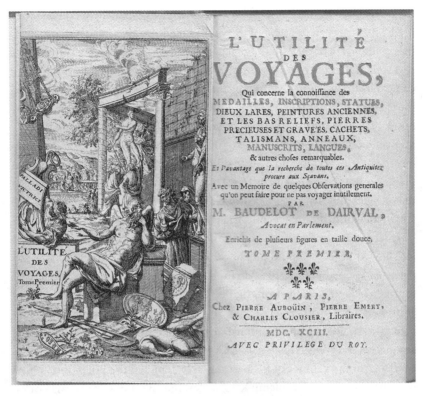

FIGURE 53. Charles-César Baudelot, *L'utilité des voyages* (Paris, 1693), title page.

de sieur Paul Lucas au Levant in two volumes.[25] Lucas was one of the men whom the king had sent to the East to bring back coins and manuscripts to Paris, and the trip to the Levant was just the second of five trips altogether to the Orient. Baudelot took the manuscript travel report as his basis but added well-informed notes and massive editorial interventions to make a book that could meet the demands and needs of European scholarly readers.[26]

Baudelot, however, had laid the foundations for his activities in 1686 when, at the age of thirty-eight and no longer young, he wrote his book *De l'utilité des voyages*. He had held off a long time from contributing anything substantial to classical studies, so this was his entry ticket to the Republic of Letters, using

25. *Voyage de Sieur Paul Lucas au Levant*, 2 vols. (Paris, 1704–5).
26. Lucette Valensi, "Lucas, Paul," in *Dictionnaire des orientalistes de la langue française* (Paris, 2008), 614.

the career strategy that Anne Goldgar has identified.[27] And he succeeded with it. The book was an example of the genre called *Ars apodemica*, advice literature on the art of travel[28]—although here the meaning was specifically the uses of travel for the study of antiquities, and therefore it dealt with learning about coin collections, statues, gems, talismans, and manuscripts. Baudelot lauded the effects that changing one's spatial and cultural position could have on one's mind. It allowed one to achieve a "veritable sagesse" (a true wisdom),[29] a consciousness also of the superiority of universal knowledge and of scholarship over merely local cults and diverse superstitions. The undeniable advances in science certainly had not made travel superfluous: "Today, my Lord, although the sciences find themselves enthroned and rule with such sovereignty in the Christian world, it is no less important to travel."[30]

In later masterpieces, such as his *Histoire de Ptolemée Auletes* of 1698, Baudelot showed how one could pull all such studies together to illuminate one particular monographic topic.[31] In the meantime he had been appointed curator of "Madame's" collection, that is, the collection owned by the wife of "Monsieur," the brother of the king. She was Liselotte, Princess of the Palatinate, and she was hardly less enthusiastic than her brother-in-law in collecting antiquities and coins. The occasion for Baudelot's study was an engraved amethyst from the cabinet of his patroness. It depicted the portrait of a man Baudelot thought was Ptolemy XII Auletes, the father of Cleopatra, because the image matched a coin in his collection.[32] "Auletes" meant flute player, and indeed in Baudelot's reconstruction the portraits were adorned with the insignias of flautists. In this way the antiquarian over the course of almost five hundred pages painted a picture of a learned king and his entourage, drawing out the parallels with the court at Versailles and society in Paris. One could even

27. Goldgar, *Impolite Learning*.

28. See Justin Stagl, *Apodemiken: Eine räsonnierte Bibliographie der reisetheoretischen Literatur des 16., 17. und 18. Jahrhunderts*, with the collaboration of Klaus Orda and Christel Kämpfer (Paderborn, 1983); idem, *Eine Geschichte der Neugier: Reisekunst 1550–1800* (Vienna, 2002).

29. Baudelot, *De L'utilité des voyages et de l'avantage que la recherche des antiquitez procure aux sçavans* (Paris, 1686); cf. the two-volume edition (Paris, 1693), 1:65.

30. Ibid., 68: "Aujourd'hui, Monsieur, que les sciences sont sur le throne, et regnent si souverainement dans le monde Chrêtien, il n'est pas moins important encore de voyager."

31. *Histoire de Ptolemée Auletes: Dissertation sur une pierre gravée antique du cabinet de Madame* (Paris, 1698).

32. On Ptolemaios XII "Auletes" (ca. 115–51 BCE), see Werner Huß, *Ägypten in hellenistischer Zeit 332–30 v. Chr.* (Munich, 2001), 671–702.

say that this work was intended as a scholarly pendant to the flute concerts given by Lully or Charpentier. To give just a glimpse of how Baudelot moved toward his goal from coin to coin, and from gem to statue, here is one tiny example.

Baudelot was looking for parallels to the flute-playing Ptolemy when, in a chapter on muses, nymphs, sirens, and Amazons, he came to Lamia, the beloved of the Diadoch Demetrius I. Poliorketes, who had died in 283 BCE, that is, two hundred years before the time of Ptolemy Auletes.[33] According to Baudelot, this Lamia was also well educated and played the flute. Baudelot reproduced a relief from his own cabinet (perhaps one that he had obtained from Nointel or Thévenot) on which a young woman and a flute can be seen (figure 54).[34] He then demonstrated that veils were often a sign of female flute players and ad-

FIGURE 54. Relief of Lamia of Athens. Charles-César Baudelot, *Histoire de Ptolemée Auletes* (Paris, 1698), 311.

duced a gem from the cabinet of "Madame," which he took to be a portrait of Lamia.[35] To prove Plutarch's claim that the Demetrius who was in love with Lamia was still a young man, Baudelot reproduced a tetradrachm from his collection, which shows him as a beautiful youth (figure 55).[36] Demetrius had even built a temple for "Venus Lamia," and although he had taken Lamia as a slave from Ptolemy I, his love had made him "the slave of his captive," to quote the gallant phrase of Baudelot.

During his lifetime Baudelot was an active participant in the Parisian milieu of antiquarian scholars. So he also supported his friends and provided them

33. See Kostas Buraselis, *Das hellenistische Makedonien und die Ägäis: Forschungen zur Politik des Kassandros und der ersten drei Antigoniden (Antigonos Monophthalmos, Demetrios Poliorketes und Antigonos Gonatas) im Ägäischen Meer und in Westkleinasien* (Munich, 1982).

34. *Histoire de Ptolemée Auletes*, 311.

35. Ibid., 319. On the cabinet, see Sigrun Paas, ed., *Liselotte von der Pfalz: Madame am Hofe des Sonnenkönigs* (Heidelberg, 1996).

36. *Histoire de Ptolemée Auletes*, 323. Tetradrachme, Amphipolis ca. 290–289 BCE. File note: Obverse: Head with crown and cattle horn; Reverse: Poseidon trident to the left, setting his right foot on a cliff, in the inner left field. Monogram in the inner right field. Newell 116, AMNG (*Die antiken Münzen Nord-Griechenlands*, ed. von F. Imhoof-Blumer, 1898–1913), III, 182.9. Baudelot speaks of Demetrios as "l'esclave de sa prisonniere."

FIGURE 55. Silver tetradrachm of Demetrios
Poliorketes, ca. 290/289 BCE, coin cabinet of the
Staatliche Museen zu Berlin, Inv. no. 18203027.

with coins as scholarly support for their works. It happened that Pierre Petit
shortly before his death in 1685 was working on the topic of the fabled Amazons. The sixty-seven-year-old Petit had originally been a physician and had
never abandoned this naturalistic foundation, even when he turned to scholarly historical topics. He argued that the prophetic Sibyls, for example, represented actual persons of the past, but he tried to reduce their multiplicity to
just one who had moved around a great deal; and, following the thinking of
Pomponazzi or Cardano, he tried to explain their prophetic activities scientifically.[37] He was also interested in ancient reports on cannibals, whom he studied as a philologist and historian but also as an anthropologist.

He made the same sort of argument about the Amazons. He began with
travel reports of Amazons perhaps still living in South America and therefore
spoke of the "Rio de las Amazonas"—that is, supposing that these people had
migrated to South America even before primeval times. He also spoke of the
Amazons in Syria who had threatened the early Christians[38] and rehearsed
the loosest speculations, like those of Jan van Gorp, according to whom such

37. Pierre Petit, *De sibylla* (Leipzig, 1686). On Petit, see Martin Mulsow, "Christian Humanism in the Age of Critical Philology: Ralph Häfner's Gods in Exile," *Journal of the History of Ideas*
70 (2009): 659–79.

38. Pierre Petit, *De amazonibus dissertatio* (Paris, 1685); I have used the edition published in
Amsterdam in 1687. According to Petit, Geronimo Mercuriale reported on Eradius, who said in
the *Vita Poemonis Abbatis* that Amazons had lived in Syria and that they had (many years after
the birth of Christ) killed many Christian fathers (42). Cardano reported that Amazons had
existed on Martinique, according to information sent from Peter Martyr to Bembo (44). Then
follows the report of Portuguese travel descriptions by Joannes dos Santos that the Amazons
lived in Ethiopia (45).

wild women had actually lived in the earliest ages.[39] As opposed to dedicated skeptics, Petit most likely believed that there had indeed been Amazons, and he tried to prove it.[40] But later he tried to curb uncontrolled speculation, and the coins that his friend Baudelot loaned him and explained to him were a help in this endeavor.[41] He now argued that the Amazons had lived among the Scythian peoples in the Caucasus and along the southern coast of the Black Sea, explaining their courage by invoking the influence of the environment. But such people survived only down to the age of Alexander the Great, after whom they ceased to exist.[42]

In his argument Petit used coins especially when he was dealing with cities that had supposedly been founded by Amazons or had had relations with them. He therefore mentioned Ephesus, with its shrine to Diana, or Smyrna, from which he could display one coin obtained from Seguin and another that he'd borrowed from Baudelot's cabinet, both of which portrayed Amazons.[43] For Petit, therefore, numismatics did not function as a tool of radically skeptical historical Pyrrhonism but not as its antidote either;[44] rather it enabled him

39. Ibid., 373ff. against Goropius et al., whose theories were "fables" that were meant to be taken rhetorically rather than philosophically.

40. Ibid., *2v.: "Mendacii esse suspecta et fabulosa censeri."

41. Ibid., *3r. Petit says in his dedicatory foreword to Baudelot that he was indebted to him, "non solum quia mihi scribendi auctor fuisti, sed maxime eorum monumentorum causa, quae partim mihi et tuo instructissimo penu literario suppediasti, partim ex aliorum Museis, atque ipsa Regis Gaza per amicos tuos utenda impetrasti."

42. Ibid., 379: "Equidem memoria repeto, me initio Dissertationis, cum de Amazonum statu agerem, quid de Thalestridis historia quisque sentire vellet, in medio reliquisse, cum utra opinio vera esset affirmantium aut negantium, parum eius disputationis interesse existimarem: nunc cum de gentis illius duratione agitur, accurantius quid mihi de hoc facto probabilius videretur, explicandum fuit, quo maxime constare posset, regnum Amazonum conservatum usque ad tempora Alexandri Magni." On the Amazons, see Hedwig Appelt, *Die Amazonen: Töchter von Liebe und Krieg* (Stuttgart, 2009); Gerhard Pöllauer, *Die verlorene Geschichte der Amazonen* (Klagenfurt, 2002).

43. Petit, *De amazonibus dissertatio*, 236ff. concerning Smyrna: "De Smyrna igitur, quod inter urbes ab Amazonibus conditas et nominatas, merito referatur, plures sunt nummi qui fidem faciant. Ac primum is, quem supra ex Petri Seguini viri eruditissimi Museo proferebamus, cum de Amazonia securi agereumus, a Smyrnaeis percussus, quem hic reponere nihil necesse est, cum cuivis promptum sit revisere eum locum, ubi eius similitudinem apposuimus, vel etiam apud ipsum Seguinum contemplari. Sed / idem alio e Gaza literaria Amici nostri confirmare libet."

44. On the relations between historic Pyrrhonism and numismatics, see Momigliano, "Ancient History."

FIGURE 56. Claude Petit, *De amazionibus dissertatio*
(Paris, 1685), 189, with an illustration borrowed from
Fortunio Liceti.

to support a moderate skepticism between too much and too little doubt, of just the sort one finds in the Dutch scholar Jakob Perizonius.[45]

Let us now leave Baudelot and Petit behind. A comprehensive history of the information concerning their practices would need to reconstruct which journeys had brought to Paris the coins that Petit used; which Parisian numismatists from Baudelot's exchange network provided Petit with coins (he mentioned Jobert,[46] Rainssant,[47] and Morell[48] as illustrators); and which other antiquarian objects he borrowed from other collections. And then one would need to study in detail how certain external and internal histories of information overlap, for example when Petit depicted an ancient lamp from Fortunio Liceti's *De lucernis antiquorum* (figure 56), a lamp from a specific collection that can actually be traced back to the specific travels or excavations that discovered and delivered them.[49] Here I can only sketch such an undertaking, which could be called a "natural history of discourse," in the sense that the individual pieces of information that support a discourse could be traced back

45. On Perizonius and his moderate historical Pyrrhonism, see Carlo Borghero, *La certezza e la storia: Cartesianesimo, pirronismo e conoscenza storica* (Milan, 1983).

46. Petit, *De amazonibus dissertatio*, 236.

47. Ibid., Praefatio *3r.

48. Ibid., 188: a medal of the Emperor Commodus depicted by Morell.

49. Ibid., 189; Fortunio Liceti, *De lucernis antiquorum reconditis libri sex* (1621; Udine, 1652).

through time and space. One could also apply that procedure to Orientalist manuscripts, if one follows their purchase during Eastern travels and possibly their mention in travel reports, their absorption into scholarly works, and the spread of specific bits of information, such as translated passages, into the European debates of the following decades.[50] One might be astonished to discover the remarkable roles certain coins or specific quotations played in the history of discourse in the seventeenth and eighteenth centuries.

Vaillant's Oriental Kings

In contrast to Baudelot, Jean Foy Vaillant actually did travel.[51] More than that, the coins he gathered on his journeys were so important to him that he swallowed them when there was a danger that they would be taken from him. Vaillant was on his second journey to the East when he was taken prisoner by pirates and hauled off to Algiers. There he got free after four months and then, when he was returning to France and was again spotted by pirates, he impulsively swallowed twenty valuable ancient gold coins weighing about 150 grams in order to save them. Nothing came of his capture, but Vaillant suffered horrible stomach pains. As nature took its course, however, he did recover his coins.

What did Vaillant do with the objects he obtained on his three trips to the East? He expanded his coin collection into comprehensive collections, which put him in a position to write books on the chronological succession and the additional names given to ancient rulers. He first treated the Seleucids in his *Historia regum Syrie* published in 1681, then after travels in Egypt and Persia he wrote a similar work on the Ptolemies: *Historia Ptolemaeorum Aegypti regum* of 1701, and finally he published a work on the Achaemenids and Parthians in 1725.[52] Under each of his illustrations he conscientiously stated whose collection a coin came from.

---

50. I have reconstructed one such story in rudimentary fashion from a passage in al-Qarafi in Mulsow, "Socinianism, Islam, and the Radical Uses of Arabic Scholarship."

51. On Vaillant, see, in addition to Veillon, "La science des Médailles antiques sous le régne de Louis XIV," Christian Dekesel, "Jean Foy-Vaillant (1632–1706): L'antiquaire du roy," in *Europäische numismatische Literatur im 17. Jahrhundert*, ed. idem and Thomas Stäcker (Wiesbaden, 2005), 69–88.

52. Vaillant, *Historia regum Syrie* (Paris, 1681); idem, *Historia Ptolemaeorum Aegypti regum, ad fidem Numismatum accomodata* (Amsterdam, 1701); idem, *Arsacidarum imperium sive regum parthorum historia, ad fidem numismatum accomodata* (Paris, 1728); idem, *Achaemenidarum*

Vaillant introduced his book on the Seleucid kings with a personal remark that tells us much about the interwoven nature of travel, diplomatic and scholarly networks, and numismatics:

> I once asked myself what the use of old coins could be and how much they could illuminate the history contained in them, when suddenly a sack full of such coins was produced. It had been sent to me by one of my friends on his return from a study trip, a friend whom I had gotten to know rather well in Byzantium when I was living there collecting coins for the Most Christian King [of France]. When I found many coins of the Syrian kings among them, it came to me that I could still gather more if I wanted to assemble a complete series of them, which might clarify the otherwise completely confusing accounts of those princes. With this resolution I began to read through the writings of the ancients, excerpting fragments from them and transferring them into one unified chronology, so to speak, in which the words of the writers were carefully quoted, so that no one could suspect me of distorting their meaning.[53]

Here we can see Vaillant's scholarly practice clearly, which also at a critical stage included important work on texts. In Constantinople he made contacts that later paid off. His networks for obtaining objects continued to function long after he was back in Paris. Vaillant obviously had what Bianca Chen found to be true for Gisbert Cuper: an ongoing mutual exchange relationship between travelers to the East and resident classical scholars in Europe.[54] In the case of the Dutchman Cuper the relationship looked like this: his acquaintance

imperium sive regum Ponti, Boshori, et Bithyniae historia, ad fidem numismatum accommodata (Paris, 1725). In the foreword to his *Histoire de Ptolemée Auletes*, xxviii, Baudelot explicitly urged Vaillant to finish his book on the Ptolemies.

53. Vaillant, *Historia regum Syrie*, praefatio, unpag. fol. **1r: "Cogitanti mihi aliquando quae sit Numismatum veterum utilitas, quantumque ad illustrandam Historiam praesidii in his positum sit, plenus ecce talium Nummorum sacculus affertur. Hunc ad me quidam amicorum notus olim Byzantii familiariter, cum illic ad Thesaurum Christianismi Regis locupletandum versarer, a perigrinatione recens mittebat. In his cum multos Regum Syriae nummos reperissem, venit in mentem quam possem plurimos colligere, si forte integram ex his seriem possem efficere, quae Principum illorum Historiae alioqui apud scriptores intricatissimae, aliquid lucis afferent. Hoc consilio veterum scripta perlegere aggressus, fragmenta ex his deprompsi, et in unum veluti Chronologiae corpus redigi, verbis ipsis auctorum ferme repraesentatis, ne quis sensum a me detortum suspicari posset."

54. Bianca Chen, "Digging for Antiquities with Diplomats: Gisbert Cuper (1644–1716) and His Social Capital," *Republics of Letters: A Journal for the Study of Knowledge, Politics, and the Arts*

Coenraad Calckberner copied inscriptions from Aleppo and the newly discovered city of Palmyra, purchased ancient coins, and then sent them to Cuper along with travel reports; and Cuper would in turn respond at once by telling Calckberner what he thought these discoveries meant. Similarly, Vaillant received coins and could send his assessments back to Constantinople.

But once he was back in Paris, he had access to the whole scholarly organization. He could create tables in which he entered excerpts from his readings, employing techniques that had just been invented for displaying such knowledge.[55] Vaillant considered the separate kings and compared them with his coin series, which had arrived at a level of remarkable completeness, using the chronology as it was then understood. For Vaillant the authoritative scholarly chronology was still the *Opus de doctrina temporum* (*The Doctrine of Times*), composed by Denis Petau in 1627. Petit had included a small chapter *De Pontificium Hebraeorum serie, ac successione* (*On the Series and Succession of the Hebrew Rulers*), correcting the list given by Joseph Scaliger and registering twenty or twenty-one kings.[56] Vaillant could do this better because of his combination of coins and texts, calling his advantage *fides numismatum* (faith in coins).[57] His form of numismatically supported history was superior in credibility (*fides*) to that provided by texts alone.

In revising these chronologies, Vaillant may have used the new manuscripts brought back from the East, such as Islamic world chronicles.[58] But so far we have not yet detected traces of any in this case. To be sure, the erudite Ezechiel Spanheim expanded Vaillant's corrections to Petau's work even further. He counted twenty-six rulers after Seleucus and was able to add many details that

1, no. 1 (2008), http://arcade.stanford.edu/rofl/digging-antiquities-diplomats-gisbert-cuper
-1644-1716-and-his-social-capital.

55. See Arndt Brendecke, "Tabellenwerke in der Praxis der frühneuzeitlichen Geschichts-vermittlung," in *Wissenssicherung, Wissensordnung und Wissensverarbeitung: Das europäische Modell der Enzyklopädien*, ed. Theo Stammen and Wolfgang E. J. Weber (Berlin, 2004), 157–89; Benjamin Steiner, *Die Ordnung der Geschichte: Historische Tabellenwerke in der Frühen Neuzeit* (Cologne, 2008).

56. Petau, *Opus de doctrina temporum* (Paris, 1627), book X, chap. 47. On modern research, see Kai Brodersen, ed., *Zwischen West und Ost: Studien zur Geschichte des Seleukidenreichs* (Hamburg, 2000).

57. See the subtitle of Vaillant's works on history (see note 51 above).

58. For such texts, see Gerald Toomer, *Eastern Wisedome and Learning: The Study of Arabic in Seventeenth-Century England* (Oxford, 1996).

he derived from the coins.[59] Especially for studies of the politically effective epithets such as *soter* (savior) or *nikator* (conqueror), which rulers gave themselves, the historical evidence of coins was clearly superior.

The Numismatist in His Cell: Morell

But can we tell the information history of numismatics with nothing more than studies of mobility or of the interaction between mobile and sedentary activities among members of the knowledge bourgeoisie? Not really, because there are also extreme cases of immobility among some members of this social group, and this immobility can lead us to see new aspects of precarity, control, and surveillance. Take the case of Andreas Morell, who was perhaps the most gifted and most ambitious numismatist in the whole Parisian milieu but also languished for many years in the Bastille.[60] Morell became famous not just because he was incredibly knowledgeable about coins but also (and especially) because no one else could depict coins as well as he did.[61] The ability to translate the original into an analytical drawing was highly prized, because a drawing could serve as the basis for a copper-plate engraving that then could be published. Interpretations of coins depended crucially on the accuracy of these copies. In addition Morell undertook—again, as just one individual— the monumental and absurd project of drawing all the known coins of the ancient world, each with a numismatic explanation, and classified according to a system. Inspired by the posthumous works of Hubert Goltzius, which he discovered in Paris, he sketched and introduced his ambitious plan in his 1683 work, *Specimen universae rei nummariae antiquiae* (*Examples of All the Coinages of Antiquity*).[62]

59. Ezechiel Spanheim, *De praestantia et usu numismatum antiquorum* (London, 1706), 1:403–47.

60. See generally Jacob Amiet, *Der Münzforscher Andreas Morellius von Bern: Ein Lebensbild aus der Zeit der Bastille* (Bern, 1883).

61. Examples of this sort of drawing can be found today in the Thuringian State Archive in Rudolstadt, Inventory "Münzkabinett Arnstadt," nos. 4–7. One finds engravings based on his drawings in the posthumous volumes *Thesaurus Morellianus*, vols. 1 and 2: *sive Familiarum romanarum numismata omnia*, ed. Sigbert Haverkamp (Amsterdam, 1734), vols. 3–5: *continens XII priorum Imperatorum Romanorum numismata*, ed. Petrus Wesseling (Amsterdam, 1752).

62. Andreas Morell, *Specimen universae rei nummariae antiquae* (Paris, 1683), and especially 1695, pp. 3–4: "Solus superiori saeculo huiusmodi institutum aggressus fuit, summae industriae vir, *Hubertus Goltzius*, cuius tamen egregium laborem invidia & praestantibus ausis inimica

After Morell arrived in Paris in 1680, he quickly established himself and made himself indispensable as a copyist.[63] He did, however, have one problem: he was a Protestant. In the embittered confessional atmosphere after Colbert's death (1683) and the rise of the Marquis de Louvois as minister, along with the Revocation of the Edict of Nantes (1685), it was no longer possible to tolerate a Protestant as the leading man in one of the most prestigious scholarly enterprises in Paris. But Louis XIV wanted Morell to be superintendent of his coin collection and he hoped he could finish his gigantic plan to depict all the coins of antiquity, all to the greater glory of France.[64] To do so Morell would have to convert. Time and again he was given the opportunity, but he repeatedly refused. That resulted in many sudden and groundless arrests by means of lettres de cachet. That was the darker side of the royal offer: he had to convert or suffer in the Bastille.

Several of Morell's letters to a friend, François Dron, have survived along with reports on Morell, which Dron passed on to Nicolas Toinard (figure 57). From these materials a bleak picture emerges. Morell was imprisoned for five years altogether (with interruptions); but when Morell's friend and patron Rainssant died in an accident in 1689, it appeared that there was no hope for even the limited freedom to meet with visitors that he had enjoyed in prison.[65]

---

mors abrupit: etenim is de omnium Imperatorum nummis aeri incidendis cogitationem susceperat; quod patet ex eius MSS. quae Vesontii apud nobilissimum Chiffletium, curiae Parlamenti consiliarium, conspexi, quaeque postea in Ludovici Magni Galliarum Regis bibliothecam nummariam pervenere; ubi totius operis istius delineandi occasio mihi data est." This second expanded edition appeared in 1695. It was increased in value by a series of detailed expert reports by Spanheim, which took the form of letters to Morell and were attached to the book. On Goltzius, see Cunnally, *Images of the Illustrious.*

63. See the posthumously collected evidence of Morell's efforts at depicting and explaining all the coins and medals in the royal cabinet in *Comptes des Batiments du Roi sous le regne de Louis XIV*, ed. Jean-Jacques Guiffrey, 5 vols. (Paris, 1881–1901), 1684, col. 538; 1688, col. 123; 1689, cols. 267, 304; 1690, cols. 123, 385.

64. On Louis's self-dramatization, see Burke, *The Fabrication of Louis XIV.*

65. Dron to Toinard, June 17, 1689, in Forschungsbibliothek [Research Library] Gotha, Ch. B. 1749, 2 vols., *Lettres numismatiques ecrites par Messieurs Dron, Vaillant et Morel a Mr. Toinard (1687–1690)*, 2:37: "Il n'y a plus de liberté pour Mr. Morell depuis la mort funeste de Mr. Rainsant qui a eté trouvé noyé dans un bas[s]in de l'orangerie. Le lendemain de ce facheux accident Mr. de Villacerf alla le trouver a la bastille pour lui offrir la charge de la part du Roy s'il vouloit se convertir. Ce qu'ayant refusé de faire, nous sçavons qu'on ne le voit plus, et rien d'avantage. Il l'avoiy vû deux jours auparavant, et l'avoit disposé a vous donner les desseins des medailles que vous pouriez lui demander. Vous verrez par son raisonnement qu'il n'est pas encore bien tué."

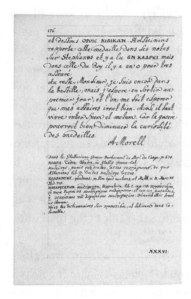

FIGURE 57. Andreas Morell, letter.
Forschungsbibliothek Gotha,
Ch. B. 1749.

His comprehensive knowledge concerning the royal coin collection had become precarious knowledge.

It is fascinating to see that Morell, thanks to his web of connections with numismatic friends, continued to function as an expert on coins. Although Dron often had to decline assignments and inquiries because Morell had no access to necessary materials, expert opinions, drawings, and advice continued to find their way out of his prison cell to his friends, and constant floods of new material were smuggled in for his learned opinion.[66]

It was significant that this enforced scholarly immobility corresponded with an accelerating movement and circulation of the people around Morell: among Protestants and those Catholics who were weary of Louis XIV's intolerant regime. In a letter from Morell to Leibniz we can see that Morell had contacts with Henning Meyercrone, the Danish ambassador.[67] Meyercrone and his embassy chaplain Gustav Schrödter were book and coin collectors, but they also secretly harbored Huguenot refugees and helped to smuggle them out of the country. When the Maurist Mathurin Veyssière La Croze fled from Paris in 1695, he succeeded only because of his contacts with the Danish embassy and with Protestant scholars on study visits, such as Gabriel Groddeck or Frederik Roostgaard, who had set up a meeting place in the embassy.[68] We do not know if the lettres de cachet against Morell were a result of such activities or were maybe just a way to increase the

66. See also the fragment of Morell's correspondence available in vol. Ch. B. 1730, found in the Research Library in Gotha: letters to Morell from correspondents with the initials M to T. Among the Paris friends these were mainly Nicaise (fols. 35–69) and Toinard (fol. 318), who are represented here, but also Spanheim, with many letters (fols. 128–213). No one has yet fully evaluated this large and important body of correspondence.

67. Morell to Leibniz, October 3, 1701; in this letter Morell asks Leibniz to distribute some copies of a work to friends in Paris, including Meyercrone. Leibniz: AA, Reihe I, vol. 20: *Allgemeiner und gelehrter Briefwechsel 1701–1702* (Berlin, 2006), no. 292, p. 498.

68. Mulsow, *Die drei Ringe*, 19–28; idem, *Die unanständige Gelehrtenrepublik*, 235ff.

pressure on Morell to convert to Catholicism. But there is no doubt that the situation was dangerous. Meyercrone was murdered in 1707.

In this way the precariat extended up into the highest circles of scholarly and diplomatic life. The extremely high symbolic capital possessed by numismatics in the Paris of 1700 led almost inevitably to high-stakes confessional imbroglios. One could not be separated from the other. So to that extent one had to be vigilant, and the tactics used did not leave numismatics untouched. When Morell refused to convert to Catholicism, his friends (or were they spies?) such as the Jesuit Jobert turned away from him, or even possibly conspired against him; and Father Hardouin, who plagiarized him, used Morell's knowledge of coins in order to denounce (in an almost paranoid manner) virtually all the writings of antiquity as spurious and to approve as authentic only the few that were favorable to his Jesuit order.[69]

Surveillance

Morell was too close to the center of power. But what if a numismatist was far away, on travels to the edge of the world, separated by oceans from the dense rivers of information of central Europe? For them entirely new problems presented themselves. By exploiting the attempts of the kings of Spain to monitor their transatlantic empire, Arndt Brendecke has described the techniques of rule necessary to maintain contact with subjects in distant lands. He speaks of "surveillance triangles," which were set up between the ruling center on the one hand and at least two emissaries on the other hand: "On the periphery at least two persons must be there, who appear either as actor or observer (although the functions of acting and observing change back and forth). Both must also have the ability to communicate with the ruling center independently, so that they can each report the loyalty or disloyalty of the other one. Thirdly, both the actor and the observer must also be close enough to each other that they can watch and judge the other. . . . Communication does not have to be constant, but it must be regular. . . . Each actor has to reckon that an observer might report to the center about him. The incentive for doing so becomes all the greater the more the center succeeds in preserving its monopoly over rewards and punishments."[70]

69. Anthony Grafton, "Jean Hardouin: The Antiquary as Pariah," *Journal of the Warburg and Courtauld Institutes* 62 (1999): 241–67; Mulsow, *Die drei Ringe*, 36–44.

70. Brendecke, *Imperium und Empirie*, 181ff.

Brendecke make it clear that surveillance triangles were often undermined or simply did not work. That also happened in the case of numismatic travels to the Levant, even if these naturally had a different status than trying to control huge areas under imperial rule. Let us examine a well-documented case, that of Johann Michael Wansleben.[71] From the end of the 1650s, Wansleben specially trained at the expense of the court of Saxe-Gotha to undertake a journey to Ethiopia. The reasons for such an expedition were the political and religious interests of the Saxon duke in Gotha, but above all the fact that the first Ethiopian grammar had just been created through the collaboration of the Saxon court scholar Job Ludolf and an exiled Ethiopian, Abba Gregorius.[72] That led to sensing that a foreign policy advantage was available that should not go unexploited. Wansleben traveled in 1663 to Egypt and from there in 1664 up the Nile. But he did not get farther than Upper Egypt because a war made the journey too dangerous. In 1665 Wansleben began his return and got off his ship in Leghorn but had no further means to continue his trip to Gotha. So he decided to remain in Italy and to convert to Catholicism. For the zealous Lutherans in Gotha, that was the worst possible outcome: a scholar especially trained for the transfer of knowledge defecting to one's confessional enemy. As in the case of Morell, the confessional dividing line proved to be political as well.

From Gotha an inquiry concerning Wansleben was sent to Johann Philipp Fleischbein, a Frankfurt patrician with mercantile interests in Italy, whose son was living in Venice.[73] Thus the information-seeking tentacles stretched out toward Italy, in the hope of at least finding out what the renegade emissary was doing there. Had Wansleben ever been in Egypt at all or had he just faked the whole thing while actually squandering his money on a debauched lifestyle in Italy? A file was begun into which all available reports on this matter were

71. On Wansleben, see Alexandre Pougeois, *Vansleb savant orientaliste et voyageur: Sa vie, sa disgrace, ses oeuvres* (Paris, 1869); Hans Stein, "Die Biographie des Orientreisenden Johann Michael Wansleben (1635–1679): Eine 'chronique scandaleuse'?" in *Ernst der Fromme: Staatsmann und Reformer 1601–1675*, ed. Roswitha Jacobsen and Hans-Jörg Ruge (Bucha, 2002), 177–94; Alastair Hamilton, *The Copts and the West, 1439–1822: The European Discovery of the Egyptian Church* (Oxford, 2006), 143–51; Collet, *Die Welt in der Stube*, 132–65.

72. See Johannes Paul Flemming, "Hiob Ludolf: Ein Beitrag zur Geschichte der orientalischen Philologie," *Beiträge zur Assyriologie und vergleichenden semitischen Sprachwissenschaft*, vol. 1 (Leipzig, 1890), 537–82 (Leipzig, 1891), vol. 2 (Leipzig, 1894), 63–110.

73. Research Library of Gotha, Ch. A 101, fols. 73a–76b. See Stein, "Biographie," 182.

deposited.[74] There could, however, be no thought of more effective surveillance because the small German principality had too feeble a foreign policy network to stay on the trail of the stubborn scholar.

That changed when Wansleben entered the service of the French court in 1670. France was obviously a power that maintained diplomatic and economic relations with the Levant, and when Colbert sent Wansleben on another journey to Egypt and Ethiopia in 1671, the Catholic side could certainly hope to keep the man under better control this time. But this time too things did not really go satisfactorily for his employer. Wansleben tried in 1673 to get to Upper Egypt and from there farther south, but again he had to return. He went on his own initiative to Constantinople because manuscripts and coins could be more easily purchased there; after all, that was another part of his commission. Bad weather forced him to stay longer on Chios and in Smyrna than he had planned. He then stayed twenty months in Constantinople but found a cool reception among the French there and did not always receive his pay.[75] Once again he was urged to travel to Ethiopia.

From the standpoint of information history, this journey was better structured than the Gotha enterprise. Pierre de Carcavy sent Wansleben clear instructions regarding what he had to do.[76] Those instructions were checked by Colbert, who criticized them for neglecting the political goal of reaching Ethiopia while emphasizing the many scholarly tasks that Carcavy had described.[77] Wansleben was urged to keep an exact diary during his journey;[78] through constant correspondence he could be monitored concerning where and what he was doing.[79] Even surveillance triangles were sporadically set up, using ambassadors such as the Marquis Nointel along with the many French consuls in the Ottoman port cities. These men were also in regular correspondence with Paris so that they could report on their meetings with Wansleben.

74. The dossier is catalogued as Ch. A 101 in the Research Library Gotha.

75. On the diverse contacts among merchants, scholars, and diplomats in Constantinople, see John-Paul Ghobrial, "A World of Stories: Information in Constantinople and Beyond in the Seventeenth Century" (PhD diss., Princeton University, 2010).

76. Printed in Omont, *Missions*, 56–63.

77. Ibid., 63.

78. Published later as *Nouvelle Relation en forme de Iournal, d'un voyage fait en Égypte . . . en 1672 et 1673* (Paris, 1677).

79. The letters among Carcavy, Colbert, and Wansleben are partially printed in Omont, *Missions*, 54–174.

Wansleben bought a great many Arab, Persian, and Turkish manuscripts; he investigated the customs and history of the Coptic Christians in Egypt (which he was not exactly supposed to do); but he also bought coins, and the lists for them still survive.[80] Moreover he presented his financiers in Paris two "beautiful images of the gods of the ancient Egyptians made of terracotta, an amulet, . . . a written amulet, a seahorse that was found off the coast of Smyrna, and certain interesting fish called 'veloni' [i.e., *belone*, or garfish] that are found in the sea off Chios. Mr. Arnoul has the invoice for the expenditures."[81]

He rejected accusations that he had paid too much attention to "superstitious and forbidden sciences," which probably meant magical and talismanic writings and objects:[82] "I found myself not only in a land where these [forbidden sciences] originate, [but] was living with a people who hold them in the highest esteem and use them assiduously; with almost every step [I took] I saw traces of them and heard almost constant talk of their supernatural effects."[83] Wansleben had difficulty making it clear to his masters in Paris what it meant to live in a culture saturated with magic and to adapt the categories of his curiosity to the conditions he found there. We see again the

80. Omont, *Missions*, 916: "Lista delle medaglie che hò comprate in Scio, e mandatele con la medesima commodità à M. Arnoul, tutte di ramo mediocre." These were mostly Roman provincial coins with Greek inscriptions. Wansleben's book drew on Coptic research: *Histoire de l'église d'Alexandrie, fondée par S. Marc, que nous appelons des Jacobites-Coptes d'Égypte* (Paris, 1677).

81. Omont, *Missions*, 916: "Di più hò mandato due belli idoli delli antichi Egitti, di terra cotta. Un amuletto. Due perri di pietra della scola di Homero in Scio. Una scrittura amuletica. Un cavallo marino, che si è trovato nel mare di Smirna et certi pesci curiosi, detti veloni, che si trovano in gran quantità nel mare die Scio. Mons. Arnoul hà il conto delle spese."

82. On this, see chapter 12.

83. Omont, *Missions*, 943: "Il me semble que c'est icy l'endroit, où il faut que je fasse quelque petite apologie pour moy, pour me garantir des reproches, qu'on me pourroit faire de ce que j'ay témoigné tant de curiosité dans les sciences superstitieuses de défendues parmy nous.... Je me trouvay dans un païs d'où non seulement elles ont eu leur origine et je demeuray parmi un peuple chez lequel elles avoient été en tout temps en très grande estime, et étoient encore actuellement fort en usage, j'en voyois presque à chaque pas quelque vestige, et j'entendois presque à tous momens parler de leurs effets surprenants." Wansleben continued: "de plus, la curiosité m'avoit porté à parcourir tous les endroits de l'egypte, à bien apprendre la langue du pays et à rechercher avec exactitude la croyance de son people, et après tout cela, n'aurois-je pas osé témoigner encore quelque peu de curiosité touchant leurs sciences extraordinaires, ne m'auroit-il pas été avantageux de profiter de la commodité qui se présentoit, ou est-ce qu'un petit scruple devroit ainsi borner ma curiosité?"

ambivalence and revulsion concerning magic that we discussed in chapter 12. "Finally, if I had sent Your Majesty's library only books of theology, history or similar disciplines, which would be appropriate only for schools, wouldn't scholars then have had reason to complain that I was not considering their needs?"[84] Other complaints included the charge that Wansleben had interfered in the affairs of the consuls and had acted as their monitor and censor.[85] Here we can see the levels of distrust that surveillance triangles could generate. Both Wansleben and the consuls had to reckon with the likelihood that their activities would be reported back to Paris. Despite all of these complaints, however, Wansleben was unsuspecting and in a good mood when he arrived in Paris in 1676 after being recalled. But once there, he was given the cold shoulder. He had been dropped.

Conclusion

Numismatics is an extremely dialogical science because coins cannot be read like manuscripts and books; instead they need to be compared with many other objects in order to make any sense. Therefore numismatic writings, more than other scholarly activities, are a mirror of the networks from which they emerge, which is reflected in the dedications, treatises in the form of letters, descriptions of provenance, and expressions of thanks attached to illustrations. From these traces we can see that numismatics in Paris around 1700 stood in a complex relation to travel and travel reports. Coins were first obtained on travels that were undertaken not least for just this purpose. Such journeys were precarious affairs: insecure, fascinating, and characterized by differing interests. The coins were mentioned in travel descriptions and sometimes copied in drawings as well, even if not so accurately or carefully as with unmovable inscriptions. The scholars working in Paris had become well informed during such travels and then sometimes evaluated the coins they brought back, which were then used in connection with travel reports (or as with Petit used to correct travel reports) for broader analyses. The small spaces of circulation in Paris were thus superimposed on the huge spaces of journeys to the East. The mobility of numismatists oscillated—in

84. Ibid.: "Si à la fin je n'eusse envoyé à la Bibliothèque de Sa Majesté que des livres de théologie, d'histoire ou d'autres semblables, qui ne sont propres que pour l'école, les curieux n'auroient ils pas eu raison de se plaindre de moy, si je n'avois pas encore songé à eux?"

85. See Stein, "Biographie," 188.

the most various of ways—between these two poles. A central problem was that of surveillance, that is, the supervision of travelers and the verification of their efforts. That activated specific nodes in the networks that constituted surveillance triangles. This sort of supervision went so far at times that numismatists (such as Morell) were arrested in order to control the flow of information to and from them and to put pressure on them. That forced them into the knowledge precariat.

14

Microscripts of the Orient

NAVIGATING SCHOLARLY KNOWLEDGE FROM NOTEBOOKS TO BOOKS

Microscripts

"Microscripts" is the title that was given to the notes that the poet Robert Walser created between 1924 and 1933: he explained that they were "from the pencil zone," stories that required a magnifying glass just to decipher them. Walser developed a tiny form of writing with a script that was only one or two millimeters high so as to outsmart himself: "They should learn," he wrote to Max Rychner, "that I began about ten years ago first to sketch out everything that I produce shyly and devoutly with pencil. . . . For the writer of these lines there was, in fact, a time when he hated his pen so vehemently, so horribly, that he wearied of it . . . , and in order to free himself from this weariness with this writing pen, he began to pencil."[1]

I will use the term "microscripts" also for the notes with which Johann Christoph Wolf filled his reading notebooks. Born in 1683, Wolf was a pupil at the academic gymnasium in Hamburg and then studied theology in Wittenberg. From 1712 until his death in 1739 he was a professor of Greek and Hebrew at the academic gymnasium and pastor of St. Catherine's Church in Hamburg;

---

1. Robert Walser, *Aus dem Bleistiftgebiet: Mikrogramme 1923–1933*, ed. Bernhard Echte and Werner Morlang, 6 vols. (Frankfurt, 2003). Robert Walser to Max Rychner, June 20, 1927, in Robert Walser, *Briefe*, ed. Jörg Schäfer with collaboration of Robert Mächler (Frankfurt, 1979), 300ff. I am grateful to Elke Matthes of the State and University Library of Hamburg, who dedicatedly helped me to locate the texts that I'm treating here. An earlier, slightly different version of this chapter appeared in Denis Thouard, Friedrich Vollhardt, and Fosca Mariani Zini, eds., *Philologie als Wissensmodell* (Berlin, 2010), 345–95.

we met him briefly in chapters 4 and 5. He is known today for his five-volume *Curae philologicae et criticae* (*Philological and Critical Efforts*) on the New Testament and his editions of Libanius's letters and of many Greek, Byzantine, and Hebrew texts, as well as his works on religious history, especially on the gnostic-Manichaean tradition. Wolf was also a great book collector; his roughly twenty thousand books and countless manuscripts form the core of today's State and University Library of Hamburg.[2]

Wolf wrote his notes like microscripts, not with a pencil but with a sharp quill pen. At that time writing one's reading notes in a script no more than two or three millimeters tall was not unheard of, but "penciling" of this sort had both an aesthetic and a psychological side. Using a tiny script is not just a matter of practicality, of saving paper; it was also a form of appropriating knowledge, assimilating books and information into something of one's own. If we look, for example, at Wolf's personal copy of Johannes Leusden's *Ono-masticum sacrum* (*List of Sacred Names*), we find tiny entries not only on the inner jacket page but also all over the title page, wherever there was so much as a square centimeter of empty space (figure 58).[3] That was more than just an

2. On Wolf (1683–1739), see Johann Wilhelm Götten, *Das jetzt noch lebende Europa* (Braunschweig, 1735), 1:142–58; Johannes Moller, *Cimbria litterata* (Copenhagen 1744), 2:1010–15; F. L. Hoffmann, "Hamburgische Bibliophilen, Bibliographen und Litterarhistoriker XIV: Die Brüder Wolf," *Serapeum* 21 (1863): 321–33 as well as 22 (1863): 337–48 and 23 (1863): 353–60; Simone Hinträger, "Die Entstehungs- und Rezeptionsgeschichte der Bibliotheca Hebraea Johann Christoph Wolfs—unter besonderer Berücksichtigung der hebräischen Handschriftensammlung der Hamburger Staats- und Universitätsbibliothek" (unpublished typescript, Bremen, 2002); Mulsow, "Johann Christoph Wolf." See Wolf, *Bibliotheca Hebraea, sive notitia tum autorum haebraeorum, cujusque aetatis, tum scriptorum, quae vel hebraice primum exarata vel ab aliis conversa sunt, ab nostram aetatem deducta; Vol. I : Index codicum Cabbalist. MSS, quibus Jo. Picus, Mirandulanus Comes, usus est* (Hamburg, 1715); *Vol. II: Historiam scripturae sacrae . . . Talmudis item utriusque, tum vero bibliothecam Iudaicam et Antiiudaicam . . . , scripta iudeorum anonyma* (Hamburg, 1721); *Vol. III: complectens accessiones et emendationes ad volumen primum totum, et partem secundi, quoad de scriptis anonymis exponit, pertinentes* (Hamburg and Leipzig, 1727); *Vol. IV: complectens accessiones et emendationes inprimis ad volumen secundum tum vero ad totum opus pertinentes una cum indicibus auctorum et rerum* (Hamburg, 1733); idem, *Curae philologicae et criticae,* vol. 1: *SS. Evangelia Matthaei, Marci, et Lucae* (Hamburg, 1725); vol. 2: *In Evangelium S. Iohannis, et Actus apostolicos* (Hamburg, 1725); vol. 3: *In IV. priores S. Pauli epistolas* (Hamburg, 1731); vol. 4: *In X. posteriores S. Pauli epistolas* (Hamburg, 1734); vol. 5: *In SS. Apostolorum Jacobi, Petri, Judae et Joannis epistolas huiusque apocal.* (Hamburg, 1735).

3. Staats- und Universitätsbibliothek Hamburg (SUBH) Cod. hist. litt. 8° 46. Johannes Leusden, *Onomasticum sacrum, in quo omnia nomina propria Hebraica, Chaldaica, Graeca, & origine*

FIGURE 58. Johann Christoph Wolf's private copy of Johannes Leusden,
Onomasticum sacrum (Leiden, 1684). State and University Library of Hamburg,
Cod. hist. litt. 8° 46.

efficient use of writing space—there was no need for such parsimony—this
was more: it was taking ownership.

In understanding the taking of ownership through annotation, consider the
following question: How was the world of the ancient Orient "read" within
the philological culture of Hamburg around 1700?[4] In a certain sense the Orient itself was precarious, not because the study of Egyptians, Chaldeans, or

*Latina, tam in V. & N.T., quam in libris apocryphis occurrentia, dilucide explicantur, & singula
propriis suis typis describuntur* (Leiden, 1684).

4. Research on early Oriental studies and the first histories of religion in Germany is still
very sparse. I cite only a few titles: Georg Behrmann, *Hamburgs Orientalisten* (Hamburg, 1902);
Dominique Bourel, "Die deutsche Orientalistik im 18. Jahrhundert. Von der Mission zur Wissenschaft," in *Historische Kritik und Biblischer Kanon*, ed. Henning Graf Reventlow et al. (Wiesbaden, 1988), 113–26; Jan Loop, "Kontroverse Bemühungen um den Orient. Johann Jakob Reiske und die deutsche Orientalistik seiner Zeit," in *Johann Jacob Reiske—Leben und Wirkung:
Ein Leipziger Byzantinist und Begründer der Orientalistik im 18. Jahrhundert,* ed. Hans-Georg
Ebert and Thoralf Hanstein (Leipzig, 2005), 45–86; Mulsow, "Den 'Heydnischen Saurteig.'"

Phoenicians was forbidden in some way. Wolf was a good Christian and meant no harm, but the East was imponderable and fascinating. Scholars had begun to learn its languages, to the extent that they could be deciphered—hieroglyphs were still unreadable, even though Athanasius Kircher thought he had divined the fundamental meaning of these signs; people were now collecting manuscripts and wondering what meaning might be hiding within the mythical names and doctrines.

Recently I discovered that a series of notebooks in the Hamburg library, catalogued simply as "Collectanea," were actually Wolf's reading notes; they were similar to the notebooks that Christoph August Heumann had sent to Johann Jakob Brucker, the ones we examined in chapter 11. Such notebooks provide insights into Wolf's reading, his manner of excerpting, and how he digested information. Could the heaping up of layers of scholarly knowledge in these reading notebooks be interpreted as a sort of bookish journey into the world of the ancient religions? How did this "microscript-journey" proceed? Wolf's notebooks offer a rare opportunity to follow the erudite religious reading of a learned scholar step by step.

A Culture of Facts

I do not intend my reconstruction, however, to be merely another version of Anthony Grafton and Lisa Jardine's article entitled "How did Gabriel Harvey Read His Livy?" which examined how scholars behaved when they read and appropriated something.[5] I would also like to embed these questions in the context of recent discussions concerning the role of scholarly facts. If we are interested in philology as a form of scholarship, it is not sufficient to study only the broad polyhistorical understanding of philology in the early modern period by examining such scholars as Guillaume Budé, Johan von Wowern, or Gerrit Janszoon Vos (Vossius).[6] It can also be important to discern specific local models of philologically distinct scholarly cultures. Hamburg around

5. Anthony Grafton and Lisa Jardine, "Studied for Action: How Gabriel Harvey Read His Livy," *Past and Present* 129 (1990): 3–51.

6. See the important collection of essays by Ralph Häfner, ed., *Philologie und Erkenntnis: Beiträge zu Begriff und Problem frühneuzeitlicher "Philologie"* (Tübingen, 2001); Luc Deitz, "Ioannes Wower of Hamburg, Philologist and Polymath: A Preliminary Sketch of His Life and Works," *Journal of the Warburg and Courtauld Institutes* 58 (1995): 132–51; Helmut Zedelmaier, *Bibliotheca Universalis und Bibliotheca Selecta: Das Problem der Ordnung des gelehrten Wissens in der Frühen Neuzeit* (Cologne, 1992).

1700 possessed such a culture of scholars, including great names like Vincent Placcius, Abraham Hinckelmann and the two Edzardis (Esdras and Sebastian), Johann Albert Fabricius and Johann Christoph Wolf, and then later Hermann Samuel Reimarus and Johann Melchior Goeze.[7] Did they possess a special character within a culture whose core was the academic gymnasium and the chief pastors of Hamburg's Lutheran church?

Barbara Shapiro has tried to identify a specific "culture of fact" in England, in which starting with Francis Bacon a kind of common law thinking combined with new ideas of the natural sciences. Common law thinking turned investigations of "matters of fact" over to laymen, sworn as jurors; this procedure had a striking similarity to invocations of "scientific facts" in the seventeenth century. In arguing this way, Shapiro has built on what Lorraine Daston had described as Bacon's "strange facts": Bacon had used reports of miracles, monstrosities, and unusual natural phenomena in order to undermine the Aristotelian system of knowledge; it seemed to Bacon that such peculiar and erratic individual facts could not be explained within Aristotle's system and so they had to be arranged in a new and hypothetical manner. Bacon promoted just such new and open arrangements, and from them he tried to create a science that proceeded inductively.[8]

But can we speak of the culture of philologists as a "culture of fact"? I think yes, and would emphasize that Bacon also proposed the founding of a "Historia literaria."[9] For a learned culture "facts" are the units of information that are obtained from books, units that are brought into order and are tested for

7. On the culture of Hamburg, see Johann Otto Thiess, *Versuch einer Gelehrtengeschichte von Hamburg* (Hamburg, 1783); Kopitzsch, *Grundzüge einer Sozialgeschichte der Aufklärung in Hamburg und Altona*; Erik Petersen, *Johann Albert Fabricius: En Humanist i Europa*, 2 vols. (Copenhagen, 1998); Ralph Häfner, "Philologische Festkultur in Hamburg im ersten Drittel des 18. Jahrhunderts: Fabricius, Brockes, Telemann," in *Philologie und Erkenntnis*, ed. idem, 349–78; Mulsow, *Between Philology and Radical Enlightenment*; Wieckenberg, *Johann Melchior Goeze*.

8. Barbara J. Shapiro, *A Culture of Fact: England, 1550–1720* (Ithaca, 2000); Lorraine Daston, "Baconian Facts, Academic Civility and the Prehistory of Objectivity," *Annals of Scholarship* 8 (1991): 337–64; eadem and Park, *Wonders and the Order of Nature*. In addition: Simona Cerutti and Gianna Pomata, eds., *Fatti: Storie dell' evidenza empirica = Quaderni storici* 36, no. 108 (2001); Pomata and Siraisi, *Historia*.

9. Francis Bacon, *De dignitate et augmentis scientiarum* II,4 (English: "Of the Dignity and Advancement of Learning," trans. Robert L. Ellis, in *Works*, ed. von J. Spedding et al. [London, 1857–74], 8:404–15, but see also 418–21). On this work, see Zedelmaier, *Bibliotheca*, 304ff.

their validity. In the realm of the natural sciences Lorraine Daston has spoken of "small facts," emphasizing the ways that these minimal bits of information can be isolated and combined.[10]

Those aspects describe a scholarly disposition that promoted bibliography, like what we find in Hamburg's "culture of facts." Placcius compiled his large lexicon of anonymous and pseudonymous authors, Fabricius his *Bibliotheca graeca*, and various other *Bibliothecae*, Wolf his *Bibliotheca hebraea*. For Placcius I have shown how this bibliographical hunt for facts went hand in hand with an exchange of correspondence through a whole network of scholars and with certain practices for managing masses of information.[11] We can also recognize similarities to certain juridical forms of thought and to Joachim Jungius's experiments with the combinability of chemicals or logical statements. All of that created a culture of facts in Hamburg.[12]

I would, however, like to point out one more parallel to what Shapiro and Daston have said about the natural scientific culture of fact. Bacon's facts were at first mainly "strange facts." In the world of scholars and polyhistors strange facts were something rather different from sea monsters. They preferred to speak instead about rare and "paradoxical" books, forbidden and burned writings, or scandals involving heretics. Jakob Friedrich Reimmann was fully aware of adapting this insight for literary history: rare, odd, and extreme books were essential for "historia literaria" because they allowed an appraisal of the whole extent of knowledge. A book like the treatise on "The Three Impostors," on Moses, Jesus, and Mohammed, generated avid discussion throughout the learned world, regardless of its infamy. Reimmann thought it constituted an essential cornerstone for the literary historian.[13]

Just as Bacon's monstrosities wound up in cabinets of wonders (*Wunderkammer*), so the scholarly monstrosities that horrified Reimmann were

10. Lorraine Daston, "Perché i fatti sono brevi?" in *Fatti*, ed. Cerutti and Pomata, 745–70.

11. Martin Mulsow, "Wissenspolizei: Die Entstehung von Anonymen- und Pseudonymen-Lexika im 17. Jahrhundert," in idem, *Die unanständige Gelehrtenrepublik*, 217–45.

12. On Jungius, see Hans Kangro, *Joachim Jungius' Experimente und Gedanken zur Begründung der Chemie als Wissenschaft* (Wiesbaden, 1968); Stephen Clucas, "In Search of 'The True Logick': Methodological Eclecticism among the 'Baconian Reformers,'" in *Samuel Hartlib and Universal Reformation*, ed. Mark Greengraas, Michael Leslie, and Timothy Raylor (Cambridge, 1994), 51–74. I have expanded this sketch in "Entwicklung einer Tatsachenkultur."

13. Jakob Friedrich Reimmann, *Eigene Lebens-Beschreibung oder Historische Nachricht von sich selbst, nahmentlich seiner Person und Schriften* (Braunschweig, 1745), 174ff. See Mulsow, "Die Paradoxien der Vernunft," 44.

registered in book collections of "Rarissima" (most rare materials) and "Clandestina" (hidden works). Placcius, Fabricius, Wolf, and their colleagues had libraries that devoted special attention to rare and extremist books. Not because they secretly harbored heretical views, but because they understood the use of such strange facts for the polyhistor, who was trying to assess the whole field of knowledge.[14]

Thus strange facts belonged as much to literary history as to the history of fascination in the early modern period. Of course, a book like *De tribus impostoribus* possessed a natural fascination, just as did Arabic manuscripts from Yemen or the *Apotelesmatica* manuscript of Manetho, who was regarded as a most ancient Egyptian priest.[15] This sort of fascination among Hamburg Orientalists is on display in Abraham Hinckelmann, one of the forerunners of Wolf as pastor of St. Catherine's, whose precarious family situation we should recall from chapter 10. In 1693, on the basis of Greek neo-Platonic, Arabic Sufi, and Hebrew Kabbalistic manuscripts, Hinckelmann outlined over a few dozen pages a history of the ancient Persian doctrine of two cosmic principles, following it from antiquity through mystical and gnostic currents into the various religions of the Middle Ages and down to Jakob Böhme.[16] With some justice one could call Wolf the heir of Hinckelmann and Placcius. He inherited from Placcius his bent for bibliography and book lore; from Hinckelmann, his skill as an Orientalist and historian of religions. Wolf turned Hinckelmann's sketch into a five-hundred-page book, which we will examine shortly, the *Manichaeismus ante Manichaeos*. Like Hinckelmann and in the tradition of Lactantius, he saw Manichaeism as the history of an error.[17]

14. On Wolf, see Mulsow, "Johann Christoph Wolf." For Peter Friedrich Arpe, see chapter 4.

15. On the contemporary fascination with *De tribus impostoribus*, see Margot Faak, "Die Verbreitung der Handschriften des Buches 'De imposturis religionum' im 18. Jahrhundert unter Beteiligung von G. W. Leibniz," *Deutsche Zeitschrift für Philosophie* 18 (1970): 212–28; Mulsow, *Enlightenment Underground*, 78–109; on the fascination of the Manetho manuscript, see Häfner, *Götter im Exil*, 503ff.; Mulsow, "Den 'Heydnischen Sauerteig,'" 21ff.

16. Hinckelmann, *Detectio*. See Mulsow, "Den 'Heydnischen Sauerteig.'"

17. Johann Christoph Wolf, *Manichaeismus ante Manichaeos, et in Christianismo Redivivus* (Hamburg, 1707). On this work, see Ralph Häfner, "Die Fässer des Zeus: Ein homerisches Mythologem und seine Aufnahme in die Manichäismusdebatte in Deutschland am Beginn des 18. Jahrhunderts," *Scientia poetica* 1 (1996): 35–61. On Lactantius: *Divinae Institutiones* lib. II: "De origine erroris," in idem, *Opera*, ed. Servatius Gallaeus (Leiden, 1660), 136–230.

The Notebooks

Let's have a look at Wolf's notebooks. There are six paper-bound volumes, which except for the first volume are catalogued under the subject heading "Theology" in the Hamburg State and University Library. The first volume seemed to be lost initially but turned up under the subject heading "Philosophy."[18] The volumes are about 15 × 20 cm (ca. 6 × 8 inches) and comprise about 400 pages each (volume 1 has 500 pages). So altogether there are about 2,500 closely written pages full of notes. From volume 3 onward, Wolf paginated the volumes continuously. Clearly he kept these volumes with his other reference books so that he could have easy access to a piece of scholarly information whenever he wanted it. In addition to his notebooks, his reference books included a few printed books, in which Wolf also entered his annotations. These were mainly bibliographies, and especially an interleaved copy of the two thick folio volumes of Georg Matthias König's *Bibliotheca vetus et nova* (*Old and New Library*), which had appeared in 1668.[19] This was a compendium of short biographical articles on authors and their most important works. Wolf had had his copy interleaved with blank pages and then used them to expand the entries with his own information, whenever he hit upon anything relevant. In an age before Jöcher's *Lexicon of Scholars* (*Gelehrten-Lexikon*) scholars found it necessary to create their own reference works like this, and many scholars did so privately and in handwritten form: biographical compendia, lists of anonymous and pseudonymous works, compendia on libraries and their treasures.[20] Wolf's copy of König's *Bibliotheca* is an extreme example of this practice. Sometimes the masses of additional information burst the

18. Cod. theol. 2234, 2235, 2236, 2237, 2238. These are vols. 2–6 of Wolf's volumes of excerpts. It turned out that vol. 1 was catalogued entirely differently as Cod. philol. 409.

19. Cod. hist. lit. 2° 29. Georg Matthias König, *Bibliotheca vetus et nova* (Nuremberg, 1678). Only vol. 1 with entries A–H has been preserved. Vol. 2 has been missing since the end of World War II, which means that it is probably still somewhere in the area of the former Soviet Union. On volumes with interleaved pages, see Arndt Brendecke, "'Durchschossene Exemplare': Über eine Schnittstelle zwischen Handschrift und Druck," *Archiv für Geschichte des Buchwesens* 59 (2005): 50–64.

20. As an example, see Christian Theophil Unger's voluminous research for a biographical lexicon, which was partially added to Wolf's collection after Unger's death. Many scholars also created their own lists of anonymous and pseudonymous authors, especially before the publication by Placcius, but even afterward. On this, see Mulsow, "Wissenspolizei," 232ff. For Wolf, see, e.g., the occasional entries in Cod. theol. 2238: "Anonymi Pseudonymi."

capacity of the microscopically inscribed interleaved pages. Then he added extra pages or slips in order to record the remaining extra material—this happened, for example, with the entry on "Le Clerc" (*Clericus*), because Jean Le Clerc's productivity was so great that twenty or thirty extra entries were completely inadequate (figure 59).[21]

The heart of his personal reference collection, however, was his notebooks. We can tell exactly when Wolf began taking these notes. He was fourteen years old and a pupil at the Hamburg Johanneum (the city Latin school next to the academic gymnasium) when in 1697 he began reading Jeremias Drexel's *Aurifodina artium et scientiarum* (i.e., "Gold Mine of the Arts and Sciences"). The Munich Jesuit intended his book as an encouragement for pupils and students to create notebooks of excerpts, and it described exactly how to excerpt properly.[22] Wolf took this advice personally and meticulously. He even punctiliously followed Drexel's recommendation that these volumes be formatted in quarto. Wolf entitled the very first entry "Memoria" (Memory), and transcribed what Drexel had written about the problem of forgetting and the necessity of remembering: "Memory is a great good, but also a fragile one, exposed to all the harms of forgetting."[23] Therefore, Drexel said, it is needful to add artificial supports for memory, namely excerpts.

21. On Le Clerc, one must still consult Annie Barnes, *Jean Le Clerc (1657–1736) et la République des Lettres* (Paris, 1938).

22. Jeremias Drexel, *Aurifodina artium et scientiarum omnium: Excerpendi solertia, omnibus litterarum amantibus monstrata* (Munich, 1638); see Florian Neumann, "Jeremias Drexels Aurifodina und die Ars excerpendi bei den Jesuiten," in *Die Praktiken der Gelehrsamkeit in der Frühen Neuzeit*, ed. Helmut Zedelmaier and Martin Mulsow (Tübingen, 2001), 51–61; Alberto Cevolini, *De arte excerpendi: Imparare a dimenticare nella modernità* (Rome, 2006), esp. 118ff. If the practice at the Hamburg Johanneum of teaching pupils how to excerpt is not even older, it arose at the latest with Vincentius Placcius, who wrote an *Ars excerpendi* (Hamburg, 1689). Probably excerpting was taught much earlier, e.g., by Placcius's teacher Joachim Jungius, who was much interested in such techniques. See Christoph Meinel, "Enzyklopädie der Welt und Verzettelung des Wissens: Aporien der Empirie bei Joachim Jungius," in *Enzyklopädien in der Frühen Neuzeit*, ed. Franz M. Eybl et al. (Tübingen, 1995), 162–87; see also Helmut Zedelmaier, "Buch, Exzerpt, Zettelschrank, Zettelkasten," in *Archivprozesse: Die Kommunikation der Aufbewahrung*, ed. Hedwig Pompe and Leander Scholz (Cologne, 2002), 38–53.

23. Cod. philol. 409, p. 1: "Memoria bonum grande, sed bonum fragile et ad omnes oblivionis injurias expositum." See Drexel, *Aurifodina*, part I, chap. II. Wolf continued: "Aurifod. Memoria vas multorum capax, sed rimarum plenum, hac atque illac perfluit. id. ibid. Memoria necessarium maxime vitae bonum, nec tamen aliud est aeque fragile in homine, morborum casus et injurias atque etiam metus sentiens. Memoria bonum grande sed bonum fragile, et ad omnes

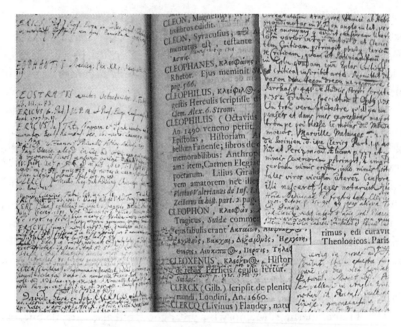

FIGURE 59. Johann Christoph Wolf's private copy of Georg Matthias König, *Bibliotheca vetus et nova* (Nuremberg, 1678). State and University Library of Hamburg, Cod. hist. lit. 2° 29, detail with inserted notes on Le Clerc: 1043.

With the help of these six volumes we can follow Wolf's reading exactly, along with the growth in his knowledge and the interests he showed in his choice of subject headings. Indeed, whenever he began his first entry under a particular heading, he often revealed the source that lay at its foundation, so that his choice of topics in their succession allows us to see his progress in reading one work and the transition to the next one. When reading, he noted all the topics of interest, made a first entry, and left as much empty space as he

---

oblivionis injurias expositum. Divinitatis argumentum, eloquentiae gazophylacium, eorum quae discimus reconditorium memoria est. De memoriae felicitate videatur Drexel. Aurifod. Part I. Chap. II." Drexel emphasized that knowledge could not be acquired through collections of compilations and florilegia but by reading original writings, which would then be excerpted. He recommended dividing excerpts into three classes: *Lemmata*, *Adversaria*, and *Historica*. In Wolf's notebooks we obviously have *lemmata* (subject headings) combined with *adversaria* because the *lemmata* were to contain short, more or less bibliographical data on the locations of each topic, while the *adversaria* were to give definitions of concepts. Wolf did both in his notebooks. And so he gave this as the title of his first volume: "Lemmata et adversaria a Iohanne Christopho Collecta anno 1697."

thought necessary for later findings that would be classified under the same topic.[24] In order to find a lemma or topic later, it was also necessary at the end of a volume to make an alphabetical list of all the lemmata with a reference to the page numbers. Then it was no real problem if in later reading the same lemma was (perhaps intentionally) created again. Later we will, for example, see that Wolf filed notes on the topic "Sibylline Oracles" in at least four places. In his first two volumes Wolf wrote his indexes in the relevant volume, but the lemmata for the rest of his notebooks must have had a separate index, but it's gone missing.

After Wolf became adept at excerpting, his script shrank from 8 to about 3 millimeters, and the notebook took on the appearance of a microscript. The pupil of 1697 made entries under such conventional lemmata as "Amicus," "Pudicitia," "Robur," "Homo quid?" and "Mulieres loquaces" (friend, modesty, strength, what is man?, talkative women), which set up writing space for excerpts taken from the moral dicta of ancient philosophers, still drawing on his reading of Drexel.[25] Then he obviously read Sallust because we now find entries on "Voluptas," "Imperium," and "Respublica" (i.e., pleasure, empire, republic)[26] but followed soon by the much less common reading of Marcello Palingenio Stellato's poem entitled *Zodiacus Vitae* (*The Zodiac of Life*).[27] Wolf's concern with the question of what an "atheist" was began as early as page 29 in 1697. And this sort of *Atheus* lemma appeared over and over in the succeeding volumes.[28] In 1700 atheism was a specter that haunted both theology and society. But along with such entries, his school reading proceeded with Lipsius and other moralizing and historical authors. Later, perhaps

---

24. On early modern reading notebooks in general, see Ann Moss, *Printed Commonplace-Books and the Structuring of Renaissance Thought* (Oxford 1996); Blair, "Note Taking as an Act of Transmission"; eadem, "Reading Strategies for Coping with Information Overload ca. 1550–1700," *Journal of the History of Ideas* 64 (2003): 11–28.

25. Cod. philol. 409, pp. 2ff.

26. Sallust was still one of the authors whom Drexel excerpted and whom he recommended.

27. *Marcelli Palingenii Stellati Zodiacus Vitae, hoc est, de hominis vita, studio ac moribus optime instituendis libri duodecim* (Basel, 1543), and many later editions. See Cod. philol. 409, p. 172: "Paling. Sagit. v. 664." On Palingenius Stellatus, see Franco Bacchelli, "Note per un inquadramento biografico di M. P. Stellato," *Rinascimento* 25 (1985): 275–92. For the pedagogical use of the book, see Foster Watson, *The Zodiacus Vitae of Marcellus Palingenius Stellatus: An Old School Book* (London, 1908).

28. See e.g., Cod. theol. 2235, p. 128; Cod. theol. 2236, pp. 418, 716. See later Wolf (praes.)/ Peter A. Boysen (resp.), *Atheismi falso suspecti vindicati* (Wittenberg, 1710; 2nd ed., 1717).

during his theological studies in Wittenberg beginning in 1703 or perhaps even earlier in response to theological readings at his gymnasium, he added more entries with theological content.[29]

Absorbing the Orient

So when and how did Wolf discover the Orient? It obviously happened before 1707 because that is the year that he, as a twenty-four-year-old adjunct in the philosophical faculty at Wittenberg, published *Manichaeismus ante Manichaeos* (*Manichaeism before the Manichees*), in which he set forth the full richness of current scholarship concerning the religious history of the ancient world.[30] Entries relating to the topics in this book appear first in volume 3 of his notebooks—on page 57. Up to then Wolf had read only theological works that he organized under topic headings "Concordiae," "Ceremoniae," "Fides," and "Libri apocryphi" (i.e., [religious] agreements, ceremonies, faith, and apocryphal books). But then we find a new entry on "Atomistic atheists." And later he added material under "The Idea of God," polytheism, the "Persian philosophers," Apollonius of Tyana, the Sibylline Oracles, Egypt, Orphic theology, and so forth. What sort of book was it that Wolf was then reading that inspired him to create such headings? It appears to have been an apologetic work that stretched far back into the religions of the ancient Near East. There is essentially one work that fits this profile: Ralph Cudworth's 1678 *True Intellectual System of the Universe*.[31] This gigantic work examines the history of the pagan religions, especially in the fourth chapter, where Cudworth mainly used the materials cited by Vossius in *De theologia gentili*.[32] Cudworth did so to prove

29. Near the end of the first notebook the entries are on: sepultura, miracula, papatus papistae, compendium, intentio animi.

30. Wolf, *Manichaeismus ante Manichaeos*.

31. Ralph Cudworth, *The True Intellectual System of the Universe: The First Part; wherein, All the Reason and Philosophy of Atheism is Confuted; and its Impossibility Demonstrated* (London, 1678). On this, see Günter Frank, *Die Vernunft des Gottesgedankens: Religionsphilosophische Studien zur frühen Neuzeit* (Stuttgart, 2003); *Grundriss der Geschichte der Philosophie: Die Philosophie des 17. Jahrhunderts*, vol. 3, ed. Jean-Pierre Schobinger (Basel, 1988), partial vol. 1, pp. 267–72, with further literature.

32. Richard H. Popkin, "Cudworth," in idem, *The Third Force in Seventeenth-Century Thought* (Leiden, 1992), 333–50; Gerhard Johannes Vossius, *De theologia gentili, et physiologia christiana; sive de origine ac progressu idololatriae; deque naturae mirandis, quibus homo adducitur ad Deum libri IX* (Amsterdam, 1668). On Vossius's idolatry project, see Häfner, *Götter im Exil*, 224–48.

that the ancients already had the idea of God and even traces of the Trinity. Clearly the seventeen- or eighteen-year-old Wolf had no trouble reading the English text, an ability that was by no means common in the Germany of 1700. If we look closely at the contents, we see that Wolf had mainly concerned himself with this fourth chapter. Down to page 87 the lemmata of his notebook follow roughly the topics of Cudworth's book, and then after small interruptions from page 93 onward the reading notes from Cudworth again predominate. Now for the first time Wolf read the first chapters in which various forms of atomism were identified and where Cudworth distinguished between "hylozoistic" atheists and other types.[33] These were chapters that Wolf had initially ignored after his first entry on atomistic atheists. After another interruption from page 123 onward there are further sporadic topics drawn from Cudworth: the "Theologia gentium," "Causae Polytheismi ethnici," "Mundus," "Metempsychosis," "Ideae Platonici," and "Sabii" (i.e., "The Theology of the Gentiles," "The Causes of Pagan Polytheism," "The World," "Transmigration of Souls," "Platonic Ideas," and "The Sabaeans").[34]

There is, however, a problem in dating these entries. Volume 2 of the reading notes contains numerous excerpts from manuscripts and books of English origin and should therefore probably be dated to Wolf's *peregrinatio academica* (i.e., "academic study tour") in 1708–9.[35] But if the entries from volume 3 came after this journey to England, then the Cudworth readings that generated the lemmata I just mentioned would have to have represented a second reading. His first reading must have occurred sometime before 1707 because Cudworth was one of the central authors referred to in Wolf's *Manichaeismus*; but if so, that reading seems to have left no traces in his notebooks, which seems unlikely to me. I therefore think that Wolf placed his separately paginated but later reading notebook (vol. 2) from his England trip before the continuously paginated later volumes in order to avoid interrupting their order.

33. Cudworth, *True Intellectual System*, 6ff. on atomism; 63ff. on the different arguments for atheism; and 104ff. on the different forms of atheism.

34. Cod theol. 2235, pp. 102, 107, 123, etc.

35. Cod theol. 2234. See, e.g., p. 197: *Historia literaria anglorum*; p. 200: *The Naked Gospel* [by Arthur Bury]; other entries on Toland, on English deists, etc., with many English excerpts. On p. 331 it says in the first-person singular: "Vidi in Bibl. Publ. Cantabrig. Bernardi Ochini Senensi Dial. 30." [Bernardino Ochino, *Dialogi XXX in duos libros divisi, quorum primus est de messia, secundus est . . . potissimum de trinitate* (Basel 1563)]. Is that eyewitness evidence of his journey, or had Wolf been in England earlier?

How might Wolf have come to read Cudworth? To find a precise answer one should examine his correspondence from before 1707.[36] But without even doing that we can suspect that Wolf's teacher Johann Albert Fabricius played a role in recommending such works. From 1699 on Wolf was studying at the academic gymnasium, and in preparation for the second volume of Fabricius's *Bibliotheca graeca*, that is, before 1706, Fabricius gave Wolf a manuscript from Oxford containing Eustathius's *Commentaries on Homer* and charged him with evaluating it.[37] So in this way Wolf would have gained knowledge of Fabricius's other topics as treated in volume 1 of the *Bibliotheca*, and especially the critical survey of the supposedly early wisdom teachings from Hermes, Orpheus, the Sibyllines, and others.[38] If he had made his notebook entries on these topics as late as 1705, then the first entry would probably have read, "vid. Fabricius Bibl. graec. vol. 1." But Wolf based himself instead on Cudworth. And so I suspect that Fabricius recommended Cudworth to Wolf at the very beginning of his studies at the gymnasium and that Wolf's reading notes on him can therefore be dated to the years around 1700–1701.

Sibyls

Let us follow Wolf's method of excerpting with one example—and in the process follow his reading "conquest" of the Orient and of ancient religion. In the third volume of his notebooks the lemma on page 71 reads "Sibyllina Oracula" (figure 60). The first entry at the top of the empty page reads: "De iis vide . . . Cudw. in system. c. 4. p. 281–284."[39] Indeed, on pages 281–84 Cudworth did write about the Sibylline Oracles. He started by noting that opinions diverged dramatically on these ancient prophecies: "As for the Sibylline Oracles, there may . . . be Two Extremes concerning them: One, in swallowing down all that

36. Wolf's correspondence is preserved mostly in the State and University Library of Hamburg; for the early period, see, e.g., the letters from and to Valentin Ernst Löscher, Edzardi, etc.

37. "Index scriptorum ab Eustathio in Commentariis ad Homerum citatorum accommodatus ad paginas editionis romanae," in Johann Albert Fabricius, *Bibliotheca graeca* (Hamburg, 1706), 2:306–29. On the *Bibliotheca graeca*, see Petersen, *Fabricius*.

38. Fabricius, *Bibliotheca graeca*, vol. 1 (Hamburg, 1705); see above all the alphabetically organized book I, with entries on Hermes and the Hermetic writings (cap. VII–XII), Orpheus and the Orphic writings (cap. XVIII–XX), Sibyl and the Sibylline oracles (cap. XXIX–XXXIII), and Zoroaster and Zoroastrian oracles (cap. XXXVI).

39. For the following: Cod. theol. 2235, p. 71. [Translation of Wolf's Latin: "On them see . . . Cudworth, in his *Systema*, chap. 4, pp. 281–284."]

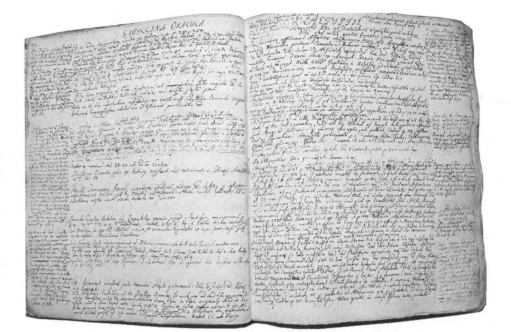

FIGURE 60. Johann Christoph Wolf, *Oracula Sibyllina*. State and University
Library of Hamburg, Cod. theol. 2235, p. 71.

is now extant under that Title, as Genuine and Sincere. . . . The Other Extreme
may be, in concluding the whole business of the Sibylline Oracles (as any ways
relating to Christianity) to have been a mere Cheat and Figment; and that
there never was any thing in those Sibylline Books . . . , that did in the least
predict our Saviour Christ or the Times of Christianity."[40] Cudworth himself
tried to take up a middle position and to make distinctions. He thought that
only a few early Christians had approved the oracles or had used them for their
own purposes. There may in fact have been authentic oracles, he conceded,
but what we possess today is mostly corrupt and spurious.

---

40. Cudworth, *True Intellectual System*, 281ff. On the Sibylline oracles, see Jane L. Lightfoot,
The Sibylline Oracles (Oxford, 2007); Rieuwerd Buitenwerf, *Book III of the Sibylline Oracles and
Its Social Setting* (Leiden, 2003); Mariangela Monaca, *La sibilla a Roma: I libri sibillini fra religione
e politica* (Rome, 2005). See generally Wolfgang Speyer, "Religiöse Pseudepigraphie und liter-
arische Fälschung im Altertum," in idem, *Frühes Christentum im antiken Strahlungsfeld* (Tübingen, 1989), 21–58.

As a student Wolf seems to have used Cudworth's work not so much for
Cudworth's own views but as a quarry and as a way to access topics of this sort.
Within the Sibylline literature much was controversial: their dating, their origins, their status as authentic or fraudulent prophecy, and finally their value
for proving the truth of Christianity, because they apparently announced the
birth of the Savior. One of the circumstances that made the topic of pagan
prophecies of Christian truth so difficult for early modern scholars was that
they offered "spurious contexts" but "true contents"; they also displayed the
tension between reason (which was indispensable for the critical evaluation
of the phenomenon of prophecy) and the "suprarational" claims of the prophecies. Wolf took note of Cudworth's references under the subject heading but
did not go any further into Cudworth's views on the matter. Instead the references formed a prelude for further notations that would gradually fill the
whole page. But what levels of reading over the following thirty or more years
did Wolf add to this first entry? Did they show an awareness of the whole
complex discussion that raged around the sibyls in the seventeenth and early
eighteenth centuries, as described by Ralph Häfner?[41]

Wolf's second entry points to a passage in the *Shepherd of Hermas*, which
he had found in Cotelier's new edition published by Jean Le Clerc in 1698. In
his note to this passage Cotelier (or Le Clerc) argued against David Blondel
and the theories he had set out in 1649, which granted that Hermas may have
composed the Sibylline Oracles.[42] Then follows a reference to Johann

41. Häfner, *Götter im Exil*, 249–422.

42. SS. *Patrum Qui Temporibus Apostolicis Floruerunt, Barnabæ, Clementis, Hermæ, Ignatii, Polycarpi Opera Edita Et Inedita, Vera, & supposititia/J. B. Cotelerius . . . ex Mss. Codicibus eruit, ac correxit, versionibusque & notis illustravit. Accesserunt In Hac Nova Editione Notæ Integræ alio-rum virorum Doctorum . . . Recensuit & Notulas aliquot adspersit Ioannes Clericus* (Antwerp, 1698); David Blondel, *Des Sibylles celebrées tant par l'antiquité payenne que par les saincts peres . . .* (Cha-renton, 1649), esp. book 2, chap. 7. Blondel belonged to those interpreters who declared them-selves in favor of philological tests for authenticity, without declaring that the practice of "pious" pseudepigraphy was necessarily fraudulent. Häfner, *Götter im Exil*, 275ff.: "Blondel doubtless made the most important contribution on the problem of the Sibylline Oracles in the first half of the seventeenth century; his voluminous accounts were combined with a harsh critique of the careless use made by early Christian thinkers of the Sibylline forgeries; Clement of Alexan-dria especially fell victim to self-deception when he held that the pagan prophecies were clearer and more enlightening that those of the Old Testament prophets." For a critique of Blondel's attributions to Hermas, see also Fabricius, *Bibliotheca*, chaps. XXXIII, XVI.

Christian Nehring's German translation of the Oracles, published in 1702.[43] Each new entry appears in a different ink so that we can tell that these notes were not written all at once. We find, for example, notes on a celebratory oration by Georg Wilhelm Kirchmaier and another set of notes on Thomas Hyde, which were clearly added in 1703 because Kirchmaier was Wolf's Greek professor when he began his studies at Wittenberg.[44] So the notebook has moved from Hamburg to Wittenberg. Kirchmaier had led a dialogue with mathematicians in Wittenberg, which was memorialized in the notebook from that first semester. Thomas Hyde, for his part, had in 1700 just published his epoch-making book on the ancient Persian religion—a book that was avidly discussed in Wittenberg[45]—and had also discussed the problem of the Sibylline Oracles. But it is not clear whether Wolf already had Hyde's book in hand.

Hyde obviously considered the prophecies to be nothing but fables. The Sibyl was a virgin, and Hyde noted that among the Arabs and Persians the sign for Virgo among the heavenly constellations was a staff, which she holds in her hand, a staff called "Súmbul" or "Súmbula." According to Hyde, the virgin was therefore identified with her staff, and both the Phoenicians and the Chaldeans had used the word "Sibbula" when they meant the heavenly virgin. They ascribed prophetic powers to this virgin. Because they had turned the observation of the stars into a science of prophecy, they transferred this characteristic to the virgin.[46] In this way the myth of the "Sibyls" made its way to the Greeks

43. Johann Christian Nehring, *Oracula Sibyllina oder Neun Bücher Sibyllinischer Weissagungen, anjetzo wegen vieler darinnen enthaltenen erbaulichen, auch diese letzte Zeiten betreffender wichtigen Dinge zum erstenmahl auß der Griechischen in die Teutsche Sprache mit besonderem Fleiße übersetzet* (Essen, 1702). See Häfner, *Götter im Exil*, 254–57. The third entry on this page allows us to date it as no earlier than 1702.

44. "Varia . . . de Sibyllinis erudita programma exponit J. Guilh. Kirchmaier." Georg Wilhelm Kirchmaier, *"De Orac[ulis] Sibyll[inis],"* in *Clariss. Virorum Ad Georg. Casp. Kirchmaierum, . . . Ex Museo Georg. Guil. Kirchmaieri, . . . Programmata Duo, Alterum De Fantasiai Orat. Alterum De Oracul[is]. Sibyll[inis]* (Wittenberg, 1703). From 1701 on Kirchmaier was the successor to Schurtzfleisch, the professor for Greek language at the University of Wittenberg.

45. See the somewhat later dissertations: Heinrich Gottlob Schneider (praes.)/Johannes David Mulert (resp.), *Dissertatio historico-philologica prima . . . de nomine et vita Zoroastris* (Wittenberg, 1707); Heinrich Gottlob Schneider (praes.)/Michael Wippert (resp.), *De aetate et magia Zoroastris* (Wittenberg, 1707); Heinrich Gottlob Schneider (praes.)/Georg Rudolf Habbe (resp.), *De oraculis Zoroastris* (Wittenberg, 1708).

46. Thomas Hyde, *Historia religionis veterum Persarum eorumque Magorum* (Oxford, 1700), chap. 32. I have used the 1760 Oxford edition; see pp. 398ff.: "Apud Arabes et Persas, hoc Signum Synecdochice vocatum est Súmbul, seu Súmbula, i.e. Spica; quae tamen proprie, et absque

and Romans. Hyde's thesis was proof that this new kind of Oriental studies as practiced by the Dutch and the English had an extraordinary potential. It showed this power, for example, if one wanted to connect the oldest forms of star-worship—ascribed to the legendary "Zabaeans" or "Sabaeans"—to the later European culture of idolatry. It also showed that the method (developed by Christian Rave and Samuel Bochart) of using a knowledge of Arabic to reconstruct older and now barely accessible Semitic root words was extremely promising.[47]

Next in Wolf's notes we find a sentence emphasizing that certain oracles were clearly written at the time of Emperor Hadrian.[48] Wolf remarked that Henricus Valesius (Henri de Valois) had already made this point in his commentary on Eusebius's church history.[49] Meanwhile—it may now have been 1704—Wolf had long since arrived at a point where one lemma or subject heading intersected others on a related topic. He was now studying theology and had therefore possibly read Eusebius's church history, which could lead to lemmata such as "Haeretici" (Heretics) and similar topics.

But then comes the next entry in microscript. Wolf noted to himself in a long passage an important argument of Isaac Vossius from 1685 that one part of the Sibylline documents was of Jewish origin.[50] Wolf added references to

---

figura, est tantum primaria hujus Signi Stella, Spicarum Fasciculum repraesentans. Et haecce Virginalis Signi Pars (nomine tamen totius, Virgo subinde vocata,) toti huic Signo exprimendo sufficiebat, cum plura, vel pingere, vel verbis prolixius describere, non esset necessarium. Chaldeis et Phoenicibus Sibulla, est Coelestis Virginis Signum: unde (cuique hoc perpendenti) Fabula Sibyllarum tam obvia est, ut quisque forte dolebit quod, sine me monente, haud citius rem perceperit. Vocem quod attinet, eadem est quae in S. Bibliis Sibbóleth, quae quidem Forma quibusdam forte videatur aliquantulum diversa." On Hyde, see Stausberg, *Faszination Zarathushtra*, 2:680–718. Wolf noted: "De Sibyllis singularis et ante [?] inaudita opinio a Thom. Hyde in cap. 32 de religio. veterum Persar." See also Fabricius, *Bibliotheca graeca*, vol. 1, cap. XXIV, XI.

47. See Christian Rave, *A Discourse of the Oriental Tongues* (London, 1649); Samuel Bochart, *Geographia sacra*, vol. 1: *Phaleg*, vol. 2: *Chanaan* (Caen, 1646). On Rave, see Toomer, *Eastern Wisedome and Learning*, 187ff.

48. See the references, e.g., in books V and book VIII of *The Sibylline Oracles*, trans. and ed. Milton Terry (New York, 1899).

49. Hadrian had been "predicted" in the third book of the Sibylline Oracles. See Buitenwerf, *Book III*.

50. Isaac Vossius, *De Sibyllinis aliisque quae Christi natalem praecessere Oraculis* (Oxford, 1679). See David S. Katz, "Isaac Vossius and the English Biblical Critics, 1650–1689," in *Scepticism and Irreligion in the Seventeenth and Eighteenth Centuries*, ed. Richard H. Popkin and Arjo Vanderjagt (Leiden, 1993), 142–84. Häfner, *Götter im Exil*, 366–77.

the controversies concerning this thesis. Vossius had provoked deep and wide-spread indignation because the idea that the Jews could have composed the prophecies contradicted the popular notion that outside the Christian tradition there might yet be divine revelations that offered independent proof of God's plan for salvation.

Today we recognize that the oracles, especially those in the first group (books I–VIII), do in fact go back partially to Jewish material and that ca. 160 BCE an Alexandrian Jew had begun to rewrite parts of the oracles, introducing Jewish elements.

Again, and with a different ink, Wolf's next line on this page contains a reference to Jakob Perizonius. Another entry took up the question of the attitude of the church fathers to the oracles.[51] At this point Wolf was probably still a theology student in Wittenberg, working his way deeply into patristics. His further entries here circle around the question of the authenticity of the Sibylline documents. For example, Wolf noted that the Cumaean Sibyl was said to be the daughter of the Chaldean priest Berosus (a claim found in Baronius's *Annales ecclesiastici*), but he immediately added Casaubon's critique of this view voiced in the *Exercitationes*: "a glossatore inepto ea verba inserta esse" (that these words were inserted by a brainless glossator) in Casaubon's words.[52] In this way Wolf discovered the late antique uses of supposedly much more ancient documents: passages from Berosus (3rd century BCE) that had been transmitted through Alexander Polyhistor (ca. 65 BCE) to Eusebius and Josephus; but quite apart from their problematic value as a source, they had also been the basis for later interpolations and forgeries all the way down to Giovanni Nanni's (Annio da Viterbo's) great forgery in the late fifteenth century.[53] Later Wolf added that various forged and bogus oracles could also be found in John Malalas (d. 578 CE) and he named his source for that information: Bentley's *Epistola ad Millium*, page 7.[54] Bentley had specifically

51. "Sibyllina oracula alii ex patribus applaudunt [?], alli reiiciunt."

52. Isaac Casaubon, *De rebus sacris et ecclesiasticis exercitationes XVI* (Geneva, 1614). On Casaubon's critique of Baronius, see Anthony Grafton, "The Lamentable Deaths of Hermes and the Sibyls," in *The Uses of Greek and Latin*, ed. A. Carlo Dionisotti et al. (London, 1988), 155–70.

53. See Wilhelm Schmidt-Biggemann, "Heilsgeschichtliche Inventionen: Annius von Viterbos 'Berosus' und die Geschichte der Sintflut," in *Sintflut und Gedächtnis. Erinnern und Vergessen des Ursprungs*, ed. Martin Mulsow and Jan Assmann (Munich, 2006), 85–111.

54. Richard Bentley, *Epistola ad Joannem Millium* (Oxford, 1691). On the Byzantine universal chronicle by Johannes Malalas, see Herbert Hunger, *Die hochsprachliche profane Literatur der*

written his famous letter to John Mill on the occasion of Mill's edition of Malalas's universal chronicle.

Wolf follows this with a reference in a different ink to Jean Robertet's French translation of the Sibylline Oracles from the late fifteenth century.[55] In König's *Bibliotheca* there was a lemma for "Robertet," which Wolf had expanded in manuscript. Thus Wolf was so meticulous that with the mention of Robertet he wrote a reference to this entry in his notebook: "vid. q[uod] scripsi ad König sub Robertet" (See what I wrote in König's *Bibliotheca* under Robertet).[56] The various components of his reference collection of books were thus connected by cross-references.

Like annual tree rings, Wolf's notes on his reading laid themselves down around the original core of Cudworth, and so we can follow the maturation of his intellectual experience. We are now at a point in the notebooks that is well past Wolf's Wittenberg period, for he went briefly to Flensburg in 1707, but Wolf then laid them aside for two years when he took his study trip to Holland and England. During this period other notebooks took their place: a small octavo volume that served as a diary, which he could easily place in a coat pocket,[57] many supplementary folders with excerpts from the Bodleian Library and other libraries,[58] and—if I'm right about the order of his manuscript works—the notebook that was later called volume 2, in which we find many notes on English authors. An alternative interpretation of this volume could conclude that it comes exactly in the order we would expect from the later volumes, namely from the period between volume 1 (1697–98) and volume 3

Byzantiner (Munich, 1978), 1:319–25; generally on these chronicles and the archaic elements they contain, see William Adler, *Time Immemorial: Archaic History and Its Sources in Christian Chronography from Julius Africanus to George Syncellus* (Washington, DC, 1989). On Bentley, see Kristine Haugen, *Richard Bentley: Poetry and Enlightenment* (Cambridge, MA, 2011).

55. The translation of Robertet ("Les ditz prophetiques des sibilles tires du latin & composes par feu messire iehan robertet") follows that of Symphorien Champier ("Les prophéties ditz & vaticinations des sibilles *translatez* . . . par maistre simphorien *champier* . . .") in the latter's work: *La nef des dames vertueuses* . . . (Lyon, 1503; 2nd ed., Paris, 1515; 3rd ed., Paris, 1531). Cf. the critical edition: Symphorien Champier, *La Nef des dames vertueuses*, ed. Judy Kem (Paris, 2007). See also *Essais de litterature pour la connoissance des livres* (The Hague, 1702, 1703). Cf. issues for September 1702 and February 1703.

56. See State and University Library of Hamburg, Cod. hist. lit. 2° 29. Because the second volume of Wolf's copy of König is missing, the entry can no longer be checked.

57. State and University Library of Hamburg, Cod. geogr. 84.

58. On the rich crop of excerpts from (mostly) English libraries, see Mulsow, "Johann Christoph Wolf," 92ff.

(1700–1701), in other words from roughly 1699 to 1700. One might then explain the many English quotations by pointing out that Wolf at this time in his
life, at about sixteen years of age, was intensively learning English and reading
English books. In his gymnasium there was no English instruction, but in a
port city like Hamburg there were certainly ways to learn the language privately from an Englishman. That could explain Wolf's ability to study Cudworth in the original. There was no translation of the work, only the French
summary that Jean Le Clerc published in his *Bibliothèque choisie*—and that
only from 1703 on, and therefore well after the time when Wolf entered his
Cudworth quotations into his notebook.

What year are we now up to in the notebook entries about the Sibylline
Oracles? It seems to be 1715, at a time with Wolf had already been a professor
for three years at the academic gymnasium in Hamburg. He was also getting
ready to become pastor of St. Catherine's and thus join the Hamburg establishment. This was also when he had his portrait painted.[59] The latest entry on
the page devoted to the Sibyls dealt with William Whiston. As a follower of
Isaac Newton and an amateur historian of early Christianity, Whiston had
published a *Vindication of the Sibylline Oracles, to which are added the genuine
oracles themselves.*[60] He cultivated a very peculiar view of early Christianity,
regarding Athanasius as a great forger and the apocryphal Acts of the Apostles
as the true gospel. According to Wolf, Whiston was responding to John Floyer's English translation of the oracles from 1713. Floyer himself was a devoted
Christian who had vehemently defended the authenticity of the Sibyllines
against the charges leveled by Vossius. For him they even proved that God had
revived the "old antediluvian religion," after the corruptions of this religion
brought by the star and hero cults of the Chaldeans, Egyptians, and Greeks.[61]
The sibyls were thus a pagan counterpart to the renewal of religion brought by
the Jewish prophets, and it was obviously important for Floyer to keep this
alternative channel of salvation for mankind open. Vossius's thesis that the

59. Today the portrait hangs in the reading room of the State and University Library of
Hamburg; it was painted by Johann Salomo Wahl. I would date it to 1716, especially because his
ordination as pastor would have been an appropriate occasion for it.

60. William Whiston, *A Vindication of the Sibylline Oracles* (London, 1715). On Whiston, see
James H. Force, *William Whiston: Honest Newtonian* (Cambridge, 1985).

61. Sir John Floyer, *The Sibylline Oracles* (London, 1713), dedication: "I here present to you
in these Oracles the old Antediluvian Religion, and all the Moral Precepts communicated to
Japhet's Family, which also contain many Prophesies concerning the Changes which would
happen in the Kingdom of Japhet's Posterity." See Katz, "Isaac Vossius," 162ff.

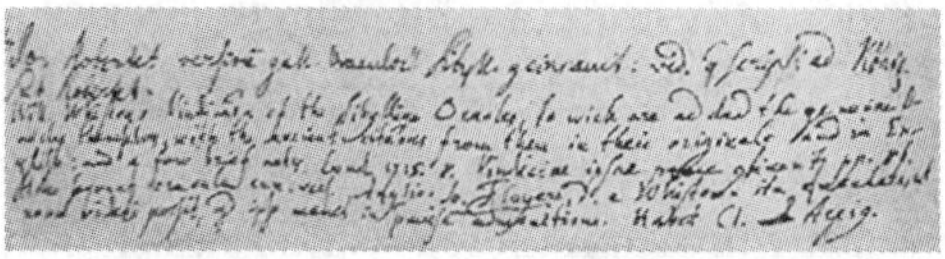

FIGURE 61. *Oracula Sibyllina*, detail: "Habet Cl.
Arpius." State and University Library of Hamburg,
Cod. theol. 2235, p. 71.

oracles were of Jewish origin would concentrate the entire providential plan
on the Jews only.

Whiston, however, did not want to exclude the possibility that Vossius had
been right. Yet he too was concerned to show that divine inspiration had been
distributed throughout the whole world and not just among one people, a
claim that strengthened the argument for the worldwide validity of Christianity. Wolf managed to reduce all of these grand ideas to a short sentence with
just one pointed reference, for the purpose of his lemmata was only to set
down short entries and not to transcribe longer passages.

What Wolf wrote about Whiston's work was simply: "Habet Cl. Arpius"
("M. Arpe owns this") (figure 61). Little inconspicuous remarks like this provide a surprising glimpse of the trading relations that supported his practice
of annotation. Naturally Wolf could not personally own all the books that he
excerpted. He borrowed some from Fabricius or—and especially if they were
heterodox books—from his friend Peter Friedrich Arpe. Arpe was one of his
suppliers for "strange facts": he was interested not just in magic and Hermetics
but also in forbidden writings of all sorts, works with which he sympathized
at least to some extent.[62] If Wolf was copying out clandestine works or if he
purchased such manuscripts from Uffenbach, he would occasionally compare
them with the copies that Arpe owned.[63] And when he placed these clandestine writings in his bookcase, he used the one that he marked with a green
letter "R."[64] That was his cabinet of poisons. That was where he placed the

62. On Arpe (1682–1740), see chapter 4.

63. See Mulsow, "Johann Christoph Wolf," 102ff.

64. This green number appears to have been chosen for a specific species of rare and often
forbidden books. Even though the texts are now catalogued differently in the State and University Library of Hamburg, in many cases Wolf's old number can still be seen on them. For example, they decorate Wolf's edition of *De tribus impostoribus* (R34), Guillaume Postel's *Les
Très-merveilleux victoires des femmes du nouveau monde* (R13), the Koran (R11), Pseudo-Vallée's

most heterodox works, just as Arpe surely did as well with a special section of his own library.

But let's return to the lemma "Sibyllina Oracula." By now Wolf's whole page was covered in writing. But the margin measuring about 3.5 cm (1 3/8 inches) was still empty. So his next and final entries took over the margin. That's where we find a reference to Morhof's *Polyhistor*, and farther down a more precise explanation of Vossius's position with regard to the Sibylline problem.[65] Often enough, when such marginal notes referred to literature that had already been mentioned on the main body of the page, Wolf would draw a diagonal line with his pen across the page pointing to the reference. He did that also with a note placed at the bottom of the margin, for he connected it with a reference in the main body; it was a citation of a French passage that mentioned Floyer's translation of the Sibyllines and that Wolf had already referred to in connection with Whiston.[66]

But what could he do if he got even more information about the Sibyls from his advancing reading? Then he needed a new lemma entry. So in the same volume of the notebooks, on page 132, we find another lemma for "Sibyllina Oracula." And other related entries occasionally appeared in later volumes.

With these late entries, whether here or elsewhere, Wolf no longer referred unfailingly to the original English edition by Cudworth but cited Johann Lorenz Mosheim's Latin translation of 1733 instead.[67] Because this edition, in contrast to the original, had an index, Wolf could in the last decade of his life content himself with a reference to the index of the work. These entries (e.g., "vid. Cudw. ed. Mosheim in indice") (i.e., "See Cudworth as edited by Mosheim, in the index") prove that Wolf used his notebook system that he had begun at the age of fourteen throughout his whole life.

Indeed, on the early empty pages in König's *Bibliotheca vetus et nova* Wolf inscribed a microscopically tiny entry entitled "De libris Sibyllinis." To the extent that we can decipher what he wrote there, it refers to the Romans, their state secrets, and the connection to the Sibylline books.

Ars nihil credendi (R16), John Toland's *Pantheisticon* (R 32), Michael Servetus's *Dialogus de trinitate* (R 5), and some of Andreas Dudith's (antitrinitarian) letters (R14)—these were all small octavo volumes that fit into a narrow cupboard for special manuscript "rara."

65. Daniel Georg Morhof, *Polyhistor* (Lübeck, 1708), I,I,10,18–22 = vol. 1, pp. 98ff. Morhof had positioned the Sibyls in his chapter entitled "De libris mysticis et secretis."

66. "Les oracles des Sibylles traduites . . . par le Cheval. Floyer."

67. Cudworth, *Systema intellectuale huius universi* (Jena, 1733).

Becoming a Book

What was the relationship was between Wolf's notes and his printed works, especially his book on Manichaeism? Excerpts and notes were intended to aid in the making of a new work: to help move from reception to production. To answer this question, let's take a short look at several lemmata. In the Manichaeism book Wolf spends the first 250 pages describing the ancient religion, following Hinckelmann's proposal to establish the genealogy and the universality of the "error" from its two fundamentally opposed principles, good and evil.[68] He dealt with the Chaldeans, Zoroaster, the magi, the cult of Mithras, Egypt, the Sabaeans, Orpheus, the Pythagoreans, Plato, the early Christian gnostics, and Mani—topics that recall not so accidentally both Cudworth and also the lemmata in Wolf's notebooks. And indeed Cudworth was the most often quoted author on these pages, but of course he was supplemented with all the other names from Huet to Spencer, from Dickinson to Hyde, from Kircher to Vossius, from Scaliger to Le Clerc, whom one also finds in his notes. A less common name, though frequently cited, was that of Thomas Gataker, the Presbyterian minister from Rotherhithe, who in 1652 had published a famous edition of the *Meditations* of Marcus Aurelius.[69] In the overabundant notes to this edition Gataker provided (just as Hinckelmann had done for Böhme) a treasure trove of philological and religious-historical insights.

The basic thesis of Wolf's book was that the contemporary discussion concerning the two basic principles of the world, God and matter, had a long prehistory reaching back to well before the phenomenon of Manichaeism. He held that one had to research Persian Zoroastrianism (or what was then understood under that term) and the neighboring Near Eastern cultures if one really wished to understand the debates that had started with Böhme or the rather different debates that erupted with Bayle. They had concentrated on the Christian-mystical and gnostic traditions. Along with Hinckelmann and his supporters Wolf was rooting these modern debates in an ancient Persian and

---

68. See Häfner, "Die Fässer des Zeus"; Mulsow, "Johann Christoph Wolf."

69. *Marci Antonii Imperatoris de rebus suis, sive de eis quae ad se pertinere censebat, libri XII, locis havd pavcis repurgati, suppleti, restituti: versione insuper Latina nova; lectionibus item variis, locísq[ue] parallelis, ad marginem adjectis; ac commentario perpetuo, explicati atque illustrati, studio operaqe Thomæ Gatakeri Londinatis* (Cambridge, 1652). On Gataker (1574–1654), see Thomas Webster, *Godly Clergy in Early Stuart England: The Caroline Puritan Movement, c. 1620–1643* (Cambridge, 1997).

Sabaean past and contributing to the "Orientalization of Christianity," that is, to the embedding of the Judeo-Christian tradition in an ancient Oriental context.[70] That explains the broader importance of Wolf's book, which could perhaps be considered more a symptom than as the achievement of original research. And therein lies the deeper reason why Wolf's literary appropriation of the Orient should interest us. We can see here how scholarly research into religion of the seventeenth and early eighteenth centuries, by engaging in a long process of taking ownership, gradually incorporated ancient Oriental studies with such fascinating related topics as magic, polytheism, and belief in the power of the stars.

This phase was not yet the "Orientalism" that Edward Said described for the nineteenth century, and it was no longer the age of miracle tales from the East that Stephen Greenblatt has depicted.[71] It was an intermediate phase, a story of appropriation but also of fascination, in which objective research mixed with instinctive Christian apologetics. Although the East was not yet an object to be colonized, it was still what it had long been, the region of "idolatry," that is, of false belief.[72] Scholars studying topics connected to "idolatry" often involuntarily revealed the strength of the spell that this foreign world had cast upon them. In this sense Wolf's microscripts with their tiny writing were an attempt to exorcize the forces within this foreign, past world by confining them to the pages of a notebook.

Returning to the question of how Wolf's notes migrated into the text of a book, let us rephrase our inquiry: How did this appropriation of something fascinating get translated into a set of written theories? The path Wolf took was surprisingly short. Both the distance from the notebook to the printed work and from appropriation to expression took just one tiny step. If one compares

70. On this concept, see Häfner, "Die Fässer des Zeus."

71. Said, *Orientalism*. It is surely a weakness of Said's book that he begins with Silvestre de Sacy and Renan and continues with British authors, so that he neglects the seventeenth and eighteenth centuries and German contexts as well. At least as far as the German scene goes, a remedy is offered by Suzanne Marchand (*German Orientalism in the Age of Empire*), but she too focuses on the nineteenth century; Stephen Greenblatt, *Marvelous Possessions: The Wonder of the New World* (Chicago, 1991), esp. chap. 2 on Mandeville's travels.

72. On the semantics of idolatry, see Joan-Pau Rubiés, "Theology, Ethnography, and the Historicization of Idolatry," *Journal of the History of Ideas* 67 (2006): 571–96; Jonathan Sheehan, "Sacred and Profane: Idolatry, Antiquarianism, and the Polemics of Distinction in the Seventeenth Century," *Past and Present* 192 (2006): 35–66; Mulsow, "John Seldens *De Diis Syris*"; Stroumsa, *A New Science*.

the lemma "Zabii" (Sabaeans) in Wolf's notebooks with the almost four published pages on the legendary Zabaeans or Sabaeans—the people whose astral worship Maimonides regarded as the paradigmatic form of original idolatry[73]—then we discover that the printed text was barely more than a reworking of the notes.[74] The authors mentioned and the sources quoted are almost identical: the Scaliger letter no. 62; Herbelot with his *Bibliotheca orientalis*; John Spencer; Hottinger; Huet; Le Clerc; Simon; Stanley; Casaubon; Pocock; Stillingfleet; and naturally Hinckelmann, who had even contrived to discover Sabaeans in Europe in the form of the Druids and the Celtic bards.[75] Since in his notes Wolf had already sketched the problems he had with this research, and especially with Spencer's claim that the age of the Sabaeans extended past the time of Mohammed, he now merely had to pull his notes together into a coherent text. Spencer had contributed a controversial article to the journal *Observationes selectae*, and Wolf had taken notes on it, but he left that out of his book on Manichaeism and devoted a separate dissertation to Spencer's ideas on the Sabaeans.[76] The burning fascination that I sense lurking behind all of Wolf's notes with their dogged intensity was transmuted in Wolf's printed book into a polemic against recent "hypotheses."

We find the same picture if we look at the lemma "Egyptii" (Egyptians). The Egyptians played a special and dishonorable role in the universal history of idolatry because Noah's son Ham, the founder of Egypt according to

73. See Maimonides, *The Guide for the Perplexed*, book III, chap. 29; for research on the Sabaeans, see Daniel W. Chwolson, *Die Szabier und der Szabismus* (St. Petersburg, 1856; reprint, Hildesheim, 1965); Michel Tardieu, "Sabiens Coraniques et 'Sabiens' de Harran," *Journal Asiatique* 274 (1986): 1–44.

74. The lemma entry is in Cod. theol. 2235, p. 123.

75. Wolf, *Manichaeismus*, 85ff.: "Ad ZABIOS jam accedo, qui in acie hujus cohortis collocandi erant, si in eruditorum plerumque sententia de eorum antiquitate acquiescere animus fuisset. Constat enim plerosque & in primis Arabas ad ultimam remotissimamque antiquitatem eorum referre origines, adeo ut non dubitent cum Sabais perantiqua illa gente, quae a Saba sive . . . Chusi filio nomen tulit, Arabiamque felicem incoluit, Zabios non esse distinguendos, inter quos numero HOTTINGERUM Histor. Orient. lib. 1. c. 8. p. 170. recte ideo notatum a SPENCERO p. 212. de Legg. Hebr. Ritual. Et sane vel ex sola scriptionis diversitate, quae in utroque nomen Sabaeorum scilicet & Zabiorum observatur, Vir doctissimus non invalide confutari potest, quae causa etiam permovit CASAUBONUM, ut ep. 223. haec verba consignata reliquerit: . . ." etc. See Hinkelmann, *Detectio*, 111.

76. *Observationes selectae* (Halle, 1700ff.). Wolf, *Ex antiquitate orientali, Spenceriana de Zabiis hypothesis . . . ceu dubia . . . excussa* (Wittenberg, 1706). See John Spencer, *De legibus hebraeorum ritualibus* (The Hague, 1686), book II, chap. 1, pp. 211ff.

contemporary notions, had spread idolatry there and had spread it from there to the whole world.[77] But at the same time Egyptian culture had venerated "the hidden one god," and Cudworth saw in that a perfect example for his apologetic purposes.[78] Cudworth had written about the Egyptians on pages 311ff. of his book, and Wolf took four whole pages of notes on them (fols. 73–75b), and in his Manichaeism book from 1707 the topic again took up pages 36–39 and 71–85. These passages were part of Wolf's discussion of polytheism, which we can follow from Cudworth to Wolf's notebooks and then into the book. Under the lemma "Polytheismus," Wolf had recorded information about the two principles of good and evil, including among the Egyptians, ideas that he also drew from Kircher's *Oedipus aegyptiacus* (who was drawing on Plutarch); these passages reappear in their own section in the Manichaeism book where Wolf was discussing Egypt.[79] Of course, there were also adjustments, but the general use that Wolf made of his notebooks leaves no doubt that they were crucial.

But that's just the practical side. Speaking psychologically, this whole topic concealed a deeper ambivalence. Egyptian culture was repellent, for it was polytheist, idolatrous, evil. But Egypt was also attractive because it had cultivated the hidden God and thus suggested an alternative path to true belief. Perhaps Egyptian culture was attractive precisely because it incorporated the idolatrous world—but that would be just speculation. The same was true of the Sibylline Oracles: they stood for false prophecy, deceit, pagan religious culture, but on the other hand they seemed to represent the miracle of a true pagan prophecy of Christ. I would suggest that this ambivalence undergirds the early modern phase of "Orientalism" and is also the reason that such scholars were so close to the precariat.

In their printed books scholars could sometimes no longer contain the explosive energy bound up in their ambivalence, which might then burst forth in polemics or in a rage for wild conjectures (*Hypothesenwut*). The seventeenth and early eighteenth centuries were a time of rash speculations about the

77. Cod. theol. 2235, p. 73. See Guy G. Stroumsa, "Noah's Sons and the Religious Conquest of the Earth: Samuel Bochart and His Followers," in *Sintflut*, ed. Mulsow and Assmann, 307–18.

78. See Assmann, *Moses the Egyptian*, 80–91, 140–42.

79. Cod. theol. 2235, p. 66b; *Manichaeismus*, 80; Cudworth, *True Intellectual System*, 160; Kircher, *Oedipus aegyptiacus*. On Kircher's image of Egypt, see Wilhelm Schmidt-Biggemann, "Hermes Trismegistos, Isis und Osiris in Athanasius Kirchers *Oedipus Aegyptiacus*," *Archiv für Religionsgeschichte* 3 (2001): 67–88.

ancient East, all of them (by our standards) resting on an extremely weak basis; after all, neither hieroglyphics nor cuneiform writing had yet been deciphered, and the Avesta was still unknown.[80] It was also an age of harsh polemics against everything that did not lead to orthodox Christianity. Oriental studies were therefore locked in battle against Socinians, deists, neo-Manichees, Pietists, separatists, and atheists. But Orientalists stared with dread fascination at their central subject.

The Cycle of Navigation

When scholarly thought makes the jump from notebook to the text of a book, it sometimes concentrates itself into an argument but often enough remains nothing more than a bibliographical statement or a description of the state of research. Books like Wolf's *Manichaeismus ante Manichaeos* steer the reader like a passenger on a ship through an ocean of theories and scholarly studies. On dozens of pages they only depict what others thought, but then the author may turn in a specific direction and develop an argument. Almost every second line mentions an author or quotes a passage. "Navigation" and "orientation" are the keywords that describe this sort of text better than concepts like the "writing of history," "theorizing," or "the storage of knowledge." They constitute what was then called "Historia literaria." Let us recall the close association of literary history and eclecticism. Francis Bacon, one of the founders of this sort of *historia*, actually embraced the metaphor of navigating unknown waters.[81] Keeping a notebook was in this way a preparation for navigation, in which an author accumulated masses of information. The resulting book was then the actual navigation. However, between these two points lay the lecture. Was the lecture also tied into the cycle of bibliographical navigation?

To answer this question, let us choose a lecture by Wolf's and Fabricius's model student, the precarious Hermann Samuel Reimarus, whom we have already met frequently in this book. During the 1740s Reimarus lectured often

80. See Michael Stausberg, "Von den Chaldäischen Orakeln zu den Hundert Pforten und darüber hinaus: Das 17. Jahrhundert als rezeptionsgeschichtliche Epochenschwelle," *Archiv für Religionsgeschichte* 3 (2001): 257–72.

81. On Bacon, see Paolo Rossi, *Francis Bacon: From Magic to Science* (London, 1968). On literary history, see Grunert and Vollhardt, *Historia literaria*. In that book, on Bacon, see Annette Syndicus, "Die Anfänge der Historia literaria im 17. Jahrhundert. Programmatik und gelehrte Praxis," 3–36.

at the academic gymnasium in Hamburg on topics drawn from ancient biblical history.[82] The text he was lecturing on was Conrad Iken's *Antiquitates hebraicae*, a textbook that had been often reprinted since its publication in 1732.[83] At the very beginning, commenting on § 4 of the "Prolegomena," in which Iken mentioned John Spencer, Reimarus alerted his students to scholarly discussions of Spencer. In 1685, in *De legibus hebraeorum ritualibus* (i.e., "On the Ritual Laws of the Hebrews") the English Orientalist had investigated the possible reasons why the Jews had established their many, often bizarre, ritual laws. He suspected that these laws were partly an imitation, but partly an inversion, of the older Egyptian ritual laws, against which the Jews were defining their own culture.[84] There was no avoiding Spencer even if in Hamburg—as we have seen with Wolf's treatment of the Sabaeans—there were severe reservations about Spencer because awarding Egyptian culture the title of being more ancient seemed to threaten the primacy of the sacral Judeo-Christian order.

We are here less interested in what Reimarus said about Spencer than *how* he said it. How did such lectures appear? What was their relationship to the culture of keeping notebooks with the excerpts and annotations that we have learned about? Can we watch the professor at work?[85] "Spencer's hypothesis about the origin of Hebrew rituals was favored not just by John Marsham, as we see in his *Canon chronicus* of 1698 (in quarto)," Reimarus told his students

82. Ms. orient. 71, University Library of Rostock. I thank Ulrich Groetsch for generously sharing his copy of the manuscript. On Reimarus, see chapters 1 and 10.

83. Conrad Iken, *Antiquitates hebraicae, secundum triplicem Judaeorum statum, ecclesiasticum, politicum et oeconomicum breviter delineatae* (Bremen, 1732).

84. John Spencer, *De legibus Hebraeorum ritualibus et earum rationibus* (Cambridge, 1685). See Assmann, *Moses the Egyptian*, 54–80; Mulsow, *Enlightenment Underground*, 61–77.

85. Ms. orient. 71, pp. 4ff.: "Spenceri hypothesis de origine rituum Hebraeorum placuit non solum Joh. Marshamo in canone chronico, Londini 1698 in 4, sed et Joh. Tolando in origg. Judaicis, Hagae comit. 1709, 8, et dudum Maimonidi in More Nebuchim, parte III c. 32 et 45, quem vindicans contra Nachmanidem Abarbanel cap. IV exord. in Levit. etiam Talmudicis et Rabboth loca, huic sententia faventia, adducit. Placuit et patribus eccles. christianae, quos vide apud Buddeum in Hist. eccl. V. T. part. I pag. 668seqq. et Outramum, de sacrificiis cap. 22 § 1 et 2. De Jo. Spencero ejusq. hypothesi et adversariis cf. B. J. A. Fabricium in Bibliograph. antiq. cap. 15 § 3 et Jo. Fabricium in hist. biblioth. suae part. I p. 354sq. praecipue vero Christ. Matth. Pfaffium in fronte recentioris edit. libr. Spenceri de legibus Hebraeorum ritualibus. Contra hanc hypothesin in primis urgeri debet 1) antiquitas et institutio divina praecipuorum rituum, sabbathi, sacrificiorum, circumcisionis, aliorum plurimorum. Viguisse adeo apud Patriarchas ante Mosen demonstrare conatus sum in Disp. de ritibus Moaicis ante Mosen."

in tidy Latin and with a scrupulous bibliographical reference, "but also by John Toland in his *Origines Judaicae*, The Hague, 1709 (in octavo)." Perhaps we can hear a slight murmur rippling through the lecture room because Toland was notorious as a freethinker. "And even earlier," Reimarus continued, with perhaps a touch of irony in his voice, "Maimonides favored it as well, in Part III of his *More Nebuchim*, in chapters 32 and 45.[86] Abarbel defended him against Nachmanides on this point in Chapter IV of his Introduction to Leviticus, and he cited passages from the Talmud and the [Midrash] Rabboth to support his view." So Reimarus was making it clear to his students that Spencer's theory was by no means original but had been discussed in the Jewish Middle Ages and even earlier with textual references that went far back into early rabbinic Judaism. "The early Christian Church Fathers also liked this notion, on which one can inform oneself in Budde's *Historia ecclesiastica Veteris Testamenti* ('Ecclesiastical History of the Old Testament') Part I, pages 668 ff., and in Outram's *De Sacrificiis* ('On Sacrifices') Chapter 22, § 1 and 2."[87] His students must have eagerly taken notes. Their professor was evidently demoting Spencer historically, as had been done in the case of Budde's *Spinozismus ante Spinozam* (1701) or Wolf's *Manichaeismus ante Manichaeos* (1707), and as Reimarus himself had done in his *Machiavellismus ante Machiavellum* (1729).[88] These hotly discussed "innovators" were not so entirely new after all; they were old hat, but at the same time he was showing them who knew history and who did not. The business of true scholars was to "demote" currently trendy topics, that is, to position them farther back in the depths of history; and to do that it was helpful if one had studied the whole (Western) tradition intensively as well as that of the ancient Near East; and that was much easier if one had been taking notes for decades on the Arabic, Talmudic, Byzantine, Syriac, Greek, ancient Persian, and ancient Egyptian roots of current discussions.

Reimarus, however, was by no means finished with his bibliographical advice: "On John Spencer, his hypothesis, and its opponents, see also the late Johann Albert Fabricius in his *Bibliotheca antiquaria*, Chapter 15, § 3, and

86. Reimarus's teacher Wolf had already noticed Spencer's borrowing from Maimonides. See Wolf, *Manichaeismus*, 87.

87. He was referring to William Outram, *De sacrificiis libri duo, quorum altero explicatur omnia Judaeorum, nonnulla gentium profanarum sacrificia; alterum sacrificium Christi* (London, 1677), a work attacking the Socinians.

88. Johann Franz Budde, *De Spinozismo ante Spinozam* (Halle, 1701); Hermann Samuel Reimarus, *Dissertatio schediasmati de Machiavelismo ante Machiavellum* (Hamburg, 1729).

Johann Fabricius [the Helmstedt scholar, whom Hamburg students would have naturally distinguished from their own Hamburg professor, who had died in 1736] in his *Historia bibliothecae suae* ('History of His Own Library') Part I, pages 354 ff., but above all Christoph Matthäus Pfaff at the beginning of his new edition of Spencer's book, *De legibus Hebraeorum ritualibus*." Indeed, the Tübingen theologian Pfaff had published an expanded edition with a new introduction to Spencer's work in 1732.[89] Reimarus instructed his students, moreover, that "against [Spencer's] hypothesis one should emphasize the age and the divine origin of the most important Jewish rites, the sabbath, sacrifices, circumcision, and many other rites."

We can see here that a lecture at the Hamburg gymnasium was always an apologetic exercise as well. Even if Reimarus by this point was no longer a sincere supporter of Orthodox Christianity, he had to arm his young students with arguments against the threats coming from the new religious scholarship in England. And he could do just that because of his own preliminary work, for he had himself published a treatise in 1741 entitled *De legibus Mosaicis ante Mosen* (*On the Mosaic Laws before Moses*), which was a sort of "On Spencerianism before Spencer."[90] "In a disputation *On the Mosaic Ritual Laws Before Moses* I tried to show that [these rites] existed among the pre-Mosaic patriarchs."

If we compare such passages with Wolf's notebooks, we may be struck by the fact that instruction by lecture was not so very different from keeping a notebook of reading notes. Lectures too were a navigation through the literature, a taking of the students by the hand and introducing them to the world of the Bible and its Oriental context. Students in turn wrote it all down and then at home copied out neat versions of their lecture notes, which were directly comparable to their volumes of reading excerpts. Armed with this knowledge they could roam their school library, the Johanneum, looking up the cited references and deepening their knowledge. The Helmstedt scholar whom Reimarus mentioned, the polyhistor Johannes Fabricius, even went so far as to set forth his multivolume history of scholarship

---

89. John Spencer, *De legibus Hebraeorum ritualibus* (Tübingen, 1732). Pfaff based his edition on the 1727 edition by Leonard Chappelow, which was in turn based on Spencer's manuscript.

90. Hermann Samuel Reimarus (praes.)/Christian Ziegra (resp.), *De legibus Mosaicis ante Mosen cogitationes, . . . publico examini in Gymnasio Hamburgensi ad. d. XI. April. A. MDCCXLI subiicient* (Hamburg, 1741). See esp. pp. 4ff. on Spencer.

as a description of his own library, as a detailed navigation down the ranks of his own bookshelves.[91]

Circulations

We are therefore looking at a world in which facts circulated. Philology was first a form of polymathy, a form of knowing all that was known,[92] and well before it had the function of critique or interpretation, it had at its base the excerpting, *inventio* (i.e., discovery), and classification of the smallest elements of knowledge. Books were read and excerpted, notebooks with lemmata were kept in which the conquered "small facts" were listed, which were also sometimes "strange facts," because they dealt with fascinating distant pasts in the East, with prophetesses, idols, and pharaohs, but also with the wild and bold hypotheses of Isaac Vossius, John Spencer, and Athanasius Kircher. These "facts" were laid down in sublimated form in bibliographies that were an indirect form of scholarly assertion, deposited like annual tree rings in the notebooks, one on top of another. But they could at any moment be liberated from mere potentiality, and their ambivalent potential could be transformed into "social energy," to use the term of Stephen Greenblatt.[93] This energy, no matter how sharply restrained, found expression when such notes were transformed into lectures or published books. This process of transformation could be "weak" and "cold," if there was hardly any change from the notes, or it could be "strong" and "hot" if they were consolidated into arguments or even into daring or original theses about the East. Above all the book then became the launch pad for new excerpts by other readers, and the process of circulation took on a new course.

Perhaps Hamburg in the period between the baroque and the Enlightenment was the most extreme example of such a scholarly culture of circulating facts. Even if the collecting of "knowledge units" was characteristic of the whole early modern culture of *Historia*, it was especially pronounced in the

91. Johannes Fabricius, *Historia Bibliothecae Fabricianae*, 6 vols. (Wolfenbüttel, 1717–24).

92. I am playing on the definition given by August Böckh: "Accordingly the real task of philology is the knowledge of what the human mind has produced, i.e., of what is known. Philology presumes that there is everywhere a given knowledge, which it must recognize again." *Enzyklopädie und Methodenlehre der philologischen Wissenschaften*, 2nd ed. (Leipzig, 1886; reprint, Darmstadt, 1966), 10.

93. See Stephen Greenblatt, "The Circulation of Social Energy," in idem, *Shakespearean Negotiations: The Circulation of Social Energy in Renaissance England* (Berkeley, 1988), 1–20.

Hamburg of the great polyhistorical bibliographers. I doubt that such a culture of appropriation and reproduction was in a position to create genuinely new knowledge—in the sense of Kuhn's paradigm shifts—but that difficult question is not under discussion here. I can only suggest that Reimarus, who did produce such a paradigm shift as he moved from being a Christian apologist to being a critic of revelation, needed much more than just an internal increase in his knowledge of the ancient Orient. It was the cool rationality of Wolffianism and the calculating spirit he took from natural science and technology that gave him the distance he needed to look in from the outside at the Hamburg circulation of information.[94]

Wolf's book on Manichaeism was still very much indebted to these factual circulations. It certainly did contain a basic thesis and advance an argument, but it overflowed with bibliographical knowledge. The book was—and this was both a positive and a negative—a mirror of Wolf's notebooks, a run-on arrangement of short, one- to five-page sketches of the current state of knowledge on topics in the history of ancient religion. One could almost read the book as a series of lemmata: on idolatry (33ff.), Egypt (36ff.), the Jews (40ff.), the Chaldeans (45ff.), Zoroastrians (48ff.), fire worship (50ff.), the magi (55ff.), the two principles (58ff.), Mithras (62ff.), the god of the Egyptians (71ff.), the Sabaeans (85ff.), and so forth. To that extent the book was a typical early work: it displayed the enormous learning of the twenty-four-year-old and his ability to process enormous amounts of information. This trait drowned out any more mature form of discussion of the topics he treated, which we can see if we compare his book with Isaac de Beausobre's more thoughtful (and later) book, *Histoire critique de Manichée et du Manicheisme*.[95] Wolf's book was, however, much closer to another work with which it shared the same urgent cause: Mosheim's peculiar and monumental translation of Cudworth. It was peculiar because Mosheim overwhelmed the text with notes that make up nine-tenths of the book and that often run completely counter to Cudworth's argument.[96] Despite that, Mosheim's work bolstered Cudworth's text with

94. Martin Mulsow, "From Antiquarianism to Bible Criticism? Young Reimarus Visits the Netherlands," in *Between Philology and Radical Enlightenment*, ed. idem, 1–39.

95. Isaac de Beausobre, *Histoire critique de Manichée et du Manicheisme*, 2 vols. (Amsterdam 1734, 1739); on that book, see Häfner, "Die Fässer des Zeus"; Sandra Pott, "Critica perennis: Zur Gattungsspezifik gelehrter Kommunikation im Umfeld der Bibliothèque Germanique (1720–1741)," in *Praktiken der Gelehrsamkeit*, ed. Zedelmaier and Mulsow, 249–73.

96. See Sarah Hutton, "Classicism and Baroque: A Note on Mosheim's Footnotes to Cudworth's *The True Intellectual System*," in *Johann Lorenz Mosheim (1693–1755): Theologie im*

many layers of supplemental information, just as Wolf's notebooks took lemmata from Cudworth but then enriched them with additional information. If one opens Mosheim's version of Cudworth to pages 304ff., at the entry for "Apollonius Tyanaeus," one finds (to no surprise) partly the same names as in Wolf's entry in his notebooks.[97] But the forty-year-old Mosheim spoke from a much richer philological experience than the young man Wolf.[98]

The layers of information that Wolf added to Cudworth had, in their bibliographical agglomeration, the character of independent entities, of complex modules, or even of "implicit stories." Just how much these entries function as implicit stories or learned modules becomes evident if we cast one last glance at another page from the notebook, the one with the lemma *Metempsychosis* (i.e., "Transmigration of Souls").[99] The page brims over with documented knowledge, and it was precisely the compactness on a single page that gave this knowledge its intrinsic bias toward expansion: it was a severely compressed research report, knowledge that desperately needed to be explained and told as a story.

An essential element here was the very materiality of the record. Along with the interleaved copies of books, such notebooks were instruments of appropriation, of taking ownership. And I suggested earlier that this appropriation needs to be seen within the context of a history of fascination despite the lingering deep ambivalences about the Orient, which both attracted and repelled the intellectuals of northern Europe. Now I can expand the point. They were also part of a scholarly consumer culture, of a material acquisition of knowledge in collections of thousands of books, manuscripts, and ancient

Spannungsfeld von Philosophie, Philologie und Geschichte, ed. Martin Mulsow, Ralph Häfner, Helmut Zedelmaier, and Florian Neumann (Wiesbaden, 1997), 211–28; Marialuisa Baldi, "Confutazione e conferma: L'origenismo nella tradizione latina del True Intellectual System (1733)," in *"Mind Senior to the World": Stoicismo e origenismo nella filosofia platonica del seicento inglese*, ed. idem (Milan, 1996), 163–204.

97. Cudworth, *Systema intellectuale*, 304ff.; Cod. theol. 2235, p. 71b; Philostratus, *The Life of Apollonius of Tyana*, ed. and trans. Christopher P. Jones, 3 vols. (Cambridge, MA, 2005). On Apollonius of Tyana, see Dzielska, *Apollonius of Tyana in Legend and History*.

98. Mosheim, for example, voiced considerable reservations over the credibility of the information in Philostratus. See Mosheim, "De existimatione celeberrimi Philosophi, Apollonii Tyanaei," in idem, *Observationum sacrarum et historico-criticarum liber I* (Amsterdam, 1721), 260–382. On that, see Mulsow, "Eine Rettung des Servet und der Ophiten? Der junge Mosheim und die häretische Tradition," in *Mosheim*, ed. idem et al., 45–92, esp. 68ff.

99. Cod. theol. 2235, p. 106b. On the topic of metempsychosis, see Zander, *Geschichte der Seelenwanderung in Europa*.

objects. Cultural consumption shaped identities, formed "taste," and was translated into conversation and status markers.[100] That was even true of the rather specialized acquisitions of scholars like Fabricius and Wolf. These people were sitting in the midst of their gigantic libraries, letting their contents flow into their notes. Sometimes their book worlds intersected with those of colleagues, with the collections of Arpe, Winckler, Uffenbach, or Morhof. If they published a book, as the young Wolf did, then it was not "conspicuous consumption," as Veblen might have called it, but "conspicuous production."[101] The history of fascination with the ancient Orient was a branch within this complex but aesthetically loaded culture of consumption and communication that took ownership of foreign worlds in four steps: purchase, reading, excerpting, and transformation into scholarly texts.[102] The history of such fascination was generally implicit in this process, which the English and Americans often call "bookish." But travel reports or even personal travel experiences played virtually no role in the German part of this story. In chapter 13 we saw how the first travelers of the seventeenth century created a new sort of stimulus, but in Germany that was extremely uncommon, and this picture changed only over the course of the eighteenth century. The only "external" stimulus in Germany came at first just from Lutheran Orthodox clerics who launched a furious campaign against dangerous "fanatics" (i.e., Pietists) by dissecting their "errors" historically.[103] But that campaign was enough to keep the scholarly engine stoked, so that books would produce ever more books, creating monuments of erudition that can still astonish us today. The social energy embedded deeply in these cycles of circulation rarely burst out into the open: in polemical failures, in scholarly indecencies, or in crazy theses like those of Huet or

100. On the theory of cultural consumption, see John Brewer and Roy Porter, eds., *Consumption and the World of Goods* (London, 1994); Martin Mulsow, "Kulturkonsum, Selbstkonstitution und intellektuelle Zivilität: Die Frühe Neuzeit im Mittelpunkt des kulturgeschichtlichen Interesses," *Zeitschrift für historische Forschung* 25 (1998): 529–47.

101. Thorstein Veblen, *The Theory of the Leisure Class: An Economic Study in the Evolution of Institutions* (New York, 1899).

102. Stephen Greenblatt provides an interesting typology of appropriations in his "Circulation of Social Energy," esp. 9–11.

103. See Thomas Kaufmann, "Nahe Fremde—Aspekte der Wahrnehmung der 'Schwärmer' im frühneuzeitlichen Luthertum," in *Interkonfessionalität—Transkonfessionalität—binnenkonfessionelle Pluralität. Neue Forschungen zur Konfessionalisierungsthese*, ed. Kaspar von Greyerz et al. (Heidelberg, 2003), 179–241; Lehmann-Brauns, *Weisheit in der Weltgeschichte*.

Hardouin.[104] But mostly this social energy remained buried in scribbled marginalia while the circulation of information continued running at its normal operating speed. One thing is clear: the books that were annotated over and over in tiny ink, the notebooks filled to bursting with microscripts, occupied a key position in this process. Travel to the Orient proceeded through a "pencil zone" of the same sort that restored to Robert Walser enough light-heartedness that he was able to conjure up his novels out of it.

104. On these topics, see my book *Die unanständige Gelehrtenrepublik*, 1–26; on Hardouin, see also chapter 13.

Concluding Word

IT MIGHT SEEM tempting to end a book on precarious knowledge on a melancholy note. There are paintings, still lives, that portray books and manuscripts—that is, the embodiments of human knowledge—as transitory. These books, yellowed and warped, appear next to burned-down candles, soap bubbles, skulls, and worm-eaten flowers as symbols of ephemerality, of *vanitas*. Especially in the Netherlands of the early seventeenth century such still lives depicting books were popular, notably in Leiden, the university town in which so much knowledge was strenuously produced, but also in Haarlem and other towns too. The culture of Calvinism, torn between economic success and strict morality, between the desire to display one's material wealth and the bad conscience of owning so much, fell for this genre of painting, which combined both.[1] Pieter Claesz was one of the painters who specialized in still lives with books. In one painting from the year 1630, which hangs today in the Mauritshuis in The Hague, one sees a skull displayed with grim directness, resting on a book (figure 62). The pocket watch has run down, the lamp has burned out, the glass has tipped over, the pen

---

1. On this ambivalence, see Simon Schama, *The Embarrassment of Riches: An Interpretation of Dutch Culture in the Golden Age* (New York, 1987). On the art of the still life, see as an introduction, Claus Grimm, *Stilleben: Die niederländischen und deutschen Meister* (Stuttgart, 2001); still-life images of books are numerous in the catalog *Leselust: Niederländische Malerei von Rembrandt bis Vermeer* produced by the Schirn Art Exhibition Hall in Frankfurt, Stuttgart, 1993. See esp. the contribution by Görel Cavalli-Björkman, "Hieronymus in der Studierstube und das Vanitasstilleben," 47–53. I am grateful to Eckhard Leuschner for this reference.

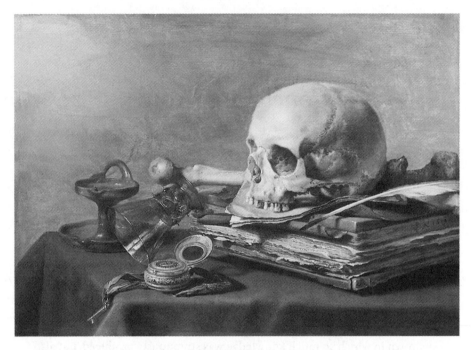

FIGURE 62. Pieter Claesz, *Vanitas Still Life*. Mauritshuis Den Haag.

has been laid aside.[2] The author of the book would appear to be dead; what remains of his knowledge?[3]

A painted still life with books by Jan Davidszoon de Heem from 1628 was not so explicit but still played with the same theme of transience (figure 63).[4] De Heem placed a disorderly heap of books on a table, with no ornamentation

2. See Martina Brunner-Bulst, *Pieter Claesz—der Hauptmeister des Haarlemer Stillebens im 17. Jahrhundert: Kritischer Oeuvrekatalog* (Lingen, 2004); Pieter Biesboer et al. eds., *Pieter Claesz: (1596/7–1660), Meester van het stilleven in de Gouden Eeuw. (Aust.kat.: Frans-Halsmuseum Haarlem 2005)* (Zwolle, 2004).

3. Very occasionally the skulls represented in paintings bear a laurel wreath. That leaves room for the hope that scholarly achievements and fame would not be all for naught. See, e.g., David de Heem, *Vanitas*, depicted in *Leselust*, 211. Certain painters, e.g., Jacques de Gheyn II, reveal a closeness to Neo-Stoicism. See B. A. Heezen-Stoll, "Een vanitasstilleven van Jacques de Gheyn II uit 1621: Afspiegeling van neostoische denkbeelden," *Oud Holland* 93 (1979): 217–45.

4. Sam Segal, *Jan Davidsz de Heem und sein Kreis* (Braunschweig, 1991); Quentin Buvelot et al., eds., *A Choice Collection: Seventeenth-Century Dutch Paintings from the Fritz Lugt Collection* (Zwolle, 2002), 96–101.

FIGURE 63. Jan Davidszoon de Heem, *Still Life with Books*. Fondation Custodia,
Collection Frits Lugt, Paris, Inv. No. 183.

or accessories, the pages all opened and damp, as if owned by an old antiquarian who has not cared for them. The titles of some of the books are visible, and
one can tell from them that the theme of friendship among young people who
have died lurks in the background. De Heem painted such works in Leiden
from the mid-1620s onward. The Synod of Dort at which the strict Calvinists
were victorious had just finished. Such still lives with books may have been
intended to temper the pride of Leiden professors and poets, especially if they
had given themselves over to erotic fantasies (one of the books in the background is the Dutch translation of the neo-Catullan love poems entitled *Basia*
[i.e., "Kisses"], a precarious work because it was so controversial).[5] Youth,
pleasure, knowledge—all were vanities.

5. Johannes Secundus [Johann Nico Everaerts], *Basia* (Utrecht, 1539). See Edmund Dorer,
Johannes Secundus, ein niederländisches Dichterleben (Baden, 1854); Thomas Borgstedt, "Kuß,

I did not write this book, however, to spread melancholy. It is dedicated not to some diffuse, general transitoriness of all human knowledge but to the very specific conditions under which thoughts, ideas, and theory could be endangered because of their dependence on material carriers. It has studied human responses to this endangerment: the habitus that they developed, the tactics they used, their attempts to rehabilitate forbidden knowledge and to recover lost knowledge. Does this produce an alternative intellectual history in the early modern period?

This intellectual history is "alternative" in three respects. First, it represents a change of perspective, shifting our focus away from well-known and secure teachings to those that were controversial, insecure, endangered. One might think that this would result in a "history from below," in the style of Marxist or post-Marxist historiography. But that's not necessarily true. We have seen that the precariat (even if it's in the form of "fragility") extended up into the established levels of the educated and learned. That is why this shift of perspectives under the categories of security versus insecurity produces an alternative history. Second, there are no great minds in the foreground of this history but figures of the second or third rank. That means presenting an intellectual history not as the story of innovations, in which a succession of new thoughts and theories appears, but rather a history of appropriations, extrapolations, and rehabilitations. Wolf did not invent the practice of excerpting; he was one of many who occupied themselves with copying, transforming, and reformulating. Arpe was not a revolutionary freethinker; he was interested in making the radical theses of atheists palatable to the German public around 1700. Third, and finally, this intellectual history departs from the usual doxographical accounts in that here we have consistently treated ideas, theories, and debates as embedded in emotions, mental attitudes, values, and collective perceptions, and not least in fears, defensive reactions, and ambivalences; but also incorporated in practices, tactics, and strategies; and finally embodied in institutions, in ways of communicating, and in the very preconditions of communication—including even the postal system.

I emphasized at the beginning that I would be able to present various aspects of such an "alternative" intellectual history only by trying out diverse possibilities, posing unconventional questions, or presenting little-known

Schoß, Altar: Zur Dialogizität und Geschichtlichkeit erotischer Dichtung (Giovanni Pontano, Joannes Secundus, Giambattista Marino and Christian Hofmann von Hofmannswaldau)," *Germanisch-romanische Monatsschrift*, n.s., 44 (1994): 288–323.

materials. And yet at the end the question remains, whether something can be said about the changes and development of precarious knowledge during the long phase from the fifteenth to the eighteenth century that we are used to calling the "early modern period." Yet that very expression, used especially by historians, breathes an air of caution. It does not speak of the Renaissance or of the Enlightenment but instead uses a neutral expression, which leaves its neutrality behind only when it declares its connection to "modernity." An alternative term would be "premodern," an expression that connects our period to the Middle Ages and that distinguishes itself only from the genuinely modern post-1800 world.

So is there now a history of precarious knowledge in the early modern period? We have certainly suggested many *small* histories that remain to be written: A history of "problematic" ways of expressing oneself; a history of maskings; a history of the ways knowledge could be appropriated on note cards that could easily be lost; a history of scholarly correspondence that followed the rhythm of trade fairs and the opportunities for transportation; a history of visual self-stylizations and of covert emblematic hints; a history of epistemic encouragement, disappointment, and ambivalence; a cultural history of truth between trust and distrust; a history of scholarly mobility and immobility; a history of the generational transfer of embarrassing knowledge. I do think that an alternative intellectual history of the early modern will have to include all of these many small histories, and it will have to deal with their interconnectedness. The present book has therefore proceeded like an episodic film. Protagonists from one chapter return in lesser roles in another; topics that took pride of place in certain chapters reappear unexpectedly elsewhere. The director Robert Altman has spoken of using a "multi-character-form" to depict this interconnectedness.[6]

There are certainly contrary tendencies in such an "episodic film," tendencies that point to topics like modernization, secularization, and the emergence of the "public" but also others that suggest a withdrawal or a yearning for the ancient. If, however, the urge cannot be repressed to seek some broad lines of development—despite all our current skepticism about teleologies, fantasies of modernization, and grand narratives, despite our resistance to prematurely sweeping microhistories together into some new general story—then most

6. See, e.g., David Thompson, ed., *Altman on Altman* (London, 2006). See above all the film *Short Cuts* based on the book by Raymond Carver.

likely an intellectual history of precarious knowledge will be part of two large histories: the history of freedom and the history of security.

An increase in freedom means that individuals carrying subversive knowledge around with them no longer have to hide. They can be authentic, they can sign their own names, publish openly, and in this way lend some permanence to their thoughts. If the modern period has brought some progress in freedom, then the problem of precarious knowledge has diminished. To what extent that has actually happened is not our topic here. The history of samizdat literature in the twentieth century shows us that knowledge is still repeatedly suppressed. And the flood of information in the present allows us also to see that knowledge can also disappear if it drowns in a vast ocean.

Nor is this the place to decide whether the course of modern history has brought with it a growth in security. Yes, from about 1700 onward a "secure normal society has taken shape,"[7] in which many kinds of precarity have declined, where we can insure ourselves against many risks, and where packages are reliably delivered. And yet even under these conditions truly rare knowledge still sometimes escapes despite protections. Can knowledge be insured? Many external difficulties against which the early modern protagonists of this book had to struggle have indeed been eradicated; and yet, as I mentioned at the outset, the most recent storage media have opened up new forms of insecurity. And social insecurities, even among scholars, are every bit as present in our postindustrial society as they were earlier. So the history of precarious knowledge has clearly not yet reached its end.

7. Zwierlein, *Der gezähmte Prometheus*; for the nineteenth century, François Ewald, *Der Vorsorgestaat* (Frankfurt, 1991).

INDEX

Abano, Pietro d', 279
Abraxas, 178, 336, 339–40
Abu-Ma'shar, 343
Accademia Carrara, 173–74, 188
Accademia degli Incogniti, 174–76, 181–99, 270, 278
Accademia degli Investiganti, 275
Accademia della Fama, 176
Accademia Veneziana, 269–70
Acta eruditorum, 300–301
Acta philosophorum, 297–300, 304–6
Agrippa, Heinrich Cornelius, von Nettesheim, 250, 258, 279, 335–36, 343, 349
Agustin, Antonio, 361
Aikema, Bernard, 175–87, 196, 247, 268–69
al-Fārābi, 41
Albertus Magnus, 49
alchemy and alchemists, 10, 75, 86, 98, 137, 180, 202, 218–19, 257–59, 262–63, 267, 270, 274–75, 279, 300
Alethophiles, Society of the, 227–33, 236
Algiers, 369
Alsted, Johann Heinrich, 259, 270, 280n113
Altdorf, 285, 290
Altman, Robert, 421
Altona, 33, 39
Amazons, 365–67
Anaximander, 119
Andreae, Johann Valentin, 87, 104n11, 256
Ansbach, 38, 202, 218, 220, 299
Anton Ulrich, duke of Brunswick-Wolfenbüttel, 214

Apamea, Phrygia, 358
Apinus, Sigmund Jakob, 308–10
Apollonius of Tyana, 352, 392, 414
Aretino, Pietro, 171–73, 89, 197n65
Aristotle and Aristotelian, 22, 28, 49, 54, 182, 198, 220, 225, 245, 252–53, 259–61, 270, 274, 279, 306, 342, 385
Arnold, Gottfried, 28, 104–5, 110, 113, 143, 154, 165
Arpe, Peter Friedrich, 24, 29, 37, 105–6, 109–38, 148–63, 240, 350–53, 402–3, 415, 420; *Apologia pro Vanino*, 105–6, 110, 112–33, 150, 163–64
atheism and atheists, 5, 20–21, 33, 41, 56–62, 65n64, 77, 95, 101–17, 125–30, 156, 158, 391–93, 408, 420
atheism, 33, 58, 103, 105–6, 109, 115, 117, 125–27, 129, 158, 391, 393n33
Augsburg, 301–2, 308, 320–21
August Wilhelm, duke of Brunswick-Wolfenbüttel, 201
Aumont, Louis Marie Victor, Duke d', 362
Averroes and Averroists, 13, 49–53, 58, 64, 341
Avila, miraculous bells of, 344n45

Baader, Franz von, 201
Bacon, Francis, 22, 181, 189, 385–86, 408
Baronio, Cesare, 339
Basel, 359
Bassewitz, Count Adolf Friedrich von, 145–46
Bassewitz, Count Henning von, 144, 146–47, 149

Bateson, Gregory, 11
"Bath, Mutianus de," 134
Baudelot de Dairval, Charles-César, 24, 359–60, 362–68
Bayer, Siegfried Theophil, 146
Bayle, Pierre, 104, 110, 143, 156, 358, 404
Bayreuth, 311
Beausobre, Isaac de, 413
Becanus, Goropius (Jan van Gorp), 206
Becher, Johann Joachim, 75, 80, 86, 90, 99
Beck, Ulrich, 164
Behler, Ursula, 323
Benedetti, Natalitio, 339–40
Benivieni, Girolamo, 48
Bergamo, 173, 176–77, 182, 185, 188
Berlin, 132, 134, 145, 220, 227, 231, 235–36
Bern, 360
Beverland, Adrian, 32, 69–73, 84, 135
Bianchi, Luca, 54
biblical criticism, radical, 38, 40, 293
Bibliotheca Vulcani (Library of Burned Books), 135, 139, 143–44, 150–57, 161, 164, 166
Bignon, Jean Paul, Abbé, 360
Bissendorf, Johann, 153
Bisterfeld, Johann Heinrich, 259–60
Blankenburg, 319
Blondel, David, 396
Blount, Charles, 66, 135
Blumenberg, Hans, 24
Bocchi, Achille, 187–89, 210–11
Bodin, Jean, 131–32, 160
Boethius of Dacia, 54
Böheim, Hans (the Piper of Niklashausen), 78
Böhme, Jakob, 244, 287–90, 387, 404
Böhmer, Henning, 159–60
Bologna, 51, 217
Bonifacio, Baldassare, 185n31, 189, 194–95
Bonifacio, Giovanni, 173, 252
book burning, 140, 153–54; *bibliotheca vulcani* (library of burned books) 30, 135, 139–66
Boszormenyi-Nagy, Ivan, 283–84

Bourdieu, Pierre, 34–35
bourgeoisie, intellectual, 9–10, 22–24, 29, 143, 165, 240–41, 245, 281, 324, 328, 333
Boyle, Robert, 187, 190
Brackenhoffer, Elias, 348
Brandenburg, court of, 220, 360
Brandom, Robert, 20
Brandt, Reinhard, 257
Breckling, Friedrich, 143, 151
Bremen, 271
Brendecke, Arndt, 329, 375–76
Brockes, Barthold Hinrich, 120, 126, 144
Bronisch, Johannes, 230
Brucker, Johann Jakob, 37–38, 295n1, 301–14, 318, 320–24, 384
Bruno, Giordano, 120, 132, 136, 151, 189, 258, 267, 310, 336–38
Brunswick, 308–10, 312–14, 318, 320–22
Budde, Johann Franz, 119, 298, 410
Budé, Guillaume, 384

Calabria, 177, 336
Calckberner, Coenraad, 371
cameralism, 34, 39, 78–84, 88–91, 95
Camillo, Giulio, 269
Campanella, Tommaso, 44, 119, 337–38
Carcavy, Pierre de, 360, 377
Carpzov, Johann Benedikt, 288
Casaubon, Isaac, 338, 399, 406
Castel, Robert, 23, 31
Cauz, Constantin Franz von, 227
Cavaillé, Jean-Pierre, 191–92
Cecco d'Ascoli, 337
Celle, 202
censorship, 15
Certeau, Michel de, 29–30
Chaldeans, 306, 338, 383, 399, 401, 404, 413
Charles XII, king of Sweden, 145
Charron, Pierre, 104n11, 118, 124
Chartier, Roger, 34–37
Chazzim. *See* Engelberger
Chen, Bianca, 370
Child, Josiah, 80
Chios, 377–78

Christian August, Duke of Palatinate-Sulzbach, 278

Christian August, prince bishop of Lübeck, 144, 149

Claesz, Pieter, 417–18

clandestinity, 5–6, 9, 31–33, 37–45, 108–9, 131–38

Clavicula Salomonis, 279

Clavius, Andreas, 202–3, 212, 220–23

Cleopatra, 364

Coburg, 151

Colbert, Jean-Baptiste, 360, 362, 373, 377

Colerus, Johann Christoph, 203

collecting of books and manuscripts, 20, 106–8, 111, 129, 163, 326, 351, 357, 384, 412

collecting of magical objects, coins, and other materials, 20, 207, 299, 326–27, 335–36, 347–49, 357, 364, 370

Colli, Ippolito de', 208–9, 222

Collins, Anthony, 61, 130–31, 135

Comenius, Jan Amos, 256, 259, 284–85, 289

Conring, Hermann, 161

Constance, Council of, 151

constellations, intellectual and social, 240, 296, 298, 326

Copenhagen, 109–10, 146, 351

Coptic Christians, 378

Cotelier, Jean-Baptiste, 396

Cremona, 343

Crusius, Christian August, 236

Cudworth, Ralph, 125, 392–96, 400–401, 403–4, 407, 413–14

Cuffeler, Abraham Johannes, 135

Cuper, Gisbert, 206n20, 208, 370–71

Curtis, Mark H., 34–35

Cymbalum mundi, 131–32

Dale, Antonius van, 160

Damme, Stéphane Van, 328, 355

Danzig, 271

Darwin, Erasmus, 294

Daston, Lorraine, 22, 385–86

De tribus impostoribus, 14, 127, 132, 135, 156, 157n52, 387

deism and deists, 39–40, 59, 66, 98, 125, 127, 160, 161, 408

Delrio, Martin, S. J., 340

Delumeau, Jean, 294

Demetrius I. Poliorcetes, Diadoch, 365

Democritus, 93–94, 119

Denmark, 136n114, 145, 149

Dew, Nicholas, 358

Dickinson, Edmund, 404

Dippel, Johann Konrad, 79, 98, 135

dissimulation as tactic, 9, 30, 41, 47, 54–56, 83, 93, 106, 122, 129, 181, 190–93, 208n30, 214

distrust, culture of, 18, 63, 168, 189–97, 379, 421

Dodsley, Robert, 290, 292

Doni, Antonfrancesco, 193

Dooley, Brendan, 191

Döring, Detlef, 228–30, 233, 236, 247

Dorn, Gerhard, 180

Dort, Synod of, 235, 419

double truth, idea of, 49, 52–54, 175

Dresden, 73, 75, 134

Dron, François, 360, 362, 373–74

Dryden, John, 73

Durand, David, 112

Dyck, Daniel van den, 175

Eckhard, Johann Georg, 158

eclecticism, 40–41, 61n44, 62, 64–66, 68, 99, 116–20, 130–33, 142, 160, 165, 408

"economy of secrets," 263–64, 275–80

Edelmann, Johann Christian, 79, 108n24, 134, 136

Edinburgh, 291

Edzardi, Esdras, 385

Edzardi, Sebastian, 153, 385

Egypt, 206, 210–11, 216, 306, 346, 369, 376–78, 383, 387, 401, 404, 406–7, 409–10, 413

Eisenach, 300, 323

Eisenstein, Elizabeth, 15

Eisleben, 318

Elcha ben David, 343

emblems, 75, 86–97, 173, 179, 211–14, 217, 221, 229, 235

Emerald Tablet, 262–63

Engelberger, Ferdinand Franz, 153

Engels, Friedrich, 290

Enlightenments, radical, moderate, and orthodox, 10–11, 33, 36, 42, 75, 77–79, 83, 100, 129, 142, 163–65, 233, 352–53

Epicurus and Epicurean, 8, 28–29, 98, 119, 194n57

Erfurt, 33

Erlangen, 290

esotericism, 98n81, 189, 205, 212, 217, 222–23, 326–27

Esprit de Spinosa, 134, 156–57

Essenes, 229, 307

Ethiopia, 19, 306, 376–77

Eusebius, 398–99

Eustathius, 394

explosiveness, inferential, 13, 20–22

Fabricius, Johann (of Helmstedt), 411

Fabricius, Johann Albert (of Hamburg), 111, 126, 129, 131, 134, 143, 145, 163, 297, 323, 385–87, 394, 402, 408, 410–11, 415

Fairs, trade, 307–10, 324, 421

Falconieri, Ottavio, 358–59

family systems therapy, theory of, 241, 283, 289

fascination, communities of, 222–23, 325–29, 387, 405, 414–15

Firpo, Luigi, 226–28, 232–33

Fleischbein, Johann Philipp, 376

Flensburg, 400

Floyer, John, 401, 403

Fludd, Robert, 229–30, 259

Fogel, Martin, 107

footnotes, as niche for knowledge, 13–14

Forli, Marcolino da, 171

Foucault, Michel, 17, 84, 168, 200

Franckenau, Georg Franck von, 119n27, 351–52

Franco, Nicolò, 193

Frankfurt, 31–32, 56, 77–78, 97, 100, 132, 134, 297, 301, 309, 324, 376

Frederick II of Prussia, King, 132, 231

Frederick William I of Prussia, King, 220, 285

Freemasonry, 76, 223

freethinking and freethinkers, 23, 69, 73, 76, 77, 106, 109, 118, 156, 198, 227, 232–33, 275, 410

Frevert, Ute, 325

Friedrich August, Duke of Oldenburg, 149

Frisch, Johann Leonard, 145

Fritsch, Christian Friedrich, 75

Fritsch, Kaspar, 157

Furly, Benjamin, 156–57

Gaffarel, Jacques, 24, 342–45, 352

Galland, Antoine, 360, 362

Gassendi, Pierre, 104, 227–28, 234–35

Gataker, Thomas, 404

Gemma, Cornelius, 261n55, 267

George, Stefan, 282

German studies, as a field, 158–61

gestures, 73, 176–79, 184, 186–88, 204–6, 214, 216, 222, 236, 252, 336; knowledge and, 17–18, 169, 204

Giddens, Anthony, 38, 190

Gierl, Martin, 141

Gießen, University of, 203

Gilio, Giovanni, 193

Gimma, Giacinto, 270

Ginzburg, Carlo, 211, 233–35

Giovine, Palma, 182–83

Giovio, Paolo, 193, 197n65, 198

Gladigow, Burkhard, 67

gnosticism and gnostic gems, 206, 288, 339–40, 346, 382, 387, 404

Goertz, Baron Georg Heinrich von, 144

Goethe, Johann Wolfgang, 68

Goeze, Johann Melchior, 136, 385

Goldenbaum, Ursula, 66

Goldgar, Anne, 132, 364

Goltzius, Hubert, 361, 372

Görlitz, 287

Göttingen, 24, 304, 308, 310, 312–13, 323;
    university of: 232, 316–18
Gottsched, Adelgunde Luise, 203, 219
Gottsched, Johann Christoph, 227–31, 301,
    308, 311–12, 314–22
Gottsched, Johann Christoph, 37–38
Grafton, Anthony, 384
Grandier, Urbain, 151
Greenblatt, Stephen, 405, 412, 415n102
Gregorius, Abba, 376
Großschedel, Johann Baptist, 250–52, 264,
    269
Gundling, Jacob Paul, 285
Gundling, Nikolaus Hieronymus, 61,
    285–86, 289
Gundling, Wolfgang, 286

Habermas, Jürgen, 212
Häfner, Ralph, 340, 396
Hague, The, 97, 156, 417–18
Halevi, Judah, 346
Halle, 28–29, 40, 73, 104, 142, 151, 159, 230,
    246, 256, 267, 285, 289, 298, 300, 308
Hamahalzel, 343, 345
"Hambourg," 154–55, 157
Hamburg, 10, 24, 38–39, 63, 75, 105–9, 126,
    128–29, 133–37, 143, 149, 151, 153, 157, 163,
    281, 286–94, 318, 329. 381–90, 397, 401,
    409, 411–13
Hanover, 146, 298, 312, 318
Hardouin, Jean, S. J., 360, 375, 416
Hardt, Hermannn von der, 134, 201–3,
    212–17, 220, 297, 349–50
Harpocrates and Harpocratism, 209–23
Hatzfeld, Johann Conrad Franz von, 135
Haude, Ambrosius, 232
Heem, Jan Davidszoon de, 418–19
Hegel, Georg Wilhelm Friedrich, 104, 169
Heinsius (postmaster), 314–15, 318, 320, 322
"Heiseishe, Brenno Vulcanus," 154
Helmont, Franciscus Mercurius van,
    276–80
Helmont, Jan Baptist van, 276–77
Helmstedt University, 201, 349, 411

Hemmerling, Wiebke, 317
Herbelot, Barthelmy d', 360, 406
Herbert of Cherbury, Edward, 125
Herder, Johann Gottfried, 201
Herford, 270
Hermes Trismegistos, 211, 244, 262–63, 273,
    394
Heubel, Johann Heinrich, 24, 135, 144–65,
    301
Heumann, Christoph August, 24, 203,
    297–324, 384
Hildesheim, 134, 153
Hinckelmann, Abraham, 286–89, 328, 347,
    385, 387, 404, 406
Hinckelmann, Benedikt, 287
Hippocrates, 270–75
Hobbes, Thomas, 32, 40, 56, 59–60, 81, 89,
    160, 167, 229, 307
Hoffmann, Adolph Friedrich, 236
Holbein, Hans, 265
Holstein, 146–47, 149, 157, 159
Hopi Indians, 331–32
Höpken, Daniel Niclas von, 136n114, 146
Horace, 113, 135, 226–37, 231–42, 234, 236
Horb, Johann Heinrich, 288
Horus, Egyptian god, 206
Hottinger, Johann Heinrich, 338, 406
Houssayes, Amelot de, 14
Huet, Pierre-Daniel, 404, 406, 415
Huguenots, 80n24, 103, 132, 156, 374
Hunter, Ian, 27–29, 102
Hus, Jan, 151
Hyde, Thomas, 397–98, 404

Ibn Ezra, Abraham, 346
Iken, Conrad, 409
images, knowledge and, 17–18
Index of Prohibited Books, 8, 140, 278n111
indifferentism, 129, 131, 165–66
"intellectual field," 205, 223
intellectual history, new kind of, 9–11, 17,
    23–24, 101, 173, 191, 295–96, 420–22
intellectuals, alienated, 34–36
Isaac of Troki, 121

Israel, Jonathan, 163–66
Issy, 362

Jablonski, Daniel Ernst, 284, 288–89
Jandun, Jean de, 54
Jardine, Lisa, 384
Jefferson, Thomas, 128
Jena, University of, 245–46, 303, 347
Jerome of Prague, 151
Jerome, Saint, 115
Jobert, Louis, S. J., 360, 362, 368, 375
Johns, Adrian, 15
Jordan, Charles Etienne, 132–34
Jorio, Andrea de, 177–78, 336
Josephus, 307, 399
Jungius, Joachim, 99, 386, 389n22

Kabbalah and Kabbalism, 19, 44, 120, 230,
    246, 249–72, 276, 279, 287–89, 306, 328,
    335, 342–43, 387
Kant, Immanuel, 60–61, 65, 104, 225–26,
    231–33, 236
Kantorowicz, Ernst, 46–47, 67
Karl Friedrich, duke of Schleswig, 144–45
Kaufbeuren, 301, 310, 323
Keckermann, Bartholomäus, 209
Ketzermacherei (the manufacture of
    heretics), 104, 141, 150
Khomer, Rabbi, 343
Kiel, 24, 37, 105, 109, 120, 147–48, 153–54, 159,
    162, 271
Kircher, Athanasius, 206, 208–11, 261–62,
    347, 384, 404, 407, 412
Kirchmaier, Georg Wilhelm, 397
Kittsteiner, Heinz Dieter, 294
Klingemann, August, 46
knowledge: definition of, 2–3, 7, 15; tacit, 17;
    loss of, 3–4; withholding of, 12–13;
    precarious, 42–45, 166
"knowledge bourgeoisie," 9–10, 24, 29, 143,
    164–65, 240–41, 245, 281, 324, 328, 333, 372
Knutzen, Mattthias, 79
Koblig, Johann Sigismund, 334, 348, 350, 353
Koerbagh, Adriaan, 135

Konarski, Stanislaw, 231
König, Georg Matthias, 388, 390
Königsberg, 33, 73, 75
Konsequenzenmacherei (hunting for
    supposedly dangerous implications), 20
Koran, the, 121–22
Koselleck, Reinhart, 149, 194n56, 223
Kreuzlingen, Sanatorium Bellevue in, 331–32
Kreyssig, Georg Christoph, 134
Kuhlmann, Quirinus, 151
Kuhn, Thomas S., 167, 413
Kulpis, Johann Georg von, 159
Kurland (Kurzeme in Latvia), 80

La Croze, Mathurin Veyssière, 105, 132, 297,
    374
La Mettrie, Julien Offrey de, 135
La Mothe le Vayer, François, 47–49, 54, 56,
    62, 64, 66, 104–5, 120
La Peyrère, Isaac, 22
La Vie de Spinosa, 154–57
Lactantius, 387
Lafitau, Jean-François, S. J., 332–33
Lahire, Bernard, 198
Laisné (traveler to the Orient), 360
Lamia, portraits of, 365
Lancelot, Antoine, 135, 150
Landucci, Sergio, 54
Lar, Persia, 358
Latour, Bruno, 10
Lau, Philipp, 96
Lau, Theodor Ludwig, 11, 24, 30–34, 39–44,
    56–68, 73–100, 125–28, 130–33, 135, 138,
    160, 173, 220
Le Clerc, Jean, 40, 389–90, 396, 401, 404, 406
Le Petit, Claude, 151
Leibniz, Gottfried Wilhelm, 24, 38, 135, 158,
    202, 217, 220, 222, 230, 243, 245, 249, 301,
    374
Leiden, 71, 338, 417, 419
Leipzig, 37, 43, 147, 218, 222, 227, 229, 235–36,
    245–47, 249, 271, 280, 300–301, 308–22, 324
Lely, Peter, 177
Lessing, Gotthold Ephraim, 136, 232, 292

Leusden, Johannes, 382–83
Levier, Charles, 156–57
Libanius, 382
libertines and libertinism, 12, 24, 29, 30, 48, 54, 56, 64, 66–67, 71, 73, 98, 102–6, 111, 112, 113, 118–19, 168, 175, 186, 228; Venetian, 174–75, 182, 191–98, 275, 278
Liceti, Fortunio, 347, 352, 368
lies and lying, 52–54
Lipsius, Justus, 179, 209, 235, 391
Liscow, Christian Ludwig, 219, 223
Liselotte, Princess of the Palatinate, 364
Locke, John, 24, 40, 63–64, 79–80, 360
Loredano, Giovan Francesco, 175, 182–83, 192, 195
Löscher, Valentin Ernst, 109, 203, 328, 348, 350
Lossau, Christian Joachim, 135–37, 152
Lotter, Johann Georg, 308–11, 315, 317
Loudun, 151
Louis XIV, King, 356–60, 373–74
Louvois, François-Michel le Tellier, Marquis de, 373
Löwenstein-Wertheim-Virneburg, Countess of, 10
Lübeck, 144, 149
Lucania, 337
Lucas, Jean-Maximilien, 155
Lucas, Paul, 360, 363
Lucian, 113, 123, 193
Lucretius, 98
Ludewig, Johann Peter, 158
Ludolf, Job, 376
Ludovici, Carl Günter, 219, 223
Luhmann, Niklas, 11, 190

Mabillon, Jean, O.S.B., 161
Machiavelli, Nicolo and Machiavellianism, 14, 99, 203, 208, 410
MacIntyre, Alasdair, 225
Magdeburg, 308
magic, 19–20, 24, 37, 103, 151, 177–79, 188, 195, 264, 326–28, 331–53, 378–79, 402, 405
magic, knowledge and, 19–20

Magnusson, Arni, 146
Maimonides, Moses 41, 339, 347, 406, 410
Manetho, 387
Manichaeism and Manichaeans, 151, 382, 387, 392–93, 404–13
"mano in fica" (the fig sign, a magical and obscene gesture), 173, 176–78, 185, 193
Manteuffel, Count Ernst Christoph von, 227, 230–32, 236
"manu cornuta" (the sign of the horns, a magical gesture), 173, 176–77, 185, 336
Marana, Giovanni Paolo, 293
Marchand, Prosper, 156–57
marginalia, as niche for knowledge, 14
Marino, Giambattista, 182
Marsham, John, 409
Martino, Ernesto de, 337
Marx, Karl, 289–90
Mastricht, Gerhard, 107
Maupertuis, Pierre Louis Moreau, 291
Mauss, Marcel, 27
May, Johann Friedrich, 315
May, Johann Heinrich, Jr., 299
Melanchthon, Philipp, 227, 235
Melm, Gottfried, 107
Memmingen, 301
Mencke, Johann Burkhardt, 147, 149, 158, 219, 300–301, 324
Merian, Matthias, 229
Merseburg, 318
Mersenne, Marin, 261
Merz (Augsburg book dealer), 321
Meslier, Abbé Jean, 123
metempsychosis. See transmigration of souls
Meyercrone, Henning, 374–75
Michelangelo Buonarotti, 193
microcosm and macrocosm, 245, 273–74
microscripts, 381–84, 391, 395, 398, 405, 416
Minder, Robert, 13–14
Mirandola, Giovanni Pico della, 48, 260, 342
Mittau (Jelgava in Latvia), 75
Molesworth, Robert, 14

Molinos, Miguel de, 203

Monçeau, François de, 344

Monceaux, André de, 360

Monnoye, Bernard de la, 135, 150

Montaigne, Michel de, 181

Montesquieu, Charles Louis de Secondat, Baron de, 293

Montfaucon, Bernard de, 178, 336

Montmarquet, James, 225

Mordente, Fabrizio, 263, 267

Morell, Andreas, 360, 362, 368, 372–76, 380

Morhof, Daniel Georg, 109, 111, 403, 415

Moscherosch, Johann Michael, 94–95

Moscow, 151, 176

Mosheim, Johann Lorenz von, 124, 135, 144, 148, 297, 315, 317, 352–53, 403, 413–14

Mourgues, Michel, 125

Müller, Jan, 209, 210

Münchhausen, Gerlach Adolf, Baron von, 319–20

Murray, Johann Philipp, 232

Mylius, Christlob, 232

Nanni, Giovanni, 399

Naples, 44, 177, 270, 275, 336

Naudé, Gabriel, 24, 104–5, 110–11, 118, 120, 143, 341–44, 352

Negri, Salvatore de', 279

Nehring, Johann Christian, 397

Nelson, Benjamin, 141

Neo-Stoicism, 179, 192n48, 234–35

Newton, Isaac, 10, 73, 217, 401

Nicaise, Claude, 360, 362, 374n66

niches for knowledge, 11–14, 30, 79n18

Nicolas Fréret, 38–39

Niklashausen, Piper of, 77–78, 100

Nizolio, Mario, 12

Nointel, Charles Ollier de, 362, 365, 377

Nolte, Thomas Zacharias, 349–50

Northern War, Great, 144, 148

numismatics, 24, 231, 236, 299–300, 326–27, 355–80

Nuremberg, 308–9, 312, 318–19

Nystad, Peace of, 146

obscenity, uses of, 94, 173, 176–78, 184, 188–89, 194–95, 199, 244

Olearius, Johann Gottfried, 105

Orthodoxy, Lutheran, 9–10, 20, 40, 54, 58, 85n40, 86, 104n11, 109, 122–23, 136–37, 142, 165, 201, 203, 233, 236, 286–88, 328, 348, 411, 415

Owens, John, 311

Padua, 198, 268–71, 338, 359

palingenesis, doctrine of, 77n13, 96, 98

Pallavicino, Ferrante, 195

Palmyra, 371

Panofsky, Erwin, 332

pansophy and pansophists, 181, 246–47, 249, 252, 264–65, 268–71, 279–80

pantheism and pantheists, 9, 68, 76, 89, 100, 102, 208, 211, 216n49

Paracelsism and Paracelsists, 180–81, 244, 251, 258

Paris, 12, 14, 53–54, 58, 149–50, 338, 358–68, 370–79

Patin, Charles, 359

Patin, Guy, 104, 136n114, 160, 361

Patrizi, Francesco, 270

Peignot, Gabriel, 143

Peiresc, Nicolas-Claude Fabri, 207, 297, 338–39

Perizonius, Jakob, 368, 399

persona: sociological and psychological meanings of, 27; radical, 29–30; double or twin, 46–49, 66; moral, 56–57, 95; of the philosopher, 29, 102, 204

Petau, Denis, 371

Peter the Great, of Russia, 146–47

Petit, Claude le, 151

Petit, Pierre, 366–67

Petrarch, Francesco, 53

Pfaff, Christoph Matthäus, 411

Phoenicians, 306, 384, 397

physicotheology, 40, 90, 111, 125–27

Picatrix, 346
Pietism and Pietists, 98, 113, 134, 141–43, 205, 212n43, 222, 282, 286–98, 298, 408, 415
Pignoria, Lorenzo, 69n1, 206, 338
Pinelli, Gianvincenzo, 297
Placcius, Vincent, 107, 109, 111, 300, 385–89
Plato, Platonic, and neo-Platonic, 2, 28, 48–51, 64, 180–81, 185n33, 188, 194, 198–99, 216, 218, 229–30, 236, 251–53, 258, 269, 298, 306, 335, 387, 404
pluralization, crisis of, 66–67, 140, 142, 164, 166, 173, 197n66
Plutarch, 206, 208, 365, 407
Pocock, Edward, 406
Pomponazzi, Pietro, 48–53, 103, 175, 341–42, 352, 366
Pona, Francesco, 278–79
Ponickau, Johann August von, 134
Porta, Giambattista della, 337
portraits, self-presentation and, 69–76, 87–96, 181, 188, 198, 234–35, 248–80
postal system and routes, German, 16, 23, 295n1, 307–10, 312–15, 318–22, 324
Postel, Guillaume, 135, 343
precariat, 8–10, 17–18, 22–23, 32n5; intellectual 8–10, 164, 241, 278, 420; clandestine 31–45, 142–43, 324, 375, 380
precarity, 4–5, 7–8; knowledge transmitters and, 5–6; social status and, 6; forms of expression and, 7–8; knowledge transfers and, 14–15
precarization, 139–42
proof, kinds of, 253–56
pseudonyms, 7, 15, 33, 47, 107–8, 154, 287, 300, 361n22, 386, 388
Ptolemy Auletes, 364–65, 369–70
"public sphere," 60–61, 63, 65–68, 212
Pufendorf, Samuel, 56–57, 59, 61, 64, 86
Pythagoreanism, 188, 202, 217–19, 222, 246, 257, 259–60, 267, 272, 279, 309, 341, 402

quaternaries, 257, 259, 265–66
quietism, 120, 130, 203–4, 222
Qumran, 229

Radical Reformation, 77–78, 86
radicalism, 40, 109, 119–20; sublimated, 24, 131, 354; spiritualist, 79, 86, 104, 282–83, 298
Raimondi, Francesco Paolo, 112–13,
Rainssant, Pierre, 360–62, 368, 373
Ratke, Wolfgang, 99, 256
Raulff, Ulrich, 282
Rawls, John, 101, 128
Rechenberg, Adam, 43
Reddy, William, 325
Reemtsma, Philipp, 194
Reichelt, Julius, 347, 352
Reimarus, Albert Hinrich, 291–94
Reimarus, Elise, 291–93
Reimarus, Hermann Samuel, 10–11, 38–40, 121, 137, 281, 291–94, 385, 408–13
Reimmann, Jakob Friedrich, 43, 109, 116, 297, 386–87
Reinbeck, Johann Gustav, 227
Republic of Letters, 17, 60n43, 106–7, 132, 300, 324, 363
rescue operations, philosophical, 104, 111, 120, 243, 154, 163, 165, 172, 240, 341
Reuchlin, Johannes, 257, 342
Richter, Christoph Gottlieb, 290
Riposio, Donatella, 193
Robertet, Jean, 400
Rocco, Antonio, 186, 187n34, 192, 196
Roche, Daniel, 146, 328, 355
Rochester, John Wilmot, Second Earl of, 71–73
Rome, 151, 197, 277
Rorty, Richard, 101n1, 106, 128
Rosa, Salvator, 54–56
Rosenwein, Barbara, 325
Rousseau, Jean Jacques, 67
Ruar, Martin, 285
Rudbeck, Olof, 145
Rüdenskjold, Baron von, 231
Rudolph August, duke of Brunswick-Wolfenbüttel, 213–14
Ruschi, Francesco, 175, 182–84
Russia, 145, 147n25, 149

Russiliano, Tiberio, 52
Rychner, Max, 381

Sabaeans, 338–39, 347, 393, 398, 404–6, 409, 413
Sachsenspiegel, 162
Sadducees, 307
Said, Edward, 327, 362, 405
Saint-Hyacinthe, Themiseul de, 219
Sala, Angelo, 278
Salzburg, 139–40
samizdat literature, 5, 15, 422
"sapere aude" (dare to know), 65, 168, 225–36
Sarmant, Thierry, 359
satire, 37, 73, 79, 94, 139–40, 150, 154, 186, 219, 290, 315
Savonarola, Girolamo, 151
Saxe-Gotha, ducal court of, 376–77
Saxl, Fritz, 172, 189, 332
Scaliger, Joseph Justus, 103, 338, 371, 404, 406
Schaffer, Simon, 167
Schelhorn, Johann Georg, 301–2
Schelling, Friedrich Wilhelm Joseph, 201
Schickhardt, Wilhelm, 265
Schimpfer, Batholomäus, 267, 279
Schmidt-Biggemann, Wilhelm, 306
Schmidt, Johann Lorenz, 10, 39
Schöne, Albrecht, 86, 211
Schoonhoven, Florentius, 179–80, 233–35
Schorer, Leonhard, 75, 96
Schott, Kaspar, 265
Schramm, Johann Moritz, 105
Schröder, Winfried, 228
Schröter, Wilhelm, 80, 91
Schupp, Johann Balthasar, 99
Schwabe, Johann Joachim, 232
Scotland, 292
Seckendorf, Veit Ludwig von, 80, 301
secrecy, 15, 33, 206, 208. *See* "economy of secrets"
Seguin, Pierre, 359, 367
Selden, John, 338–39, 347
self-fashioning, 47, 83n32, 108
Semler, Johann Salomo, 59n42

Seneca, 113, 118, 179, 196
serenity, philosophy of, 118, 123, 127–31, 137, 164, 166
Servetus, Michael, 1, 21–22, 103, 131–32, 135, 142–43, 148, 151
Severino, Marco Aurelio, 275–76
Shaftesbury, Anthony Ashley Cooper, Third Earl of, 63–65, 227, 231–32, 235
Shapin, Stephen, 167–68, 189–90, 198, 294
Shapiro, Barbara, 385–86
Shepherd of Hermas, 396
Sholem, Gershom, 229
Sibyls, Sibylline Oracles, 151, 366, 391–92, 394–403, 407
Sidau, Christian, 75
Siger of Brabant, 54
Silenus, 178, 336
Simon, Richard, 406
skepticism, 15, 28, 47, 71, 119–20, 129–30, 164, 189, 191, 198n69, 227, 367–68, 421
Smith, Pamela, 75
Smyrna, 367, 377–78
Socinians, 283
Socinians, 283–86, 408
Soissons, Congress of, 149, 151
Soll, Jacob, 14
Soner, Ernst, 285
Sorbière, Samuel, 227–28, 234–35
Sosa, Ernest, 224–25
Spalding, Almut, 291
Spalding, Johann Joseph, 231, 235
Spanheim, Ezechiel, 300, 357, 360, 361–62, 371–72, 374n66
Spark, Geraldine, 283–84
spells, magical, 177, 336
Spencer, John, 404, 406, 409–12
Spener, Philipp Jakob, 141
Spinoza, Baruch, 11, 24, 32, 40, 41, 43–44, 56, 81, 89n54, 104, 119–20, 129–30, 143, 155, 157–58, 160, 191, 229–30, 298
Spon, Jacques, 207–8, 216, 359, 361
St. Peter's Abbey, Salzburg, 139, 151, 154
St. Petersburg, 145–46, 311
Stanley, Thomas, 300, 406

Stauffenberg, Claus Schenk, Count of, 282

Steinwehr, Wolf Balthasar von, 315–18

Stillingfleet, Edward, 406

Stockholm, 145–46

Stoics and Stoicism, 47–49, 56, 63–64, 119, 129, 179, 204, 216, 234–35, 298

Stolberg, 318–19

Stolle, Gottlieb, 297

Strauss, Leo, 30, 41, 122

Strimesius, Johann Samuel, 146

Struve, Burkhard Gotthelf, 158

Stübner, Friedrich Wilhelm, 311–22

Sweden, 54, 144–46, 149

Symbolum Sapientiae, 81, 132, 134–35, 240n6

Tabula Smaragdina. See *Emerald Tablet*

Tachenius, Otto (Otto Taken), 24, 40, 254, 270–80

Tacitus, 14, 160, 208

talismans, 19, 333–39, 342, 345, 348, 350–53, 364, 378

Taylor, Charles, 205

Telesio, Bernardino, 276, 307, 338

Tentzel, Wilhelm Ernst, 158, 300

ternaries, 255–60, 266n72

Tertullian, 159, 335

tetractys, Pythagorean, 217, 257, 264–66, 271, 279

Theophrastus redivivus, 5–6

Thévenot, Melchisédech, 362, 365

Thomasius, Christian, 24, 28–29, 34, 36, 40–41, 43, 57–62, 66, 86, 95, 104–5, 110, 117–18, 125, 131, 141, 159, 236, 285, 307

Thomasius, Jacob, 28, 119, 125, 298

Ticino, 282

"time to understand," 34, 36–37, 39–40, 45

Tindal, Matthew, 161

Titel, Basilius, 267, 279

Titian, 176

titles, false, 15

Toinard, Niccolas, 360, 373–74

Toland, John, 14, 32, 56, 76, 81, 119, 135, 410

toleration, idea of, 15, 67,101, 103, 118, 121, 125, 127–28, 130–33, 142, 229, 280, 284, 374

Torre, Giorgio, 278

Traité des trois imposteurs, 124, 156–58, 163

transfers, cultural, 16, 24, 239–41, 289; risky 14–17, 281

translation, 16, 91, 97n78, 104–5, 121, 189, 231–32, 369, 372, 405

transmigration of souls, 77–78, 98, 393, 414

Turin, 226

two bodies, kingship and, 46–47; libertines and, 46–68

Ubaldino, Roberto, 117

Uffenbach, Conrad Zacharias, 132, 134, 213, 297–301, 324, 402, 415

Uppsala, 145

Vaillant, Jean Foy, 356, 359–62, 369–71

Valesius, Henricus (Henri de Valois), 398

Valle, Pietro della, 358

Vallée, Geoffroy and Pseudo-Vallée, 131, 135

Valvasense, Francesco, 195–96

Vanini, Lucilio ("Giulio Cesare"), 32, 56, 58, 81, 102–6, 137, 143, 151, 153, 160, 240

Vasoli, Cesare, 102–3

Vecchia, Pietro della, 24, 173–89, 191–92, 194–99, 233, 247–52, 263, 265, 268–80, 336

Veillon, Marie, 359

Venice, 24, 168, 177, 189–99, 240, 249, 269–72, 275–76, 278, 280, 336, 376

Venturi, Franco, 226–27, 231–32

Verona, 278

Versailles, court of, 364

Vicenza, 176–77, 269

Vico, Enea, 361

Vienna, 151, 153, 271

Vilnius, 271

Vilthat (licentiate), 320

Viterbo, Annio da. *See* Nanni, Giovanni

Vogel, Johann, 285–86, 289

Vogt, Johann, 148

Vois, Ary de, 70–71

Völkel, Markus, 193, 198

Vossius, Gerrit Janszoon, 71, 347, 384, 392

Vossius, Isaac, 398–99, 401–4, 412

Wachter, Johann Georg, 37, 44, 135, 145–46, 158, 228–31, 233, 235–36

Wagenseil, Johann Christoph, 121–22, 153

Wagner, Gabriel, 36, 38, 43

Wagner, Georg, 256

Wagner, Heinrich Theodor, 203–4

Walser, Robert, 381, 416

Walther, Balthasar, 287

Wansleben, Johann Michael, 24, 360, 376–79

Warburg, Aby, 331–33

Wassertrüdingen, 202

Weigel, Erhard, 99, 245–82

Weißmüller, Siegmund Ferdinand, 202–3, 212, 217–23

Wekhrlin, Wilhelm Ludwig, 38

Wepfer, Johann, 278

Werner, Thomas, 140

Wernsdorf, Gottlieb, 203

Wertheim, 311

Westphal (postmaster), 319–20

Whiston, William, 401–3

Wichmann, Christian August, 227

Wilde, Jacob de, 300

Williams, Bernard, 13, 53, 168

Winckler, Johann, 415

Wind, Edgar, 188–89, 332

Wittenberg, 144, 203, 227, 348, 381, 392, 397, 399–400

Wolf, Johann Christoph, 24, 111, 133–34, 143, 145, 152, 163, 296–97, 303, 323, 328, 381–415, 420

Wolff, Christian, 88, 119, 201, 217, 230

Wolff, Jacob, 347

Wolff, Johann Heinrich, 219

Wolffians, 35, 98, 218, 219, 227, 230–32, 236, 413

Woolf, Daniel, 356

Wowern, Johan von, 384

Wulfila, 158

Zagzebski, Linda, 168, 225

Zähinger, Georg Wilhelm, 322

Zeidler, Johann Gottfried, 79

Ziegler, Christina von, 315

Zimmermann, Johann Jakob, 301

Zoroaster and Zoroastrianism, 202, 342, 344, 394n38, 404, 413

Zschackwitz, Johann Ehrenfried, 151

A NOTE ON THE TYPE

This book has been composed in Arno, an Old-style serif typeface in the
classic Venetian tradition, designed by Robert Slimbach at Adobe.